A PRACTICAL GUIDE TO APPELLATE ADVOCACY

A Practical Guide to Appellate Advocacy

Mary Beth Beazley
Associate Professor of Law
Moritz College of Law
The Ohio State University

ASPEN
PUBLISHERS

1185 Avenue of the Americas, New York, NY 10036
www.aspenpublishers.com

Permissions
Aspen Publishers
1185 Avenue of the Americas
New York, NY 10036

Printed in the United States of America

3   4   5   6   7   8   9   0

ISBN 0-7355-2406-8

Library of Congress Cataloging-in-Publication Data

Beazley, Mary Beth, 1957–
    A practical guide to appellate advocacy / Mary Beth Beazley.
      p. cm.
    Includes bibliographical references and index.
    ISBN 0-7355-2406-8
      1. Briefs—United States. 2. Appellate procedure—United States. I. Title.

KF251 B42 2002
347.73'8—dc21   2001058382

About Aspen Publishers

Aspen Publishers, headquartered in New York City, is a leading information provider for attorneys, business professionals, and law students. Written by preeminent authorities, our products consist of analytical and practical information covering both U.S. and international topics. We publish in the full range of formats, including updated manuals, books, periodicals, CDs, and online products.

Our proprietary content is complemented by 2,500 legal databases, containing over 11 million documents, available through our Loislaw division. Aspen Publishers also offers a wide range of topical legal and business databases linked to Loislaw's primary material. Our mission is to provide accurate, timely, and authoritative content in easily accessible formats, supported by unmatched customer care.

To order any Aspen Publishers title, go to *www.aspenpublishers.com* or call 1-800-638-8437.

To reinstate your manual update service, call 1-800-638-8437.

For more information on Loislaw products, go to *www.loislaw.com* or call 1-800-364-2512.

For Customer Care issues, e-mail CustomerCare@aspenpublishers.com; call 1-800-234-1660; or fax 1-800-901-9075.

Aspen Publishers
A Wolters Kluwer Company

To my parents,
who made it possible;

to David,
who made it probable;

and to Betsy and Annie,
who make it all worthwhile

Summary of Contents

Contents

CHAPTER TEN

SIX DEGREES OF LEGAL WRITING: MAKING YOUR DOCUMENT READER-FRIENDLY   135

CHAPTER ELEVEN

EXPLOITING OPPORTUNITIES FOR PERSUASION   149

APPENDIX A
FOR REFERENCE: CITATION FORM AND PUNCTUATION INFORMATION   215

APPENDIX B
UNITED STATES SUPREME COURT RULES   229

APPENDIX C
SAMPLE BRIEFS   241

Using the Examples in This Book

This book is meant to guide law students and others who are new to writing appellate briefs. It attempts to make the writing process easier by examining the various decisions a brief-writer must make, and by articulating criteria that will help the writer to make those decisions. The book contains numerous excerpts from student-written appellate briefs that illustrate various aspects of brief-writing. Although following examples too closely can be dangerous, I know that many good writers learn through imitation. Therefore, I offer the following caveats:

1
SOME EXAMPLES ARE "BAD" EXAMPLES

Do not presume that the principle illustrated in each example applies to the brief you are currently writing. First, the examples in the book are not meant to represent the current law on any subject. They come from a variety of student briefs written over the last several years. Some of the cases cited in the examples are fictional. Second, some of the examples are "bad examples," that is, they were adapted to show how *not* to do something. Unfortunately, some students, in a hurry to complete a project, will consult a textbook and imitate its examples slavishly, including "bad examples." To try to avoid this problem, the bad examples are carefully labeled—with the words "bad example" and with a downward arrow—so that you will not mistake a bad example for a good example. Most, if not all, of the bad examples are paired with a good example to show how to address the problem illustrated in the bad example. These are labeled with the words "good example" and an upward arrow.

The examples that are not paired are labeled with the words "example" and an arrow pointing to the example. Virtually all of these examples are good examples, but even these examples must not be followed unquestioningly. Just as the same law applies differently to different fact situations, the guidelines in this book may apply differently to briefs addressing different issues. For that reason, I have used examples from a variety of cases; no one case aptly illustrates every type of brief-writing problem. The majority of the examples in the text come from student briefs written for four Supreme Court cases: *Minnesota v. Carter*, 524 U.S. 975 (1998); *Knowles v. Iowa*, 525 U.S. 113 (1998); *Miller v. Albright*, 523 U.S. 420 (1998); *Rubin v. Coors Brewing Co.*, 514 U.S. 476 (1995) (argued as *Bentsen v. Adolph Coors Co.*). There are also scattered examples from student briefs written for *Ohio v. Robinette*, 519 U.S. 33 (1996); *City of Chicago v. Morales*, 527 U.S. 41 (1999); *Holloway v. United States*, 526 U.S. 1 (1999); and *City of Indianapolis v. Edmond*, 531 U.S. 32 (2000).

Even the good examples may not be perfect, but they represent good attempts by law students to write effectively. The sample briefs in Appendix C contain marginal notes that point out passages that are particularly effective, as well as passages that might be made even more effective if the writer had made certain decisions differently. Some marginal notes try to explain why certain peculiarities about the case may have led the writer to choose a certain writing or organizational technique. Thus, when you are deciding whether to imitate an example, you should first consider whether the example is effective; second, decide whether your case presents the same types of writing concerns as the case used in the example.

2
NOTE THE TONE AND WRITING STYLE CONVENTIONS IN THE GOOD EXAMPLES

Generally, you should imitate the tone and writing style in the good examples and not in the text itself. Tone and writing style should change to reflect the needs of particular types of documents and of particular audiences, and only the examples are written in appellate brief style. Your writing teachers may already have told you not to imitate judicial writing styles because the needs of judges and clerks (the audience for an appellate brief) differ from the needs of the readers of judicial decisions. Similarly, you should not model your brief-writing style after the writing style of the *text* in this book. Unlike the good examples in this book, I did not write the *text* material in appellate brief style. Although I followed many conventions that also apply in appellate briefs, I used a tone and writing style that is more like the one that I use when I write comments on student papers. I use contractions, attempt humor, and use unusual metaphors, many of which could easily hinder the effectiveness of an appellate brief. Thus, you should use a particular writing technique only when that technique is consistent with the rules and conventions of the court to which you are writing.

Bearing these caveats in mind, the examples should provide an opportunity for you to see how various writing decisions play out in the context of real cases and real (student) briefs. I hope that you find them helpful.

Acknowledgments

I would like to recognize and thank the following people who helped me in many different ways as I worked on this book:

Those of us who teach legal writing are blessed by the existence of a strong corps of supportive colleagues. I am grateful to the founders of the Legal Writing Institute, Anne Enquist, Laurel Currie Oates, and Christopher Rideout, of Seattle University. They were instrumental in the profound changes that have occurred in the teaching of legal writing over the past 20 years; without those changes I would not be teaching legal writing or writing about it. I also thank the colleagues whose work first taught me that there is a doctrine of legal writing that can be analyzed and communicated to others: Elizabeth Fajans, Jill Ramsfield, Mary Barnard Ray, Marjorie Rombauer, Helene Shapo, and Marilyn Walter. At Legal Writing Institute Conferences and, later, at conferences of the Association of Legal Writing Directors, I have been able to learn and grow through the exchange of ideas with colleagues who became friends: Coleen Barger, Linda Edwards, Richard Neumann, Terri LeClercq, Grace Tonner, Christy Nisbett, Sue Liemer, JoAnne Durako, Steve Johansen, Terry Seligmann, Jane Kent Gionfriddo, Ellen Mosen James, Anita Schnee, Steve Jamar, and Jan Levine. I am grateful to Judy Stinson and Samantha Moppett, who field-tested the book with their students, to my first colleagues, Julie Jenkins and Mary Kate Kearney, and to my first teachers of legal writing and how to teach it, Nancy Elizabeth Grandine and Teresa Godwin Phelps.

I thank my current and former colleagues at Ohio State who provided support, read drafts of this document, and gave advice early and often: Doug Berman, Debby Merritt, Camille Hébert, Chris Fairman, Nancy Rapoport, Cre Johnson, Terri Enns, Steve Huefner, Kathy Northern, and Ruth Colker. I also thank the three Ohio State deans who have affected my life in significant ways: Frank Beytagh, who hired me; Gregory H. Williams, who appointed me to the tenure track; and our current dean, Nancy Hardin Rogers, who provided critical support at a crucial time in my career. Liz Cutler Gates, Art Hudson, and Loraine Brannon provided technical support, and Nancy Darling, Shirley Craley, Carol Peirano, and Michelle

Whetzel-Newton provided administrative support. Finally, I would like to recognize Kimberly Town Abels, now of the University of North Carolina at Chapel Hill, who suggested that the "macro-micro-final draft" method would be suitable for legal writing, and Jacqueline Jones-Royster, Associate Professor of English and Vice Chair for Rhetoric and Composition at the Ohio State University, who suggested that I develop a self-grading instrument for my students.

I have been teaching legal writing since 1982, and I have learned so much from my students over that time. Students at Ohio State have been field testing versions of this text for the past two years, and versions of the self-graded draft since 1993. I want to especially thank the students at Ohio State who have allowed me to use and adapt their work for the examples in this text: RonNell Jones, Tiffany C. Miller, Peter Nealis, Timothy G. Pepper, Rebecca Woods, Bridget Hayward Kahle, Steven Webb, Michael Duffy, Andrew Kruppa, and Christopher Snyder. I am also grateful to the students whose work gave me insight into appellate advocacy, and who sent me examples of good and bad writing after they entered the practice of law, including Glenda Gelzleichter, John Lowe, Peter Rosato, Kevin Kessinger, Angelique Paul, Kathleen Lyon, Cynthia Roselle, Yvonne Watson, and Sean Harris. I particularly thank Jen Manion, research assistant extraordinaire.

I have learned something from each of the many adjuncts with whom I have worked over the years, but especially from Robert Burpee, Peggy Corn, Cynthia Cummings, Hilary Damaser, Ken Donchatz, Rita Eppler, Sean Heasley, Dan Jones, Randy Knutti, and Stephen Wu.

I thank the people at Aspen who guided and encouraged me along the way, including Lynn Churchill, Betsy Kenny, Carol McGeehan, Jay Boggis, Michael Gregory, Peggy Rehberger, and George Serafin. I am also grateful to the anonymous reviewers who gave helpful advice about the manuscript.

Finally, I thank the people at the home front who helped and supported me, including my parents, Ben and Pat Beazley; Trish and Dick Sanders, Mike and Julie Beazley, Marlene and Rick Fields, Mary Slupe, Laura Sanders, and Laura Williams; and of course, my daughters, Betsy and Annie Pillion; and my dear husband, David Pillion.

A PRACTICAL GUIDE TO APPELLATE ADVOCACY

INTRODUCTION

1.1
BEFORE WE BEGIN

Before we begin, let's get one thing straight: This book is not about how to write the "perfect brief." Even if that were an attainable goal, I don't know too many attorneys who have the time to spend attaining it. This book is about the practical side of appellate advocacy, about recognizing the limits that every legal writer works with — factual limits, legal limits, and time limits. It's also about recognizing and understanding the important decisions that you make every time you write a brief, so that you can do a better job making those decisions.

We all make thousands of decisions every day, both consciously and unconsciously. On some level, you have decided that your eyes are going to move across this page to read these words, and that at the end of each line, you will move your eyes to the left to start reading the next one. These decisions may have been inspired by a faculty member or by your own interest in the subject, but they are decisions just the same. Many of your decisions are unconscious, or become unconscious, and they need to — you would go crazy if you had to decide consciously to read every word or to take every step when you walk.

What we need to do when we write, however, is to identify the important decisions that must be made, so that we can make them consciously and thus more effectively. Too many of us go into default mode when we write. We don't think about which issue we want to argue first, second, or third. We don't consciously decide what our best points are, and so we don't take care to state them as effectively as we can or to put them in the places in the document where we know that readers will be paying the most attention.

And that's the other thing most of us don't think about, either: the people who read our briefs. We know that we're writing a brief to a court, but too many of us, I fear, have some vague, dreamy notion that our brief is being read by a panel consisting of Oliver Wendell Holmes, Thurgood Marshall, and Sandra Day O'Connor at the peak of their judicial and intellectual powers and on a free day with nothing to do but wonder at the fascinating complexities of our arguments.

Well, life's not like that. First of all, many of your briefs will be read by law clerks as well as judges, and sometimes by law clerks alone. Your readers will be real people with real lives. People who have phones that ring, and computers that bring them e-mail messages, and colleagues who knock on their doors and interrupt their work. People with families and deadlines. People a lot like you, except they're a little further down the road than you are now, if you're a law student. Or they took a different road from yours, if you're a practitioner.

So instead of reveling in the complexities of your argument or throwing a bunch of authorities at a busy law clerk, you have a different job to do. You have to look at those complexities and make them easy. You need to find the rules and policies that govern your argument and state them in simple terms, so clearly that the judges will wonder why they didn't notice before how obvious the answer is. You'll follow the law, of course — it's no good writing clearly about legal rules that don't exist. And you'll follow the court's rules, too, so that it won't be distracted from your tight, clean argument by stupid mechanical errors. And you'll use honest persuasive techniques to make sure that your readers get the best opportunity to read and understand your arguments.

And when you write, you'll be practical about your own behavior as a writer, too, and recognize that in addition to your reader's needs, you have to pay attention to your own needs as a writer and self-editor. You'll learn how to identify the important decisions that you have to make, and to take steps that will help you to recognize what information you've included and what you've left out of your argument.

By being practical about both the reader's needs and your needs, you can learn how to use the resources available to create documents that are easy to read and easy to use.

1.2
KNOW YOUR AUDIENCE

The first thing to realize as you prepare to write an appellate brief is that you are writing to a busy reader. The United States Supreme Court, for example, hears 75 to 100 cases per term. Consider that each case requires reading several documents. The petitioner submits a brief accompanying the petition for writ of certiorari, and the potential respondent often submits a brief in response. If the Court grants the petition, there will usually be three briefs on the merits: petitioner's brief on the merits, respondent's brief on the merits, and petitioner's reply brief on the merits. Furthermore, various parties may submit amicus briefs, and counsel for the parties will submit documents to support or oppose the various motions that may accompany Supreme Court practice.

Thus, even estimating conservatively that each case generates about seven documents, Supreme Court Justices and their clerks are reading 500 to 700 documents per year. Of course, this statistic does not take into account the reading required when the Justices review the joint appendix (selected elements of the case record) and the statutes, cases, and other sources cited in the briefs. It also does not take into account the time spent reviewing the thousands of certiorari petitions that are ultimately denied or — by the way — the time spent writing opinions.

The numbers are equally impressive in the lower courts. Judge Boyce F. Martin, Jr., of the United States Court of Appeals for the Sixth Circuit, has noted that the average judge on the Sixth Circuit sits on 32 panels and hears 192 cases a year. In addition, the average Sixth Circuit judge sits on 110 cases that are decided without oral argument.[1] At the state court level, an average intermediate appellate judge writes 56 to 60 opinions each year.[2] Presuming that these judges sit on three-judge panels and that the opinion-writing duties are evenly spread, this average state appellate judge hears 168 to 180 cases per year. An Associate Justice in Maine's highest court noted that during her first six months on the court, she and her colleagues heard 114 oral arguments and conferenced 181 cases on briefs alone in addition to reviewing 120 petitions for review of workers' compensation matters.[3] While cases submitted to lower courts may not generate the same number of documents as cases submitted to the United States Supreme Court, the number is still daunting: An average intermediate court judge may read 600 briefs per year, while an average federal circuit judge may read as many as 900 briefs per year.

Even if we strike a conservative average of 20 pages per brief, our busiest judge is reading 18,000 pages per year, or about 75 pages each workday, in the unlikely event that the reading is spaced out evenly over the year. Even less busy judges are reading 12,000 pages per year, or an average of 50 pages *just of attorney briefs* per day.

Remember these statistics when you make every decision — from whether to file an appeal,[4] to the number of issues to argue, to, particularly, how to organize and write the brief. Your goal should be to produce

---

[1] Boyce F. Martin, Jr., *In Defense of Unpublished Opinions*, 60 Ohio St. L.J. 177, 182 (1999).

[2] Daniel J. Foley, *The Tennessee Court of Criminal Appeals: A Statistical Analysis*, 66 Tenn. L. Rev. 427, 442 (1999) (citing National Ctr. for State Cts., Court Statistics Project, State Court Caseload Statistics, 1994, at 133-36 (1996)).

[3] Leigh Ingalls Saufley, *The Judicial Process: Amphibians and Appellate Courts*, 51 Me. L. Rev. 18, 19 (1999).

[4] This book is meant to advise on methods of brief-writing and oral argument. For advice on preserving issues for appeal and deciding whether to appeal, you may want to consult a reference geared to the jurisdiction in which you are practicing. *See, e.g.*, Ulrich, Kessler & Anger, P.C. and Sidley & Austin, *Federal Appellate Practice: Ninth Circuit* (2d ed. 1999); G. Ronald Darlington, Kevin J. McKeon, Daniel R. Schuckers & Kristen W. Brown, *Pennsylvania Appellate Practice* Lawyers Co-op, (2d ed. 1995).

a document that can be understood by a busy reader the first time through without reference to outside sources.

1.3
FOLLOW AN EFFECTIVE WRITING PROCESS

Because your reader is so busy, you should base your brief-writing decisions on these four policies:

(1) The *law* upon which you base your argument should be complete and accurate. No judge wants to waste time considering arguments that must be rejected. Furthermore, if you have failed to identify a significant legal authority or an important legal, ethical, or policy argument, you should presume that no one else will dig it up either.

(2) Your arguments must be *organized and written* in a way that makes them easy to read and understand. Write with your reader in mind, and presume that your reader is intelligent but ignorant of the specifics of your case. If your point can't be understood without a struggle, it probably won't be understood at all.

(3) You must avoid *mechanical* problems of all types. First, follow the local rules of the court about format requirements and other ancillary matters. In some courts, failure to follow the rules will get a case dismissed; in others, it may result in your brief being returned to you so that you can try again to comply with the rules. Even if you escape these sanctions, you hurt your credibility with the court when you make technical mistakes.[5] Second, proofread carefully to avoid typographical errors, citation form errors, and mistakes in citations (e.g., transposed page numbers). While these errors may not seem legally significant, they waste time and hence annoy the reader.

(4) You should use *persuasive techniques* that make the most of your facts and your arguments but that do not violate ethical rules or otherwise hamper your credibility with the court. If your persuasive methods go too far, all of the work you have devoted to writing a legally valid, well-organized, and error-free document will be wasted. The court may well discount your arguments, or even stop reading your brief, if it believes that you cannot be trusted.

Not coincidentally, these four policies represent four different focuses in the writing process. It is impossible to make each of these focuses totally separate. For example, you cannot help but notice your content while you are reviewing your organization. By forcing yourself to pay special attention to each of these areas, however, you make it easier to create an effective brief.

---

[5] *See generally* Judith D. Fischer, *Bareheaded and Barefaced Counsel: Courts React to Unprofessionalism in Lawyers' Papers*, 31 Suffolk Univ. L. Rev. 1, 20-36 (1997).

1.4
How to Use This Book

In this book, you will learn about techniques that will help you to advance each of the policies noted above and thus to write a better appellate brief. (If you have never seen an appellate brief before, you may want to turn briefly to Appendix C to see what a complete appellate brief looks like.) Although you are writing with the complete end product in mind, your end product will usually be better if you follow a writing process that focuses your attention on only one task at a time.

As you begin your writing process, focus your attention on gaining an understanding of the legal issues that your case presents and of the legal authorities that govern those issues. Get to know the facts of the case, and plan and execute your research. Chapter Three will give you advice on getting to know your record and planning your research.

When your research is fairly complete, focus your attention on how to structure your argument. You might even write a rough draft of your argument as a method of trying to understand how the law and the facts relate. After you have gained an understanding of how the legal issues of your case relate to the legal authorities, use the rewriting stage of the writing process to think about how best to organize the document so that your reader will be able to understand the legal issues as well as you do. You can do this by writing a draft of just the argument section of the document that (1) uses the arguments and authorities that you think are necessary, (2) uses an effective large-scale organization, and (3) includes a full analysis of each legal issue. Because this type of draft is focused on "large-scale" concerns, you may wish to think of it as a "macro draft." Chapters Four and Five will help you as you rough out your argument and plan its structure.

After you have created a macro draft of some kind, review and revise your written argument a few times, focusing on these two important features of content and organization. Check your authorities and supplement your research if necessary. Eliminate weak arguments, and devote your attention to the strong ones. Make sure that each section of the argument is focused on just one point. Chapter Six will help you to examine your use of authority, while Chapter Seven will help you to review your argument for focus and completeness.

Next, create a draft of the entire document, including everything from the cover page to the certificate of service. Because this type of draft broadens its focus to include smaller-scale concerns, you may wish to think of it as a "micro draft." Chapter Eight identifies and describes the format requirements that are common to most appellate briefs.

After you have created your micro draft, review the way that you have presented your arguments. For example, make sure that you have laid out your arguments clearly and organized them well. Take a look at the signals you are sending to the reader through your headings, roadmaps, and topic sentences, and revise them as needed. Evaluate your statement of the case to verify that it presents the facts in a positive light without stretching the truth. Review each element of the brief in this way to make sure that you are presenting an accurate and effective legal argument. Chapter Ten will help you to make your document more reader-friendly, while Chapters Nine and Eleven will help you to use persuasive writing techniques both in the argument and in those "special" elements such as the question presented, statement of the case, and the summary of the argument.

In the polishing stage of the writing process, pay attention to sentence structure, grammar, citation form, and format details so that you create a final draft that is complete, well-structured, and free from distracting technical errors. Chapter Twelve will give you guidance on objective techniques you can use to make your document error-free.

Even before you are finished writing the brief, you should be considering the oral argument. Of course, the brief will in large measure dictate the oral argument, but a practice oral argument can help you write your brief. You may want to hold a "moot court" while you are still writing the brief, perhaps even while you are working on the first draft of your argument. Preparing for an oral as opposed to a written presentation will force you to confront your issues and arguments from a different point of view. As you argue, you may realize the strengths of certain arguments and the weaknesses of others. The process can result in significant substantive or structural changes in your written product. Chapter Thirteen gives you advice on preparing an effective oral argument; Chapter Fourteen addresses using oral argument and brief-writing skills in Moot Court competitions.

As you work on all of these tasks, you might keep in mind one of Aesop's lesser-known fables about an argument between the sun and the wind:

> The Wind and the Sun were disputing which was the stronger. Suddenly they saw a traveler coming down the road, and the Sun said: "I see a way to decide our dispute. Whichever of us can cause that traveler to take off his cloak shall be regarded as the stronger. You begin." So the Sun retired behind a cloud, and the Wind began to blow as hard as it could upon the traveler. But the harder he blew the more closely did the traveler wrap his cloak round him, till at last the Wind had to give up in despair. Then the Sun came out and shone in all his glory upon the traveler, who, finding it too hot to walk with his cloak on, soon took it off.

The moral of this fable is that "Kindness effects more than severity,"[6] or to put it another way, "you catch more flies with honey than with vinegar." Like the sun and the wind, you are trying to get someone to do something when you act as an appellate advocate. To be most effective as

---

[6] *See http://www.pacificnet.net/~johnr/aesop/*, visited on February 10, 2001.

an advocate, however, you must be both the sun *and* the wind. As the wind, you use the law and the facts to show the court that it *must* reach a decision in your client's favor. As the sun, you use persuasive writing techniques to help the court realize that it *wants* to reach that decision.

1.5
SUMMARY

No process can guarantee a perfect result, but it is practical to use a process that requires you to focus your attention on certain aspects of the document at the appropriate time. Just as you would probably not paint the trim of a house before deciding what color to paint the walls, you should not fuss with grammar problems and format concerns before you have decided which authorities and arguments will be most effective in your case. By following an effective writing process, you help to ensure that — given the inevitable limitations of the law, the facts, and the deadlines — you will submit the best possible brief that you can.

CHAPTER TWO

APPELLATE JURISDICTION AND STANDARDS OF REVIEW

Understanding some basic principles about the various courts of appeals and their powers will help you to make decisions as you prepare your written and oral arguments. Your arguments will be different if you are writing to an intermediate court of appeals as opposed to a court of last resort. Intermediate courts of appeals must hear every appeal (with few exceptions)[1] and must follow the decisions of the courts above them. Courts of last resort, on the other hand, usually have the authority to decide which cases they will hear[2] and the authority to make new law. In addition to considering the type of court that is hearing the argument, you must also know and understand the standards of review that a court applies to different types of decisions under its review.

---

[1] *See, e.g.,* Ohio Rules of Appellate Procedure, Title II, Rule 3; Federal Rules of Appellate Procedure, Rule 3.

[2] *See, e.g.,* Ohio S. Ct. Prac., Rule II, § 1 (listing "appeals as of right," "claimed appeals as of right," "discretionary appeals," and "certified conflict cases"). *See also* Rules of the United States Supreme Court, Rule 10.

2.1
JURISDICTION IN COURTS OF LAST RESORT

A "court of last resort" is the highest court in a particular legal system. It is the last court to which plaintiffs or defendants can resort when seeking resolution of a legal issue. In the federal system, the United States Supreme Court is the court of last resort, and the vast majority of its cases come from the United States Courts of Appeals of the various circuits. In state systems, the highest court of appeals — often called the "Supreme Court" — is the court of last resort. Generally, the United States Supreme Court will hear appeals from state courts of last resort only if the issue is a matter of federal law. For example, the Court may hear an appeal in order to determine whether the state court has interpreted a federal law or state law in a way that may have conflicted with the United States Constitution.

Most courts of last resort are not merely courts of error; that is, they do not take cases simply because one party claims that there was an error of law in a lower court decision. For example, Rule 10 of the Rules of the Supreme Court of the United States explicitly says that "[a] petition for a writ of certiorari [the main method for gaining access to the Court] is rarely granted when the asserted error consists of erroneous factual findings or the misapplication of a properly stated rule of law." Instead, a Court of last resort takes cases in order to resolve pressing issues, and it may refuse to take cases unless or until it believes that its intervention is necessary.[3] Two factors make it more likely that the Court will grant a petition for a writ of certiorari. First, the Court frequently grants certiorari if a state court or a lower federal court of appeals is misinterpreting or misapplying the Court's jurisprudence. Second, and more commonly, the Court will grant certiorari when two courts are in conflict over an interpretation of the federal constitution, or when two federal courts are in conflict over any question of federal law.[4]

Interestingly, the Court does not always grant certiorari immediately when either of these factors is present. It is not uncommon for the Court to let a conflict simmer for a few years, with many different lower courts writing decisions either way. The Court may use this method purposefully, to benefit from the analysis and reasoning of several different lower courts. By allowing several opinions to be written on a subject, the Court can assess several different resolutions and analyses of the same issue.

---

[3] The Ohio Supreme Court, for example, distinguishes between "claimed appeals as of right" and "discretionary appeals." Ohio S. Ct. Prac., Rule II, § 1. It then decides whether to grant each type of appeal, depending on whether the appeal meets the court's standards, e.g., whether the appeal involves any "substantial constitutional question" (one standard for claimed appeals as of right) or asserts a "question of public or great general interest" (one standard for discretionary appeals). Ohio S. Ct. Prac., Rule III, § 6.

[4] *See generally* Rules of the Supreme Court of the United States, Rule 10.

Perhaps for these reasons, the Court attaches no precedential value to the denial of a petition for a writ of certiorari. That is, a denial of certiorari does *not* indicate that the Court approves of the decision below. Rather, it means only that the Court did not believe, for whatever reason, that it was a case that was worthy of its review *at that time*.

2.2
JURISDICTION IN INTERMEDIATE COURTS OF APPEALS

The rules are somewhat different in intermediate courts of appeals. Generally, state and federal intermediate courts of appeals will hear any appeal *of a final order* if the appellant has met specified procedural guidelines.[5] The United States Courts of Appeals have jurisdiction over appeals from all final decisions of the United States District Courts.[6] The Courts of Appeals also have jurisdiction to hear appeals from a variety of other judicial and quasi-judicial bodies, including, for example, appeals to enforce or challenge orders of the National Labor Relations Board.[7]

Federal Intermediate Courts of Appeals have and exercise the discretion to decide cases without oral argument. Although, according to the rules, oral argument is presumed, a three-judge panel can vote unanimously that oral argument is unnecessary in a given case for any of the following three reasons:

(A) the appeal is frivolous;

(B) the dispositive issue or issues have been authoritatively decided; or

(C) the facts and legal arguments are adequately presented in the briefs and record, and the decisional process would not be significantly aided by oral argument.[8]

What this rule means in practice is that a large percentage of cases is assigned to the so-called Summary Docket, and many of those are decided based on memoranda submitted by law clerks and staff attorneys who have reviewed the party briefs. The Courts' statistics indicate that in 2000, a typical year, almost 65 percent of the appeals terminated on the merits

---

[5] *See, e.g.*, Ohio Rules of Appellate Procedure, Title II, Rule 3; Federal Rules of Appellate Procedure, Rule 3. Appeals of interlocutory orders and certain criminal appeals may have to meet different standards. *See, e.g.*, Ohio Rules of Appellate Procedure, Title II, Rule 5; Federal Rules of Appellate Procedure, Rule 5, regarding "appeal by permission." Generally, federal courts of appeals have full discretion whether to hear interlocutory appeals. *See Coopers & Lybrand v. Livesay*, 437 U.S. 463, 475 (1978).

[6] 28 U.S.C. § 1291.

[7] 29 U.S.C. § 160 (e), (f).

[8] Federal Rules of Appellate Procedure, Rule 34(a)(2).

were decided without oral argument.[9] When cases are on the summary docket, some judges make their decisions based on staff memoranda and may not read the briefs in full at all. Thus, your first goal as a writer may be to write a brief that will convince the judges' clerk that your case is worth hearing.

2.3
APPELLATE STANDARDS OF REVIEW

Whether a court is an intermediate court of appeals or a court of last resort, whether it hears an appeal as of right or as a matter of discretion, it agrees only to *review* the decision below. Hearing an appeal does not mean that the court will re-try the case. Instead of observing the examination and cross-examination of witnesses, hearing opening and closing arguments, and seeing the attorneys present various evidentiary exhibits all over again, the court *reviews* important evidence (whether findings of fact, testimony, or exhibits) and the attorneys' written arguments — in the form of briefs to the court — about the significance of that evidence. During the oral argument on appeal (if any), the court questions the attorneys about the sufficiency of the evidence, the significance of the arguments, or the impact of a holding one way or the other. The court then decides whether to affirm, to reverse, to reverse and remand, or to vacate the decision below.

When reviewing the decision of any lower court, the court — explicitly or implicitly — applies a certain appellate standard of review to that decision. The *appellate standard of review*[10] is a label that a reviewing court puts on the level of **deference** it gives to the findings of the court below. The appellate standard of review tells the court how "wrong" the lower court has to be before it will be reversed.

The appellate standard of review that the court will choose to apply depends on which aspect of the case is under review: an evidentiary ruling, a finding of fact, a legal ruling, or some other type of decision. Some decisions can be reversed simply if the reviewing court disagrees with the lower court. Others can be reversed only if the reviewing court can identify a serious error on the part of the court below. Generally, courts give high deference to decisions about facts — that is, they are loathe to upset a finding of fact — and low deference to conclusions of law.

---

[9] Federal Judicial Center, *U.S. Courts of Appeals — Appeals Terminated on the Merits After Oral Hearings or Submission on Briefs during the 12-month period ending September 30, 2000, http://www.uscourts.gov/judbus2000/tables/s01sep00.pdf* Table (accessed August 21, 2001); *See also* Patricia M. Wald, *19 Tips from 19 Years on the Appellate Bench,* 1 J. App. Prac. & Proc. 7, 9 (1999) (Estimating that 60 percent of cases nationwide are decided without oral argument).

[10] For the sake of clarity, I have used the label *appellate standards of review* to refer to these standards. However, as I note below, courts use the label *Standard of Review* to refer to appellate standards of review, government action standards of review, and motion standards of review.

Because the particular appellate standard of review can significantly affect the arguments that you make to the court, you should consider this issue early in your research process and decide what standard the court is likely to apply to the decision you seek to have reversed, or hope to have affirmed.

2.3.1
PURPOSE AND MEANING OF APPELLATE STANDARDS OF REVIEW

Various public policies support the competing appellate standards of review.[11] Courts use a low deference appellate standard of review for decisions about the law because they believe that those who must use the law benefit from uniformity.[12] Low deference standards give reviewing courts an opportunity to create a consistent body of law, which may be particularly important for issues of constitutional rights.[13]

A high-deference appellate standard of review, on the other hand, promotes judicial economy and finality of certain types of decisions. A single case may contain many different types of decisions, such as the denial of a motion to suppress, the overruling of an objection, or a decision that a defendant is liable to a plaintiff. If each one of these decisions had a good chance of being reversed, then every little decision would be appealed and the already-burdened court system would become even more so.

A high-deference standard is also based on the premise that the trial court is in the best position to understand evidence. Particularly in the case of witness testimony, a trial court judge or jury has an opportunity that the court of appeals doesn't have. The judge or jury can observe the witnesses' demeanor, their tone of voice, and body language, and use its best judgment based on those intangibles when it makes findings of fact.

Although many advocates ignore the standard after (or even instead of) articulating it, the appellate standard of review is really the context within which the entire argument rests. Because there is often no controversy about which standard applies, some litigators are lulled into complacency on this subject and may miss fertile ground for legal argument.[14]

---

[11] For an interesting discussion of the policies behind certain appellate standards of review, *see* Michael R. Bosse, *Standards of Review: The Meaning of Words,* 49 Me. L. Rev. 367, 374-84 (1997).

[12] *See, e.g., Ornelas v. United States,* 517 U.S. 690, 698 (1996).

[13] *See generally* Bosse, *supra* note 11, at 383, 397.

[14] The appropriate appellate standard of review for significant legal issues was a factor in a recent United States Supreme Court decision, *Ornelas v. United States,* 517 U.S. 690 (1996) (holding that determinations of "reasonable suspicion" and "probable cause" should be reviewed de novo by appellate courts). *See also Koon v. United States,* 518 U.S. 81 (1996) (holding that appellate court should apply abuse of discretion standard to trial court's decision about application of federal sentencing guidelines). The standard of review was also famously debated in *Bose Corp. v. Consumers Union of United States, Inc.,* 466 U.S. 485 (1984) (de novo review appropriate in case in which court was bound to make an independent review of the record), and in *Miller v. Fenton,* 474 U.S. 104 (1985) (holding that issue of voluntariness of a confession is not a finding of fact). *See generally Bosse, supra* note 11, at 374-84 (discussing *Ornelas, Bose Corp.,* and *Miller*) and Kelly

As a practical lawyer, you should devote serious attention to the appellate standard of review early in the research process in order to determine whether it will be a significant factor in your case. The discussion that follows describes the most significant appellate standards of review, using the labels most commonly used in federal courts. Although, of course, you must rely on research rather than a textbook to provide support for any appellate standard of review argument, the state courts apply standards that are similar to the federal standards.

a. Clearly Erroneous

A **clearly erroneous** standard applies to findings of facts. Rule 52(a) of the Federal Rules of Civil Procedure provides: "Findings of Fact, whether based on oral or documentary evidence, shall not be set aside unless clearly erroneous, and due regard shall be given to the opportunity of the trial court to judge the credibility of the witnesses." This standard reflects the attitude that the fact-finder is often in the best position to observe the presentation of the facts. The United States Supreme Court has commented on the importance of the trial judge's opportunities:

> The rationale for deference to the original finder of fact is not limited to the superiority of the trial judge's position to make determinations of credibility. The trial judge's major role is the determination of fact, and with experience in fulfilling that role comes expertise. . . . [T]he trial on the merits should be "the 'main event' . . . rather than a 'tryout on the road.' " . . . When findings are based on determinations regarding the credibility of witnesses, Rule 52(a) demands even greater deference to the trial court's findings; for only the trial judge can be aware of the variations in demeanor and tone of voice that bear so heavily on the listener's understanding of and belief in what is said.[15]

The clearly erroneous standard is a high hurdle for the petitioner or appellant to overcome. The Seventh Circuit has observed:

> [t]o be clearly erroneous, a decision must strike us as more than just maybe or probably wrong; it must, as one member of this court recently stated during oral argument, strike us as wrong with the force of a five-week-old, unrefrigerated dead fish.[16]

Although not all courts use such vivid language to describe their reactions, all courts are extremely hesitant to overturn findings of fact.[17]

Kunsch, *Standard of Review (State and Federal): A Primer*, 18 Seattle U.L. Rev. 11, 25 (1994) (discussing *Bose*).

[15] *Anderson v. City of Bessemer City*, 470 U.S. 564, 574, 575 (1985).

[16] *Parts & Elec. Motors, Inc. v. Sterling Electric Inc.*, 866 F.2d 228, 233 (7th Cir. 1988).

[17] Note that all federal (and most state) jury findings, which may be hard to separate into separate questions of law and fact, are usually reviewed under the "substantial evidence" standard per the Seventh Amendment to the United States Constitution, which provides that "no fact tried by a jury shall be otherwise re-examined in any Court of the United States, than according to the rules of the common law." Those "rules of the common law" generally provide that such a finding must only have a "reasonable basis in the law" and have "warrant in the record." *NLRB v. Hearst Publications*, 322 U.S. 111, 131 (1944). Commentators have noted that courts are extremely reluctant to find that there is not "substantial evidence" to support a jury finding. Kunsch, *supra* note 14, at 43.

b. De Novo

Because most decisions that come before appellate courts are based on questions of law, the most commonly applied standard is the **de novo** standard. The de novo standard is a low-deference standard — or, more aptly, a no-deference standard — that applies when courts are reviewing the meaning or application of the controlling law. De novo review is sometimes referred to as "plenary review," no doubt because it allows the court to give a full, or plenary, review to the findings below. When courts apply the de novo standard, they look at the legal questions as if no one had as yet decided them, giving no deference to any findings made below. When this standard is applied, the reviewing court *is* willing to substitute its judgment for that of the trial court or the intermediate court of appeals.

Courts apply the de novo standard not only to questions of law, but also to mixed questions of law and fact. A mixed question of law and fact is often characterized as a question about whether certain agreed-upon facts meet a legal standard. In *Ornelas v. United States*, for example, the United States Supreme Court decided that de novo was an appropriate appellate standard of review when it reviewed a trial court's determination as to whether a police officer had indeed had probable cause based on the undisputed facts.[18] The Court justifies the de novo standard in mixed question situations, as it does when it reviews other questions of law, with the goal of unifying precedent and stabilizing legal principles.[19]

Because the de novo standard is so common, appellate advocates must recognize that the legal findings of the courts below have *no weight* other than their intrinsic validity. Thus, it is illogical to justify a conclusion that you want the appellate court to accept by citing to the case that is being appealed. You may appropriately argue that the decision below is correct, but you must support that assertion with citations to other authorities that the appellate court may find to be valid.

c. Abuse of Discretion

The **abuse of discretion** standard is typically used to review a judge's procedural rulings during a trial and other discretionary decisions. These decisions might include decisions on motions, objections, admissibility of evidence, or general conduct issues.[20] Commentators have noted that language such as "the court may" or "for good cause" are often predictors of an abuse of discretion standard of review.[21] Like the clearly erroneous standard, this standard presumes some expertise on the part of the trial court judge. Some judges see the standard in the same light as the clearly erroneous standard. For example, the United States Court of Appeals for the First Circuit has noted that, as to evidentiary rulings, "[o]nly

---

[18] *Ornelas, supra* note 12, at 695.
[19] *See generally id.* at 697.
[20] *See, e.g.,* Kunsch, *supra* note 14, at 34-5.
[21] Kunsch, *supra* note 14, at 35 (citing Maurice Rosenberg, *Judicial Discretion of the Trial Court, Viewed from Above,* 22 Syracuse L. Rev. 635, 655 (1971)).

rarely — and in extraordinarily compelling circumstances — will we, from the vista of a cold appellate record, reverse a district court's on-the-spot judgment concerning the relative weighing of probative value and unfair effect."[22]

d. Other Standards

Review of administrative agencies decisions is governed by the Administrative Procedure Act, which distinguishes between informal agency actions (reviewed under the **arbitrary and capricious** standard) and formal, "record-producing" agency actions (reviewed under the **substantial evidence** standard).[23]

2.3.2
IDENTIFYING THE APPROPRIATE APPELLATE STANDARD OF REVIEW

Of course, knowing the standards is only the first step. You must then decide which standard or standards apply in your case. Some issues are obviously questions of fact (e.g., Did the defendant hit the victim? Did the officer ask a certain question of the defendant?), while others are obviously questions of law (e.g., Did the court apply the correct legal standard? Is a supervisor an "employer" under the terms of the statute?). Mixed questions are more difficult to identify; courts generally identify a mixed question of law and fact as one that is based on how a legal principle applies to established or agreed-upon facts.

Using one standard over another — for example, a clearly erroneous appellate standard of review rather than a de novo standard — can lead to a vastly different review of the same case. Accordingly, you should study the record below carefully. Identify the decisions, rulings, and/or findings that are at the crux of your client's case. First, identify who made the ruling. The standard of review may vary if the decision maker was a judge, a jury, or an administrative body. Second, focus on what kind of decision was made. If it was a ruling on an evidentiary matter, the abuse of discretion standard will apply. If it was a finding of fact, the court will apply the clearly erroneous standard. If, as is most likely, it was a decision of law, the court will apply a de novo standard when it reviews the decision below. If you are arguing to a court of last resort, you may look to the court of appeals decision to see what appellate standard of review it applied. If no standard is mentioned in the decision (and the standard is often not mentioned), the court probably applied a de novo standard. Of course, you need not accept as correct the court's decision as to the appellate standard of review.[24]

---

[22] *Freeman v. Package Mach. Co.*, 865 F.2d 1331, 1340 (1st Cir. 1988).

[23] *See, e.g.,* Kunsch, *supra* note 14, at 40-1.

[24] *See generally Ornelas, supra* n.12, at 698-99 (noting that the court below erred when it applied a deferential appellate standard of review).

If you are in doubt as to the appropriate standard of review for the legal issue your case presents, do a little research. You may find precedent as to the standard of review for the narrow legal issue in your case. In addition to conducting primary research, you may find secondary sources helpful as well. Many "practice manuals" are geared to attorneys practicing within the courts of a specific jurisdiction; some of these address appellate standards of review as they apply to particular legal issues.[25] Although the appellate standard of review is usually not controversial, at times it is at the heart of the appellate decision.[26]

If the standard of review in your case is de novo, it will have almost no impact on your argument. You will address the standard of review — either in the introductory section or in a separate, labeled section — and then you will spend the rest of the argument discussing the appropriate legal standards and how the appellate court should apply those standards.

If your case could or should be reviewed with a more deferential standard, however, that standard will have a significant impact on your argument. Even if the court you are writing to asks for the standard to be announced in a separate section, you must still incorporate it into your argument. For example, if the clearly erroneous standard applies, your argument must identify the particular finding of fact that you assert to be clearly erroneous, and cite to the record. Then, you must show how the evidence indicates that the finding was clearly erroneous, and show how it changed the outcome of the case. Alternatively, if you must assert that the judge abused his or her discretion, you must identify the particular decision the judge made in error, why it was wrong, and why it changed the outcome of the case.

As you must with any legal argument, make appellate standard of review arguments honestly. Do not create an appellate standard of review issue where none exists. If the standard genuinely makes a difference in the case, however, you can and should use it to demonstrate the justice of the result you seek.

2.3.3
FORMAT CONSIDERATIONS

During recent years, many courts have begun using their local rules to ask for a separate statement of the appellate standard of review. The local rules of the Third Circuit, for example, require a formal statement of the "standard or scope of review" to appear "under a separate heading placed before the discussion of the issue in the argument section."[27] If the

---

[25] *See, e.g., Sixth Circuit Federal Practice Manual* 34-68 (2d ed. 1999).

[26] For an interesting discussion of using policy concerns to drive the discussion of appellate standard of review, see Bosse, *supra* note 11, at 374 et seq. If the appropriate appellate standard of review is controversial, you can and should justify your argument with references to policies served by choosing the standard you favor.

[27] 3d Cir. LAR [Local Appellate Rule] 28.1(b) (1997).

local rules do not demand a separate statement, the standard should usually be included in introductory material within the argument. No matter what method is used, you should cite to authority for the standard of review, just as you would for any legal proposition.

In most situations, the statement of the appellate standard of review requires no more than a paragraph. If the standard is controversial, however, or if it is otherwise significant to the attorney's argument, it should be treated like any other major issue, with appropriate point headings and text used to make the point. This method should be used even if the local rules require a separate, formal statement of the standard.

2.3.4
AVOIDING CONFUSION

Unfortunately, courts do not always use the term *standard of review* precisely. Although I have used the phrase *appellate standard of review* throughout this text, courts often use the phrase *standard of review* to mean the same thing — and to mean other things. Besides its use to refer to appellate standards of review, courts commonly use the phrase *standard of review* in two other contexts: (1) to describe the level of scrutiny that a court may use to review the constitutionality of a state statute or other government action, and (2) to describe the standard that a court uses when deciding whether to grant or deny a motion to dismiss or a motion for summary judgment.

The easiest way to keep the standards straight is to remember that only appellate courts use appellate standards of review. However, because all three types of standards may be used in appellate advocacy, you should understand all three uses of the term.

a. Standards for Reviewing the Constitutionality of Government Action

Courts usually use the phrase *standard of review* to describe the standard that a court will use to review the constitutionality of a state statute or other government action. Some actions will be reviewed under a "strict scrutiny" standard, while others will be reviewed under a "rational basis" standard. Although strict scrutiny and rational basis are *standards*, and they are used to *review*, they are not the same thing as appellate standards of review.

All types of courts, from the trial court on up through the United States Supreme Court, may use a strict scrutiny or rational basis standard to review the constitutionality of a government action. Thus, if your client's case involves the constitutionality of a government action, your argument may include a reference to this "level of scrutiny" or *"government action* standard of review," as well as to the appellate standard of review.

b. Standards for Deciding to Grant or Deny Certain Motions

In addition, the term *standard of review* is frequently used when describing the court's analysis of the validity of certain motions. The standard of review for a motion to dismiss, for example, has been articulated as follows:

> A motion to dismiss for failure to state a claim pursuant to Rule 12(b)(6) should be granted only if it "appears beyond doubt that the plaintiff can prove no set of facts in support of his claim that would entitle him to relief." *Cooper v. Parsky*, 140 F.3d 433, 440 (2d Cir. 1998) (quoting *Conley v. Gibson*, 355 U.S. 41, 45-46, 78 S. Ct. 99, 102, 2 L. Ed. 2d 80 (1957)). The factual allegations set forth in the complaint must be accepted as true, *see Zinermon v. Burch*, 494 U.S. 113, 118, 110 S. Ct. 975, 979, 108 L. Ed. 2d 100 (1990), and the court must draw all reasonable inferences in favor of plaintiff.[28]

The standard for a motion for summary judgment under Federal Rule of Civil Procedure 56(c), on the other hand, requires the court to grant the motion only when there is no genuine issue as to any material fact and when the moving party is entitled to judgment as a matter of law.[29]

Because motions to dismiss and motions for summary judgment are made at the trial court level, it is obvious that trial courts may use these standards. However, an appellate court may *also* have to apply one of these standards. For example, if a trial court grants a motion to dismiss and that decision is appealed, the appellate court must analyze whether the trial court applied the motion standard of review properly, and it would therefore have to use that standard in its analysis.

Although the use of the same term for three different meanings may be confusing, keep the distinguishing factors in mind: (1) Trial courts may **not** use appellate standards of review. *Only courts of appeals* may use appellate standards of review when they review *lower court decisions*; (2) *Any* court (trial or appellate) may use a *government action* standard of review to review *actions by governmental entities*; (3) *Any* court (trial or appellate) can use a *motion* standard of review to decide or review the validity of a decision on a *motion*.

Just to make things interesting, it is entirely possible for an appellate court to use all three types of standards of review in the same case. For example, if a trial court granted a motion for summary judgment in a case in which the constitutionality of a state statute was at issue, the appellate court would use a de novo appellate standard of review to analyze the two questions of law the case would present: (1) Did the trial court properly apply the proper legal standard to review the constitutionality of the

---

[28] *See generally In Re Motel 6 Securities Lit.* 93 Civ. 2183 (JFK) (S.D.N.Y. 2000) 2000 U.S. Dist. LEXIS 3824.
[29] *See generally Virginia Soc'y for Human Life, Inc. v. FEC*, 83 F. Supp. 2d 668, 671 (E.D. Va. 2000).

TYPE OF STANDARD OF REVIEW:	MOTION STANDARD OF REVIEW	GOVERNMENT ACTION STANDARD OF REVIEW	APPELLATE STANDARD OF REVIEW
Type of court that may use this standard:	Trial Court Intermediate Court of Appeals Court of Last Report	Trial Court Intermediate Court of Appeals Court of Last Report	Intermediate Court of Appeals Court of Last Report
Example(s) of this type of standard:	"Plaintiff wins unless he or she can prove no set of facts that will entitle him or her to relief"	"Strict Scrutiny" "Heightened Scrutiny" "Rational Basis"	"No Novo" "Clearly Erroneous" "Abuse of Discretion"
What the court uses this standard to decide:	Whether it's appropriate to grant or deny a **motion**	Whether certain **government action** is constitutional	Whether to affirm, reverse, or vacate a **decision** of a court below

government action at issue? (2) Did the trial court properly apply the proper legal standard for a summary judgment motion?

2.4
SUMMARY

The type of court that hears your case, and the standard of review that court applies, can make a significant difference in the way that you structure your arguments. You do not have to decide whether your case is heard by an intermediate court of appeals or a court of last resort — that decision is made for you. While you will not decide what the standard of additional review *is* — that decision is up to the court — you *will* decide what the standard *should be*, and you must keep that standard in mind as you conduct the rest of your research and write your brief. It is likely that most of the appellate cases you argue will be reviewed under a de novo standard. But do not make this decision on automatic pilot. Carefully consider the record, the issues, and the relevant appellate standards of review so that you can make an informed decision about which standard applies to your case.

CHAPTER THREE

BEFORE YOU WRITE

3.1 Creating an Abstract of the Record
3.2 Planning Your Research
  3.2.1 Begin at the Beginning: Decide What Questions You Need to Answer
  3.2.2 Broadening Your Horizons (You *Can* Compare Apples and Oranges)
  3.2.3 The Abstraction Ladder
  3.2.4 Using the Abstraction Ladder in Legal Research
  3.2.5 Identifying Valid Authority
    a. Relevant Facts
    b. Relevant Legal Issues
    c. Relevant Sources
      i. Legal Sources
      ii. "Extra-Legal" Sources
  3.2.6 Using What You Already Know
  3.2.7 Knowing When to Stop
3.3 Summary

Naturally, you would not expect to be able to receive an appellate brief assignment and immediately begin to draft the brief. Nor should you expect that you can immediately go to the library and begin your legal research. Just as you plan before you write by conducting legal research and by outlining, you must also plan before you begin your formal legal research. The first step is to become thoroughly familiar with the facts of the case and the issues that the case presents. Next, decide what questions you need to answer and what types of authorities are best suited to provide those answers. You need not always restrict your research to cases and statutes. Sometimes, courts can be effectively persuaded by reference to "extra-legal" authorities.

3.1
CREATING AN ABSTRACT OF THE RECORD

The first thing you should do as you prepare to write an appellate brief is to get to know the case to which you have been assigned. Although as a lawyer you may well have worked on the case since it began, in law school (and sometimes in real life) you are coming in at the middle. Your job now is to get to know the facts and the procedure as if they had happened to you. Thus, you should carefully study the "record" of the case. The record can consist of many different elements, depending on the case. These elements will always include the decision(s) below; they may also include transcripts of trial testimony, reproductions of exhibits or other evidence offered at trial, transcripts of depositions, and other items.

Many appellate courts either require or allow a joint appendix prepared by the petitioner and perhaps supplemented by the respondent. The joint appendix is a printed document that includes record elements that one or both of the parties would like the appellate court to have before it while the court is making its decision. Technically, the joint appendix does not take the place of the record: The court may always refer to the complete record if it wishes. As a practical matter, however, most judges do not go beyond the joint appendix when reviewing decisions below. You should certainly plan the joint appendix and, later, write your brief, as if the joint appendix *is* the entire universe of information to which the judges will refer.

The joint appendix always contains certain procedural information; it also contains information that one or both of the parties believes is relevant to the appeal. For example, United States Supreme Court Rule 26.1 provides:

> The joint appendix shall contain: (1) the relevant docket entries in all the courts below; (2) any relevant pleadings, jury instructions, findings, conclusions, or opinions; (3) the judgment, order, or decision under review; and (4) any other parts of the record that the parties wish to bring to the Court's attention.

Thus, the joint appendix may contain the text of the decisions below (particularly unpublished decisions), excerpts of trial testimony, excerpts of other documents submitted into evidence (e.g., depositions), or reproductions of exhibits used in the case. The joint appendix can therefore give the court access to sufficient knowledge about the case without forcing the judges to wade through an enormous record.

If you are at the intermediate level, you may be creating the joint appendix as you work on your brief. If you are arguing to a court of last resort, you may be able to start from a joint appendix that was created for the intermediate court.

Whether your record is a joint appendix, a "raw" record and opinions below, or just the opinions below, your job at this early stage of the writing process is to identify the important facts of the case. One of the best ways to organize this process is to create an abstract of your record. An *abstract* in this sense is a referenced summary of the information contained in the record. The purpose of an abstract is to help the lawyer — or whoever is working on the case — to easily find important information from the record throughout the writing process.

Even though a joint appendix itself usually consists of excerpted information, it may be lengthy. Reading the joint appendix and the decisions below carefully a few times and creating a good abstract will enable you to learn more about your case now and to find important information in the record while you are conducting legal research or writing the brief.

Like conducting legal research, preparing an abstract is often a recursive process. It is difficult to understand the significance of the case's facts until you know what law applies to the case, but it's difficult to understand the significance of the law of the case until you know the facts. Therefore, as preparation for creating an abstract, read over the lower court opinions first to familiarize yourself with the major issues that the case presents. Then, read through any other materials two or three times. You may wish to abstract information as you go through it each time, or you may wish to wait until you have read the document through once before you begin to abstract the details that you think are important. After you abstract the information in the joint appendix, reread the opinions below at least twice to abstract the information and arguments contained in them.

To create the actual abstract, make a chart — either on paper or on the word processor — and summarize the important information found in each part of the record or joint appendix as you read through it. Some things to look for and to record:

1. Page cites for positive facts, testimony, and other evidence
2. Page cites for negative facts, testimony, and other evidence
3. Page cites for segments of the appendix (e.g., each separate pleading or other type of document); If a formal joint appendix has been created, this information may appear in its table of contents
4. Page cites for evidence that establishes needed elements of the crime or cause of action
5. Page cites for findings of fact in the opinions below
6. Page cites for legal findings in the opinions below
7. Page cites for major arguments that each side has made below
8. Page cites for concessions that either side has made below (e.g., in pleadings or in stipulations)
9. Page cites for information that may support any policy arguments you plan to make
10. Page cites for any information you think is important even if you are not yet sure why it is important[1]

A section of an abstract of the joint appendix in the case of *Adolph Coors Co. v. Bentsen* (later decided as *Rubin v. Coors Brewing Co.*, 514 U.S. 476 (1995)) might look like the example below. In that case, counsel for Coors was arguing that the First Amendment allowed beer manufacturers to

---

[1] *See generally* Michael R. Fontham, *Written and Oral Advocacy* 25-34 (1985) (discussing "preparing to write the brief").

print on beer labels the percentage of alcohol in the beer and that therefore the prohibition-era regulation that forbade this information was unconstitutional. The joint appendix was over 350 pages long and contained excerpts of various depositions as well as photographic reproductions of several trial exhibits.

In the excerpts below from two different parts of the abstract, the attorney has recorded the page number from the abstract in the left-hand column. In the right-hand column, the attorney has described the information that can be found on that page. The comments in brackets are what an attorney for Coors might write as a way of using the abstract to think about potential arguments in the case. When the attorney is actually writing the brief, he or she could scan through the abstract to find references to information that might be helpful; the attorney could then quickly find the appropriate page in the joint appendix or opinion below and find specific language, citations, or other information to include in the brief itself.

Excerpts from Abstract

PAGE #	INFORMATION
135	First page of Deposition of Timothy Ambler, Alcohol Mktg. expert from England.
139–40	Testimony re: mandatory disclosure of alcohol on beer labels in Britain and the European Community: [Any precedent for following international precedent?] . . . .
284	Plaintiff's Exh. 3A — Chart showing Alcohol % by weight of various beers [Use to show low range of variation among most beers?]
289	U.S. Dept. of HHS, Inspector General's survey on Youth and Alcohol: "Do they know what they're drinking?"
294	Survey findings: "⅔ students can't distinguish alcoholic beverages from non-alcoholic beverages" [use to show public benefit of putting alcohol percentage on the label?].

Creating an abstract may sometimes be time-consuming (especially if the record is long), but it can actually save time in the long run. The process of creating an abstract helps you get to know the realities of your case, lets you rely on recorded information instead of memory, and, during brief-writing, makes it easier for you to support your arguments with citations to the record.

3.2
PLANNING YOUR RESEARCH

3.2.1
BEGIN AT THE BEGINNING: DECIDE WHAT QUESTIONS YOU NEED TO ANSWER

Effective legal research begins before you go to the library or type in your computer-research password. Of course, when you write an appellate brief, you should follow the same research methods that are relevant to any type of legal research. Be thorough. Take good notes. Be sure to check the validity of your authorities. This section will address some basic methods of legal research and some methods that are particularly appropriate to researching appellate briefs.

A good method to use before starting to research any legal issue is to analyze the facts that you have at hand and begin to identify possible search words and possible legally significant categories.[2] Then, create "research questions" based on what you know about the case so far.

Like all statements of legal issues, your research questions should be focused on how the relevant law applies to the legally significant facts. A popular structure for these questions is the so-called Under-Does-When structure.[3] The "under" part of the question identifies the law that governs the legal issue, the "does" part identifies the narrow, yes-or-no legal question that you are trying to answer (whether it is about liability, guilt, or some other legal status or form of legal responsibility), and the "when" part identifies the legally significant facts that relate to the legal issue. Thus, a format for your research question is "Under [relevant law], does [legal status] exist when [legally significant facts] exist?"

Let's presume that you are conducting research on the *Coors* case. From reading the decisions below and the joint appendix, you know that this case is about the constitutionality of a federal statute that prohibits printing alcohol content information on beer labels. If that were all you knew, you'd have a pretty broad "under" clause:

Under the United States Constitution . . .

But of course, when you created your abstract, you read the lower court decisions, and so you know that this is a First Amendment case, and that

---

[2] *See, e.g.,* Mary Barnard Ray & Jill J. Ramsfield, *Legal Writing: Getting It Right and Getting It Written* 258-62 (2d ed. 1993) (citing Christopher Wren & Jill R. Wren, *The Legal Research Manual: A Game Plan for Legal Research and Analysis* (2d ed. 1986)).

[3] *See, e.g.,* Mary Barnard Ray & Jill J. Ramsfield, *Legal Writing: Getting It Right and Getting It Written* 243-44 (2d ed. 1993); Laurel Currie Oates, Anne M. Enquist, & Kelly Kunsch, *The Legal Writing Handbook* 118-23 (2d ed. 1998). Although your research questions may be similar in format to questions presented, you should not expect that your research questions will be identical to the formal question presented.

the issue is not a matter of political speech but of commercial speech. Thus, your "under" clause can be a little more focused:

> **Under the First Amendment's freedom of speech provisions as they pertain to commercial speech . . .**

The "does" part of the research question refers to the legal question that your research will answer. In this part of the question, you ask a yes-or-no question — which may or may not begin with the word "does" — that often focuses on the question that the case is about, as in the following example:

> **Is 27 U.S.C. § 205(e)(2) constitutional when . . .**

Of course, your reading of the arguments in the lower courts might lead you to address more narrow questions related to the then-existing commercial speech test, and thus you might try to articulate questions that reflect your current understanding of that test and of the relevant arguments, as in the following examples:

> **does prohibiting the printing of alcohol content information on a beer label sufficiently advance the government's interest in preventing strength wars when . . .**

> **does prohibiting the printing of alcohol content information on a beer label directly advance the government's interest in preventing consumers from having misleading information when . . .**

These core questions help you to focus your research merely by forcing you to articulate the narrow questions that your research is designed to answer.

In the "when" part of the question, you list the legally significant facts that you (or your opponent) will use to demonstrate that the legal issue should be resolved in a certain way. One caveat about the "facts" part of the research question — what is a "fact" in a legal question may vary from case to case. In a statutory analysis case like *Coors*, for example, some (or perhaps all) of your "facts" may consist of the requirements of the statute. For example, if your "does" element had asked merely "is 27 U.S.C. § 205(e)(2) constitutional?" then your "when" element should at least describe what the statute requires, as in the following example:

> **when the statute prohibits beer manufacturers from printing truthful alcohol content information on their beer labels**

If your "does" section had been more detailed, your "when" section might be written as follows, based on your predictions as to which pieces of evidence the Court would find to be most important:

> **when there is no evidence of strength wars in states or countries in which alcohol content information is allowed to be printed on beer labels**

> when it is now possible to accurately measure alcohol content in beer
> and thus the statute is preventing publication of truthful information

These details may or may not be important later, but right now the writer is using them to help plan the research for the case.

Of course, in a case in which statutory language is not at issue, your questions would be different. For example, in *State v. Knowles*, 569 N.W.2d 601 (Iowa 1997), the issue was the constitutionality of the behavior of an officer who conducted a complete search of a vehicle stopped for a traffic violation. In that situation, the "when" part of the question could have more details about the parties in the case, as in this example:

> when the officer had no indication that the defendant had broken any
> law other than a traffic law before he initiated the search of the defen-
> dant's car

The "when" part of the question helps to focus your research by helping you to identify relevant authorities. The more familiar you are with the legally significant facts, the more quickly you can identify cases and statutes that are and are not relevant to your client's case.

Putting all of the pieces together, here are three sample research questions for the *Coors* case. The first question could be used alone, while the second and third questions might reveal two different aspects of the case, and thus could be used together:

> Under the First Amendment's freedom of speech provisions as they per-
> tain to commercial speech, is 27 U.S.C. § 205(e)(2) constitutional when
> the statute prohibits beer manufacturers from printing truthful alcohol
> content information on their beer labels?

> Under the First Amendment's freedom of speech provisions as they per-
> tain to commercial speech, does prohibiting the printing of alcohol
> content information on a beer label sufficiently advance the govern-
> ment's interest in preventing strength wars when there is no evidence
> of strength wars in states or countries in which alcohol content infor-
> mation is allowed to be printed on beer labels?

> Under the First Amendment's freedom of speech provisions as they per-
> tain to commercial speech, does prohibiting the printing of alcohol
> content information on a beer label directly advance the government's
> interest in preventing consumers from having misleading information
> when it is now possible to accurately measure alcohol content in beer
> and thus the statute is preventing publication of truthful information?

A complete sample question for *Knowles v. Iowa* might look like this:

> Under the Fourth Amendment's search and seizure limitations, does a
> police officer have the authority to conduct a complete vehicle search
> of a car that has been stopped for a traffic violation, when the officer
> had no indication that the defendant had broken any law other than a
> traffic law before he initiated the search of the defendant's car?

One more caveat. At this early stage of the writing process, don't worry about perfect form or perfection in any way. The important thing is to get some information down in a useful format.

3.2.2
BROADENING YOUR HORIZONS (YOU *CAN* COMPARE APPLES AND ORANGES)

After you have formulated your research questions, you should make one more decision before you hit the books or the computer. Decide in advance what you're looking for. What are your "ideal" authorities and your "practical" authorities? That is, if you could invent an ideal authority, what would it be? On the other hand, if the ideal authority isn't out there (and it probably isn't), you should decide what types of authorities would be useful in your client's case.

This step is important because the problem many people have with legal research is not that they can't *find* relevant authorities, it's that they don't *recognize* relevant authorities when they see them. Even people who can *eventually* recognize relevant authorities often don't recognize them during the initial phase of their research. They are looking for the perfect match, and they ignore every authority that is not identical, factually and in every other way. After they realize that they're not going to find the ideal case, they have to retrace their steps to pick up those imperfect authorities that now look a lot better.

Many researchers are able to recognize those imperfect authorities the first time through if they try to identify both ideal and practical authorities before they begin their research. Identifying the ideal authority is simple: It would be great to find a constitutional provision that mandates a decision in your favor. Being only slightly more realistic, it would be wonderful to find a Supreme Court opinion that is on point and in your favor. Finding your ideal authority may be difficult, because the United States Supreme Court and other courts of last resort frequently take up issues that they haven't decided before. Accordingly, you must consider what non-ideal or practical authorities would support your argument and be acceptable to the court.

To identify practical authorities, broaden your horizons. If your client is a nun who was bitten by an aardvark, don't pass by a case about an antelope that bit a priest. That is, instead of looking at the narrow facts of your case, look for legally significant categories that you can use to characterize the parties, events, or issues in your case and that will help you recognize potentially relevant authorities.

3.2.3
THE ABSTRACTION LADDER

Many legal writers use a theoretical device called the "abstraction ladder" to help them identify relevant categories. The abstraction ladder is based on the concept that everything in the world can be thought of at various levels of abstraction or concreteness.

First, let's define our terms. The word "abstract" has several meanings and is sometimes hard for people to understand. We used it earlier to talk about a written summary of the information in the record or joint appendix. The meaning of "abstract" in the abstraction ladder has perhaps a more familiar definition. In this sense, art is abstract if two people could see different things in the same painting. A word is abstract if two people could perceive two (or more than two) different meanings from the same word.

For example, if someone asked you what you did before you came in to school or work this morning, you might answer, somewhat abstractly, "I ate." Different people might conjure up different mental images of what kind of food you had from your rather abstract reply. You might be a little less abstract and say, "I had breakfast." Even with this description, some people might picture yogurt, while others would think of bacon and eggs. Or you could be a little more concrete and say, "I had some cereal." Or even more concrete and say, "I had some Cheerios." Or you might be even more concrete and say, "I had one and one quarter cups of Cheerios and three-quarters of a cup of skim milk." Thus, the words you use to describe something can be placed on a ladder between the extremes of "most abstract" and "most concrete." You might think of the ladder growing wider as it grows taller; the more abstract something is, the more other things share the same rung.

Moving in the other direction, from most concrete to most abstract, you can think of a cow by thinking of Bossy, a particular cow. Or you can be a little more abstract and think of a Holstein. Or you can be a little more abstract and just think of cows in general. Or you could move up the abstraction ladder — or several abstraction ladders — and think of farm animals, or mammals, or farm property, or assets, or wealth. At the top of this (and every) abstraction ladder, you can think of a cow as a "thing."[4]

This concept is important to legal analysis because abstract reasoning helps lawyers to identify analogous authorities. Once you recognize that facts and issues can be put into broader, more abstract categories, you may be better able to see legal similarities between your client's case and relevant authorities. Very frequently, the tension in a legal argument is about whether a rule applies to a broad category that includes a certain person,

---

[4] S. I. Hayakawa, *Language in Thought and Action* 155 (4th ed. 1978) (discussing the abstraction ladder in general and the cow example in particular).

thing, or event, or whether the rule applies to a narrower group that ex-cludes a certain person, thing, or event. You can use the abstraction ladder to identify categories that may be significant to your argument.

3.2.4
USING THE ABSTRACTION LADDER IN LEGAL RESEARCH

The good news is that if you move up the abstraction ladder high enough, you can almost always identify some connection between two sets of facts. For example, you could analogize a cow to a horse because they are both farm animals. Or you could analogize a cow to a wheat field because they are both income-producing property for farmers. You could even analogize a cow to a tractor because they are both farm property. Or you could analogize a cow to a pet dog because both are mammals.

The bad news is that after asking whether there is an analogy, you must then ask whether the analogy is legally significant. For example, if a rule governs licensing of pet dogs and cats, that rule will probably not apply to cows on a dairy farm even though cows, dogs, and cats are all mammals. If, however, a rule governed additives to cow feed, you might be able to argue that the same rule or a similar rule should apply to fer-tilizers on wheat fields because both cow feed and wheat field fertilizer may affect food that consumers purchase. One hint about using the ab-straction ladder — try to go "up" (i.e., to a more abstract level) only as far as you need to in order to find a legally significant analogy and no farther. For example, a goat and a cow are both mammals, but their more legally significant connection in most cases would probably be lower on the ab-straction ladder: They are both animals that produce milk that may be sold for human consumption.

Thus, before you go to the library, look at your case and at your re-search question(s) and decide what types of authorities you're looking for. If you were researching the *Coors* case, for example, you should plan what to do if you don't find any cases dealing with regulation of beer labels. Going up the abstraction ladder, you might look for regulations about labels of any kind. Or going up farther, you might look for regulations about any kind of advertising.

But "any kind of advertising" might be too broad a concept. What is significant about beer advertising as opposed to the general definition of advertising? One obvious answer is that there are lots of restrictions on beer — as one of my students put it, it's a vice that government regulates. Thinking in terms of "vices" that the government regulates would broaden your horizons to looking for cases about regulation of advertising about liquor, gambling, smoking, or pornography because they are all legal activities subject to significant governmental regulation ("vices").

Broadening your horizons in this way can make the research process easier because you will be more attuned to the cases that are relevant and helpful even though they are not 100 percent on point. By being more practical about the potential results of your research, you will be more likely to recognize relevant authorities.

3.2.5
IDENTIFYING VALID AUTHORITY

When you are writing a brief to a court, you are trying to convince it to do something. On a basic level, your argument consists of assertions that will convince the court to decide in your favor — if it agrees with those assertions. The court will be much more likely to agree with your assertions if it believes in the validity of the authorities you cite as support for your assertions.

The "validity" of each authority depends on several factors. When you are deciding what authorities to cite, realize that most judges are not interested in breaking new ground or making new law: They are interested in not getting reversed. Thus, part of your job is to reassure them that the result you seek is consistent with the mandatory authorities that govern their jurisdiction. Every time you cite to an authority that is not mandatory, the judge may be thinking, "Why do I care about this?" If you are writing to a court of last resort, like the United States Supreme Court, realize that — even though that court has the power to make new law — its first instinct is to look to its own decisions for authority rather than to lower court authorities.

The more valid the authorities you cite, the more weight the authority will have with the court. Because each case is decided based on the facts and issues unique to it, the validity of an authority can vary from case to case. Therefore, when assessing the validity of authorities during your research, keep several different aspects of authorities in mind.

a. Relevant Facts

First, consider what types of facts might be relevant, and look for authorities that relate to those types of facts. Some cases with similar facts will be easy to recognize, but you need to think about different levels of similarity. This is where the lessons of the abstraction ladder become important: Thinking about your facts at various levels of abstraction can help you to recognize facts from other cases whose relevance is not apparent. If your client is seeking to ban smoking in the workplace, for example, you might look for cases dealing with other types of toxic fumes in the workplace or other types of dangers in the workplace.

b. Relevant Legal Issues

Second, consider what types of legal issues might be relevant. If your issue involves the meaning of a federal statute, for example, cases interpreting the statute would certainly be relevant. But you might also consider looking for cases that have interpreted other statutes that either use similar language or govern similar legal problems. If your case has several possible sub-issues, authorities that address a sub-issue might be highly relevant — for that sub-issue — even though they might not be relevant to every issue in your case. For example, if you are analyzing a torts issue, a case addressing foreseeability might be relevant to your case even if the particular tort at issue in that case is irrelevant.

c. Relevant Sources

i. *Legal Sources*

Finally, consider what types of sources might be relevant. The most obvious source for legal authority is a court of law, but some courts will have more validity with the reviewing court. Thus, if you are writing to an Indiana Court of Appeals, opinions of the Indiana Supreme Court would have high relevance. The simple rule is that mandatory authorities from the relevant jurisdiction will have the most validity with the court.

If there is no mandatory authority exactly on point, however, find out how close your jurisdiction has come to the relevant issue and build your argument on those authorities. If you must also cite to nonmandatory authority, those authorities will have more validity if you tie them to mandatory authorities or to rules from mandatory authorities in your jurisdiction. Thus, if you find that there are few opinions addressing the issue in your case, and none that are on point, first find the opinions in your "mandatory court" that are most on point. If you also wish to cite to a nonmandatory authority, you could begin your discussion of that issue by citing to the mandatory authority and then bringing in any non-mandatory authorities, noting that those cases are "consistent with" or are "applying a rule very similar to" mandatory rules. Although, of course, the court is not obligated to follow these cases, you have laid groundwork that will help the court to find the authorities valid.

Some non-court authorities can also be valid. If you are asking a court to decide on the meaning of federal legislation, the opinion of a federal agency would be relevant if that agency was involved in drafting regulations, enforcing the legislation, or suing to have the legislation enforced. If the area of law is particularly novel, you may have difficulty finding on-point cases or other authorities. If that is the situation, consider whether any law review articles have been written on the subject. Although most courts would rather rely on cases in which courts have considered the impact that their decision would have on real-life parties, they can and do refer to law reviews when case authorities are few or inadequate.[5] If you can cite to a prestigious professor from a prestigious law

---

[5] *See generally* Deborah J. Merritt & Melanie Putnam, *Symposium on the Trends in Legal Citations and Scholarship: Judges and Scholars: Do Courts and Scholarly Journals Cite the Same Law Review Articles?* 71 Chi.-Kent. L. Rev. 871 (1996).

school, so much the better, but most courts are more interested in the legal analysis that the article presents than in the pedigree of its author.[6]

ii. "Extra-Legal" Sources

And don't limit your research to traditional legal sources. If your case concerns an issue of public significance — and many cases argued to courts of last resort fit that definition — you may want to give the court information that will help it understand how this issue affects the public, not just the parties that are before the court.[7] Although traditionally courts are restricted in their use of information to facts that have been admitted into evidence, in recent years courts have shown more and more willingness to consider "extra-legal" or "legislative facts."[8] Courts consider facts outside the record by taking "judicial notice" of those facts, under Federal Rule of Evidence 201.

For example, suppose you are representing the state in a Fourth Amendment case about the constitutionality of a state law that gives police officers the authority to order all passengers out of a vehicle at a traffic stop. If you are counsel for the state, you might be making a policy argument that the court should find the law constitutional because it will promote officer safety. To support that argument, you could look for statistics about the dangers that police officers face when conducting traffic stops, noting how often passengers in the stopped vehicles became violent or caused other problems. These authorities might persuade the court to agree with your assertion that traffic stops are dangerous situations for police officers, and thus make it more likely to decide that the state law is a valid exercise of police power.

In the *Coors Brewing* case discussed above, one reason the government gave for banning alcohol percentages on beer labels was its fear that consumers, especially young consumers, would base their beer-purchasing choices on the percentage of alcohol in the beer. One of the parties might cite a reputable study that analyzed beer-buying patterns of young people in states or countries in which alcohol percentages *were* on the label. The conclusion of that study might convince the court that alcohol percentages on beer labels either helped or hindered consumers' abilities to make good choices when purchasing beer. That in turn might affect the court's decision in the case.

Of course, many of these "extra-legal" facts could be submitted into evidence at the trial court, but trials are usually focused on the individual parties. Often, arguments about the broad impact of the case become significant only at the appellate level. Just as with legal authorities, extra-legal authorities will be more or less valid depending on the source. The

[6] *Id.* at 890-92.
[7] *See generally* Ellie Margolis, *Beyond Brandeis: Exploring the Uses of Non-Legal Materials in Appellate Briefs*, 34 U.S.F.L. Rev. 197 (2000).
[8] *Id.* at 199 (citations omitted).

reputation of the source, whether a newspaper article or a university study, will doubtless have an impact on the court's attitude toward the validity of the information from that source. Therefore, when deciding whether to use extra-legal information, consider the source carefully.

Assessing the possible relevance of the facts, the legal issues, and the sources of the authorities you plan to cite can help you to predict which authorities the court will find more valid, and to decide where and how to concentrate your research.

3.2.6
USING WHAT YOU ALREADY KNOW

As the author of an appellate brief, you have some of your research work done in advance. The lower court or courts that have previously considered the legal issues will certainly have cited some of the relevant authorities. Still, you should always plan on doing some independent research. Of course, it makes sense to read the significant authorities cited in the lower court opinions, and you may well use some or all of them in your brief. You may also discover, however, that the lower court did not consider some of the arguments that may be most effective for your client. Often, the arguments that end up winning the case at the appellate level either were not considered or were considered and rejected by the lower court.

Consider, too, that the lower courts may have been persuaded by authorities that would not persuade the United States Supreme Court or another court of last resort. For example, if at the intermediate appellate level you (or the attorney then working on the case) were arguing to a federal court of appeals, you might have used on-point authorities from that court or from other federal courts of appeal. When you must write a brief on that same issue to the United States Supreme Court, you should do more research to see what Supreme Court cases have addressed this issue — or at least how "close" the Supreme Court has come to that issue — and thus you may discover a variety of authorities that were not explored in the lower courts. Therefore, although you can begin your research with the authorities cited by the court being appealed, those authorities should be only a starting point.

Consider two cases that may or may not be representative. In *Rubin v. Coors Brewing Co*, 514 U.S. 476 (1995), the United States Supreme Court cited approximately ten cases (other than the case being reviewed) in its majority opinion. The United States Court of Appeals for the Ninth Circuit, whose opinion the court affirmed, cited only three. *Adolph Coors Co. v. Bentsen*, 2 F.3d 355 (9th Cir. 1993). In *Knowles v. Iowa*, 119 S. Ct. 484 (1998), the United States Supreme Court cited approximately 18 cases (other than the case being reviewed) in its unanimous decision. All but three of these cases were U.S. Supreme Court decisions. The Iowa Supreme Court, whose opinion the court reversed, cited approximately half a dozen, none of them U.S. Supreme Court decisions. *State v. Knowles*, 569 N.W.2d 601 (Iowa 1997).

When you are writing to the United States Supreme Court, there are some well-worn paths that can be fruitful when using a lower court decision as the starting point for your research. First and most obviously, you should carefully consider any U.S. Supreme Court decisions cited in that opinion. If there are other decisions cited — e.g., decisions of U.S. Courts of Appeal — read those decisions and see if *those decisions* cite to the United States Supreme Court. If you want to use the rules or holdings from those lower court decisions, you may be able to find a Supreme Court "hook" in the decisions themselves. If you cannot find any Supreme Court authority in those decisions and you still want to use the legal principles, use your research skills (and your abstract reasoning) to search for Supreme Court decisions that govern the same or similar points.

If your case presents an issue of statutory or constitutional construction, you should probably conduct some research in the text versions of the United States Code Annotated or the United States Code Service. With these hard-copy sources, it is easier and faster to survey a wide array of authorities that have cited the relevant statute or constitutional provision. In addition, remember that courts are interested in hearing about interpretations of similar statutes, or even different statutes that use similar phrases or clauses. For example, if your case involves the federal Age Discrimination in Employment Act, you might look for similar language in Title VII, which deals with sex and race discrimination, or in the Americans with Disabilities Act, which deals with discrimination against people with disabilities. If your analysis focuses on the meaning of a particular word or phrase, try using one or more words from the phrase as a search term, and search in a United States Code database to see if you can find any other statutes with the same or similar language. You may then be able to use authorities that interpret those other statutes when making your arguments.

In essence, when looking for authority on the meaning of statutes, you should consider the three branches of government. First, the executive — has this statute been interpreted by a relevant federal agency? If so, then the court may defer to the agency's interpretation under the *Chevron* rule.[9] Second, consider the legislative branch: Is there any relevant legislative history? (Keep in mind, however, that many courts look at legislative history with a jaundiced eye.) Finally, and often most importantly, consider the judicial branch: Has a relevant court interpreted this lan-

---

[9] See *Chevron U.S.A., Inc. v. Natural Resources Defense Council, Inc.*, 467 U.S. 837, 842-44 (1984) (holding that courts must defer to a federal agency interpretation of an ambiguous statute if it is based on a "permissible construction" of the statute). Note that federal agencies sometimes interpret statutes in documents other than formal rulings.

guage or analogous language? When you look for interpretations from all three points of view, you may discover analysis that may help you argue that your interpretation is the correct one.

3.2.7
KNOWING WHEN TO STOP

Most lawyers have a hard time ending their research, perhaps because they don't want to start writing. Researching is fun, and you don't have to make any hard decisions — if you think a case or other authority may be useful, you print it and keep on going. I find that research is like dating and writing is like marriage. You want to keep researching forever because you hope that if you keep going, you'll find the perfect match right around the next corner. With writing, you just have to take what you have, and try to work it out.

Accordingly, when doing your research, you should consciously decide when to stop. No matter how diligent your research, your writing will probably reveal some gaps that need to be filled. Don't try to fill those gaps *before* you start writing. Instead, let the writing reveal the gaps to you and help to direct your follow-up research. Think in terms of a partial stop and a full stop. You should come to a partial stop when you have followed a good research process, updated your authorities, and you're not finding anything new — you keep encountering again and again those almost-relevant cases that you've rejected once or twice before.

This is a good time to take a break from researching and start to draft your document. Invariably, as you write, you will discover new avenues that you wish to explore, and you can make tactical strikes on the library to grab cases or other authorities to support the points that come up. The time to come to a full stop in your research is determined by outside forces — the due date of your document.

3.3
SUMMARY

In order to write an effective brief, you must follow an effective research process. In order to follow an effective research process, you need to know your case thoroughly and plan your research accordingly. Before you research, get to know the facts of your client's case by abstracting the decisions below and any other record materials. Identify the questions that your research must answer, and be realistic about the types of authorities you can expect to find. When assessing the validity of authorities, use the abstraction ladder to identify those that address analogous facts and issues. Weigh the validity of the source of the authority, and be willing to look beyond legal authorities. Be practical, too, about the percentage of your available time that you spend on researching. Set a deadline for research that allows you sufficient time to work on the actual writing of your brief, for the process of writing the brief will often reveal gaps in your research.

FACING THE BLANK PAGE

The hardest thing about writing is writing. Writing is harder than researching before you write, and it's harder than revising after you've written. But to use the research, and to have something to revise, you must actually write a draft of your document at some point.

Two techniques can make it easier for you to face the blank page: (1) deciding on some sort of structure before you begin to write and (2) using a method to record your concerns about problems with the draft as you write it.

4.1
FINDING STRUCTURE

At this stage, you should have a stack of authorities that you plan to use in support of your client's case. Now, you must make the move from that stack of paper to some sort of an outline. Effective legal arguments are usually best organized around issues, rules, and arguments rather than around authority cases. The court's major concern is not whether the cases you have found are analogous to your client's case. Instead, the court wants to know the issues that your case presents, the rules that govern those issues, and how it should apply those rules to your case. Of course, you will probably use cases to *illustrate* or *explain* the rules that you identify, but the *rules*, rather than the cases, should be the focus of your analysis.

If the rules that govern your case are well established and you must argue how those rules apply, you can structure your argument around those established rules.[1] Unfortunately, not every case is governed by well-established rules. Even when a case is governed by an established rule, some writers are able to discover and/or articulate the legal rules only after they have begun to write. If you are still struggling to find some or all of the rules that govern your case, or you can't decide how to structure your argument, let your research help you.

4.1.1
LET YOUR RESEARCH HELP YOU STRUCTURE YOUR DOCUMENT

Look at that stack of authorities. Each one of those authorities made it into the "chosen" pile on your desk because it appeared to support your argument as to some aspect of your case. Some authorities may support more than one, or even several, aspects of your case. Take each authority and write out the ways in which the authority supports your case. Ideally, that "support" will take the form of assertions that the court would have to agree with to decide in your favor, or rules that the court would need to apply to decide in your favor. Don't worry about making the statements in perfect rule format, or even in formal language. Just use some method to record the reasons that you thought that authority would be helpful to your argument. You might also write down the assertions that you believe you need to make in order to convince the court to decide in your favor.

Although many good writers compose at the computer keyboard, the computer might not be the best place to use this method. You might want to write the assertions on index cards, so that you can shuffle them around later. You might want to write them on a big piece of paper, so you can think about how the statements from one authority connect to the statements from another authority.

Let's use the case of *Miller v. Albright*, 523 U.S. 420 (1998), for an example. The petitioner in *Miller* was the foreign-born daughter of a United States serviceman. The daughter wanted to become a United States citizen based on her status as the daughter of a United States citizen, but her parents had never married. 8 U.S.C. § 1409(a) imposes strict requirements for citizenship on foreign-born children of unmarried U.S. citizen fathers and foreign mothers. Because it imposes almost no requirements for citizenship on foreign-born children of unmarried U.S. citizen mothers and foreign fathers, the daughter sued to have the statute declared unconstitutional.

Let's presume that you are researching *Miller v. Albright* on behalf of the petitioner, and you have reached a "partial stop" in your research. You have before you a stack of authorities that (you think) support your argument. You might come up with the following list of assertions that you believe the court has to agree with to decide in your favor:

---

[1] *See, e.g.,* Linda H. Edwards, *Legal Writing: Process, Analysis, and Organization* 29-36 (Aspen 2d ed. 1999); Richard Neumann, *Legal Reasoning and Legal Writing* 95-111 (Aspen 4th ed. 2001).

List of points that court must agree with:

1. Court should reverse decision below.
2. Statute is unconstitutional.
3. Statute discriminates on the basis of gender.
4. Court should scrutinize statutes that discriminate based on gender under intermediate level of scrutiny.
5. Statute fails the intermediate scrutiny test.
6. Statute is even unconstitutional under rational basis-type scrutiny.
7. Court should not defer to Congress even though this is an immigration law.
8. The statute is not substantially related to the achievement of the government's objective.
9. There is not an "exceedingly persuasive justification" for the distinction between the children of the two types of parents.
10. It is not rational to distinguish between children of U.S. citizen fathers and children of U.S. citizen mothers.
11. Stopping gender discrimination and "illegitimacy" discrimination is more important than allowing Congress control over immigration.
12. Someone who is a child of a U.S. citizen is not an "immigrant" and so a statute that regulates such a person is not an immigration statute.
13. Biological parent-child relationships are important.
14. A statute that applies differently to citizens of different genders can only be upheld if it passes a significant level of scrutiny.

After making the list, try to identify relationships between and among the points. For example, points 1 and 2 are really two sides of the same coin: If the statute is unconstitutional, the decision below must be reversed. Some of the points may be repetitive of other points, and so they can be eliminated, or the two repetitive points can be synthesized into one point, for example, points 4 and 14. Some points may be parts or sub-parts of other points, and so they should be grouped accordingly, for example, points 5, 8, and 9. Some points may be threshold issues, so you may decide that they should be addressed first.

If you have listed these points on index cards, you might try moving the cards around to identify the relationships between and among the points. You might stack the cards that seem to make the same point. If you have listed these points on a piece of paper, you might try drawing lines or circles to connect related points, or to identify a hierarchy among the assertions.[2]

4.1.2
CREATE A REVERSE ROADMAP

Another method of identifying structure is to create an outline in paragraph form. Start with the ultimate point that you want the court to agree with, and then ask yourself what point or points the court must

---

[2] *See, e.g.,* Elizabeth Fajans & Mary R. Falk, *Comments Worth Making: Supervising Scholarly Writing in Law School,* 46 J. Leg. Educ. 342 (1996).

agree with in order to agree with *that* point, moving in reverse until you are at the smallest part of any test you might ask a court to apply. This method is more complicated because you must already have some relationships between and among your points in mind as you develop the points. The method might result in several branching paragraphs rather than just one. For example, if you were working on *Miller v. Albright*, the case described above, part of your roadmap-outline might look like this:

> **This court should reverse the decision below. In order to decide to reverse, they have to agree that 1409 is unconstitutional.**
>
> **In order to agree that 1409 is unconstitutional, they either have to agree that it violates the intermediate scrutiny test or that it violates the rational basis test.**
>
> **In order to agree that it violates the intermediate scrutiny test, they first have to agree that the intermediate scrutiny test applies. In order to agree that the intermediate scrutiny test applies, they have to agree that the statute discriminates on the basis of gender.**
>
> **They would also have to agree that this is not an immigration statute, so they don't have to defer to Congress and therefore apply an easier test, OR they have to agree that even if it is an immigration statute, the fact that it discriminates on the basis of gender is more significant.**
>
> **Now, in order to agree that the statute *fails* the intermediate scrutiny test, they have to agree both that there's no substantial relationship between the discrimination in the statute and the achievement of the government's goals *and* that there's no exceedingly persuasive justification for the statute.**
>
> **In order to agree that it violates the rational basis test, they first have to agree that this is the correct test to apply, which means that they think that immigration law is more important than gender law. In order to agree that it violates the rational basis test, they first have to agree that Congress had no rational reason for the law.**
>
> **It might help them agree that 1409 is unconstitutional if they agree that biological parent-child relationships are important, or reuniting parents and children are important.**

As with the "list of assertions" method, this method might be more effective with pen and paper than with a computer. The ability to pick up an index card and move it around, or to draw lines connecting two or more paragraphs with each other, is often easier to do on paper than on a screen.

4.1.3
THE WORKING OUTLINE

Once you have written your points down somehow and analyzed how they relate to each other, you might come up with a working outline like the one below. (Note that these headings are not in perfect "point heading" form):

Working Outline

I. **This court should reverse because 1409 is unconstitutional.**
   A. **This court should apply an intermediate scrutiny test.**
      1. **The statute discriminates on the basis of gender.**
      2. **This is not an immigration statute, so no special deference to Congress is needed.**
      3. **Even if it is an immigration statute, fighting gender discrimination and "illegitimacy" discrimination trumps immigration.**
   B. **This statute fails the intermediate scrutiny test.**
      1. **There's no substantial relationship between the discrimination in the statute and the achievement of the government's goals.**
      2. **There's no exceedingly persuasive justification for the statute.**
   C. **Even if this court applies the rational basis–type test, the statute still fails because there's no rational relationship between encouraging ties between parents and children and requiring a father to establish ties in a different way than mothers do.**

Of course, this outline is not carved in stone. As you write, you may discover that some arguments are incomplete, while others are not worth making. As with the research questions, your goal is not perfection; it's to create an outline that is complete enough to get you started on your writing.

If *any* type of pre-writing outline is too difficult for you, you may want to try writing *before* you outline. Keep your paragraphs to a reasonable length, and then, after you have written your argument, use the advice in Chapter Ten to write an effective topic sentence for each paragraph. Those topic sentences will reveal the main points you have made and the order in which you have made them. You can then use the topic sentences to evaluate the relationships among your points and to plan your large-scale organization.

Deciding to Use Rules Based on Policy

Legal writing is based on rules, and usually rules provide the best structure for legal analysis. Some writers, however, focus so much on the structure that the rules provide that they miss important policy arguments.

Policy Arguments are based on a special kind of rule called a "Public Policy." In law, "Public Policy" can be roughly defined as a societal rule about how people should behave or how things should work in our society. For example, over the past 25 years, laws about smoking in public places have changed based on the public policy or societal belief that one person should not cause harm to another. In many legal arguments, the policy arguments are implicit in the more formal legal rules that apply to the issues in the case, and they need not be addressed separately. Sometimes, however, the court will be more likely to agree with your ultimate conclusion if it can also be convinced — or reminded — of the importance of a policy that underlies your argument.

In a Fourth Amendment case, for example, you might include a separate point addressing either the dangers of police work (and therefore the need to allow police officers wide latitude in their work) or the importance of the right to privacy (and therefore the need to limit the abilities of police officers to invade that privacy).

In an argument based on the *Miller v. Albright* case, counsel representing Miller might make a separate argument based on the notion that parent-child relationships are fundamental and must be promoted, no matter when that relationship is formed. This argument might not be based on rational basis or strict scrutiny; it could be a separate point that might make the court more willing to apply strict scrutiny, or to hold that the statute violates the rational basis test.

Even if you make a policy argument separately from more traditional legal arguments, you should not treat the policy argument differently. You do not need to label them as "public policy" or "policy" arguments (e.g., you need not say, "For reasons of public policy, this court should. . . ."). Furthermore, policy arguments can and should be supported by references to outside authorities. Although policy arguments might be more likely to include citations to extra-legal sources, whenever possible, you should include citations to and analysis of cases in which courts referenced certain policies when deciding similar legal issues.

4.2
USING "PRIVATE MEMOS" TO QUIET YOUR INNER DEMONS AND PREVENT WRITER'S BLOCK

Even if you have created a good outline, you may still face writer's block at this stage of the process if you worry so much about avoiding mistakes that you are afraid to write a word. As Ray and Ramsfield have noted, a crisis can result when the "id" of creativity bumps into the "superego" of criticism.[3] As we write, we hear a critical voice yammering away inside our heads, asking, "What about the res ipsa issue? Do I have enough cases on this point? Shouldn't that second issue come before this one?" and so on. The writer freezes, and writing comes to a stop.

Hearing your critical voice is not a bad thing in itself. After all, writing is a method of learning. While you write, you may discover aspects of your case that you hadn't noticed before, avenues of research, and even whole arguments that didn't occur to you while you were researching or outlining. That's why it's important to leave yourself enough time to write: You should presume that your first couple of drafts will be "thinking drafts" or "learning drafts" that will teach you a lot about your case.

If you stop writing every time your critical voice reminds you of something, however, you may never finish a draft. Instead, allow yourself to write an imperfect first draft, and record the questions or criticisms that

---

[3] *See* Mary Barnard Ray & Jill J. Ramsfield, *Legal Writing: Getting It Right and Getting It Written* 212 (2d ed. 1993).

occur to you. Instead of freezing up, use a method called "private memos."[4] As the critical voices chatter in your head, drop a footnote and write down what those voices are saying: "Do I need more research here?" "Should I talk about the other issue first?" In this way, you can silence your critical voice by preserving the concern that you're worried about, but you avoid writer's block because you don't interrupt your writing process. Plan to review your private memo footnotes during the rewriting stage of your writing process. You may find some points were irrelevant after all; on the other hand, some of the private memos may lead you to new and more effective arguments.

4.3
SUMMARY

You will be able to draft your argument much more effectively if you take the time to create a working outline for the argument. While drafting the argument, be ready to recognize and record any questions that you have about your research, your organization, or other aspects of your argument.

---

[4] *See* Mary Kate Kearney & Mary Beth Beazley, *Teaching Students How to "Think Like Lawyers": Integrating Socratic Method with the Writing Process*, 64 Temple L. Rev. 885, 894-97 (1991).

CHAPTER FIVE

ONE PIECE AT A TIME: DRAFTING THE ARGUMENT

5.1
USING AN ANALYTICAL PARADIGM

As indicated above, good legal writing is organized around issues and assertions rather than around cases. When you wrote your outline or your "reverse roadmap," you were focusing on the conclusions that you want the court to agree with. Now, you must flesh out your argument by writing a complete argument for each of the points in your outline.

Many first-year law students learn "IRAC" (Issue-Rule-Application-Conclusion) as a method of organizing legal analysis. IRAC and similar paradigms can be helpful because they force writers to answer vital questions about their arguments. Your outline has identified the issues that you think the court needs to address. For each of those issues, you must answer four questions:

(1) What rule governs this issue?
(2) What does this rule mean?
(3) Why should it be applied (or not applied) in a certain way in this case?
(4) What impact does that application have on the court's decision in this case?

We can illustrate how this paradigm works with a familiar syllogism:

Issue: Is Socrates mortal?
Rule: All human beings are mortal.
Application: Socrates is a man.
Conclusion: Socrates is mortal.

You may notice a problem in this paradigm. The rule application is supposed to show the connection between the rule and the legally significant facts, but that connection is not explicit in this example. It needs to be rewritten with an explanation of what the rule means in this context:

Issue: Is Socrates mortal?
Rule: All human beings are mortal.
Explanation: Human beings include men and women.
Application: Socrates is a man.
Conclusion: Socrates is mortal.

The rule explanation shows the reader how the rule about mortality connects to the facts about Socrates. Admittedly, rule explanation gets more complicated when we get beyond the question of simple mortality. Nevertheless, the pattern remains the same, with one major change for advocacy writing. Instead of beginning the argument by stating the legal issue as a question, we state it as an assertion, or a conclusion. Therefore, our paradigm changes from IRAC to CREXAC and now looks like this:

Conclusion: Socrates is mortal.
Rule: All human beings are mortal.
EXplanation: Human beings include men and women.
Application: Socrates is a man.
Conclusion: Socrates is mortal.

You should complete a CREXAC analysis for every significant part of your argument.

Some writers have a hard time understanding the CREXAC paradigm. They may try to make the whole argument section one long CREXAC, or they can't decide which elements are worthy of a CREXAC analysis and which elements are not. At this stage of the writing process, let your outline dictate your structure. See Illustration 5.1 for a guideline you can use to identify where you need to supply a CREXAC analysis within your argument. Each element of the CREXAC paradigm is explained more fully below.

5.1.1
STATE YOUR ISSUE AS A CONCLUSION

In the first "conclusion" element of the paradigm, the writer articulates the specific issue that is being addressed, or articulates the problem

Illustration 5.1

Sample Argument Structure

I.   This court should reverse because first major assertion
     [introductory material and roadmap to Sections I.A & I.B].
     A. First major assertion is true because first reason is true
         [CREXAC analysis of A].
     B. First major assertion is true because second reason is true
         [introductory material & roadmap to sections I.B.1 & I.B.2].
         1. Second reason is true because first sub-reason is true
             [CREXAC analysis of I.B.1].
         2. Second reason is true because second sub-reason is true
             [CREXAC analysis of I.B.2].
II. Even if first assertion is not true, back-up assertion is true
     [CREXAC analysis of II].
III. This court should reverse because policy reason is true
     [CREXAC analysis of III].

(or part or sub-part of the problem) that is being "solved" in this section of the document. The writer could articulate an issue from *Miller v. Albright* by stating affirmatively what the issue is:

> **Under the intermediate scrutiny test, the first issue that must be decided is whether 8 U.S.C. § 1409(a) is "substantially related" to the achievement of the government's objective.**

While this method effectively tells the court the issue (and is preferable to neglecting to articulate the issue at all), it is not the best choice in a brief to a court because it is not argumentative. Generally, in persuasive writing, you should make your arguments as if they are the only reasonable resolution to the issues before the court. Therefore, it is generally best to state your issues as conclusions:

> **8 U.S.C. § 1409(a) is not "substantially related" to the achievement of the government's objective because it is unconstitutionally over-inclusive.**

If your issue is more complicated, the conclusion may be longer than just a simple sentence as it is in the following example, from *Minnesota v. Carter*. In that case, the Court was asked to determine whether an officer violated the Fourth Amendment when he observed criminal activity through the window of a basement apartment:

> **Because Thielen was located outside the curtilage of the apartment, he was free to observe any scene in plain view. Respondents' activities within the apartment were in plain view from Thielen's lawful vantage point. Thus, Thielen's observation violated no reasonable expectation of privacy and did not constitute a Fourth Amendment search.**

By stating your issue as a conclusion, you begin to focus your reader not only on the issue that you will be addressing in this section of the argument, but also on the result that your analysis of the issue will reveal.

Will My Writing Be Boring if I Use the Same Paradigm in Each Section?

The CREXAC paradigm does not provide one rubric that governs the whole argument section. Instead, it provides a rubric that will be used over and over again, anytime the writer has some point to explain or prove. Some writers worry that their writing will be boring or overpredictable if they follow a paradigm like CREXAC in each section of their document. This worry is unfounded for a couple of reasons.

First, CREXAC does not tell you *what to say*. Instead, it recommends a particular *organization* for the information that readers traditionally need when analyzing legal issues. Most legal readers want to know the rule first, then understand the rule's meaning, and then see how it applies to the facts. Most judges want a simple organization; they don't want to have to struggle to find a rule that a writer "creatively" saved for the end of his or her analysis of a legal issue.

The second reason not to worry is related to the first. CREXAC is only an organizational structure. With no extra effort on your part, each section of your argument will vary from the section before according to the *substance* of the argument itself and the particular demands of the issue. Every issue needs a rule, but sometimes the rule is a simple quote from a statute, while at other times it is a common law rule, and at other times it is a cluster of rules that end on the particular rule that governs the narrow legal issue that is the focus of that section of the document. Similarly, the explanation of the rule and application of the rule to the facts will also vary from issue to issue.

Even if CREXAC is not the most perfect organization for the analysis of a particular legal issue or sub-issue, it will probably still be an *effective* organization. Thus, it is probably most *practical* for an attorney to assume a CREXAC organization rather than to spend precious time trying to determine what is the "best" structure for analyzing a legal issue.

Whatever organizational method you use, the elements of CREXAC provide a good checklist. In every section of the argument, the reader will always need to know the issue you're addressing, the rule that governs the issue, what the rule means, and how it applies in this case.

5.1.2
PROVIDE THE RULE

After you have focused the reader's attention on the issue being addressed, you should articulate the "rule" that governs the issue. If your rule comes from a statute or a well-established common law test, stating the rule may be simple. Stating the rule can be controversial, however, if there is controversy about which rule applies, or if you must use inductive reasoning to "find" your rule.

a. Stating Established Rules

First, let's define our terms. A rule essentially says that "if a certain condition exists, then a certain legal status results." For example:

> If you are a human being [certain condition], then you are mortal ["legal" status].

> If you have a duty, breach a duty, and cause compensable harm [certain condition], then you are liable in negligence [legal status].

Most rules in a brief will not be stated in "if-then" terminology. However, using the if-then structure can help you to test the rules that you include in your brief.

You may state the rule in a variety of ways. If the rule is derived from a statute or other enacted law, you may simply quote the pertinent language, as in this example:

> 26 U.S.C. § 5861(d) provides that "[i]t shall be unlawful for any person to receive or possess a firearm which is not registered to him in the National Firearms Registration Transfer Record."

Similarly, if the rule is a well-accepted common law rule derived from a well-known authority, you may simply articulate the rule in its familiar language:

> While a person's home is, for most purposes, a place where he expects privacy, activities that are exposed "to the 'plain view' of outsiders are not protected" under the Fourth Amendment. <u>Katz v. United States</u>, 389 U.S. 347, 361 (1967) (Harlan, J., concurring).

If your case is more complex, stating one rule may not give the reader enough context. Some writers articulate the rule that governs a narrow situation by providing a "rule cluster" that starts with a well-accepted general rule and moves to the more narrow rule that is the focus of that section of the argument. The following example is from the argument section of *Minnesota v. Carter*, a Fourth Amendment case. This section of the argument is focused on the narrow issue of whether the alleged intrusion by the government agents constituted a "search." Notice how the writer moves the reader from the general rule — the Fourth Amendment — to the narrow rule at issue, which will be the focus of this section of the argument (which, by the way, will include two sub-sections):

> The Fourth Amendment to the United States Constitution guarantees "[t]he right of the people to be secure in their persons, houses, papers, and effects, against unreasonable searches and seizures." U.S. Const., Amend. IV. A search occurs only when governmental agents intrude upon an area in which a person has a reasonable expectation of privacy. <u>California v. Ciraolo</u>, 476 U.S. 207, 212 (1986). This Court will find that a Fourth Amendment search occurred only if two factors exist: (1) the location from which the observation occurred was within a complainant's zone of privacy, and (2) the government agents used extraordinary measures to accomplish the observation. <u>See</u> <u>id.</u> at 213.

Thus, although the paragraph lists three rules, the writer is focusing the reader's attention only on the last rule in the list.

b. Choosing Among Two or More Rules

As noted in an earlier chapter, some cases are governed by well-established rules, and the court needs to decide only how, or whether, a particular rule applies to the facts of the case. Sometimes, however, a major issue in the case is the debate as to which of two or more rules the court should apply to the situation. If you have to convince the court to choose the rule that you want, as opposed to the rule that your opponent wants, you must include a section in your argument devoted to proving that "your" rule is the best rule to apply. Of course, that "rule-choice" argument must be based on a rule, as well.

If a court has chosen a particular rule to apply to a situation, it has done so because it has decided that the case has certain factors or raises certain issues that the chosen rule best addresses. Sometimes, courts state the "rule-choice rule" explicitly. For example, everyone who has taken a constitutional law course knows that when courts have to decide whether certain governmental action is constitutional, they have at least three choices. They can apply the "strict scrutiny test" (which they apply when certain fundamental rights are implicated or the rights of a suspect class are affected); they can apply the "intermediate or heightened scrutiny test" (which they apply in a variety of situations, including situations in which laws make gender-based distinctions); or they can apply the "rational basis test" (which they apply when a law does not affect fundamental rights or make questionable distinctions). Thus, if your case is about the constitutionality of a governmental action, your first order of business is to argue about which rule applies, using the "rule-choice rule" that governs strict scrutiny and rational basis. For example, if you believed that strict scrutiny was appropriate, that section of your argument would be based on the following "rule-choice rule":

> **If a statute makes distinctions based on suspect classifications, then the strict scrutiny test applies.**

If there are two or more competing rules and the courts have not yet labeled the "rule-choice rule," your job is to find and articulate that rule. You "find" the rule by reasoning inductively from one or more cases in which a court has made the rule-choice decision.

c. Using Inductive Reasoning to Find and Articulate Legal Rules

As many a frustrated first-year law student can attest, courts sometimes decide cases without explicitly articulating the rule that they are applying. Furthermore, sometimes the rule that they are applying can be accurately stated more narrowly or more broadly. If the cases that are analogous to your case do not contain a clear rule, or if the applicable rule as it is currently envisioned would dictate a bad result for your client, you may have to "induce" a rule. Using inductive reasoning is appropriate for finding rules of all types, not just rule-choice rules. It is not accurate to say that you are labeling a "new" rule when you use inductive reasoning. The rule was there all along; inductive reasoning simply lets you recognize it, label it, and present it more effectively to the court.

When you use inductive reasoning to find a rule, you are trying to read between the lines of court opinions, to notice patterns that always or never predict certain results, or results that occur *only* when certain patterns are present. Authors of law review articles might observe these patterns in a vacuum, but you have a head start because you know the type of pattern you are looking for. In an advocacy document, inductive reasoning frequently begins when you distinguish your case from the cases that apparently apply.

For example, in the case *Ohio v. Robinette*, 519 U.S. 33 (1996), the issue was the constitutionality of an officer's request to conduct a drug search of a car that had been stopped for speeding. The government argued that the defendant had been free to refuse the officer's request, and so his consent was voluntary and constitutional. Many of the cases used as authority involved officers stopping people in airports and asking for permission to search for contraband. One student-attorney, writing on behalf of Robinette, noticed a distinguishing factor between Robinette's case and the so-called airport cases, and she used that distinction to help her to induce a more precise rule:

> There are two types of situations in which police request consent to search — those in which the police-citizen encounter begins consensually, and those in which the police-citizen encounter begins by an assertion of legal authority. When police-citizen encounters begin consensually, courts will find the consent request valid if there was nothing in the record to suggest "that the [citizen] had any objective reason to believe that she *was not free* to end the conversation [with the officers] . . . and proceed on her way," United States v. Mendenhall, 446 U.S. 544, 555 (1980) (emphasis added). On the other hand, when police request consent to search after a police-citizen encounter that began with an assertion of legal authority, the Court should use a different test, and should analyze when the defendant would have an objective reason to believe that he or she *became free* to end the conversation and proceed on his or her way. Because Newsome and Robinette's encounter began with an assertion of legal authority, and because there was no clear end to this assertion of legal authority despite Newsome's return of Robinette's license, this Court should apply the totality of the circumstances test to this case.
>
> Courts use the totality of the circumstances test to ascertain when police behavior rises to the level of a detention. See Florida v. Bostick, 501 U.S. 429, 434 (1991) ("[t]he encounter [between an officer and a citizen] will not trigger Fourth Amendment scrutiny unless it *loses its consensual nature*.") (emphasis added). Courts have failed to note, however, that when a police-citizen encounter already involves legitimate force

over that citizen, an inquiry as to when the encounter "rises" to the level of a detention is inapposite. . . .

. . . Thus, when a police-citizen encounter begins with the police officer's assertion of legal authority over the citizen, a subsequent request to search is part of a "consensual encounter" only if the citizen has objective knowledge either (a) that the legal detention has ended, or (b) that he or she is free to refuse consent to search.

Legal readers expect to hear about the rule as soon as they learn about the legal issue. However you find your rule, be sure to state it explicitly early within the appropriate section of the argument. In this way, you satisfy the reader's expectations and allow him or her to understand your analysis more easily.

5.1.3
EXPLAIN THE RULE

After you have articulated the rule, you must provide your reader with any needed "Explanation" of the rule. Before you explain the rule, however, you must decide which part of the rule you are focusing on in the particular sub-section of your argument. Usually, controversies about whether or how a rule applies will focus on certain words or phrases that are at the heart of the controversy regarding that rule. Some legal writers call these words or phrases the "key terms";[1] I refer to each as a "phrase-that-pays." By focusing on one or two "phrases-that-pay" within each sub-section of the document, you ensure that you are focusing on one issue or sub-issue at a time. Thus, after you have articulated your rule, scrutinize that rule and decide what words or phrases are the "phrases-that-pay" for that section of the document.

The phrase-that-pays is important because you often explain your rule by defining the phrase-that-pays, showing how it has been applied in the past, or both. You will decide how much explanation to provide for the phrase-that-pays, depending on the language of the phrase-that-pays itself and its significance in your argument.

a. Identifying the "Phrase-That-Pays"

In each section of your argument, you will have one or two phrases-that-pay that are the focus of analysis, usually because you are trying to prove that the phrase-that-pays exists or does not exist, has been met or has not been met, etc.

You can almost always identify the phrases-that-pay by turning your rule into an if-then statement.[2] As noted, an "if-then" rule says, for in-

---

[1] *See, e.g.,* Oates, Enquist & Kunsch, *The Legal Writing Handbook* 539 (Aspen 2d ed. 1998).
[2] Note that you should not necessarily articulate your rule as an if-then statement in the argument itself; this technique is merely a method for identifying your phrase-that-pays.

stance, "if a certain condition exists, then a certain legal status results." The "phrase-that-pays" is almost always the "condition" that you are trying to prove the existence (or non-existence) of. Your explanation section would explain what the phrase-that-pays means so that you could show, in your application section, why the phrase-that-pays exists or does not exist in your client's case.

The phrase-that-pays is almost always contained in the "if" clause; that clause usually contains the narrow point that the writer is trying to explain or prove. For example, a rule might be written in a brief as follows:

> **While a person's home is, for most purposes, a place where he expects privacy, activities that are exposed "to the 'plain view' of outsiders are not protected" under the Fourth Amendment.** <u>Katz v. United States</u>, 389 U.S. 347, 361 (1967) (Harlan, J., concurring).

The same rule stated as an if-then statement would read:

> **IF a person exposes activities to the plain view of outsiders, THEN those activities are not protected against observation by the Fourth Amendment's search and seizure limitations.**

This writer is trying to prove that the defendant's activities occurred within the plain view of police officers. Thus, "in plain view" is the phrase-that-pays.

Identifying the phrase-that-pays for each section of your document can help you to focus your writing: Once you have identified your phrase-that-pays, you can test the analysis in each section to make sure that it relates somehow to that phrase-that-pays. In your explanation section, for example, you should define the phrase that pays, explain its meaning, and/or show how it has been interpreted in earlier cases. In the application section of the paradigm, you should show how it applies in this situation.

b. Deciding How Much Explanation Is Necessary

If the phrase-that-pays is unambiguous and/or not controversial in your case, you may not need to provide much explanation at all. For example, if your client was a homeowner whose dog had bitten a person who was committing a burglary, the following rule would need no explanation because its phrase-that-pays ("committing a trespass or other criminal offense") is clear, and its application would not be controversial:

> **Ohio Revised Code § 111.1111 (1995) provides that a dog owner is not liable for the dog's attack on "a person who is committing a trespass or other criminal offense on the dog owner's property at the time of the attack."**

Presumably, all of the issues analyzed in an appellate brief will be controversial; if they were not controversial, they would not need to be analyzed.[3] When a phrase-that-pays is ambiguous, controversial, or both, you should "explain" its meaning by illustrating how it has been applied in one or more authority cases. In the example below, the writer is arguing that an officer's behavior did not violate the Fourth Amendment because the observed activities were in plain view. The writer explains the rule by showing how the concept of "plain view" — the phrase-that-pays — has been interpreted in other cases. Notice how the writer has used the phrase-that-pays (underlined in this example) in each paragraph to help the reader understand how the paragraph connects to the analysis of the legal issue:

> 2. No Fourth Amendment search occurred because the apartment interior was in <u>plain view</u> from the officer's lawful vantage point.
>
> Because Thielen was located outside the curtilage of the apartment, he was free to observe any scene in <u>plain view</u>. Respondents' activities within the apartment were in <u>plain view</u> from Thielen's lawful vantage point. Thus, Thielen's observation violated no reasonable expectation of privacy and did not constitute a Fourth Amendment search [note statement of conclusion here].
>
> The Fourth Amendment protection of the home "has never been extended to require law enforcement officers to shield their eyes when passing by a home on public thoroughfares." <u>California v. Ciraolo</u>, 476 U.S. 207, 213 (1985). While a person's home is, for most purposes, a place where he expects privacy, activities "that he exposes to the '<u>plain view</u>' of outsiders are not protected." <u>Katz v. United States</u>, 389 U.S. 347, 361 (1967) (Harlan, J., concurring) [note statement of rule here].
>
> Illegal activities in <u>plain view</u> from outside the curtilage are not protected even if the police observation is specifically directed at identifying illegal activity. <u>United States v. Dunn</u>, 480 U.S. 294 (1987) (holding that an officer's observation into a barn was not a Fourth Amendment search, and stressing it was irrelevant that the observation was motivated by a law enforcement purpose); <u>Ciraolo</u>, 476 U.S. at 212, 213. In <u>Ciraolo,</u> the defendant was growing marijuana in a 15-by-25 foot plot in his backyard. He surrounded the yard with a 6-foot outer fence and a 10-foot inner fence. <u>Id.</u> at 209. Officers flew over the defendant's house in a private airplane and readily identified the illegal plants using only the naked eye. <u>Id.</u> The government in <u>Ciraolo</u> argued that the observation was analogous to looking through a knothole or an opening in a fence: "If there is an opening, the police may look." <u>Id.</u> at 220. This Court agreed with the government, holding that the observation was not a Fourth Amendment search. <u>Id.</u> The airspace was outside the curtilage of the apartment, and the Court reasoned that the scene would have been in <u>plain view</u> to any member of the public flying in the same airspace. Thus, the officers had violated no reasonable expectation of privacy. <u>Id.</u> at 213-14.

---

[3] See discussion of introductions and roadmaps in Chapter Ten below, for examples of how to deal with issues that are not controversial, but that must be included in the analysis in some way because they are necessary elements of a statute, test, or other legal rule.

The length of your explanation will vary depending on how abstract and/or controversial the rule is. Probably the best way to fully illustrate the meaning of a rule is to use at least one authority that illustrates what the rule does mean in the context of facts that are similar (or nearly similar) to the facts at bar, and at least one authority that illustrates what the rule does *not* mean in the context of facts that are similar to the facts at bar.[4] In the example above, if the writer had found a case in which the court had held that certain activities in a home were *not* within plain view, the reader would have a fuller understanding of why this case must fall within the definition.

Illustrating what the phrase-that-pays means and does not mean sets the boundaries of the phrase-that-pays, and gives the application of law to facts more validity. See Chapter Six for a discussion of how to use authority cases effectively in your explanation section.

5.1.4
APPLY THE RULE TO THE FACTS

After you have articulated the rule and explained it as needed, it's time to "apply" the rule to the facts (some legal writers say "applying the facts to the rule" to mean the same thing). In this step of your analysis, you are trying to show the reader how the phrase-that-pays intersects with the facts. How do the elements that the rule requires exist (or not exist) in your case? You should never substitute synonyms for the phrase-that-pays in any section, but particularly not in the application section.

You should begin the application section of your analysis by stating affirmatively how the rule does or does not apply to the facts. Essentially, you begin by saying "Phrase-that-pays equals (or does not equal) our case facts." If your case is not controversial, a short passage might be enough:

> **In this case, Mr. Burglar was "committing a trespass or other criminal offense" when he was bitten. Mr. Burglar was convicted of the crime of burglary in connection with the events of January 8. Burglary is considered a "criminal offense" under Ohio Rev. Code § 111.1111.**

This writer showed the reader how the rule and its explanation intersected with the client's facts by explaining that burglary "equals" a "criminal offense" under Ohio Revised Code § 111.1111.

If the issue is at all controversial, you should be sure to provide details about the record facts[5] that support your assertion about how the law applies to the facts, as in this example:

---

[4] *See also* Oates, Enquist & Kunsch, *The Legal Writing Handbook* 134 (Aspen 2d ed. 1998)
[5] Be sure to cite to the record so that the court can verify each referenced fact. Rules about and methods for citing to the case record are discussed in a later chapter.

> In the case at bar, Officer Thielen merely observed a scene that was in plain view from his lawful vantage point. The area in which Officer Thielen stood was outside the curtilage of the apartment. While standing outside the curtilage, the officer plainly viewed Respondents' unlawful activities. <u>See</u> Record E-2. While Officer Thielen did go to the common area outside the apartment window in response to the report from the informant, <u>see</u> Record G-11, his motivation is irrelevant. The illegal activity was in plain view regardless of Officer Thielen's motivation.

You may also wish to expand your application section by drawing analogies between your client's case and the cases that you cited for authority in your explanation section:

> Like the officers in <u>Ciraolo</u>, who did not need to shield their eyes from what could be seen while traveling in public airways, Officer Thielen did not need to refrain from viewing what could be seen from the public area outside Thompson's window.

While drawing analogies is not always necessary, analogizing and distinguishing relevant authorities can help to cement the reader's understanding of how a rule does or does not apply to your client's case.

5.1.5
RE-STATE YOUR CONCLUSION

After you have applied the rule to the facts, you should re-state the conclusion as to the issue in that section. You may not need to begin a new paragraph if the application has been brief and the conclusion is straightforward. For example,

> Therefore, because Mr. Burglar was committing a burglary when he was bitten, Mr. Angell cannot be held liable for his injuries under O.R.C. § 111.1111.

Stating your conclusion explicitly at the end of your analysis is an important part of the paradigm. Even though you stated a conclusion at the beginning of your analysis, the conclusion at the end of the analysis serves a different purpose. It makes the reader aware of your conclusion, yes, but it also tells the reader that your analysis of this part of the discussion is finished and that you will soon be moving on to another point.

If the particular section of your argument is about a dispositive point, you can and should make the connection between that point and the ultimate result you seek. In any case, make certain the conclusion connects your analysis of the phrase-that-pays to the point that was at issue in that section of the argument:

> Activities that Respondents exposed to the plain view of outsiders were not protected by the Fourth Amendment. Because Respondents' activi-

ties within the apartment werc in plain view from Thielen's lawful vantage point, Thielen's observation violated no reasonable expectation of privacy.

This conclusion ties the writer's point about the phrase-that-pays — "plain view" — to the point of the section, which is whether the respondents had a reasonable expectation of privacy.

5.2
SUMMARY

By using the CREXAC paradigm to analyze every controversial element in your argument, you give the court the information it needs to understand the validity of each element of your argument. This information, in turn, increases the chances that the court will understand why the law demands the result that you seek.

CHAPTER SIX

PRACTICE POINTERS: USING CASE AUTHORITY EFFECTIVELY

One of the brief's most important jobs is showing the court that the law that supports your argument is valid and that the law that supports your opponent's argument is either invalid or not on point. Accordingly, your argument should address both the authorities that support your argument and the main authorities that support your opponent's argument. Furthermore, the brief should include enough information about the case authorities cited so that anyone can understand their significance. In addition, however, it must use citations effectively so that those who want to consult your cited authorities will be able to do so easily.

The practical brief writer should assume that none of his or her readers will read anything other than the brief itself before deciding the case. Admittedly, at least the judge who writes the opinion, or his or her law clerk, will probably look up each cited case and review it to test whether it adequately supports your argument. Some readers may also conduct additional research to test the validity of the parties' arguments. Because your audience is all of the judges who will be voting, however, your brief should include enough information to be useful to those who want to go beyond it, but to be understandable and credible to those who do not.

With these concerns in mind, brief writers need to pay attention to several different aspects of using case authority: (1) they must deal with negative authorities; (2) they must provide the reader with an appropriate amount of information about the cases they do cite; (3) they must use quotations effectively; (4) they must use language precisely when they are analogizing and distinguishing cases; (5) they must use unpublished decisions properly; and (6) they must use citations in a way that makes it easy for the judge or the judge's clerk to verify the validity of the rules and authorities in the argument.

6.1
ADDRESSING NEGATIVE AUTHORITIES

Some legal writers are tempted to leave out negative authorities, perhaps hoping that their opponents will leave them out, or that the court will not notice the gap. Judge Hamilton of the Fourth Circuit notes that the best briefs "[address] head-on the opponent's best responsive argument, best supporting case law or statutory authority, and, if at issue, the opponent's listing of contrary evidence."[1] If these authorities are missing, the judge may draw negative conclusions, as Judge Parker of the Second Circuit has observed:

> I would also like to recommend that all advocates distinguish contrary authority, even in their opening brief. If there is bad precedent out there for your case, you can assume your adversary will cite it to us, or we will independently find it. If the first time I see an adverse case is in the answering brief, then my initial reaction is that the appellant does not have a good explanation as to why that case is inapposite. While a response in the reply brief may dispel this initial impression, it may not. Therefore, by failing to mention contrary precedent in the opening brief, the advocate makes that precedent more weighty than it perhaps should be.[2]

Addressing negative authorities does not necessarily mean that you have to focus certain sections of your argument on your opponent's authorities. Rather, it means that you must make sure that your argument addresses your opponent's most significant arguments and authorities in some way.

Often, your opponent's authorities will arise naturally, with no special

---

[1] Clyde H. Hamilton, *Effective Appellate Brief Writing*, 50 S.C.L. Rev. 581, 582 (1999).
[2] Fred I. Parker, *Foreword: Appellate Advocacy and Practice in the Second Circuit*, 64 Brooklyn L. Rev. 457, 463-464 (1998).

effort on your part. For example, you may both agree which rules and which cases are relevant, but you disagree as to the meaning of those rules and authorities and their application to your client's facts. In that situation, your argument and analysis may well include all of the authorities that you need to bring up to counter your opponent's argument. Of course, you may wish to pay special attention in your analysis to addressing what the rules or authorities do *not* mean or do *not* say, and to justify your decisions. However, you need not highlight your opponent's arguments, as in this example:

▽ **BAD EXAMPLE**

The Respondent may argue that the <u>McGuffin</u> case applies here.

Instead of arguing defensively, starting with the admission that you are trying to contradict the respondent's argument, you may want to address the point offensively:

△ **GOOD EXAMPLE**

The <u>McGuffin</u> case does not apply here for two reasons. First . . .

In other situations, you may refute your opponent's argument just by making your own argument. For example, if you are arguing that the rational basis test applies, but your opponent is arguing that the strict scrutiny test applies, you can refute your opponent's argument as part of your argument. To do so effectively, however, you must do more than make conclusory statements about which rule applies. Explain why your side of the case is correct, taking into account the arguments that your opponent will probably make.

For example, in the case of *Romer v. Evans*, counsel for the state of Colorado was arguing (unsuccessfully) in favor of a constitutional amendment that prohibited any unit of government from enacting any type of antidiscrimination law that would protect citizens who were identified as homosexual, gay, or lesbian. The lower court had found the statute unconstitutional under the strict scrutiny test, saying that the amendment infringed on the "fundamental right to participate in the political process." The United States Supreme Court held that the amendment failed even the deferential rational basis test.[3] Counsel for the state of Colorado, however, could have believed that the amendment had its best chance under the rational basis test and certainly had to argue against the strict scrutiny test, which the court below had applied. It would have been ineffective, however, merely to state in a conclusory way that the rational basis test applies:

▽ **BAD EXAMPLE**

This Court should apply the rational basis test because this case involves a governmental action, and, contrary to respondent's assertion,

---

[3] *Romer v. Evans*, 517 U.S. 620, 632 (1996).

> none of the factors are present that would call for the application of in-termediate or strict scrutiny.

Instead, counsel should unpack both the reasons that support the application of the rational basis test *and* the reasons that argue against application of the strict scrutiny test. Doing so would create a more complete argument that would directly attack the other side's contentions, but in an offensive rather than a defensive way:

⚠ GOOD EXAMPLE

I.   **This court should examine Amendment 2 under the rational basis standard.**
   A.   **Amendment 2 does not infringe upon the fundamental right to vote.**
   B.   **This court should not expand the reach of the Due Process Clause of the Fourteenth Amendment by recognizing a new fundamental right to participate equally in the political process.**
   C.   **Amendment 2 does not affect a suspect class.**

Notice that these headings do not mention the opponent, nor do they mention the concept of strict scrutiny (although the concept may well have been mentioned in the argument). Instead, they directly attack the substance of the opponent's arguments in favor of strict scrutiny.

The way in which you address negative issues or authorities will depend on the particulars of your case. The important thing is that you address your opponent's arguments.

6.2
PROVIDING APPROPRIATE DETAIL
IN CASE DESCRIPTIONS

Analyzing authority cases is an essential part of effective written advocacy. Many legal writers neglect this important task, presuming wrongly that citations alone provide adequate support for the assertions in the brief. They seem to have the mistaken impression that judges have all of the needed law at their mental fingertips and that the brief writer needs only to allude to some of the relevant authorities, drop in some favorite quotations, or provide a string cite of the cases that might have some bearing on the case at bar — certainly the judge and the clerks can fill in the rest. Most readers, however, need more information than the citation can give.

I gladly agree with the premise that all appellate judges are extremely intelligent and very knowledgeable about the law. However, there is a difference between the general knowledge that they possess and the specific knowledge that is needed to decide a case intelligently. Most judges know and understand the general rules that apply to commonly encountered legal issues. This means that you do not need to discuss the British practice of writs of assistance in the colonies when arguing a Fourth Amendment case or cite to *Marbury v. Madison* if you are asking the court to declare a statute unconstitutional. Having the general knowledge to understand what rules mean and how they apply does *not* suggest, however, that all judges know the particular details of every case that you cite, and why and how each is relevant to your legal argument.

When you cite a case in a brief, it will mostly likely be for one of two reasons. You may be using the case to provide "rule authority": that is, you are citing the case to provide authority for the existence of a rule. More likely, however, you are citing the case as "illustrative authority": that is, you believe that the case effectively illustrates how the rule should be applied. While the depth of your case description may vary depending on whether it is being used as a rule authority or an illustrative authority, you should provide some description for every case you cite. As a former deputy solicitor general has noted, "[e]very case that is worth citing . . . is worth discussing sufficiently to show why it is particularly on point or sheds analogous light on the question at hand."[4]

The question remains, what is "sufficient" discussion? Generally, if you are citing a case, the reader should be able to glean four elements from your case description. Notice that I say that the reader should be able to *glean* these four elements. I am not saying that you must devote a sentence to each of these elements or even that you must say all of these elements aloud. Your decisions as to which elements to say aloud and which to leave unsaid will depend, as do most decisions, on the context in which the case descriptions appear.

With that warning, here are the elements:

(1) **The issue.** Be sure that the reader can identify which of the case's many issues and sub-issues you are using the case to illustrate. You should also provide the legal context in which the court analyzed that issue, *if it is different from the context of the case at bar or the cases under discussion in that section of your argument.* If you will be analogizing or distinguishing the case based on the details relevant to the legal issue, be sure to provide sufficient detail so that the reader can understand your analysis.

(2) **The disposition.** Make clear how the court disposed of that narrow issue and, if relevant, how it disposed of the entire case.

(3) **The facts.** Include enough of the legally significant facts for the reader to understand how the court applied the law to reach its holding on the issue and how the case is analogous to the case at bar. If you wish

---

[4] James vanR. Springer, *Symposium on Supreme Court Advocacy: Some Suggestions on Preparing Briefs on the Merits In the Supreme Court of the United States,* 33 Cath. U.L. Rev. 593, 601 (1984). (The author was a deputy solicitor general of the United States from 1968 to 1971.)

to draw an analogy to these facts or to distinguish your case based on its facts, provide more detail.

(4) **The reasoning.** Include enough information to give the reader a basic understanding of why the court decided the issue before it in the way that it did. If either the case or the reasoning behind the court's decision is significant, provide more detail.

Including these four elements in a case description is not all that the effective brief writer must do, however. In order to ensure that the brief is effective, you must be sure that your case description is as succinct as possible; you must use verb tenses accurately; and you must use parenthetical case descriptions effectively and appropriately.

6.2.1
MAKING CASE DESCRIPTIONS AS SUCCINCT AS POSSIBLE

Including the issue, the holding, the facts, and the reasoning in a case description may seem to require a long description. Actually, all four of these elements can often be conveyed in a parenthetical description and certainly in a textual description of two sentences. Of course, if the case is significant, or if the argument is controversial, your case description will be lengthier.

There are two keys to succinct case descriptions. The first key is focus. You must understand the focus of the argument you are currently making, and make sure that the case description has that same focus. The second key is efficient use of language. Too many case descriptions begin with a wasted sentence that does little more than announce that the case exists. Use your subjects and verbs with care to convey the most information in as few words as you can.

a. Focus

The case descriptions below are from a discussion about the illegality of gender-based classifications in a brief written in support of the petitioner's argument in *Miller v. Albright*. Notice how they efficiently include each of the necessary case description elements (signaled by a number after each of the elements appears):

⚠ GOOD EXAMPLE

① Issue
② Disposition
③ Facts
④ Reasoning

As noted above, the <u>VMI</u> Court discredited **②** governmental justifications for gender-based classifications **①** as to state-supported military schools **③** because the justifications were based on overbroad generalizations about the different capabilities of men and women **④**. 116 S. Ct. at 2275. The <u>J.E.B.</u> Court also categorically rejected **②** such broad assumptions about men and women's relative capabilities **④** when it struck down **②** a state's use of gender-based peremptory challenges to exclude all men from a jury **①** & **③**. 511 U.S. 138-40.

One method you can use to test the focus of your case descriptions is to look for the phrase-that-pays that you are focusing on in that section of the document. If you have used the phrase-that-pays, chances are good that you have at least focused the description on the right legal issue. For example, in the previous example, "gender-based classifications" was the phrase-that-pays. In the "plain view" argument discussed in Chapter 5, the brief writer discussed cases in which the Court allowed or disallowed certain searches based on whether or not the officers were looking at things that were in "plain view." The brief writer took care to connect the words "plain view" to each of the two case descriptions in the following illustration:

⚠ **GOOD EXAMPLE**

> **Illegal activities in plain view [phrase-that-pays] from outside the curtilage are not protected even if the police observation is specifically directed at identifying illegal activity. United States v. Dunn, 480 U.S. 294 (1987) (finding that an officer's plain view [phrase-that-pays] ④ observation into a barn ③ was not a Fourth Amendment search ③ & ②, even though the observation was motivated by a law enforcement purpose ③); Ciraolo, 476 U.S. at 212, 213. In Ciraolo, the defendant was growing marijuana in a 15-by-25 foot plot in his backyard. He surrounded the yard with a 6-foot outer fence and a 10-foot inner fence ③. Id. at 209. Officers flew over the defendant's house in a private airplane and readily identified the illegal plants using only the naked eye ③. Id.**
>
> **   The government in Ciraolo argued that the observation was analogous to looking through a knothole or an opening in a fence: "If there is an opening, the police may look." Id. at 220. This Court agreed with the government, holding that the officers violated no expectation of privacy and that the observation was not a Fourth Amendment search ① & ②. Id. at 215. The airspace was outside the curtilage of the apartment, and the Court reasoned that the scene would have been in plain view [phrase-that-pays] to any member of the public flying in the same airspace ④. Id. at 213-14.**

① Issue
② Disposition
③ Facts
④ Reasoning

If the court has not been thoughtful enough to use the phrase-that-pays that you have identified for that section of the argument, you can make the connection yourself, as long as you do it honestly. If you do make the connection yourself, be sure to justify the connection in the way you describe the case, or with language that you quote, as in this illustration of a description of the court's reasoning in a fictional case:

⚠ **GOOD EXAMPLE**

> **The court apparently believed that the search was justified by the fact that the defendant was smoking marijuana in plain view [phrase-that-pays] of the arresting officer, because it noted that "police officers need not turn away when they encounter illegal behavior right under their noses." Ohio v. McGuffin, 101 U.S. 101, 103 (2013).**

When trying to decide how much detail to give the reader, first assess how you are using the case. If you are using the case as rule authority and you plan to discuss it in depth in your "explanation" section, you may give only a "naked cite." On the other hand, you may be using a case as rule authority only because it is from a court of mandatory jurisdiction or it is well-known as the source of a particular rule, rather than because of its relevance to your client's case. (Presumably, you plan to use other cases to illustrate the rule.) If that is the situation, you should provide a parenthetical description, as indicated in the writer's use of the <u>Dunn</u> case on page 67 above.

b. Using Language Effectively

Even when using a textual case description and even when you must give the reader more detail, your case description should not be needlessly long. Provide only the information that the reader needs about each of the four elements. The description of the <u>Ciraolo</u> case on page 67 above is somewhat lengthy, but its length is concentrated in the facts and the reasoning. The plain-view issue is fact-specific, and thus the details about cases in which plain view was or was not established were particularly important in that case.

In many case descriptions, writers run into trouble in the first sentence. One way to avoid this trouble is to concentrate on the subject-verb combination. The first sentence you write about a case should tell the reader something that the court did in that case or something about the reasoning. It should *not* tell us what the case "involved," "regarded," or "concerned," or what the court "addressed," "considered," "examined," or "dealt with." Notice how the first sentence in the following case description wastes the reader's time and (scarce) energy:

▽ BAD EXAMPLE

> In <u>J.E.B. v. T.B.</u>, 511 U.S. 127 (1994), **this Court examined the issue of sex discrimination in the selection of jurors.**

This sentence leaves the reader in suspense, and suspense is the enemy of good legal writing. Instead of saying only that the court "examined" the issue, the writer should say something about a court's ultimate ruling or, if relevant, a particular finding in the case. Verbs like "held" and "found" are more likely to get your reader to the point of the case:

△ GOOD EXAMPLE

1 Issue
2 Disposition
3 Facts
4 Reasoning

> **This Court has held that sex-based ❶ peremptory challenges ❸ violate ❷ jurors' rights to equal protection ❶. <u>J.E.B. v. T.B.</u>, 511 U.S. 127, 138-40 (1994).**

The bad example told the reader only the issue that the court addressed in *J.E.B.* The good example, on the other hand, tells the reader the issue, the legally significant facts, and the disposition of the issue. The writer can add any needed reasoning in a second sentence.[5]

c. Verb Tense in Case Descriptions

Many writers get confused as to the appropriate verb tense when describing cases. This confusion results when courts mix general rules, which are properly stated in the present tense, with case facts, findings, and holdings, which are properly stated in some form of the past tense.[6]

Within a case description, use some form of past tense to describe the events that happened before the case began as well as events that happened in the case. The court's holdings as to specific parties should also be described using the past tense:[6]

⚠ **GOOD EXAMPLE**

The plaintiff claimed that the defendant had assaulted him.
The advertisement had not specified the need for a college education.
Defendant had sought outside counsel before deciding to terminate the
**   plaintiff.**
The plaintiff alleged . . .
The defendant argued . . .
The court found . . .
The court reasoned . . .
The court held that Officer Thielen had violated the Fourth Amend-
**   ment when he observed the defendants through a gap in a window**
**   blind.**

When you are stating a general rule that the court articulated, however, use the past tense only to describe the court's action, and use the present tense for the rule itself:

⚠ **GOOD EXAMPLE**

The Court held that police officers do not violate the Fourth Amend-
ment when they are able to observe criminal activity from a lawful
vantage point without the aid of special equipment.

The correct verb tense may not make or break your argument, but using the wrong verb tense distracts the reader at best. At worst, it confuses the reader and slows down his or her comprehension.

6.2.2
WRITING AND USING EFFECTIVE PARENTHETICAL DESCRIPTIONS

Many writers use parenthetical case descriptions to give the reader information about authority cases more efficiently. Parenthetical descrip-

---

[5] For information on avoiding wordiness generally, *see* Anne Enquist & Laurel Currie Oates, *Just Writing: Grammar, Punctuation, and Style for the Legal Writer* 110-26 (Aspen 2001).

[6] A detailed discussion of the sequence of tenses is beyond the scope of this book; for an excellent explanation of how verb tenses are used in legal writing, *see* Anne Enquist & Laurel Currie Oates, *Just Writing: Grammar, Punctuation, and Style for the Legal Writer* 176-81 (Aspen 2001).

tions can save both space and the reader's time, and they are often a good choice. However, it is just as important to keep the principles of focus and completeness in mind when writing parenthetical descriptions as it is when writing textual descriptions. Ineffective parentheticals tend to give the reader a snippet of information, but not enough to make the case useful to the reader who must decide whether the cited case provides authority for a ruling in the case at bar:

▽ **BAD EXAMPLE**

> <u>See generally</u> <u>VMI</u>, 116 S. Ct. at 2275 (discussing gender-based classifications in state-run military schools); <u>J.E.B. v. T.B.</u>, 511 U.S. at 138-40 (male juror challenged peremptory challenge based on his sex).

These parentheticals tell the reader something about the issue (gender-based classifications) and the facts (the classifications occurred in a military school and in peremptory challenges to jury selection), but they do not tell the reader how the court resolved the issue or why the court resolved it the way it did. An effective parenthetical gives the reader information about the issue, the disposition, the facts, and the reasoning:

△ **GOOD EXAMPLE**

① Issue
② Disposition
③ Facts
④ Reasoning

> <u>See generally</u> <u>VMI</u>, 116 S. Ct. at 2275 (rejecting ② governmental justifications for gender-based classifications ① as to state-supported military schools ③ because justifications were based on "overbroad generalizations about the different capabilities of men and women" ④); <u>J.E.B. v. T.B.</u>, 511 U.S. 138-40 ("categorically" rejecting broad assumptions about relative capabilities of men and women ④ and striking down ② gender-based ① peremptory challenges in jury selection ③).

As with textual descriptions, using language effectively and focusing on the phrase-that-pays can help to make the description more useful.

Knowing how to write effective parenthetical case descriptions is important, but the writer must also know *when* to use a parenthetical description. Deciding whether to use a textual or a parenthetical description for a cited case is really a question about how much detail to provide. If little detail is needed, as when you are citing to a case only for rule authority, you can easily use a parenthetical description. Ultimately, your decision will be based on the answers to two questions: (1) How is the case significant to your argument? (2) What information does the reader need to have in order to understand the case's significance? The more significant an authority case is, and the more important it is for the reader to understand its facts and reasoning, the more detail you need to provide *in your argument*. If the issue or the authority case is more straightforward, on the other hand, you can provide a shorter textual description or a parenthetical description.

As noted in Chapter Five, the ideal explanation section within each unit of discourse in your argument will include at least one case in which the court found that the rule applied to a certain set of facts, and at least one case in which the court found that the rule did *not* apply to a certain different set of facts. In most situations, you will want to provide a textual description of both of those cases. A sensible compromise is to provide one or two more detailed case descriptions, followed up — when needed — by citation to one or more illustrative cases with merely parenthetical descriptions.

Do not use this method as an excuse to bombard the reader with eight authorities where one would suffice. Cite an additional authority only when it illustrates some aspect of the case that your previous authorities did not illustrate, or when it proves that the interpretation you are illustrating is well established. (See the discussion about avoiding string cites, in Section 6.6.3, about limiting your citations.)

The following example is an excerpt from a Respondent's brief in *Minnesota v. Carter*. The brief writer is using four cases to explain the rule that a person has a legitimate expectation of privacy in a location if that person can demonstrate an expectation that his or her activities would be private, and if society will accept that expectation as reasonable. This example shows the "Conclusion, Rule, Explanation" part of the paradigm. The writer begins by articulating the rule and citing to authority, and follows by stating in a summary fashion how the rule should apply to the client's facts. The writer then proceeds to explain the rule, using the rule authority and other cases. In one of the cases, the Court found that no legitimate expectation of privacy existed. Notice how the writer gives details from the Court's reasoning in that case that he can use to distinguish the case from that of his clients, who are claiming an expectation of privacy in an apartment that they visited for the purpose of packaging illegal drugs:

⚠ **GOOD EXAMPLE**

This Court has held that people will be recognized as having a legitimate expectation of privacy if they demonstrate an expectation that their activities are treated as private, and if it can be shown that society will find that expectation to be reasonable in a given situation. Katz v. United States, 389 U.S. 347, 361 (1967) (Harlan, J., concurring) **1**. In this case, respondents demonstrated their expectation of privacy when they lowered the blinds to the apartment's window. Society should be prepared to recognize this expectation of privacy in a friend's apartment as reasonable.

1 Rule authority that will be used later in this section as illustrative authority and then described in full.

This Court has allowed Fourth Amendment protections to extend beyond the home when the defendants have legitimate expectations of privacy and society can accept those expectations as legitimate. See, e.g., Minnesota v. Olson, 495 U.S. 91, 98 (1990) **1**. In Olson, this Court held that the unwarranted arrest of defendant, an overnight guest, was an illegal seizure. Id. The Court recognized that overnight guests have a sufficient interest in the privacy of the host's home to be free from unwarranted search and seizure. Id. at 96-97. Furthermore, the defendant's subjective expectation of privacy was found to be reasonable because society is

1 illustrative authority

known to recognize the social custom of staying overnight in an-other's home: "We will all be hosts and we will all be guests many times in our lives. From either perspective, we think that society recognizes that a houseguest has a legitimate expectation of pri-vacy in his host's home." Id. at 98. The Court specifically noted that it is a "mistaken premise" that a place "must be one's 'home' in order for one to have a legitimate expectation of privacy there." Id. at 96.

   Indeed, this Court has consistently found that legitimate ex-pectations of privacy exist outside the home, as long as the cir-cumstances are those in which most people would normally expect to enjoy a feeling of privacy. Olson, 496 U.S. at 96–97. Ac-cordingly, this Court has found that defendants did not have a le-gitimate expectation of privacy in the contents of a car in which they were merely passengers, and where they had expressed no ex-pectation of privacy in the areas of the car searched. Rakas v. Illi-nois, 439 U.S. 128, 148-49 (1978). The Rakas Court specifically refused to make a finding as to whether guests in houses or apart-ments would be treated similarly, noting that "cars are not to be treated identically with houses or apartments for Fourth Amend-ment purposes." Id. at 148 (citations omitted). See also Katz v. United States, 389 U.S. 347, 348 (defendant found to have legiti-mate expectation of privacy in conversations in a closed phone booth); McGuffin v. United States, 362 U.S. 257, 265 (1960) (defendant has standing to challenge a search warrant used to ar-rest him while in a friend's apartment).

Thus, when describing authority cases, (1) make sure to provide sufficient information about the issue, disposition, facts, and reasoning; (2) focus the information on the issue currently under discussion; (3) use language efficiently to avoid unnecessary wordiness; and (4) use parentheticals as needed for rule authorities or less-significant cases.

6.3
USING QUOTATIONS EFFECTIVELY IN CASE DESCRIPTIONS

First of all, you should usually paraphrase rather than quote lan-guage from authorities. Quotation marks draw the reader's attention, and you want to save that special attention for important statements. Gener-ally, use direct quotations only when you are stating rules or other lan-guage at issue, or when you are justifying a conclusion you have drawn about the meaning of an authority.

Writers' problems with quotations from cases tend to fall into the two categories of "not enough" and "too much." Some writers drop quotations into their arguments without giving the reader enough information about the case. Without sufficient context, the quotation is meaningless. Other writers give the reader too much quoted language, leaving the reader to sift through the language and sort out its meaning. Police your writing to avoid both kinds of problems.

6.3.1
NOT ENOUGH CONTEXT

Legend has it that Marie Antoinette once said, "Let them eat cake!" If you don't know the context of that remark, she sounds like a pretty nice person. She sounds a lot less friendly, however, once you learn that she supposedly said it while looking down at the peasants in the street who were crying for bread.

Keep Marie in mind when you are tempted to drop a pithy quote from an obscure case into the middle of your rule explanation section. If the judge doesn't know what that court was looking at — i.e., the issue, the rule, and the facts — when it made that statement, he or she can't begin to understand the significance of the quote without looking the case up. And since most judges don't have time to read the cases cited in the briefs, the quote may have a negative impact because the judge will be annoyed at being given insufficient or misleading information.

Thus, when using a quotation from a case, be sure you have provided the reader with the type of context mentioned in Section 6.2 above. Do not drop a quotation into your argument like a chocolate chip into batter:

▽ BAD EXAMPLE

> This Court has noted that generalizations "concerning parent-child relations . . . become less acceptable as the age of the child increase[s]." Caban v. Mohammed, 441 U.S. 380, 382 (1979). Thus, the gender-based generalizations in this case are invalid.

An altered quotation with an unaccompanied citation does not fill the court with confidence about the validity of your argument. Instead, include the details that will give context for the quotation:

△ GOOD EXAMPLE

> As far back as 1979, this Court struck down a statute that characterized parent-child relationships between unwed fathers and their children differently from those of unwed mothers. Caban v. Mohammed, 441 U.S. 380, 382 (1979). While conceding that unwed mothers might be closer to their children at birth, the Court stated that the generalization would become "less acceptable as a basis for legislative distinctions" as the age of the child increased. Id.

Quotations can also be used effectively in a parenthetical:

△ GOOD EXAMPLE

See, e.g., <u>Caban v. Mohammed</u>, 441 U.S. 380, 382 (1979) (striking down statute that distinguished on the basis of unwed mothers' and fathers' relative relationships with their offspring, noting that any generalizations would become "less acceptable as a basis for legislative distinctions" as the child grew older).

By making a quotation part of a coherent case description, you make it more likely that the quotation will do the job of convincing the court that the case stands for the proposition you say it does.

6.3.2
TOO MUCH QUOTED LANGUAGE

Some writers are so enamored with the court's language that they are loathe to paraphrase. Instead, they simply provide page after page of excerpted quotes and let the reader determine the significance of the quoted language. "Over-quoting" creates two problems. First, the writer is not doing his or her job. The writer is not supposed to provide the raw material to the readers and let them sort out what it all means. Instead, the writer should research the law, synthesize the available information, and write up the analysis in a way that allows the reader to understand the situation with a minimum of effort.

The second problem is related to the first. A reader who is constantly asked to consume and digest lengthy quotations may lose the thread of the argument. As a practical matter, many readers (including some of the people reading this book) skip long quotations. Judges who are reading briefs know that the quotation says nothing about the case currently before the court; instead, it talks about another case, which must somehow be connected to the current case. Writers who overuse long quotes frequently do so because they have not figured out that connection and thus cannot make the connection within the argument. They compensate by giving the reader background reading that may, with luck, allow the reader to reach the conclusion that the writer espouses.

The following example is from a student-written brief written in the case of <u>Chicago v. Morales</u>. In that case, the City of Chicago argued in favor of the constitutionality of a statute that allowed the arrest of people who "loitered" with gang members and who refused to disperse on police order. The writer of the following example apparently wanted the reader to use the quoted language to draw the conclusion that laws that promote "peace and quiet" are constitutional:

▽ BAD EXAMPLE

This Court has provided almost absolute protection to speech of a political nature. In 1969, the Court found the arrest of demonstrators for disorderly conduct to be unconstitutional under the First Amendment.

Gregory v. Chicago, 394 U.S. 111, 116 (1969). The Court made this find-ing in favor of political speech even though the picketers' actions led to a disruption of the peace and quiet of a neighborhood by picketing in front of the mayor's home. Id. at 111. A concurring opinion stressed the lawfulness and peacefulness of the demonstration as well as the peti-tioners' First Amendment right to engage in that activity. Id. at 121 (Black, J., concurring). However, Justice Black also declared:

> Plainly, however, no mandate in our Constitution leaves States and governmental units powerless to pass laws to protect the public from the kind of boisterous and threatening conduct that disturbs the tranquility of spots selected by the people either for homes, wherein they can escape the hurly-burly of the outside business and political world, or for public and other buildings that require peace and quiet to carry out their functions, such as courts, libraries, schools, and hospitals.

Id. at 118 (Black, J., concurring). Therefore, even if loitering were treated as a fundamental right, Petitioner possesses a significant, legiti-mate interest in limiting criminal street gang members' right to loiter for no purpose.

Readers who skipped the quote would have no way of knowing where the writer's "therefore" came from. Even readers who read the quote would have to figure out for themselves the significance of the quoted language. If you are tempted to use a lengthy quotation, try one of two tactics to help ensure that your readers will understand your message.

The first and perhaps most obvious solution is to try to shorten the quote. Start by underlining the language that is most significant to your argument:

> Plainly, however, <u>no mandate in our Constitution</u> leaves States and gov-ernmental units powerless to pass laws to protect the public from the kind of boisterous and <u>threatening conduct</u> that <u>disturbs the tranquility</u> of spots selected by the people either for homes, wherein they can es-cape the hurly-burly of the outside business and political world, or for public and other buildings that require peace and quiet to carry out their functions, such as courts, libraries, schools, and hospitals.

Then, quote only the underlined material, and incorporate a paraphrase of the rest into your argument:

⚠ GOOD EXAMPLE

This Court has provided almost absolute protection to speech of a polit-ical nature. In 1969, the Court found the arrest of demonstrators for disorderly conduct to be unconstitutional under the First Amendment. Gregory v. Chicago, 394 U.S. 111, 116 (1969). The Court made this find-ing in favor of political speech even though the picketers' actions led to a disruption of the peace and quiet of a neighborhood by picketing in front of the mayor's home. <u>Id.</u> at 111. A concurring opinion stressed the lawfulness and peacefulness of the demonstration as well as the petitioners' First Amendment right to engage in that activity. <u>Id.</u> at 121 (Black, J., concurring). However, Justice Black also declared that "no mandate in our Constitution" prevents states from passing laws that protect the public from "threatening conduct" that "disturbs the tranquility" of homes or certain public buildings. <u>Id.</u> at 118 (Black, J., concurring). Therefore, even if loitering were treated as a fundamental right, Petitioner possesses a significant, legitimate interest in limiting criminal street gang members' right to loiter for no purpose.

In the alternative, you may determine that the lengthy quote is absolutely necessary for your argument. If this is the case, promote the effectiveness of the quotation by articulating the conclusions you want the reader to draw from it and putting those conclusions into the body of your argument. I recommend using what I refer to as a "Tom Brokaw Introduction" before the quotation.

A Tom Brokaw Introduction is an introduction that focuses the reader's attention on the point the writer is using the quotation to prove or establish. I call it that because Tom Brokaw and other newscasters constantly introduce little snippets of interviews or public events in the same way that a long quote is a little snippet of an opinion or other legal document. Legal writers, unfortunately, often give readers unfocused introductions like "The Court noted," or, as in the illustration above, "Justice Black also declared." In contrast, newscasters almost never give introductions like "The President said," or "The Senator noted." Instead, they give the audience some context and essentially tell them what to listen for when they hear the quoted language.

The illustration below is from a newscast in which Tom Brokaw excerpted pieces of his interview with Senator Daniel Inouye. Senator Inouye is a Japanese-American who served in the United States Military during World War Two despite having been interned as an "enemy alien" after the Japanese bombed Pearl Harbor. Notice how the language leading up to the quotation prepares the audience for what is to come:

⚠ GOOD EXAMPLE

Suddenly, Inouye and every other Japanese-American were suspects — even though many had lived in this country all their lives.

"We were considered enemy aliens right after December 7," says Inouye.[7]

In the same way, you should introduce your quotation by stating the conclusion you want the reader to draw from the quotation:

[7] NBC Nightly News with Tom Brokaw, Interview with Senator Daniel Inouye (June 21, 2000): *http://www.msnbc.com/news/423871.asp* (accessed 9/6/01).

⚠ GOOD EXAMPLE

However, Justice Black also pointed out that governments can prohibit certain behaviors in public places to protect the public:

> Plainly, however, no mandate in our Constitution leaves States and governmental units powerless to pass laws to protect the public from the kind of boisterous and threatening conduct that disturbs the tranquility of spots selected by the people either for homes, wherein they can escape the hurly-burly of the outside business and political world, or for public and other buildings that require peace and quiet to carry out their functions, such as courts, libraries, schools, and hospitals.

Id. at 118 (Black, J., concurring). Therefore, it is possible for municipalities to protect both the Constitution and the peace and quiet of their communities with appropriate legislation.

Use a "Tom Brokaw Introduction" to help the reader to get the most out of lengthy quotations. The focused introduction will encourage the reader to read the quote by directing his or her attention and making it easier to understand the point of the quotation. Even if the reader does skip the quote, the writer has still made the point of the quotation in a way that the reader can understand.

6.4
USING LANGUAGE PRECISELY WHEN ANALOGIZING AND DISTINGUISHING CASES

Analogizing and distinguishing relevant authority cases can be a vital part of the application sections of your argument. By showing the reader how a case is like or unlike a relevant case, a writer can convince the reader to apply the rule in a way that will achieve the desired result. Note that your application section should not *begin* with the analogy or distinction. Instead, begin with an explicit assertion about how the law applies to the facts (generally, "phrase-that-pays equals or does not equal case facts"). Use the relevant cases to support that assertion.

Do not begin your application this way:

▽ BAD EXAMPLE

This case is like McGuffin.

Instead, begin by telling the reader how the law applies to the facts:

⚠️ GOOD EXAMPLE

Mr. Pillion had a reasonable expectation of privacy. Like the defendant in McGuffin. . . .

Your case analogies and distinctions will be most effective if they are *precise*. Do not analogize a specific fact to a whole case:

🔻 BAD EXAMPLE

Like Robinson, the Defendant here had committed an arrestable offense.

This comparison is inapt because one defendant, by definition, cannot be "like" a whole case. Make your analogy or distinction specific. Compare defendants to defendants, and other actors to their specific counterparts in the authority case. These illustrations, from the sample brief in Appendix C, make the comparisons explicit:

⚠️ GOOD EXAMPLE

In the present case, Respondents, like the defendants in Lewis and Hicks, were present on property for the sole purpose of conducting criminal business.

⚠️ GOOD EXAMPLE

Like the officer in Lewis, Officer Thielen observed only activities that were a necessary part of Respondents' illegal business. During the entire time Officer Thielen watched the apartment occupants, the occupants did nothing but divide and package cocaine. See Record at E-2, G-14.

⚠️ GOOD EXAMPLE

Thus, like the defendant in Riley, Respondents were completely undisturbed by the officer's observations. Like the defendant in Riley, Respondents cannot claim the officer took extraordinary measures. Officer Thielen did not violate any reasonable expectation of privacy.

These examples also provide details from the client's case that make the analogies vivid. The writer must do more than make the bare statement that "this case is like (or unlike) McGuffin" if the reader is to see the connection or the disconnect between the two cases. In the example below, the writer takes care to provide the details that will clarify the distinctions between the two cases:

⚠️ GOOD EXAMPLE

Unlike the defendant in Katz, who argued that he sought privacy by closing the door to his phone booth, Respondents introduced no evidence of conduct that demonstrated an intent to keep their activity private. Though the blinds were drawn, there is no indication that Respondents drew them. See Record at E-2, E-10. On the night in question, Respondents were present in a first-floor apartment that had sev-

eral windows at ground level. Record G-26. The windows faced a public area that apartment residents and nonresidents frequented. Record G-69, G-70. As darkness fell in early evening, Respondents sat illuminated under a chandelier light at a table directly in front of one of these windows. Record G-13. Only a pane of glass and a set of blinds that featured a series of laths, Record G-50, separated Respondents from the adjacent common area. On the night in question, the blinds, though drawn, had a gap in them; the gap was large enough for a citizen who passed by and an officer who stood a foot or more from the window to view easily the entire illuminated interior scene. Record G-13.

An individual in Respondents' position would have known and expected that a passerby could look through the gaps in the blinds and see into the illuminated kitchen. Thus, Respondents could not have actually expected that their illegal activities would go unnoticed. Absent a subjective expectation, Respondents do not have a legitimate expectation of privacy and cannot assert a Fourth Amendment challenge to an alleged search of the premises. Therefore, this Court must reverse.

This application is somewhat long, but the details are necessary for the reader to understand how the law applies to the facts. When you analogize and distinguish cases, first make sure that your analogy or distinction focuses on the specific aspects of the case that you want to compare. Second, make sure that you provide the details that allow the reader to understand both the comparison and the application of law to facts.

6.5
DEALING WITH UNPUBLISHED DECISIONS

In recent years, the "publication" and use of unpublished decisions has become controversial, with some courts forbidding their citation, others allowing it with some restrictions, and one court holding that rules limiting use of unpublished decisions are unconstitutional.[8] When deciding whether to cite to unpublished decisions, you must follow the rules of the court to which you are writing.

All U.S. Supreme Court opinions are published, as are virtually all opinions of state Supreme Courts. State and federal trial courts and intermediate appellate courts, however, designate a significant percentage of their opinions as "unpublished." Actually, because of the availability of opinions on the Internet and research services like Lexis and Westlaw, the decisions are not "unpublished" in the real sense. Instead, they are decisions that the court has decided to designate as unpublished, perhaps because the judges believe that they address routine issues that will not

[8] *Anastasoff v. United States*, 223 F.3d 898 (8th Cir. 2000).

add significantly to the body of law.[9] The First Circuit, for example, has used its local rules to explain that it issues unpublished opinions "in the interests both of expedition in the particular case, and of saving time and effort in research on the part of future litigants," and that such opinions "are likely not to break new legal ground or contribute otherwise to legal development."[10]

Most federal circuit courts allow citation to unpublished decisions, but only as persuasive authority.[11] Some of the rules that allow citation to these decisions specifically state that their use is "disfavored." For example, Rule 36.3 of the United States Court of Appeals for the Tenth Circuit provides:

> (A) Not precedent. Unpublished orders and judgments of this court are not binding precedents, except under the doctrines of law of the case, res judicata, and collateral estoppel.
> (B) Reference. Citation of an unpublished decision is disfavored. But an unpublished decision may be cited if:
>> (1) it has persuasive value with respect to a material issue that has not been addressed in a published opinion; and
>> (2) it would assist the court in its disposition.
> (C) Attach copy. A copy of an unpublished decision must be attached to any document that cites it. If an unpublished decision is cited at oral argument, the citing party must provide a copy to the court and the other parties.

In contrast, some courts absolutely forbid the use of unpublished opinions and would be correct to chastise counsel if they were used. For example, Rule 36(b)(2)(F) of the United States Court of Appeals for the First Circuit provides:

> (F) Unpublished opinions may be cited only in related cases. Only published opinions may be cited otherwise. Unpublished means the opinion is not published in the printed West reporter.

Because a search on the internet or on Westlaw or Lexis may turn up unpublished opinions, you must know what the rules are in the court to which you are writing. If you don't know the rules, find out. Check the library or the court's Web site, or call the clerk of the court. If the court does allow citation to unpublished opinions, and you cite any in your brief, be sure to attach copies of them to the briefs that you serve on the court and on opposing counsel.

Unpublished opinions require different citation forms. The *ALWD Citation Manual* (Aspen 2000), Rule 12.18, for example, requires that the

---

[9] *E.g.,* K. K. DuVivier, *Are Some Words Better Left Unpublished? Precedent and the Role of Unpublished Decisions,* 3 J. App. Prac. & Process 397, 399 (2001).
[10] Rule 36(a) of the United States Court of Appeals for the First Circuit.
[11] *DuVivier, supra* n.11, at 404.

author provide the case name, the docket number, the court abbreviation, and the exact date of disposition:

> Operator Serv. Co. v. Croteau, No. CL961672Al (Fla. Cir. Ct. 15th Dist. Aug. 5, 1996).

Particularly if the case is a recent decision, you may decide to provide additional parenthetical material to distinguish a decision that is unpublished because it is so recent from a decision that is unpublished because the court designated it as unpublished:

> McGuffin v. Coleman, No. LCW25890856 (Fla. Cir. Ct. 85th Dist. Jun. 13, 2001) (court-designated unpublished decision) (copy attached).

In addition or in the alternative, you may want to state explicitly that you are citing to an unpublished decision in the text of your argument:

> The 98th District Court of Appeals, in an unpublished decision, endorsed just this interpretation in 1992. Pillion v. McGuffin, No. AB9123561A4 (Ohio App. 98th Dist. Jan. 24, 1992) (copy attached).

Use your judgment when deciding whether to add this information, but it is usually better to err on the side of giving too much information if there is a possibility that the court will presume you are violating court rules.

6.6
USING CITATIONS EFFECTIVELY

6.6.1
WHEN TO CITE

The first challenge for many legal writers is figuring out when citations are necessary. Generally, you *must* include a citation at the end of every sentence in which you state a legal proposition, refer to a new authority, or state what a court held, found, reasoned, or decided. One of the few occasions on which you may *omit* a citation is when you have already analyzed an authority and are applying that authority's rule to your case. For example, the statement that "the *McGuffin* rule applies here" does not need a citation in a discussion in which the writer has already introduced and cited *McGuffin*.

Some legal propositions are so basic that they may seem self-evident. If you are asking a court to apply such a legal principle to your client's case, however, you should cite an authority that controls in that court's jurisdiction. Legal writing is referenced writing, and readers expect frequent citation. Use short citation forms and effective sentence structures to keep your writing readable.

6.6.2
USING EFFECTIVE SENTENCE STRUCTURES TO ACCOMMODATE CITATION FORM

Many writers instinctively introduce a new case by beginning a sentence with a long-form citation:

▽ BAD EXAMPLE

> In <u>J.E.B. v. T.B.</u>, 511 U.S. 127, 138-40 (1994), this Court held that sex-based peremptory challenges violate jurors' rights to equal protection.

This sentence is difficult to read because the citation takes up a lot of space within the sentence. Furthermore, this structure puts too much emphasis on the citation and not enough emphasis on the substance of the sentence. To solve this problem, some writers would mistakenly separate the case name from the rest of the sentence:

▽ BAD EXAMPLE

> In <u>J.E.B. v. T.B.</u>, this Court held that sex-based peremptory challenges violate jurors' rights to equal protection. 511 U.S. 127, 138-40 (1994).

This "separated long-form" structure is also not acceptable. First, no citation rule condones this separation.[12] Second and more importantly, it may confuse the reader, who could be expecting a long-form citation because she does not recall reading about the case earlier. The best way to write a readable sentence and still use correct citation form is to put the citation in a separate citation sentence:

△ GOOD EXAMPLE

> This Court has held that sex-based peremptory challenges violate jurors' rights to equal protection. <u>J.E.B. v. T.B.</u>, 511 U.S. 127, 138-40 (1994).

Thus, instead of focusing the attention in your sentence on the citation, you focus it on the Court that took the action, or, as in this next example, on the rule itself:

△ GOOD EXAMPLE

> Sex-based peremptory challenges violate jurors' rights to equal protection. <u>J.E.B. v. T.B.</u>, 511 U.S. 127, 138-40 (1994).

This structure lets the citation do its work of telling the reader the name of the case, the Court, and the year of decision, but keeps it from intrud-

---

[12] *See, e.g., ALWD* Rule 44.1(c), illustrating long-form embedded citations and lamenting that they make sentences difficult to read. *See also ALWD Citation Manual* 444-45 (Aspen 2000) (illustrating a legal memorandum without using any "separated long-form" citations).

ing on the sentence itself. Including a case name alone in your sentence is only appropriate *if* you have already cited the case in full in that same discussion:

⚠ GOOD EXAMPLE

> This Court has held that sex-based peremptory challenges violate jurors' rights to equal protection. <u>J.E.B. v. T.B.</u>, 511 U.S. 127, 138-40 (1994). In <u>J.E.B.</u>, the court reasoned that the peremptory challenges were based on broad assumptions about men's and women's relative capabilities. <u>Id.</u>

Thus, structure your sentences so that all citations, and particularly long-form citations, can be placed in their own citation sentences. You can accomplish this goal by keeping the focus on the court or the rule rather than on the citation.

6.6.3
AVOIDING STRING CITATIONS

Judges are almost uniformly against the use of string citations. As Judge Boyce Martin notes, "When I read a lengthy string cite in a brief or slip opinion, I often find that I have lost the gist of the argument after fighting through line after line of gobbledygook."[13] Admittedly, string citations can be useful on rare occasions. For example, if you need to illustrate a trend in the law, give a brief overview of a still-developing area of law, or establish that multiple authorities in a variety of jurisdictions have followed or not followed a particular rule, a string citation may be appropriate. Two warnings: First, most cases you write briefs for will not present any of these situations, so presume that you will not need a string cite; second, the longer the string cite, the less likely it is that anyone will look at it except the unfortunate judge's clerk who has been assigned to review all of the cited cases. You will make more friends if you have fewer string cites.

When a string cite is unavoidable, put as much information as possible into the sentence preceding the string cite. Most readers will not be able to pick up much information in phrases and clauses interspersed among the citations. One problem with a string citation is that it inevitably creates a very long sentence, and, psychologically, the reader tries to keep that sentence "going" in his or her brain. A sentence with text and citations interspersed is probably the hardest thing for a reader to read:

▽ BAD EXAMPLE

> Several courts of appeals have considered the issue of whether a transient visitor has a legitimate expectation of privacy while within the

---

[13] Boyce F. Martin, Jr., *Judges on Judging: In Defense of Unpublished Opinions*, 60 Ohio St. L.J. 177, 193 (1999).

> residence of another, <u>see, e.g.</u>, <u>United States v. Gale</u>, 136 F.3d 192 (D.C. Cir. 1998), and they have considered this issue in a variety of contexts and using a variety of factors in reaching their decisions, including the frequency of rent payments, <u>id.</u> at 193; the lack of an overnight stay, <u>United States v. Maddox</u>, 944 F.2d 1223, 1234 (6th Cir. 1991); the use of another's hotel room, <u>United States v. Carr</u>, 939 F.2d 1442, 1446 (10th Cir. 1991); the lack of evidence of connection to the residence, <u>United States v. Antone</u>, 753 F.2d 1301, 1313 (5th Cir. 1985); and mere presence in a hotel room, <u>United States v. Irizarry</u>, 673 F.2d 554, 558 (1st Cir. 1982).

To make this information easier to digest, write a sentence informing the reader of the significance of the cases, and then end it with a period. The string citation can be placed in a footnote; even if it is in the text, it will be easier for the reader to read:

> Several courts of appeals have decided that a transient visitor has no legitimate expectation of privacy while within the residence of another, whether the residence was a home or a hotel room, when the visitor did not have sufficient connection to the residence. <u>See, e.g.</u>, <u>United States v. Gale</u>, 136 F.3d 192, 193 (D.C. Cir. 1998) (current day visitor's one rent payment seven months ago not enough to establish sufficient connection); <u>United States v. Maddox</u>, 944 F.2d 1223, 1234 (6th Cir. 1991) (attendance at drug party without overnight stay does not establish sufficient connection); <u>United States v. Carr</u>, 939 F.2d 1442, 1446 (10th Cir. 1991) (guest in another's hotel room does not have sufficient connection); <u>United States v. Antone</u>, 753 F.2d 1301, 1313 (5th Cir. 1985) (fingerprints on book not enough to establish daytime visitor's connection to residence); <u>United States v. Irizarry</u>, 673 F.2d 554, 558 (1st Cir. 1982) ("mere presence" in hotel room not sufficient to establish connection).

The best solution is one that avoids the string cite entirely. If you are using the string cite to point out the well-established fact that many courts have already agreed with a legal rule, you may be able to use a parenthetical to accomplish the goal of the string cite. Often, one of the most recent cases in a "string" will have addressed the fact that the rule is well-established, and may have cited most or all of the other cases. In that situation, you may tell the reader that the cases exist and give him or her access to those cases by citing only the most recent one:

⚠ GOOD EXAMPLE

> Since 1978, every Ohio court that has addressed this issue has decided in favor of the employee. <u>See, e.g.</u>, <u>Sanders v. McGuffin Corp.</u>, 101 Ohio St. 3d 111, 122, 901 N.E.2d 911, 933 (1999) (citing cases).

This citation supports an accurate statement — that every Ohio court has decided a certain type of case in a certain way — and it allows the judge or the judge's clerk to find all those decisions if needed by citing to a decision that cites them. Use this method with care. It cannot be used unless the text of your argument accurately reflects what the cited case has said about the list of cases cited. When it is appropriate, however, the legal writer is able to simultaneously avoid a string cite and give the reader access to multiple authorities that support his or her argument.

6.6.4
CASES THAT CITE OTHER CASES

A citation dilemma for many legal writers is what to do when citing an excerpt of a case that has cited another case. Both *ALWD* Rule 48.7(c)(2) and *Bluebook* Rule 5.2 indicate that the writer should cite the original source, as the writer does in the following example:

▽ BAD EXAMPLE

> A person possesses a reasonable expectation of privacy, and thus a search occurs when an officer makes an observation from a location within the curtilage of a private home. See Oliver v. United States, 466 U.S. 170, 180 (1984). Curtilage, "the land immediately surrounding and associated with the home," is "the area to which extends the intimate activity associated with the 'sanctity of a man's home and the privacies of life.' " Id. (quoting Boyd v. United States, 116 U.S. 616, 630 (1886)).

Although this guideline may be appropriate for law review articles and other publications, it is not always the best rule for brief writing. In this situation, it is doubtful that the court needs to know about an 1886 case that is the origin of the "sanctity" language.

Granted, a legal writer may want to cite the original source to give added credence to a discussion of a case decided by a nonmandatory court. In the example below, from a petitioner's brief in *Minnesota v. Carter*, the writer is discussing a California case that applied *Minnesota v. Olson*, a significant United States Supreme Court case that had been previously cited in that same section of the brief:

△ GOOD EXAMPLE

> In 1992, a California court found that a defendant who moved to suppress items seized at his brother's apartment while the defendant was babysitting there had a legitimate expectation of privacy. People v. Moreno, 3 Cal. Rptr. 2d 66, 70 (Cal. Ct. App. 1992). The court cited Olson and indicated that, "[l]ike 'staying overnight in another's home,' babysitting 'is a longstanding social custom that serves functions recognized as valuable by society.' " Id. at 70 (quoting Olson, 495 U.S. at 98).

Noting that the California court was basing its decision on United States Supreme Court authority may have given that California decision more weight in a brief written to the United States Supreme Court. Thus, if knowing the origin of the cited language could affect the Court's understanding of your argument, identify that source. This situation does not occur regularly in legal writing; generally, if the origin of the language were significant, the writer would go to the original source and cite that authority instead. It is only when the relationship between the two sources is significant — as it is when an on-point case applies a rule from a mandatory court — that the reader is likely to be interested in the origin of the quoted language.

In most other situations, however, judges looking at the citations supporting an argument want to know only that a valid court made that statement in an analogous case. They usually have little or no interest in the original source of particular words or phrases. If the cited opinion is a valid authority for that quote, it matters only that *that court* made the statement in its majority opinion and that the statement is not dicta. Even if that court misinterpreted the original language, what matters is that the court believed that the language was appropriate to apply to the particular set of facts that was before it. Thus, determine whether the court you are writing to would better understand your argument if it knew the original source of the quoted language. If knowing the source would not improve the court's understanding, you can omit the citation, as long as you inform the court that you are doing so:

⚠ GOOD EXAMPLE

> Curtilage, "the land immediately surrounding and associated with the home," is "the area to which extends the intimate activity associated with the 'sanctity of a man's home and the privacies of life.' " Id. (citation omitted).

Substituting the "citation omitted" parenthetical phrase for the full citation will allow those who wish to track the original language the opportunity to do so. Most judges and clerks, however, will be grateful that you have not cluttered the brief with irrelevant citations.

6.6.5
IMPORTANCE OF PINPOINT CITATIONS

A "pinpoint citation" or "pinpoint cite" is a citation to the specific page on which quoted or cited language appeared. Some legal writers use the phrase "jump cite" to mean the same thing. You must include pinpoint citations *every time* you cite to a case.

Do not try to convince yourself that you are citing the case only "generally" and thus do not need to include a citation to the specific page. If you want your readers to be able to verify that the authorities you cite stand for the propositions you say they do, you must make it incredibly easy for them to do so. Remember that the clerk of the judge who is writing the opinion will often be given the task of verifying the truth of the assertions in the briefs. If you do not give pinpoint citations, you may force the clerk to wade through 30- or 40-page opinions, trying to find the legal principle that you said was in there. If you cite a case for its main holding, find the page on which the court articulated that holding: That is the pinpoint page. Even if you are citing to the first page of the opinion (a rare event, since many reporters contain "non-cite-able" editorial information that completely fills the first page), you must still provide a pinpoint citation:

⚠ GOOD EXAMPLE

McGuffin v. Wood, 101 F.3d 115, 115 (6th Cir. 2015).

Think of the judges and your clerks whenever you are making a citation decision. Whenever you can make it easier for them to understand your argument by putting a little more information into the brief, you should do so.

6.7
SUMMARY

The practical brief writer has a lot to remember when trying to use case authorities effectively. Remembering the needs of the judges and clerks who must use your brief will help you (1) to include all of the authorities that are necessary, (2) to give enough information about those authorities, but not too much, (3) to present that information in a helpful way, and (4) to cite that information in a way that provides sufficient information without needlessly intruding on the text.

CHAPTER SEVEN

SEEING WHAT YOU HAVE WRITTEN

7.1
FOCUSING YOUR REVISION: USING THE SELF-GRADED DRAFT[1]

The etymology of the word *revision* means "to see again." You can revise your writing most effectively if you can figure out a way to "see it again."

After completing a good draft of your document and checking your use of authority, the next step you should take is to check the document's content and large-scale organization. One way to check content, of course, is to review your substance. If you have not yet Shepardized and KeyCited your authorities, now is a good time to do so.[2] While reviewing your authorities, you may wish to follow up on any unexplored leads to verify that you have marshaled the best arguments and authorities in your client's favor.

After you have checked the validity of the points you are trying to make, the next step is to review your writing — the way in which you

---

[1] Some of the material in this section comes from Mary Beth Beazley, *The Self-Graded Draft: Teaching Students to Revising Using Guided Self-Critique*, 3 Legal Writing 175 (1997).

[2] The best course is not to rely on either Shepard's or KeyCite alone, but to use both.

have made those points in your brief. At this stage, you should review the argument for structure, focus, and completeness. Of course, it is often difficult for people to review their own writing because they lack the psychological distance necessary to distinguish between the information on the printed page and the information still "inside their heads." Using an exercise like the "self-graded draft" is one way to combat these difficulties.

The self-graded draft is an exercise that requires you to review your argument and to complete eight fairly simple tasks (such as marking certain elements in the margin or highlighting certain elements) within each analytical segment of the document. Although you could complete many different types of self-grading tasks, this chapter will illustrate the method by describing common analytical requirements and their purposes. Each of the eight tasks should help you with one or more of the areas of structure, focus, and completeness.

The eight tasks require you to use both objective methods (highlighting) and subjective methods (marginal notes) to find and label the most important elements of the CREXAC paradigm (Conclusion, Rule, EXplanation, Application, Conclusion) within *each* analytical section of the document.

7.1.1
BACKGROUND

The self-graded draft is an objective, focused, critiquing exercise that allows little room for the self-delusion that often interferes with self-editing. Essentially, the exercise asks you to find, mark, and evaluate individual elements within each part of your document. The process of finding the elements and of labeling them or highlighting them encourages you to focus your attention on one element of the document at a time. This focus often helps to provide enough psychological distance to allow you to conduct an objective evaluation of your writing and then improve it.

An "objective" or focused critiquing method is particularly helpful in legal writing because of the predictable structure of legal documents and the predictable behavior of legal readers and legal writers. Most legal documents have a set format, and they require analytical elements that are usually found at predictable "intellectual locations" within the format. In a brief, for example, "intellectual locations" would include elements within each analytical segment of the document: the statement of the rule, the explanation of that rule, and the application of the rule to the facts.

Most of us lack focus when we sit down to edit. We may review our writing by reading and re-reading the document with no definite goal in mind. We may focus on typographical errors or grammar mistakes, hoping that substantive problems will leap out at us as we read. Essentially, we are reviewing the document and asking ourselves, "Is this okay?"

The self-graded draft addresses this lack of focus by concentrating your attention on various parts of the document and then asking focused questions. For example, instead of looking at a *sentence* and asking yourself "Is this okay?" you will be asked to look at the *application of law to facts* within a particular section and ask yourself, "Did I use the phrase-that-pays when I applied law to facts? Did I include all of the legally significant facts?" This improvement in focus often helps to improve your ability to self-edit.

The second, and more difficult, problem self-editors face is the problem of psychological distance. Many of us find it psychologically impossible to really see what we have written. Those of us who have reviewed our own writing several weeks, months, or years after "polishing" it have had the experience of discovering glaring mistakes, inconsistencies, or other weaknesses. We are aghast; how could we have missed those mistakes? And yet the phenomenon is not that surprising.

When we write, we are, naturally, thinking about our complete message. When we later revise and edit, we see the words we wrote, and these (often inadequate) words remind our short-term memories of the complete message we had in mind when we were writing. The short-term memory then "tells" the brain the complete message, and we presume that the words we wrote contained the message. Actually, the short-term memory often fills in the blanks. The complete message may never have made it into the written word.[3] This phenomenon creates a sort of brain eclipse.[4] The short term memory "passes between" the written document and our brain, "blocking" us from seeing and understanding the words that we actually wrote.

Self-grading can address your brain eclipse by requiring you to look at individual words, sentences, and elements (for example, elements of CREXAC), instead of at the document as a whole. The self-grading exercise does not ask you *whether* you included an element; it asks you to *mark* the very words that comprise the element. This marking forces you to discover for yourself what words and ideas actually made it onto the paper, and what words and ideas are still inside your brain. The self-graded draft does not create the message; it simply helps you to discover whether the document includes the complete message. If part of the message is not written down, you will not be able to find and mark it during the self-grading. In this way, you will discover what parts of the message are missing, and you will be in a better position to make revision decisions.

In addition to helping you discover what analytical elements are missing, self-grading helps revision simply by focusing your attention. After you have marked the places in the document in which you applied the

---

[3] *Cf.* Joseph M. Williams, *Style: Ten Lessons in Clarity and Grace* 63 (5th ed. 1997).
[4] I am grateful to Dean Nancy Rapport of the University of Houston Law Center for suggesting this term to describe this mental phenomenon.

rule to the facts, for example, you can focus your attention on that aspect of analytical writing and critically review your work.

7.1.2
COMPLETING THE SELF-GRADING

Some writers like to complete their self-grading section by section, completing their marking of each section's "CREXAC" before moving on to the next. Others prefer to find each element throughout the whole document before moving on to the next element (e.g., first finding all of the rules that serve as the "focus" for each section of the document, then finding all of the phrases-that-pay, etc.) because they believe that this method helps them to be more objective. Whichever method you use, at some point you should review the self-grading for each "unit of discourse" separately. In addition, keep a separate sheet of paper (or an empty word processor screen) handy so that you can note any questions or concerns that arise as you self-grade, record any possible revisions that you find necessary, and write a final comment.

Each of the self-grading tasks is listed below, followed by an explanation of what the writer is to do or why the writer is to do it.

7.2
COMMON SELF-GRADING TASKS
AND EXPLANATIONS

7.2.1
IDENTIFY THE FOCUS OF EACH UNIT OF DISCOURSE

Within each point heading section or sub-section, write "focus" in the margin next to the sentence(s) in which you articulate the rule, policy, or thesis *that is the focus* of that section or sub-section. Do *not* write "focus" next to every statement that could be called a rule.

A helpful self-grading task is identifing the point you are focusing on in each section of your document. Usually, you will be focusing on a rule that governs the issue that you are discussing, but sometimes you may be focusing on a policy or some other thesis. Every section of the document should be focused on *something;* identify the first place in which you articulate that something and mark it in the margin as the "focus" of that section. If you find that you cannot find a focus in a given section, take a moment and draft a sentence that articulates the section's focus.

7.2.2
CREATE A SEPARATE FOCUS LIST

After you have identified or drafted all of your focuses, create a separate document in which you list each "focus" in order of appearance. You can use this list to determine if your brief addresses the appropriate issues and to review your large-scale organization.

After you have identified the focus of each section, make a "focus list" that records the focus of each section of your document. The focus list can help you to evaluate the completeness of your document because it will remind you of which points you have discussed. You can check this list against your initial research or your follow-up research to see if you have addressed all of the points that you need to address. The list can also help you to evaluate structure. Note whether you are addressing your most important arguments first and whether you have addressed your arguments in a logical order. Finally, note whether you can link each point to your ultimate thesis.

7.2.3
IDENTIFY THE PHRASES-THAT-PAY WITHIN EACH UNIT OF DISCOURSE

Within the sentence that articulates each focus, identify its phrase-that-pays and highlight that phrase-that-pays in PINK. Highlight each phrase-that-pays wherever it appears throughout its section or sub-section.

As you find each rule or focus (or after you have completed your focus list), identify the phrases-that-pay that are the focus of your analysis within each section of your document, and highlight them wherever they appear within the section. Remember that in most briefs, each section will have a different phrase-that-pays because each section will be focused on a different rule, policy, or other thesis. Take some time with this task; it is important to identify the phrases-that-pay for each section accurately.

Usually, you can find the phrase-that-pays by identifying what you are trying to prove in that section. One method for identifying the phrase-that-pays is to manipulate the language of your rule and then analyze that language: (1) mentally restate the rule as an if-then proposition (NOTE: Do *not* presume that rules should be stated as if-then statements in the document itself), then (2) look in the "if" clause to identify what you are trying to prove. That thing that you are proving usually constitutes the main phrase-that-pays.

As noted earlier in this text, an "if then" rule says, "If **Condition (phrase-that-pays)** exists, then **Legal Status or Legal Consequence** occurs." Your explanation of that rule would try to show what the phrase-that-pays means so that, in your application section, you can predict whether the phrase-that-pays (Condition) exists in your client's case. Once you establish that the phrase-that-pays does or does not exist, you can argue in your conclusion section that the Legal Consequence should or should not occur.

For example, if you were writing about whether or not the victim of a dog bite could recover damages from the owner of the dog, you might have a statutory rule that says, among other things, that the owner cannot be held liable if the victim of the dog bite was committing a trespass or other criminal offense on the dog owner's property at the time of the attack. You could turn that proposition into an "if-then" rule as follows:

> **IF the victim of a dog bite is committing a trespass or other criminal offense on the dog owner's property at the time of the attack, THEN he or she cannot recover damages for any injury or loss.**

Looking in your "if" clause, you see several items that could be the focus of analysis in a legal document. For example, the writer could be trying to prove (1) that the dog-bite victim was committing a trespass or other criminal offense, (2) that the dog-bite victim was on the dog owner's property, or (3) that the trespass or criminal offense was being committed at the time of the attack. Your goal is to identify what language of the rule is at issue in the particular section you are focusing on. Let's presume that, in this section, you are trying to prove that a civil trespass is included in the types of trespass described in the statute. Thus, your phrase-that-pays or phrases-that-pay would be "committing a trespass or other criminal offense," and your explanation section would be devoted to establishing the meaning of that phrase.

Finding and highlighting the phrase-that-pays in each section of the document can help you to evaluate whether your analysis is focused: Ideally, you should see the phrase-that-pays several times within the section. It should appear within the focus, within the explanation of that focus, within the application of that focus to the facts of your client's case, and within the internal conclusion or mini-conclusion to that section. Marking each of these elements (rule, explanation, application, conclusion) in the margin is a helpful part of self-grading.

7.2.4
IDENTIFY CITED AUTHORITIES

Highlight each citation (or reference to authority, even if not in a formal citation) in GREEN.

After you have identified the phrases-that-pay, a useful task is to highlight all citations to authorities that you have used to support your arguments. Be sure to highlight all kinds of citations: long form, short form, and *Id.* citations. This task helps you to analyze the completeness of your document. You will review your authorities for quantity (do you have enough support for each point?) and for validity (do you cite mostly mandatory authority? Does each non-mandatory authority have a reason for being included?) You should also review your analysis of each authority (have you provided the reader with enough information about each case?).

7.2.5
IDENTIFY THE EXPLANATION OF EACH FOCUS

Write the word "Explanation" in the margin next to the paragraphs in which you *explained* the focus. Generally, you will have one or more paragraphs containing only pink and green highlights because in those paragraphs, you will be explaining the meaning of the phrases-that-pay according to various authorities.

Looking for green citations and pink phrases-that-pay should help you to find the explanation within each section of your argument. Usually, your explanation will consist of discussions of definitions of the phrase-that-pays, or descriptions of cases in which the phrase-that-pays has been applied in the past. The task of labeling the explanation is another step in evaluating the completeness of your analysis.

7.2.6
IDENTIFY THE APPLICATION OF EACH FOCUS TO YOUR CLIENT'S FACTS

Throughout the entire argument section, highlight any references to *your* case facts in BLUE. (Remember, if the language of enacted law is at issue, that language may sometimes act as your "facts.") Within each point heading section and sub-section, write "Application" in the margin next to the sentences in which you discuss how the focus for that section applies or does not apply to those facts.

This is broken down into two parts. First, highlight the facts of your client's case wherever they appear within the section. Although this task is usually a simple one, it can be complicated if your case involves the analysis of a statute or another legislative provision. In that situation, part of your "facts" may be the language of the provision, for you may be applying a "rule" of statutory interpretation to the "facts" of the provision's language.[5]

After you have highlighted all of the facts in blue, write "Application"

---

[5] As with any of the self-grading tasks, if you have any problem identifying your facts within a heading section, you may want to drop a private memo note so that you can ask for help if needed.

in the margin next to the sentences or paragraphs in which you applied the law to the facts *in each section of the argument*. Looking for paragraphs that contain both blue facts and pink phrases-that-pay should reveal where you applied the law to the facts, and allow you to analyze both the focus and the completeness of this part of your document. Ideally, you will find a sentence that says, in essence, "phrase-that-pays equals [or does not equal] my case facts." Of course, your application will often be much more detailed than this, particularly if the issue is a controversial one.

7.2.7
IDENTIFY THE INTERNAL CONCLUSIONS

Within each point heading section and sub-section, write the word "Conclusion" in the margin next to the sentence in which you explicitly state your internal conclusion or "mini-conclusion"[6] — that is, the internal conclusion for that section or sub-section. Highlight the conclusion in YELLOW. Do *not* highlight a conclusion at the beginning of the sub-section even though you may begin with a conclusory statement. Highlight a conclusion *only* at the end of the section or subsection.

An easy task is finding and labeling the sentence(s) in each section of your argument in which you state the internal conclusion for the section (also known as the "mini-conclusion"). Note whether the conclusion contains the phrase-that-pays for the section and whether you have connected the phrase-that-pays to the next link in the chain, or, if appropriate, to your ultimate thesis. If you cannot find an explicit conclusion, take a moment and write one.

7.2.8
WRITE A FINAL COMMENT

By now, you should have an idea of some of the areas you want to concentrate on in your revision. List the two or three most important elements or sections that you plan to revise. You may also want to note the areas of your brief that you believe are strongest.

No matter how many self-grading tasks you complete, your final task is to review the self-grading you have completed on your entire document and write a final comment. What two or three aspects of your document need the most revision? What elements of the document are particularly effective? Recording this information now, while the impressions are strong in your mind, will help you later as you tackle the important step of revising your document with your reader in mind.

---

[6] *See generally* Oates, Enquist & Kunsch, *The Legal Writing Handbook*, Chs. 5-6 (Aspen 2d ed. 1998).

7.3
SUMMARY

Use the self-graded draft exercise to separate yourself from your text so that you can see what is really on the printed page. By looking for specific analytical elements and asking yourself focused questions, you can begin to see your writing through your reader's eyes. Now is the time for you to shift your focus. Your first focus must always be on gaining an understanding of the case: what the facts are, what the relevant rules and authorities are, and how they work together in your argument. Now you must start to think about how the reader will perceive your argument and, more importantly, how you can craft your argument to increase the reader's understanding of your case.

FOLLOWING FORMAT RULES

Although fulfilling your brief's format requirements is a much less intellectually demanding task than writing the argument, it is nonetheless important. Rightly or wrongly, many readers form an impression of your credibility based on your ability or willingness to conform to the minutiae of court rules. More significantly, you may suffer sanctions — from having to fix offending portions of the brief to having your case dismissed — for failure to follow certain rules.[1]

Most state and federal courts of appeals in the United States are governed by at least two sets of rules. The more significant rules are the rules of procedure that govern all of the courts within a certain jurisdiction, for example, the Federal Rules of Civil Procedure, the Federal Rules of Appellate Procedure, or the Ohio Rules of Appellate Procedure. Be aware, how-

---

[1] Judith B. Fischer, *Bareheaded and Barefaced Counsel: Courts React to Unprofessionalism in Lawyers' Papers*, 31 Suffolk U.L. Rev. 1, 31 et seq. (1997) (this article also contains several examples of courts' reactions to misstatements of law and facts and other failings).

ever, that most courts also have so-called local rules that may deal with requirements such as filing requirements, page length, certificates of service, service on opposing parties, citations, etc. Whenever you are asked to file a brief, make sure that you have copies of all of the rules that apply to documents submitted to that court.

This chapter will explain the format requirements that are common to most appellate briefs. While it will usually refer to Supreme Court rules, most of the requirements are common in other appellate courts. Of course, you should follow the rules of the court to which you are writing, or of your professor.

8.1
LENGTH REQUIREMENTS

Probably the most significant format mistake that lawyers make is to fail to follow required page limits. Unfortunately, some lawyers see an imposed page limit as a sort of challenge, and they turn the page limit into a goal. Realize that most courts design their page limits to accommodate even complex cases that require lengthy analysis of each issue. Your goal as a writer should be to write enough about each issue to give your answer to that issue and to provide enough support for your answer so that the court understands why it should agree with that answer. Lawyers do not win any points from judges for padding simple arguments, making the same point in two or three different point heading sections, or describing five cases where one would make the point. On the contrary, most judges are grateful to read a brief that makes its points effectively and then stops.[2]

All of this is not to say that you should give the court only a cursory description of your arguments. Presume that your readers are intelligent, but that they are ignorant of the particulars of the case currently before the court. Your brief should give enough details about your case, and about the cases and other authorities that you cite, for the members of the court to understand your analysis without having to resort to other documents. Of course, they might understand things more deeply if they read all of the cases or reviewed the entire record, but your job is not to give them the same in-depth knowledge of the case that you have. Rather, you should perform a cost-benefit analysis vis-à-vis the information that you provide. For example, a brief case description will give the court a reasonable understanding of the authority and will take two or three sentences. A lengthy case description may take two or three paragraphs, but in most situations, it will not provide any more needed insight than a two-or-three sentence description.

---

[2] *See generally* Fischer, *supra* note 1, at 22.

8.2
TYPEFACES AND MARGINS

Some lawyers have tried to evade length requirements by using smaller margins, smaller fonts, or other techniques that computers allow. Many courts have responded by specifying margin and font requirements, or by imposing word limits or even character limits in place of page limits.[3] For example, the Federal Rule of Appellate Procedure 32(a)(5) designates typeface requirements, and Federal Rule of Appellate Procedure 32(a)(7) designates length requirements with both page limits and word limits. Most computer programs can provide information about a document's word and character counts. (In both Wordperfect® and Microsoft Word®, choose "File" on the toolbar and then "Properties," after which you should consult the "information" or "statistics" folders, respectively.)

If the court to which you are submitting your brief does not specify anything beyond page limits, presume standard margins (one-inch all around) and a standard font size (12-point, non-proportional spacing).

8.3
NUMBER OF COPIES

United States Supreme Court Rule 29.2 does not require that multiple copies be filed with the court; however, Rule 29.3 does require that if counsel is filing a bound document (most briefs are bound in booklet format per Rule 33.1), he or she must serve three copies "on each other party separately represented in the proceeding."

In contrast, Rule VIII, Section 5 of the Rules of Practice of the Supreme Court of Ohio requires that counsel file 18 copies of the brief. Similarly, Local Appellate Rule 31.1 of the Third Circuit Local Appellate Rules requires that counsel "file ten (10) copies of each brief with the clerk and serve two (2) copies on counsel for each party separately represented." Whenever you file a document with a court, make sure that you are filing a sufficient number of copies, both with the court and with any opposing counsel.

---

[3] *See* Fischer, *supra* note 1, at 31.

8.4
DOCUMENT FORMAT REQUIREMENTS
AND SERVICE REQUIREMENTS

The United States Supreme Court rules specify exactly what elements are to be included in every type of brief submitted to it, from a brief petitioning for a writ of certiorari to a petitioner's reply brief on the merits. This chapter will address the document requirements of a petitioner's brief on the merits, which are described in Supreme Court Rule 24. In most appellate advocacy courses, students on each side of the case are required to complete all elements of the document for pedagogical reasons. In practice, however, courts usually allow the Respondents to omit some elements if they agree with the Petitioner's version.

8.4.1
COVER PAGE

Supreme Court Rule 34.1 lists the elements that must be included on the cover page of a brief, including the docket number of the case, the name of the court in which the case will be heard, the caption of the case, the court of origin of the case, the type of document, and the name of the counsel of record.

8.4.2
QUESTION PRESENTED

The question presented appears all alone on the first page after the cover page. As noted in Rule 24.1(a), the brief may not raise additional questions or change the substance of the questions raised in the petition for the writ of certiorari; however, "the phrasing of the questions presented need not be identical with that in the petition for a writ of certiorari." A later chapter will discuss methods for writing an effective question presented. Note that if your case has multiple questions, you should number the questions. Note also that the page number of this page should be written in lower-case roman numerals (i.e., the question presented appears on page "i"), and that this method of pagination continues through the Table of Authorities (see section 8.4.5). Arabic numbering of the pages begins with the Opinions Below (see section 8.4.6).

8.4.3
PARTIES TO THE PROCEEDING

In many cases, all of the parties to the proceedings have been listed in the caption on the cover page. In some cases, however, the parties are too numerous to list on the cover page, or the parties have changed since the decision of the case below. In either of these situations, Rule 24.1(b) requires you to include a separate page labeled "Parties to the Proceeding," which (1) lists all parties not listed on the cover sheet and (2) explains the absence of any parties who were parties to the proceeding in the court whose judgment is under review. If any of the parties is a company with parent companies or non-wholly-owned subsidiaries, you may need to add corporate disclosure information about that company here. *See* Rule 29.6.

8.4.4
TABLE OF CONTENTS

Rule 24.1(c) requires a table of contents for all briefs that exceed five pages. Generally, the table of contents contains a list of every element of the brief that has a title, from the Question(s) Presented, the Opinions Below, the Argument *and* its sections that are labeled with point headings, to the Conclusion, the Certificate of Service, and the Appendix (if any). The table of contents should list only the first page on which each element appears.

8.4.5
TABLE OF AUTHORITIES

Rule 24.1(c) also requires a table of authorities for all briefs that exceed five pages. Rule 34.2 requires that the table of authorities include "cases alphabetically arranged, constitutional provisions, statutes, treatises, and other materials." Attorneys list their cited authorities in this order, noting *each* page on which an authority is cited. If an authority is cited so frequently that listing the individual pages would not help the court to find particular discussions of the authority, the table of authorities may note *passim* (Latin for "throughout") instead of listing individual pages. *Passim* is often necessary to refer to a statute that is at issue, because the statute may well be referenced on every page of the argument. Take care to use *passim* only when absolutely necessary; it is not an excuse for being too lazy to search through the brief to find the particular pages on which the citations appear.

8.4.6
OPINIONS BELOW

With this page, the writer begins arabic page numbering, and most writers reprint the caption of the case before this element (although Rule 24.1 does not specify this requirement).[4] The writer's goal in the "Opin-

---

[4] *See* the sample brief at page 1 for an example of this type of internal caption.

ions Below" section, according to Rule 24.1(d), is to inform the court where it can find the "official and unofficial reports of the opinions and orders entered in the case by courts and administrative agencies." If official citations exist, the writer should provide them; if the opinions are also (or only) available in the Joint Appendix or some other document submitted to the court, the writer should make that clear as well, e.g., "The decision of the Second Circuit Court of Appeals can be found at 101 F.3d 101 and at page 73 in the Joint Appendix."

8.4.7
JURISDICTION

In Supreme Court briefs, the jurisdictional statement, required by Rule 24.1(e), is usually rather straightforward. The attorney should include the date on which the judgment being reviewed was entered, the date on which the petition for certiorari was filed, and the date on which the petition was granted. These items are necessary because they show that a final decision has been entered and that the petitioner has followed the necessary procedural steps. The brief should also include the statute or statutes that give the Supreme Court the authority to hear this type of appeal.[5] Although jurisdiction is rarely an issue before the United States Supreme Court, it can be raised for the first time at any point in the proceedings; thus, in practice, be sure that you understand the court's jurisdiction in your client's case.

8.4.8
RELEVANT ENACTED LAW

Rule 24.1(f) requires the attorney to set out — "verbatim with appropriate citation" — the constitutional provisions, treaties, statutes, ordinances, and regulations involved in the case. Label this element according to what it contains, e.g., "Relevant Constitutional Provisions" or "Relevant Statutes" or "Relevant Constitutional and Statutory Provisions." If printing the entire text of the relevant provisions would take up too much space (more than a page), simply include the citations here and explain that the full text is reprinted in the appendix.[6]

8.4.9
STATEMENT OF THE CASE

Rule 24.1(g) asks for a "concise statement of the case, setting out the facts material to the consideration of the questions presented." Although

---

[5] *See* the Jurisdictional Statement in the sample brief, and accompanying footnote text, for a discussion of the most common relevant statutes.
[6] *See* Section 8.4.16 below for discussion of Supreme Court rule requirements for the Appendix.

writing effective statements of the case will be addressed in a later chapter, for now you should keep in mind that the statement usually includes both facts and procedure and always includes citation to the record or the joint appendix.[7]

8.4.10
SUMMARY OF THE ARGUMENT

Writing the summary of the argument will be addressed in a later chapter. The formal requirements are few, but some are quite particular. Rule 24.1(h) specifically notes that "mere repetition of the headings under which the argument is arranged is not sufficient."

8.4.11
THE ARGUMENT

Much has already been written about the argument; I will simply note here that Rule 24.1(i) asks that the argument exhibit "clearly the points of fact and of law presented and [cite] the authorities and statutes relied on."

8.4.12
THE CONCLUSION

The only requirement that the Court imposes on the conclusion, in Rule 24.1(j), is that it "[specify] with particularity the relief the party seeks." At a minimum, your conclusion should tell the court what you want it to do: affirm, reverse, reverse and remand, or vacate the decision below. Many lawyers write only one sentence as a conclusion, as in this example:

GOOD EXAMPLE

For the foregoing reasons, this court should reverse the decision below.

It can be effective to make the conclusion more specific to your case. Even if you wish to do so, you should avoid writing a lengthy conclusion. Instead, substitute your best reason(s) for the opening clause, as in this example:

GOOD EXAMPLE

Because the First Amendment should never be interpreted in a way that keeps truthful information from consumers, this court should affirm the decision below.

[7] *See* the sample brief for examples of correct citations within the statement of the case.

Some courts will have little patience for a conclusion that is much longer than a paragraph.

8.4.13
SIGNATURE

The rules of the United States Supreme Court do not specifically require that attorneys sign briefs; however, Rule 34.3 requires that the body of every document (i.e., information before any certificate of service or appendix) "shall bear at its close the name of counsel of record."

Other appellate courts do require a signature. For example, Rule VIII, Section 3 of the Rules of Practice of the Supreme Court of Ohio requires that "[t]he original of every pleading, memorandum, brief, or other document filed in the Supreme Court shall be signed by an attorney representing the party on whose behalf the document is filed. A party who is not represented by an attorney shall sign the document being filed." Likewise, the Third Circuit's Local Appellate Rule 46.4 provides that "[a]ll papers, motions and briefs must be signed by an attorney or by a party appearing pro se."

8.4.14
CERTIFICATE OF SERVICE

Most courts require that litigants who serve papers on the court also certify that they have served copies of those documents on opposing counsel. Supreme Court Rule 29.5 specifies that "proof of service . . . shall accompany the document when it is presented to the Clerk for filing and shall be separate from it." The rule specifies several methods of certifying service, including "a certificate of service, reciting the facts and circumstances of service . . . and signed by a member of the Bar of this Court representing the party on whose behalf service is made." Consult the sample brief to see an example of a certificate of service.

8.4.15
CERTIFICATE OF COMPLIANCE

The certificate of compliance is a fairly new requirement; it seems to serve as an alternate to page-length requirements. For example, Federal Rule of Appellate Procedure 32(a)(7) requires that a brief must either comply with a page limit or with a word limit that is verified in a certificate of compliance. Federal Rule of Appellate Procedure 32(a)(7)(C) requires that the certificate must state either the number of words in the brief or the number of lines of monospaced type in the brief. Although the United States Supreme Court does not require a certificate of compliance, one sample brief includes one because some courts do and because some law professors require them in appellate advocacy courses.

8.4.16
APPENDIX

The Supreme Court rules do not *require* an appendix. As noted above, however, Rule 24.1(f) suggests an appendix when legislation is too lengthy to reprint in the body of the brief. Do not attach copies of statutes printed from Lexis or Westlaw. Instead, retype the statutes in a readable format, or download the text into a word processing system and reformat the text, using typefaces and margins that increase readability.

Counsel should also consider including in the appendix any information to which the court may need to refer while it considers the case (and which has not been included in the Joint Appendix). E.g., counsel may include unpublished decisions, copies of documents (or segments of documents) that are at issue, etc.[8]

8.5
SUMMARY

Format requirements are not intellectually demanding, but they do take time. Whenever you must file a brief, make sure that you have access to all relevant rules, and be sure to allow yourself time to read and understand their requirements.

---

[8] *See, e.g.,* Carole C. Berry, *Effective Appellate Advocacy: Brief Writing and Oral Argument* 107 (1999); Ruggero J. Aldisert. *Winning on Appeal* 84-89 (rev'd 1st ed. 1996).

CHAPTER NINE

SPECIAL TEAMS: QUESTIONS PRESENTED, STATEMENT OF THE CASE, SUMMARY OF THE ARGUMENT, POINT HEADINGS

In football, coaches organize several different types of practices. The offense and the defense must prepare differently, just as you must prepare a petitioner's brief differently from the way you prepare a respondent's brief. Most football coaches also have practices for what they call "special teams," the teams that handle certain expected types of plays during the game. For example, coaches will hold a separate practice for kickoffs, for kickoff returns, and for the onside kick. Coaches do this because each of these plays presents special situations not part of the regular play of the game, and each has special rules that govern it. Because these situations are opportunities to score points, or at least create opportunities to score points, time focused on special teams may mean the difference between victory and defeat.

In appellate brief writing, most of the attention goes, properly, to the argument section. But brief writers must pay attention to their "special teams," too. Different rules apply to various sections of appellate briefs, and the writer must bring different skills to bear in these sections. Furthermore, even though most of these sections are not part of the argument per se, they can have an impact on the argument, either by encouraging the reader to reach certain conclusions before reading the argument, or by persuading the reader to take a more sympathetic view of the argument. While appellate advocacy is not a game, you can use your special teams to help the court to understand your arguments better. In this way, these sections of the document can have a significant impact on the outcome of the case.

9.1
WRITING THE QUESTION PRESENTED

Judge Patricia Wald of the United States Court of Appeals for the District of Columbia notes that counsel should spend some time on the issue because it "provides the lens through which the judge-reader filters the rest of the brief."[1] For most judges, the question presented provides the first image of the case, and each time they consider a new angle of the case by reading a new brief, they gain a new image (or regain an old image) by reading the question presented first. Practical lawyers exploit this opportunity and make sure that the image conveyed in the question presented is one that they want the court to see.

9.1.1
FORMAL REQUIREMENTS

Supreme Court Rule 14.1(a), which governs the questions as they appear in the petition for the writ of certiorari, and which is referenced in Rule 24.1(a), requires that each question be "expressed concisely in relation to the circumstances of the case, without unnecessary detail." The rule further requires that the question be "short" and that it "should not be argumentative or repetitive." For briefs on the merits, Supreme Court Rule 24.1(a) requires that the brief contain "the questions presented for review under Rule 14.1(a)." Although this language appears to require that the attorney repeat the exact language of the question(s), the rule later states explicitly that the attorney may rewrite the language:

> The phrasing of the questions presented need not be identical with that in the petition for a writ of certiorari or the jurisdictional statement, but

---

[1] Patricia M. Wald, *19 Tips from 19 Years on the Appellate Bench*, 1 J. App. Prac. & Process 7, 12 (1999).

the brief may not raise additional questions or change the substance of the questions already presented in those documents.

Supreme Court Rule 24.1(a). Supreme Court Rule 14.1(a) specifically notes that "[t]he statement of any question presented is deemed to comprise every subsidiary question fairly included therein." Thus, the question presented written to the Court is generally a broad question that addresses the ultimate issues that the Court must consider in order to decide how to dispose of the case. Counsel for either party may decide to rephrase the questions to give the Court what it considers to be a more accurate snapshot than the other side is capable of.

9.1.2
DRAFTING CONSIDERATIONS

a. Elements to Include

Generally, writers should include three elements when writing a question presented: the question itself — expressed as a yes-or-no question — the relevant law, and the legally significant facts. Two formats that writers commonly use are the "under-does-when" format and the "whether" format. The under-does-when format essentially asks, "under relevant law, does a certain legal status exist when these legally significant facts exist?" The whether format contains the same elements, but the information can be arranged in a different order: "Whether a certain legal status exists when relevant law governs the situation and these legally significant facts exist?" A whether question could also be arranged differently: "Whether a certain fact situation results in a certain legal status under this relevant legal standard?"[2] Here is an example of the same question, written once in "under-does-when" format and once in "whether" format:

> **Under the Fourth Amendment's privacy guarantees, does an invitee into a residence have a legitimate expectation of privacy when the invitee's sole purpose for being present is to assist the resident in an illegal activity?**

> **Whether an invitee into a residence has a legitimate expectation of privacy under the Fourth Amendment to the United States Constitution when the invitee's sole purpose for being present in the residence is to assist the resident in an illegal activity?**

Some writers use the question presented to ask a question about a substantive legal issue, essentially asking:

---

[2] People who are particular about grammar often cringe at the "whether" format, because lawyers use it as if it is a complete sentence, even though it is technically a sentence fragment. (If you wanted to use the format "correctly," from a grammar viewpoint, you would write, "The issue is whether . . ." and end the sentence with a period.) Lawyers, however, have adopted the whether format as a valid sentence (using either a question mark or a period), and seem unlikely to change.

> Under relevant law, does a certain legal status exist when these legally significant facts are present?

as in this example:

> Consistent with the Fourth Amendment, can a state promote the interest of officer safety by enacting a statute that gives police officers authorization to conduct a search of a motor vehicle when they issue a citation to a person who has committed an offense that allows arrest?

Other writers put the legal issue in the context of the decision that the court is being asked to reverse, essentially asking,

> Whether the court below was correct when it held that under the relevant law, a certain legal status existed when these legally significant facts were present?

as in this example:

> Whether the Iowa Supreme Court correctly held that states can, consistent with the Fourth Amendment, promote the interest of officer safety by enacting a statute that gives police officers authorization to conduct a search of a motor vehicle when they issue a citation to a person who has committed an offense that allows arrest?

In addition to deciding whether to focus on the legal issue or the correctness of the decision below, you must also decide how to structure the question. The "whether" structure often moves the core question to the beginning of the question:

> Whether the court below erred when it held that this law applied in this way to the legally significant facts?

or

> Whether legal status exists when these legally significant facts exist and when this law applies?

The under-does-when format, on the other hand, puts less emphasis on the core question, putting the law at the beginning. It also allows the writer to shift the legally significant facts to the end of the question, which may help to emphasize positive facts, as in this example:

> Under the Fourth Amendment's privacy guarantees, does an invitee into a residence have a legitimate expectation of privacy when the invitee's sole purpose for being present is to assist the resident in an illegal activity?

When deciding which format to use, consider what information you would like in the positions of emphasis within the question. Generally, the beginning and the end of the question are positions of emphasis, with the end of the question being the strongest position.

b. Persuasive Questions Presented

When choosing both the format and the type of question that you ask, consider which drafting method will allow you to emphasize your point of view. The practical lawyer does more than merely write a question that includes all three of the needed elements. Karl Llewellyn has noted the importance of "controlling" the legal issues in a case:

> Of course, the first thing that comes up is the issue and the first art is the framing of the issue so that if your framing is accepted the case comes out your way. Got that? Second, you have to capture the issue, because your opponent will be framing an issue very differently. . . . And third, you have to build a technique of phrasing your issue which will not only capture the Court but which will stick your capture into the Court's head so that it can't forget it.[3]

Conventional wisdom has it that the advocate should draft a question so that a "yes" answer is favorable to his or her case. This advice is valid, but it often does not result in a question that grabs the reader's attention and allows the reader to see the case from the advocate's point of view. The better path is to ask yourself how you would describe your client's case in a nutshell. What facts are most important? How would you characterize the issue? Look at the differences between the following two questions. They were written from the opposite sides of *Minnesota v. Carter*, a case about the constitutionality of an arrest that was based on an officer's observation of two apparent drug dealers in a colleague's apartment as they "bagged" some drugs for sale:

> **Was the Minnesota Supreme Court correct when it found that respondents, as social guests, had a reasonable expectation of privacy in the home they were visiting?**

> **Whether the Fourth Amendment gives invitees into a residence a legitimate expectation of privacy while in the residence when their sole purpose for being present is to assist the resident in an illegal activity?**

Note that the writer of the first wants the reader to answer "yes," to agree with the assertion that social guests have a reasonable expectation of privacy in the home in which they are visiting. The second is also an effective question, but the drafter of that question has essentially asked the question "do invitees have a legitimate expectation of privacy when they are doing something illegal?" and hopes that the reader will answer "of course not!"

The writers of both of these questions are trying to influence the Court's image of the case by including what Judge Ruggero Aldisert calls "enthymemes" — unspoken premises that support their arguments.[4]

---

[3] Karl N. Llewellyn, *A Lecture on Appellate Advocacy*, 29 U. Chi, I,. Rev 627, 630 (1902), cited in Bryan A. Garner, *The Deep Issue: A New Approach to Framing Legal Questions*, 5 Scribes J. Leg. Writing 1, 11 (1994-95).

[4] *See* Ruggero J. Aldisert, *Winning on Appeal* 142-43 (rev. 1st ed. 1996).

While the best enthymemes are based on legal premises that any court would agree with, some effective enthymemes can be based on policy premises, or even common-sense premises. Some enthymemes are conveyed through the focus of a question on a particular angle of the case, while others may be conveyed merely by the choice of one word over another.

In the first example above, the writer is basing his or her arguments on at least three unstated premises: (1) that the Supreme Court should give some deference to the Minnesota Supreme Court, (2) that "homes" are private places, and (3) that "social guests" have expectations of privacy.

The second example, written from the government's point of view, is based on some opposite premises: (1) that "invitees" have less of an expectation of privacy than "social guests," (2) that "residences" are less private than "homes," and, most importantly, (3) that people who participate in illegal activities have no expectation of privacy. The writer is hoping that these premises are so strong that the reader will immediately think "of course not" in answer to the question.

If you can base your question on a premise that is both valid and applicable, you can go a long way toward getting the Court to agree with your argument before it has even read your first point heading. Often, both sides will have valid and applicable premises on which to base their questions, as in the following examples from the employment discrimination case of *Hishon v. King and Spaulding*:

PETITIONER'S QUESTION

Whether King and Spaulding and other large institutional law firms that are organized as partnerships are, for that reason alone, exempt from Title VII of the Civil Rights Act of 1964, and are free (a) to discriminate in the promotion of associate lawyers to partnership on the basis of sex, race, or religion; and (b) to discharge those associates whom they do not admit to partnership based on reasons of sex, race, or religion under an established "up-or-out" policy.

RESPONDENT'S QUESTION

Whether law partners organized for advocacy are entitled to constitutionally protected freedom of association.[5]

The Petitioner's question is based on the premise that employment discrimination based on race, sex, or religion is illegal; the reader is prompted to answer "of course not" when asked, in essence, if law firms have a right to discriminate. The Respondent's question is based on the premise that freedom of association is legal, and prompts the reader to answer "of course" to its simple statement of the issue. The attorneys on each side of

---

[5] Reprinted in Laurel Currie Oates, Anne Enquist & Kelly Kunsch, *The Legal Writing Handbook* 277-78 (2d ed. 1998).

the case have done an excellent job of framing the issue to reflect their own points of view about the case.

When writing the question, remember that readers naturally pay more attention to information that appears in certain natural positions of emphasis — usually beginnings and endings — and try to put your best points in the beginning and especially at the end of the question presented. By planning your question in advance, noting what elements are most important and least important, you can structure your sentence to highlight your best points.

c. Problems to Avoid

i. Assuming Elements at Issue

When writing questions presented, include facts and law that will help the readers to reach the conclusion you want them to reach. Avoid, however, assuming as true an element that is at issue in the case. A question that assumes an element at issue often asks, in essence:

▽ BAD EXAMPLE

Will this court find that condition *X* exists when all of the factors necessary for condition *X* have been proven?

Even though you may firmly believe that all of the factors are there, your question should not assume away elements that your opponent legitimately disputes. Instead, include the facts and the law that you can use to prove that the court should decide in your favor.

For example, in the following question, the writer has assumed that no fundamental right has been violated:

▽ BAD EXAMPLE

Do voter-initiated, state constitutional amendments that prohibit the enactment of legislation desired by an identifiable class comply with the Equal Protection Clause of the Fourteenth Amendment when such amendments do not violate a fundamental right?

Because the other side argued that the amendment *did* violate a fundamental right, the question assumes an element at issue. Instead, the writer should include the facts and law that he or she plans to use to show that no fundamental right has been violated:

△ GOOD EXAMPLE

Do voter-initiated, state constitutional amendments that prohibit the enactment of legislation desired by an identifiable class comply with the Equal Protection Clause of the Fourteenth Amendment when the amendments do not inhibit the right to vote?

This question focuses on the fact that the writer thinks is most important. whatever else the amendments may do, they do not inhibit the fundamental right to vote.

In the following example, a different version of a question appropriate in *Minnesota v. Carter*, the writer has assumed that the issue of whether or not the defendant had a "reasonable expectation of privacy" has been met:

▽ **BAD EXAMPLE**

Whether citizens have a constitutionally protected right to be free from a police officer's covert observation into a private dwelling when that citizen reasonably expected and took measures to ensure that his activities would be shielded from the public's view.

Instead of including the citizen's "reasonable expectation" as a fact, the writer should include only the facts that he or she will use to prove that the expectation of privacy was reasonable:

△ **GOOD EXAMPLE**

Under the Fourth Amendment, does a citizen have a right to be free from a police officer's covert observation into a private dwelling when the citizen was sitting in a kitchen and the blinds on the windows had been closed against the public's view?

This question still makes effective use of the enthymemes "citizens have a right to privacy," "private dwellings are private," and "covert observations are illegal," but it doesn't sabotage itself by assuming the crucial element at issue.

In addition to violating rules of logic, questions that assume elements at issue needlessly annoy the judge or justice reading the brief, and fail to do the job of the question presented — to enlighten the court as to the issue or issues before it. The Honorable Fred I. Parker of the United States Court of Appeals for the Second Circuit has noted that questions that assume the element at issue "serve no useful purpose."[6] Furthermore, he notes, they may prejudice the judge against an attorney who would write such a useless question:

> [A]fter reading such a statement, my natural instinct is to believe the actual issue probably involves [some other legal question], which the writer of the brief was not nice enough to clearly state for me and has instead left me to figure out on my own. I am, therefore, immediately less than sanguine about the brief and, consequently, the advocate and his or her client. Further, in failing to quickly be able to ascertain what the issues are, I may resort to the other brief for help.[7]

Thus, by avoiding the trap of assuming elements at issue, you can both preserve your credibility with the court and incline the judge or justice to rely on your brief for a fair analysis of the case.

---

[6] Fred I. Parker, *Foreword: Appellate Advocacy and Practice in the Second Circuit*, 64 Brooklyn L. Rev. 457, 461 (1998).
[7] *Id.*

ii. Overlong Questions

Writers who try a variety of persuasive techniques may also fall into the trap of writing a question that is too long. Questions that are too long are not read carefully — if they are read at all — and so any individual points that the writer may make in the question are lost to the reader, as in the following question, written for one of the parties in *Rubin v. Coors:*

▽ **BAD EXAMPLE**

> **Should the Supreme Court of the United States affirm both the District Court and Tenth Circuit Court of Appeals decisions to enjoin enforcement of that portion of 27 U.S.C. § 205(e)(2) and its pertinent regulation 27 C.F.R. § 7.26, which prohibit labeling malt beverages with their accurately measured and truthful alcoholic content and thus allow the plaintiff and other brewers of malt beverages to better inform the consumers of their products by placing the percentage of alcohol contained in the beverage on the beverage container's label?**

This question includes several valid premises — truthful information is good, informing consumers is good, it is legal to give accurate information to people — but the question's length reduces its effectiveness. This question covers some of the same ground, but more briefly:

△ **GOOD EXAMPLE**

> **Does the First Amendment allow a prohibition against labeling malt beverages with their alcohol content when including the content on the label would allow consumers to have access to accurate and truthful alcohol content information?**

d. Summing Up

When writing the question presented, strive to control the picture that the court has of your case by deciding what question you want it to focus its attention on and by using appropriate writing techniques, including (1) giving the court a complete picture of the issue by including the legal context, the core legal question, and the relevant facts; (2) using appropriate enthymemes in the question; (3) structuring the question to highlight the positive aspects of the question; (4) avoiding assuming elements at issue; and (5) keeping the question at a reasonable length.

9.2
STATEMENTS OF THE CASE

9.2.1
FORMAL REQUIREMENTS

Rule 24.1(g) provides that a brief on the merits for a petitioner or an appellant[8] shall contain a

> concise statement of the case, setting out the facts material to the consideration of the questions presented, with appropriate references to the joint appendix, e.g., App. 12, or to the record, e.g., Record 12.

An effective statement of the case will make it unnecessary for the Court to resort to the record or the joint appendix, providing a "universe of facts" to which the Court can refer. At the very least, the statement should include in sufficient detail any fact even *referenced* in the Argument. In addition to the facts needed for the argument, however, the statement of the case should include necessary procedural facts and relevant background information. The advocate should tell the story of the events that gave rise to the litigation and how it progressed through the court system on up to the current hearing.

The statement should also include citations that will allow the reader to verify the information cited. Most of the information will come from a joint appendix or a record, and that information should be cited according to Rule 24.1(a). Information that comes from the lower court opinions in the case, as well as any statutes that may be included in the fact statement should be cited according to appropriate citation rules.

Citations in the fact statement are vital because many judges will not trust facts without an appropriate citation. Judge Clyde H. Hamilton, of the United States Court of Appeals for the Fourth Circuit, counts missing citations as one of the major problems with fact statements:

> [The importance of] appropriate citations to the appendix. . . . cannot be overemphasized. Little else makes my blood boil quicker than reading an appellate brief that lacks appropriate citations to the appendix in the statement of facts and the argument components. Apparently, the parties submitting these briefs are under the serious misimpression that appellate judges have endless hours to spend combing the appendix in an effort to match up scattered pieces of evidence with a party's unreferenced factual assertions.[9]

---

[8] Supreme Court Rule 24.2 permits respondents and appellees to omit several items from the brief (questions presented, the list of parties to the proceedings, opinions below, jurisdictional statement, statutes involved, and statement of the facts) "unless the respondent or appellee is dissatisfied with their presentation by the opposing party." In most Appellate Advocacy courses, however, all students are required to include all elements of the brief.

[9] Clyde H. Hamilton, *Effective Appellate Brief Writing*, 50 S.C.L. Rev. 581, 586 (1999).

Thus, your goal as a writer should be to include citations at *a minimum* at the end of every paragraph, and certainly to include a citation at the end of *every sentence* in which you have referenced a different page of the record.

9.2.2
ORGANIZING THE FACT STATEMENT

A good fact statement begins by providing the reader with the necessary context. Too many writers begin the statement with the first happening in the case's chain of events, as in the following example from a fact statement written in the case of *Rubin v. Coors*:

▽ BAD EXAMPLE

> In 1987, Coors Brewing Company submitted an application to the Bureau of Alcohol, Tobacco and Firearms requesting approval for the labels that disclosed the alcohol content of their Coors and Coors Light Beers. App. 60-65.

While this sentence makes reference to the controversy — whether beer manufacturers can put alcohol content on their labels — it does not identify the controversy for the reader. The following example provides better context:

△ GOOD EXAMPLE

> This Court is being asked to affirm a decision of the Ninth Circuit Court of Appeals that found that 27 U.S.C. §§ 205(e)(2) and 205(f)(2) violate the First Amendment to the United States Constitution. Those provisions prohibit labels or advertisements disclosing the alcohol content of malt beverages unless disclosure is required by state law.

These two sentences set both the procedural and legal context, and will better enable the reader to understand the significance of the rest of the information in the statement.

After providing context, the writer must decide how to organize the rest of the fact statement. Although chronological organization is often favored, sometimes a topical organization can be more effective. For example, in a case about a car accident in which both the manufacturing process and warranties at the time of purchase were at issue, it might not make sense to begin with the first event — the manufacture of the automobile. Instead, the writer might organize the facts around three topics: (1) the accident, (2) the manufacture of the car, and (3) the warranties provided at the time of purchase. By addressing the accident first, the writer alerts the reader to the problems in the car that might have caused the accident, and better prepares him or her to review the information about both the manufacturing of the car and the warranties provided at the time of purchase. Remember that you can provide internal headings in the fact statement, especially if it is lengthy. Headings are particularly appropriate with a topical organization.

Although the writer must provide procedural as well as "factual" information, there is no requirement as to where in the fact statement this information must be included. Some writers provide the information about court proceedings immediately after giving context; others progress chronologically from the facts that happened "in the world" to the facts that happened in court. Finally, some writers include internal headings to separate their "statement of the case" (including procedural information) from their "statement of the facts" (for factual information).

9.2.3 Making the Fact Statement Persuasive

Most courts frown on the inclusion of legal arguments in the fact statement. They frown even more on lying, or on "stretching the truth" in the way that you characterize the facts. You should include all legally significant facts, even those that may hurt your case. Including all relevant facts is important for both "moral" reasons — your oath as an attorney requires it — and for practical reasons — your opponent will point out that you lied, and you will lose your credibility with the court.[10] Judge Morey L. Sear, of the United States District Court for the Eastern District of Louisiana, has noted that "[i]f a lawyer's brief . . . fudges on the content of clear testimony, credibility is immediately destroyed. In my view, credibility is one of the most important virtues a litigator can possess."[11]

Supreme Court Justice Ruth Bader Ginsburg advises that "[a]bove all, a good brief is trustworthy. It states the facts honestly."[12] Judge Parker notes that severe distortions of the facts "will actually make me stop reading the brief and go to the district court's opinion, or even the opposing brief."[13]

Nevertheless, you can make your fact statement as persuasive as possible by using persuasive writing techniques to tell the story from your point of view, to highlight the facts that are in your favor, and to lead the reader to draw favorable conclusions about your client's case.[14]

When drafting the fact statement, remember that your reader will not be a passive recipient of information, dutifully taking in whatever you have put on the page and doing nothing more with it. Most readers — yourself included — are constantly assessing, using inductive and deductive reasoning, leaping to conclusions, and, at times, leaving the text en-

---

[10] *See, e.g.,* Fred I. Parker, *Foreword: Appellate Advocacy and Practice in the Second Circuit,* 64 Brooklyn L. Rev. 457, 462 (1998).

[11] Morey L. Sear, *Briefing in the United States District Court for the Eastern District of Louisiana,* 70 Tul. L. Rev. 207, 219 (1995).

[12] Ruth Bader Ginsburg, *Remarks on Appellate Advocacy,* 50 S.C.L. Rev. 567, 568 (1999). *See also* Sarah B. Duncan, *Pursuing Quality: Writing a Helpful Brief,* 30 St. Mary's L.J. 1093, 1101 (1999); Joel F. Dubina, *How to Litigate Successfully in the United States Court of Appeals for the Eleventh Circuit,* 20 Cumb. L. Rev. 1, 5 (1998/1999).

[13] Fred I. Parker, *Foreword: Appellate Advocacy and Practice in the Second Circuit,* 64 Brooklyn L. Rev. 457, 462 (1998).

[14] For an excellent discussion of persuasive writing techniques in fact statements, *see* Laurel Oates, Anne Enquist & Kelly Kunsch, *The Legal Writing Handbook* 285-98 (2d ed. 1998).

tirely. In the argument, you will be announcing your conclusions to the reader and then, ideally, supporting them with your analysis. In the fact statement, on the other hand, you can provide information that the reader can put together to reach a conclusion. If you do it skillfully enough, the reader will have drawn a conclusion in your favor even before reaching the first page of the argument section.

For example, my father, who served in the Coast Guard in the early 1950s, tells this possibly apocryphal story about a captain and his first mate:

> One day, when the sailors took shore leave, the first mate returned to the ship drunk. The Captain recorded this event, noting "The first mate was drunk today" in the Captain's log. The first mate has the responsibility for keeping the log when the Captain is off duty, so he soon saw the note. He was furious; he had never been drunk before, he had been off duty when he was drunk, and he was one of a dozen drunk sailors, none of whose drunkenness was recorded in the log. He decided to retaliate. He knew he couldn't lie about the Captain, for the Captain would be seeing the log the very next day. So he wrote the simple truth: "The Captain was sober today."

If you read that log without knowing the details, you would no doubt jump to the conclusion that the Captain was *usually* drunk; thus, it was worth recording the rare occasion when he was sober. Realize that whenever you read, you are using deductive and inductive reasoning, and your own knowledge and prejudices, to fill in details and jump to conclusions.

More commonly, readers jump to conclusions based on information that is not included. For example, while I was in the middle of reading a novel set in and written in the nineteenth century, a new male character was described as "clean-shaven." I suddenly realized that all of the *other* male characters must have had "whiskers." I had pictured them as clean-shaven, because that fit with my "default" image of adult males: Presume no facial hair unless told otherwise. The author did not believe that whiskers were worth mentioning, for in her world whiskers were the default mode for adult men.

Thus, when you are writing your statement of the facts, ask yourself what legal conclusions you want the reader to draw, and how those legal conclusions relate to the facts. Recognize conclusions that you might want to lead your readers to, and conclusions you want the reader to avoid. Consider what presumptions, or "default images" your readers might bring to the case generally, and to people like your client or your opponent in particular. For example, has your client had several drug arrests? Do your readers have certain presumptions about police officers that you want to reinforce or rebut? You can do this by giving details that contradict or support your readers' presumptions.

If you want the reader to believe that your client's procedural rights were violated, it might help the court to decide in your favor if it believes that your client got a "raw deal" from the government and that your client is conscientious. Include the details that will help the reader reach these conclusions independently.

For example, in the case of *Holloway v. United States*, counsel for Mr. Holloway had to convince the Court that it should overturn a conviction under the federal carjacking statute. The controversy centered on whether Holloway's participation in the carjacking constituted sufficient "intent to cause death or serious bodily harm." Holloway (Petitioner at the Supreme Court) had, admittedly, been part of the carjackings, and a carjacking is a frightening crime to most people. One (student) counsel for Holloway tried to give details in the facts that would contradict the presumption that someone who would participate in a carjacking would be a violent person:

⚠ GOOD EXAMPLE

> **Vernon Lennon recruited the petitioner to steal cars with him. Record 156. Lennon showed Holloway the revolver that Lennon planned to carry during the commission of the robberies. Apparently, it was Holloway's job to drive the "getaway" car. Id. There is no evidence in the record that Lennon told Holloway that he planned to shoot the victims. Holloway never carried a gun during any of the robberies.**
>
> **On October 14, 1994, Lennon and Holloway stole a car in Queens. Record 83-84. The car's owner sustained no injuries. The next day, the two men stole a Toyota and a Mercedes-Benz. Record 84. Holloway never even approached the driver of the Toyota; like the first driver, he escaped unharmed. Id. Lennon and Holloway both advanced toward the driver of the Mercedes-Benz, and Lennon produced his gun and threatened to shoot. Record 84. When the driver hesitated momentarily, Holloway stepped in and struck him once, before Lennon could take any action. Id. At this point, the driver surrendered his keys and fled, essentially unharmed. Id.**

These details emphasize that Holloway never carried a gun, that none of his victims were shot, and that Holloway may have prevented Lennon, his accomplice, from shooting one of the victims.

After you have considered the conclusions you want the reader to draw, make a list of all of the facts that are relevant to your case. You may consult the abstract of the record, the record itself, the lower court decisions, and even the argument to come up with all of the legally (and emotionally) significant facts. (Be certain, of course, *not* to use facts that were offered into evidence and rejected.) Perhaps divide your list into three parts — neutral facts, positive facts, and negative facts. You can use some or all of the following persuasive techniques to highlight the positive facts and "lowlight" the negative ones.

a. Positions of Emphasis

An easy and effective way to highlight information is to put it into positions of emphasis within the document. As will be explored in more depth in a later chapter, scientists have learned that readers subconsciously pay more attention to information that appears before or after a mental or physical break within the document. Thus, both the beginning and the ending of the fact statement are positions of emphasis, as are the beginnings and endings of any heading sections within the facts, and even the first and last sentences of paragraphs.

When writing your fact statement, strive to put your "positive facts" into positions of emphasis. You may even create positions of emphasis by inserting topical headings, by creating paragraph breaks, or by using headings to separate the introduction from the fact statement or the fact statement from the statement of the "case" (i.e., the description of the proceedings below).

b. Context

Another way to control the way your reader sees information is to put the information into the appropriate context. When making your list of facts, use the "buddy system" for your bad facts. Try to make sure that every bad fact that must be included in the statement is paired with a good fact that explains (or neutralizes) its presence. Certain negative facts will look better if they are juxtaposed with a good fact, or even a neutral fact that either explains why the negative fact occurred or why it doesn't affect the outcome of the case. For example, in the case of *Miller v. Albright*, Ms. Miller, who was born in the Philippines, was trying to establish United States citizenship through her relationship with her father, a U.S. citizen. Her father had not been listed on her birth certificate, a "bad fact" that needed to be addressed. One writer tried to put that fact into a good context in the following way:

⚠ GOOD EXAMPLE

> **Ms. Miller was born in the Philippines on June 20, 1970. App. 15. Although her birth record did not include her father's name, a voluntary paternity decree issued on July 27, 1992, by a Texas state court established Charlie R. Miller, a U.S. citizen, as her biological father. App. to Pet. for Writ of Cert. at 37.**

Thus, the reader learns that even though the father's name was not on the birth certificate, he was willing to have paternity established by a *voluntary* paternity decree.

c. Spending the Reader's Time, Saving the Reader's Energy

To make sure that your readers remember the positive facts in your case, make the reader spend more time and less energy on them. Use several sentences to make a point instead of crowding the information into one sentence. Be as concrete as you can be when describing a positive fact so that the reader doesn't have to figure out what happened. Conversely, when you want to de-emphasize a fact, don't spend much time on it, don't go into a lot of detail, and don't use concrete language. For example, in *City of Indianapolis v. Edmonds*, a case about the constitutionality of drug interdiction roadblocks, counsel for the City of Indianapolis might describe the police procedure succinctly:

> **Traffic stops consist of two simple steps: Officers verify the driver's license and registration, and then conduct a quick walk-around of the car with a narcotics-sniffing dog. Record 57a. They conduct a more thorough search *only* if the narcotics dog, plain-view, or plain-smell observation reveals a suspicion of narcotics possession, or if the driver gives explicit consent to search. Record 57a, 53a.**

These two rather long sentences give a complete, but not detailed, account. The reader would have to expend energy to identify the details that this brief description implies, and more than likely would not do so. Counsel for the Respondent, on the other hand, might describe the police procedure in greater detail:

> **Upon entering the checkpoint, an automobile's driver and occupants are subjected to a number of examinations, which are conducted by Indianapolis police officers. Record 57a. First, the officers approach the vehicle, and the driver is asked to produce both a valid driver's license and the registration for the vehicle. Record 57a. After one officer examines and verifies this documentation, other officers scrutinize the vehicle in two ways. First, they use plain-view detection techniques, looking through the vehicle's windows. In addition, they use plain-smell methods, sniffing the air around the car as they walk around it. Both of these techniques are used to determine whether or not the officers can discover probable cause that would allow them to conduct a more invasive search of the automobile and its occupants. Record 57a. Furthermore, if the officers can persuade the driver to consent to a search, they can conduct an even more extensive search of the vehicle. Record 53a. One other method of search is used during even routine stops: A narcotics detection dog is walked around the exterior of the vehicle, in a final attempt to discover probable cause to search the vehicle for narcotics. Record 57a.**

Notice how the writer has "unpacked" the sentences to state explicitly information that is implicit in the first example. In the first example, the officers "verify license and registration." These words imply request, retrieval, handing over, and inspection; the second example provides these details. The second example uses this detail to create an impression of significant intrusion on the driver and the passengers. The writer provides every detail, leaving nothing for the reader to figure out on his or her own. The numerous sentences, the level of detail, and the word choice all work to create an image of a long, intrusive stop. If the reader believes in minimal police intrusion without probable cause, he or she could be halfway to a favorable conclusion merely after reading the statement of facts, for it will have created a concrete picture in the reader's mind of precisely what a "routine stop" entails.

Of course, as with any persuasive method, use good judgment. Being either too succinct or too detailed can negatively impress the court.

To sum up, when writing your fact statement, you should (1) decide what conclusions you want the reader to draw after reading the facts and noting which presumptions the reader might bring to the fact statement; (2) collect the facts, noting which facts are positive, negative, and neutral vis-à-vis the conclusions you want the reader to draw; (3) organize the facts; (4) make the facts persuasive by exploiting positions of emphasis, context, level of detail, and specificity; (5) take care not to violate ethical or logical rules; and (6) make sure that you cite to the record as needed.

9.3
SUMMARY OF THE ARGUMENT

The summary of the argument follows the statement of the facts, and it signals an abrupt change. Up until this point, the writer has been describing the case, including its issues, the opinions below, and the facts. Now the writer begins to argue.

Supreme Court Rule 24.1(h) provides that the brief must include

> A summary of the argument, suitably paragraphed. The summary should be a clear and concise condensation of the argument made in the body of the brief; mere repetition of the headings under which the argument is arranged is not sufficient.

At the very least, the summary can serve as a roadmap to the argument as a whole. The writer should succinctly state the major arguments relied upon in the brief, in the order in which they appear in the argument section. Some writers use the summary to present a "holistic" picture of their case, focusing more on policy and equity than on black-letter law.

Judge Hamilton notes that the summary of the argument is "significant on several levels":

> First, it is the party's first opportunity to put a legal gloss on the facts. Second, it is the party's first opportunity to orient the appellate judges assigned the appeal to the theme of the party's argument. Third, and most importantly, it serves as the party's official opening statement, previewing and summarizing the key legal points the party wants to make in the argument component of the brief.[15]

A good summary should grab the reader's attention in its opening paragraph. While the statement of facts should open with a somewhat objective statement of what the case is about, the summary of the argument can be more dramatic, identifying the underlying issues that the

---

[15] Clyde H. Hamilton, *Effective Appellate Brief Writing*, 50 S.C.L. Rev. 581, 586-87 (1999).

case presents. In the case of *Rubin v. Coors*, for example, counsel for the United States (Rubin) might open the summary with a declarative statement about the result being sought:

▽ **BAD EXAMPLE**

Section 205(e)(2) of the Federal Alcohol Administrative Act, prohibiting alcohol content disclosure on malt beverage labels, does not violate the Free Speech clause of the First Amendment.

While this opening is appropriately argumentative, it doesn't grab the reader's attention. To create a more dramatic opening, counsel might begin the summary by reminding the reader of the original purpose of Section 205(e)(2). The statute was drafted shortly after Prohibition ended; the government was seeking to prevent strength wars among brewers, and to prevent beer drinkers from "forum shopping" for the most powerful beer. Counsel for the United States might bring that purpose up to date by opening the summary of the argument like this:

△ **GOOD EXAMPLE**

"Prohibition" is not just a time in history that ended 60 years ago. Every day is the end of Prohibition for someone who reaches the legal drinking age.

In *Miller v. Albright*, in which the issue before the Court was whether a statute could constitutionally distinguish between so-called illegitimate children of U.S. citizen fathers and those of U.S. citizen mothers, the attorney representing Ms. Miller could have opened the summary of the argument by reminding the Court of the harsh reality of the statute's distinction:

△ **GOOD EXAMPLE**

The issue before this court is whether Congress may use an irrebuttable gender stereotype to impose an arbitrary time limit on the relationship between a father and his daughter.

Each of these openings grabs the reader's attention and makes him or her want to learn more about the client's argument.

Many writers clog up the summary of the argument with too much detail. This part of the document is meant to provide a *summary*. It should focus more on rules and how they apply rather than on detailed explanations.

In the excerpt below, from the summary of the argument in a petitioner's brief in *Minnesota v. Carter*, the author summarized a 30-page argument in two pages. The case had two main points. After introducing those points in the opening paragraph, the writer used one paragraph to lay out the first rule, then two paragraphs to apply it, followed by one paragraph on the second rule, and another paragraph to apply that rule.

She ends the summary by telling the Court how she wants it to decide the case:

⚠ GOOD EXAMPLE

Respondents did not have a reasonable expectation of privacy when they bagged cocaine in front of a partially covered window in a basement apartment. The Minnesota Supreme Court incorrectly reversed the trial court's denial of Respondents' motion to suppress. First, it erroneously ruled that Respondents had a legitimate expectation of privacy while in another's apartment for the sole purpose of illegally bagging cocaine. Second, it wrongly held that an officer conducted a search when he merely observed criminal activity in plain view from an area outside the apartment's curtilage **1**.

1 Note how the writer lays out the two issues that the argument, and thus the summary, will address.

This Court's Fourth Amendment jurisprudence demonstrates that the Minnesota Supreme Court's ruling was erroneous. In order to invoke the Fourth Amendment's protections, an individual must prove that he had a legitimate expectation of privacy. An individual possesses a legitimate expectation of privacy when he demonstrates that he has both a subjective expectation of privacy and an expectation of privacy that society is prepared to view as reasonable **2**.

2 In this paragraph, the writer lays out the basic rule that governs the first issue, identifying two sub-issues. She does not cite to authority, which is an acceptable convention in the Summary of the Argument.

Respondents were sitting at an illuminated kitchen table facing a window of a ground-floor apartment and packaging cocaine. Respondents should have realized that a passerby could have looked into the apartment and noticed the illegal activity occurring within the apartment. Thus, Respondents can claim no subjective expectation of privacy **3**.

3 In this paragraph, the writer connects the facts to her legal conclusion that the Respondents can claim no subjective expectation of privacy.

Additionally, any subjective expectation of privacy Respondents possessed is not one that society is prepared to recognize as reasonable in light of longstanding social customs that serve functions recognized as valuable by society. As non-overnight guests, they lacked the connection with the premises that legitimizes an expectation of privacy. Even if shorter-term guests can claim the protection of the Fourth Amendment, only those short-term guests who are present for socially permissible and valuable reasons qualify for Fourth Amendment protection. Respondents were present only to conduct criminal business activities and therefore did not have an expectation of privacy that was reasonable in light of longstanding social customs that serve functions recognized as valuable by society **4**.

4 In this paragraph, the writer gives the factual details that show why society is not prepared to recognize Respondents' expectation of privacy as reasonable. These reasons reflect the organization of her argument.

Furthermore, even assuming that Respondents are entitled to invoke the Fourth Amendment's protections, no Fourth Amendment search occurred. A search occurs only when governmental agents intrude upon an area in which an individual has a reasonable expectation of privacy. A reasonable expectation of privacy is violated when an officer intrudes upon the home or its curtilage, the area immediately surrounding the home that shares the same private characteristics as the home. Conversely, there is no violation of a reasonable expectation of privacy, and therefore no search, when an officer merely stands outside the curtilage of a residence and observes what is in plain view **5**.

In this case, the officer stood in a publicly accessible common area outside the apartment's curtilage. The officer used only his natural senses to observe what was in plain view. He conducted his observation without physical intrusion, without the use of any device, and in a manner that any member of the public could have employed. The officer's conduct violated no reasonable expectation of privacy and therefore was not a Fourth Amendment search. **6**

For these reasons, this Court should hold that Respondents had no legitimate expectation of privacy in the apartment and that the observations of the officer did not constitute a search. This Court should reverse the Minnesota Supreme Court's judgment. **7**

Most effective summaries of the argument do not contain numerous citations to authority. If a statute, constitutional provision, or other authority is at issue, it will of course be mentioned; likewise, if the case is largely controlled by a particular authority, that authority may be mentioned as well. Usually, however, the focus is on legal principles rather than on the authorities that are the source of those principles.

To summarize, the summary of the argument should (1) signal the writer's theme, (2) signal the writer's major arguments and the order in which those arguments will appear, (3) focus on rules and their application rather than detailed explanations, and (4) avoid most citations to authority.

9.4
POINT HEADINGS

9.4.1
FORMAT AND FUNCTION

The Supreme Court rules do not give much guidance about point headings. Rule 24.1(h) mentions them in passing, noting that an effective summary of the argument should not merely repeat "the headings under which the argument is arranged." Nevertheless, well-drafted point headings can help the writer to organize the argument and help the reader to use the argument effectively.

Point headings are used as headings and subheadings within the argument section of a brief. They are also reprinted in the table of contents; they are useful there as a concise summary of your major points and as a tool to help the reader find those points.

Point headings serve three functions in the body of the argument. First, they give the court easy access to the writer's basic argument. The

---

**Format Requirements for
Point Headings**

Major contentions are labeled with roman numerals. Sub-points under roman numerals are labeled with capital letters. Sub-points under upper-case letters are labeled with arabic numerals. Sub-points under arabic numerals are labeled with lower-case letters. Thus:

I.
    A.
        1.
            a.
            b.
        2.
    B.
    C.

Conventional wisdom is that you should never have a "I" without a "II," an "A" without a "B," etc. While this advice is valid, there is an exception in appellate advocacy. If your argument relies on one dispositive point, that point can be labeled as a "I" even though there is no "II." (Some writers, in the alternative, simply do not label their main argument with a roman numeral at all.) Note that the *only* exception to this point is at the roman numeral stage. You *must* have at least a "B." heading if you have an "A." heading.

Although traditionalists use all capital letters for their roman numeral point headings and underline their capital letter point headings, these traditions no longer make sense. They come from the days before word processors; typewriters did not allow much flexibility. Unless court rules require otherwise, you should consider putting *all* headings (both point headings and section headings — e.g., The Summary of the Argument) in **bold-faced type** to increase their visibility and thus help the reader to find particular segments of the brief.

---

point headings are thesis statements of the writer's argument in each section and sub-section of the brief. Point headings are particularly effective as concise statements of the writer's best points because they occur in a "position of emphasis" within the document. Anytime the reader takes a break between one segment of a document and another (whether those segments are sentences, paragraphs, or sections) his or her attention peaks. A bold-faced heading spikes the reader's attention and makes it likely that he or she will pay attention to the information in the heading. The writer gains maximum benefit from this position of emphasis when his or her major contentions appear in the headings.

The second function of the point headings is organizational. The point headings help the reader to understand the relationships between and among the different sections of the argument, for example, that these A and B points are part of the argument related to the roman II point heading, or that the writer has three main arguments as expressed in romans I, II, and III. On a less substantive but equally important note, the point headings help the reader to find the particular argument that he or she wants to read about. Often, readers do not read through a brief from beginning to end. Even if they do once read the brief straight through, after that initial reading the readers will use the brief like a reference work, and they will use the point headings to help them to find what they are looking for.

The third function of the point heading is its simplest: The point heading provides a graphic break for the reader between sections of the brief. By inserting a heading or sub-heading, the writer tells the reader, "you are finished with the previous point, and now you are moving on to the next point." Because reading briefs can be a daunting task, effective use of point headings can help break a long argument up into easy-to-understand (or easier-to-understand) segments. Remember that judges are more likely to be persuaded by briefs that they can easily understand. Therefore, to promote understanding, try not to have more than three or four pages without a point heading or sub-heading.

At this stage of the writing process, you should have already identified the main assertions you plan to make to convince the court to decide in your favor. When deciding how to arrange these assertions into headings, identify the relationships between and among those assertions. First, group the assertions that are related; second, identify the major assertions. In particular, identify the assertions that are dispositive: that is, if the court agrees with this assertion, it must decide the case in your favor.

When you first try to identify the relationships between and among your headings, your roman numeral point headings should be only dispositive assertions. This method is the most logical, and it is most likely to display an argument whose main points track the brief's questions presented. Many good attorneys do not follow this advice, however. If a case is complex, with many sub-issues related to the one dispositive assertion, the brief could end up with sub-sub-sub-sub-heads. In that situation, it would be preferable to eliminate the single dispositive heading and "promote" all of the other headings. Your starting point, however, should always be to identify the points that are dispositive.

9.4.2
DRAFTING THE POINT HEADINGS

A classic point heading is a concise, persuasive statement of
(1)
    (a) a conclusion that you want the court to accept **or**
    (b) an action that you want the court to take
PLUS
(2)   the reason that the court should take that action or agree with that assertion.

To draft your point headings, first consult your list of ultimate assertions and identify something you want the court to **do** or something the court must **conclude** or **agree with** in order to decide in your client's favor. Next, identify the reasons that support taking those actions or reaching those conclusions. If the reasons are the sub-parts of an argument, make each reason a separate point heading. If there are no sub-parts in that section of the document, "add" the reason(s) to the assertion, often with a "because."

For example, this point heading, from a respondent's brief in *Knowles v. Iowa*, is based on something the writer wants the court to do:

> I.   This Court should extend the search-incident-to-arrest exception to the Fourth Amendment's warrant requirement to situations in which an officer is issuing a citation in lieu of arrest.

The same point could be written in a different way, as an assertion that the writer wants the court to agree with:

> I.   The search-incident-to-arrest exception to the Fourth Amendment's warrant requirement should include situations in which an officer is issuing a citation in lieu of arrest.

The three sub-headings below show the "reasons" that support the writer's assertion:

> A.   The situation contemplated by Iowa Code § 805.1(4), where an officer issues a citation in lieu of arrest, presents the same policy concerns as when an actual arrest takes place.
>
> B.   The search incident to arrest exception should be extended to cover citations in lieu of arrest because the public interests advanced by such a search substantially outweighs the extent to which such a search intrudes upon individual privacy rights.
>
> C.   Outlawing a warrant exception for a search incident to a citation in lieu of arrest would encourage police officers to arrest more people in order to conduct searches.

Note how the "B" point heading above includes the "because clause" within the heading. Because that clause makes the heading a bit long, the writer could restructure to allow sub-headings to show the reasons:

> B.   The search incident to arrest exception should be extended to cover citations in lieu of arrest.
>
>   1.   Allowing a search incident to a citation in lieu of arrest advances the substantial government interest in officer safety.
>
>   2.   Conducting a search incident to a citation in lieu of arrest represents a minimal intrusion upon individual privacy rights.

Of course, this technique works only when the "because clause" consists of two or more reasons worthy of analysis.

A good point heading should: (1) indicate the issue being discussed, (2) indicate your position on the issue, and (3) indicate the basic reason(s) for that position. Accordingly, your point headings should be full sentences, not phrases. They should be statements about how the law applies to the people or entities in your case, not abstract pronouncements about the law generally.[16] As a test, see if you could "recycle" your point heading in another brief on the same point. If so, you probably need to be more specific. In particular, you need to be more specific if your point heading could be used in your *opponent's* brief. For example, don't write, "The First Amendment protects freedom of speech." Instead, write "Because the First Amendment protects freedom of speech, Mr. Johnson should be allowed to distribute homemade, anonymous leaflets at a public rally."

9.4.3
THE RELATIONSHIPS BETWEEN AND AMONG POINT HEADINGS

There can be many different types of logical relationships between and among point headings, but four are particularly common. One type of relationship exists when the main heading describes a multipart test, and the sub-headings discuss each of the parts in turn. For example, this set of point headings for the Petitioner in *Miller v. Albright* shows how the writer believes that two parts of the intermediate scrutiny test should be applied:

III. **The use of an irrebuttable gender stereotype in 8 U.S.C. § 1409(a) is not "substantially related" to the achievement of the government's objective, and there is no "exceedingly persuasive justification" for the stereotype's use.**

    A. **8 U.S.C. § 1409(a) is unconstitutionally overinclusive, and, therefore, is not "substantially related" to the achievement of the government's objective 8 U.S.C. § 1409(a).**

    B. **There is no "exceedingly persuasive justification" for the use of an irrebuttable gender stereotype in 8 U.S.C. § 1409(a) because less discriminatory methods would achieve the government's objective.**

In the second type of relationship, the main heading makes an assertion, and the sub-headings provide legal support that may or may not be formal "sub-parts" of the main assertion. In this excerpt from a petitioner's brief in *Minnesota v. Carter*, note how the A, B, C, and D headings make legal arguments that support heading I. Although they are not all necessary sub-parts of a "reasonable expectation or privacy" argument, the reader will be more likely to agree with heading I if he or she agrees with sub-headings A, B, C, and D:

I.   **As temporary business invitees present in another's residence for the sole purpose of packaging drugs, Respondents had no legitimate ex-**

---

[16] *See, e.g.,* Lynn B. Squires, Marjorie Dick Rombauer & Katherine See Kennedy, *Legal Writing in a Nutshell* 292-93 (2d ed. 1996).

pectation of privacy and, thus, may not invoke the Fourth Amendment's protections.

A. Respondents failed to meet their burden of proving that they had a legitimate expectation of privacy because they introduced absolutely no evidence regarding their status in Thompson's apartment.

B. Respondents had no legitimate expectation of privacy because any subjective expectation they might have had while temporarily in another's home for the sole purpose of conducting illegal business was not one society recognizes as reasonable.

C. Respondents may not claim a legitimate expectation of privacy, because by engaging in criminal acts in a well-lit room, directly in front of a window facing a widely used common area, they exhibited no subjective expectation of privacy.

D. This Court should maintain its reluctance to expand the class of individuals who may claim a legitimate expectation of privacy and invoke the exclusionary rule.

In the third type of relationship, the main heading makes an assertion, and the sub-headings focus on how particular facts support the main assertion.

2. Even if the _Olson_ rule extends to non-overnight guests, Respondents' expectation of privacy is unreasonable because they were present only to conduct illegal business that is not valuable to society.

a. Illegal drug distribution is not a longstanding social custom that serves functions recognized as valuable by society.

b. Respondents were present for a purely commercial purpose and were not entitled to the Fourth Amendment protection associated with the home.

The fourth common type of relationship is a relationship between "equal" headings rather than between a main assertion and its sub-headings. In this relationship, the headings present alternative arguments, as in this example from a petitioner's brief in _Minnesota v. Carter_:

⚠ GOOD EXAMPLE

1. The _Olson_ rule dictates that only overnight guests have a connection to a premises that gives rise to a legitimate expectation of privacy.
2. Even if the _Olson_ rule extends to non-overnight guests, Respondents' expectation of privacy is unreasonable because they were present only to conduct illegal business that is not valuable to society.

Using "even if" language in the second alternative point heading can help the Court to understand the relationships between the headings more quickly. Despite the concerns of some students, alternative arguments are perfectly acceptable, as long as the law and the facts could reasonably support both arguments.

9.4.4
SUMMING UP

When drafting your point headings, (1) base the headings on actions you want the court to take or assertions you want the court to accept, (2) make sure that the point headings reflect logical relationships between and among the issues in your case, and (3) make your point headings concrete assertions that incorporate the facts and law at issue in your case.

CHAPTER TEN

SIX DEGREES OF LEGAL WRITING: MAKING YOUR DOCUMENT READER-FRIENDLY

An appellate brief is a functional document, and it is used in different ways at different stages in the decision-making process. If there is an oral argument, the judges will use the brief before the argument to understand how the law and the facts support that argument. After the argument, one or more of the judges and their clerks may use the brief to help them write the opinion. Your readers will have different needs at different times, and your brief must meet these different needs. The first time the readers read the brief, it is important for them to understand how the different parts of your argument work together to support the conclusion you want the court to reach. Later, it is important for them to be able to find the points and authorities that they are interested in.

When most readers use your brief, they will not be reading it the way you might read a favorite novel. Instead, they will be trying to find the parts they care about. As one commentator noted in the *Harvard Law Review* back in 1959, the brief writer cannot expect the complete and undivided attention of every judge:

> [W]ritten arguments filed with the Court are not documents like law review essays which the author is entitled to expect each of his readers to peruse carefully and reflectively from beginning to end. Perhaps the writer of an opinion reads a brief this way. But for other members of the Court these documents necessarily serve a different function than the communication simply of a connected line of thought. They are documents from which busy [people] have to extract the gist in a hurry. . . . Briefs on the merits need not only tell their story to one who takes the time to read all the way through them, but to be so organized that they

can be used, like a book of reference, for quick illumination on any particular point of concern.[1]

Because your document will be *used*, not just *read*, it must not only *be* focused and well-organized, it must *highlight* that focus and organization for the reader.

Even after you have written a complete draft that says what you want it to say, it may still be only a "writer-based document." That is, it is a document that only the writer can understand and use effectively. At this stage of the writing process, it is time to move to a "reader-based document," a document that is written and organized to promote understanding by others. Two vital steps in turning your document into a reader-based document are (1) making sure that the reader understands how each part of the argument supports your thesis and (2) making sure that the reader can easily find information within the document.

10.1
FIND YOUR "KEVIN BACON"

A few years ago, Craig Fass, Michael Ginelli, and Brian Turtle created the game "Six Degrees of Kevin Bacon." The game is based on the concept at the heart of the 1990 John Guare play *Six Degrees of Separation:* We are all connected to everyone else in the world through no more than six people. The game's premise is that "Kevin Bacon is the center of the entertainment universe"[2] and that he can be connected to any other actor through no more than six movies. For example:

Oprah Winfrey was in *The Color Purple* with Danny Glover;
Danny Glover was in *Places in the Heart* with Sally Field;
Sally Field was in *Punchline* with Tom Hanks; and
Tom Hanks was in *Apollo 13* with Kevin Bacon.

Now, what does all of this have to do with legal writing? Every legal document should have a Kevin Bacon, that "center of the universe" to which everything else in the document connects. With a well-written legal document, the reader should be able to throw a dart at any sentence in the document and get back to the document's "Kevin Bacon" just as easily as we moved from Oprah Winfrey to Kevin Bacon in the paragraph above.

---

[1] Hart, *The Supreme Court, 1958 Term, Forword: The Time Chart of the Justices*, 73 Harv. L. Rev. 84, 94 (1959) (cited in James VanR. Springer, Symposium on Supreme Court Advocacy: Some Suggestions on Preparing Briefs on the Merits in the Supreme Court of the United States, 33 Cath. U.L. Rev. 593, 593-94 (1984)).

[2] To play the game and learn more about it, you may want to visit "The Oracle of Bacon" Web site at <http://www.cs.virginia.edu/oracle/>. I will note that when I submitted "Oprah Winfrey," I learned that she has a "Bacon Number" of two. (Oprah Winfrey was in *Native Son* (1986) with Matt Dillon; Matt Dillon was in *Wild Things* (1998) with Kevin Bacon.) Since a Bacon number of four provides a better teaching tool, I will leave my example as is.

When writing a brief, you should decide what the center of your brief's "universe" is: That's your Kevin Bacon.

In *Minnesota v. Carter*, for example, one of the petitioner's dispositive arguments was that people who come to an apartment for the sole purpose of bagging cocaine cannot invoke Fourth Amendment protections. The "Kevin Bacon" of that brief, as for all petitioners' briefs, would be the assertion that the decision below should be reversed. If we throw a theoretical dart at the brief, we find the assertion that "the respondents were in the apartment solely to conduct commercial activity." The reader should be able to "Kevin Bacon" that point back to the ultimate assertion this way:

Respondents were in the home only to conduct illegal commercial activity;

Because the activity was an illegal commercial activity, it is not an activity that is recognized as valuable by society;

Because their activity is not recognized as valuable by society, respondents can have no legitimate expectation of privacy when conducting that activity;

Because the respondents have no legitimate expectation of privacy when conducting that activity, they cannot invoke the Fourth Amendment; and

Because the respondents cannot invoke the Fourth Amendment, this Court must reverse.

Thus, in a brief, the "links" in the "Six Degrees of Legal Writing" game are the assertions that you are focusing on in the various sections of your document, and "Kevin Bacon" is your ultimate conclusion. Knowing that the links are there is only half the battle, however. You must be sure to make the connections in the text of your brief so that the reader will be as aware of the connections as you are.

For example, in a petitioner's brief in *Minnesota v. Carter*, the following paragraph would *not* do a good job of making the links explicit:

▽ BAD EXAMPLE

Because society does not value the respondents' illegal business activity, this Court must reverse.

Instead, the writer must "Kevin Bacon" her point about illegal business activity to the conclusion that the Court must reverse by making the connections explicit:

△ GOOD EXAMPLE

Thus, Respondents, who were conducting a purely commercial activity, were not visitors to a "home" and were not engaging in longstanding social customs that serve functions recognized as valuable by society. While Respondents may have been legitimately in the apartment, in the sense that Thompson permitted their presence, Respondents did not

have any legitimate expectation of privacy in the apartment because they were present only to conduct illegal business. Because Respondents' expectation of privacy was not one that society recognizes as reasonable, they cannot claim the Fourth Amendment's protections, and this Court must reverse.

Although the example above shows a concluding paragraph, the more common location for making "Bacon links" explicit is in the beginning of a section or sub-section. In the illustration below, notice how the writer "Kevin Bacons" sub-section B.2 to sub-section B.1 and to the "B" point heading. She then provides a roadmap to the two sub-points to section B. I have included all of the relevant headings so you can see how the writer makes the connections clear:

> B. Respondents had no legitimate expectation of privacy because any subjective expectation they might have had while temporarily in another's home for the sole purpose of conducting illegal business was not one society recognizes as reasonable. . . .
>
> 1. The <u>Olson</u> rule dictates that only overnight guests have a connection to a premises that gives rise to a legitimate expectation of privacy. . . .
>
> 2. Even if the <u>Olson</u> rule extends to non-overnight guests, Respondents' expectation of privacy is unreasonable because they were present only to conduct illegal business that is not valuable to society.
>
> > If <u>Olson</u> does not stand for the proposition that only overnight guests may assert a Fourth Amendment challenge, it at least stands for the proposition that only a very limited category of guests may do so. The limited category includes only those guests whose connections to the home give rise to an expectation of privacy that society is prepared to recognize as reasonable. <u>See Olson</u>, 495 U.S. 91, 95. Respondents failed to demonstrate that their expectation of privacy was one society is prepared to recognize as reasonable.
> >
> > The Minnesota Supreme Court found that Respondents demonstrated an expectation of privacy that society is prepared to recognize as reasonable because they were present in the apartment "to conduct a common task." <u>State v. Carter</u>, 569 N.W.2d 169, 176 (1997). This Court should reverse the decision of the Minnesota Supreme Court because (1) the distribution of drugs is not a longstanding social custom that serves functions recognized as valuable by society and (2) Respondents were not "guests" in a home but rather were business invitees on the property for a purely commercial purpose, and therefore lost the Fourth Amendment protection normally associated with the home.
> >
> > > a. Illegal drug distribution is not a longstanding social custom that serves functions recognized as valuable by society.

    b. **Respondents were present for a purely commercial purpose and were not entitled to the Fourth Amendment protection associated with the home.**

When you revise, consider how each section of your document relates to the other sections and to your overall thesis. If the connection is not obvious, see if you can make the connection obvious by adding a sentence or a paragraph in which you make the connection explicit. If you cannot figure out how to connect the point to your overall thesis, decide whether the section really belongs in your argument.

You should "Kevin Bacon" the points in each section to the other relevant points and, when necessary, to your overall thesis. By doing so, you save the reader's time and effort and increase his or her understanding of your argument.

10.2
INSTALL A SYMBOLIC TEMPLATE TO HELP YOUR READER *USE* YOUR DOCUMENT

Many of us have used little plastic templates that fit over the function keys on our computer keyboards to help us find the function keys we need. In an appellate brief, give your reader a symbolic "template" by using headings, roadmap paragraphs, and topic sentences, and by explicitly stating mini-conclusions about each issue and sub-issue before going on to the next issue or sub-issue. A template of this kind helps in three ways. First, creating the template forces you to break your argument into smaller parts, and this lightens the reader's burden. Second, readers can use the template to skip the parts of the document they don't need and to find the parts they do need. Finally, readers will look for "Kevin Bacon" connections in the template items so that they can understand how each section of the document relates to the other sections or to your overall thesis.

The template can be created in a four-step process. First, identify or write topic sentences for every paragraph. Second, as needed, use the topic sentences to identify your large-scale organization and insert headings that reveal that large-scale organization to the reader. Third, use the headings to create as many roadmap paragraphs as are appropriate. Finally, insert internal conclusions or "mini-conclusions" at the end of each section and sub-section.

10.2.1
TOPIC SENTENCES

Although most of us learned in grade school that the topic sentence could be the first, second, or last sentence in the paragraph, in legal writing the topic sentence should come first. Putting the topic sentence first is vital because most legal readers decide whether or not to read the paragraph based on the first sentence of the paragraph. If the first sentence shows the reader how the paragraph is relevant to the issue under discussion, the reader will continue. If not, many readers will skip down to the next paragraph, looking for more relevant information. In addition, when topic sentences are the first sentence in each paragraph, they easily reveal the document's organization to both the reader and the writer.

To check your topic sentences, review the first sentence of each paragraph. If any sentence doesn't reveal how that paragraph relates to the thesis of that section or of the whole document, write a new first sentence in place of or in addition to the current first sentence. Many writers waste the beginning of a paragraph with a sentence about the facts of an authority case, as in this example (from a brief about the *Coors* case):

▽ BAD EXAMPLE

> **In <u>Posadas</u>, the owner of a casino gambling operation sued to enjoin enforcement of a restriction on casino advertising. 101 U.S. at 101.**

This sentence tells the reader that the paragraph is about the *Posadas* case. While on some level that may be true, the paragraph is probably really about the *principle* from the *Posadas* case, and that principle — and its phrase-that-pays — should be the focus of the topic sentence:

△ GOOD EXAMPLE

> **This Court has continuously held that state legislatures have more latitude to regulate speech in areas of socially harmful activity. <u>Posadas</u>, 101 U.S. at 101.**

In this way, the writer focuses the reader's attention on the true point of the paragraph: the legislature's ability to "regulate speech," which is the focus of that section of the document. The reader then knows that this paragraph will explain something further about conditions under which states may "regulate speech." In the first example, in contrast, the reader knew only that the writer would be talking about the *Posadas* case.

After you have written an effective topic sentence for each paragraph and verified that each sentence in the paragraph is focused on that point, make a "topic sentence outline" to check your organization. You can create a topic sentence outline by blocking and copying the first sentence of each paragraph into a new document.

Review the topic sentence outline as a method of checking your organization. Ideally, your topic sentences will be logically grouped; first, you will find several sentences relevant to your first point, then several sentences relevant to your second point, and so on. To the extent that you find sentences that are out of place, decide whether to fix the sentence, move the paragraph to a new location, or remove the paragraph from the brief.

One objective method you can use to check your topic sentences is to look for your phrase-that-pays. For example, the following list of topic sentences comes from a section of a brief for the petitioner in *Minnesota v. Carter*. In this section of the brief, the writer is trying to get the Court to accept a bright-line rule that only overnight guests have an expectation of privacy in another's home, and "overnight guests" was the writer's phrase-that-pays. Notice how the word "overnight" appears in every topic sentence:

> This Court established the rule that "status as an **overnight guest** is alone enough to show that [the defendant] had an expectation of privacy in the home that society is prepared to recognize as reasonable" in Minnesota v. Olson, 495 U.S. 91, 96-97 (1990).

> Though some lower courts have been confused as to the scope of the Olson rule, the reasoning in Olson and this Court's emphasis on Olson's **overnight** status indicate that the holding does not extend to invitees who are not **overnight guests**.

> In establishing the rule that **overnight guests** have a legitimate expectation of privacy sufficient to challenge a Fourth Amendment search, the Olson Court repeatedly emphasized the **overnight** nature of the defendant's stay, thus illustrating that the holding does not cover a shorter-term guest.

> The Olson Court discussed at length the social custom of staying **overnight** with friends or family when traveling to a strange city and the concomitant expectation of privacy that comes with seeking **overnight** shelter in another's home.

> The factors that gave Olson the right to challenge a search of the residence all hinged on his **overnight** status.

> Furthermore, a significant number of courts that have examined Olson have applied the Olson rule narrowly, refusing to find an expectation of privacy for non-**overnight** visitors.

> Additionally, a number of lower courts have flatly declined to extend Olson to casual or temporary visitors who did not stay **overnight**.

> In the present case, the record bears no evidence that Respondents were invited **overnight** guests.

> The Minnesota Supreme Court conceded that "it is undisputed that Carter failed to produce any evidence that he was a 'guest' of Thompson's, let alone an '**overnight guest**.' "

Using the phrase-that-pays in each topic sentence tells the reader that the paragraph is worth reading because it will provide more information about the word or phrase that is crucial in that section of the document.

On rare occasions, you may use words other than the phrase-that-pays to show the paragraph's focus on the key topic, but do so carefully. In the example below, from another section of a *Minnesota v. Carter* petitioner's brief, the writer was arguing that the respondents did not have an expectation of privacy in the apartment in which they were bagging drugs because they were there only for a commercial purpose, so "commercial purpose" was the phrase-that-pays. In the list of topic sentences below, the phrases that substitute for "commercial purpose" are in bold-faced type.

> Respondents were not present in a "home," but were on property for a purely **commercial purpose**.

> This Court has recognized that **business premises** invite lesser privacy expectations than do residences.

> In <u>Lewis</u>, this Court held that a defendant who used his home for the felonious **sale of narcotics** could not claim a violation of any reasonable expectation of privacy when an undercover officer entered the home to purchase marijuana.

> Utilizing the same reasoning, the D.C. Circuit held that a visitor who used another's apartment solely to **conduct drug transactions** could not claim Fourth Amendment protection.

> In the present case, Respondents, like the defendants in <u>Lewis</u> and <u>Hicks</u>, were present on property for the sole purpose of **conducting criminal business**.

> Like the apartments in <u>Lewis</u> and <u>Hicks</u>, the property in the present case had been converted into a **commercial center** to which outsiders were invited for **purposes of transacting unlawful business**.

> Thus, Respondents, who were conducting a **purely commercial activity**, were not visitors to a "home" and were not engaging in longstanding social customs that serve functions recognized as valuable by society.

This method requires the reader to do some work. In this example, the reader must recognize that "business," "sales," and "drug transactions" are all related to the concept of "commercial purposes." While most readers would be able to make this connection, your argument should not require the reader to put two and two together. You should do the work of putting the phrase-that-pays into the topic sentence to signal to the reader that the paragraph will say something meaningful about the phrase-that-pays. In the list below, notice how small revisions allow the writer to incorporate the phrase-that-pays:

> Respondents were not present in a "home," but were on property for a purely **commercial purpose**.

> This Court has recognized that **business premises**, which exist for **commercial** rather than domestic activity, invite lesser privacy expectations than do residences.

> In Lewis, this Court held that a defendant who used his home for the **commercial purpose** of **selling illegal narcotics** could not claim a violation of any reasonable expectation of privacy when an undercover officer entered the home to purchase marijuana.

> Utilizing the same reasoning, the D.C. Circuit held that a visitor who used another's apartment solely for the **commercial purpose** of **conducting drug transactions** could not claim Fourth Amendment protection.

> In the present case, Respondents, like the defendants in Lewis and Hicks, were using the property for a **commercial purpose**: they were present on the property for the sole purpose of **conducting criminal business**.

> Like the apartments in Lewis and Hicks, the property in the present case had been converted into a **commercial center** to which outsiders were invited for **purposes of transacting unlawful business**.

> Thus, Respondents, who were conducting a **purely commercial activity**, were not visitors to a "home" and were not engaging in longstanding social customs that serve functions recognized as valuable by society.

As a general rule, the small amount of work it will take to incorporate the phrase-that-pays is worth the trouble. Using the phrase-that-pays in a topic sentence increases the likelihood that the reader will actually read the paragraph. Readers who read your entire argument are much more likely to understand and agree with it.

10.2.2
HEADINGS

Effective point headings were discussed in Chapter Nine. I raise them here only as a practical matter. By this stage of the writing process, most writers will have identified where their headings belong, and will have begun to draft headings as well. On those unusual occasions when you must churn out a brief without time for revision, however, you might use the template method to help you to turn a stream-of-consciousness draft into a readable document.

Inserting headings is one of the simplest steps a writer can take to improve readability because they allow the reader to find the most important parts of the document. In an objective document, the headings can be simply a word or phrase that accurately describes the subject of the section or sub-section. For example, "Damages," "Breach of duty to provide due care," and the like. Because the writer is usually not pushing one conclusion or another, the headings can be merely objective labels. When writing an argument, however, resist the temptation to take the easy way out: Use argumentative point headings instead of objective labels.

Argumentative point headings are an important part of your template because they are so highly visible. To make them most effective, I recommend using bold-faced type unless local rules forbid it. Most of us unconsciously follow "typeface customs" that we have observed in printed materials throughout our lives, and in briefs throughout our legal careers. Most of these customs evolved during the age of the typewriter, when bold-faced fonts did not exist. Of course, you should find out if the local judges forbid bold-faced fonts, but I believe that most judges would welcome being able to find new point headings easily as they page through the argument. Similarly, headings made up of all capital letters should be reserved for the title of the document (which local rules often require to be written in all capital letters) and for segment headings such as "Statement of the Case" and "Question Presented." In the examples below, note how much more readable the bold-faced heading is:

▽ BAD EXAMPLE

ILLEGAL DRUG DISTRIBUTION IS NOT A LONGSTANDING SOCIAL CUSTOM THAT SERVES INTERESTS RECOGNIZED AS VALUABLE BY SOCIETY.

△ GOOD EXAMPLE

Illegal Drug Distribution Is Not a Longstanding Social Custom That Serves Functions Recognized as Valuable by Society.

If you have not yet broken your argument into segments at this point, consult your topic sentence list. In a well-organized document you should see several paragraphs about one issue, then several paragraphs about the next issue, and so on. When your topic sentences indicate that you have shifted to a new topic, it's time to insert a new heading.

10.2.3 Roadmaps and Mini-Roadmaps

Effective analytical documents usually include a roadmap paragraph within the introduction to any complex section of the document. I do not mean to imply that the writer should label either the "introduction" or the "roadmap" as such. Rather, by "the introduction," I simply mean the material that introduces a part of the argument — for example, the material after the "I" heading but before the "A" heading should introduce the A and B headings. In introductory material, the writer generally includes any information that is common to all of the sub-points or that will "Kevin Bacon" the sub-points to the writer's thesis. Illustration 10.1 shows where introductory material and roadmaps should be used.

Roadmap paragraphs are important because they help confirm, and

Illustration 10.1

I.   **First Major Point**
     [introductory material relevant to A, B, &
     C and roadmap foreshadowing A, B, &
     C]
     A.
     B.
     [introductory material relevant to 1 & 2
     and mini-roadmap foreshadowing 1 & 2]
          1.
          2.
     C.
II. **Second Major Point**
     [introductory material relevant to A & B
     and roadmap foreshadowing A & B]
     A.
     B.
III. **Third Major Point**
     [no subpoints, so no roadmap]

sometimes establish, the writer's expectations for the document. By writing an effective roadmap paragraph, the writer tells the reader how "far" the document extends — how many points does the writer talk about before stopping? In addition, an effective roadmap lays out the document's large-scale organization by telling the reader the order in which the writer will address the main points. Even a poorly-organized document will be easier to understand if the writer has provided a good roadmap.

Although many writers are familiar with the law review style of roadmap paragraph (e.g., "this article will address three issues"), roadmaps in court documents can and should be more sophisticated. A simple technique is to introduce the legal problem (using only as much detail as is appropriate) and then use the decision maker's needs as the focus of the roadmap,[3] as in the following example, based on *Miller v. Albright*:

I.   Section 1409(a) is an Unconstitutional Denial of Equal Protection as Guaranteed by the Fifth Amendment's Due Process Clause.

The statute at issue in this case, 8 U.S.C. § 1409(a), classifies foreign-born children of a U.S. citizen and a non-citizen into three groups: (1) those who are "legitimate," (2) those who are "illegitimate" and have a U.S. citizen for a mother, and (3) those who are "illegitimate" and have a U.S. citizen for a father. Children in the first two groups — those who are "legitimate" and those with a U.S. citizen mother — are U.S. citizens by birthright. See 8 U.S.C. § 1401(g). Children in the last group — those "illegitimate" children with U.S. citizen fathers — may receive their fathers' citizenship only after clearing several statutory hurdles.

Even when paternity has been established by "clear and convincing evidence," and even assuming that the father was a U.S. citizen at the time of the child's birth, a child in this third group will still be denied citizenship unless (1) the father agrees in writing to support that child until age 18, *and* (2) either the child is "legitimated" before he or she reaches the age of 18, *or* the father acknowledges paternity before the child reaches the age of 18, *or* the father's paternity is estab-

---

[3] *See* Laurel Currie Oates, Anne M. Enquist & Kelly Kunsch, *The Legal Writing Handbook* 530-32 (2d ed. 1998).

lished by adjudication before the child reaches the age of 18. § 1409(a)(4).

These first two paragraphs provide context for all of Section I by laying out what the statute does, and why it is controversial.

Section 1409(a) illegally discriminates against children of U.S. citizens based on their legitimacy and on the sex of their citizen parent. For more than twenty-five years, this Court has consistently applied a heightened scrutiny to state statutes or state constitutional provisions which have classified persons based on gender. See, e.g., J.E.B. v. Alabama, 511 U.S. 127, 140 (1994) (citing cases). Similarly, for almost twenty years, this Court has applied a heightened scrutiny to those state statutes which have classified persons based on their "illegitimacy." See, e.g., Pickett v. Brown, 426 U.S. 1, 6-9 (1983) (citing cases). In reviewing federal legislation, this Court has also demanded that Congress satisfy a higher standard than the traditionally deferential one for classifications based on either illegitimacy, see id. at 8 (quoting Trimble v. Gordon, 430 U.S. 762, 767 (1977)), or based on gender. See, e.g., Rostker v. Goldberg, 453 U.S. 57, 66-70 (1981).

In this paragraph, the writer provides the legal basis for the arguments she will make in Section I. Unlike the Summary of the Argument, introductory material typically includes citations to authority as appropriate.

Because of its questionable classifications, § 1409(a) should be subjected to a heightened scrutiny despite the great deference normally due Congressional authority to enact immigration legislation. Section 1409(a) cannot survive this level of scrutiny because neither its gender-based classifications nor its legitimacy classifications are supported by "exceedingly persuasive" justifications, nor does either classification substantially further an important governmental interest.

In this paragraph, the writer foreshadows the three points that will be addressed in Section I. Although this writer did not use enumeration, enumeration is often helpful in roadmap paragraphs.

Notice that the writer prefaced the roadmap with some general information relevant to the case as a whole. The roadmap paragraph then indicated that the writer would first address which test applies and then address the argument that neither classification within the statute — the classification based on gender nor the classification based on illegitimacy — can survive the test. Notice how the roadmap foreshadows the points made under the three sub-headings within that section of the document:

A. This Court should apply a heightened scrutiny to Section 1409(a) consistent with the Fifth Amendment's equal protection guarantee.

B. Section 1409(a) does not survive the heightened scrutiny that this Court has applied to gender-based classifications.

C. Section 1409(a) does not survive the heightened scrutiny that this court has applied to illegitimacy-based classifications.

Some writers provide a roadmap to the entire argument within the Summary of the Argument. They then provide mini-roadmaps — as the writer in the example above has done — to each complex section of the document (i.e., each section of the document that has further subparts). The structure of the headings will dictate the structure of the roadmap paragraphs. If there are two main headings, there should be two points in the overall roadmap. If a main heading section contains three sub-sections with sub-headings, then the mini-roadmap that introduces that section should have three points.

Review your headings and your roadmaps to make sure that the road-maps predict exactly the points you will address and that the roadmaps use the language that you will use when you address each point. The roadmap will create expectations in the reader; by using similar language in the roadmap and the headings, you can reassure the reader that you are fulfilling those expectations.

10.2.4
EXPLICIT MINI-CONCLUSIONS

Just as the headings helped the writer to craft any needed roadmap paragraphs, they can also help the writer to check for needed explicit conclusions. The last paragraph before a new heading is a strong position of emphasis, and stating a strong conclusion is a good way to exploit that position of emphasis. The writer can easily check for explicit conclusions by looking for each new heading or sub-heading and then checking the paragraph above that heading; unless it is a roadmap, the paragraph should end on the writer's explicit conclusion as to the point under discussion within that heading or sub-heading.

Although some writers end a point heading section by foreshadowing the next issue, this technique is usually not necessary in a document with explicit headings. If making the connection between the points in two sections or sub-sections is important, try reaching back to the earlier section instead of reaching forward to the later section.

For example, in a sub-section about part one of a two-part test, some writers will end the sub-section by saying, in essence, "Petitioner meets part one of the test. Next, it will be shown that petitioner meets part two of the test." To use positions of emphasis more effectively, the writer could end the first sub-section by saying "Petitioner meets part one of the test." After an appropriate, persuasive point heading, the next sub-section's text can begin by saying, e.g., "In addition to meeting part one of the test, petitioner can also meet part two. . . ." In this way, the writer has shown a connection between the two parts of the test, but has also exploited the position of emphasis at the end of the first sub-section by focusing on the point made in that sub-section.

The guidelines are slightly different if the point is dispositive, that is, if that point alone can result in a victory for your client. In that situation, you may want to use your conclusion to "Kevin Bacon" the point to your overall thesis and tell the court what it must do:

⚠ GOOD EXAMPLE

Thus, Respondents, who were conducting a purely commercial activity, were not visitors to a "home" and were not engaging in longstanding social customs that serve functions recognized as valuable by society. While Respondents may have been legitimately in the apartment, in the sense that Thompson permitted their presence, Respondents did not

have any legitimate expectation of privacy in the apartment because they were present only to conduct illegal business. Because Respondents' expectation of privacy was not one that society recognizes as reasonable, they cannot claim the Fourth Amendment's protections, and this Court must reverse.

If the point is not dispositive, exploit the position of emphasis that a section ending provides to articulate an internal conclusion that hammers home the point you wish to make in that section.

10.3
SUMMARY

To make your document reader-friendly, first be sure that *you* understand how the parts of your argument fit together. Then, make sure to tell the reader explicitly how the pieces fit together, and make it easy to find the various sections of your argument. Use roadmaps, headings, topic sentences, and mini-conclusions to show the reader both where each section of the argument is and how each section relates to the whole.

CHAPTER ELEVEN

EXPLOITING OPPORTUNITIES FOR PERSUASION

11.1
OPPORTUNITIES FOR PERSUASION

In the game of Scrabble®, players use letter tiles to spell words in a crossword puzzle pattern on a game board. They score points based on which letter tiles they use — the infrequently used "X" is worth 8 points, while the more common "T" is worth only 1 point. Players earn bonuses, however, if a letter is placed on a special space on the board. Some spaces are "double letter score" or "triple letter score" spaces, which allow the player to double the points of the letter on that square. Even better, some spaces are "double *word* score" or "triple word score" spaces, which allow the doubling or tripling of the points for the whole word.

When you write an appellate brief, you will "score points" with your reader just based on your "tiles" — the strength of the arguments you make about the law or the facts. In addition, however, there will be opportunities for persuasion that arise at various times as you write the brief. These "opportunities for persuasion" in both the brief and the brief-writing process, like the colored squares on the Scrabble® board, allow you to make the most of what you have.

The opportunities for persuasion addressed in this chapter are based on knowledge about how readers use legal documents. Practical advocates exploit this knowledge and base their writing decisions on it. Every writing decision you make — from which issues to argue, to how you structure your sentences, to what typeface to use — can affect how the reader understands and perceives your argument. Some decisions will affect the reader's impressions of you as a credible advocate and a reliable reporter of the law and the facts. Others will affect the reader's ability to identify and comprehend the most important parts of your argument. All must be made with care, and with the reader in mind.

11.2
HOW NOT TO PERSUADE

The first and most important point to make is that persuasion is not about lying. There are two reasons not to misstate the facts or the law in your case. The first reason is simply because it is wrong. The ethical canons in every state forbid it. For example, Rule 3.3 of the Illinois Rules of Professional Conduct provides:

Rule 3.3 Conduct Before a Tribunal

(a) In appearing in a professional capacity before a tribunal, a lawyer shall not:

(1) make a statement of material fact or law to a tribunal which the lawyer knows or reasonably should know is false;

(2) fail to disclose to a tribunal a material fact known to the lawyer when disclosure is necessary to avoid assisting a criminal or fraudulent act by the client;

(3) fail to disclose to the tribunal legal authority in the controlling jurisdiction known to the lawyer to be directly adverse to the position of the client and not disclosed by opposing counsel. . . .

Furthermore, Rule 46(c) of the Federal Rules of Appellate Procedure allows a court of appeals to discipline attorneys for "for failure to comply with any court rule," and the local rules of many federal courts specifically prohibit misrepresenting the law or the facts. Local Rule 46.5(b) of the

United States Court of Appeals for the Tenth Circuit, for example, provides that an attorney's signature on a document gives several assurances to the court:

1. [that] the paper is not being presented for any improper purpose, such as to harass or to cause unnecessary delay or expense in the litigation;
2. [that] the issues presented are warranted by existing law or by a non-frivolous argument for extending, modifying, or reversing existing law or establishing new law; and
3. [that] the factual contentions or denials are supported in the record.

Courts will sanction counsel for misrepresentations of law and of fact.[1]

The second reason not to lie to the court is that it hurts your credibility. After an academic life filled with anonymous grading, many law students forget that the practice of law is not anonymous. Judges can and do remember attorneys who have lied to them, and so an attorney's credibility with the court is a valuable asset. Judge Parker notes that an attorney's clients suffer from the attorney's loss of credibility, because the loss "ultimately . . . inhibits that advocate's ability to persuade."[2] In contrast, if you write a strong, reliable brief, you help not only your current client, but future clients as well. Judge Duncan notes that "a Quality brief — that is, one that is accurate, concise, and logically analyzed and organized . . . not only increases a lawyer's chance of winning an appeal, but (more important in the long run) transforms that lawyer into becoming a permanent friend of the court."[3]

Judge Saufley of the Maine Judicial Court warns attorneys not to "squander" their credibility:

> Do not ever misquote cases or the record. Be absolutely vigilant about such practices in your office. Failure to do so may lose much for your clients and your reputation. It is never worth it.[4]

Another "persuasive" tactic that usually fails is an attack on opposing counsel or the judges in the court(s) below. Because law students do not usually fall into this trap, given their hypothetical cases and clients, law school may be the best time to learn that judges are not persuaded by ad hominem arguments. Judge Pregerson notes that attorneys injure themselves and their client's cases if they "vilify or belittle [their] opponents. . . . A shrill tone in a brief diminishes its persuasive force."[5] Judge Saufley worries that too may attorneys rely on the old adage: "If the law is with you, argue the law; if the facts are with you, argue the facts; if neither is

---

[1] *See generally* Raymond T. Elligett, Jr. and John M. Scheb, *Professional Responsibility of Appellate Advocates*, 1 Fl. Coastal L.J. 101 (1999) (citing cases).

[2] Fred I. Parker, *Appellate Advocacy and Practice in the Second Circuit*, 64 Brooklyn L. Rev. 457, 462 (1998).

[3] Sarah B. Duncan, *Pursuing Quality: Writing a Helpful Brief*, 30 St. Mary's L.J. 1093, 1101 (1999).

[4] Leigh Ingalls Saufley, *Amphibians and Appellate Courts*, 51 Me. L. Rev. 18, 22 (1999).

[5] Harry Pregerson, *Appellate Brief Writing and Other Transgressions*, 34 U.C.L.A. L. Rev. 431, 436 (1986).

with you, call the other guy names." She points out that name-calling has a negative effect on the brief-writer: "As soon as I see an attack of any kind on the other party, opposing counsel, or the trial judge, I begin to discount the merits of the argument."[6] Supreme Court Justice Ruth Bader Ginsburg notes that a "top-quality brief" "scratches put-downs and indignant remarks about one's adversary or the first instance decision-maker" because they will "more likely annoy than make points with the bench."[7]

Persuasion is a subtle art. It consists of creating an image of yourself as a competent, credible, helpful, reliable advocate — the kind of person whose brief the court can't wait to read. It also consists of taking advantage of opportunities at every stage of the brief-writing process to highlight your strengths and "low-light" your weaknesses.

11.3
CHOOSING ISSUES RESPONSIBLY

One of the first ways that advocates establish their credibility is by appealing only those issues — and cases — that are worthy of appeal. Most law students cannot choose which issues to argue, but they can choose how many arguments to make. Soon, they will be choosing the issues, as well as deciding whether the appeal is even worth pursuing. You should appeal any case and make any argument that has a credible chance of resulting in a reversal, but use good judgment when making those decisions, and remember the busy courts to whom you are arguing. A marginal appeal weakens the advocate's present and future credibility; a brief that addresses fewer issues argued well is better than a brief with many issues argued poorly.

Judge Patricia Wald, of the U.S. Court of Appeals for the District of Columbia Circuit, notes: "Confident counsel should almost always go for broke and rely on their one or two best arguments, abandoning the other 9-10 wish-list entries. . . . The fewer arguments you make the more attention they will get from us in preparing and disposing of your case."[8] Judge Pierce has noted that trial judges make "relatively few mistakes" and that a brief that asserts a half-dozen or more key points of error may "needlessly divert" the judge's attention from the more compelling grounds, with the result that the court's ability to recognize the validity of any one of the grounds "decreases significantly."[9]

Similarly, former Chief Justice Burger has noted that "a brief that raises

---

[6] Saufley, *supra* n.4, at 23.
[7] Ruth Bader Ginsburg, *Remarks on Appellate Advocacy*, 50 S.C.L. Rev. 567, 568 (1999).
[8] Patricia M. Wald, *19 Tips from 19 Years on the Appellate Bench*, 1 J. App. Prac. & Process 7, 11 (1999).
[9] Lawrence W. Pierce, *Appellate Advocacy: Some Reflections from the Bench*, 61 Fordham L. Rev. 829, 835-36 (1993).

every colorable issue runs the risk of burying good arguments."[10] Judge Wiener advises that counsel should "[d]ecide which legal arguments are key to resolving the issues of the case in your client's favor," and should "[f]orce" themselves to "omit fringe issues and far-out theories; they will only dull the thrust of your appeal and obscure the potentially winning points."[11] Finally, Judge Parker notes that you do a disservice to your client when you raise too many issues on appeal, noting that if you raise 20 issues and give them all "equal [time] — and therefore, short-shrift," you may fail to convince the court that the district court "committed just one error which justifies some relief for your client."[12]

Thus, when choosing issues and arguments, restrict your brief to those that are best supported by both the law and the facts. Not every error is worthy of appeal, or even of argument. Before arguing about an error in the trial court, identify a causal link between the error and the court's judgment against your client; without that link, the error is irrelevant. Further, remember that the validity of each individual argument has an impact on the whole brief. Every specious argument chips away at your overall credibility. When all the arguments are legitimate, on the other hand, the stock of the whole brief and of counsel rises.

11.4
EXPLOITING POSITIONS OF EMPHASIS

Within the brief itself, the practical advocate exploits physical positions of emphasis. Your words will have more impact if you place them in certain physical locations within the brief. Scientists called psycholinguists have learned that readers pay more attention to certain physical positions in a document. Any time there is extra white space in a document — at the beginning or ending of a paragraph, for example, or more importantly, at the beginning or ending of a document element such as a heading section or the summary of the argument — readers subconsciously pay more attention.[13] Just as Scrabble® players angle to put certain letters or words in certain positions on the game board, you should angle to put your strongest arguments and statements in certain positions in your brief.

A reader's attention peaks to varying degrees when reading all titles and headings, as well as when reading the first and last paragraphs in document segments (e.g., the Statement of the Case, the Argument), the

---

[10] Jones v. Barnes, 463 U.S. 745, 751-52 (1983).
[11] Jacques L. Wiener, Jr., *Ruminations from the Bench: Brief Writing and Oral Argument in the Fifth Circuit*, 70 Tul. L. Rev. 187, 194 (1995).
[12] Fred I. Parker, *Appellate Advocacy and Practice in the Second Circuit*, 61 Brooklyn L. Rev. 457, 460 (1998).
[13] *See generally* Robert P. Charrow and Veda R. Charrow, *Making Legal Language Understandable: A Psycholinguistic Study of Jury Instructions*, 79 Colum. L. Rev. 1306 (1979).

first and last paragraphs in point heading sections, and even the first and last sentences in paragraphs. To a lesser degree, information at the beginning or ending of a sentence is also in a position of emphasis,[14] as is a short sentence, particularly when it is placed within a group of longer sentences. Finally, within a sentence itself, the reader pays more attention to the information expressed in the subject-verb combination, with particular emphasis on the verb.[15]

Positions of deemphasis are positions that are away from white space, away from the natural breaks that the reader takes while reading. In other words, "middles": the middle of a point heading section, a paragraph, a document. A series of long sentences slows down comprehension by making the reader work harder to assemble the information in the sentences. Within a sentence, moving information from a verb to a noun, or removing an actor (that is, the person or thing that "verbed") by using passive voice, also deemphasizes information.

Thus, to make your brief more persuasive, focus your attention. Decide (a) what information you want to emphasize and (b) what information you want to deemphasize. Exploit the positions of emphasis by making sure that you "fill" them with the information that is most important to the case and/or the reader. Lessen the impact of negative information by placing it in positions of deemphasis. The various positions of emphasis present many opportunities for persuasion in your brief.

11.4.1
PERSUADING WITH LARGE-SCALE ORGANIZATION

To exploit the reader's peak attention at the beginning of the argument section, begin the argument with your best point rather than starting with a weak point and "leading up" to a strong point. Judge Coleman advises you to "[p]resent your strongest points first to try to capture votes early."[16] When you start your argument with a weak point, your reader may think, "Is this the best they can do?" That bad impression can taint the rest of the argument. On the other hand, when you start your argument with a strong point, the reader's first thought is "This is a good argument," and that impression can carry over to the rest of the points that you make.

The only exception to this guideline is a case that could be governed by a threshold issue. If you are arguing a standing or jurisdictional issue

---

[14] *See, e.g.,* Joseph M. Williams, *Style: Ten Lessons in Clarity and Grace* 107-09, 146-51 (5th ed. 1997); *see also* Laurel Currie Oates, Anne M. Enquist & Kelly Kunsch, *The Legal Writing Handbook* 292-94, 608-12, 619-22 (2d ed. 1998).

[15] This point is now a staple for most legal writing teachers. It was famously articulated by Richard Wydick in a law review article that later became a book: Richard Wydick, *Plain English for Lawyers* 23-32 (3d ed. 1994). *See also* Joseph M. Williams, *Style: Ten Lessons in Clarity and Grace* 41-70 (5th ed. 1997). *See* Section 11.4.4(2), *infra* for specific examples.

[16] James H. Coleman, Jr., *Appellate Advocacy and Decisionmaking in State Appellate Courts in the Twenty-First Century*, 28 Seton Hall L. Rev. 1081, 1083 (1998).

in addition to a substantive issue, for example, logic would dictate that the substantive issue should come second. It could be ludicrous to argue for several pages about a legal error as to one of the case's issues, and then move to the point that the court should not be hearing the case at all.

Particularly in a lengthy brief, your last argument is also in a position of emphasis. For example, if you have decided that you must include a desperation argument in your brief, you may *not* want it to be the last thing the court reads. Just as you want to start with a good impression, you also want to leave the court with a good taste in its mouth. Whenever possible, move that weak argument to the second-to-the-last position to help keep your image as a credible, responsible advocate.

11.4.2
PERSUADING WITHIN EACH ISSUE

Exploit natural positions of emphasis within each heading section as well. Make sure that the first paragraph in the section articulates the point you are proving in that section. The CREXAC paradigm recommends using the first paragraph in the section to state your conclusion as to the issue addressed in that section. Similarly, end the section by restating your conclusion on that point. In this way, your point is driven home in the precise locations where the reader is likely to be paying the most attention.

In general, state your conclusion as if it is the truth, not as if it is one of many possible ways for the court to rule. Do not begin any section of your argument by stating the issue as a question that must be resolved:

▽ BAD EXAMPLE

The next issue turns on whether an officer issuing a citation in lieu of arrest should have the same authority to search as an officer who is placing a suspect under arrest.

Instead, articulate the issue as an assertion:

△ GOOD EXAMPLE

Officers who issue citations in lieu of arrest and officers who actually arrest should have the same authority to search for weapons that might be used against them.

Similarly, do not label your arguments as your arguments. The Petitioner should never make a statement like "The Petitioner argues. . . ." If you do this with any argument, you might as well start every argument with that statement, for the entire brief consists of the Petitioner's arguments. The entire document is labeled as "Brief for the Petitioner," so the court knows that it will be made up of Petitioner's arguments. Do not remind the court of your partisan slant by labeling individual arguments within the brief.

Finally, if practical or ethical requirements require you to discuss cases or arguments that do not support your client's case, you may decide to deemphasize them by including them in the middle of a point heading section rather than highlighting them in a separate section. For example, in the example below, the writer of a respondent's brief in *Minnesota v. Carter* is trying to emphasize connections to cases in which the Court found that a privacy right existed, and to deemphasize cases in which the privacy right was found not to exist. Notice how the topic sentence (the first sentence in the paragraph) states the rule in a way that is favorable to her clients before the writer discusses a case in which the Court found no expectation of privacy:

> **Indeed, this Court has consistently found that legitimate expecta-tions of privacy exist outside the home, as long as the circumstances are those in which most people would normally expect to enjoy a feeling of privacy. <u>Olson</u>, 496 U.S. at 96-97. Accordingly, this Court has found that defendants did not have a legitimate expectation of privacy in the contents of a car in which they were merely passengers, and where they had expressed no expectation of privacy in the areas of the car searched. <u>Rakas v. Illinois</u>, 439 U.S. 128, 148-49 (1978). The <u>Rakas</u> Court specifically refused to make a finding as to whether guests in houses or apartments would be treated similarly, noting that "cars are not to be treated identically with houses or apartments for Fourth Amendment purposes." <u>Id.</u> at 148 (citations omitted).**

Of course, "hiding" a contrary authority in the middle of a paragraph or section will not turn a losing case into a winner. You must also show why the substance of your argument is more effective. Using positions of em-phasis and deemphasis simply makes it easier for the reader to see and understand the validity of your points. In the example above the writer takes care to emphasize the Court's distinction between cars and houses, and ends her paragraph on that point, rather than on the negative point about the passengers' expectations of privacy.

11.4.3
PERSUASIVE PARAGRAPH STRUCTURE

Within the argument, review the topic sentences to make sure that you are not wasting the first sentence in a paragraph on a case citation or a description of authority case facts. Instead, exploit these positions of emphasis by using them to state rules or make favorable assertions about the result you want the court to reach. If you must deal with a negative authority, you may wish to sandwich it between positive assertions. See Chapter Ten for more information about writing effective topic sentences.

In addition to considering structure within paragraphs, you can use a short paragraph to create a position of emphasis. Although conventional wisdom frowns on one-sentence paragraphs, on rare occasions, one or two-sentence paragraphs can effectively make a dramatic statement. Con-versely, you can bury a negative point in a long paragraph to lessen its impact. Take care when using this tactic, however; if the paragraph is so long that it distracts or annoys your reader, you will cancel out any benefit from the persuasive technique.

In this example, the writer applies the law to the facts in one long paragraph that provides the details to establish that Respondents did not manifest a subjective expectation of privacy:

▽ BAD EXAMPLE

> In the case at bar, both Respondents' behavior and their location within the apartment indicate that they had no actual, subjective expectation of privacy. Respondents manifested at most a hope that no one would observe their unlawful pursuits inside Thompson's apartment. Unlike the defendant in Katz, Respondents introduced no evidence of conduct that demonstrated an intent to keep their activity private. Nothing in the record indicates Respondents took any action to preserve their privacy. Though the blinds were drawn, there is no indication that Respondents drew them. See Record at E-2, E-10. On the night in question, Respondents were present in a first-floor apartment that had several windows at ground level. Record G-26. The windows faced a public area that apartment residents and nonresidents frequented. Record G-69, G-70. As darkness fell in early evening, Respondents sat illuminated under a chandelier light at a table directly in front of one of these windows. Record G-13. Only a pane of glass and a set of blinds that featured a series of laths, Record G-50, separated Respondents from the adjacent common area. On the night in question, the blinds, though drawn, had a gap in them large enough for a citizen who passed by and an officer who stood a foot or more from the window to view easily the entire illuminated interior scene. Record G-13.

The only difference in the following example is that the writer has provided paragraph breaks to draw attention to the fact that respondents did not take action to preserve their privacy. The white space creates a position of emphasis that highlights not only the one-sentence paragraph, but also the paragraphs around it, particularly the paragraph after the one-sentence paragraph.

△ GOOD EXAMPLE

> In the case at bar, both Respondents' behavior and their location within the apartment indicate that they had no actual, subjective expectation of privacy. Respondents manifested at most a hope that no one would observe their unlawful pursuits inside Thompson's apartment. Unlike the defendant in Katz, Respondents introduced no evidence of conduct that demonstrated an intent to keep their activity private.
>
> Nothing in the record indicates Respondents took any action to preserve their privacy.
>
> Though the blinds were drawn, there is no indication that Respondents drew them. See Record at E-2, E-10. On the night in question, Respondents were present in a first-floor apartment that had several

windows at ground level. Record G-26. The windows faced a public area that apartment residents and nonresidents frequented. Record G-69, G-70. As darkness fell in early evening, Respondents sat illuminated under a chandelier light at a table directly in front of one of these windows. Record G-13. Only a pane of glass and a set of blinds that featured a series of laths, Record G-50, separated Respondents from the adjacent common area. On the night in question, the blinds, though drawn, had a gap in them large enough for a citizen who passed by and an officer who stood a foot or more from the window to view easily the entire illuminated interior scene. Record G-13.

As you might imagine, use this method sparingly. A one-sentence paragraph is a dramatic technique; if overused, it will lose its drama and annoy the reader.

11.4.4
PERSUADING WITH SENTENCE STRUCTURE

There are many ways that sentence structure can create positions of emphasis; this chapter will address three that most legal writers can conquer. First, by using active voice and strong verbs rather than passive voice and nominalizations, you can focus the reader's attention on subjects and verbs that emphasize actors and actions that support your argument. Second, you can alternate independent and dependent clauses in sentences to emphasize the information in the independent clauses and deemphasize the information in the dependent clauses. Finally, using short sentences in the middle of a series of long sentences can draw the reader's attention.

a. Subject-Verb Combinations

Just as readers pay more attention to information at beginnings and endings of documents and sections, they also place subconscious emphasis on the information in the verb position of a sentence. They also subconsciously look for the verb's actor — that is, the noun that is "doing" the action of the verb. You can control what information is in the subject position and the verb position, and where (or whether) you include information about the verb's actor.[17] How you arrange that information will affect how your reader comprehends your message. To take a simple example:

> The dog bit the child.
> The child was bitten by the dog.
> The child was the victim of a dog bite.
> A dog bite occurred.
> A bite occurred.

Most of these sentences convey exactly the same information. You have a dog, you have a child, and the child gets bitten. In some of the sen-

---

[17] *See, e.g.,* Joseph M. Williams, *Style: Ten Lessons in Clarity and Grace* 41-70 (5th ed. 1997).

tences, however, the reader has to work harder to get that information; in others, even when working hard, the reader can get only a vague idea of what is happening.

Thus, the way you arrange the information within a sentence can have a big impact on how quickly the reader understands the message. Information arrangement can sometimes have an impact on how the reader feels about the message as well. Take a look at these two versions of a sentence that might appear in a letter from a law school to its students:

We have decided to raise your tuition by $5,000 per year.

It has been decided that a $5,000 tuition increase is necessary.

The first sentence is more likely to make the student angry at the law school faculty and administration. Through their use of subjects and verbs, they have taken direct responsibility for the tuition increase. The reader instantly understands the message, and its clarity may intensify the reader's reaction. The second sentence is a more typical example of how to deliver bad news. No one takes responsibility for the dramatic tuition increase; it seems to come from the outside, somehow. Thus, the clarity that is helpful when easy understanding is beneficial ("the dog bit the child") has quite a different impact on those rare occasions when the writer wants to blunt the impact of our message ("we have decided to raise your tuition").

Writers can learn a wide variety of techniques to control the clarity of a sentence. Two of the most important are: (1) using or avoiding nominalizations and (2) using or avoiding passive voice.

i. Nominalizations

A "nominalization" is, quite simply, a verb that has been turned into a noun. Turning a verb into a noun does not violate any rules of grammar, but it does slow down the reader's comprehension of the information in that word. For example, the word "decision" is a nominalization of the verb "decide." When you move the word "decide" from the verb position into the noun position, you lessen the impact of that verb.

We decided to raise your tuition.

We made a decision that a tuition increase is necessary.

Look at these two different ways of describing the actions of a police officer looking into the windows of a basement apartment from a distance of 12 to 14 inches. Notice how nominalizations in one illustration and concrete verbs and other language in the other may change the perception of what the officer did:

Under the Fourth Amendment, does an officer's warrantless and purposeful sight observation into a home, made while standing within

> **inches of the apartment and peering through gaps in the covered window of the apartment, constitute an unlawful invasion of curtilage?**

> **Under the Fourth Amendment, does an officer invade the curtilage of an apartment house when he stands a foot or more from the building and looks through a gap in the blinds of a basement apartment?**

Neither sentence is wrong; they are just different ways of conveying the same information, depending on what the writer wants to emphasize.

You can often find nominalizations by looking for words that end in "-ment" or "-ion." In the alternative, review your sentences (particularly overlong sentences) and circle just the verbs. When you find sentences in which all of the verbs are weak words without a lot of concrete meaning — e.g., "was," "is" (or other "to be" verbs), "had," "made," "occurred," "existed," etc. — look for verbs that are "hidden" in nominalizations in that sentence.

When deciding whether or how to revise, ask yourself whether you want to put more emphasis on the information that you nominalized. The answer may not always be yes. Sometimes, as in the tuition letter example above, you may want to deemphasize certain negative information. Usually, though, there will be no reason to use nominalizations. When that is the case, identify your hidden verbs, find the actor that is "verbing" (i.e., "doing" the action of that verb), and create a stronger, more easily comprehensible sentence.

When looking for nominalizations, you might find a sentence like this:

> **This case is a recognition of the coercion that may happen during an arrest.**

Once you identify the hidden verbs "recognize" and "coerce," you can work on making the sentence more clear:

> **In this case, [someone] recognized that [someone] may coerce [someone] during an arrest.**

Revising to avoid nominalizations provides a hidden benefit: You may realize when information is missing from the sentence. Thus, your next step might be to include some of the missing information.

> **In this case, the Court recognized that police officers may coerce citizens during an arrest.**

Knowing how nominalizations can affect your writing can help you to make your points more explicitly when clarity is your goal and to blunt your message when it is appropriate to do so.

ii. Active and Passive Voice

Most writers know about "tense" as it relates to verbs; they consciously decide, for example, whether to write in present tense or past tense. Many, however, are unfamiliar with the concept of "voice." No matter what its tense, a verb can be cast in active or passive "voice." Voice relates not to the tense of the verb, but to whether the verb's actor is in the subject position of the sentence or clause. If the verb's actor is in the subject position, the verb is said to be cast in "active voice"; if the verb's actor is not in the subject position, the verb is said to be cast in "passive voice."

In almost every case in which the verb is cast in passive voice, the subject of the sentence is receiving the action of the verb rather than doing the action of the verb. Thus, in most cases the subject of an active voice sentence or clause is "verbing"; the subject of a passive voice sentence or clause is "being verbed." Think of the subject passively receiving the action of the verb to help you remember the meaning of "passive voice."

> **The court decided the case (active voice; the subject [court] is verbing [deciding]).**

> **The case was decided by the court (passive voice: the subject [case] is being verbed [being decided]).**

As are nominalizations, both passive and active voice verbs are grammatically correct. Because active voice verbs can be understood more quickly, however, you should use active voice unless you have a specific reason to use passive voice. Passive voice is preferred on occasion:

1. if you don't know who the actor is or you want to hide or deemphasize the actor ("a decision was made not to offer you a job"),
2. when you want to emphasize the object of the verb rather than the subject ("she was hit by a car"), or
3. when your sentence just works better with the object of the verb in the subject position (e.g., when the subject is unusually long).[18]

Look at these examples of similar information included in passive voice and active voice sentences. Try to decide which sentence might be "better" given various rhetorical situations:

> **The statute was designed to limit the number of aliens who can bypass INS-mandated citizenship procedures.**

> **Congress designed the statute to limit the number of aliens who can bypass INS-mandated citizenship procedures.**

> **The evidence in question was obtained by observations made by a police officer looking into the window of an apartment.**

> **A police officer obtained the information for the warrant when he looked into the window of the apartment.**

> **A person's home, the place where he lives, has been recognized by this Court as the most important place in which to invoke Fourth Amendment protection.**

---

[18] For more information, *see* Mary Barnard Ray & Jill J. Ramsfield, *Legal Writing: Getting It Right and Getting It Written* 343-44 (2d ed. 1993).

> This Court has recognized that a person's home, the place where he lives, is the most important place in which to invoke Fourth Amendment protection.

As at least two of these illustrations show, using active voice results in shorter, more direct sentences. The point of this section, however, is not to say that you must eliminate all nominalizations and all uses of passive voice; rather, that you should use nominalizations and passive voice only when you have a good reason to do so. When there is no reason to use them, use more direct, easier-to-understand subjects and verbs.

b. Independent and Dependent Clauses

The second way that a writer can use sentence structure to persuade is by using dependent clauses to "hide" information that the writer wants to deemphasize. In grammatical terms, an independent clause is a clause that can stand on its own as a sentence, while a dependent clause cannot. Readers subconsciously put more emphasis on information in independent clauses and less emphasis on information in dependent clauses. It may help to think of information in a dependent clause as being in parentheses: The reader often sees it as a less important part of the sentence. Notice how switching information between the dependent and the independent clauses subtly changes the impression that the sentence gives the reader:

> First, although the area where the officer stood is close to Thompson's apartment, the communal nature of the grounds makes the claim of curtilage less valid.

> First, even though the officer stood in a communal area, the place where he stood was so close to Thompson's apartment that it increases the validity of the curtilage claim.

> Though the blinds were drawn at the time of the alleged search, there is no indication that Respondents drew them.

> Although there was no testimony at the trial about who closed the window blinds, the fact remains that at the time of the search the blinds were drawn.

> On the night in question, the blinds, though drawn, had a gap in them large enough for a citizen who passed by and an officer who stood a foot or more from the window to view easily the entire illuminated interior scene.

> On the night in question the blinds had been drawn to cover the entire window, even though a small gap remained.

Again, all of these sentences are grammatically correct. The sentence you choose to write will depend on which information you want to emphasize and deemphasize.

c. Using Short Sentences for Emphasis

One guideline for sentence structure and length is the same for legal writing as for any kind of expository writing: Sentence variety is good. One short sentence can be effective. More than two short sentences are not. Compare the two examples below, and notice the impact of a short sentence and concrete language as compared to a long sentence and more abstract language:

> Thus, Society will be prepared to recognize Respondents' expectation of privacy in Thompson's apartment as reasonable only if they were present on the premises for a purpose society deems permissible and valuable. Respondents, who introduced no evidence that they were anything other than temporary, transient visitors on the premises for the sole purpose of conducting illegal business, simply do not belong to the class of individuals who have an expectation of privacy that society is prepared to recognize as reasonable.

> Thus, Society will be prepared to recognize Respondents' expectation of privacy in Thompson's apartment as reasonable only if they were present on the premises for a purpose society deems permissible and valuable. Respondents were there to bag cocaine. They simply do not belong to the class of individuals who have an expectation of privacy that society is prepared to recognize as reasonable.

To make the point even more emphatic, put the short sentence in a position of emphasis at the end of a paragraph:

> Thus, Society will be prepared to recognize Respondents' expectation of privacy in Thompson's apartment as reasonable only if they were present on the premises for a purpose society deems permissible and valuable. Respondents were there to bag cocaine.

Use this persuasive technique with care. If you use too many short sentences in your document, they will lose their dramatic effect.

11.4.5
EFFECTIVE WORD CHOICE

When it comes to word choice, the effective advocate must make decisions carefully. Certainly, it makes sense to choose words that have connotations that are more positive for your client's side. Think in terms of "claimed" instead of "stated"; "admitted" instead of "said." Once again, however, you must take care. It is easy to push this method into ridiculousness.

▽ BAD EXAMPLE

> The officer was able to peer into the private window of the apartment because he abandoned the sidewalk, marched across the grass, and wedged himself behind bushes placed 24 to 48 inches away from the window. Record G-43.

△ GOOD EXAMPLE

The officer was able to approach a window belonging to the apartment by leaving the sidewalk leading up to the building, walking onto the grass and behind bushes located two to four feet away from the window. Record G-43.

Most writers know enough not to use exclamation points to emphasize points or to write in all capital letters to draw attention to a point. Yet many writers try to intensify their arguments with words that are just as ineffective as these techniques. "Clearly," "obviously," "of course," and "it is evident that" have been so overused that they go beyond having no meaning to having a negative meaning. Many writers refer to them as "negative intensifiers."

Instead of using a negative intensifier, identify and use "positive intensifiers." Positive intensifiers include "precisely," "exactly," "specifically," "significantly," and "explicitly." These words are positive intensifiers because they signal that the writer will be giving the reader concrete information about what happened to parties before the court or in a case, about what a rule says, or about how a rule relates to the client's facts. Note the differences between the two examples below:

▽ BAD EXAMPLE

Second, the drawn blinds on the window of the apartment through which the police officer peered clearly indicated that the apartment was not open to public observation.

△ GOOD EXAMPLE

The blinds were drawn in the apartment precisely because the occupants did not want the apartment to be open to public observation. Whoever drew the blinds, that person was taking steps to prevent members of the public — and the police — from looking through the windows.

Of course, if you use a positive intensifier you have to follow it up with the specifics that it promises, lest it become a negative intensifier:

△ GOOD EXAMPLE

The court specifically noted that its holding was not predicated on antiquated notions about the relative abilities of men and women; rather, the holding was predicated on the objectively verifiable fact that women could not serve in combat roles in the United States armed forces.

Whenever you use a positive intensifier, ask yourself how the law or the facts show that this information is "precisely," "specifically," or "significantly" true, and then include those details in your writing.

11.4.6
PERSUASIVE PUNCTUATION

Writers use punctuation marks to organize sentences and the words within sentences. They also use punctuation to show relationships between and among phrases and clauses within sentences. Legal writers can use punctuation marks to emphasize information and to imply relationships when argument is inappropriate. Three types of punctuation marks can be particularly helpful: the semicolon, the dash, and the colon.

a. The Semicolon

The grammar rules governing semicolons dictate that they can be used in two circumstances. First, semicolons punctuate a list when items in the list contain internal commas. In legal writing, this situation occurs most frequently when writers cite multiple cases in support of a proposition. Second, semicolons can be used to separate two independent clauses. This technique is frequently used to highlight some sort of relationship between the two clauses, as in the following examples.

> **GOOD EXAMPLE**
>
> Section 1409(a) does more than legislate on the basis of this stereotype beyond infancy; it applies this stereotype *forever.*

> **GOOD EXAMPLE**
>
> The Supreme Court has allowed a warrantless search when a custodial arrest is performed largely because the suspect already will be subject to substantial interference with individual liberties; similar intrusions exist when a citation is issued in lieu of an arrest.

Semicolons can also be used to juxtapose information in a way that will lead the reader to draw a conclusion. In *Minnesota v. Carter*, for example, the petitioner might want the reader to draw the conclusion that the respondents did not have a legitimate expectation of privacy in the apartment in which they were bagging cocaine. This conclusion could be supported by the lack of a connection between the respondents and Thompson, who lived in the apartment. In the statement of facts, it is inappropriate to argue, but the writer could use a semicolon to juxtapose two facts that might lead the reader to the desired conclusion:

> **GOOD EXAMPLE**
>
> Nothing in the record indicates any personal or social relationship between Thompson and the Respondents; none of Respondents' personal effects were found in the apartment, and they did not present any evidence that they were overnight guests. <u>See</u> Record E-4, E-7, and G-2.

Because you can state conclusions rather than imply them within the argument, this method is used to greatest effect in the statement of the case. But you can always use semicolons to make clear a close relationship between two ideas. In any case, it is a good idea to be able to write sentences in a variety of ways. Proper use of semicolons separates sophisticated writers from unsophisticated ones; it's a good idea to learn to use them properly.

b. The Dash

Mary Barnard Ray and Jill Ramsfield refer to the dash as "the gigolo of the punctuation world,"[19] and too many dashes may give your writing an inappropriately casual tone. The dash can be used effectively, however, to highlight information in the middle of a sentence. Proper use of the dash consists of a space, two hyphens, and another space (at which point many word processing computers properly convert the two hyphens to a connected line called an em-dash). When you use a dash on either side of an interrupting phrase, it creates white space on either side of the phrase and thus creates a position of emphasis within the sentence. Notice how the writer of a *Miller v. Albright* brief uses the dash to highlight a comparison between how the law treats the foreign-born children of U.S. citizens in different relationships:

⚠ GOOD EXAMPLE

Children in the first two groups — those who are "legitimate" and those who have a U.S. citizen mother — are U.S. citizens by birthright. <u>See</u> 8 U.S.C. § 1401(g) (1994). Children in the last group, however — those "illegitimate" children with U.S. citizen fathers — may receive their fathers' citizenship only after clearing several hurdles.

To avoid making your writing sound too casual, don't overuse the dash, and use it only to set off an interrupting phrase in the middle of a sentence rather than as a means to add an afterthought at the end of a sentence.

c. The Colon

The colon is my favorite way to use punctuation for emphasis. Most writers use it only to introduce a long quotation or list, and it is properly used for that purpose. But it can be very effectively used within sentences both to highlight information and to explain or elaborate on the information that came before the colon, as in these examples:

⚠ GOOD EXAMPLE

Through gaps in the drawn horizontal mini-blinds on the window, Officer Thielen observed the same scene the informant had described to

---

[19] Mary Barnard Ray & Jill Ramsfield, *Legal Writing: Getting It Right and Getting It Written* 103 (3d ed. West 2000).

him: two males and one female sitting at a kitchen table handling a white powdery substance. Record E-2.

 GOOD EXAMPLE

In <u>Chimel</u>, this Court examined the search incident to an arrest exception to the warrant requirement and made note of the two major policy justifications for the search: preserving officer safety and preventing the destruction of evidence by the suspect. 395 U.S. at 763.

 GOOD EXAMPLE

The cases in which no substantial relation was found have one common element: They reject gender stereotypes that are little more than vestiges of past discrimination.

The shorter the phrase or sentence after the colon, the more emphatic the use of the colon is. Note the differences among these examples: As the phrases get shorter, the sentence gets more emphatic.

 GOOD EXAMPLE

As illustrated by the plight of Lorelyn and Charlie Miller, these burdens can become insurmountable: Section 1409(a) will prevent Mr. Miller and Ms. Miller from ever legally proving that they have a close family relationship unless this court refuses to accept the irrebuttable gender stereotype in Section 1409(a).

GOOD EXAMPLE

The government argued that the observation was analogous to looking through a knothole or an opening in a fence: "If there is an opening, the police may look."

GOOD EXAMPLE

The record indicates that Respondents engaged in only one activity while inside Thompson's apartment: bagging cocaine.

Grammatically, the information that precedes the colon should be a complete sentence. The information that comes after need not be. Do not capitalize the first word after a colon unless the information after the colon could be a separate sentence; even then, you may choose to leave it uncapitalized. If, like me, you fall in love with the colon, you should still avoid overusing it.

11.5
AVOIDING SPELLING, GRAMMATICAL, AND TYPOGRAPHICAL ERRORS

Avoiding mechanical errors does not really present an opportunity for persuasion. Your reader will not particularly notice or remark upon a brief that is free of these problems: Perfection on small things is a minimal expectation. Unfortunately, however, mechanical errors will have a negative effect. Many readers presume that someone who writes a document with mechanical errors cannot be trusted to conduct sound legal analysis. While the logic behind this attitude may be questionable, it's unmistakable that the attitude is there, and it provides one more reason why you should proofread diligently.

Chapter Twelve talks about effective proofreading methods, and Appendix A addresses common punctuation mistakes.

11.6
CREDIBILITY THROUGH DOCUMENT DESIGN

The way your document looks also creates an opportunity for persuasion. If it is neat, clean, visually easy-to-read, and complies with all local rules, you will impress the court with your competence, and your credibility will rise. Many small decisions can affect the ease with which the reader can read your brief, and thus your credibility.

11.6.1
TYPEFACE

Even your choice of typeface can make a difference in the readability of your brief. Readers can more easily read typefaces that have "serif," that is, small lines as part of the beginning or ending strokes of each letter. The serifs help the reader to connect the letters and thus move through the text more quickly and easily. Typefaces that do not have serif are called "sans serif" ("without serif"), and are a little more difficult to read. Here are some serif and sans serif typefaces:

1. Times New Roman is a serif typeface.

2. Garamond is a serif typeface.

3. Bookman old style is a serif typeface.

4. Courier New is a serif typeface.

5. Arial is a sans serif typeface.

6. **Futura Md BT is a sans serif typeface.**

Although some people get emotionally attached to their "favorite" typefaces, you should base your decision on the reader's needs rather than your own preferences.

11.6.2
CITATIONS AND EMPHATIC TEXT: <u>UNDERLINING</u>, *ITALICS*, **BOLD-FACED TYPE**, AND CAPITALIZATION

Both the *ALWD Citation Manual* and the *Bluebook* allow the writer to choose between underlining and italics when citing cases and other titles. Although both underlining and italics have the same meaning vis-à-vis citation form, they are not equal in the eyes of the reader. An underlined word or phrase jumps out at the reader as soon as the page is turned, while an italicized word is noticed only upon closer inspection. Try flipping through this textbook, which uses examples with underlined citations, and note how the underlining jumps out at the eye. Even if you cannot read the words immediately, the underlining catches your eye and draws it to the underlined words. A busy judge or a clerk who is looking for your analysis of a particular case will have a much easier time finding that discussion if you use underlining instead of italics to designate case names and other titles.

Whether you use underlining or italics for citation form, you should be consistent throughout all of your citations and all of the parts of your citations. For example, don't use italics for signal words but underlining for case names:

▽ **BAD EXAMPLE**

See, e.g., <u>Fairman v. McGuffin</u>, 101 U.S. 101, 105 (2014).

△ **GOOD EXAMPLE**

<u>See, e.g.,</u> <u>Fairman v. McGuffin</u>, 101 U.S. 101, 105 (2014).

On the other hand, you may decide to use underlining for citations, but to use italics and bold-faced type for emphasis. This suggestion is somewhat radical; many readers expect a document to contain underlined words or italicized words, but not both. I believe, however, that this expectation is a mistaken carryover from the rule that underlining or italics should be used consistently in all *citations*. As a practical matter, you should use the graphic technique that will help the reader understand your point with minimal distraction. Because underlining provides such strong emphasis, you may distract the reader if you underline words that should receive only slight emphasis. Of course, as with many writing techniques, too little is better than too much. If you emphasize too many words, even with the subtle emphasis of italics, you will distract or annoy your reader and lose the benefit of the emphasis.

Bold-faced type, which provides the strongest emphasis, should generally be reserved for headings. On extremely rare occasions, however, you may use bold-faced type for emphasis within your text. For example, if you have decided to include a long quotation of the text of a statute, you may be worried that your reader will skip the quotation. In that situation, italics would do little to show the reader the significant statutory language:

▽ BAD EXAMPLE

Section 1409(c) gives immediate citizenship to a foreign-born child of unmarried parents if the child's mother is a United States citizen at the time of birth:

> Notwithstanding the provision of subsection (a) of this provision [which requires fathers to meet certain requirements to establish the citizenship of their children], *a person* born, after December 23, 1952, outside the United States and out of wedlock *shall be held to have acquired at birth the nationality status of the mother, if the mother had the nationality of the United States at the time of such person's birth*, and if the mother had previously been physically present in the United States or one of its outlying possessions for a continuous period of one year.

8 U.S.C. § 1409(c) (1994) (emphasis added).

If you use bold-faced type for the most crucial language in the statute, however, even readers who skip the quotation would be sure to see it:

△ GOOD EXAMPLE

Section 1409(c) gives immediate citizenship to a foreign-born child of unmarried parents if the child's mother is a United States citizen at the time of birth:

> Notwithstanding the provision of subsection (a) of this provision [which requires fathers to meet certain requirements to establish the citizenship of their children], **a person** born, after December 23, 1952, outside the United States and out of wedlock **shall be held to have acquired at birth the nationality status of the mother, if the mother had the nationality of the United States at the time of such person's birth**, and if the mother had previously been physically present in the United States or one of its outlying possessions for a continuous period of one year.

8 U.S.C. § 1409(c) (1994) (emphasis added).

As the example shows, this technique can also be used to allow the reader to read a complete phrase or clause without being distracted by language that is irrelevant to the issue under discussion.

Finally, a word about using capitalization for emphasis: Don't. In fact, unless court rules require it, you can write a very effective brief using no "all-caps" words. Words written entirely in capital letters are more difficult to read. Of course, many writers use all capital letters to designate element headings such as "SUMMARY OF THE ARGUMENT" or "QUESTIONS PRESENTED." Most readers can tolerate this use reasonably well, but writing more than a few words in all capital letters will usually drive the reader to a new paragraph.

11.6.3
JUSTIFICATION

"Justification" refers to the alignment of the text. In most legal documents, text is aligned along the left side of the page, or "left-justified." Some information, like page numbers in tables, is "right-justified" or aligned along the right side of the page. Many word-processing programs allow writers to use "full-justification." Full-justified text is aligned evenly along the left and the right side of the page. Sometimes, using full justification allows the writer to fit more words on the page because a program will compress some words to make them fit into a line. Unfortunately, the variable spaces in full-justified text interfere with readability. Although full-justified text may look more attractive from a distance, it is also more difficult to read. Notice the difference between these two versions of text from a Securities and Exchange Commission handbook promoting the readability of disclosure statements filed with the Commission:

△ GOOD EXAMPLE

> Research shows that the easiest text to read is left justified, ragged right text. That is, the text is aligned, or flush, on the left with a loose, or ragged, right edge. The text in this handbook is set left justified, ragged right. Fully justified text means both the right and left edges are flush, or even. When you full justify text, the spacing between words fluctuates from line to line, causing the eye to stop and constantly readjust to the variable spacing on each line. Currently, most disclosure documents are fully justified. This, coupled with a severe shortage of white space, makes these documents visually unappealing and difficult to read.

▽ BAD EXAMPLE

> Research shows that the easiest text to read is left justified, ragged right text. That is, the text is aligned, or flush, on the left with a loose, or ragged, right edge. The text in this handbook is set left justified, ragged right. Fully justified text means both the right and left edges are flush, or even. When you full justify text, the spacing between words fluctuates from line to line, causing the eye to stop and constantly readjust to the variable spacing on each line. Currently, most disclosure documents are fully justified. This, coupled with a severe shortage of white space, makes these documents visually unappealing and difficult to read.[20]

Most word processing programs have flush left, ragged right as their default justification. Do not be tempted to use full justification to save

---

[20] *A Plain English Handbook: How to Create Clear SEC Disclosure Documents* 44 (Securities and Exchange Commission 1998) (paragraphing altered). The handbook is also available at *http://www.sec.gov/pdf/handbook.pdf*.

space or to "clean up" a ragged right edge. That ragged right edge helps your reader to read the document more efficiently.

11.6.4
EFFECTIVE TABLES

Because judges and clerks who read briefs often consult the Tables of Contents and Authorities, it is important that these tables look good as well as contain accurate information. One of the four basic principles of design is alignment,[21] and effective alignment is crucial in making tables look good. Page numbers and document elements should be aligned consistently, so that readers can easily find the information that they need.

In this excerpt from a table of contents, note how none of the elements are aligned; the reader's eye bounces all over the page to look for information:

▽ BAD EXAMPLE

---

[21] Robin Williams, *The Non-Designer's Design Book* 14 (Peachpit Press 1994).

To improve the table, the writer "double-indented" each heading so that each category and sub-category is aligned. Page numbers are aligned along the right-hand margin:

⚠ GOOD EXAMPLE

ARGUMENT.. 8

    I. As temporary business invitees present in another's residence for the sole purpose of packaging drugs, Respondents had no legitimate expectation of privacy and, thus, may not invoke the Fourth Amendment's protections 8

        A. Respondents failed to meet their burden of proving that they had a legitimate expectation of privacy because they introduced absolutely no evidence regarding their status in Thompson's apartment... 10

        B. Respondents had no legitimate expectation of privacy because any subjective expectation they might have had while temporarily in another's home for the sole purpose of conducting illegal business was not one society recognizes as reasonable 11

            1. The <u>Olson</u> rule dictates that only overnight guests have a connection to a premises that gives rise to a legitimate expectation of privacy... 12

            2. Even if the <u>Olson</u> rule extends to non-overnight guests, Respondents' expectation of privacy is unreasonable because they were present only to conduct illegal business that is not valuable to society.. 16

                a. Illegal drug distribution is not a longstanding social custom that serves functions recognized as valuable by society... 16

                b. Respondents were present for a purely commercial purpose and were not entitled to the forth Amendment protection associated with the home 19

        C. Respondents may not claim a legitimate expectation of privacy, because by engaging in criminal acts in a well-lit room, directly in front of a window facing a widely used common area, they exhibited no subjective expectation of privacy.................. 21

You may presume that you need not worry about design because in practice you will have an administrative assistant who will type and print the document. You should not presume, however, that your assistant will know or care about document design. You must take responsibility for what your document says and for how it looks because you will have to face the consequences for the impression it makes.

11.7
SUMMARY

Persuasive writing techniques cannot change bad law or weak facts to make a losing case a winner. They can, however, increase your chances of victory in a close case, and, when used properly, establish and maintain your credibility with the court.

POLISHING

Unfortunately, many writers lose interest when they read advice about polishing the mechanics of a document because they think that people do not notice mechanics or that their administrative assistants will take care of mechanical problems. First of all, people do notice "the small stuff." Judge Wald, of the D.C. Circuit, recommends that counsel "proofread with a passion":

> You cannot imagine how disquieting it is to find several spelling or grammatical errors in an otherwise competent brief. It makes the judge go back to square one in evaluating the counsel. It says — worst of all — the author never bothered to read the whole thing through, but she expects us to.[1]

Fairly or unfairly, many readers see mechanical mistakes as a sign of overall incompetence; too many typographical errors may lead the judge to mistrust the validity of the legal analysis. Justice Ginsburg notes that if a brief is "sloppy" in regard to mechanics, "the judge may suspect its reliability in other respects as well."[2] In a 1994 case, a federal district judge dismissing a complaint ordered a sanctions hearing for the plaintiff's attorney, noting that the attorney's mechanical errors were evidence of a lack of due care:

> [Counsel] continues to submit documents to this Court with grammatical errors and misstatements. . . . Moreover, throughout the Amended Complaint [the attorney] repeatedly refers to his client as "he" instead of "she." These types of errors strongly suggest that Mr. Williams has not taken the appropriate care to avoid errors before submitting documents to this Court.[3]

---

[1] Patricia M. Wald, *19 Tips from 19 Years on the Appellate Bench*, 1 J. App. Prac. & Process 7, 22 (1999).

[2] Ruth Bader Ginsburg, *Remarks on Appellate Advocacy*, 50 S.C. L. Rev. 567, 568 (1999).

[3] *Styles v. Philadelphia Electric Co.*, No. CIV.A.93-4593, 1994 WL 245469, at *3 (E.D. Pa. June 6, 1994) (cited in Judith D. Fischer, *Bareheaded and Barefaced Counsel: Courts React to Unprofessionalism in Lawyers' Papers*, 31 Suffolk U.L. Rev. 1, 27 (1997)).

The second reason you must learn polishing skills is that you cannot afford an assistant who can do this kind of polishing. You must take responsibility for polishing the mechanics of your legal documents because your document reflects on your client and on your competence.

Polishing is hard for the same reason that revision is hard. Most people don't really see their writing when they review it. Instead, they see the document that they meant to write; their short-term memory interferes with their ability to see typographical errors or other problems. For that reason, this chapter identifies some objective methods for polishing that will help you to break up that relationship between your short-term memory and your document, and help you to catch mistakes in both your writing and your analysis.

The best way to proofread effectively is to put your writing away for a while. If you've ever gone back and read a document that you wrote last year, or even last month, you've probably noticed several mistakes or style problems that you missed when you wrote it. If you are trying to polish a document that you wrote this morning, your short-term memory makes it hard for you to see your mistakes. It knows what you wanted to say, and it tends to gloss over the mistakes. Therefore, if you can get a draft done a week before your deadline, *don't* reread it and edit it every day. Instead, wait three days and do a thorough edit, and then wait three more days and do a final edit. Even a little time can make some difference. In a crunch, that might mean taking a 15-minute walk and then coming back to edit, but taking some time can make a difference.

A second effective polishing technique is to "start in the middle" when reviewing your work. Most writing teachers find that mechanical mistakes and other weaknesses show up more often in the second half of the document than in the first half. That's because many writers get bored with editing or polishing as they get closer to the end of the document; many give up before finishing the job. Even conscientious editors should give "fresh eyes" to different parts of the document at different times.

Generally, it is ineffective to proofread by reading the entire document very slowly once or twice, trying to catch every type of error. Instead, you should read the document through several times on the computer and several times in hard copy form. Make surgical strikes, focusing on only one or two aspects of the document at a time. This chapter will address methods to use on both the computer and your hard copy that will help you to find common errors and other problems.

12.1
METHODS TO USE ON THE COMPUTER

When reviewing your document while it is still in electronic form, you can use the "search" or "find and replace" function to your advantage.

Although your eyes get tired, the computer never misses on a search, presuming you are searching precisely.

1. **Pronoun search**. Use the "find and replace" function to search for "he," "she," "it," "they," and so on. Stop when you hit a pronoun and scrutinize it to make sure that reader will have *no doubt* as to the noun you are referring to (the "antecedent"). Also, make sure that you have not mistakenly used "they" in place of "it." For example, both courts and corporations should be referred to in the singular as "it."

2. **Apostrophe search**. If you tend to use too many apostrophes, use the "find and replace" function to search for [s'] or ['s] so that you can scrutinize whether you've used the apostrophes correctly. If you use too few apostrophes, your task is a little harder. You could use the search function to find words that end in "s" by searching for "s[space]" or "s.[space]." Once you are zeroed in on the potential problem words, consult grammar guidelines to see if you are using apostrophes correctly. Appendix A includes advice about the most common apostrophe problems.

3. **Quotation Mark Search**. The rule in American English is that periods and commas *always* go inside quotation marks, even if you are quoting only one word or one letter.

▽ BAD EXAMPLE

Judge Wald noted that finding errors in a brief makes her "go back to square one in evaluating the counsel".

△ GOOD EXAMPLE

Judge Wald noted that finding errors in a brief makes her "go back to square one in evaluating the counsel."

▽ BAD EXAMPLE

The word "Aspen", which refers to both trees and a publisher, begins with the letter "A".

△ GOOD EXAMPLE

The word "Aspen," which refers to both trees and a publisher, begins with the letter "A."

To find errors of this type, use the find and replace function to search for quotation marks, and check your punctuation. Also, check to make sure that each beginning quote has an ending quote.

4. **Citation Search.** To review your citations, search [begin underline] or [begin italics] or even "v." to help you find citations and scrutinize them in isolation. Three types of errors are particularly common: (1) incorrect volume or page numbers, (2) misspelled party names, and (3) incorrect citation form

5. **Spell-check.** Run the spell-check early and often, but keep a few things in mind. First, keep your hand away from the mouse, or your finger

off the button, so that you don't hit "replace" or "skip" by mistake. Second, don't hit "skip" as soon as you see a party name or a case name; make sure that you've spelled them properly and consistently.

Third, after completing spell-check, use the "find and replace" function to search for typos that the spell-check function won't catch. In every document, look for "statue" for "statute," "untied" for "united," "form" for "from" (and vice versa) "reasonable" for "reasonably" (and vice versa), and "probable" for "probably" (and vice versa). You might consider setting your "quick correct" function to change "pubic" to "public" to avoid that potentially embarrassing error. If your document is about "probable cause" or "reasonable doubt," it is even more important to do this kind of search. I have read several briefs in which students claim that there was no "probably cause" for the defendant's arrest, or that the defense could not establish "reasonably doubt." Because both forms of the word could appear in the text, search for each form separately and make sure each use is proper.

As you can see, the find and replace function can help you to proofread on the computer in many different ways. You may be able to figure out other ways to make the computer's tireless brain work for you.

12.2
METHODS TO USE ON THE HARD COPY

Plan to print out a hard copy a few times before you must file the document. Because your brain works differently when you are looking at a computer screen than when you are looking at a hard copy, you will undoubtedly find errors on the hard copy that you missed when reading the document on the computer.

1. **Check paragraph length.** You may have created some overlong paragraphs as you revised; they will be evident on the hard copy. Remember that there are two reasons to create a paragraph break: substance and graphics. Even if you have not moved on to a new subject, the reader may need the brief visual rest that a paragraph break provides. If you must create an artificial paragraph break in this way, you may need to add a topic sentence to ensure that the reader can instantly understand how the paragraph is relevant to the point under discussion.

2. **Check sentence length.** If you have a problem with overlong sentences, edit for them by just looking for periods. Take a pencil and make a slash mark at every period; you can do this without even reading the text. When you're done, review the slash marks. If you see several sentences in a row that are over four lines long, review them and try to shorten at least one. One good way to shorten long sentences is to look for verbs. If you have three verbs in one sentence, try giving each verb a subject and its own sentence. If you see several sentences that are only

one line long — and you're not using short sentences for occasional, dramatic effect — try to combine a couple of the short sentences.[4]

3. **Review the verbs.** Readers subconsciously pay more attention to information in the verb position. Thus, go through your document and circle all of your verbs, trying not to read the sentences. You should scrutinize all vague verbs, including "is," "are," "was," "were," "made," "involved," "concerned," "had," and the like. Unless you are using them designedly — e.g., in a persuasive document to de-emphasize information, or because you are using passive voice to avoid an unusually long subject — you should look for the better verb hidden in the sentence and revise accordingly.

4. **Review the signals to the reader**. The best way to review signals to the reader is to review the "template items" identified in Chapter Ten above. Look at the first paragraph (or two) of each heading section for either a roadmap paragraph or some other sort of introduction. Look at the last paragraph of each heading section for a conclusory statement about the point being covered within that heading section. Scan the first sentence of each paragraph to see how often your paragraphs begin with main points and include the phrase-that-pays. Scan through the document to make sure there are enough headings. If you go more than three or four pages without a new heading, scrutinize that section. Can you break that section down into two sub-sections? Or have you gone onto a new point without labeling it with a heading?

Similarly, review each roadmap and mini-roadmap, and then compare it to your headings. The roadmap should predict precisely the headings that follow.

5. **Do a ruler-read**. After you have taken these steps, read a hard copy aloud (as slowly as you can) backwards and forwards **with a ruler under each line as you read it.** Using the ruler helps to separate you from your text, breaking up that cozy relationship between your short-term memory and your document. When doing this "ruler-read," include all extraneous materials like cover pages and tables; these sections often get short shrift when it comes to proofreading.

6. **Repeat any or all of the above as needed**. If you keep finding new mistakes when using these techniques, you need to keep proofreading. Do not print the final version of the document until you can read it through and find *no* mistakes.

12.3
PROOFREADING YOUR REVISIONS

Word processors have greatly improved the quality of written documents, but they are also responsible for a new type of editing error. In

---

[4] *See* Mary Barnard Ray & Jill J. Ramsfield, *Legal Writing: Getting It Right and Getting It Written* 279 (2d ed. 1993).

the past, when a writer revised a document, someone had to type the whole thing over again, and so it was fairly easy to substitute the new words and to leave the old words out. Now, with the constant editing that word processors allow, and the "find and replace" functions that are widely available, it is not uncommon to see both old and new versions of a phrase within a document: The writer typed the new version in and forgot to delete the old one. Writers who use the "find and replace" function carelessly frequently find sentences like this in their writing:

▽ **BAD EXAMPLE**

On Saturday, the Mr. Johnson returned home.

The best way to avoid these types of errors is, once again, to focus your proofreading. After each round of edits, print out the hard copy and highlight the words, lines, or paragraphs in which edits occurred. Read those sections in isolation, so that you don't get caught up in the meaning of the words. In addition, *never* use the "replace all" function; doing so causes mistakes like the one above because it's difficult to envision all of the contexts in which a word or phrase might appear. Instead, look at each use of the word you are replacing to avoid mistakes.

12.4
THE LAST THING TO DO WITH THE DOCUMENT

This section is really about the second-to-the-last thing to do with the document. The last thing you should do is file it with the court. But the last proofreading method you should use with your document is to read it aloud, out of order. Either start in the middle, start on the last page and then read the second to the last page, and so on, or mix up the pages and read them in a random order. Whichever method you use, your goal is to pay attention to individual words and sentences rather than getting swept away by your no doubt fascinating discussion of the law.

12.5
SUMMARY

In practice, you will often need to write and file documents in a hurry, without time to polish and proofread in a leisurely way. Take the time now to develop an effective polishing process that will give you the best chance of avoiding distracting technical errors.

ORAL ARGUMENT

Supreme Court Rule 28.1 provides that oral argument "should emphasize and clarify the written arguments in the briefs on the merits. Counsel should assume that all Justices have read the briefs before oral argument. Oral argument read from a prepared text is not favored."

Although most law students think of the oral argument first when they think of appellate advocacy, most judges agree that the brief is more important than the oral argument. Justice Ginsburg has noted that "[a]s between briefing and argument, there is near-universal agreement among federal appellate judges that the brief is more important."[1] In many federal courts, most cases are decided without oral argument. Justice Ginsburg has noted that the Fourth, Tenth, and Eleventh Circuits dispense with oral argument in about 70 percent of cases, while Judge Wiener has pointed out that almost two-thirds of the appeals filed in the Fifth Circuit are decided without oral argument.[2] Even in cases in which oral argument occurs, the brief usually has more to do with the outcome of the case. A 1986 article conducted a limited study of three appellate

---

[1] *See, e.g.,* Ruth Bader Ginsburg, *Remarks on Appellate Advocacy*, 50 S.C. L. Rev. 567, 567 (1999).

[2] Ginsburg, *supra* note 1, at 568; *see also* Jacques L. Wiener, Jr., *Ruminations from the Bench: Brief Writing and Oral Argument in the Fifth Circuit*, 70 Tul. L. Rev. 187, 189 (1995).

judges and noted that oral arguments changed the views they held before the oral argument in 31 percent, 17 percent, and 13 percent of the cases heard.[3]

This is not to say that oral argument is unimportant. The late Justice Brennan has observed, "I have had too many occasions when my judgment of a decision has turned on what happened in oral argument, not to be terribly concerned for myself were I to be denied oral argument."[4] Judge Bright, of the Eighth Circuit, has noted that "oral argument is an essential component of the decisionmaking process."[5] It is certainly responsible for generating more adrenalin.

13.1
PURPOSE OF ORAL ARGUMENT

The purpose of the oral argument is not to give an impressive speech. Rather, your goal as an oral advocate is simply to highlight your best arguments and to answer any questions that the judges have about the case. Judge Pierce has noted that oral arguments give judges "the opportunity to discuss . . . the issues they consider dispositive or particularly troublesome — issues that may not have been briefed or at least not briefed fully."[6] Justice Ginsburg has observed that questions during oral argument "give counsel a chance to satisfy the court on matters the judges think significant, issues the judges might puzzle over in chambers, and resolve less satisfactorily without counsel's aid."[7]

Many judges form a sort of rebuttable presumption about how the case should be decided after reading the briefs and relevant authorities. They use the oral argument to test that presumption and to probe the case's limits, strengths, and weaknesses by asking counsel to clarify difficult issues or to speculate on the impact of a decision on future cases. Because of their intimate knowledge of the facts of the case and the relevant law, counsel for the parties are uniquely qualified to help the judges as they wrestle with the issues presented by the case.

---

[3] *See* Myron H. Bright, *The Power of the Spoken Word: In Defense of Oral Argument*, 72 Iowa L. Rev. 35, 40 nn.32-33 (1986).

[4] *Commission on Revision of the Fed. Court Appellate Sys., Structure and Internal Procedures: Recommendations for Change*, 67 F.R.D. 195, 254 (1975) (quoting Justice Brennan's comments at the 1972 Third Circuit Judicial Conference) (quoted in Lawrence W. Pierce, *Appellate Advocacy: Some Reflections from the Bench*, 61 Fordham L. Rev. 829, 833 (1993)).

[5] Bright, *supra* note 3, at 36.

[6] Pierce, *supra* note 4, at 833-34.

[7] Ginsburg, *supra* note 1, at 569. *See also* Wiener, *supra* note 2, at 199 (noting that oral argument "further crystallize[s] the issues [and] enhance[s] the court's] understanding of the factual and legal details, subtleties, and nuances of the case").

13.2
FORMAT

In appellate arguments, the petitioner (or appellant) argues first. He or she may reserve some of the allotted time for rebuttal. Counsel for respondent (or appellee) follows, after which counsel for petitioner may present a rebuttal. Time allotted to each side for argument varies from 10 to 30 minutes; in many courts, each side is allotted 15 minutes, and counsel for petitioner may reserve one, two, or three of those 15 minutes for rebuttal. Counsel for respondent does not have the opportunity for rebuttal.

13.3
INTELLECTUAL PREPARATION: WHAT DO YOU NEED TO KNOW?

You complete the most important preparation for the oral argument when you write the brief, for it is in writing the brief that you gain an understanding of the facts, issues, and authorities that control the case. Nevertheless, there are two practical things that you must do in specific preparation for the oral argument. First, you must decide what points to argue and then prepare your argument. Second, you must gather the information that the court will expect you to know — to have at your mental fingertips — when you are at the podium.

13.3.1
DECIDING WHAT POINTS TO ARGUE

Your job on oral argument is not to present a summary of your brief.[8] You will not have time to discuss all of the issues and arguments that you raised in the brief. When planning your oral argument, identify the two or three points that are most necessary to convince the court of the justice of the result you seek. Frequently, these points will be those that could be resolved in favor of either party,[9] and thus, spending time on these points in oral argument will be particularly important. As you take notes on the points you will present to the court, write down citations to cases and statutes that support your assertions. Although you will not be read-

---

[8] *See, e.g.,* Karen J. Williams, *Help us Help You: A Fourth Circuit Primer on Effective Appellate Oral Arguments,* 50 S.C. L. Rev. 591, 595 (1999).
[9] *Id.*

ing from your notes, the act of writing down the points and their supporting authorities will help cement them in your mind.[10]

In your brief, you may have followed a "CREXAC" (Conclusion, Rule, Explanation, Application, Conclusion) model of analysis. When planning your oral argument, a pared-down version of that model can be useful. That is, first, you should state the point — or the conclusion — that you want the court to agree with. Then support that conclusion by stating the rule that governs the issue. If the case or statute is significant to your argument, you may mention it, but in oral argument, the rule is frequently more important than the citation to authority for that rule. On the other hand, you must be thoroughly familiar with all of the relevant authorities so that you may answer questions about them. In addition, in some cases the relevant authorities become an important part of the argument.

Generally, the "explanation" part of the formula that was so important in the brief may be all but eliminated in the oral argument. The judges' eyes may glaze over during any lengthy recitation of authority case facts and holdings unless it is given in response to a specific question. How much support you should give for the rule varies from issue to issue. If the rule is a readily accepted one, you may not need to do more than mention the rule, or perhaps the name of the relevant authority. If the rule is controversial, however, you may need to mention more than one authority or explain how a particular authority supports the rule. If the rule is a statute whose meaning is in controversy, you may wish to spend some time discussing pertinent legislative history.

After you have stated the rule and supported it (if needed), apply the rule to the facts by naming the particular facts that mandate the result that you seek. While your explanation will often be shorter in an oral argument, do not stint on the application of law to facts. The judges will be particularly interested in why the facts of the case mandate the application of the rule in the manner that you suggest. Similarly, they will benefit from a detailed explanation of the result that occurs when the rule is applied to your facts.

While planning your argument is useful, realize that you will rarely be permitted to proceed through the argument of an entire point without interruption.[11] Nonetheless, you should outline a full discussion of each of the points you plan to make during the argument. Doing so teaches you more about your case as you prepare to face the panel.

13.3.2
GATHERING INFORMATION

After you have planned your argument, make sure that you know the case, the issues, and the relevant authorities well enough to answer the

---

[10] *See, e.g., id.* at 594.
[11] *See, e.g., id.* at 598.

court's questions. Although you should limit your prepared presentation to only two or three points, the court will probably ask you about other issues. You must be prepared for all relevant — and some irrelevant — questions from the bench.

First, renew your acquaintance with the facts and procedure of the case. You should be able to answer the court's questions about the details of any relevant facts and be able to tell the court where in the record, the decisions below, or the joint appendix certain facts have been recorded. Make sure that you understand all of the details surrounding the legally significant facts; very often, these factual details can make a legal difference. Judge Wald notes that counsel's familiarity with the record can play a crucial role in the argument:

> The more arcane the subject matter . . . the more intimate with the record the advocate needs to be. All the questions of fact . . . that the brief may have raised in the judges' minds will surface at argument, and nothing frustrates a bench more than an advocate who does not know the answers. Your credibility as a legal maven spurts as soon as you show familiarity with the facts of the underlying dispute.[12]

Similarly, make sure you know the procedural details of the case. The judges may rely on you to clear up momentary confusion about what happened in the courts below.

Second, familiarize yourself with all filed briefs and the authorities cited in those briefs. You should be able to tell the court the facts, holding, or reasoning of any significant authority cases, and you should be able to explain how your case is similar to or distinguishable from those cases. Likewise, if you are asking the court to apply a multipart test, make sure that you understand all of the parts of the test, even those that are not controversial.[13]

Finally, and perhaps most importantly, figure out what you are asking for. What rule are you asking the court to create, or apply? What will be the impact of that rule on future cases? (Knowing the impact of a decision in your favor will enable you to respond effectively to hypotheticals posed by the court.) On a related note, try to anticipate what concessions you may be asked to make. For example, you may be asked to concede that the rule in the case applies to a certain type of plaintiff or defendant, or that your client has or has not met all or part of the standard your opponent espouses. You should know which points you would (or should) concede immediately (those that have little or no effect on your argument), which points you can concede if pressed by the court (those that are important to your argument, but that do not determine victory), and which points you can never concede (any point that would cause you to lose the argument).

¹² Patricia M. Wald, *19 Tips from 19 Years on the Appellate Bench*, 1 J. App. Prac. & Process 7, 19-20 (1999).
¹³ Williams, *supra* note 8, at 597.

Not all judges try to force counsel to concede either minor or significant points, but it is wise to be prepared for the ones who do. Justice Ginsburg has noted that "questions are sometimes designed to nail down a concession that will show up in an opinion, perhaps in a footnote that reads: 'At argument, counsel conceded thus and so.' That doesn't mean lawyers should avoid concessions as inevitably damaging. As Judge Wald has observed, a concession once in a while can enhance a lawyer's credibility."[14]

Judge Karen Williams, of the Fourth Circuit, has also noted that judges may ask questions that try to get attorneys to "concede away [their] case[s]," stating that counsel should listen carefully to questions that seek concessions, to ensure that "the judge has accurately restated your argument. The judge may be leading you down the slippery slope to an absurd result. At the same time, nothing hurts an advocate's credibility with the court more than the failure to concede an obvious point."[15]

To sum up, at the end of your "intellectual preparation" for the argument, you should have a command of both what you plan to say and what you need to know.

13.4
PHYSICAL PREPARATION: WHAT SHOULD YOU BRING TO THE COURTROOM?

At a minimum, the well-prepared oral advocate should bring two things to the courtroom: the briefs that have been filed in the current hearing of the case, and the joint appendix or other record materials that are before the court. In the unusual (but not unheard of) event that the court should ask you to consider information on a particular page in the record or a brief, you want to have the materials there with you. You may leave them at counsel table if it is close by and if you will easily be able to retrieve them.

It is also appropriate to bring an outline or some form of notes up to the podium, but you should plan to make these materials succinct. Judge Wiener, of the Fifth Circuit, has noted that counsel should not "bring lots of documents to the lectern — shuffling books and papers and reading from them interrupts the flow of your presentation and paints a picture of an unprepared or bumbling advocate."[16]

It is the tradition at many law schools for students to use a manila folder for their notes; the students either write their notes on the four

---

[14] Ginsburg, *supra* note 1, at 569.
[15] Williams, *supra* note 8, at 599.
[16] Wiener, *supra* note 2, at 204.

sides of the folder, or prepare them on a word processor and tape or staple them in place. The advantage of a manila folder is that it gives the advocate four pages that stay in order even if dropped. Also, four pages is about the maximum number that the oral advocate should try to look at. Many students use the interior of the folder for their main outline, and store information about facts and cases, to be referred to if needed, on the outside.

Some students who want a more professional look use a three ring binder instead of a manila folder. While this may look better on the way to and from the podium, the pages may be more difficult to turn. Furthermore, having a three-ring binder, which allows multiple pages, may tempt the advocate to write a more detailed outline, or even to write out the text of the argument.

Although the anxious advocate may believe that writing out a prepared speech will be a tonic to the nerves, reading from a prepared text is certain to antagonize the court. Supreme Court Rule 28.1 notes, delicately, that "[o]ral argument read from a prepared text is not favored." Judge Williams makes the point more directly. She believes that reading the argument can hurt both its style and its substance:

> The worst thing you can do is deliver a stiff presentation by attempting to read your argument verbatim. Such a presentation style is tedious and makes it difficult for you to answer questions from the bench. If you spend your time looking down at the podium reading your argument, you are likely to miss signals from the bench, and you cannot engage in a dialogue with the judges. Try to argue extemporaneously, or at least leave us with the impression that you are.[17]

Thus, when preparing materials to bring up to the podium, think in terms of words, phrases, and lists, rather than sentences, paragraphs, or pages. If you write full sentences, you will be tempted to read them because you will presume that a prefabricated sentence will sound better than an off-the-top-of-your-head remark. Remember, however, that the judges expect the oral argument to be, to some extent, a spontaneous dialogue. Most judges would rather hear an imperfect sentence from an advocate who is engaged in conversation with the court than perfect prose from a reader. Read the transcripts from a few oral arguments (they are available on some legal research databases) and you will see that the argument is full of half-finished sentences and apparent lapses in grammar. This is because an oral argument is a conversation, not a speech.

Write your outline on full-sized paper rather than index cards, and use felt-tipped markers or large, bold-faced fonts to make your points easy to read. List your points in the order in which you plan to address them, and list supporting authorities under each point. You may want to write

---

[17] Williams, *supra* note 8, at 598

key words, or even the main 'phrases-that-pay' in bold-faced type across the top of the outline so that the words will jump out at you and remind you of your main contentions, even if you just glance at the page.

Some advocates create a case list, on which they list the name, citation, and relevant information (facts, reasoning, etc.) about each case. Creating such a list is a good idea, even if you never consult it during the argument. Both creating and studying the list provide excellent opportunities to help you to commit important information to memory.

13.5
PRESENTING THE ARGUMENT

13.5.1
INTRODUCTION

Although your introductory material should be short (often less than a minute, and always less than two minutes), the introduction fulfills several important functions. A good introduction should tell the court what is happening procedurally — who you are, who your client is, and what your client wants; it should provide sufficient factual context, it should outline the argument and tell the court why you are asking for the result that you seek, and it should grab the court's attention by focusing the court on your theme.

Traditionally, advocates begin their arguments by saying, "May it please the court," although "good afternoon, your honors" or any other respectful greeting will be acceptable to most judges.[18] Of course, you should review local rules to see if they require any particular opening, and, whenever possible, observe some arguments in that court before your debut so that you can learn the court's customs. In the United States Supreme Court, for example, advocates traditionally begin by addressing the Chief Justice directly, saying, "Mr. Chief Justice, and may it please the Court."

Your next task is to introduce yourself and your case. Judge Wiener recommends opening with "a short, simple introduction: tell the panel your name, the name of your client, your client's role in the appeal . . . and in the trial . . . but refrain from blowing a lot of 'smoke' at the court . . . [b]egin your presentation with a short, attention-getting 'simple and direct' introduction of the points you plan to make."[19] Judge Williams notes that the only uninterrupted time most oral advocates will have is at the beginning of the argument, and that they must use this time "to succinctly present the issue and explain to the court the most important

---

[18] Wiener, *supra* note 2, at 203.
[19] Wiener, *supra* note 2, at 201, 203.

reason why [they] should prevail. [They] may wish to use this time to give an outline of the points" to be covered during the argument.[20]

Many advocates spend too much time providing factual context. An oral argument does not have a formal "statement of the case" the way a brief does. You can presume that the court has read your brief and the joint appendix. The Internal Operating Procedures of the United States Court of Appeals for the Third Circuit, for example, require that briefs and appendices be "distributed sufficiently in advance to afford at least four (4) full weeks' study in chambers prior to the panel sitting." Internal Operating Procedures, U.S. Court of Appeals for the Third Circuit, 1.1 (2000). Rule 1.2 lays out the "Responsibility of Panel Prior to Scheduled Sitting," noting that "[t]his court has the tradition of carefully reading briefs and reviewing appendices prior to oral argument or conference."

Thus, you should spend only one or two sentences on the relevant facts. Ideally, the court should not even realize that you are laying out facts; if it does, it should do so only at the moment you move to your argument. Of course, later in the argument, you should discuss facts in detail as they relate to your points or in answering questions; in the introduction, however, you must be succinct.

Presenting a roadmap of the points you plan to cover has two advantages. First, it gives you at least one opportunity to make those points. With some "hot" courts, that opportunity may be the only one. Second, a roadmap provides the obvious benefit of telling the court the points you plan to address and the order in which you plan to address them. Some courts will let you proceed with your argument if you have named the points that the court is interested in; if you do not provide a roadmap, on the other hand, the judges may interrupt quickly to make sure that you discuss an issue that has provoked their interest. You should not state the points in your roadmap objectively (e.g., don't say, "first, I will address whether the statute passes the heightened scrutiny test"). Instead, state your points argumentatively and use the roadmap to explain why you are asking for the result you seek.

If you are the petitioner, you may wish to grab the court's attention in the manner in which you describe the case, or in your roadmap. Although you should not be overdramatic, you can be argumentative. If you are the respondent, you may wish to grab the court's attention by referring specifically to a question that one of the judges asked of the petitioner and explaining its significance to the case. There is no formula for what you should say in order to grab the court's attention. You must review your case and decide what aspect of the facts, the law, or your argument epitomizes the injustice you seek to have corrected. This is the time to tell the court the theme of your argument. Identify the common-sense reason why the court should decide the case in your favor.

The sample introduction below is from a petitioner's argument in *Mil-*

---

[20] Williams, *supra* note 8, at 598.

ler v. Albright. Note that the advocate introduces herself, asks for rebuttal time, tells the court what she is asking it to do, describes the case in practical terms, and outlines the points that she will address in the argument:

> May it please the Court, I am Glenda Gelzleichter, and I represent the petitioner, Ms. Lorelyn Penero Miller. At this time I would like to reserve three minutes for rebuttal. Ms. Miller, who was the plaintiff below, is asking this Court to reverse the decision of the United States Court of Appeals for the District of Columbia Circuit. That court upheld the constitutionality of 8 U.S.C. § 1409(a), which governs the citizenship of children born outside the United States to unmarried parents when only one of the parents has U.S. citizenship. Section 1409(a) distinguishes among these children based solely on the gender of the child's citizen parent.
>
> Section 1409(a) wrongly uses an irrebuttable gender stereotype to put a time limit on the relationship between a father and his children. This Court should find Section 1409(a) unconstitutional and reverse the decision below for two reasons. First, Section 1409's requirement that only fathers prove a close, personal relationship before their children can be declared citizens is premised on overbroad generalizations abut the relative capabilities of men and women, and thus violates the standard that this Court laid down in the VMI case just last year. Second, even if this Court should apply a less stringent test, Section 1409(a) is still unconstitutional because its concern with unreliable proof of paternity is neither facially legitimate nor rational in 1997.

In the second paragraph above, the writer has identified her broad themes: The statute should not use irrebuttable gender stereotypes, and it should not impose an arbitrary time limit. Her roadmap lays out the legal support behind these themes and tells the Court the order in which she plans to proceed.

The respondent need not ask for rebuttal time and can spend much less time introducing the case. Respondent should, however, strive to grab the court's attention by showing that he or she is "responsive" to the court's concerns. For example, a respondent representing the other side in the case of *Miller v Albright* might begin the argument like this:

> May it please the Court, I am Bradley Walent, and I am counsel for the respondent, Secretary of State Madeline Albright. A moment ago, Justice Vargo asked counsel for petitioner whether Section 1409(a) is or is not an immigration statute. Your honors, that question is at the very heart of this argument. This Court has consistently refused to interfere in Congress's decisions about immigration law, and this case is not the time to start. This Court should affirm the decision of the District of Columbia Court of Appeals precisely because Section 1409(a) *is* an immigration statute, and this Court has traditionally applied a deferential standard when reviewing federal immigration legislation. Furthermore, under that deferential standard, Section 1409(a) is facially legitimate, and it is rationally related to Congress's goal of promoting close, early family ties with U.S. relatives.

> **Identifying the Theme of Your Argument**
>
> Intermediate appellate courts must follow the mandatory authorities of the Court(s) above them, if any on-point authority governs the case. Courts of last resort, however, and intermediate appellate courts deciding cases of first impression, are more likely to consider the impact that their decision will have on real-world situations.
>
> Accordingly, you must know the common sense-reason behind what you are asking the Court to do. Why would a decision in your favor be fair or just? In the case of *Miller v. Albright*, counsel for the young woman seeking citizenship could focus on the inherent unfairness of gender stereotypes, or on the problems with imposing an arbitrary time limit on father-daughter relationships. Counsel for the government, on the other hand, might focus on Congress, and the importance of respecting Congress's decisions in certain limited areas of law.
>
> The theme is particularly important in oral argument. Having a theme in mind can help you keep the Court focused on the reason for a decision in your favor. Frequently, when questions have led you away from the point of your argument, you can recover by returning to your theme. This does not mean that you can avoid answering a question. Instead, answer the question, and then remind the Court of your theme. For example, if counsel for the government were asked about the irrebuttable gender stereotype in the statute, he or she could provide a substantive answer, but then say, e.g., "this Court has never examined this type of claim in an immigration statute, because the Court defers to Congress in this area."

Although the speaker did not use a traditional "first, second, third" road-map, his introduction revealed his theme (deference to Congress), the two points that he planned to make, and the order in which he planned to make them: first, he planned to address the requirement that the Court use a deferential standard; second ("furthermore"), he planned to explain what happens when that deferential standard is applied.

The introduction will take up only a small percentage of your argument time, but you should plan it carefully so that you can obtain optimal benefits.

13.5.2
THE ARGUMENT ITSELF

After you have finished the introduction, you should simply move to your first point. Do not wait for the court to tell you to go on. Although many advocates provide a full sentence of transition between introductory material and the argument, rarely is such a formal shift necessary. Instead of saying, "Now that I have laid out the issues, I will address the first of the three points of my outline," it is usually more effective to be briefer, e.g., "turning to the first issue . . ." or even "First. . . ." A shorter transition saves both time and the Court's patience.

If you have prepared effectively you can proceed to your first point, the rule governing it, the support for that rule (if needed), and the discussion of how that rule applies to the facts. Handling questions from the bench will be discussed in Section 13.6 below.

13.5.3
THE CONCLUSION

Although the court will often control the amount of time you spend talking about particular points, the good advocate is aware of the passage of time and tries to provide an effective conclusion to his or her argument. In many courts, a podium light system is used: A green light is displayed throughout most of the argument; a yellow light signals that time is running short (how short may vary from court to court — e.g., there may be two to five minutes remaining when the light turns on); and a red light signals that time is up. Counsel should never stop the court from asking questions in order to conclude. However, if the court is quiet, and the yellow light is on, counsel may decide to conclude rather than to launch into his or her final (and presumably weakest) point.

Like the conclusion to a brief, the conclusion to an oral argument should be short and sweet. At a minimum, it should tell the court what you want it to do with the decision below: affirm it, reverse it, or reverse and remand it. If more time is available, counsel may want to recap the main reasons that support his or her conclusion, as in the following conclusion that might be appropriate for petitioner in *Miller v. Albright*:

> Even in the area of immigration, Congress does not have the authority to pass a law that violates the Equal Protection Clause of the Constitution. Section 1409(a) denies equal protection to children of men who are U.S. citizens. Rather than promoting family ties between a father and a child, 1409(a) prevents those ties from developing further. For all of these reasons, this court should reverse the decision of the District of Columbia Court of Appeals. Thank you.

If you are still in conversation with the court when your time elapses, you must acknowledge that time has run out and ask for permission to continue. If the court is asking you a question when your time elapses, pay careful attention to the question and plan your answer. Before answering, however, inform the court that time is up and ask if you may have time to answer the question. Almost every court will give you permission. Unless you are asked still more questions, segue from your answer into your conclusion. Even if you have a strong, dramatic conclusion planned, do not use it if time has already elapsed, even if the court has given you permission to continue. This is the time to move to a one-sentence conclusion, e.g., "Therefore, because Section 1409(a) makes unconstitutional distinctions based on gender stereotypes, this Court should affirm the decision below. Thank you."[21]

---

[21] For more information on making your conclusion effective, see § 14.5.3 below.

13.6
HANDLING QUESTIONS FROM THE BENCH

All of the hard work that you have completed to prepare you for the argument should have one purpose: enabling you to answer the court's questions.[22] Some questions may be answered by your argument itself — that is, you will have anticipated the court's concerns — but many others will come up the old-fashioned way: The court will interrupt your presentation and demand your attention. How you handle these interruptions says everything about your skill as an oral advocate and may even determine whether you win or lose your case.

The first thing you must do is *let* the court interrupt you. As Justice Ginsburg has noted, some attorneys — foolishly — try to squelch the court's questions by talking louder and more quickly when a judge tries to speak:

> A race the lawyer is bound to lose is the press-straight-on run when a judge attempts to interject a question. More than occasionally, I have repeated a lawyer's name three times before he gives way to my inquiry. Despite his strong desire to continue orating, the lawyer should stop talking when the judge starts.[23]

Remember that your job is not to "get through your stuff." Instead, you are there to find out what the judges are interested in, and so you should stop talking immediately when one of them tries to reveal an area of interest by asking a question. Judge Williams has noted that, "[q]uestions are not interruptions, they are opportunities. The questions from the bench are the only indication of what issues are bothering the judges[,] and [the questions] may clue you in on what is preventing them from seeing the case your way."[24]

Thus, maintain eye contact so that you can see any nonverbal signals that one of the judges has a question. Speak slowly enough to allow the judges time to interject. If one of the judges makes the slightest noise or attempts to interrupt, you should stop speaking to give the judge a moment to ask a question. Use every technique possible to let the court know that you welcome their questions.

Do not presume that all questions will be hostile. Judges frequently "use" counsel to advance an argument that they already agree with, in hopes of gathering more votes. Justice Ginsburg admits that "[s]ometimes we ask questions with persuasion of our colleagues in mind, in an effort to assist counsel to strengthen a position."[25] Judge Williams advises that

---

[22] *See* Richard H. Seamon, *Preparing for Oral Argument in The United States Supreme Court*, 50 S.C. L. Rev. 603 (1999), for advice on preparing for oral argument primarily by anticipating and planning answers for the court's questions.

[23] Ginsburg, *supra* note 1, at 569.

[24] Williams, *supra* note 8, at 599.

[25] Ginsburg, *supra* note 1, at 569.

"you may encounter a judge who is in favor of your position and spends time asking you easy questions that lead you to an even stronger version of your position."[26]

Second, you must listen to the question. Do not rush to give an answer. Oral argument is not a quiz show, in which you must beat your opponent to the buzzer. Instead, listen carefully to make sure that you understand what the court is trying to do. Some questions ask for a concession. At other times, as noted above, a judge may try to advance your point of view by asking a question designed to reveal your best arguments. Some questions ask you to identify or explain a policy supporting your thesis, or seek information about a case or other authority. Some questions focus on the point you are addressing, while others show that the court has moved on to a new issue. Listen to the question, and assess what the court is asking before you try to answer.

If you do not understand the question, you should ask the court to clarify the question for you. Ideally, you should try to articulate what you think the court has asked, e.g., "I'm not sure that I understand your question, Judge Lowe. Are you asking whether this Court has ever invalidated an immigration statute?" Many questions occur to the court during the argument, and thus are asked in a rather rambling style. Few judges will take offense at being asked for clarification, as long as counsel does so in a respectful way.

Third, you should answer the question directly. Judge Williams recommends that advocates "[r]espond immediately to a question with a 'yes,' 'no,' 'it depends,' or 'I don't know.' "[27] Some advocates, perhaps fearful that a direct answer will reveal a weakness in the case, try to launch into an explanation of the significance of the answer before they give the answer itself. This tactic is a mistake, because the court doesn't hear the explanation; it hears only that counsel has refused to answer a direct question with a direct answer. Furthermore, you risk forgetting to answer the question directly or, more commonly, being interrupted before you can do so. The court will be much better able to listen to your explanation if you first satisfy the court's need for an answer to its question. Of course, it is very important that you *give* the explanation. Many attorneys refer to this kind of exchange as a "yes, but" answer. You must agree with the fact or legal rule that the court has laid before you, but you disagree as to its significance. It is perfectly appropriate to make a concession and then explain why that concession does not affect your argument.

Fourth, you should tie your answer to your argument. Judge Williams advises, "Follow your short answer with a concise explanation and citation to the record or precedent as necessary."[28] You must decide whether to return to the point you were making, or continue on to another point.

---

[26] Williams, *supra* note 8, at 599.
[27] *Id.*
[28] *Id.*

If the court has asked a question that moves you to your second issue while you were still addressing your first, for example, you may be wise to continue with other support for that second point. The court may have been signaling you that it is not interested in the first issue, either because it already agrees with you or because there is no way that it will ever agree with you. In either circumstance, time is better spent on an issue in which the court has shown its interest.

If the court has asked you about an issue that you believe is irrelevant to the case, you must still answer the question, if you are able. You may let the court know that you think the question is irrelevant by respectfully pointing out the fact, legal rule, or other information that shows that the resolution of your case does not require resolution of the issue that it asked about, e.g., "Yes, your honor, that is true. However, in this case, Officer O'Donnell testified that he had no reason to believe that Mr. Richardson was violating any laws when he conducted the search."

Similarly, do not dismiss hypothetical questions without an answer. Justice Ginsburg has expressed her dismay over advocates' repeated dismissals of hypothetical questions with the pat answer, "that is not this case, your honor": "[the judge] knows, of course, that her hypothetical is not this case, but she also knows the opinion she writes generally will affect more than this case. The precedent set may reach her hypothetical."[29] When judges pose hypotheticals, they are testing the boundaries of the rule you suggest. The good advocate knows the boundaries of the rule he or she recommends, and so is able to explain which hypotheticals will be governed by the new rule, and which will not.

13.7
REBUTTAL

Counsel for the petitioner should not reserve important *arguments* for rebuttal. Supreme Court Rule 28.5 provides that "counsel making the opening argument shall present the case fairly and completely and not reserve points of substance for rebuttal." In the United States Supreme Court, counsel may not *set aside* time for rebuttal; counsel can reserve time for rebuttal only by stemming the tide of the justices' questions before his or her allotted time has elapsed. Be sure you understand your own local rules as to rebuttal before the day of your argument.

Although final decisions about what to say in rebuttal must be made on the spot, there are some guidelines you can follow to make your rebuttal more effective. First, remember that rebuttal is for rebuttal only.[30] Any point you make on rebuttal should be a response to a point made by

---

[29] Ginsburg, *supra* note 1, at 569-70.
[30] *See, e.g.,* Wiener, *supra* note 2, at 199, 202.

counsel for the respondent. Many courts will interrupt counsel who try to use rebuttal to "finish up" the main argument, saying, "Counselor, do you have any rebuttal to offer?"

Second, even though you must use rebuttal to respond to statements that opposing counsel has made during the argument, you should prepare for rebuttal as you prepare your argument. You can reasonably anticipate many of the points that your opponent will make. In a moot court argument, you should identify the points to which you have a "clean" response — that is, a response that will not draw painful questions from the bench. In real life, of course, you should identify the points that are most crucial to your argument, for you must address those points even if they result in painful questions.

Plan ahead, even make an outline, and then, during the argument, note which points your opponent actually makes. You might even jot down a word or phrase from your opponent's presentation to make your point more effective, e.g., "Your honors, counsel for respondent stated that Ms. Miller's attempts to establish a relationship with her father were 'too little, too late.' This time limit on family relationships is precisely what is wrong with section 1409(a)."

Third, don't sweat the small stuff. Unless an otherwise small error has legal significance in your case, rebuttal is not the time to point out that your opponent has given the wrong year in a case citation, confused the parties' names, or made some other picayune error. Rebuttals of this type hurt the petitioner more than they do the respondent.

Finally, make your points and then sit down. While this advice holds true at all stages in the argument, it is particularly important on rebuttal. When you stand up to give your rebuttal, address the court and then tell it how many points you plan to make, e.g., "Your honors, I have two points on rebuttal. First, counsel for respondent stated. . . . This is irrelevant because. . . . Second, counsel cited. . . . That case does not apply here because. . . . Thank you."

Be aware that many courts do not listen passively to a rebuttal. Thus, you must be as prepared to answer questions during the rebuttal as you were during your main argument. It is important, therefore, to let the court know how many points you intend to make; courts that have this knowledge may allow you to make all of your points, even if they have used up your time with questions.

13.8
PUBLIC SPEAKING TIPS

This point appears last because the most important public speaking tips — don't read to the court, and maintain eye contact with the court — have already been made. The court is much more interested in the law and the facts of the case than it is in a professional oratorical style. That said, there are a few general pieces of advice that can help to make your presentation more effective.

First, speak loudly enough and slowly enough to be heard and understood. Visit the court before the day of your argument to find out what kind of amplification system, if any, is in use, and how effective it is. If you see several arguments in which the court is easily able to understand counsel who speak normally in front of a microphone that is six to eight inches from them, you can presume that you do not need to hold the microphone up to your lips in order to be understood. Make sure, however, to adjust the microphone so that it is pointing at your face, rather than your shirt front or the air above your head.

Second, avoid distracting gestures or other mannerisms. Most courts appreciate normal hand gestures. They are distracted, however, by both arms waving at once, or hands that go beyond the boundaries of the podium (e.g., pointing at the judges). Generally, it is good advice not to touch your face or your clothes; don't adjust your collar or tie, run your fingers through your hair, scratch your ear, or jingle the keys in your pockets. If you are unsure whether you have any of these mannerisms, ask a colleague to videotape a practice argument, and then run through it at high speed. Any overused mannerisms will become obvious.

Third, just as you should use sentence variety when writing, try to use vocal variety when speaking. Vary your tone of voice — don't speak in the monotone that the actor Ben Stein has made famous — and your speed. You can pause occasionally to let an important point sink in. Likewise, if a point is important, speaking slowly will draw the court's attention to it.

Finally, maintain a professional posture before, during, and after your time at the podium. While at the podium, stay *at the podium*. Most judges expect that the attorney will stand behind the podium for the entire argument, and recording systems presume that they will. Realize also that you are "on stage" even while you are at counsel's table, and act professionally there as well. Judge Wiener aptly illustrates the unprofessionalism of an attorney who overreacts to his or her opponent's argument:

> Don't "act out" while seated at the counsel table during your opponent's turn at the lectern. Most judges resent being distracted by seated counsel's body language and nonverbal comment — shaking or nodding your head, rolling your eyes, grimacing, squirming in your chair, and the like — in response to your opponent's remarks from the lectern or our questions from the bench. Just sit still and pay attention to opposing counsel and the court. Likewise, don't make a big production out of taking notes while your opponent is arguing. When you must look at your papers or take notes, do so unobtrusively and discreetly.[31]

Because your goal on oral argument is to convince the court to adopt your point of view, you must take pains at every stage of the argument to impress the court with your credibility and your professionalism.

---

[31] Wiener, *supra* note 2, at 205.

13.9
SUMMARY

All of this detailed advice may seem overwhelming to the new attorney, but it really boils down to a few points: Know what you're asking the court to do, and what the impact of its holding will be. Know the facts and authorities behind your case so that you can answer questions about it. Treat the oral argument like a conversation, let the court interrupt you, and be willing to answer all of the court's questions. Act professionally.

You should also know that the most common remarks I hear after a law student's first oral argument are (1) "they didn't even ask me about everything I know!" and (2) "I want to do that again."

You'll do fine.

MOOT COURT COMPETITIONS

Each year, dozens of interscholastic moot court competitions take place around the country. There are two reasons to participate in a competition: to learn and to win. Everyone who participates in a moot court competition learns a great deal about the subject matter at issue and quite a bit about the practice of law. Nevertheless, despite the many tangible and intangible benefits of learning for the sake of learning, most teams still want to win. If you are a team member on an interscholastic moot court team, this chapter is meant to help you to enhance your learning experience in the hopes that it may help you to win.

Appellate advocacy is about mastery. You must master the facts in the case so that you can research and write effectively. You must master the law at issue so that you can explain why the law dictates the result that you seek. Moot court competitions are about demonstrating your mastery of the law and the facts through the vehicles of briefs and oral arguments.

Like the writing process generally, moot court competitions are also about making decisions. You and your teammates may be able to decide which competition to join, or which side to argue. You will definitely have to decide how to divide your workload, how to assign the issues that the case presents, how to write the brief, and how to conduct the argument.

Like real practitioners, you will be able to seek advice, to greater or lesser degrees, from colleagues or mentors. Ultimately, however, you must decide which advice to take, and which advice to leave alone.

Every year, when I meet for the first time with my team, and when I judge practice arguments for other teams, I tell them that they must decide whether they agree with my advice or not. I explain my suggestions, but they will be the ones at the podium during the competition. No matter whose advice they follow, they may well be victims of what I call "pet peeve-itis": Someone will deduct points from their score because they did or did not do something that happened to be a pet peeve of one of the judges. Therefore, they must sift through the often conflicting advice they will receive from the many people who judge their practice arguments and decide which advice best fits their theory of the case and their performance style.[1]

Since law practice is full of real-life decision making, one of the many benefits of moot court competitions is that they give students practice in making decisions in a context in which there will be real consequences: their victory or defeat in an argument round. The information in this book is meant to help you make those decisions, but it is *advice*. Only you and your teammates can decide how to use this advice.

14.1
TYPICAL COMPETITION REQUIREMENTS

The typical moot court competition requires a team of two or more students to complete a brief and participate in a series of oral arguments. Competitors are usually provided a record of some kind, with varying amounts of factual and procedural information (e.g., depositions or affidavits, stipulations, complaints) and complete or excerpted "decisions below." They must then write a brief and file it with the competition by a date certain. Many competitions also require teams to file copies with the host of the competition and all of their potential opponents. Then, after some time to allow for practice arguments and for scoring of the briefs by the competition's representatives, the teams gather for oral argument rounds.

Unlike real-life attorneys, students in moot court competitions often argue both sides of the case, although they usually complete only one brief. The score in each round is typically based on a combination of the team's brief score and oral argument score. In real life, the brief usually has much more impact than the oral argument, but in most moot court competitions the oral argument is worth a higher percentage of the score.

---

[1] *See also* Sanford N. Greenberg, *Appellate Advocacy Competitions: Let's Loosen Some Restrictions on Faculty Assistance*, 49 J. Leg. Educ. 545, 555 (1999).

That said, however, the brief score is often dispositive: if the brief scores are spread over a broad range, in a close oral argument the team with the higher brief score will win.

The requirements as to faculty participation vary; usually, the amount of outside help the students may receive during the briefing process is more limited than the help available after the brief is turned in. Sadly, some competitions even limit the amount of help students may receive during practice arguments. For many students, the learning that takes place during these practice arguments is invaluable. They learn not only about their own case, but also, by listening to the stories the practice argument judges tell about their real-life experience with cases of this type, they learn much about the practice of law. Thus, if you have a choice as to which competitions your school may enter, or as to which team you wish to try out for, you may want to review the rules of the competitions you are interested in or talk to the coaches to see which competition's rules will give you the best possible experience.

Once you are on a team, your first task on receiving the materials for the competition should be to read the rules with a highlighter. In addition to typeface and page limit requirements, you should note requirements as to (1) the type of assistance that may be given, and (2) when that assistance may be given. A typical requirement is that no assistance may be given until after the brief has been submitted.

Do not rely on your coach to read the rules for you. You are the one who will be competing, and you must know the rules intimately. They are your "rules of civil procedure" for the competition, and you need to be aware of how they operate. Of course, you can consult your coach to answer questions or to decide if it is necessary to ask the competition administrator to interpret a rule. But you, as a team member, must take ultimate responsibility for your role in the competition.

14.2
DIFFERENCES BETWEEN MOOT COURT COMPETITIONS AND "REAL LIFE"

Although moot court competitions are meant to simulate real-life legal issues, no simulation experience can perfectly replicate real life. First, both your procedural facts and the client's case facts are limited to what you have been given. If your research reveals an issue that would be affected by a fact that has inadvertently been left out of the "record," you cannot do more investigation to discover that fact, as you would in real life. The best you can do is make a realistic assumption based on other facts in the record, and include that presumption in your argument (e.g., "Presuming that Ms. Johnson had graduated from high school. . . ."). Naturally, you should *not* make presumptions that will significantly affect the issues in the case. (e.g., "Presuming that the police did not provide Mr. Smith with valid *Miranda* warnings. . . ."). If a fact gap could create or dispose of a significant issue, you should contact the competition administrator as soon as possible so that he or she can issue a clarifying memorandum to all of the competitors.

Second, in a moot court competition, there are some expectations about what you will argue and what you will not argue. Many competitions provide the parties with the questions presented; others will include a grant of certiorari that allows the parties to argue "all issues fairly raised by the record," but will include a lower court opinion that clearly identifies two major issues.

Finally, in a moot court competition style is often as important as substance. It is not *more* important — most judges will notice significant misstatements of the law — but it has a much larger role in moot courts than it does in real life. In real life, the law and the facts will usually dictate the outcome even though oratorical style may play a role in some extremely close cases. In moot court competitions, in contrast, the substantive points are earned not based on which side has the *better* substance, but on which side is best-acquainted with the substantive arguments in the case, and which side can best express themselves to the court when explaining that substance. Since most students become fairly well acquainted with the legal issues that the case presents, the only significant distinctions between some competitors may be style differences.

I should stress at this point that not all students need to aim for the *same* style. Over my many years of judging and coaching moot court competitions, I have seen several different effective styles. Students who speak softly (but loudly enough to be heard) can be as effective as students who speak loudly; students who gesture can be as effective as more sedate students. The main points of an effective style — maintaining eye contact, speaking loudly enough to be heard, listening when the court speaks, answering questions directly, supporting answers with reference to law and facts, and integrating answers into the argument — work with many different kinds of speaking styles.

14.3
CHOOSING WHICH SIDE TO BRIEF

If your school sends two teams to a particular competition, the rules usually dictate that one team must act as petitioner and one team must act as respondent. In that case, your choice of side will probably depend on a coin flip or some other arbitrary method. If your school sends only one team, however, you may be allowed to choose which side of the case to brief. Because you will be arguing both sides of the case at the competition, make this decision based mainly on how it relates to the brief. Presuming that there is no deadline for your decision (other than the brief deadline), you may want to begin researching and writing based on your gut instinct, but allow yourself to change sides if you later decide that the other side would be better.

Do not agonize too much over this decision, because you cannot control how the judges will react to each side of the case. If the judges think that one side is much easier than the other, they may consciously or unconsciously award more points to what they perceive to be the most challenging side. On the other hand, if the judges are not overly perceptive of the relative difficulties of the two sides, they may award more points to the briefs that seemed to make the better arguments. Thus, you should choose the side that you think will allow you to write the better brief. If you think you have chosen the easier side, be careful. Do not fall into the trap of failing to adequately brief issues because they seem "easy" or "obvious" to you.

14.4
WRITING THE BRIEF

The research, organization, and writing guidance throughout this book applies to any appellate brief. In a moot court competition, however, you will be working collaboratively, and so other issues may arise. Most moot court competitions allow three students on a team. Some schools choose to have one person write the brief and the other two argue, but I do not recommend this structure. While it may make for an easier writing process, I believe that the final product is usually better if all three team members participate. More importantly, all three team members learn much more about their case, and about writing and oral argument, when all three participate in both writing the brief and arguing the case.

14.4.1
DIVIDING UP THE WORK

Because research and writing are parts of the analytical process necessary to fully understand the issues in a case, the people doing the arguing will be better prepared if they participate in the writing process. No less an authority than Chief Justice Rehnquist has noted the importance of the oral advocate's participation in the drafting of the brief:

> The questions you get in an oral argument are often ones that are not squarely covered in the brief — indeed that is probably the reason for the question from the bench. So an advocate who has not gone beneath the surface of the brief to understand how its parts fit together into a coherent

> argument will be at a considerable disadvantage. Even an advocate who
> has all but memorized the brief will be at this kind of disadvantage, if he
> has done no more than memorize it.[2]

Thus, if you are the one who conducted research, chose some cases to
include in your argument and rejected others, and hammered out the
analysis, you will be much better able to understand and respond to the
questions from the bench. If you must argue an issue that you did not
brief, try to read more than the cases that are cited in the brief. Get to
know the area of the law thoroughly, so you can explain why certain
authorities are relevant or irrelevant.

There is no one best way for two or three people to collaborate on
writing a brief. Since revising and polishing should be team efforts, the
first decision to be made is how to complete the first draft. Some teams
divide up the two major issues — giving two of the team members one
issue each, and then having the third member handle the "extras" such
as the statement of the case, the summary of the argument, the table of
contents, and other format requirements. If one of the two issues is much
more challenging than the other, however, you may wish to divide that
issue between two people, have the third person handle the second issue,
and collaborate on the extras.

The most demanding method, and perhaps the most effective, would
be to have all three team members conduct separate initial research on
both issues with a short deadline. At that time, the team could meet and
discuss the issues. Since three heads are better than one, this method
would make best use of the intellectual strengths of all three team members. After the meeting, the team members could decide how best to divide up the continued research and the drafting of the arguments, and
each writer would have the benefit of input from the other team mem-
ber(s).

Even at this early stage of the writing process, it is important that you
have a specific understanding of length and typeface requirements. For
example, it wastes time to draft in Times Roman font if your final draft
must be in Courier font. Similarly, if your competition requires that your
citations follow ALWD format, you should make sure that all of the citations are in that format from the very beginning. Find out the specific
requirements of your competition, and write with those in mind from the
start. Recording necessary citation information as you take your notes,
and observing length limitations from early in your writing process, will
help to prevent last-minute editing crises.

Completing multiple drafts guarantees a higher quality product.
Whatever method is used to divide up the work, it is important to have
a date certain for the first draft to be completed. Even if your faculty
advisor cannot critique your brief before it is filed, he or she can require

---

[2] William H. Rehnquist, *From Webster to Word-Processing: The Ascendance of the Appellate Brief*,
1 J. App. Prac. & Process 1, 5 (1999).

you to turn in drafts at certain times during the time allotted for writing. Decide how and when you are going to work together on critiquing the drafts.

14.4.2
CRITIQUING YOUR TEAMMATES' WORK

Often, teams that have begun the competition with much good will fall apart at the critiquing stage. Either their work doesn't progress because they don't meet regularly, or they are angered by the "stupidity" or the "rudeness" of their teammates. Do not let your desire to win the competition rob you of your basic good manners and civility. Remember that you will have to work with colleagues in this way when you practice law, and that you must treat them politely if you wish to keep your job. Treat your teammates with that same respect.

First, you must decide how to conduct your critiques. Some team members trade briefs and read each others' work separately, trading written comments with each other. Some teams find it more efficient to meet together and review each team member's contribution as a group. A combination of these two approaches may be best. If the team members exchange their work and review it separately, someone with questions about the law or the facts may review the record or research a narrow point in order to answer the question before the team meets. This is much more efficient than interrupting the discussion to hop on line or run to get a book (although you may end up doing this anyway, as the critique progresses).

Second, you must decide when to conduct your critiques. Plan ahead, and be aware of each team member's needs. While many teams are comfortable with the "all-nighter" method of collaboration, do not presume that this method will work for every member of the team. If one team member is on law journal and has another deadline during the brief-writing time, plan around that date. If another team member has family responsibilities, plan to meet during the day if at all possible.

Finally, you must conduct the actual critiques with tact and respect. In practice, you will often be asked to critique the work of others (as well as deal with critiques of your own work). Start now to act like a professional. Some of the advice here is obvious. Avoid words with extreme negative connotations, such as "wrong," "stupid," etc. Your critiques will be easier to take — and will accomplish more — if they presume the writer is intelligent, but that you are having trouble understanding something.

Try to ask questions and to have your questions be as specific as possible about what is confusing you. Instead of saying "this argument is wrong," ask, "how does this argument support a reversal?" Hearing your teammate's explanation may convince you of the validity of the argument and may inform all of you as to what further information needs to be included in the brief. On the other hand, if the argument is not valid, your teammate may recognize its weakness himself or herself when trying to explain it to you. By talking each argument out among the three of you, the team can get a good idea of the strengths and weaknesses of the various arguments, and revise accordingly.

Although you must be polite to each other, you also have an obligation to raise issues that are bothering you. Effective collaboration is a balancing act. Each member of the team must feel comfortable raising questions about anything that is troubling. Once, after a competition, I was discussing an issue that I thought had not been briefed effectively with one of the team members. He told me that he, too, had seen the problem, but was self-conscious about raising it, since "the other two seemed to think everything was okay." Each team member has a responsibility to point out possible problems or mistakes. That is the best way to get the full benefit of three collaborators working on a brief.

On the other hand, you cannot beat an issue to death. After the team has fully considered a problem or concern and decided what action to take (or not to take), that should be the end of it. Even if you disagree with the outcome, don't sulk, and don't second-guess. Once the decision is made, it's over, unless new "evidence" appears.

14.4.3
POLISHING THE BRIEF

Particularly if you are not allowed to seek faculty assistance, you must work hard to see the brief through others' eyes as you edit and polish. Imagine that your most demanding law professor is reading the brief. What would he or she say? Where would he or she find weaknesses, unsupported arguments, or inadequate analysis? When you are proofreading, imagine your most demanding editor — perhaps a parent, a legal writing professor, or a significant other.

The polishing advice given in Chapter Twelve applies here, but in some ways perfection is even more important for a moot court brief than for any *one* professional brief. While your reputation will suffer over the long term if you consistently have small errors in your briefs, it would be extremely unusual for you to lose a case because of typographical errors, wrong font size, or some other minor error (of course, remember that cases can and have been dismissed because counsel missed deadlines or violated other more significant "format" rules of the court). In a moot court competition, in contrast, a few points off for citation form errors or for using the wrong font size can mean the difference between victory and defeat in a close round.

Thus, take care with your proofreading. Be sure to leave enough time to allow you to reprint the brief after correcting errors. Also, be sure to read the brief from beginning to end, from the docket number to the certificate of service.

14.5
PRACTICE ARGUMENTS

Hold as many practice arguments as you can. Practice arguments do two things: First, they teach you about your case by presenting new questions to you and giving you a chance to consider your answers. Second, they give you needed practice to polish your performance for the competition.

Ideally, your practice arguments should begin well before you complete your brief. Although most rules prohibit, or at least limit, coaching during the brief-writing process, nothing prevents the three members of a team from conducting an "internal moot." Review the authorities relevant to your teammates' issues, and grill each of them in turn. Challenge the assumptions inherent in their arguments, and probe their knowledge of the relevant authorities. You could even spur their research by asking about the existence of other relevant cases, e.g., "Is there any case in which the court has held . . . ?" Besides the obvious substantive benefits, an internal moot can help the team to rev up the sometimes dry process of churning out the brief.

As for practice arguments after the brief has been turned in, recruit as many judges as you can beg, borrow, or steal. The more different judges you have, the more different questions you will be exposed to, and the less frequently you will face an unexpected question at the competition. At each practice, one of the team members not at the podium should be assigned the task of recording all of the questions that are asked. The team can study them later to identify questions that require more research or thought. Furthermore, you will discover which questions are the most common, and you can take the time to develop strong answers to those questions you will almost certainly be asked.

The typical format for a practice argument is to treat it like a regular moot court: to time it in the way that it will be timed at the competition and to hold a critique after the argument. This format will be fine for most of your practices. For at least some practices, however — perhaps those with just your coach acting as judge — you may want to break the mold. If you get a question that stumps you, stop the clock and talk it out. Confer with your teammates or your coach as to the best way to handle the question. If you think you need to do more research, jot down ideas to help you get started.

Although in real life judges do not particularly care about diction, an advocate whose arguments are easier to understand will score more points than one who struggles to put his or her thoughts into words. If you have a good answer but cannot phrase it effectively, stop and take the time to figure out the best way to make your point. Strong subject-verb combinations and concrete language are even more important to easy comprehension in oral argument than they are in writing. Instead of saying, e.g., "The concerns over officer safety that justified the search incident to an arrest also justified the lesser intrusion presented by the issuance of a citation," say, "The search was justified because police officers are in as much danger when they give a driver a ticket as when they put a driver under arrest."

In addition to planning how you will answer questions, you should use your practice arguments to practice for "positions of emphasis" in the oral argument: The Introduction and the Conclusion. In addition, plan how to deal with predictable problems, like a cold court or your opponent's misstatements.

14.5.1
The Introduction

Because virtually every moot court competition features two oralists on each team, the first speaker on each team faces another challenge. Instead of the usual introduction, he or she must introduce the case and explain which issues each team member will address. Doing so is courteous, for it helps the court to understand how things are organized. It is also smart, because it reduces the chances that one team member will be asked about another's issues.

There are two common ways to present your introduction. The first method is the objective method:

> "May it please the court. My name is Jennifer Manion, and along with my co-counsel, Stephen Webb, I represent the Petitioners, Stitt & Gallagher, Inc. At this time I would like to reserve two minutes for rebuttal. Your honors, we are asking this court to reverse the decision of the Eighteenth Circuit Court of Appeals, which held that Stitt & Gallagher violated Mr. Jasiunas's constitutional rights when it fired him. I will be addressing the privacy issue, and Mr. Webb will be addressing the issue of the applicability of the <u>McGuffin</u> test. [pause] Your honors, Stitt & Gallagher, Inc., did not violate Mr. Jasiunas's right to privacy when it dismissed him because of the contents of his e-mail messages. . . ."

On the other hand, you could deliver the same information in a more argumentative style:

> "May it please the court. My name is Jennifer Manion, and along with my co-counsel, Stephen Webb, I represent the Petitioners, Stitt & Gallagher, Inc. At this time I would like to reserve two minutes for rebuttal. Your honors, this court should reverse the decision of the Eighteenth Circuit Court of Appeals for two reasons. The first reason,

which I will explain, is that Stitt & Gallagher, Inc., did not violate Mr. Jasiunas's right to privacy when it dismissed him because of the contents of his e-mail messages. The second reason, which Mr. Webb will explain, is that plaintiffs such as the Respondent are not entitled to recover under the <u>McGuffin</u> test. [pause] Your honors, the Respondent has no privacy right in e-mails that he sends on company time.

Although both introductions do the job and get the message across, the second example is more argumentative and may be seen as more persuasive. You must identify the introduction that works best for you.

14.5.2
PLANNING FOR AWKWARD MOMENTS

a. The Cold Court

Most practice arguments are before "hot" courts, that are well prepared and pepper the team with questions. You should also practice, however, for a cold court. In real life, a cold court is not a problem. You can make the points you think are most important and sit down, even if only a few minutes of your time has elapsed. In a competition setting, however, a quiet court is a problem; you will have less of a chance to demonstrate your vast knowledge of the case and its governing authorities. Further, some competitions require that you spend at least ten minutes of your time at the podium, and deduct points if you fail to do so. Thus, during your practice arguments, figure out what to do if you have a panel that has nothing to say to you.

Essentially, you must impress every panel with your skill as an orator and your knowledge of the law. If you have a quiet panel, the first thing to do is to slow the pace of your speech. While many advocates could benefit by speaking more slowly, talking too fast is even more of a problem with a quiet court. If you are talking quickly, you are going through your material quickly, and you may not have enough to say to use up the minimum time required. Also, if you talk more slowly, you provide more opportunities for the judges to interrupt you. On a silent panel, the judges may be too intimidated by their own silence to break into a rat-a-tat delivery. If you pause fairly often — but not so often as to be noticeable — a judge may venture into the breach with a question.

Second, you must develop a strategy for impressing the quiet court. You impress a hot court when the judges ask you tough questions and you answer them. But how do you impress a court that won't ask you any tough questions? One method is to go out of your way to refer to authority for the legal propositions you state. Give details from the cases that show why they support your assertions. Cite to the record whenever you mention a particularly significant fact.

Another way to impress a quiet court is to "ask yourself" the tough questions. In your practice rounds, identify any apparently tough questions for which you have a strong answer. Keep those questions in mind for when you have a quiet court. For example, let's say that one of your practice judges asked, "Won't allowing foreign-born children to establish parentage at any time discourage early bonds between fathers and children?" You could "ask yourself" that question by stating, "Allowing foreign-born children to establish parentage at any time will not discourage early bonds between fathers and children. First, as this Court noted in McGuffin. . . ."

Some advocates try to wake up a quiet court by making bombastic statements in the hope that someone on the court will rise to the bait and challenge the assertion. While this technique may loosen the logjam if it succeeds, it is a risky proposition. If no one challenges your assertion, you may end up sounding foolish or ignorant.

b. Dealing with Opponents' Misstatements of Law or Facts

Oral arguments serve a different purpose in moot courts than in real life. In real life, as noted above, judges often read the briefs before the argument and form a rebuttable presumption as to how the case will turn out. They will often question the attorneys about specific points made in the briefs, and attorneys may challenge specific points that the other party has made in a brief.

Furthermore, in real life the oral argument is only a small part of the decision-making process. After the oral argument, the judges may cast an initial vote on the outcome of the case and justify that decision with a written opinion. Claims made in the oral argument or the brief will be tested by the research and analysis of the judges and their clerks. Finally, a majority opinion and, perhaps, concurring or dissenting opinions, will convey the court's decision on the issue.

In a moot court argument, on the other hand, the judges have often not seen any briefs in the case; they are relying only on the record and on bench materials. They may question counsel on very narrow points of law, but they cannot challenge specific statements that appeared in the briefs. Furthermore, the oral argument ends the decision-making process. The brief will have received a score earlier, and that score will be combined with a score that the judges give on the spot, right after the argument. If either side makes claims about the law or the facts, those claims will be evaluated immediately, without reference to cases cited, or, most likely, the record (even though judges will usually have the record with them).

This difference between moot courts and real arguments makes detailed mastery of the law and the facts even more important for moot courts than for real life arguments. In real life, if your opponent innocently misstates a fact or misinterprets the meaning of a case, there is a good chance that the error will be discovered during the decision-making process, and that your opponent's misstatement will have no impact on the decision. In a moot court, however, if the two sides contradict each other as to the facts or the law, the judges must make a decision on the spot as to which one is to be believed. Some students try to prevail in this battle merely by contradicting their opponents, sometimes forcefully. I believe that the best signals of credibility are citations to the record or the opinions at issue.

Thus, if your opponent mistakenly mischaracterizes a fact that is crucial to the argument, you can best correct it — professionally and politely — with a citation to the record:

> Counsel for the respondent stated that the arrest occurred at 6:45 P.M. While that is true, that is not the crux of petitioner's argument. If I may direct the court's attention to page three of the record; on that page, in the second paragraph, Officer Perek explicitly stated that defendant was "taken into custody" after church "that morning." This is the time when Miranda warnings should have been given.

If your opponent mischaracterizes an authority case, your best bet is to counter that characterization with language from the opinion that shows that your interpretation is the correct one:

> Counsel for the petitioner has said that the McGuffin Court limited the impact of Miranda to the time after "arrest." This is inaccurate. On page 372 of the decision, the McGuffin Court specifically noted that Miranda warnings must be given not only upon arrest, but before any custodial interrogation.

At first glance, memorizing specific page numbers may seem to be a daunting task. However, you will discover that throughout your practices, you are memorizing many "sound bites" about the facts and authorities relevant to your case. Get in the habit of including the page number when you talk about these elements. After all, the page number is just one more word to remember, and its benefits in credibility are worth the slight cost of brainpower. Of course, you must decide whether your performance arguments should include page numbers every time you mention a crucial fact, or a crucial point from an authority case. While the specific page numbers can be effectively used to contradict an opponent's misstatement of the law or the facts, using them throughout the argument can look like showboating. On the other hand, some judges are duly impressed by counsel's ability to provide such specific support for statements about the law and the facts.

Keep in mind that, although citations to cases are unusual in real life, citations to the record are not. If you have had the opportunity to observe more than a couple of oral arguments, you have probably seen a judge ask counsel where a particular fact can be found in the record. Upon receiving the answer, most judges turn to the page to start reviewing the facts immediately. Thus, memorizing certain page numbers can be a skill worth developing.

Perhaps the best way to prepare for this situation is to make a "cheat sheet" for both the law and the facts. Make a chart of the most significant facts, and note their location in the record. Similarly, identify the two or three cases that are most significant to each argument, and identify a statement from the case that crystallizes the point you are using the case to make. Doing so will help you to learn the law and the facts, and will give you a ready reference to take to the podium if needed.

14.5.3
THE CONCLUSION

Although the argument's conclusion may take less than a minute of your time, it is important to do it right because it represents the last impression that the court will have of you. To make life more interesting, your conclusion should be structured differently depending on what is happening when your time runs out or is about to run out. Your first job is to be aware of your time. At the competition, talk to the bailiff before the round, and make sure that he or she is sitting where you can see the time cards. If the bailiff is planning to sit in an inconvenient place, don't be shy about asking for a change in seating arrangements. The whole purpose of keeping time is for the participants and the judges to know how much time has elapsed.

Second, during the argument, pay attention to the time cards. In real life, many courts give extra time at the podium only grudgingly; in some courts, your microphone will be turned off when time elapses. You *must acknowledge the end of your time* when your time elapses and ask the court's permission if you wish to continue speaking. You should plan ahead and have a few different "exit strategies" planned for the various possible scenarios.

First, you may have a quiet panel. In this case, after you see the two-minute card (or a while after you have seen the five-minute card), transition into a rather lengthy conclusion. State your two or three best points affirmatively, and then say "for these reasons, this court should affirm [or reverse] the decision below. Thank you."

Second, you may have a panel that keeps you frantically answering questions every minute of your time. If you have lost track of your time and see the "stop" card as you pause after answering a question, *don't* go into a lengthy formal conclusion. I have seen too many oralists stop a stirring colloquy to turn to a wooden, obviously prefabricated conclusion. If you are surprised by the "stop" card, you may simply say, "I see that my time is up. Thank you." If you are a little braver, *most* courts will let you get away with a little more: "I see that my time is up. We ask that the court affirm [or reverse] the decision below. Thank you." Do not presume that you must end by asking for relief. As long as you have asked for it at some point in your argument, it is perfectly appropriate — and often effective — to end with a simple "thank you."

A sidebar on handling an active court — saying the words "in conclusion" will cause many courts to stop paying attention and look to their score sheets. While this is generally not advised, it may be helpful if you have a relentless court. Saying "in conclusion" (when you see that you have only a minute or so left) may quiet the court enough to allow you to end on a strong point. In the alternative, one of my moot court team members used to see the two-minute sign and then say "I see that my time grows short." This always made the judges sit up and take notice of the time, and often, they relaxed and let him finish the argument in peace.

Third, you may be in the middle of answering a question, or the court may be in the middle of asking a question, when the time elapses. If the court is talking, wait until the question is asked before noting the end of your time. If you are speaking, stop immediately. In each case, say, "I see that my time is up. May I answer [or finish answering] your question?" Almost every court will allow you to answer. I do *not* recommend asking for time to conclude in this situation. Instead, finish your answer with a few words that encompass one of your assertions, and then segue to a brief "and therefore, this court should reverse the decision below."

14.6
PROFESSIONALISM

Naturally, you will treat the court and your opponents with respect at all times. You may certainly address a judge as "your honor," but it is more realistic, and more effective, to use names. Ask the bailiff if there will be name plates, or if he or she can tell you who will be sitting where. Of course, it is much better to call a judge "your honor" than to use the wrong name; one of the counsel for the Florida Secretary of State provided an unintended moment of levity during the 2000 election oral arguments by addressing Justice Stevens — twice — as "Justice Brennan." Justice Brennan had retired from the bench in 1990 and died in 1997.

You should dress professionally, as well. My general guideline is to dress as if you are interviewing for an important job. Unfortunately, your choices are rather limited; men are expected to wear conservative colors, with no distracting accessories. Long hair on a man, a pant suit on a woman, or a pierced tongue or lip on anyone, may be frowned upon. You may decide that this personal choice is important to you, and so you may go ahead and wear the pants or forgo the haircut. As long as you look professional, most reasonable judges will not change your score for this type of choice. Some judges may want to discuss your appearance during the critique. If this happens, listen respectfully, thank the judge for his or her opinion, and then continue to make your own decisions. This advice holds true for the entire critique. Polite disagreement is appropriate, and you may certainly ask a question to clarify advice that a judge gives you, but it is both unprofessional and fruitless to argue with the court on a point of law or a method of presentation.

Finally, you must deal with your opponents professionally. Before the argument, it is courteous to introduce yourself, shake hands, and wish them luck. After the round, you should shake hands again and congratulate your opponents before conducting any private post-mortems with your coach or teammates.

Whatever the result of the round, accept the news with dignity. If you win, don't high-five your teammates or shoot your fist into the air. If you lose, don't lay your head on the table (as I have seen people do!). Again, shake hands with your opponents, congratulate them on a job well done, and wish them luck or accept their good wishes, as appropriate.

Through my many years of coaching I, alone, have gained the unique insight that *people do not like to lose*. In every competition, every team but one has to lose at some point. It is all right to feel bad when you lose a round or are eliminated from a competition. But don't get carried away. Don't berate yourself, your teammates, or your coach. Some post-mortem analysis is to be expected, and may be helpful, but post-mortems are best in moderation. Especially if you lose in a preliminary round, don't let it knock you for a loop, for you may still advance in the tournament. If you get too upset over an early loss, however, you may hurt your performance in a later round, and ensure your elimination from the competition.

14.7
SUMMARY

Even though moot court competitions do not replicate the practice of law, participating gives you practice in collaboration and decision making as well as in legal writing and oral argument. If you win, be grateful and excited; savor the moment. If you lose, give thanks that this is *moot* court. In any case, take full advantage of the learning opportunities that the competition presents.

For Reference: Citation Form and Punctuation Information

Because even lawyers still make grammatical and citation form mistakes, this appendix provides basic information about these pesky problems. Review it now, and keep it handy when you are polishing your final draft.

A.1
Putting Citations in Their Place

Sections A.1 to A.4 will address four basic concerns about citations: (1) when to cite and not to cite, (2) information to include in "long-form" and "short form" citations, (3) how to adjust your sentence structure to accommodate citation form, and (4) statutory citations.

A.1.1
When to Cite

There are four common occasions that call for a citation:

(1) When you are either **quoting** or **paraphrasing** language from another source, you must cite the source of the language.

(2) When you state a legal proposition, you must cite to authority for that proposition. This rule applies even when the legal proposition could be part of a lawyer's general knowledge. In a formal document, all legal propositions must be supported by a citation to authority, preferably authority from the controlling jurisdiction.

(3) The first time you tell the reader about an authority — whether by quoting language from it, by paraphrasing a summary of it, or by referring to it generally — you must cite to that authority in full.

(4) *Each time* you tell the reader — through a quote or a paraphrase — what a court held, found, reasoned, decided, or stated, you must cite to the page to which you refer.

A.1.2
WHEN NOT TO CITE

Naturally, there are many times when you need not cite to an authority. There are two occasions, however, that present dilemmas to many legal writers.

(1) You usually don't cite to authority within the summary of the argument, within point headings, and within a question presented even though you might be stating legal propositions here. Of course, there are exceptions to this guideline, as well.

(2) When you are comparing the facts of your case to the facts of an authority case that you have already introduced and explained within the same general discussion, you usually don't need to cite to the authority again. Citations are also omitted when you refer to a common-law rule that you've already cited, e.g., "Thus, the rule in McGuffin should apply in this case."

A.2
COMMON CASE CITATION FORMATS

A.2.1
LONG FORM

The guidelines below are based on both ALWD and Bluebook citation rules.[1] ALWD Rule 12.1 illustrates "full citation" or "long form." The typical long-form case citation includes five elements:

(1) **The case name.** (See ALWD Rule 12.2 or Bluebook Rule 10.2.1.) For most cases, the name of the case consists of one name on each side

---

[1] For complete ALWD guidelines, consult Darby Dickerson, *The ALWD Citation Manual* (Aspen, 2000). For complete Bluebook guidelines, consult *The Bluebook: A Uniform System of Citation* (The Harvard Law Review Association, 17th ed. 2000).

of the "v." Do not use a party's first name (unless it is part of a corporate party name, e.g., "Larry King, Inc.") and do not use more than one name, even if there are multiple plaintiffs and defendants. To use abbreviations precisely, consult ALWD Rule 12.2(e) and Appendix 3 or Bluebook Rule 10.2.2. Never abbreviate the first word in a party name; never use *et al.* in a citation. Case names should be underlined or italicized. Some writers mistakenly underline or italicize an entire citation, whether to a case or a statute, because they have seen entire citations underlined in hypertext or a website or another on-line resource. Statutory citations are *never* italicized or underlined; in cases, *only* the case name (e.g., "*Smith v. Jones*") should be italicized or underlined. Because the eye is drawn to underlined words but not to italicized words, I recommend underlining.

(2) **Where the case and the information cited to can be found.** (See ALWD Rules 12.3-12.5 and Appendix 1, and Bluebook Rule 10.3.1 and P.3 and Table T.1, regarding which reporters to cite.) This element is the most important part of the citation for a reader who is actually looking up a case that you've cited. Provide the volume of the reporter, the designated reporter abbreviation, and the page on which the case begins.

(3) **The pinpoint citation.** (See ALWD rule 12.5.) With every cite, you should include the specific page to which you are citing ("pinpoint cite"). Although it is tempting not to bother with the pinpoint cite, realize that you may be frustrating or angering a busy clerk when you leave it out. Some writers tell themselves that pinpoints are unnecessary because they are just citing to the case "generally." This excuse is usually a cop out. In almost every situation, you are at least citing to the case's holding. Make the clerk's life easier — and increase the chance that the judge will agree that the case stands for the point you say it does — by providing pinpoints that take the clerk to the parts of the case that prove your argument.

In some jurisdictions, you will be asked to provide "parallel cites," that is, citations to two different reporters that contain the same case. Although providing parallel citations is not fun for the writer, take it seriously if it is required. If you don't, you can bet that one of your readers will. ALWD Rule 12.4(c) addresses parallel citations.

(4) **The year of decision.** (ALWD Rule 12.7, Bluebook Rule 10.5.) This element is the simplest; simply put the year of the decision into parentheses. Even readers who aren't fussy about minor citation form errors care deeply when you leave the date of decision out of a long-form citation. Because the date of a decision affects its current validity, readers always want to know the year in which authority cases were decided.

(5) **Which court decided the case.** (ALWD Rule 12.6, Bluebook Rule 10.4.) If the reporter title conveys this information "unambiguously," you don't need to include this information elsewhere within the citation. For example, "Ohio St. 3d" publishes only decisions of the Ohio Supreme Court, so no further information is needed. "F.3d," however, publishes decisions of all the federal courts of appeal. When citing to decisions in F.3d, put the correct circuit into the parentheses with the date.

Knowing which court decided the case is vital in knowing whether a case is controlling. Therefore, even readers who are not fussy about citation form are vitally interested in knowing which court decided the case. Make sure to include this important element in your citation. Unlike the *Bluebook*, ALWD Rule 12.6(b)(2) requires information on districts and divisions when citing state law cases. Many attorneys include this information regardless of citation rules because the district or division can affect the weight the case will have with the court you are citing to.

Examples of correct long-form ALWD citations:

<u>Donchatz v. Corn</u>, 101 U.S. 101, 105 (1999).
<u>Ohio v. Burpee</u>, 101 F.3d 122, 128 (6th Cir. 1999).
<u>Jackson-Forbes v. Tuch</u>, 101 F. Supp. 122, 128 (N.D. Ohio 1999).
<u>Brown v. Blasko</u>, 101 N.E.2d 122, 128 (Ohio 1999).

A.2.2
SHORT FORM

ALWD Rule 12.21 and Bluebook Rule P.4 give examples of correct short form citations. The most basic guideline is that you should leave out the date and court information. Otherwise, use of short form depends on context.

If you are citing again to the last-*mentioned* authority, you may use the <u>Id.</u> form. "Id." replaces the name of the case, the volume of the reporter, and the abbreviation of the reporter. Thus, if you cited again to the case of <u>Donchatz v. Corn</u>, you could use the following short form if you were citing to a different page in the opinion:

<u>Id.</u> at 107.

If you were citing to the same page, of course, you could use "<u>Id.</u>" alone.

If you are citing to an already-cited opinion, but (a) you have cited to or *mentioned* another authority in the meantime, *or* (b) there is any doubt that the reader will know to which authority you are referring, use a short form that identifies the name of the case. Make sure to use an identifiable case name; if one of the parties is a governmental entity, for example, use the name of the other party in the short-form cite. If you were citing again to <u>Ohio v. Burpee</u>, but there had been an intervening cite, use either of the following formats:

<u>Burpee</u>, 101 F.3d at 125.
<u>Ohio v. Burpee</u>, 101 F.3d at 125.

Note that it is *never* appropriate to use <u>supra</u> when citing cases in a brief, nor is it appropriate to use a case name cite without including reporter information. Thus, the two examples below are both wrong:

▽ BAD EXAMPLE

Jackson-Forbes, supra, at 126.

▽ BAD EXAMPLE

Brown at 135.

Important Reminder

Unless your citation indicates otherwise, the reader will presume that you are citing to a majority opinion. Thus, when you cite to a plurality opinion, a concurrence, a dissent, etc., you *must* indicate as much in a parenthetical after the citation.[2] This is true even if you have mentioned the type of opinion cited in your text; it's also true for both long-form and short-form citations. Thus, the following citations are all correct:

Donchatz v. Corn, 101 U.S. 101, 125 (1999) (plurality opinion).
Id. at 155 (Williams, J., dissenting).
Brown, 101 N.E.2d at 135 (Moyer, C.J., concurring in part and dissenting in part).

A.3
CHANGING SENTENCE STRUCTURE TO ACCOMMODATE CITATION FORM

Many writers instinctively begin sentences with a citation:

In McGuffin v. Consolidated Ice Cream Board, 44 N.E.2d 33, 39 (Ind. 1981), the court found that ice cream is a "traditional dessert" within the meaning of the Mousse Statute.

This sentence is hard to read because the citation takes up a lot of space within the sentence. In addition, this structure puts too much emphasis on the citation and not enough emphasis on the substance of the sentence. To solve this problem, some writers would separate the case name from the rest of the citation:

▽ BAD EXAMPLE

In McGuffin v. Consolidated Ice Cream Board, the court found that ice cream is a "traditional dessert" within the meaning of the Mousse Statute. 44 N.E.2d 33, 39 (Ind. 1981).

But this technique creates another problem because separating the case name from the rest of a long form citation violates both ALWD and Bluebook rules. There is a way to write a readable sentence and still use correct citation form:

---

[2] Consult ALWD Rule 12.11(a) or Bluebook Rule 10.6 for more information.

⚠ GOOD EXAMPLE

Ice cream is a "traditional dessert" within the meaning of the Mousse Statute. <u>McGuffin v. Consolidated Ice Cream Bd.</u>, 44 N.E.2d 33, 39 (Ind. 1981).

This sentence emphasizes the rule itself. If you wanted to emphasize the court that decided the case, you could write the sentence this way:

⚠ GOOD EXAMPLE

The Indiana Supreme Court has held that ice cream is a "traditional dessert" within the meaning of the Mousse Statute. <u>McGuffin v. Consolidated Ice Cream Bd.</u>, 44 N.E.2d 33, 39 (Ind. 1981).

Thus, write the sentence in a way that lets you put the citation in a separate sentence at the end. Ideally, you should look at all of your citations to make sure that as few as possible are within textual sentences. Your sentence structure will change depending on what you want to emphasize, but you rarely want to emphasize the citation itself. Three of the four sample sentences above are technically correct, but they each emphasize something different.

Of course, if you have already cited to a case and wish to refer to it again, it is appropriate to use the case name only, as in the following example:

⚠ GOOD EXAMPLE

Ice cream is a "traditional dessert" within the meaning of the Mousse Statute. <u>McGuffin v. Consolidated Ice Cream Board</u>, 44 N.E.2d 33, 39 (Ind. 1981). In <u>McGuffin</u>, the court examined the ingredient lists for the plaintiff's product before finding that it was a traditional dessert. 44 N.E.2d at 39.

Opening the second sentence with "In <u>McGuffin</u>" provides an effective transition. Because the case name is in the sentence, a "just the numbers" short form is permissible.

A.4
STATUTORY CITATIONS

The first thing to remember about statutory citations is to consult the appropriate charts in either the ALWD manual (Appendix 1) or the *Bluebook* (Table T.1). Look up the jurisdiction that you are citing to and check the recommended method. Note that, although the *Bluebook* illustrates statutory citations using so-called "Big and little caps," Rule P.1 says that only two typefaces are used in legal briefs and memoranda — underscoring and italics — and Rule P.1(h) provides in pertinent part that you should "Print . . . statutory material . . . in ordinary roman type." The ALWD guide requires all citations to be printed in ordinary roman type.

The second thing to remember about statutory citations is that you must include a date for the statute, and that the date required is the date on the book and/or pocket part (supplement) that the language appears in. (Neither citation guide contemplates citing statutory material to a computer database.) ALWD Rule 14 and Bluebook Rule 12 address statutory citations.

Thus, a correct citation to a statute that appears partially in a bound volume dated 1997 and partially in a pocket part dated 1999 would be as follows:

> **Okla. Stat. tit. 19, § 222.22 (1997 & Supp. 1999).**[3]

If the entire statute appeared in the pocket part (or at least the entirety of what the writer referenced), the citation would be as follows:

> **Okla. Stat. tit. 29, § 122.22(h) (Supp. 1999).**

If the language cited appeared entirely in the bound volume, the citation would be as follows:

> **Okla. Stat. tit. 15, § 111.22(a) (1997).**

Note that, although your instinct may be to provide the date of enactment or amendment, that information is not required. You may decide to add this information if you think it is relevant to your analysis:

> **Okla. Stat. tit. 19, § 222.22 (1997 & Supp. 1999) (effective May 27, 1987).**

Finally, the third thing to remember about citing statutes is that you can use short form to refer to statutes. The statute cited in the first example above could be cited later in the discussion by title and section number, as in "tit. 19, § 222.22," or simply by section number, as in "§ 222.22."

Of course, you should never start a sentence with an abbreviation or a symbol. If you wish to open the sentence with a short form reference to a statute, spell out the first word, e.g., "Title 19, § 222.22 provides . . ." or "Section 222.22 provides. . . ."

A.5
COMMON PUNCTUATION PROBLEMS

Unfortunately, many legal writers still have problems with basic punctuation; perhaps even more unfortunately, others will judge their

---

[3] Note that the supplements to the United States Code are numbered; thus, you might have a cite like this: 29 U.S.C. § 122 (1993 & Supp. II 1999).

intelligence based on punctuation mistakes. This section addresses some of the most common punctuation problems and gives common sense advice on how to avoid them.

A.5.1
APOSTROPHE PROBLEMS

Many apostrophe problems are caused by mixing homonyms (words with different meanings that sound alike), while others are caused by a misunderstanding of the rules of possessives. This section will address each in turn.

a. Common Homonym Problems

Many writers confuse "their," "theirs," and "they're," while others confuse "its" and "it's" and "your," "yours," and "you're." Making one of these errors is a sure way to anger your reader and give an impression of carelessness. It's worth the time to study these explanations and make sure you understand the differences.

"Their," "theirs," and "they're"

Use "their" to modify a noun that belongs to more than one person or entity.

△ **GOOD EXAMPLE**

This animal is their dog.

Use "theirs" to stand alone as a possessive pronoun when the noun possessed is in another part of the sentence or is in a previous sentence.

△ **GOOD EXAMPLE**

This animal is theirs.

"Theirs" **never** takes an apostrophe.
    "They're" is a contraction meaning "they are."

△ **GOOD EXAMPLE**

They're happy to admit that this animal is their dog. The fleas are also theirs.

"It's" and "its"

"It's" is a contraction of "it is" and, less often, of "it has."

△ **GOOD EXAMPLE**

It's time to go.

△ **GOOD EXAMPLE**

It's been a long day.

"Its" is the possessive form of the pronoun "it."

⚠ GOOD EXAMPLE

The company formed its board of directors within one week of incorporation.

NOTE: There is no good reason why "its" does not have an apostrophe in its possessive form. The "it's/its" rule is easier to remember if you *don't* apply logic. Just remember that someone made the arbitrary rule that the possessive of "it" does *not* take an apostrophe. Perhaps an easier rule to remember is that the *only* time "it" *does* take an apostrophe is when the word is used as a *contraction*. Because contractions are rare in formal legal writing, you probably shouldn't be using "it's."

To find and correct it's/its problems, use your search function to search the word "it's" and then "its" and check them both against this handy reference (or any grammar reference).

"Your," "yours," and "you're"

A your/you're mistake is particularly grating to fussy readers. Use "your" to modify a noun belonging to "you."

⚠ GOOD EXAMPLE

This animal is your dog.

Use "yours" to stand alone as a possessive pronoun when the noun possessed is in another part of the sentence or is in a previous sentence.

⚠ GOOD EXAMPLE

This animal is yours.

"Yours" **never** takes an apostrophe.
"You're" is a contraction meaning "you are."

⚠ GOOD EXAMPLE

You're sure that this animal is your dog? Well, then, the fleas are also yours.

b. Rules of Possessives

Making a singular noun possessive

If you wish to make a singular noun possessive, add an apostrophe and then an "s." Typically, the word following the possessive noun will be the thing that belongs to the noun; on rare occasions, the thing belonging to the noun will be implied. Examples:

⚠ GOOD EXAMPLE

This house belongs to Bill (no possessive noun, so apostrophe not needed).

⚠ GOOD EXAMPLE

This is Bill's house *(possessive form needed; "owned" noun in sentence).*

⚠ GOOD EXAMPLE

This house is Bill's *(possessive needed; "owned" noun implied).*

Although there is some controversy on this point, most formal writers (including the *New York Times*) add an "apostrophe s" to make a singular noun plural *even when the singular noun already ends in "s."*

⚠ GOOD EXAMPLE

This house belongs to Mr. Burns.

⚠ GOOD EXAMPLE

This is Mr. Burns's house.

⚠ GOOD EXAMPLE

This house is Mr. Burns's.

⚠ GOOD EXAMPLE

The delay in the vote was Congress's fault.

⚠ GOOD EXAMPLE

The delay in the vote can be blamed on Congress.

⚠ GOOD EXAMPLE

The fault was Congress's.

Adding "apostrophe s" when making any singular noun possessive is preferable because most people pronounce the added "s" without any problem. Furthermore, as a practical matter, one rule is easier to remember than two.

Making a plural noun possessive
About this point there is no controversy. When you are making a plural noun possessive, *and that plural noun already ends in "s,"* add an apostrophe without an "s."

⚠ GOOD EXAMPLE

This house belongs to the Dukes.

⚠ GOOD EXAMPLE

This is the Dukes' house.

⚠ GOOD EXAMPLE

This house is the Dukes'.

If the plural noun does not end in "s" (e.g., "children"), add "apostrophe s."

⚠ GOOD EXAMPLE

These toys belong to the children.

⚠ GOOD EXAMPLE

These are the children's toys.

⚠ GOOD EXAMPLE

These toys are the children's.

A.5.2
SEMICOLON USE

Effective use of semicolons separates sophisticated writers from unsophisticated ones; it's worth taking a little time to learn to use them properly. Here are a few basic semicolon rules:

1. Use a semicolon to separate independent clauses[4] *not* joined by a *coordinating conjunction.*[5] For example:

⚠ GOOD EXAMPLE

Mr. Sanders refused to transfer to the production room; the salary of production room workers is $5,000 per year less than Mr. Sanders's current salary.

Writers often use semicolons to imply a relationship between the points made in each of the two independent clauses. In the example above, the writer is implying the reason that Mr. Sanders refused the transfer to the production room.

2. Use a semicolon when two independent clauses *are* joined with a *conjunctive adverb.*[6]

⚠ GOOD EXAMPLE

The salary of production room workers is $5,000 less per year than that of copy editors; therefore, Mr. Sanders refused an opportunity to transfer to the production room.

Note: Do not assume that every conjunctive adverb separates two independent clauses and therefore needs a semicolon; instead, realize that conjunctive adverbs can also appear in many other sentence structures.

3. Always use semicolons to separate items in a series if one or more of the items has internal commas. For example:

---

[4] An "independent clause" is a clause that could stand on its own as a sentence.
[5] The seven "coordinating conjunctions" are "and," "but," "or," "for," "nor," "yet," and "so,"
[6] The most common "conjunctive adverbs" are "accordingly," "also," "besides," "consequently," "furthermore," "hence," "however," "indeed," "instead," "likewise," "meanwhile," "moreover," "nevertheless," "still," "then," "therefore," and "thus." For more information, *see* Anne Enquist and Laurel Currie Oates, *Just Writing* 171 (Aspen 2001).

> ⚠️ GOOD EXAMPLE
>
> **The plaintiff has owned residences at 5 Main Street, Quechee, Vermont; 4560 Hickory Street, Mishawaka, Indiana; and 303 Jackson Street, Columbus, Ohio.**

You may use a couple of different techniques to search for semicolon problems. If you use too *many* semicolons, use the search function on your computer to search for and scrutinize your semicolons. If you use commas where semicolons belong, first, train your reader's "ear" by reading about and doing exercises on semicolon use. Second, scrutinize your longer sentences and/or your lists.

A.5.3
COMMON COMMA PROBLEMS

Although the simple little comma arrives on the punctuation scene with the baggage of many rules, I will address only three of the most common problems here. Two rules concern when you *should* have a comma, and the other rule concerns where you should *not* have a comma.

1. Use commas between items in a series of more than two items. Make sure to put a comma before the conjunction, as in "tall, dark, and handsome."

Some informal writers swear that you should eliminate the comma after the second-to-the-last item in a series (in our example, after the "dark"), but this advice is bad for legal writing. There have been law cases in which a will, a contract, or a statute had to be litigated because of a missing comma. Thus, in legal writing, make sure to include the comma before the conjunction.

> ▽ BAD EXAMPLE
>
> **Mr. Johnson is tall, dark and handsome.**

> ⚠️ GOOD EXAMPLE
>
> **Mr. Johnson is tall, dark, and handsome.**

> ▽ BAD EXAMPLE
>
> **Ms. Gomez researched the law, wrote the motion and filed the motion.**

> ⚠️ GOOD EXAMPLE
>
> **Ms. Gomez researched the law, wrote the motion, and filed the motion.**

2. Place a comma before a coordinating conjunction separating two independent clauses.

As I have already noted, "and" and "or" are the most common coordinating conjunctions. When a coordinating conjunction creates a compound noun or verb, there is only one independent clause, and no comma is necessary.

△ GOOD EXAMPLE

Mr. Johnson is tall and handsome.

△ GOOD EXAMPLE

John laughed all the way to the bank and then made a large deposit.

However, if the two parts of the sentence are independent clauses, they should be separated with a comma.

△ GOOD EXAMPLE

Mr. Johnson is tall, and he is handsome, too.

△ GOOD EXAMPLE

John laughed all the way to the bank, and then he made a deposit.

For most people, the hard part about using this comma properly is correctly identifying an independent clause. Usually, you can identify an independent clause by looking for an independent subject and a verb, as long as the clause is not introduced by a subordinating conjunction. In the sentence "John laughed all the way to the bank and then made a deposit," there is a verb ("made") after the "and," but there is no separate subject — the subject from the first, independent, clause carries over into the second, dependent, clause. However, in the sentence "John laughed all the way to the bank, and then he made a deposit," you find a separate subject ("he") for the verb ("made") in the second clause, which means that it is an independent clause. Although this rule is not foolproof, it can help you separate the dependent clauses from the independent clauses.

   3. Unless a clause intervenes, do NOT put a comma between a subject and a verb.

▽ BAD EXAMPLE

The infamous rule against perpetuities, is hard to understand.

△ GOOD EXAMPLE

The infamous rule against perpetuities is hard to understand.

△ GOOD EXAMPLE

The infamous rule against perpetuities, which is the bane of many lawyers, is hard to understand.

This appendix is by no means comprehensive. If you have problems that are not covered here, you may wish to consult Anne Enquist and Laurel Currie Oates, *Just Writing* (Aspen 2001) or Mary Barnard Ray and Jill J. Ramsfield, *Legal Writing: Getting It Right and Getting It Written* (3d ed. West 2000).

UNITED STATES SUPREME COURT RULES

Excerpted below are the Rules of the United States Supreme Court that are most relevant to the writing of briefs on the merits and to oral argument. They appear in order of significance. To review all rules, consult: *<http://www.supremecourtus.gov/ctrules/ctrules.html.>*.

You may also wish to review the Federal Rules of Appellate Procedure (e.g., at *<http://www.ck10.uscourts.gov/circuit/rules/99contents.htm>*) or State Appellate Rules (e.g., at <http://www.sconet.state.oh.us/Rules/>).

Rule 24
BRIEFS ON THE MERITS: IN GENERAL

1. A brief on the merits for a petitioner or an appellant shall comply in all respects with Rules 33.1 and 34 and shall contain in the order here indicated:

(a) The questions presented for review under Rule 14.1(a). The questions shall be set out on the first page following the cover, and no other information may appear on that page. The phrasing of the questions presented need not be identical with that in the petition for a writ of certiorari or the jurisdictional statement, but the brief may not raise additional questions or change the substance of the questions already presented in those documents. At its option, however, the Court may consider a plain error not among the questions presented but evident from the record and otherwise within its jurisdiction to decide.

(b) A list of all parties to the proceeding in the court whose judgment is under review (unless the caption of the case in this Court contains the names of all parties). Any amended list of parent companies and non-wholly owned subsidiaries as required by Rule 29.6 shall be placed here.

(c) If the brief exceeds five pages, a table of contents and a table of cited authorities.

(d) Citations of the official and unofficial reports of the opinions and orders entered in the case by courts and administrative agencies.

(e) A concise statement of the basis for jurisdiction in this

Court, including the statutory provisions and time factors on which jurisdiction rests.

(f) The constitutional provisions, treaties, statutes, ordinances, and regulations involved in the case, set out verbatim with appropriate citation. If the provisions involved are lengthy, their citation alone suffices at this point, and their pertinent text, if not already set out in the petition for a writ of certiorari, jurisdictional statement, or an appendix to either document, shall be set out in an appendix to the brief.

(g) A concise statement of the case, setting out the facts material to the consideration of the questions presented, with appropriate references to the joint appendix, e.g., App. 12, or to the record, e.g., Record 12.

(h) A summary of the argument, suitably paragraphed. The summary should be a clear and concise condensation of the argument made in the body of the brief; mere repetition of the headings under which the argument is arranged is not sufficient.

(i) The argument, exhibiting clearly the points of fact and of law presented and citing the authorities and statutes relied on.

(j) A conclusion specifying with particularity the relief the party seeks.

2. A brief on the merits for a respondent or an appellee shall conform to the foregoing requirements, except that items required by subparagraphs 1(a), (b), (d), (e), (f), and (g) of this Rule need not be included unless the respondent or appellee is dissatisfied with their presentation by the opposing party.

3. A brief on the merits may not exceed the page limitations specified in Rule 33.1(g). An appendix to a brief may include only relevant material, and counsel are cautioned not to include in an appendix arguments or citations that properly belong in the body of the brief.

4. A reply brief shall conform to those portions of this Rule applicable to the brief for a respondent or an appellee, but, if appropriately divided by topical headings, need not contain a summary of the argument.

5. A reference to the joint appendix or to the record set out in any brief shall indicate the appropriate page number. If the reference is to an exhibit, the page numbers at which the exhibit appears, at which it was offered in evidence, and at which it was ruled on by the judge shall be indicated, e.g., Pl. Exh. 14, Record 199, 2134.

6. A brief shall be concise, logically arranged with proper headings, and free of irrelevant, immaterial, or scandalous matter. The Court may disregard or strike a brief that does not comply with this paragraph.

Rule 25
BRIEFS ON THE MERITS: NUMBER OF COPIES AND TIME TO FILE

1. The petitioner or appellant shall file 40 copies of the brief on the merits within 45 days of the order granting the writ of certiorari, noting probable jurisdiction, or postponing consideration of jurisdiction. Any respondent or appellee who supports the petitioner or appellant shall meet the petitioner's or appellant's time schedule for filing documents.

2. The respondent or appellee shall file 40 copies of the brief on the merits within 30 days after receiving the brief for the petitioner or appellant.

3. The petitioner or appellant shall file 40 copies of the reply brief, if any, within 30 days after receiving the brief for the respondent or appellee, but any reply brief must actually be received by the Clerk no more than one week before the date of oral argument. Any respondent or appellee supporting the petitioner or appellant may file a reply brief.

4. The time periods stated in paragraphs 1 and 2 of this Rule may be extended as provided in Rule 30. An application to extend the time to file a brief on the merits is not favored. If a case is advanced for hearing, the time to file briefs on the merits may be abridged as circumstances require pursuant to an order of the Court on its own motion or that of a party.

5. A party wishing to present late authorities, newly enacted legislation, or other intervening matter that was not available in time to be included in a brief may file 40 copies of a supplemental brief, restricted to such new matter and otherwise presented in conformity with these Rules, up to the time the case is called for oral argument or by leave of the Court thereafter.

6. After a case has been argued or submitted, the Clerk will not file any brief, except that of a party filed by leave of the Court.

7. The Clerk will not file any brief that is not accompanied by proof of service as required by Rule 29.

Rule 33
DOCUMENT PREPARATION: BOOKLET FORMAT; 8½- BY 11-INCH PAPER FORMAT

1. Booklet Format:

(a) Except for a document expressly permitted by these Rules to be submitted on 8½- by 11-inch paper, see, e.g., Rules 21, 22, and 39, every document filed with the Court shall be prepared using a standard typesetting process (e.g., hot metal, photocomposition, or computer typesetting) to produce text printed in typographic (as opposed to typewriter) characters. The process used must produce a clear, black image on white paper. The text must be reproduced with a clarity that equals or exceeds the output of a laser printer.

(b) The text of every booklet-format document, including any appendix thereto, shall be typeset in Roman 11-point or larger type with 2-point or more leading between lines. The typeface should be similar to that used in current volumes of the United States Reports. Increasing the amount of text by using condensed or thinner typefaces, or by reducing the space between letters, is strictly prohibited. Type size and face shall be consistent throughout. Quotations in excess of 50 words shall be indented. The typeface of footnotes shall be 9-point or larger with 2-point or more leading between lines. The text of the document must appear on both sides of the page.

(c) Every booklet-format document shall be produced on paper that is opaque, unglazed, 6⅛ by 9¼ inches in size, and not less than 60 pounds in weight, and shall have margins of at least three fourths of an inch on all sides. The text field, including footnotes, should be approximately 4⅛ by 7⅛ inches. The document shall be bound firmly in at least two places along the left margin (saddle stitch or perfect binding preferred) so as to permit easy opening, and no part of the text should be obscured by the binding. Spiral, plastic, metal, and string bindings may not be used. Copies of patent documents, except opinions, may be duplicated in such size as is necessary in a separate appendix.

(d) Every booklet-format document shall comply with the page limits shown on the chart in subparagraph 1(g) of this Rule. The page limits do not include the pages containing the questions presented, the list of parties and corporate affiliates of the filing party, the table of contents, the table of cited authorities, or any appendix. Verbatim quotations required under Rule 14.1(f), if set out in the text of a brief rather than in the appendix, are also excluded. For good cause, the Court or a Justice may grant leave to file a document in excess of the page limits, but application for such leave is not favored. An application to exceed page limits shall comply with Rule 22 and must be received by the Clerk at least 15 days before the filing date of the document in question, except in the most extraordinary circumstances.

(e) Every booklet-format document shall have a suitable cover consisting of 65-pound weight paper in the color indicated on the chart in subparagraph 1(g) of this Rule. If a separate appendix to any document is filed, the color of its cover shall be the same as that of the cover of the document it supports. The Clerk will furnish a color chart upon request. Counsel shall ensure that there is adequate contrast between the printing and the color of the cover. A document filed by the United States, or by any other federal party represented by the Solicitor General, shall have a gray cover. A joint appendix, answer to a bill of complaint, motion for leave to intervene, and any other document not listed in subparagraph 1(g) of this Rule shall have a tan cover.

(f) Forty copies of a booklet-format document shall be filed.

(g) Page limits and cover colors for booklet-format documents are as follows:

Type of Document	Page Limits	Color of Cover
i. Petition for a Writ of Certiorari (Rule 14); Motion for Leave to file a Bill of Complaint and Brief in Support (Rule 17.3); Jurisdictional Statement (Rule 18.3); Petition for an Extraordinary Writ (Rule 20.2)	30	white
ii. Brief in Opposition (Rule 15.3); Brief in Opposition to Motion for Leave to file an Original Action (Rule 17.5); Motion to Dismiss or Affirm (Rule 18.6); Brief in Opposition to Mandamus or Prohibition (Rule 20.3(b)); Response to a Petition for Habeas Corpus (Rule 20.4)	30	orange
iii. Reply to Brief in Opposition (Rules 15.6 and 17.5); Brief Opposing a Motion to Dismiss or Affirm (Rule 18.8)	10	tan
iv. Supplemental Brief (Rules 15.8, 17, 18.10, and 25.5)	10	tan
v. Brief on the Merits by Petitioner or Appellant (Rule 24); Exceptions by Plaintiff to Report of Special Master (Rule 17)	50	light blue
vi. Brief on the Merits by Respondent or Appellee (Rule 24.2); Brief on the Merits for Respondent or Appellee Supporting Petitioner or Appellant (Rule 12.6); Exceptions by Party Other than Plaintiff to Report of Special Master (Rule 17)	50	light red
vii. Reply Brief on the Merits (Rule)	20	yellow
viii. Reply to Plaintiff's Exceptions to Report of Special Master (Rule 17)	50	orange

(continued)

(*Continued*)

Type of Document	Page Limits	Color of Cover
ix. Reply to Exceptions by Party Other Than Plaintiff to Report of Special Master (Rule 17)	50	yellow
x. Brief for an Amicus Curiae at the Petition Stage (Rule 37.2)	20	cream
xi. Brief for an Amicus Curiae in Support of the Plaintiff, Petitioner, or Appellant, or in Support of Neither Party, on the Merits, or in an Original Action at the Exceptions Stage (Rule 37.3)	30	light green
xii. Brief for an Amicus Curiae in Support of the Defendant, Respondent, or Appellee, on the Merits or in an Original Action at the Exceptions Stage (Rule 37.3)	30	dark green
xiii. Petition for Rehearing (Rule 44)	10	tan

2. 8½- by 11-Inch Paper Format:

(a) The text of every document, including any appendix thereto, expressly permitted by these Rules to be presented to the Court on 8½- by 11-inch paper shall appear double spaced, except for indented quotations, which shall be single spaced, on opaque, unglazed, white paper. The document shall be stapled or bound at the upper left hand corner. Copies, if required, shall be produced on the same type of paper and shall be legible. The original of any such document (except a motion to dismiss or affirm under Rule 18.6) shall be signed by the party proceeding pro se or by counsel of record who must be a member of the Bar of this Court or an attorney appointed under the Criminal Justice Act of 1964, see 18 U.S.C. § 3006A(d)(6), or under any other applicable federal statute. Subparagraph 1(g) of this Rule does not apply to documents prepared under this paragraph.

(b) Page limits for documents presented on 8½- by 11-inch paper are: 40 pages for a petition for a writ of certiorari, jurisdictional statement, petition for an extraordinary writ, brief in opposition, or motion to dismiss or affirm; and 15 pages for a reply to a brief in opposition, brief opposing a motion to dismiss or affirm, supplemental brief, or petition for rehearing. The page exclusions specified in subparagraph 1(d) of this Rule apply.

Rule 34
DOCUMENT PREPARATION: GENERAL REQUIREMENTS

Every document, whether prepared under Rule 33.1 or Rule 33.2, shall comply with the following provisions:

1. Each document shall bear on its cover, in the order indicated, from the top of the page:

(a) the docket number of the case or, if there is none, a space for one;

(b) the name of this Court;

(c) the caption of the case as appropriate in this Court;

(d) the nature of the proceeding and the name of the court from which the action is brought (e.g., "On Petition for Writ of Certiorari to the United States Court of Appeals for the Fifth Circuit"; or, for a merits brief, "On Writ of Certiorari to the United States Court of Appeals for the Fifth Circuit");

(e) the title of the document (e.g., "Petition for Writ of Certiorari," "Brief for Respondent," "Joint Appendix");

(f) the name of the attorney who is counsel of record for the party concerned (who must be a member of the Bar of this Court except as provided in Rule 33.2), and on whom service is to be made, with a notation directly thereunder identifying the attorney as counsel of record and setting out counsel's office address and telephone number. Only one counsel of record may be noted on a single document. The names of other members of the Bar of this Court or of the bar of the highest court of a State acting as counsel, and, if desired, their addresses, may be added, but counsel of record shall be clearly identified. Names of persons other than attorneys admitted to a state bar may not be listed, unless the party is appearing pro se, in which case the party's name, address, and telephone number shall appear. The foregoing shall be displayed in an appropriate typographic manner and, except for the identification of counsel, may not be set in type smaller than standard 11 point, if the document is prepared as required by Rule 33.1.

2. Every document exceeding five pages (other than a joint appendix), whether prepared under Rule 33.1 or Rule 33.2, shall contain a table of contents and a table of cited authorities (i.e., cases alphabetically arranged, constitutional provisions, statutes, treatises, and other materials) with references to the pages in the document where such authorities are cited.

3. The body of every document shall bear at its close the

name of counsel of record and such other counsel, identified on the cover of the document in conformity with subparagraph 1(g) of this Rule, as may be desired.

Rule 14
CONTENT OF A PETITION FOR A WRIT OF CERTIORARI

1. A petition for a writ of certiorari shall contain, in the order indicated:

(a) The questions presented for review, expressed concisely in relation to the circumstances of the case, without unnecessary detail. The questions should be short and should not be argumentative or repetitive. If the petitioner or respondent is under a death sentence that may be affected by the disposition of the petition, the notation "capital case" shall precede the questions presented. The questions shall be set out on the first page following the cover, and no other information may appear on that page. The statement of any question presented is deemed to comprise every subsidiary question fairly included therein. Only the questions set out in the petition, or fairly included therein, will be considered by the Court. . . .

Rule 29
FILING AND SERVICE OF DOCUMENTS; SPECIAL NOTIFICATIONS; CORPORATE DISCLOSURE STATEMENT

1. Any document required or permitted to be presented to the Court or to a Justice shall be filed with the Clerk.

2. A document is timely filed if it is sent to the Clerk through the United States Postal Service by first-class mail (including express or priority mail), postage prepaid, and bears a postmark showing that the document was mailed on or before the last day for filing. Commercial postage meter labels alone are not acceptable. If submitted by an inmate confined in an institution, a document is timely filed if it is deposited in the institution's internal mail system on or before the last day for filing and is accompanied by a notarized statement or declaration in compliance with 28 U.S.C. § 1746 setting out the date of deposit and stating that first-class postage has been prepaid. If the

postmark is missing or not legible, the Clerk will require the person who mailed the document to submit a notarized statement or declaration in compliance with 28 U.S.C. § 1746 setting out the details of the mailing and stating that the mailing took place on a particular date within the permitted time. A document also is timely filed if it is forwarded through a private delivery or courier service and is actually received by the Clerk within the time permitted for filing.

3. Any document required by these Rules to be served may be served personally or by mail on each party to the proceeding at or before the time of filing. If the document has been prepared as required by Rule 33.1, three copies shall be served on each other party separately represented in the proceeding. If the document has been prepared as required by Rule 33.2, service of a single copy on each other separately represented party suffices. If personal service is made, it shall consist of delivery at the office of the counsel of record, either to counsel or to an employee therein. If service is by mail, it shall consist of depositing the document with the United States Postal Service, with no less than first-class postage prepaid, addressed to counsel of record at the proper post office address. When a party is not represented by counsel, service shall be made on the party, personally or by mail.

4.

(a) If the United States or any federal department, office, agency, officer, or employee is a party to be served, service shall be made on the Solicitor General of the United States, Room 5614, Department of Justice, 950 Pennsylvania Ave., N.W., Washington, D.C. 20530-0001. When an agency of the United States that is a party is authorized by law to appear before this Court on its own behalf, or when an officer or employee of the United States is a party, the agency, officer, or employee shall be served in addition to the Solicitor General.

(b) In any proceeding in this Court in which the constitutionality of an Act of Congress is drawn into question, and neither the United States nor any federal department, office, agency, officer, or employee is a party, the initial document filed in this Court shall recite that 28 U.S.C. § 2403(a) may apply and shall be served on the Solicitor General of the United States, Room 5614, Department of Justice, 950 Pennsylvania Ave., N.W., Washington, D.C. 20530-0001. In such a proceeding from any court of the United States, as defined by 28 U.S.C. § 451, the initial document also shall state whether that court, pursuant to 28 U.S.C. § 2403(a), certified to the Attorney General the fact that the constitutionality of an Act of Congress was drawn into question. See Rule 14.1(e)(v).

(c) In any proceeding in this Court in which the constitutionality of any statute of a State is drawn into question, and neither the State nor any agency, officer, or employee thereof is a party, the initial document filed in this Court shall recite that 28 U.S.C. § 2403(b) may apply and shall be served on the Attorney General of that State. In such a proceeding from any court of the United States, as defined by 28 U.S.C. § 451, the initial document also shall state whether that court, pursuant to 28 U.S.C. § 2403(b), certified to the State Attorney General the fact that the constitutionality of a statute of that State was drawn into question. See Rule 14.1(e)(v).

5. Proof of service, when required by these Rules, shall accompany the document when it is presented to the Clerk for filing and shall be separate from it. Proof of service shall contain, or be accompanied by, a statement that all parties required to be served have been served, together with a list of the names, addresses, and telephone numbers of counsel indicating the name of the party or parties each counsel represents. It is not necessary that service on each party required to be served be made in the same manner or evidenced by the same proof. Proof of service may consist of any one of the following:

(a) an acknowledgment of service, signed by counsel of record for the party served;

(b) a certificate of service, reciting the facts and circumstances of service in compliance with the appropriate paragraph or paragraphs of this Rule, and signed by a member of the Bar of this Court representing the party on whose behalf service is made or by an attorney appointed to represent that party under the Criminal Justice Act of 1964, see 18 U.S.C. § 3006A(d)(6), or under any other applicable federal statute; or

(c) a notarized affidavit or declaration in compliance with 28 U.S.C. § 1746, reciting the facts and circumstances of service in accordance with the appropriate paragraph or paragraphs of this Rule, whenever service is made by any person not a member of the Bar of this Court and not an attorney appointed to represent a party under the Criminal Justice Act of 1964, see 18 U.S.C. § 3006A(d)(6), or under any other applicable federal statute.

6. Every document, except a joint appendix or amicus curiae brief, filed by or on behalf of a nongovernmental corporation shall contain a corporate disclosure statement identifying the parent corporations and listing any publicly held company that owns 10 percent or more of the corporation's stock. If there is no parent or publicly held company owning 10 percent or more of the corporation's stock, a notation to this effect shall be included in the document. If a statement has been included in a document filed earlier in the case, reference may be made to the earlier document (except when the earlier statement appeared in a document prepared under Rule 33.2), and

only amendments to the statement to make it current need be included in the document being filed.

Rule 28
ORAL ARGUMENT

1. Oral argument should emphasize and clarify the written arguments in the briefs on the merits. Counsel should assume that all Justices have read the briefs before oral argument. Oral argument read from a prepared text is not favored.

2. The petitioner or appellant shall open and may conclude the argument. A cross writ of certiorari or cross-appeal will be argued with the initial writ of certiorari or appeal as one case in the time allowed for that one case, and the Court will advise the parties who shall open and close.

3. Unless the Court directs otherwise, each side is allowed one-half hour for argument. Counsel is not required to use all the allotted time. Any request for additional time to argue shall be presented by motion under Rule 21 no more than 15 days after the petitioner's or appellant's brief on the merits is filed, and shall set out specifically and concisely why the case cannot be presented within the half hour limitation. Additional time is rarely accorded.

4. Only one attorney will be heard for each side, except by leave of the Court on motion filed no more than 15 days after the respondent's or appellee's brief on the merits is filed. Any request for divided argument shall be presented by motion under Rule 21 and shall set out specifically and concisely why more than one attorney should be allowed to argue. Divided argument is not favored.

5. Regardless of the number of counsel participating in oral argument, counsel making the opening argument shall present the case fairly and completely and not reserve points of substance for rebuttal.

6. Oral argument will not be allowed on behalf of any party for whom a brief has not been filed.

7. By leave of the Court, and subject to paragraph 4 of this Rule, counsel for an amicus curiae whose brief has been filed as provided in Rule 37 may argue orally on the side of a party, with the consent of that party. In the absence of consent, counsel for an amicus curiae may seek leave of the Court to argue orally by a motion setting out specifically and concisely why oral argument would provide assistance to the Court not otherwise available. Such a motion will be granted only in the most extraordinary circumstances.

SAMPLE BRIEFS

Many writing professors worry about providing samples because some students follow them too closely, imitating structure, arguments, or style that may have been appropriate in the sample but may not be appropriate for the student. Furthermore, no sample is perfect. In the following sample student briefs, I have included annotations that identify strengths, explain possible problems, or point out unusual structures that may not be appropriate in different cases. Your professor may identify other issues that you should consider when deciding whether certain samples are effective models for certain types of briefs.

The sample briefs in this Appendix follow Supreme Court rules as to format, but in some instances they follow publishing conventions rather than word processing conventions. Thus, for example, briefs that you prepare for an appellate advocacy course may have to be double-spaced (other than headings and indented quotations), may require different margins, and may require other different spacing conventions.

No. 97-1147

IN THE SUPREME COURT OF THE UNITED STATES
FALL TERM, 1998

_____

STATE OF MINNESOTA,

Petitioner,

v.

WAYNE THOMAS CARTER and MELVIN JOHNS,

Respondents.

_____

ON WRIT OF CERTIORARI TO THE SUPREME COURT OF MINNESOTA

_____

BRIEF FOR THE PETITIONER

_____

Sarah Student
55 West 12th Avenue
Columbus, Ohio 43210
Counsel for the Petitioner

QUESTIONS PRESENTED ❶

1. Whether the Court should expand the class of individuals who can claim a legitimate expectation of privacy under the Fourth Amendment to include a temporary invitee who is present on the premises only to conduct an illegal business activity? ❷

2. Whether a police officer standing in a publicly used apartment common area, who is able to plainly see an apartment interior, should be required to shield his eyes because the observation would constitute a Fourth Amendment "search"?

❶ You are not *required* to have more than one question presented, but you may if your case presents more than one dispositive issue. <u>See</u> § 9.1 for more information on drafting questions presented.

❷ The writer uses "expand" early in the question and "illegal business activity" at the end of the question to encourage the reader to answer "of course not."

TABLE OF CONTENTS

3 This brief has no "parties to the proceed-ings" page because all parties are listed on the cover page.

4 These two subheads do not contain the word "because" — they are the "becauses" for point heading B: They show why society is not prepared to recognize the respondents' expec-tation of privacy as rea-sonable.

5 Heading 2 presents an alternative, in case the court disagrees with heading 1. These two subheads are the "be-causes" for point head-ing 2: They show why the Respondents' activ-ity was not valuable to society under the stan-dard.

6 This heading is a policy argument, noting that it's just a bad idea generally to have too many people claiming a legitimate expectation of privacy. *Note that it does not label itself as a policy argument.*

7 These two subheads are the "becauses" for point heading A: They show how the place that Officer Thielen stood proves that no Fourth Amendment search occurred.

8 These two subheads are the "becauses" for point heading B: They show how Officer Thielen's actions prove that no Fourth Amendment search occurred.

9 This brief has an unusually high number of headings and subheadings. For information about deciding how to break your argument into parts and subparts, see § 9.4.3.

10 If a case name or other authority name is particularly long, use a "hanging indent" like this so that only case names appear at the left margin.

11 Notice that the writer does not use "*passim*" with these frequently cited cases. "*Passim*" should be used *only* when citation is so frequent that listing the pages would not help the reader to find the pages on which the authority is cited. The reader can use the table of authorities to note the most significant authorities at a glance and then to find the places in the brief in which those authorities are used as support.

TABLE OF AUTHORITIES

United States Supreme Court Cases:

page

Alderman v. United States, 394 U.S. 165 (1969) 13

Boyd v. United States, 116 U.S. 616 (1886) 15

Brown v. United States, 411 U.S. 223 (1973) 13

California v. Ciraolo, 476 U.S. 207 (1985) 12, 14, 15, 17, 33, 34, 37

10 Employment Division, Department of Human Resources of Oregon v. Smith,
  494 U.S. 872 (1990) 10

First Options of Chicago v. Kaplan, 514 U.S. 938 (1995) 2

Florida v. Riley, 488 U.S. 445 (1989) (plurality) 6, 15, 19

G.M. Leasing Corp. v. United States, 429 U.S. 338 (1977) 10

Harmelin v. Michigan, 501 U.S. 957 (1991) 10

Hatch v. Reardon, 204 U.S. 152 (1907) 13

Jones v. United States, 362 U.S. 257 (1960) 6

Katz v. United States, 389 U.S. 347 (1967) 5, 6, 11, 12, 14, 17, 19 **11**

Lewis v. United States, 385 U.S. 206 (1966) 10

Minnesota v. Olson, 495 U.S. 91 (1990) 5, 7, 8, 9

Oliver v. United States, 466 U.S. 170 (1984) 15, 16

Rakas v. Illinois, 439 U.S. 128 (1978) 5, 6, 9, 13

Silverman v. United States, 365 U.S. 505 (1961) 10

Simmons v. United States, 390 U.S. 377 (1979) 6

Smith v. Maryland, 442 U.S. 735 (1979) 5, 12

Texas v. Brown, 460 U.S. 730 (1983) 18

Tileston v. Ullman, 318 U.S. 44 (1943) 13

Treasury Employees v. Von Raab, 489 U.S. 656 (1989) 10

United States v. Dunn, 480 U.S. 294 (1987) 15, 17

United States v. U.S. Gypsum Co., 333 U.S. 364 (1948) 2

United States v. Salvucci, 448 U.S. 83 (1980) 13

United States Court of Appeals Cases:

Martin v. United States, 183 F.2d 436 (4th Cir. 1950) 15

Roberson v. United States, 165 F.2d 752 (6th Cir. 1948) 15

Rozencranz v. United States, 356 F.2d 310 (1st Cir. 1966) 15

Terry v. Martin, 120 F.3d 661 (7th Cir. 1997) 8

United States v. Acevedo, 627 F.2d 68 (7th Cir. 1980) 16

United States v. Fields, 113 F.3d 313 (2d Cir. 1997) 16

United States v. Hicks, 978 F.2d 722 (D.C. Cir. 1992) 8, 10

United States v. Holland, 755 F.2d 253 (2d. Cir. 1985) 16

iv

IN THE SUPREME COURT OF THE UNITED STATES

No. 97-1147

STATE OF MINNESOTA,

Petitioner,

v.

WAYNE THOMAS CARTER and MELVIN JOHNS,

Respondents.

ON WRIT OF CERTIORARI TO THE SUPREME COURT OF MINNESOTA

BRIEF FOR THE PETITIONER

OPINIONS BELOW

The decision of the Supreme Court of Minnesota reversing the trial court's decision in State v. Carter is reported at State v. Carter, 569 N.W.2d 169 (Minn. 1997). The decision of the Supreme Court of Minnesota reversing the trial court's decision in State v. Johns is reported at State v. Johns, 569 N.W.2d 180 (Minn. 1997). The decision of the Minnesota Court of Appeals affirming the trial court's decision in State v. Carter is reported at State v. Carter, 545 N.W.2d 695 (Minn. Ct. App. 1996). The decision of the Minnesota Court of Appeals affirming the trial court's decision in State v. Johns is unreported and can be found at Record D-1. The trial court's decisions in State v. Carter and in State v. Johns, denying the motion to suppress, are unreported and can be found at Record E-1.

JURISDICTION

The judgment of the Supreme Court of Minnesota was entered on September 11, 1997. Petitioners filed the Petition for Writ of Certiorari on December 29, 1997. On March 9, 1998, this Court granted the Petition. The jurisdiction of this Court rests on 28 U.S.C. § 1257 (1997).

CONSTITUTIONAL PROVISION INVOLVED

The pertinent part of the Fourth Amendment to the United States Constitution provides: "The right of the people to be secure in their persons, houses, papers and

1

effects, against unreasonable searches and seizures, shall not be violated." U.S. Const. Amend. IV.

STANDARD OF REVIEW

The Minnesota Supreme Court erred as a matter of law when it reversed the trial court's decision. This Court accepts the trial court's findings of fact unless clearly erroneous, but decides questions of law de novo. See United States v. United States Gypsum Co., 333 U.S. 364, 395 (1948). A finding is clearly erroneous when, although there is evidence to support it, the reviewing court on the entire evidence is left with the definite and firm conviction that a mistake has been committed. Id. at 395. When the Court reviews conclusions of law de novo, it makes an independent review, and is free to arrive at its own holding. See First Options of Chicago v. Kaplan, 514 U.S. 938, 947 (1995). **12**

STATEMENT OF THE CASE

This Court is being asked to reverse a Minnesota Supreme Court judgment that Respondents were entitled to suppress evidence on Fourth Amendment grounds. The issue at hand is the constitutionality of an officer's naked-eye observation of Respondents as they bagged cocaine in an apartment in which they were neither residents nor overnight guests. **13**

On May 15, 1994, a confidential informant reported to Officer Jim Thielen that drug activity was occurring in a nearby apartment. Record E-1. The informant specified that he or she had viewed the occupants of 3943 South Valley View, Apartment 103, sitting at a table placing a white powdery substance into plastic bags. Record E-2. The informant, who also gave the officer details about a car the informant believed the apartment occupants were using, said that he or she had seen the drug activity from outside the apartment's ground-level window when the informant had walked past the window. Record G-9, G-39. **14**

At approximately 8:00 P.M., in response to the informant's report, the officer drove to the apartment complex and then walked on a grassy common area to a spot one to one-and-a-half feet from the window of Apartment 103. Record G-45, G-13. From his location in the apartment complex yard, Officer Thielen could see into the interior of Apartment 103. Record E-2. At no time during his observation did Officer Thielen place his hands along the window. Record G-13. He used no flashlight or other device to supplement his natural senses. Id. **15**

Though the grassy area on which Officer Thielen stood featured some shrubs and trees, the shrubs were not planted immediately in front of the apartment window to create an enclosure that prevented the public from gaining entrance to the area. See Record E-10. The area outside the window was one on which residents and non-residents regularly walked and interacted with others. Record G-44, G-32, G-68. Children commonly played there, and on at least one occasion a bicycle was left directly outside Thompson's window. Record G-71. **16**

Through gaps in the drawn horizontal mini-blinds on the window, Officer Thielen observed the same scene the informant had described to him: two males and one female sitting at a kitchen table handling a white powdery substance. Record E-2. One male placed the powder onto the table, then passed the substance to the second male, who placed the powder into plastic bags. Id. The second male gave the plastic bag to the female, who cut off the ends of the bag for sealing. Id. The officer observed the

12 Because the writer never discusses the significance of findings of facts in her argument, she need not draw the Court's attention to the standard of review for such findings.

13 Note that the writer provides context by telling the Court what it is being asked to decide. While the facts included are certainly more sympathetic to the petitioner's argument, they are facts and not legal conclusions, and thus are appropriately used here.

14 Note the use of the words "specified" and "details" to heighten the credibility of the informant's information.

15 Here, the writer creates a position of emphasis with a paragraph break, to emphasize the things that the officer did *not* do and which are crucial to her argument.

16 This record was a complex one; notice how the writer assembled facts from various places in the record ("E-10," "G-44, G-32, G-68"). The citations increase the reliability of the fact statement and make it easy for the Court to check the validity of the facts.

activity for 15 minutes, during which time the three individuals filled five or six bags. Record G-13, G-14.

Officer Thielen then contacted South Metro Drug Task Force Officer Kevin Kallestad, who applied for warrants to search the apartment and the car that the informant indicated may have belonged to the apartment occupants. Record F-7. At approximately 10:30 P.M., police stopped the car as it left the premises. Record E-3. Officer Thielen recognized the driver, Respondent Wayne Thomas Carter, and the passenger, Respondent Melvin Johns, as the males he had observed in the apartment. Record G-21, G-22. Officer Thielen identified Carter as the individual he had seen putting the white substance onto the table and dividing it into piles and Johns as the man who placed the piles into the bags. Id.

Respondents were arrested, and when police executed a search warrant on the vehicle, they discovered pagers, a scale, and more than 40 grams of a white mixture that later tested positive for cocaine. Record E-3. After Respondents' arrests, police returned to the apartment and arrested its occupant, Kimberly Thompson. When police executed a search warrant on the apartment, they found plastic bags and cocaine residue on the kitchen table. State v. Carter, 569 N.W.2d 169, 172 (Minn. 1997).

Both Petitioner and Respondents stipulated that the sole lessee of Apartment 103 was Kimberly Thompson. **17** Officer Thielen identified Thompson as the woman he had viewed cutting off the ends of the baggies and placing the baggies in piles. Record E-3. Nothing in the record indicates any personal or social relationship between Thompson and the Respondents. See Record E-4. No evidence was presented that Respondents lived at Apartment 103 long term, were overnight guests or were related to the leaseholder. See Record E-7. Both Respondents are residents of Chicago, Illinois, and no evidence was presented as to their status in the apartment except that the officer viewed them from outside the window for a short period of time on May 15, 1994. See Record E-3, E-4. None of Respondents' personal effects or clothing were found on the premises. See Record G-2.

At trial, Respondents moved to suppress all evidence obtained as a result of Officer Thielen's initial observation of the apartment, on the grounds that his observation constituted a warrantless search. Record E-7. On December 16, 1994, the District Court for the First Judicial District in the County of Dakota denied Respondents' motion to suppress. Record E-5. The court held that Respondents had no standing to challenge the officer's observations through Thompson's window, because Respondents failed to present any evidence that their expectations of privacy were expectations that society is prepared to recognize as reasonable. Record E-7. The district court further held that the officer's observation was not a Fourth Amendment search. The court found that Officer Thielen's observation was made from a grassy common area outside the curtilage of the apartment and that the observation was limited to scenes in plain view, and therefore, the observation did not violate any reasonable expectation of privacy. Record E-9. **18**

After Respondents were found guilty, they appealed to the Minnesota Court of Appeals. The Minnesota Court of Appeals affirmed in State v. Carter, concluding that Carter did not have standing to bring a motion to suppress the evidence. State v. Carter, 545 N.W.2d 695, 697 (Minn. Ct. App. 1996). The Minnesota Court of Appeals also affirmed in State v. Johns, concluding that the officer acted reasonably in walking to the window and in continuing to observe. State v. Johns, No. C9-95-1765, 1996 WL 310305, at *2 (Minn. Ct. App. June 11, 1996). Respondents appealed to the Supreme Court of Minnesota, which reversed the trial court's judgment. State v. Carter, 569 N.W.2d 169 (Minn. 1997); State v. Johns, 569 N.W.2d 180 (Minn. 1997). The State filed a Writ of Certiorari, arguing that Carter and Johns

17 This paragraph gives details to support the assertion that Respondents had no expectation of privacy in the apartment. The paragraph starts with a "topic sentence," focusing on the "sole lessee," and backs it up with details that will lead the reader to conclude that respondents' sole connection with the apartment was to use it to bag cocaine.

18 Notice how the writer goes into more detail on the holdings at the trial court level, which were in the petitioner's favor. Take care not to go into *exhaustive* detail; that will usually backfire.

lacked a legitimate expectation of privacy in Thompson's apartment and that Officer Thielen's observation was not a search. The Supreme Court granted certiorari to review the decision of the Minnesota Supreme Court. **19**

SUMMARY OF THE ARGUMENT

This Court should reverse the Minnesota Supreme Court's judgment. The Minnesota Supreme Court incorrectly reversed the trial court's denial of Respondents' motion to suppress. First, it erroneously ruled that Respondents had a legitimate expectation of privacy while in another's apartment for the sole purpose of illegally bagging cocaine. Second, it wrongly held that an officer conducted a search when he merely observed criminal activity in plain view from an area outside the apartment's curtilage. **20**

This Court's Fourth Amendment jurisprudence demonstrates that the Minnesota Supreme Court's ruling was erroneous. In order to invoke the Fourth Amendment's protections, an individual must prove that he had a legitimate expectation of privacy. An individual possesses a legitimate expectation of privacy when he demonstrates that he has both a subjective expectation of privacy and an expectation of privacy that society is prepared to view as reasonable.

Respondents were sitting at an illuminated kitchen table facing a window of a ground-floor apartment and packaging cocaine. Respondents should have realized that a passerby could have looked into the apartment and noticed the illegal activity occurring within the apartment. Thus, Respondents can claim no subjective expectation of privacy.

Additionally, any subjective expectation of privacy Respondents possessed is not one that society is prepared to recognize as reasonable in light of longstanding social customs that serve functions recognized as valuable by society. As non-overnight guests, they lacked the connection with the premises that legitimizes an expectation of privacy. Even if shorter-term guests can claim the protection of the Fourth Amendment, only those short-term guests who are present for socially permissible and valuable reasons qualify for Fourth Amendment protection. Respondents were present only to conduct criminal business activities, and therefore did not have an expectation of privacy that was reasonable in light of longstanding social customs that serve functions recognized as valuable by society.

Furthermore, even assuming that Respondents are entitled to invoke the Fourth Amendment's protections, no Fourth Amendment search occurred. A search occurs only when governmental agents intrude upon an area in which an individual has a reasonable expectation of privacy. **21** A reasonable expectation of privacy is violated when an officer intrudes upon the home or its curtilage, the area immediately surrounding the home that shares the same private characteristics as the home. Conversely, there is no violation of a reasonable expectation of privacy, and therefore no search, when an officer merely stands outside the curtilage of a residence and observes what is in plain view.

In the case at bar, the officer stood in a publicly accessible common area outside the apartment's curtilage. The officer used only his natural senses to observe what was in plain view. He conducted his observation without physical intrusion, without the use of any device, and in a manner that any member of the public could have employed. The officer's conduct violated no reasonable expectation of privacy and therefore was not a Fourth Amendment search.

For the above reasons, this Court should hold that Respondents had no legitimate expectation of privacy in the apartment and that the observations of the officer did not constitute a search. This Court should reverse the Minnesota Supreme Court's judgment.

ARGUMENT

I. As temporary business invitees present in another's residence for the sole purpose of packaging drugs, Respondents had no legitimate expectation of privacy and, thus, may not invoke the Fourth Amendment's protections.

Individuals invited to another's residence temporarily and for the sole purpose of conducting illegal business do not possess a legitimate expectation of privacy. Respondents, who were present in Thompson's apartment for a very short period of time and for the sole purpose of packaging drugs, have no legitimate expectation of privacy and thus, may not invoke the Fourth Amendment's protections. Therefore, this Court must reverse. **22**

23 The Fourth Amendment to the United States Constitution guarantees "[t]he right of the people to be secure in their persons, houses, papers, and effects, against unreasonable searches and seizures." U.S. Const. Amend. IV. Only individuals who demonstrate a legitimate expectation of privacy can claim the protection of the Fourth Amendment. Minnesota v. Olson, 495 U.S. 91, 95 (1990); Smith v. Maryland, 442 U.S. 735, 740 (1979).

In order to demonstrate a legitimate expectation of privacy, an individual must satisfy a two-pronged test set forth in Katz v. United States, 389 U.S. 347 (1967). First, an individual must exhibit an actual, subjective expectation of privacy in the searched premises at the time of the alleged search. Id. at 361 (Harlan, J., concurring). Second, the individual's expectation must be one that society is prepared to recognize as "reasonable." Id. The expectation must be reasonable in light of "longstanding social customs that serve functions recognized as valuable by society." Olson, 495 U.S. at 98. The proponent of a motion to suppress bears the burden of proving that he or she had a legitimate expectation of privacy. See Rakas v. Illinois, 439 U.S. 128, 130-31 n.1 (1978).

24 In the case at bar, Respondents failed to demonstrate a subjective expectation of privacy. Respondents engaged in illegal acts in a well-lit room directly in front of a window that faced a public area. Even assuming Respondents did possess a subjective expectation of privacy, Respondents failed to show that their subjective expectation of privacy was one that was reasonable in light of longstanding social customs that serve functions recognized as valuable by society. Respondents were temporary invitees whose activities within the apartment were both criminal and commercial. Bagging cocaine is not a social custom that serves functions recognized as valuable by society.

25 Respondents had neither a subjective expectation of privacy nor an expectation of privacy that society is prepared to recognize as reasonable, so they cannot claim a legitimate expectation of privacy. Having demonstrated no legitimate expectation of privacy, they may not assert a Fourth Amendment challenge. Because this Court should be extremely reluctant to expand the class of persons who can claim legitimate expectations of privacy, and because Respondents have not demonstrated that they fit within any group that has such a claim, this Court should reverse.

5

---

22 This paragraph gives a quick summary of the writer's whole argument *for this section.* Because this argument alone is dispositive, it's appropriate to state that the Court must reverse if it accepts the argument.

23 In these two paragraphs, the writer lays out the legal groundwork for her roman I argument. Note how she starts with the Fourth Amendment — the central rule at issue — and then moves to the cases that lay out the rules about "expectation of privacy," which is the rule at issue in this section (roman I) of the argument.

24 In this paragraph, the writer applies the rule to the facts in a conclusory way to support her assertion that the respondents have no legitimate expectation of privacy.

25 In this paragraph, the writer provides a roadmap to the specific arguments that will be addressed as subpoints within the roman I heading. Note that not all roadmaps must contain enumerated points.

A. Respondents failed to meet their burden of proving that they had a legitimate expectation of privacy, because they introduced absolutely no evidence regarding their status in Thompson's apartment.

Respondents bore the burden of proving that they had a legitimate expectation of privacy that entitled them to invoke the Fourth Amendment's protection. Respondents failed to introduce any evidence whatsoever regarding their status in Thompson's apartment and, therefore, failed to meet their burden of proof. Because Respondents have proved no legitimate expectation of privacy, this Court must reverse.

The proponent of a motion to suppress bears the burden of establishing that his or her own rights were violated by the challenged search. **26** Before a criminal defendant can bring a motion to suppress evidence on the basis that it was obtained in violation of the Fourth Amendment, the defendant must show that he or she is a proper party to assert the claim of illegality and to seek the remedy of exclusion. See Rakas v. Illinois, 439 U.S. 128, 130-31 n.1 (1978); Simmons v. United States, 390 U.S. 377, 389-90 (1968); Jones v. United States, 362 U.S. 257, 261 (1960) (indicating that "it is entirely proper to require of one who seeks to challenge the legality of a search as the basis for suppressing relevant evidence that he allege, and if the allegation be disputed, that he establish, that he himself was a victim of an invasion of privacy"). The defendant in a criminal trial bears the burden of proving that his or her expectation of privacy was a reasonable one. Florida v. Riley, 488 U.S. 445, 455 (1989) (O'Connor, J., concurring).

27 In the present case, Respondents made a motion to suppress on Fourth Amendment grounds, Record E-7 and therefore bore the burden of proving they had a legitimate expectation of privacy. Yet the record is entirely devoid of evidence of any connection between Respondents and the apartment that would give rise to a legitimate expectation of privacy. The trial court explicitly found that "[n]o evidence was presented as to [Respondents'] status in the apartment" other than that Officer Thielen viewed Respondents packaging cocaine inside the apartment for a very short time on May 15, 1994. Record at E-4. The record's sparseness is attributable only to Respondents' failure to introduce evidence regarding their status.

Having failed to meet their burden of proving a legitimate expectation of privacy, Respondents cannot attempt to assert a Fourth Amendment claim. This Court must reverse.

B. Respondents had no legitimate expectation of privacy because any subjective expectation they might have had while temporarily in another's home for the sole purpose of conducting illegal business was not one society recognizes as reasonable.

Even assuming that Respondents possessed a subjective expectation of privacy, Respondents failed to establish that their subjective expectation of privacy was one that society views as reasonable as required by the second prong of the Katz test. Katz v. United States, 389 U.S. at 361 (Harlan, J., concurring). **28** Respondents' expectation was not one society is prepared to recognize as reasonable because (1) society is only prepared to recognize as reasonable the privacy expectations of overnight guests and (2) even if society is prepared to recognize as reasonable the privacy expectations of non-overnight guests, society is not prepared to recognize as reasonable the privacy expectations of business invitees present only to commit the crime of packaging drugs.

26 Although a writer may sometimes violate convention by failing to cite to authority for legal assertions (more typically, as in a summary of the argument; less typically, in a roadmap, as in the paragraph above), the writer *should* have a citation to legal authority here. For guidance on when readers expect citations to authority, see § 6.6.1.

27 This argument is placed first because it must come first logically. However, because the writer has other arguments that she believes will carry more weight, she does not complete a thorough analysis of her point.

28 Even though this introduction is very minimal, it provides context for the argument and a roadmap to the subpoints.

1. The <u>Olson</u> rule dictates that only overnight guests have a connection to a premises that gives rise to a legitimate expectation of privacy.

Respondents, who introduced no evidence that they were anything other than temporary, transient visitors on the premises for the sole purpose of conducting illegal business, simply do not belong to the class of individuals who have an expectation of privacy that society is prepared to recognize as reasonable. Therefore, they do not have a legitimate expectation of privacy in Thompson's apartment and cannot assert a Fourth Amendment challenge to any alleged search of the premises.

[29] In 1990, this Court established the rule that "status as an overnight guest is alone enough to show that [a defendant has] an expectation of privacy in the home that society is prepared to recognize as reasonable." <u>Minnesota v. Olson</u>, 495 U.S. 91, 96-97 (1990) [30] In <u>Olson</u>, the Court found that a defendant suspected of driving the getaway car used in a robbery-murder had a legitimate expectation of privacy in his girlfriend's duplex sufficient to challenge a warrantless entry into the duplex. [31] <u>Id.</u> at 100. Olson, who had been at the duplex for several days, had a change of clothes at the duplex and had spent the previous night there. <u>Id.</u> at 97 n.6. [32] This Court reasoned that, because staying overnight with a host is a socially necessary practice and because all citizens share the expectation that an overnight guest's host will respect the guest's privacy, Olson had a sufficient interest in his girlfriend's home to assert a Fourth Amendment challenge. <u>Id.</u> at 98-99. His expectation of privacy was one that society recognizes as reasonable. <u>Id.</u> [33]

Though some lower courts have been confused as to the scope of the <u>Olson</u> rule, the reasoning in <u>Olson</u> and this Court's emphasis on Olson's overnight status indicate that the holding does not extend to invitees who are not overnight guests.

In establishing the rule that overnight guests have a legitimate expectation of privacy sufficient to challenge a Fourth Amendment search, the <u>Olson</u> Court repeatedly emphasized the overnight nature of the defendant's stay, thus illustrating that the holding does not cover a shorter-term guest. <u>Id.</u> at 97-100. No language in the opinion expressly states that the holding extends beyond overnight guests. The Court's reasoning and examples indicate that the Fourth Amendment protects only those who permanently reside on the premises and those who expect the same protection because they reside on the premises overnight.

The <u>Olson</u> Court discussed at length the social custom of staying overnight with friends or family when traveling to a strange city and the concomitant expectation of privacy that comes with seeking overnight shelter in another's home. The Court reasoned that an expectation of privacy arises because "[we] are at our most vulnerable when we are asleep because we cannot monitor our own safety or the security of our belongings." <u>Id.</u> at 99. While the police found Olson in his host's closet at 3 P.M., the Court's analysis indicated that he had earned the right to assert Fourth Amendment rights in the home because he was an overnight guest in the home the night before. <u>Id.</u> [34]

The factors that gave Olson the right to challenge a search of the residence all hinged on his overnight status. The overnight guest, not the shorter-term invitee, will have a "measure of control over the premises" when "the host is away or asleep." <u>Id.</u> at 99. The overnight guest, not the shorter-term invitee, is most likely not to "be confined to a restricted area of the house." <u>Id.</u> The overnight guest, not the shorter-term invitee, has a host who is "willing to share his house and his privacy with his guest." <u>Id.</u>

Furthermore, a significant number of courts that have examined <u>Olson</u> have ap-

7

[29] Here, the writer provides the rule in the topic sentence, but, appropriately saves the citation for the end of the sentence.

[30] The writer explicitly states the rule here and uses the explanation section of the paradigm to (1) demonstrate how the rule was applied in <u>Olson</u>, and (2) demonstrate that the <u>Olson</u> Court did not intend the rule to be expanded to guests other than "overnight" guests. In the application section, she will show that the respondents cannot be characterized as overnight guests and thus cannot benefit from this rule.

[31] This sentence provides reader with many of the elements necessary for a complete case description: the issue ("standing" to challenge a warrantless entry into the duplex), the disposition of that issue (his status was sufficient to allow him to challenge the entry), and some of the facts (he was in his girlfriend's duplex).

[32] Here are more details on the facts, provided because the issue of whether or not someone is an overnight guest is a fact-intensive inquiry.

[33] These last two sentences provide the Court's reasoning.

[34] The analysis of <u>Olson</u> is lengthy only because it is the source of the rule, and it illustrates one of the most controversial issues in the case.

35 The writer should identify how many circuits have decided this issue, and cite at least one that has gone the other way, so that the Court does not leave the brief to go looking for the answer.
36 Note that strong parentheticals will have three or four of the needed case description elements of issue, facts, disposition, and reasoning.
37 Disposition is indicated here.
38 Issue is indicated here.
39 Reasoning is implied here.
40 Facts are indicated here.
41 Facts are indicated here.
42 Disposition is indicated here.
43 Issue is indicated here.
44 These analyses are good, but in order to provide a complete picture, the writer should identify how many courts have decided this issue the other way. Otherwise, she is seen to be hiding the ball, and the Court may doubt the significance of these cases.
45 Facts are indicated here.
46 Disposition is indicated here.
47 Issue is indicated here.

plied the Olson rule narrowly. **35** Several courts have held that temporary, non-overnight presence for the purpose of illegal drug activity clearly falls outside of the Olson rule. See, e.g., Terry v. Martin, 120 F.3d 661, 664 (7th Cir. 1997) (**36** holding that the legitimate expectation of privacy realized by overnight guests did not extend **37** to confer Fourth Amendment standing **38** on temporary visitors **39** present in an apartment for the purpose of buying heroin **40**); United States v. Hicks, 978 F.2d 722, 724 (D.C. Cir. 1992) (holding that a guest who used an apartment to distribute cocaine **41** had no **42** legitimate expectation of privacy **43**).

Additionally, a number of lower courts have flatly declined to extend Olson to casual or temporary visitors. **44** See State v. Wise, 879 S.W.2d 494, 505 (Mo. 1994) (holding that a defendant who was in an apartment to use the telephone **45** had no **46** legitimate expectation of privacy **47**); Villarreal v. State, 893 S.W.2d 559, 561 (Tex. Ct. App. 1994) (declining to extend the Olson expectation to an invited guest who had not stayed overnight but "was welcome to stay if he wanted to"). Some courts have even declined to extend Olson to cover party guests. See, e.g., Fisher v. State, 665 So. 2d 1014 (Ala. Ct. App. 1995); Lewis v. United States, 594 A.2d 542, 546 (D.C. App. 1991). For example, in Lewis, the court held that a party guest who happened to fall asleep for several hours in a bedroom could not assert a Fourth Amendment challenge to a search of the apartment. Id. at 545. The court ruled that because Lewis offered no evidence that he had been invited to spend the night or intended to do so, he had not shown a legitimate expectation of privacy. Id. The court reasoned that a mere guest who is not spending the night is substantially different from the overnight guest who receives standing under Olson. Id.

In the present case, the record bears no evidence that Respondents were invited overnight guests. See Record E-4. Respondents were not lessees of the apartment. Record G-5. While Respondents were residents of another state, the record provides no evidence as to Respondents' status in the apartment or any link they may have had with it or with the lessee. See Record E-3. Indeed, the only evidence of Respondents' connection to the apartment is the police officer's testimony that he saw Respondents bagging cocaine inside the apartment for a period of 15 minutes. Record E-3. The sparseness of the record and the complete absence of evidence that Respondents intended to spend the night lead only to the conclusion that Respondents were temporary visitors who could not claim any parallel characteristics to the overnight guest in Olson. Record E-8.

The Minnesota Supreme Court conceded that "it is undisputed that Carter failed to produce any evidence that he was a 'guest' of Thompson's, let alone an 'overnight guest.'" State v. Carter, 569 N.W.2d 169, 175 (Minn. 1997). Given this Court's emphasis on the special privacy concerns of sleeping guests and the social custom of staying overnight, Respondents do not fall within the Olson rule and cannot claim an expectation of privacy that society is prepared to recognize as reasonable. Thus, they have no legitimate expectation of privacy and are not entitled to claim the protection of an Amendment that was not designed for their use.

2. Even if the Olson rule extends to non-overnight guests, Respondents' expectation of privacy is unreasonable because they were present only to conduct illegal business that is not valuable to society.

If Olson does not stand for the proposition that only overnight guests may assert a Fourth Amendment challenge, it at least stands for the proposition that only a very limited category of guests may do so. The limited category includes only those guests whose connections to the home give rise to an expectation of privacy that society is prepared to recognize as reasonable. See Olson, 495 U.S. at 98-99. Respondents failed to demonstrate that their expectation of privacy was one society is prepared to recognize as reasonable. The Minnesota Supreme Court found that Respondents demonstrated an expectation of privacy that society is prepared to recognize as reasonable because they were present in the apartment "to conduct a common task." State v. Carter, 569 N.W.2d 169, 176 (Minn. 1997). This Court should reverse the decision of the Minnesota Supreme Court because (1) the distribution of drugs is not a longstanding social custom that serves functions recognized as valuable by society and (2) Respondents were not "guests" in a home but rather were business invitees on the property for a purely commercial purpose, and therefore lost the Fourth Amendment protection normally associated with the home.

a. Illegal drug distribution is not a longstanding social custom that serves functions recognized as valuable by society.

Respondents, whose purpose for being on the premises was purely criminal, cannot claim that their expectation of privacy was reasonable in light of longstanding social customs that serve functions recognized as valuable by society. Therefore, they do not have a legitimate expectation of privacy in Thompson's apartment and cannot assert a Fourth Amendment challenge to any alleged search of the premises.

Society is prepared to recognize an individual's expectation of privacy as reasonable only when the individual was present on the premises for a purpose society deems permissible and valuable. Rakas, 439 U.S. at 144 n.12 (indicating that a legitimate expectation is one that is rooted in "understandings that are recognized and permitted by society"). In Olson, this Court held that an overnight guest's expectation of privacy was legitimate because the act of staying overnight is a "longstanding social custom that serves functions recognized as valuable by society." Olson, 439 U.S. at 98.

Generally, lower courts applying the Olson test have looked to the social utility of the defendants' activities when determining whether finding a legitimate expectation of privacy will promote a "longstanding social custom that serves functions recognized as valuable by society." First, in 1992, a California court found that a defendant who moved to suppress items seized at his brother's apartment while the defendant was babysitting there had a legitimate expectation of privacy. People v. Moreno, 3 Cal. Rptr. 2d 66, 70 (Cal. Ct. App. 1992). The court cited Olson and indicated that, "[l]ike 'staying overnight in another's home,' babysitting 'is a longstanding social custom that serves functions recognized as valuable by society.' " Id. at 70. **48** Because the babysitter's activity was permissible and valuable to society, society was prepared to recognize his expectation of privacy as reasonable. He therefore had a legitimate expectation of privacy and could challenge a Fourth Amendment search. Id.

48 The writer should include the Olson cite parenthetically here.

Second, in 1993, a court in the District of Columbia found that a defendant who regularly visited a home to feed and care for the homeowner's retarded adult son had a legitimate expectation of privacy "rooted in understandings that are recognized and permitted by society." Junior v. United States, 634 A.2d 411, 419 (D.C. 1993). Society benefits when a caretaker executes his responsibilities within a home. Because the activity in Junior served functions recognized as valuable by society, society was prepared to recognize the caretaker's expectation as reasonable. Thus, he had a legitimate expectation of privacy and could challenge a Fourth Amendment search. Id.

In contrast, this Court has repeatedly recognized that the possession, use, and distribution of illegal drugs represent "one of the greatest problems affecting the health and welfare of our population" and thus "one of the most serious problems confronting our society today." <u>Treasury Employees v. Von Raab</u>, 489 U.S. 656, 668, 674 (1989). The Court has expressed concern about the grave threat that illegal drugs, particularly cocaine, pose to society in terms of violence, crime, and social displacement. <u>Harmelin v. Michigan</u>, 501 U.S. 957, 1002 (1991). Certainly, this Court does not view illegal drug possession as a longstanding social custom that serves a function recognized as valuable by society. Rather, this Court has insisted that illegal drug activity is socially unacceptable and has held that the states have a great interest in prohibiting it. <u>See, e.g.</u>, <u>Employment Div., Dept. of Human Resources of Oregon v. Smith</u>, 494 U.S. 872 (1990) (holding that the Free Exercise Clause of the First Amendment does not prohibit application of Oregon drug laws to the ceremonial ingestion of peyote).

In the case at bar, Respondents cannot claim that their expectation of privacy was one that society is prepared to recognize as reasonable. The record indicates that Respondents engaged in only one activity while inside Thompson's apartment: bagging cocaine. Record at E-2. Respondents failed to introduce any evidence of any other purpose for their presence. <u>See</u> Record at E-4. Unlike the defendant in <u>Olson</u>, Respondents were not engaged in any longstanding social custom that serves functions recognized as valuable by society. Instead, Respondents were present at another's home for the sole purpose of committing a crime.

Because Respondents' criminal activity was not a longstanding social custom that serves functions recognized as valuable by society, Respondents' expectation of privacy was not one that society recognizes as reasonable. Therefore, Respondents had no legitimate expectation of privacy and cannot assert a Fourth Amendment challenge.

b. Respondents were present for a purely commercial purpose and were not entitled to the Fourth Amendment protection associated with the home.

Respondents were not present in a "home," but were on property for a purely commercial purpose. Respondents therefore are not entitled to the Fourth Amendment protection normally associated with the home and cannot claim that their expectation of privacy was one society is prepared to recognize as reasonable.

This Court has recognized that business premises invite lesser privacy expectations than do residences. <u>See</u> <u>G.M. Leasing Corp. v. United States</u>, 429 U.S. 338, 353 (1977); <u>see also</u> 1 Wayne R. LaFave, <u>Search and Seizure</u>, § 2.4(b) at 429 (2d ed. 1987). Similarly, while the home is afforded the full range of Fourth Amendment protections, <u>see</u> <u>Silverman v. United States</u>, 365 U.S. 505, 511 (1961), when the home is converted into a commercial center to which outsiders are invited to transact unlawful business, that business is not entitled to the great measure of sanctity afforded to homes. <u>See</u> <u>Lewis v. United States</u>, 385 U.S. 206, 211 (1966).

In <u>Lewis</u>, this Court held that a defendant who used his home for the felonious sale of narcotics could not claim a violation of any reasonable expectation of privacy when an undercover officer entered the home to purchase marijuana. <u>Id.</u> The Court emphasized that the officer never saw, heard, or took anything that was not contemplated and intended by the defendant as a necessary part of his illegal business. <u>Id.</u> at 210. Because the property was properly characterized as a place of business, the defendant could not contend that the officer had violated any expectation of privacy that society is prepared to recognize as reasonable. <u>Id.</u> at 211.

Utilizing the same reasoning, the D.C. Circuit held that a visitor who used another's apartment solely to conduct drug transactions could not claim Fourth Amendment protection. <u>United States v. Hicks</u>, 978 F.2d 722, 723-24 (D.C. Cir. 1992). The court reasoned that the defendant "treated the apartment as a base for his business operation, not as a sanctuary from outsiders." Id. at 724. "Hicks was not engaging in any longstanding social custom that serves functions recognized as valuable by society. Quite the opposite." Id. The court held that while the defendant may have been legitimately in the apartment, in the sense that the apartment tenant permitted his presence, the defendant did not have any legitimate expectation of privacy in the apartment, because he was present only to engage in illegal business. Id.

In the present case, Respondents, like the defendants in Lewis and Hicks, were present on property for the sole purpose of conducting criminal business. Record at E-4. As the Minnesota Court of Appeals noted, Respondents' claims that they were predominantly social guests in the apartment are "inconsistent with the only evidence concerning [their] stay in the apartment, which indicates that [they] used it for a business purpose — to package drugs." State v. Carter, 545 N.W.2d 695, 698 (Minn. Ct. App. 1996). Officers found Respondents in possession of 40 grams of cocaine, pagers, and a scale, Record E-3, illustrating that Respondents treated the apartment as a base for a business operation, not as a sanctuary from outsiders.

Like the apartments in Lewis and Hicks, the property in the present case had been converted into a commercial center to which outsiders were invited for purposes of transacting unlawful business. The business therefore was not entitled to the great measure of sanctity afforded to homes. Like the officer in Lewis, Officer Thielen observed only activities that were a necessary part of Respondents' illegal business. During the entire time Officer Thielen watched the apartment occupants, the occupants did nothing but divide and package cocaine. See Record at E-2, G-14.

Thus, Respondents, who were conducting a purely commercial activity, were not visitors to a "home" and were not engaging in longstanding social customs that serve functions recognized as valuable by society. While Respondents may have been legitimately in the apartment, in the sense that Thompson permitted their presence, Respondents did not have any legitimate expectation of privacy in the apartment because they were present only to conduct illegal business. Because Respondents' expectation of privacy was not one that society recognizes as reasonable, this Court must reverse.

C. Respondents may not claim a legitimate expectation of privacy, because by engaging in criminal acts in a well-lit room, directly in front of a window facing a widely used common area, they exhibited no subjective expectation of privacy.

Respondents, who engaged in criminal activity in an illuminated room directly in front of a window that faced a widely-used common area, manifested at most a *hope* that no one would view their unlawful acts. Respondents exhibited no actual, subjective *expectation* of privacy. Therefore, they cannot claim a legitimate expectation of privacy in Thompson's apartment and may not assert a Fourth Amendment challenge to any alleged search of the premises. **49**

An individual seeking to establish possession of a legitimate expectation of privacy must first demonstrate an "actual (subjective) expectation of privacy." Katz v. United States, 389 U.S. 347, 361 (Harlan, J., concurring). "What a person knowingly exposes to the public, even in his own home or office, is not the subject of Fourth Amendment protections." Id. at 351.

A person exhibits a subjective expectation of privacy when his or her conduct demonstrates his intent to keep activity private. See id. at 352. In Katz, the defendant exhibited a subjective expectation of privacy when he closed the door to a telephone booth to prevent being overheard. Id. Katz did not knowingly expose his activity to

49 The writer articulates her conclusion in the first paragraph; in the second paragraph, the writer articulates the rule.

11

the public; rather, his conduct demonstrated his intent to keep the activity private. Id. Therefore, the government "violated the privacy upon which he justifiably relied" when it attached an electronic surveillance device to the telephone booth. Id. Because Katz had a subjective expectation of privacy, and that expectation was one society is prepared to recognize as reasonable, he had a legitimate expectation of privacy and was entitled to assert a Fourth Amendment challenge. Id. **50**

50 The writer then explains the rule, first by talking about a case in which the phrase-that-pays was met, and then by discussing a case in which the phrase-that-pays was not met.

In contrast, when individuals in all probability know that information or activities will be revealed to others, the individuals demonstrate no actual, subjective expectation of privacy. For example, a defendant challenged the government's installation of a pen register to record his telephone calls in Smith v. Maryland, 442 U.S. 735, 736 (1979). This Court held that the defendant likely entertained no actual, subjective expectation of privacy in phone numbers he dialed, as all telephone users realize that they must convey phone numbers to the telephone company and that the telephone company records the information. Id. at 742.

Smith illustrates that even an individual who has taken cautionary measures to protect his or her activity from public exposure may fail to exhibit a subjective expectation of privacy if those cautionary measures are in fact inadequate to safeguard the activity from public inspection. See id. at 743. The Smith Court held that the defendant did not demonstrate an actual, subjective expectation of privacy merely by using his home phone rather than some other phone. The Court reasoned that the defendant's conduct, although perhaps "calculated to keep the contents of his conversation private," could not have preserved the privacy of the number he dialed. Id. Thus, despite what may have been some effort to maintain secrecy, the defendant exhibited no actual, subjective expectation of privacy as to the exposed information. Id. Similarly, in a 1984 decision, this Court suggested that a defendant who hid his marijuana crop from the public view with two fences may have "manifested merely a hope that no one would observe his unlawful gardening pursuits" and not an actual, subjective expectation of privacy. California v. Ciraolo, 476 U.S. 207, 211-12 (1985).

51 Notice how the writer applies the rule to the facts. First, she states explicitly that the phrase-that-pays does not equal her client's facts. She follows that statement with necessary details and by distinguishing her client's case from one of the authority cases cited in the explanation section.

In the case at bar, Respondents' behavior and location within the apartment indicate that they had no actual, subjective expectation of privacy. **51** Respondents manifested at most a hope that no one would observe their unlawful pursuits inside Thompson's apartment. Nothing in the record indicates Respondents took any action to preserve their privacy. Unlike the defendant in Katz, Respondents introduced no evidence of conduct that demonstrated an intent to keep their activity private. Though the blinds were drawn, there is no indication that Respondents drew them. See Record at E-2, E-10. On the night in question, Respondents were present in a first-floor apartment that had several windows at ground level. Record G-26. The windows faced a public area that apartment residents and nonresidents frequented. Record G-69, G-70. As darkness fell in early evening, Respondents sat illuminated under a chandelier light at a table directly in front of one of these windows. Record G-13. Only a pane of glass and a set of blinds that featured a series of laths, Record G-50, separated Respondents from the adjacent common area. On the night in question, the blinds, though drawn, had a gap in them large enough for a citizen who passed by and an officer who stood a foot or more from the window to view easily the entire illuminated interior scene. Record G-13.

An individual in Respondents' position would have known and expected that a passerby could look through the gaps in the blinds and see into the illuminated kitchen. Thus, Respondents could not have actually expected that their illegal activities would go unnoticed. **52** Absent a subjective expectation, Respondents do not have a legitimate expectation of privacy and cannot assert a Fourth Amendment challenge to an alleged search of the premises. Therefore, this Court must reverse.

52 In this paragraph, the writer re-articulates her conclusion, and provides "Bacon links" to other relevant parts of her argument.

D. This Court should maintain its reluctance to expand the class of individuals who may claim a legitimate expectation of privacy and invoke the exclusionary rule.

Because the arguments for limiting the use of the exclusionary rule are compelling, this Court should continue its reluctance to expand the class of persons that may invoke the rule. The Court should reverse the case at bar because doing so recognizes (1) the significant counter interests in public safety and the proper functioning of the justice system and (2) the fundamental constitutional doctrine that an individual may not assert the rights of a third party.

Each application of the exclusionary rule "exacts a substantial social cost," as "[r]elevant and reliable evidence is kept from the trier of fact and the search for truth at trial is deflected." Rakas, 439 U.S. at 138. While recognizing the deterrent aim of the exclusionary rule, the Rakas Court emphasized that "misgivings as to the benefit of enlarging the class of persons who may invoke that rule are properly considered when deciding whether to expand standing to assert Fourth Amendment violations." Id. Expanding the class of individuals who may invoke the exclusionary rule to include persons whose own rights were not violated would be harmful to our system of justice and detrimental to effective police work.

Because of the potential harm, this Court has expressly ruled that only individuals whose rights were infringed by the search itself may urge suppression of the fruits of a Fourth Amendment violation. Alderman v. United States, 394 U.S. 165, 175 (1969). The additional benefits of extending the exclusionary rule to other defendants would not "justify further encroachment upon the public interest in prosecuting those accused of crime and having them acquitted or convicted on the basis of all the evidence which exposes the truth." Id.

Under core principles of constitutional law, a person may seek a remedy for a constitutional violation only if he or she belongs "to the class for whose sake the constitutional protection is given." Hatch v. Reardon, 204 U.S. 152, 160 (1907). A person asserting a constitutional claim must show an adverse interest based upon an alleged violation of his or her own rights, rather than the violation of the rights of some third party. See, e.g., Tileston v. Ullman, 318 U.S. 44, 46 (1943). This Court has repeatedly rejected attempts to vicariously assert violations of Fourth Amendment rights. See, e.g., Rakas, 439 U.S. at 150; Brown v. United States, 411 U.S. 223, 230 (1973). In 1980, this Court held that defendants charged with crimes of possession may claim the benefits of the exclusionary rule only if their own Fourth Amendment rights have in fact been violated. United States v. Salvucci, 448 U.S. 83, 85 (1980). To allow otherwise, the Court said, "serves only to afford a windfall to defendants whose Fourth Amendment rights have not been violated," an outcome that cannot be tolerated in light of the significant public interests in curbing crime and in fairly and accurately determining defendants' guilt or innocence at trial. Id. at 95.

Extending the Olson holding to protect Respondents in the present case would afford Respondents a windfall. The apartment where Respondents were observed was not their home, see Record G-5, and, as discussed above, they had no legitimate expectation of privacy there. They simply do not belong to the class for whose sake the constitutional protection is given. Extending the right to invoke the exclusionary rule to individuals in Respondents' situation would hamper effective police work and unacceptably thwart the truth-finding functions of judge and jury. Allowing Respondents to assert third-party rights before this Court would be contrary to decades of established case law and contrary to good public policy. Therefore, this Court must reverse.

II. Officer Thielen's conduct was not a Fourth Amendment search because he stood in a location where any member of the public might have stood and observed the criminal activity in a manner any member of the public might have employed.

53 This section provides an introduction to what follows by (a) providing necessary legal context, and (b) providing a roadmap.

53 Even if Respondents may invoke the Fourth Amendment's protections to challenge a search of Thompson's residence, no Fourth Amendment search occurred in the case at bar. Because the officer's naked-eye observation from the apartment common area was not a Fourth Amendment search, this Court must reverse.

A search occurs only when governmental agents intrude upon an area in which a person has a "reasonable" expectation of privacy. See California v. Ciraolo, 476 U.S. 207, 212 (1986). A reasonable expectation of privacy exists when an individual manifests a subjective expectation of privacy in the place from which the observation occurred and demonstrates that his or her subjective expectation is one that society recognizes as reasonable. See Katz v. United States, 389 U.S. 347, 361 (1967) (Harlan, J., concurring). A "search" suggests "some exploratory investigation, or an invasion and quest, a looking for or seeking out." 1 Wayne R. La Fave, Search and Seizure § 2.1(a) at 301 (2d ed. 1987) (quoting C.J.S. Searches and Seizures § 1 (1952).

> [I]t has been held that a search implies some sort of force, either actual or constructive, much or little. A search implies a prying into hidden places for that which is concealed and that the object searched for has been hidden or intentionally put out of the way. While it has been said that ordinarily searching is a function of sight, it is generally held that the mere looking at that which is open to view is not a "search."

Id.

This Court examines two factors in determining whether a Fourth Amendment search occurred: (1) the location from which the observation occurred and (2) the manner in which the observation occurred. See Ciraolo, 476 U.S. at 213; 1 Wayne R. LaFave, Search and Seizure § 2.3(f) at 497 (2d ed. 1987). An examination of these two factors in the present case indicates that no Fourth Amendment search occurred. The observation in the present case took place from a publicly accessible location outside the apartment's curtilage, where the officer had a right to be. The officer observed in a manner that could have been carried out by any private passerby, without physical intrusion or the use of any device, and with only the aid of his natural senses to detect what was in plain view. Under these circumstances, the officer violated no reasonable expectation of privacy. Thus, Officer Thielen's observations were not a Fourth Amendment search.

A. No Fourth Amendment search occurred because the officer merely viewed what was in plain view from a publicly accessible common area outside the apartment's curtilage, where Respondents had no reasonable expectation of privacy.

54 This introductory material would be even better with just one citation to provide needed legal context.

In the case at bar, no Fourth Amendment search occurred because Respondents had no reasonable expectation of privacy in the location where the officer stood when he observed the criminal activity occurring within the apartment. **54** The officer (1) was standing on a public area, outside the apartment's curtilage and (2) viewed only what was in plain view from this lawful vantage point. Because Officer Thielen merely stood where any other member of the public might have stood and viewed what any other member of the public might have viewed, the officer's behavior was not a search.

1. The unenclosed, publicly used common are where Officer Thielen stood was not within the curtilage of the apartment.

Officer Thielen made his observation of the apartment from an unenclosed, publicly accessible location that was regularly used by tenants of a multi-unit apartment complex. Because the observation was made from an area outside the curtilage of the apartment where Respondents were located, the observation violated no reasonable expectation of privacy. Therefore, the observation was not a search.

A person possesses a reasonable expectation of privacy, and thus, a search occurs, when an officer makes an observation from a location within the curtilage of a private home. See Oliver v. United States, 466 U.S. 170, 180 (1984). Curtilage, "the land immediately surrounding and associated with the home," is "the area to which extends the intimate activity associated with the 'sanctity of a man's home and the privacies of life.' " Id. (Quoting Boyd v. United States, 116 U.S. 616, 630 (1886)). Whether an area is curtilage depends upon four factors: (1) the proximity of the area to the home, (2) whether the area is included within an enclosure surrounding the home, (3) the nature of the uses to which the area is put, and (4) steps taken by the resident to protect the area from observation. See United States v. Dunn, 480 U.S. 295, 301 (1987). The primary focus of the curtilage test is whether the area "harbors those intimate activities associated with domestic life and the privacies of home." Id. at 304.

This Court uses the curtilage concept to recognize that certain areas are so intimately linked with the home, both physically and psychologically, that privacy expectations are as heightened in those areas as they would be within the home itself. 4 William Blackstone, Commentaries 225 (1902). Courts have ruled that curtilage can include garages, Martin v. United States, 183 F.2d 436, 439 (4th Cir. 1950), barns, Rozencranz v. United States, 356 F.2d 310, 313 (1st Cir. 1966), smokehouses, Roberson v. United States, 165 F.2d 752, 754 (6th Cir. 1948), greenhouses, Florida v. Riley, 488 U.S. 445, 452 (1989) (plurality opinion), and backyards, California v. Ciraolo, 476 U.S. 207, 213 (1986). Because curtilage is afforded the same protection as the private residence, an invasion of the curtilage violates a reasonable expectation of privacy. Oliver, 466 U.S. at 180.

On the other hand, an officer violates no reasonable expectation of privacy when he or she merely observes a scene in plain view from outside the curtilage. Dunn, 480 U.S. at 304. In Dunn, officers observed a drug laboratory inside the defendant's barn while standing outside the curtilage. Id. at 304. This Court held that even if the barn itself had been within the curtilage, the defendant could claim no reasonable expectation of privacy, because the scene was plainly visible from outside the curtilage. The police officers could look into the barn without violating the Fourth Amendment. Id.

Applying the four-factor curtilage test to the location where Officer Thielen stood reveals that the location is not within the curtilage of Thompson's apartment. First, as the trial court correctly noted, although the area where the officer stood is close to Thompson's apartment, the communal nature of the grounds "detracts from the closeness of the claimed curtilage area" to Thompson's apartment. Record E-10. The trial court in the case at bar characterized the place where the officer walked as a "grassy common area." Record at E-2. Apartment complex common areas are by nature in close proximity to many apartments, and no single apartment lessee can make a special claim to them. Cases in lower courts have recognized that it is "well-settled that observations made by law enforcement officials from the common areas of multi-unit dwellings ordinarily do not violate a resident's reasonable expectation of privacy."

15

55 A parenthetical is
not needed here be-
cause the writer pro-
vides a parenthetical in
the same paragraph.

United States v. Acevedo, 627 F.2d 68, 69 n.1 (7th Cir. 1980). **55** The privacy expectation in apartment common areas "is often diminished because it is not subject to
the exclusive control of one tenant and is utilized by tenants generally and numerous
visitors attracted to a multiple occupancy building." 1 Wayne R. LaFave, Search and
Seizure § 2.3(f) at 414 (2d ed. 1987). See, e.g., United States v. Holland, 755 F.2d
253, 255 (2d Cir. 1985) (holding that individual tenants in multi-tenant buildings
have no legitimate expectation of privacy in common hallway areas, even when
guarded by locked doors); Acevedo, 627 F.2d at 69 n.1 (holding that a surveillance
officer's observation of an undercover heroin purchase while standing in a gangway
to the side of an apartment complex did not violate expectation of privacy); State v.
Hines, 323 So. 2d 449, 450 (La. 1975) (holding that apartment tenants have no reasonable expectation of privacy as to the "common yard open to the public").

Second, the location where Officer Thielen stood was not within any enclosed
area attached to Thompson's apartment. No fence surrounded the area. Record E-10.
Shrubs and bushes were planted near where Officer Thielen stood, Record G-43, but
the trial court found that none were planted "immediately in front of the window to
create an enclosure-type space that prevents the public from gaining entrance to the
area." Record E-10. The trial court found no evidence that the shrubs were planted
for privacy reasons rather than for aesthetic reasons. Record E-11.

Third, the record unquestionably indicates that the area in the case at bar was
publicly used. Officer Thielen stood in a common area open to all residents and utilized by nonresidents as well. Record E-10, G-69. Children regularly played on the
lawn. Record E-11. Passersby often left the sidewalk to walk freely across the area.
Id. The trial court found that a bicycle parked next to Thompson's window illustrated
that the public had access to the area directly in front of Thompson's apartment.
Record E-10, G-71. Indeed, the informant who reported the illegal activity to Officer
Thielen said that he had noticed Respondents when he himself was walking past the
window. Record G-39.

Finally, the record contains no evidence whatsoever that Thompson took personal
measures to protect the area outside her window as if it were her own curtilage. See
Record E-11. Indeed, as a tenant in a multi-unit complex, she could not protect the
area outside her window as her own. In this regard, the present case is distinguishable from cases involving single-family homes. Unlike the owner of a single-family
home, Thompson was only one of many individuals who could access and use the
common area outside her window. Individuals who share a building with other tenants who are entitled to use the area without giving notice or seeking permission
cannot reasonably expect privacy from uninvited individuals. See e.g., United States
v. Fields, 113 F.3d 313 (2d Cir. 1997) (holding that a police officer's observation of
defendants cooking and bagging crack cocaine through a partially covered first-floor
apartment window was not a Fourth Amendment search, and distinguishing the case
from cases involving single-family dwellings).

Thompson and her guests did not put the area outside her apartment window to private use. The area did not "harbor those intimate activities associated with domestic
life." Oliver, 466 U.S. at 180. Under the Dunn test, the area where Officer Thielen
stood does not fall within the curtilage of the apartment. An observation of a scene in
plain view from the location where Thielen stood is not a Fourth Amendment search.

2. The apartment interior was in plain view from Officer Thielen's lawful vantage point.

Because Thielen was located outside the curtilage of the apartment, he was free to
observe any scene in plain view. Respondents' activities within the apartment were

in plain view from Thielen's lawful vantage point. Thus, Thielen's observation violated no reasonable expectation of privacy and did not constitute a Fourth Amendment search.

The Fourth Amendment protection of the home "has never been extended to require law enforcement officers to shield their eyes when passing by a home on public thoroughfares." California v. Ciraolo, 476 U.S. 207, 213 (1985). While a person's home is, for most purposes, a place where he or she expects privacy, activities that the homeowner "exposes to the 'plain view' of outsiders are not protected." Katz v. United States, 389 U.S. 347, 361 (1967) (Harlan, J., concurring).

Illegal activities in plain view from outside the curtilage are not protected even if the police observation is specifically directed at identifying illegal activity. United States v. Dunn, 480 U.S. 294 (1987) (holding that an officer's observation into a barn was not a Fourth Amendment search and stressing it was irrelevant that the observation was motivated by a law enforcement purpose); Ciraolo, 476 U.S. at 212, 213. In Ciraolo, the defendant was growing marijuana in a 15-by-25 foot plot in his backyard. He surrounded the yard with a 6-foot outer fence and a 10-foot inner fence. Id. at 209. Officers flew over the defendant's house in a private airplane and readily identified the illegal plants using only the naked eye. Id. The government argued that the observation was analogous to looking through a knothole or an opening in a fence: "If there is an opening, the police may look." Id. at 220. This Court agreed with the government, holding that the observation was not a Fourth Amendment search. The airspace was outside the curtilage of the apartment, and the Court reasoned that the scene would have been in plain view to any member of the public flying in the same airspace. Thus, the officers violated no reasonable expectation of privacy. Id. at 213-14.

In the case at bar, the officer merely observed a scene that was in plain view from his lawful vantage point. As was discussed above, the area in which Officer Thielen stood was outside the curtilage of the apartment. While standing outside the curtilage, the officer plainly viewed Respondents' unlawful activities. Record E-2. While Officer Thielen did go to the common area outside the apartment window in response to the report from the informant, Record G-11, his motivation is irrelevant. The illegal activity was in plain view regardless of Officer Thielen's motivation. Just as the Fourth Amendment does not require police traveling in public airways to refrain from observing what is visible to the naked eye, the Fourth Amendment did not require Officer Thielen to refrain from viewing what could be seen from the public area outside Thompson's window.

Activities that Respondents exposed to the plain view of outsiders were not protected by the Fourth Amendment. Because Respondents' activities within the apartment were in plain view from Thielen's lawful vantage point, Thielen's observation violated no reasonable expectation of privacy. Therefore, the officer's observation was not a Fourth Amendment search. This Court must reverse.

B. No Fourth Amendment search occurred because Officer Thielen, who used only his natural senses to observe the apartment without physical intrusion, took no extraordinary measures.

56 Officer Thielen's manner of observation violated no reasonable expectation of privacy. No reasonable expectation of privacy exists when an officer takes only ordinary measures, using only his or her natural senses, to view what any private passerby could have viewed with no physical intrusion. See California v. Ciraolo, 476 U.S. 207, 213-14 (1985). Because Officer Thielen took no extraordinary mea-

56 This introductory section does a good job of (a) providing legal context and (b) providing a roadmap.

17

sures to view the inside of the apartment, his observation violated no reasonable expectation of privacy. Therefore, the observation was not a Fourth Amendment search.

As Professor LaFave has noted, when the police "resort to the extraordinary step of positioning themselves where neither neighbors nor the general public would be expected to be, the observation or overhearing of what is occurring within a dwelling constitutes a Fourth Amendment search." 1 Wayne R. LaFave, Search and Seizure § 2.3(f), at 414 (2d ed. 1987). Conversely, if police merely observe a scene in the same manner as any member of the public might have viewed it, they have taken no extraordinary measure and have violated no reasonable expectation of privacy. Texas v. Brown, 460 U.S. 730, 749 (1983). The measures taken by Officer Thielen were not extraordinary, because (1) any member of the public might have achieved the same view and (2) Officer Thielen neither used an electronic device nor physically invaded the apartment. Because the officer took no extraordinary measure, he violated no reasonable expectations of privacy and did not conduct a search. Therefore, this Court must reverse.

1. Officer Thielen did no more than any other member of the public might have done to achieve a view of the apartment interior.

Officer Thielen, who merely positioned himself to achieve a view that any other member of the public might have achieved, violated no reasonable expectation of privacy. Because the general public could have taken the same measures Officer Thielen took, the fact that the officer changed position to achieve the view is irrelevant. The officer's measures were not extraordinary. Therefore, the officer's conduct did not constitute a search.

Officers do not take extraordinary measures when they merely position themselves to achieve a particular view from a public place. Texas v. Brown, 460 U.S. 730, 749 (1983). A measure that could have been taken by a member of the public is an ordinary measure, not an extraordinary measure. So long as a member of the public might achieve the same plain view, the officer violates no reasonable expectation of privacy. Id.

In Brown, an officer on a traffic stop bent down at an angle so that he could see the inside of the defendant' car. Id. at 734. The officer changed his position to better view the interior of the defendant's glove compartment. Id. This Court held that the fact that the officer changed his position to peer into the vehicle was "irrelevant to Fourth Amendment analysis." Id. at 740. The officer did not take any extraordinary measure and did not conduct a Fourth Amendment search. Id. The Brown Court noted that "[t]he general public could peer into the interior of [the car] from any number of angles" and that there is no reason an officer "should be precluded from observing as an officer what would be entirely visible to him as a private citizen." Id. The Court held that there is no reasonable expectation of privacy shielding scenes that may be viewed "by either inquisitive passers-by or diligent police officers." Id. What mattered to the Court was not whether the officer remained in one position or whether he casually or accidentally obtained the view, but rather whether it would have been *possible* for a member of the general public to obtain the same view. Id.

It is significant to note that some ordinary measures that might be taken by members of the public are less than polite. This Court's reasoning in Brown indicates that impolite measures are not necessarily extraordinary measures. Id. "Peering through a window or a crack in a door or a keyhole is not, in the abstract, genteel behavior, but the Fourth Amendment does not protect against all conduct unworthy of a good neighbor." State v. Smith, 181 A.2d 761 (N.J. 1962). **57** Police have a duty to investigate, and "in striking a balance between the rights of the individual and the needs of law enforcement," the Fourth Amendment does not protect individuals from observations that impolite neighbors might have made. Id.

Applying the law to the case at bar, Officer Thielen's affirmative steps to obtain the best view of the interior of the apartment simply cannot be classified as extraordinary measures. See Record G-29. Looking through a gap in the blinds may not be polite behavior, but it is something a neighbor or passerby could do, which is sufficient under Brown to place the conduct outside the Fourth Amendment.

Like the officer in Brown, Officer Thielen observed a scene that could have been viewed by either inquisitive passersby or diligent police officers. The Fourth Amendment simply did not preclude Officer Thielen from observing as an officer what he could have viewed as a private citizen. Officer Thielen's movement to secure a better view, see Record G-30, is irrelevant to the Fourth Amendment analysis.

The officer's movement was not an extraordinary measure. His manner of observation did not violate any reasonable expectation of privacy and therefore did not constitute a search. Thus, this Court must reverse.

2. Officer Thielen made no physical intrusion and used no device to enhance his natural senses.

Officer Thielen's observation, which was conducted without the aid of any device and without any physical intrusion of the premises, involved no extraordinary measures. Therefore, the observation violated no reasonable expectation of privacy and did not constitute a search.

This Court has repeatedly suggested that an officer does not take extraordinary measures when he simply observes an area without physically invading it. See Florida v. Riley, 488 U.S. 445, 449 (1989) (plurality opinion); California v. Ciraolo, 476 U.S. 207, 213 (1986). Although the Katz Court indicated that the reach of the Fourth Amendment cannot turn on the presence or absence of a physical intrusion into an enclosure, Katz, 389 U.S. at 353, Katz dealt with government officers supplementing their natural senses with electronic listening devices. In subsequent cases involving officers using only their natural senses, this Court has repeatedly indicated that the home is "not necessarily protected from inspection that involves no physical invasion." Riley, 488 U.S. at 449.

In Riley, the Court held that there was no search when police observed marijuana in a defendant's greenhouse from a helicopter circling above the greenhouse. The Court emphasized that there was no evidence that the helicopter interfered with the normal use of the greenhouse, that intimate details connected with the use of the home were observed, or that there was undue noise or threat of injury. Id. at 452. Because there was no physical invasion, the Court reasoned, the officers violated no reasonable expectation of privacy. Id.

In the case at bar, the record indicates absolutely no physical intrusion into Thompson's dwelling. The observation was completely visual, never disturbing the people inside the apartment. See Record D-3. Officer Thielen used no electronic device. He did not even utilize a flashlight. Record G-13. Nothing in the record suggests that the officer removed any obstacles or disturbed any portion of Thompson's dwelling. See Record G-46. The officer stood a foot or more from the apartment window. See Record F-2. Never did he even place his hands along the window. See Record G-13. Officer Thielen could not hear the occupants' conversation. See Record G-14. No evidence suggests that the officer's presence in any way interfered with the

57 What issue was the New Jersey court looking at when it made this pronouncement? The reader should be able to relate the quotation to the relevant issue and the disposition of that issue, at the very least.

use of the home. Indeed, during the entire time Officer Thielen observed, the occupants did nothing but illegally package cocaine. <u>See</u> Record G-14.

Thus, like the defendant in <u>Riley</u>, Respondents were completely undisturbed by the officer's observations. Like the defendant in <u>Riley</u>, Respondents cannot claim the officer took extraordinary measures. Officer Thielen did not violate any reasonable expectation of privacy. Because the officer's observation was not a Fourth Amendment search, this Court must reverse.

CONCLUSION

Respondents had no legitimate expectation of privacy in Thompson's apartment and therefore cannot assert a Fourth Amendment challenge. Even if Respondents were entitled to assert a Fourth Amendment challenge, Officer Thielen's non-enhanced use of his natural senses to observe criminal activity inside the residence from a public area outside the curtilage of the residence was not a search. This Court should reverse the decision of the Minnesota Supreme Court.

Respectfully submitted,

Sarah Student

Sarah Student
55 West 12th Avenue
Columbus, Ohio 43210-1391
Counsel for the Petitioner

November 2, 1998

CERTIFICATE OF SERVICE

This document certifies hand delivery of one copy of the foregoing brief to my opponent's mailbox on this second day of November, 1998.

Sarah Student

Sarah Student

CERTIFICATE OF COMPLIANCE

This document certifies that this brief was completed using WordPerfect software, Times New Roman font, in 12-point type. It contains 12,876 words. The brief complies with the length requirements of this Court.

This document further certifies that the author of this brief has complied with all applicable honor code requirements, including the requirement that the author may not consult briefs or memoranda prepared on behalf of parties or amici to this case.

Sarah Student

Sarah Student [58]

[58] The United States Supreme Court does not yet require a Certificate of Compliance, so this sample will be the only one that includes an example of a Certificate of Compliance. This Certificate is geared toward the requirements of an appellate advocacy course. If you are asked to include a Certificate of Compliance, in school or in practice, be sure to identify and follow the requirements of the relevant local rules.

No. 97-1147

IN THE SUPREME COURT OF THE UNITED STATES

FALL TERM, 1998

STATE OF MINNESOTA,

Petitioner,

v.

WAYNE THOMAS CARTER and MELVIN JOHNS,

Respondents.

ON WRIT OF CERTIORARI TO THE SUPREME COURT OF MINNESOTA

BRIEF FOR THE RESPONDENTS

Susan Scholar
55 West 12th Avenue
Columbus, Ohio 43210
Counsel for the Respondents

QUESTIONS PRESENTED

I. Under the Fourth Amendment, does an invited guest in a private residence **1** have a legitimate expectation of privacy from government or police observation of activity occurring wholly within that private residence, where lowered venetian blinds almost completely cover the only windows to the residence?

II. Under the Fourth Amendment, does an officer's unwarranted and purposeful sight observation **2** into a clearly private residence, made while standing within inches of the apartment and peering through gaps in the covered window of the apartment, constitute an unlawful invasion of curtilage?

1 The words "invited guests" and "private residence" create an image that supports the respondents' argument that they had a legitimate expectation of privacy.

2 Notice how the writer uses the nominalized "sight observation" instead of "look" to make the police action seem more complex.

TABLE OF CONTENTS

3 This argument is not dispositive, even though it is designated by a roman numeral. The Respondents must prove both that they have standing to raise a Fourth Amendment challenge and that Officer Thielen's behavior constituted a search. Many legal writers think that only dispositive points may be the basis for Roman Numeral headings, but some good writers break that rule where, as here, each of the points is dispositive for the writer's opponent. When deciding whether to create a roman numeral heading for a non-dispositive point, you might consider (a) the significance of the point to your argument, (b) whether the point is dispositive of your opponent's argument, and (c) whether the enumeration will still reveal the logical relationships between and among your points.

TABLE OF AUTHORITIES

IN THE SUPREME COURT OF THE UNITED STATES

No. 97-1147

STATE OF MINNESOTA,

Petitioner,

v.

WAYNE THOMAS CARTER and MELVIN JOHNS,

Respondents.

ON WRIT OF CERTIORARI TO THE SUPREME COURT OF MINNESOTA

BRIEF FOR THE RESPONDENTS

OPINIONS BELOW

The order of the Minnesota District Court, County of Dakota, denying the motion to suppress evidence against Respondents Carter and Johns is reprinted in the record at E-1. The opinions of the Court of Appeals of Minnesota affirming denial of motion to suppress evidence are reported at State v. Carter, 545 N.W.2d 695 (Minn. Ct. App. 1996), and State v. Johns, No. C9-95-1765, 1996 WL 310305 (Minn. Ct. App. 1996). The opinions of the Supreme Court of Minnesota reversing denial of the motion to suppress evidence are reported at State v. Carter, 569 N.W.2d 169 (Minn. 1997), and State v. Johns, 569 N.W.2d 180 (Minn. 1997).

JURISDICTION

The judgment of the Supreme Court of Minnesota was entered on September 11, 1997. The petition for the writ of certiorari was filed on December 29, 1997, and this Court granted the petition on March 3, 1998. The jurisdiction of this Court rests on 28 U.S.C. § 1257 (1995).

CONSTITUTIONAL PROVISION INVOLVED

The Fourth Amendment to the United States Constitution provides:

The right of the people to be secure in their persons, houses, papers, and effects, against unreasonable searches and seizures, shall not be violated, and no War-

1

rants shall issue, but upon probable cause, supported by Oath or affirmation, and particularly describing the place to be searched, and the persons or things to be seized.

STANDARD OF REVIEW

This is an appeal from the Supreme Court of Minnesota's reversal of the trial court, which decided that evidence in this case is admissible under the Fourth Amendment to the United States Constitution. Interpretation of the United States Constitution is subject to *de novo* review. Ornelas v. United States, 517 U.S. 690 (1996); United States v. United States Gypsum Co., 333 U.S. 364 (1948).

STATEMENT OF THE CASE

This case involves a claim by Defendants-Respondents Wayne Thomas Carter and Melvin Johns, challenging, under the Fourth Amendment, the constitutionality of evidence used in their conviction. The evidence in question was obtained by observations made by a police officer looking into the window of an apartment where the Respondents were guests of the apartment's leaseholder. Record E-3. **4**

4 Contrast this opening with the petitioner's opening. Both are accurate, yet each highlights different information.

On May 15, 1994, Officer Jim Thielen of the Eagan, Minnesota Police Department received information from an unidentified source that the source had observed people inside a nearby apartment "bagging" a white powdery substance. Record E-2. The source also stated that a blue Cadillac parked at the apartment building belonged to the individuals inside the apartment. Record E-2. After collecting additional information from the source, Officer Thielen proceeded to the apartment in question. The officer was able to approach a window belonging to the apartment by leaving the sidewalk leading up to the building, walking onto the grass and behind bushes located two to four feet away from the window. Record G-43.

By standing approximately twelve to eighteen inches from the window, Officer Thielen was able to observe the occupants' activities inside the apartment for approximately fifteen minutes. Record E-2, G-53. Because the blinds were closed, the officer could observe the activities only by looking through a gap in the blinds. Record G-49. He then returned to his original location at a nearby fire station parking lot, where he contacted a superior officer to inform him of his findings and to request instructions. Record G-53, G-54. Officer Thielen reported that he observed two individuals bagging a powdery substance on the kitchen table of the apartment. Record E-2.

Based on Officer Thielen's observations, Officer Kallastad proceeded to obtain search warrants for the apartment and the vehicle that the informant had identified. Record E-3. Investigation of the Respondents revealed that they were guests in the apartment in question, which was leased by a Kimberly Thompson. Record E-3. Based on findings (of a substance later determined to be cocaine) from the vehicle and apartment searches, Respondents were arrested on two counts of controlled substance crime in the first degree. Record E-4. **5**

5 This information is accurate, but it purposely does not go into as much detail about the alleged crime.

At trial, the Respondents pleaded not guilty and challenged Officer Thielen's surveillance through the window of the apartment as an unwarranted search within the meaning of the Fourth Amendment, moving to suppress all evidence obtained as a result of that surveillance. Record E-5. The District Court ruled that Respondents did not have standing to challenge Officer Thielen's observations of Thompson's apartment and denied the motion. Record E-4. On September 21, 1994, Respondents were convicted in the Minnesota District Court for the County of Dakota based on evidence obtained by officers the night of May 15. Record E-3.

On appeal to the Court of Appeals of Minnesota, Respondents argued that they had proper standing to challenge the evidence under the Fourth Amendment because their status as invited house guests is a status that society is willing to recognize as legitimate for purposes of expectations of privacy. State v. Carter, 545 N.W.2d 695, 697 (Minn. Ct. App. 1996). The Court of Appeals again rejected the motion to suppress, holding that case precedent required a guest to stay overnight in order to have standing under the Fourth Amendment. Having rejected Respondents' claim of standing, the court affirmed the lower court without discussing the merits of Officer Thielen's search. Id. at 698.

The Supreme Court of Minnesota reversed the Court of Appeals, and held that the Respondents had standing to assert a Fourth Amendment challenge to the search in question because they had demonstrated an adversary interest in the outcome of the case and because Respondents had a legitimate expectation of privacy in the observed apartment. State v. Carter, 569 N.W.2d 169, 174 (Minn. 1997). The court also held that the officer's observations into the apartment did constitute a search within the meaning of the Fourth Amendment and that the search was not reasonable. Id. at 169. **6**

6 Respondents give more details about the holdings in their favor — but not exhaustive detail.

SUMMARY OF ARGUMENT

In this appeal, this Court must decide if an invited guest in another's home has a legitimate expectation of privacy that protects him from unreasonable searches and seizures under the Fourth Amendment. This Court must also decide if observations made from directly outside an apartment into the window of the apartment constitute a search within the meaning of the Fourth Amendment because of an intrusion into curtilage. The Supreme Court of Minnesota answered both questions in the positive, saying that any time a person has demonstrated an expectation of privacy that society is prepared to recognize as reasonable, he will enjoy a constitutionally guaranteed protection from unwarranted search and seizure. Carter, 569 N.W.2d. at 176. Furthermore, the court also held that any time government observations invade the curtilage of a place where there is a legitimate expectation of privacy, a search has taken place. Id. at 178.

This Court has gone to great lengths to refine its application of the Fourth Amendment. Conclusively, cases have held that government agents do not have free reign to intrude into and tamper with the private lives of citizens without probable cause or warrant. The key to this case, and others before it, is that if (1) a person has demonstrated a subjective expectation of privacy in the particular circumstances and (2) all evidence suggests that society recognizes that expectation of privacy to be reasonable, then the police cannot invade that privacy without a warrant. This Court's analysis has shown that the Fourth Amendment, perhaps once thought to primarily protect a "man in his own castle," actually extends protection to people as guests in others' homes, in their own offices and workplaces, in telephone booths, and in automobiles, from unreasonable searches of their private activities and personal effects.

The Supreme Court of Minnesota also properly labeled Officer Thielen's surveillance as an illegal search. When Officer Thielen stood within inches of a window and looked into a private residence where the victims of the search were going about their private affairs, he was conducting a search. Whether a search has taken place within the meaning of the Fourth Amendment depends on whether the officers intruded into a privately protected area, or an area so intimately connected or tied to a private place that it constitutes curtilage. If the area intruded into is curtilage, where a person has a reasonable expectation of privacy, agents may not search that area without warrant and may not enter the area of curtilage.

In this case, Respondents have demonstrated a legitimate expectation of privacy as guests in a host's home. Their host's home is a private residence and therefore enjoys protection from unwarranted physical intrusion. As a place where Respondents had a legitimate expectation of privacy, the apartment is also given protection from unwarranted observations that are conducted from immediately outside the apartment. The Respondents therefore respectfully request that this Court affirm the judgment of the Supreme Court of Minnesota.

ARGUMENT

I. **An invitee in a residence has a legitimate and reasonable expectation of privacy under the Fourth Amendment and has protection from all unwarranted searches and seizures while demonstrating an expectation of privacy from public intrusion.**

In this case, two people who had the right to be protected from unwarranted search and seizure were denied that right. Respondents' legitimate expectation of privacy was invaded when a Minnesota police officer peeked through a small opening in the window blinds of a private residence where the Respondents were guests; thus, the officer conducted a search of the activities within, without warrant. See Carter, 569 N.W.2d at 173. This Court has consistently construed the Fourth Amendment as protecting all citizens from intrusions of unreasonable searches and seizures that invade wholly private actions conducted within the sanctity of a recognizable private home. See, e.g., Minnesota v. Olson, 495 U.S. 91, 98 (1990).

Invocation of the Fourth Amendment against evidence obtained in this case is appropriate because (1) the Respondents had a reasonable expectation of privacy from unwarranted searches while invitees in an acquaintance's residence; (2) the nature of the Respondents' presence on the searched premises was such that society recognizes them as possessing a legitimate expectation of privacy; and (3) Respondents' legitimate expectation of privacy gives them proper standing to challenge evidence under the Fourth Amendment.

A. A person has a legitimate and reasonable expectation of privacy that society is prepared to acknowledge while he is an invited guest in another person's private residence.

When the Respondents left the public streets and entered the private home of their host, they had a legitimate expectation of privacy: they believed they were protected against unwarranted government observation. This Court has said that people will be recognized as having a legitimate expectation of privacy if they demonstrate an expectation that their activities are treated as private, and if it can be shown that their expectation of privacy is reasonable in the given situation. Katz v. United States, 389 U.S. 347, 361 (1967) (Harlan, J., concurring). In Katz, conversations obtained by FBI wiretapping efforts could not be used as evidence to convict a man for transmitting wagering information by public telephone because the defendant clearly demonstrated a legitimate expectation of privacy while using the public telephone. Id. at 348.

This Court reasoned in Katz that a person using a public telephone is the type of person who has a legitimate expectation of privacy because most people who enter a phone booth and shut the door assume no one else is listening to the conversation. Id. at 361. Thus, even though a phone booth is accessible to the public, it can also be a temporary private place where the occupant legitimately expects privacy.

Legitimate expectations of privacy and society's acceptance of those expectations are used by this Court to determine when the protection of the Fourth Amendment goes beyond one's own home, and in which places a person is rightfully protected from unwarranted intrusions by the government. For example, in 1990, this Court held that an overnight guest has a legitimate expectation of privacy in his host's home. Minnesota v. Olson, 495 U.S. 91, 98 (1990). The Olson Court held that Olson's unwarranted arrest was an illegal seizure because Olson, as an invited overnight guest in the apartment, had a sufficient interest in the privacy of his host's home to be free from unwarranted search and seizure. Id. at 96-97. Furthermore, that subjective expectation of privacy was found to be reasonable because staying overnight in another's home is a socially recognized custom: "We will all be hosts and we will all be guests many times in our lives. From either perspective, we think that society recognizes that a houseguest has a legitimate expectation of privacy in his host's home." Id. at 98.

Olson did not specifically require a person to be an overnight guest or even a guest in order to have a legitimate expectation of privacy.[1] The legitimacy of Olson's expectation was upheld, not specifically because he was a guest, but because the circumstances in which the police intruded upon him were the type in which most people would normally expect to enjoy a right to privacy. Id. at 96-97. This was also true in Katz, where a privacy interest was found in a person using a public phone booth, who was neither a guest nor located in a residence. 389 U.S. at 352. Thus, the facts of the particular circumstances, coupled with the overriding values and expectations of society, will determine whether the victim of a search and seizure had a legitimate expectation of privacy and, thus, should not have been searched.

This Court has also rejected the argument that a person must have a legal property interest in the premises to challenge a search. Olson, 495 U.S. at 97. Olson drew its conclusions from a similar case in which the defendant challenged a search warrant used for his arrest while a guest in a friend's apartment. Jones v. United States, 362 U.S. 257, 265 (1960) (overruled on other grounds). The government claimed Jones could not challenge the search warrant because he had no legal property interest in the premises where he was located. This Court held that Jones could challenge the search because he was "legitimately on the premises." Id. at 265. This Court later refined the Jones "legitimately on the premises" test to mean that "a person can have a legally sufficient interest in a place other than his own home," and the "Fourth Amendment protects him from unreasonable government intrusion into that place." Rakas v. Illinois, 439 U.S. 128, 141-42 (1978).

The Fourth Amendment similarly extends to the Respondents in this case. Respondents were legitimately on the premises of their host's home because they were invited guests. The Respondents, having shown a legitimate expectation of privacy

---

[1] This Court recognized that the status of overnight guest in Olson was enough to show he had a legitimate expectation of privacy. However, the analysis did not rest wholly on whether or not he was an overnight guest, but said an unlawfully searched overnight guest was one example of "a mistaken premise that a place must be one's 'home' in order for one to have a legitimate expectation of privacy there." Id. at 96. Thus, a person can have a legitimate expectation of privacy in places other than his own home, and Olson was one example where the defendant demonstrated such a legitimate expectation. Olson left open the interpretation of what other situations will demonstrate a legitimate expectation of privacy.

5

while there, had a legally sufficient interest in being safe from unreasonable government intrusion.

B. A person has demonstrated his expectation of privacy when he takes action to protect himself from public observation.

As guests in another's home, Respondents had a legitimate expectation of privacy because people expect certain protections in the home as they conduct themselves either as guests or hosts. This Court has used several factors to determine whether a socially acknowledged, legitimate expectation of privacy exists. E.g., Jones, 362 U.S. at 265 (examining how the individual used the location where the search occurred); United States v. Chadwick, 433 U.S. 1, 7-8 (1977) (looking at intention of the framers of the Constitution and Fourth Amendment and how they might react to a particular situation); Payton v. New York, 445 U.S. 573, 589 (1979) (considering common understandings among people of which areas deserve protection from government intrusion); see also Rakas, 439 U.S. at 139 (finding that no single factor can determine the legitimacy of a Fourth Amendment claim). **7**

These cases suggest that courts should, in each case, examine the conduct of the parties involved and think about the expectations and actions of ordinary people if put in similar circumstances. This Court has found that there are many situations in which Fourth Amendment protection extends beyond the scope of one's own home and even beyond private residences. For example, this Court held that a search warrant was required to search the personal belongings inside a footlocker because, by placing their personal belongings inside the double-locked footlocker, respondents manifested an expectation that the contents would be free from public intrusion. Chadwick, 433 U.S. at 9-10. This expectation was no different from that of a person who locks the doors of his home against intrusion. Id. Also, Katz extended Fourth Amendment protection to evidence obtained by eavesdropping on a conversation held in a public telephone booth. 389 U.S. at 359. Both Chadwick and Katz demonstrate that the legitimacy of a privacy interest within the meaning of the Fourth Amendment depends not solely on the location of activities or belongings, but also on whether a privacy interest will be recognized by society in the given situation. See also United States v. Jeffers, 342 U.S. 48, 52 (1951) **8** (finding that **9** since the Fourth Amendment prohibits unreasonable searches and seizures to both house and effects, **10** a judicial warrant was required to **11** search a hotel room where the defendant was staying); Mancusi v. Deforte, 392 U.S. 364, 369 (1968) (requiring a search warrant to search a business office where a legitimate expectation of privacy was demonstrated).

In the present case, the nature of the Respondents' time as guests in the searched premises establishes that they possessed a legitimate expectation of privacy. First, Respondents had the leaseholder's permission to be in the apartment, Record G-4, G-5, as did the victims of the searches in Olson and Jones. Olson, 495 U.S. at 97 n.6; Jones, 362 U.S. at 265.

Second, Respondents were inside the apartment for a minimum of 2½ hours. Record E-2, E-3. The issue of how much time must be spent in a location before a privacy right exists has been an area of some confusion. **12** Other courts have not found a legitimate privacy expectation when the defendants were only briefly present on the premises. See generally United States v. Maddox, 944 F.2d 1223, 1234 (6th Cir. 1991) (finding the defendant could not have a reasonable expectation of privacy when it was shown he was nothing more than a short-term party guest); Prophet v. United States, 602 A.2d 1087, 1091 (App. D.C. 1992) (holding that a defendant who arrived minutes before police at his friend's house could not challenge entry). These

7 Note that these parentheticals are less effective because they tell what the court *considered,* but not what the court *did.* Note also that they make the writer's roadmap harder to perceive.

8 This parenthetical is more effective because it includes the four elements that promote effective case descriptions.
9 This phrase indicates the court's reasoning.
10 This phrase indicates the issue and the disposition of that issue.
11 This phrase indicates the significant facts.

12 If this is a significant issue, perhaps it should be treated separately, with a separate heading. Generally, it burdens the reader to return to rule explanation after beginning rule application.

cases are distinguishable from the present case because in those cases the defendants were not personally authorized or acknowledged as private guests in the home, were only present at the residence for a matter of minutes, or were unable to establish any personal connection to the people or objects within the apartment. In this case, Respondents were two of only three persons present, and their presence had the personal acknowledgment of the leaseholder. Record G-5.

Finally, for the two and one-half hour period of time Respondents remained in the apartment, they engaged in activity with the leaseholder and each other. Record E-3, E-4. The type of activity engaged in by the victims of a search is wholly irrelevant to the Fourth Amendment analysis. For example, in Katz, even though agents had hard-core evidence of the defendant's criminal activity, this Court would not allow it as evidence because the evidence was, itself, obtained illegally. 389 U.S. at 355. Similarly, in this case Respondents should not be denied their Constitutionally protected right under the Fourth Amendment because evidence obtained by disobeying the order of the Fourth Amendment might prove criminal conduct. **13**

13 This ending could be even more effective if it focused on a more positive note. Generally, you should end point heading sections by restating the main assertion to that section and, if appropriate, connecting the conclusion of that section to the overall thesis.

C. A person properly asserts Fourth Amendment protection when he has an adverse interest in the outcome of the case and when there has been a violation of some protected individual right, namely privacy.

Since the Respondents have demonstrated that they had a reasonable expectation of privacy as invited guests in another's home, they have proper standing to assert their Fourth Amendment claims. Standing for a Fourth Amendment claim requires a party to establish an adversary interest or personal stake in the outcome of the case. Baker v. Carr, 369 U.S. 186, 204 (1962). A party also must show that the adversary interest is based upon the violation of some individual right, rather than the rights of some other party. Jones, 362 U.S. at 261. The adversary interest requirement is easy to meet in this case. Any criminal defendant who faces jail time because of evidence offered against him surely has an adversary interest in the outcome. For the second part, this Court has held that determination of whether a search infringed a Fourth Amendment right depends on the person claiming such a right having a legitimate expectation of privacy in the invaded place. Rakas, 439 U.S. at 143.

Furthermore, as a general policy consideration, the Fourth Amendment must equally protect all citizens, regardless of whether or not the searched activities are tainted with criminal conduct. The Fourth Amendment was not framed to extend protection only to those citizens who can prove their activities are lawful. Rather, the protection from search and seizure extends as a right to "the people," and all citizens have always enjoyed the protections of the Constitution, without distinction between the alleged criminality or noncriminality of their actions. U.S. Const. Amend. IV. This Court pointed out that the Fourth Amendment's protection of a person's security and personal liberty "has never been forfeited by his conviction of some public offense." Weeks v. United States, 232 U.S. 383, 391 (1914) (disallowing evidence of an illegal lottery enterprise that police officers obtained by searching the previously arrested defendant's home without warrant).

The policy of the Fourth Amendment is simple: illegal and unwarranted searches are not justified just because they uncover illegal activities. If the government does not conduct its affairs legally, it cannot possibly expect to demand the same of its citizens. The Fourth Amendment, therefore, unreservedly protects Respondents' right

14 Because the reader will be moving on to heading II, it would be more effective if this heading provided a more thorough conclusion as to the writer's point about the respondents' legitimate expectation of privacy.

to enter their host's home and be safe from unwarranted observation and intrusion by police officers. **14**

II. A police officer is conducting a search within the meaning of the Fourth Amendment when he observes actions taking place inside a private residence from within inches of the residence's window, because the area is so close to the home that it qualifies as part of the residence's curtilage.

The central value of the Fourth Amendment is its protection of the sanctity of a person's home from unlawful intrusion. Silverman v. United States, 365 U.S. 505, 511 (1961) (stating that the very core of the Fourth Amendment is "the right of a man to retreat into his own home and there be free from unreasonable government intrusion"). Alongside protection of the home comes protection of the area immediately surrounding the home, known as curtilage — "the area to which extends the intimate activity associated with the 'sanctity of a man's home and the privacies of life.' " Oliver v. United States, 466 U.S. 170, 180 (1983) (quoting Boyd v. United States, 116 U.S. 616, 630 (1886)).

Curtilage is a unique concept and is not always defined strictly in terms of proximity to a home. In Katz, this Court said the Fourth Amendment protects those areas where an individual has a legitimate expectation of privacy. 389 U.S. at 360 (Harlan, J., concurring). There can be no claim of a legitimate expectation of privacy in areas surrounding the home that are open fields. California v. Ciraolo, 476 U.S. 207, 213 (1986) (holding that those areas that are knowingly and clearly exposed to a public vantage point are open fields and have no protection under the Fourth Amendment). However, other areas are so intimately tied to the home that they require protection under the Fourth Amendment because people legitimately expect privacy while in those areas. See Oliver, 466 U.S. at 178 (saying that an individual may demand privacy for activities in the area immediately surrounding the home).

In the present case, Officer Thielen's behavior constituted a search for three reasons. First, the area intruded upon was so intimately tied to the apartment itself that Respondents had a legitimate expectation that the government would not intrude upon the area, and thus intrude upon their privacy. Second, the area in question is curtilage even though the apartment lessee did not have property rights in the yard. This is so because curtilage is based on whether an individual has a legitimate expectation of privacy, not on whether the individual has a legal property interest. See, e.g., Jones, 362 U.S. at 266 (rejecting lower courts' attempts to deny Fourth Amendment standing based on lack of property rights). Third, even if Officer Thielen did not intrude into the apartment's curtilage to make the observations, he conducted an unlawful search because he demonstrated awareness that the Respondents' activities were taking place inside a privately protected area.

A. The area immediately outside of the apartment where the Respondents were guests qualifies as curtilage because there can be a reasonable expectation of privacy despite lack of property rights in the building or land in question.

Protection of curtilage does not depend on the person claiming a legitimate expectation of privacy having a property interest in the intruded-upon area. This Court has specifically rejected attempts by lower courts to deny Fourth Amendment standing based on a defendant's status as a guest or invitee. Jones, 362 U.S. at 266 (holding that a defendant properly had standing to challenge probable cause of a search warrant used to seize narcotics, despite being a guest and not the owner of the searched premises). In the present case, Respondents should be afforded the same curtilage protection as a homeowner, whose home sits on private property, because a guest in a private residence has the same legitimate expectation of privacy in an apartment as a homeowner has in his home.

This Court pointed out in Katz that the belief "that property interests control the right of the Government to search and seize has been discredited." 389 U.S. at 353 (citing Warden, Md. Penitentiary v. Hayden, 387 U.S. 294, 304 (1967)). Katz set down the principle that the Fourth Amendment was designed to "protect people, not places," and that courts need to examine whether there is a legitimate expectation of privacy, not whether officers committed a technical trespass. Id. at 351. This was shown in Silverman when police officers, without warrant, stationed themselves in a neighboring home and inserted listening devices into the ground near a heating duct, allowing them to overhear incriminating gambling conversations inside the defendant's home. Silverman, 365 U.S. at 506. The officers never entered the home in question, but simply invaded the area immediately surrounding it and listened to the conversations within. Id. at 506. This Court found the officers' efforts to be an unlawful search of the defendant's home because, even though there was no actual trespass, there was still an intrusion into a "constitutionally protected area." Id. at 512.

Since protection from search and seizure does not depend on ownership or trespass of the invaded building or land, protection of curtilage likewise should not depend on ownership of an area that is normally considered curtilage. Silverman shows that a search can occur even when agents do not intrude upon private property. This Court has also said that an actual trespass is "neither necessary nor sufficient to establish a constitutional violation." United States v. Karo, 468 U.S. 705, 713 (1984). In Karo, although it was held that Karo's Fourth Amendment rights were not violated by the public installation of a monitoring beeper that Karo later carried into his house, the Court pointed out that privacy interests would be impaired by the monitoring of a beeper in a private residence without a warrant, even when agents did not physically enter private property. Id. at 713.

Additionally, Katz showed the irrelevance of property rights under the Fourth Amendment in holding that a public phone booth is protected from intrusions because the phone user has a legitimate expectation that he or she will be free from government eavesdropping. 389 U.S. at 361 (Harlan, J., concurring). This Court has also suggested that Fourth Amendment protection may extend to individuals within commercial buildings if a person has taken reasonable steps to exclude the public. E.g., See v. City of Seattle, 387 U.S. 541, 543 (1967) (holding that a businessman has a constitutional right to conduct his business and be free from unreasonable intrusion); Camara v. Municipal Court of San Francisco, 387 U.S. 523, 528 (1967) (stating that the basic purpose of the Fourth Amendment is to "safeguard the privacy and security of individuals against arbitrary invasions by government officials," regardless of location).

The extension of Fourth Amendment protection to curtilage allows the privacy and security of a privately protected place to be more fully safeguarded. In the present case, the Respondents did not have any property rights in the apartment or the property on which the apartment building was situated. Record E-7. However, as guests in a private residence, Respondents had the same legitimate expectation of privacy as a homeowner on private property. It would be inconsistent to apply the safeguard of curtilage to some places that enjoy Fourth Amendment protection and not to others. Since guests inside a rented apartment enjoy the same Fourth Amendment protection as a homeowner in a privately owned home, both deserve equal protection against unwarranted invasion into the exterior area that is closely tied to the intimacies of the home or apartment. Therefore, observations made from the immediate ex-

9

terior of the private residence where Respondents were guests should be inadmissible as evidence because the observations constitute an illegal search from within the apartment's curtilage.

B. The observations of Respondents' activities constitute an unwarranted search because the police officer invaded the curtilage of the apartment by physically being within inches of the apartment's window and walls, having left the normal walkway area to do so.

The government may only make unwarranted observations of activities that are conducted in the open and can be seen naturally by the public at large. Ciraolo, 476 U.S. at 211 (noting that officers' observations from public areas failed to constitute a search only because the defendant's activities were open for all the public to see); United States v. Dunn, 480 U.S. 294, 303 (1987) (finding that curtilage protects the activities and privacies of the home from unwarranted observation, as compared to a nearby barn where police could freely see activities within); Katz, 389 U.S. at 352 (pointing out that physical penetration of the area where privacy is claimed is no longer a requirement of the Fourth Amendment inquiry). However, in this case, the police officer's observations were made from within inches of the apartment walls. Record G-13. This constitutes an intrusion into curtilage because the officer intruded into an area where Respondents legitimately did not expect people to intrude. The officer approached so closely to the apartment that he was able to observe the activities within, even with the window blinds shut.

The Respondents' activities took place in an enclosed, shielded area and are fundamentally different from activities conducted in openly visible areas. In Ciraolo, officers' observations from an airplane of marijuana growing in the defendant's yard were held not to be an unwarranted search within the meaning of the Fourth Amendment. 476 U.S. at 214. Similarly, in Dunn, observations of drug activity inside an open barn by officers located outside of the defendant's gate did not qualify as a search because defendants did little to shield activities from public observation. 480 U.S. at 303. This Court pointed out that the barn in Dunn, even though located on private property next to the defendant's home, was not so intimately associated with the home to qualify as curtilage, and observation of such an open place from a public vantage point was not a search. Id. at 304.

The steps that Officer Thielen took to reach his vantage point show that he invaded the apartment's curtilage. The facts in these "open fields" cases are distinguishable from the present case. In Dunn and Ciraolo, the observed activities were conducted so as to be easily and readily available to observation by the public at large. This Court said that the defendants in those cases could not possibly be recognized to have any legitimate expectation of privacy when the activities were so readily accessible to the public view. Dunn, 480 U.S. at 303; Ciraolo, 476 U.S. at 213. There was, however, no public view of the activities in this case. Respondents' activities occurred only within a private residence. Record E-3. Those activities could not be observed unless a person took the extreme action of locating himself within inches of the residence's windows. It was necessary to approach the residence very closely because the window blinds were closed, and activities could only be observed by peeking through a small gap in the blinds. Record G-49.

A reasonable person should still expect a right to privacy, even though others may be able to enter onto his or her land, or even peer into his or her windows, without committing a trespass. E.g., Katz, 389 U.S. at 351 (holding that "even an area accessible to the public [sic], may be constitutionally protected"). This is the reality of any person who lives in or is a guest in an apartment. Apartment lessees

10

depend on socially accepted concepts of privacy to be protected from invasions into those areas that are innately connected to the shelter of the apartment, since ownership and control over such areas are, in most cases, impossible. It is also reasonable that apartment lessees would have the same expectation of privacy from government invasion on the immediate exterior of the apartment, as a person who actually owns the land and walls invaded upon. A person's home, the place where he lives, has been recognized by this Court as the most important place protected by the Fourth Amendment. Payton, 445 U.S. at 589 (pointing out that the Fourth Amendment protects an individual's privacy in a variety of settings, but none is more clearly defined than the protection of a person's home). If not for the police officer's entrance into the curtilage of their host's apartment, Respondents' activities could not have been observed. **15**

15 Be careful not to end a heading section with a statement that leaves a question. Instead, explain the legal significance of your assertions as they relate to the ultimate assertion in your document, or at the minimum, in that heading section.

C. It should have been evident to the police officer making the observations that he was intruding into the privacy of the home because of the circumstances under which he made the observations.

The police officer observing Respondents was on notice that his actions were an invasion of privacy for three reasons. First, the apartment was a private residence, and the officer knew it. Record G-68, G-69. Respondents' host lived there, slept there, and conducted the other daily activities of life there. Record E-7. Second, the window of the apartment through which the police officer peered clearly indicated the apartment was not open to public observation. The blinds on the window had been drawn, with the exception of one small, defective gap. Record G-49. Finally, the officer could only see the activities inside by purposefully walking onto the grass, behind a bushy area, and within mere inches of the window to look inside. Record G-13. Simply because the yard area of an apartment is open to public traffic does not mean the public is free to peer inside, nor that a leaseholder and her guests are unreasonable to expect to be free from such eavesdropping. This Court has been reluctant to accept that police officers may freely observe in any manner from areas simply because they have a legal right to be there. Florida v. Riley, 488 U.S. 445, 454, 457 (1989) (4-1-4 decision) (O'Connor, J., concurring) (Brennan, J., dissenting) (disagreeing with the Justices in the plurality, saying that the true test of legality of observation should be measured by the regularity and frequency of public intrusion into such an area).

It is socially recognized that the windows of a home are not portals through which one may observe the intimacies of life occurring within. This concept is not novel. People go into their homes, shut the doors, and close the blinds precisely because home is the place where a person may find respite from the scrutiny of the outside world. Similarly, when someone is invited, as a guest, to join in such a respite, that guest rightfully expects to enjoy the same type of escape and privacy from the outside. The case law presented supports Respondents' right to be free from the unwarranted intrusion that police conducted while they were in the sanctity of their host's home, the intrusion of which eventually led to their arrest and conviction.

CONCLUSION

Because the Fourth Amendment protects all people who, like Respondents, demonstrate a legitimate expectation of privacy to be free from unwarranted search and seizure while invited guests in a host's home, and because officers, as in this case, may not intrude into the curtilage of a privately protected area without a warrant, this

Court should affirm the decision of the Supreme Court of Minnesota granting Respondents' motion to suppress evidence collected against them in an unwarranted search.

Respectfully submitted,

Susan Scholar

Susan Scholar
55 West 12th Avenue
Columbus, Ohio 43210
Counsel for the Respondents

November 2, 1998

CERTIFICATE OF SERVICE

This document certifies hand delivery of one copy of the foregoing brief to my opponent's mailbox on this second day of November, 1998.

Susan Scholar

Susan Scholar

12

No. 96-1060

IN THE SUPREME COURT OF THE UNITED STATES

October Term, 1996

Lorelyn Penero Miller,
Petitioner,

v.

Madeleine K. Albright,
Secretary of State of the United States,
Respondent.

ON WRIT OF CERTIORARI TO THE
UNITED STATES COURT OF APPEALS
FOR THE DISTRICT OF COLUMBIA CIRCUIT

BRIEF FOR THE PETITIONER

Simon J. Scholar
1356 School Street
Metropolis, Ohio
555-555-5555

Counsel for the Petitioner

QUESTION PRESENTED

Does the irrebuttable presumption ❶ that all men are different from all women with respect to their relationships with their "illegitimate" ❷ children, codified in 8 U.S.C. § 1409(a) (1994), violate the Fifth Amendment to the United States Constitution?

❶ The writer varies the common question-presented structure to put emphasis on the negative concept of "irrebuttable presumptions," which are generally frowned upon.

❷ Word in quotation marks to show that author does not agree that children born out of wedlock should be characterized as "illegitimate."

PARTIES TO THE PROCEEDING

Petitioner Lorelyn Penero Miller and Secretary of State Warren Christopher were plaintiff-appellant and defendant-appellee, respectively, below. Respondent Secretary of State Madeleine K. Albright was substituted for Mr. Christopher when Ms. Albright succeeded Mr. Christopher as Secretary of State of the United States. Secretary Albright is responsible under 22 U.S.C. § 211(a) (1994) for granting and issuing United States passports. Charlie R. Miller, Ms. Miller's father, was added as a co-plaintiff below by Ms. Miller; the United States District Court for the Eastern District of Texas dismissed his claims for lack of standing, and Mr. Miller is not a party to the appeal before this Court.

TABLE OF CONTENTS

3 This writer, appropriately, begins with an ar-
gument about which
test to apply because
the appropriate test is in
controversy. If the *test* is
not controversial, but
how to *apply* the test *is*
controversial, a section
like this is unnecessary.

TABLE OF AUTHORITIES

No. 96-1060

IN THE SUPREME COURT OF THE UNITED STATES

OCTOBER TERM, 1996

Lorelyn Penero Miller,
Petitioner,

v.

Madeleine K. Albright,
Secretary of State of the United States,
Respondent.

ON WRIT OF CERTIORARI TO THE
UNITED STATES COURT OF APPEALS
FOR THE DISTRICT OF COLUMBIA CIRCUIT

BRIEF FOR THE PETITIONER

OPINIONS BELOW

The opinion of the United States Court of Appeals for the District of Columbia Circuit is reported as Miller v. Christopher [4] at 96 F.3d 1467 (D.C. Cir. 1996). The opinion of the United States District Court for the District of Columbia is reported as Miller v. Christopher at 870 F. Supp. 1 (D.D.C. 1994).

[4] Although providing case names is usually not necessary in this section, it is helpful where, as here, the case name was different below.

JURISDICTION

The judgment of the United States Court of Appeals for the District of Columbia Circuit was entered on October 8, 1996. The petition for the writ of certiorari was filed on January 6, 1997, and this Court granted the petition on April 28, 1997. This Court has jurisdiction pursuant to 28 U.S.C. § 1254 (1994).

STATUTORY AND CONSTITUTIONAL PROVISIONS INVOLVED

The pertinent part of the Fifth Amendment to the United States Constitution provides that "[n]o person shall be deprived of life, liberty, or property, without due process of law."

The pertinent part of the Fourteenth Amendment to the United States Constitution

1

provides that "[n]o State shall . . . deny to any person within its jurisdiction the equal protection of the laws."

Title Eight of the United States Code provides in pertinent part as follows:

The following shall be nationals and citizens of the United States *at birth*:

. . .

(g) a person born outside the geographical limits of the United States and its outlying possessions of parents one of whom is an alien, and the other a citizen of the United States who, prior to the birth of such person, was physically present in the United States or its outlying possessions for a period or periods totaling not less than five years, at least two of which were after attaining the age of fourteen. . . .

8 U.S.C. § 1401(g) (1994) (emphasis added).

Title Eight of the United States Code then modifies 8 U.S.C. § 1401(g) by providing that, in the case of a person born outside of marriage and outside of the United States to an American father and an alien mother, that person will be a United States citizen as of the date of birth *only* if the following four conditions are met:

(1) a blood relationship between the person and the father is established by clear and convincing evidence,

(2) the father had the nationality of the United States at the time of the person's birth,

(3) the father (unless deceased) has agreed in writing to provide financial support for the person until the person reaches the age of 18 years, and

(4) while the person is under the age of 18 years —

(A) the person is legitimated under the law of the person's residence or domicile,

(B) the father acknowledges paternity of the person in writing under oath, or

(C) the paternity of the person is established by adjudication of a competent court.

8 U.S.C. § 1409(a) (1994). The different treatment given to "illegitimate" children based on the gender of their U.S. citizen parents is further emphasized by 8 U.S.C. § 1409(c), which provides in pertinent part:

Notwithstanding the provision of subsection (a) of this provision [which requires fathers to meet certain requirements to establish the citizenship of their children], a person born, after December 23, 1952, outside the United States and out of wedlock shall be held to have acquired at birth the nationality status of the mother, if the mother had the nationality of the United States at the time of such person's birth, and if the mother had previously been physically present in the United States or one of its outlying possessions for a continuous period of one year.

8 U.S.C. § 1409(c) (1994) (emphasis added). **5**

STATEMENT OF THE CASE

This is an action for declaratory judgment pursuant to 28 U.S.C. § 2201 (1994). Petitioner Lorelyn Penero Miller seeks a declaration that 8 U.S.C. § 1409(a) (1994)

5 The writer uses this unusual method to emphasize the unreasonableness of the statutes by juxtaposing the statutes governing U.S. citizen fathers and U.S. citizen mothers.

violates the Equal Protection Clause of the Fourteenth Amendment to the United States Constitution, as applied to the federal government by the Fifth Amendment to the United States Constitution.

Petitioner Lorelyn Penero Miller was born on June 20, 1970, in the Republic of the Phillippines. App. 15. Her mother, Luz Penero, was a citizen of the Republic of the Phillippines. Id. Her father, Charlie R. Miller, is a citizen of the United States and was so at the time of Ms. Miller's birth. Mr. Miller and Ms. Miller's mother were never married; Ms. Miller's birth certificate does not list the name or nationality of her father as a result. App. 15. On July 27, 1992, Mr. Miller obtained a voluntary paternity decree from a court in his home state of Texas establishing that Ms. Miller is his daughter.

In 1986, 8 U.S.C. § 1409(a)(4) was amended to lower from twenty-one to eighteen the age limit that restricted a father's ability to pass his citizenship to a foreign-born child. Because of the effective date of that amendment, Ms. Miller would be able to satisfy 8 U.S.C. § 1409(a)(4) if she met its requirements before she turned twenty-one.

On February 11, 1992, Ms. Miller applied to the United States Department of State for registration as a United States citizen and for the issuance of a passport. App. 16. The State Department ultimately denied her application on November 5, 1992, because (1) Ms. Miller had failed to obtain the paternity decree before Ms. Miller's twenty-first birthday as required by 8 U.S.C. § 1409(a)(4), and (2) Mr. Miller had failed to agree in writing (while Ms. Miller was still under twenty-one) that he would financially support her until she turned twenty-one. App. 8. Mr. Miller was denied the opportunity to pass his United States citizenship to his daughter simply because he was late completing some paperwork and because he is a man. The paperwork obstacles that Mr. Miller failed to negotiate apply only to fathers; if Mr. Miller were a mother, Ms. Miller would have been a citizen from birth. **6**

6 This borders on argument, but it states only facts: It is true that these obstacles are placed only in front of fathers. Be careful not to use language that characterizes facts in a way that affects the legal issues before the court.

Ms. Miller sought relief from the United States District Court for the Eastern District of Texas on March 31, 1993, alleging that the gender and "illegitimacy" distinctions contained in 8 U.S.C. § 1409(a) violated the Fifth Amendment to the United States Constitution. App. 6, 9. Ms. Miller subsequently added Mr. Miller as a co-plaintiff, but the district court dismissed his claims for lack of standing. Miller v. Christopher, 870 F. Supp. 1, 3 (D.D.C. 1994). Based upon Secretary Christopher's residence in Washington, the district court granted the Secretary's motion to transfer venue to the United States District Court for the District of Columbia. Miller v. Christopher, 96 F.3d 1467, 1468 (D.C. Cir. 1996). On April 29, 1994, the district court found that Ms. Miller lacked standing and granted the Secretary's motion to dismiss. Id.

Ms. Miller appealed that decision to the United States Court of Appeals for the District of Columbia Circuit on June 29, 1994. App. 1. Her appeal presented three separate claims. First, she argued that the district court erred in finding that she lacked standing; second, she argued that 8 U.S.C. § 1409(a)(4) violates the Fifth Amendment's equal protection guarantees; and third, she argued that she meets the requirements of 8 U.S.C. § 1409(a)(4) because the voluntary paternity decree "legitimated" her as of her date of birth. Miller v. Christopher, 96 F.3d at 1469-70.

The Court of Appeals found that Ms. Miller did have standing to invoke federal jurisdiction, but that Mr. Miller's voluntary paternity decree did not "legitimate" Ms. Miller as of her date of birth. Id. at 1469, 1472-73. Neither of those findings is under review in this Court.

The Court of Appeals also found that the gender and "illegitimacy" distinctions contained in 8 U.S.C. § 1409(a)(4) did not violate the equal protection principles of the Fifth Amendment to the United States Constitution. Id. at 1470-73. The Court of Appeals found that the case was controlled by this Court's decision in <u>Fiallo v. Bell</u>, 430 U.S. 787 (1977).

In her opinion concurring in the judgment, Judge Wald took the unusual step of noting the inconsistency between <u>Fiallo</u> and this court's recent equal protection jurisprudence:

> <u>Fiallo</u> is a Supreme Court decision directly on point and, as a result, we have no choice but to hold section 1409(a) constitutional. Yet I think it is important to underscore the extent to which <u>Fiallo</u> is out of step with Court's current refusal to sanction "official action that closes a door or denies opportunity to women (or to men)" based on stereotypes or "overbroad generalizations" about men and women. <u>Virginia</u>, — U.S. — , 116 S. Ct. at 2275. <u>Fiallo</u> is a precedent whose time has come and gone; it should be changed by Congress or by the Supreme Court.

7 Giving this much information from the opinions below is usually not necessary or appropriate; it *is* appropriate here because a respected judge recommended overruling the main on-point decision.

<u>Miller v. Christopher</u>, 96 F.3d at 1477 (Wald, J., concurring in the judgment). **7**

This Court granted Ms. Miller's petition for a writ of certiorari on April 28, 1997.

SUMMARY OF THE ARGUMENT

The issue before this Court is whether Congress may use an irrebuttable gender stereotype to implement its policy decisions. This Court faces two tasks when deciding this case. First, the court must select the appropriate level of scrutiny to apply to the statute codifying the irrebuttable gender stereotype; second, the Court must apply that level of scrutiny to the statute. Both tasks are made easier by this court's repeated insistence that antiquated, sexist notions about the relative roles of men and women in our society have no place in our law.

The Court's first task — the selection of the appropriate level of scrutiny — is complicated by the fact that the irrebuttable gender stereotype is embedded in a naturalization statute, and the Court has traditionally given extreme deference to Acts of Congress in the naturalization arena. This complication is readily overcome.

This Court should give heightened scrutiny, not extreme deference, to the irrebuttable gender stereotypes embedded in naturalization legislation. First, this Court has refused to defer to Congress in the past when Congress has infringed on Constitutional rights via immigration and naturalization legislation, and the Court has likewise refused to defer to Congress in the past when gender stereotypes have infected legislation in areas traditionally under almost complete Congressional control. Second, there is a significant distinction between Congressional power to set policy and Congressional power to enforce that policy: the Constitution regulates implementation more closely than it regulates the formation of policy itself. Third, and finally, this Court should apply heightened scrutiny to this statute because the questionable practices of the past should not be permitted to taint today's decisions. **8**

8 This sentence is almost identical to a point heading; generally, your summary should reflect the phrases that pay and *themes* of the point headings, but not use identical phrasing.

The Court's second task — the application of the appropriate level of scrutiny to the statute — is straightforward. At the heart of the statute is a distinction between mothers and fathers that is the result of the archaic, sexist, stereotypical thinking that continues to plague our society. Section 1409(a) embodies the antiquated view of a family in which the woman's role is to nurture children and the man's role is to pay the bills. Section 1409(a) does not merely suggest that this is the case; section 1409(a) declares that this gender stereotype is true in all cases.

The plight of Lorelyn Miller and her father illustrates this problem with section 1409(a) especially well. Ms. Miller and Mr. Miller are a family and wish to live like one in the United States; section 1409(a) denies them that opportunity because they did not jump through the bureaucratic hoops quickly enough. There is absolutely nothing that they can now do to defeat the operation of the gender stereotype codified in section 1409(a). Now that Ms. Miller is over twenty-one, section 1409(a) operates as a conclusion that she and her father *cannot* have the close family relationship that allows a parent to transmit citizenship to a child.

In short, section 1409(a) declares that all women will automatically have a close family relationship with their children, and that all men will not have such a relationship unless it is established in connection with the financial support of those children before they reach the age of majority. There is no justification for the presence of this irrebuttable gender stereotype in our law. The application of heightened scrutiny is not necessary in order to rid the law of this anachronism; the choice of how closely to examine the statute will determine nothing more in this case than the degree of mismatch between the irrebuttable gender stereotype in question and the reality of the modern world. **9**

ARGUMENT

I. Introduction **10**

The statute in question in this case, 8 U.S.C. § 1409(a) (1994), classifies children born of a U.S. citizen and a non-citizen into three groups: those who are "legitimate" (i.e., those whose parents are married), those who are "illegitimate" and have a U.S. citizen for a mother, and those who are "illegitimate" and have a U.S. citizen for a father. Children in the first two groups — those who are "legitimate" and those who have a U.S. citizen mother — are U.S. citizens by birthright. See 8 U.S.C. § 1401(g) (1994).

Children in the last group, however — those "illegitimate" children with U.S. citizen fathers — may receive their fathers' citizenship only after clearing several hurdles. Even if paternity is established by "clear and convincing evidence," as required by section 1409(a)(1), and even if the father was a U.S. citizen at the time of the child's birth, as required by section 1409(a)(2), section 1409(a)(3) and (a)(4) deny citizenship to an "illegitimate" child of a U.S. citizen father and a non-citizen mother *unless* the father agrees in writing to support that child until age eighteen *and* the child is either "legitimated," the father acknowledges paternity, or paternity is established by adjudication, *before* the child reaches the age of eighteen.

This Court has previously noted that Congress made these classifications and enacted these statutory hurdles out of a concern for "a perceived absence in most cases of close family ties, as well as a concern with the serious problems of proof that usually lurk in paternity determinations." Fiallo v. Bell, 430 U.S. 787, 799 (1977).

Those "problems of proof" do not lurk in 1998 the way they did in 1977. Furthermore, this Court soundly rejected decision making based on "perceived" notions of how men and women act in United States v. Virginia, 116 S. Ct. 2264 (1996). This Court should reverse the decision of the Court below and allow Ms. Miller to receive her birthright of United States Citizenship.

II. This Court should require an "exceedingly persuasive justification" for the irrebuttable gender stereotype codified in 8 U.S.C. § 1409(a) (1994), because extreme deference to congressional use of such gender stereotypes is unwarranted.

This Court has recently reaffirmed its unwillingness to countenance the use of gender stereotypes as proxies for more rational decision-making. United States v.

9 It is also appropriate to end the summary by reminding the court of what it is asked to do (affirm or reverse). This writer has chosen to end on a dramatic note instead.

10 An "introduction" labeled as such is unusual in effective appellate briefs. A more argumentative heading might be better here.

Virginia, 116 S. Ct. 2264, 2274 (1996) (requiring "[p]arties who seek to defend gender-based government action [to] demonstrate an 'exceedingly persuasive justification' for that action" and characterizing this approach as "skeptical scrutiny of official action denying rights or opportunities based on sex"). Although naturalization legislation has traditionally been given extremely deferential review by this Court, *Fiallo*, 430 U.S. at 792, the time has come for this Court to enforce the Equal Protection Clause in all contexts and strike down irrebuttable gender stereotypes wherever they are found.

Respect for a coordinate branch of government does not require this Court to turn its back on the Constitution's demand for equal protection of the laws. The extreme deference that has historically characterized this Court's review of naturalization legislation is more the result of momentum than logic. The approach taken in *Fiallo* typifies this extreme deference. The *Fiallo* Court held that naturalization legislation is constitutional if Congress had merely a "facially legitimate and bona fide reason" for enacting it, and basing its decision on a 1972 immigration case. *Fiallo*, 430 U.S. at 792 n.4 (citing *Kleindienst v. Mandel*, 408 U.S. 753, 770 (1972) (articulating a standard of review for *First Amendment* challenges to immigration legislation).

As the *Fiallo* Court admitted, quoting Justice Frankfurter, "much could be said for the view" that Congress does not have unchecked power over immigration "were we writing on a clean slate." *Id.* (quoting *Galven v. Press*, 347 U.S. 522, 530-32)). The *Fiallo* Court then refused to examine the issue anew, however, finding itself "not prepared to deem ourselves wiser or more sensitive to human rights than our predecessors, especially those who have been most zealous in protecting civil liberties under the Constitution." *Id.*

Petitioners respectfully contend that this Court is, indeed, more sensitive to human rights than its predecessors. This Court's unflinching application of the Equal Protection Clause in *Virginia* makes that clear. Furthermore, as will be discussed in detail below, the *Fiallo* Court's alleged impediments to a more exacting review of naturalization legislation are illusory. No legal standard prevents this Court from reviewing the appropriateness of the *Fiallo* standard because the choice of standard is a decision of law, and this Court reviews decisions of law *de novo*. *United States v. Singer Mfg. Co.*, 374 U.S. 174, 177 (1963). The time has come for this Court to give the irrebuttable gender stereotypes found in naturalization legislation the same scrutiny given to irrebuttable gender stereotypes found in other areas of the law. **11**

A. 8 U.S.C. § 1409(a) should not escape meaningful judicial review merely because Congress acted at the height of its powers.

The Equal Protection Clause of the Fourteenth Amendment is applicable to Congress via the Fifth Amendment. *See, e.g.*, *Bolling v. Sharpe*, 347 U.S. 497, 505 (1954). In *United States v. Virginia*, this Court held that legislation based on gender stereotypes should receive "skeptical scrutiny" upon review. 116 S. Ct. at 2275. There is no reason to use a different standard when reviewing § 1409(a) simply because it is immigration legislation.

The first reason offered by the *Fiallo* Court for its extremely deferential standard is that " 'over no conceivable subject is the legislative power of Congress more complete than it is over' the admissions of aliens." *Fiallo*, 430 U.S. at 791 (quoting *Oceanic Navigation Co. v. Stranahan*, 214 U.S. 320, 339 (1909)). **12** The quoted statement does not address the question whether Congressional power over naturalization is free from *any* meaningful judicial review; it merely points out that this power is more complete than congressional power over other areas of the law. It is a relative statement that addresses the power of Congress over naturalization by com-

11 This paragraph illustrates a method for including standard of review information when the court rules do not ask for a separate section. The writer inserts the information into introductory material. This introductory material also serves as a roadmap in the sense that it identifies the *themes* that this section of the document will be exploring, and thus prepares the reader for what will follow. Although it is effective, a more traditional roadmap is usually more helpful to a busy reader.

12 Because knowing the origin of the quotation does not help the reader to understand its significance, this citation

paring that power to other powers. It wisely does not attempt to place any power of Congress above the Constitution, because even when Congressional power is at its apex it may not violate the Constitution. Marbury v. Madison, 5 U.S. (1 Cranch) 137, 180 (1803) (holding that the Constitution is the "supreme law of the land" and that only those laws made pursuant to the Constitution are to be recognized).

This Court has previously recognized that specific, Constitutional grants of authority to Congress do not allow Congress to ignore the rest of the Constitution. Almeida-Sanchez v. United States, 413 U.S. 266, 272-75 (1973). The Almeida-Sanchez Court struck down a statute that authorized searches and seizures without probable cause within "reasonable distances" from any external boundary of the United States. Id. at 275. The Court reasoned that the Naturalization Clause of the Constitution — Article I, section eight, clause four, which empowers Congress to "establish a uniform Rule of Naturalization" — did not permit Congress to enact a statute that violated the Fourth Amendment's guarantee against unreasonable searches and seizures. Id. at 272-75. Similarly, the Court refused to apply the highly deferential "rational basis" standard to a draft registration statute that exempted women, even though "judicial deference to such congressional exercise of authority is at its apogee when legislative action under the congressional authority to raise and support armies and make rules and regulations for their governance is challenged." Rostker v. Goldberg, 453 U.S. 57, 70 (1981).

This Court's holdings in Almeida-Sanchez and Rostker show that Congress is never free from meaningful judicial review. The draft registration statute that received heightened scrutiny in Rostker did not violate the Constitution because men and women were undeniably dissimilarly situated by operation of the ban on women in combat roles. 453 U.S. at 79. **13** A skeptical scrutiny of the gender distinction in section 1409(a) will not reveal any such statutory distinction between mothers and fathers; the distinction is based on nothing more than a gender stereotype. Congress should not be permitted to dodge this scrutiny merely because it is legislating in the area of immigration.

B. Even unreviewable naturalization policy choices may not be implemented by patently unconstitutional methods.

The power over naturalization is a fundamental sovereign attribute involving some purely political decisions. It does not necessarily follow, however, that the enforcement of those decisions must be free from judicial review as a consequence. The Fiallo Court based its deferential review on its claim that the "power to expel or exclude aliens is a fundamental sovereign attribute exercised by the Government's political departments largely immune from judicial control." 430 U.S. at 792 (citing Shaughnessy v. Mezei, 345 U.S. 206, 210 (1953)). It also noted that "the power over aliens is of a political character and therefore subject to only narrow judicial review." Fiallo, 430 U.S. at 792 (citing Hampton v. Mow Sun Wong, 426 U.S. 88, 101 n. 21 (1976)). The Fiallo Court's reluctance to apply less deferential review is not supported by this Court's decisions.

This Court has not hesitated to apply meaningful review to the implementation of political decisions. For example, the power over domestic law enforcement is also a fundamental sovereign attribute, but "[w]here rights secured by the Constitution are involved, there can be no rulemaking or legislation which would abrogate them." Miranda v. Arizona, 384 U.S. 436, 490 (1966). The result reached in Miranda recognized that the government has wide latitude in choosing which activities to criminalize, but that it may not enforce those policy choices in an unconstitutional manner.

As far back as 1896, this Court held that Congress cannot criminally penalize ali-

Margin notes:

might best be replaced with the notation "(citation omitted)." If the writer wants to discount the *Fiallo* Court's reasoning by showing that it is relying on ancient authority, he should do so more directly.

13 This analysis goes beyond the focus of section II, which is merely to establish which test *should* be applied, rather than to apply the test.

ens without due process. See Wong Wing v. United States, 163 U.S. 228, 240 (1896) (distinguishing Congress's authority to control borders from constitutional limits on criminal penalties). As recently as 1954 this Court admitted that "[p]olicies pertaining to the entry of aliens . . . are peculiarly concerned with the political conduct of government," but noted that "in the enforcement of these policies, the Executive Branch of the Government must respect the procedural safeguards of due process." Galvan v. Press, 347 U.S. 522, 531 (1954) (holding that aliens must receive due process when the executive branch seeks to enforce the law against them). These cases addressed *due process* concerns in the implementation of policy. This Court should address *equal protection* concerns in the implementation of policy, as well. To hold otherwise would bifurcate the Constitution into one part that must be obeyed and another part that may be ignored with impunity.

Furthermore, this Court has the authority to review acts of the other branches of the federal government to ensure that they comply with the Constitution. See Marbury v. Madison, 5 U.S. (1 Cranch) 137, 150 (1803). This authority springs from the fact that the people of the United States — not the federal government — are sovereign. McCulloch v. Maryland, 17 U.S. (4 Wheat.) 316, 403-05 (1819) ("The government proceeds directly from the people. . . . In form, and in substance, it emanates from them.") The people are the collective holders of the power over naturalization. They have created a federal government to exercise that power, but they have done so through a Constitution that requires the government to adhere to specified norms. One function of this Court is to watch over the other branches of government and to ensure, on behalf of the people, that the Constitution is obeyed. To conclude that legislation can escape meaningful review in this Court when Congress acts in politically sensitive areas is to conclude that Congress itself is sovereign, and that this Court has no power to review its actions on behalf of the people.

Such a conclusion must be rejected because it would artificially place Congress above the Constitution. The Constitution gives Congress the power to set naturalization policy; but, as Marbury v. Madison made clear, Congress may never act in violation of the Constitution. In this case, this Court must use a heightened standard when reviewing Congress's decision to require close family ties before allowing some U.S. citizens — but not others — to pass on their citizenship to their foreign-born children.

C. Past practices in violation of the Constitution should not be permitted to corrupt today's decisions.

As Judge Wald noted in her concurring decision below, "Fiallo is out of step with [the] Court's current refusal to sanction 'official action that closes a door or denies opportunity to women (or to men)' based on stereotypes or 'overbroad generalizations' about men and women." Miller v. Christopher, 96 F.3d 1467, 1477 (1996) (Wald, J., concurring) (citing United States v. Virginia, 116 S. Ct. at 2275). Judge Wald went on to state explicitly that "Fiallo is a precedent whose time has come and gone; it should be changed by Congress or the Supreme Court." Miller, 96 F.3d at 1477 (Wald, J., concurring).

The Fiallo Court tried to justify its holding by noting that "in the exercise of its broad power over immigration and naturalization, 'Congress regularly makes rules that would be unacceptable if applied to citizens.'" 430 U.S. at 792 (quoting Mathews v. Diaz, 426 U.S. 67, 80 (1976)). To the extent that this reasoning indicates that the Fiallo Court deferred to the weight of past practice when enforcing the Constitution, the Fiallo Court erred, and Petitioner respectfully contends that this Court would err if it continued to follow the Fiallo line of cases.

8

This Court did not hesitate to end a long history of constitutional abuse when it enforced the Equal Protection Clause and first struck down a statute based upon an antiquated gender stereotype. Reed v. Reed, 404 U.S. 71 (1971) (unanimously striking down state law requiring that men be chosen over similarly situated women when selecting estate administrators). Likewise, this Court should not hesitate to end another long history of constitutional abuse by striking down the use of irrebuttable gender stereotypes in naturalization legislation.

Even the extremely deferential Fiallo Court noted that this Court's cases "reflect acceptance of a limited judicial responsibility under the Constitution even with respect to the power of Congress to regulate the admission and exclusion of aliens." Fiallo, 430 U.S. at 794 n.5. This Court's responsibility to enforce the Constitution goes beyond merely checking to see if Congress had a "facially legitimate and bona fide reason" for legislating on the basis of an irrebuttable gender stereotype.

In the twenty years since Fiallo was decided, our society has grown to more fully appreciate the fundamental flaw inherent in creating legislative distinctions based on gender. It is time to enforce the Equal Protection Clause across the board and apply "skeptical scrutiny" to any use of irrebuttable gender stereotypes. Without an "exceedingly persuasive justification," the use of these stereotypes in any context undermines this Court's pronouncement in Virginia that gender-based classifications "must not rely on overbroad generalizations about the different talents, capacities, or preference of males and females." Virginia, 116 S. Ct. at 2275.

Because § 1409(a) is a federal law that makes a distinction based on gender, it should be reviewed using the "skeptical scrutiny" standard that this Court set forth in United States v. Virginia.

III. The use of an irrebuttable gender stereotype in 8 U.S.C. § 1409(a) is not "substantially related" to the achievement of the government's objective, and there is no "exceedingly persuasive justification" for the stereotype's use.

This Court recently clarified the level of scrutiny applicable to gender-based classifications. See United States v. Virginia, 116 S. Ct. 2264 (1996). [14] The government must now show "at least that the challenged classification serves important governmental objectives and that the discriminatory means employed are substantially related to the achievement of those objectives." Virginia, 116 S. Ct. at 2275 (internal punctuation and citations omitted). Furthermore, the Court will apply "skeptical scrutiny," and "parties who seek to defend gender-based government action must demonstrate an exceedingly persuasive justification for that action." Id. at 2274 (internal punctuation omitted).

Petitioner Lorelyn Miller does not challenge the government's important objective of allowing U.S. citizenship to flow only through close family relationships. Petitioner does challenge, however, the government's assertion that there is an exceedingly persuasive justification for the use of an irrebuttable gender stereotype in the statutory scheme devised to achieve that objective.

The government's use of an irrebuttable gender stereotype in section 1409(a), as explained by the Fiallo Court and the court below, is predicated on two erroneous assumptions: (1) that all men, without exception, will not form close family ties with their "illegitimate" children unless that relationship is formed as a by-product of the financial support of those children, and (2) that proof of the paternity of an "illegitimate" child is much less reliable than proof of maternity of that child. See Miller v. Christopher, 96 F.3d 1467, 1472 (D.C. Cir. 1996); United States v. Fiallo, 430 U.S. 787, 797-800 (1977).

[14] Generally, it is more effective to begin point heading sections with a more argumentative statement of an assertion you want the court to agree with.

9

Congress concluded from these assumptions that the United States should make it more difficult for American fathers to pass their citizenship on to their "illegitimate" children by establishing procedural hurdles (in § 1409(a)) that (1) burden all of these fathers and their children regardless of whether they have close family ties, and (2) burden all of these fathers and children regardless of how accurately paternity can be proven. As illustrated by the plight of Lorelyn and Charlie Miller, these burdens can become insurmountable: § 1409(a) will prevent Mr. Miller and Ms. Miller from ever legally proving that they have a close family relationship unless this court refuses to accept the irrebuttable gender stereotype in § 1409(a).

A. 8 U.S.C. § 1409(a) is unconstitutionally overinclusive and, therefore, is not "substantially related" to the achievement of the government's objective.

The first inquiry under the <u>Virginia</u> test is whether congressional use of the irrebuttable gender stereotype found in section 1409(a) is "substantially related" to the government's concededly legitimate objective of conditioning citizenship on close family ties. This Court's equal protection jurisprudence makes it clear that very few gender-based distinctions are "substantially related" to the governmental objectives they purport to advance.

The cases in which no substantial relation was found have one common element: They reject gender stereotypes that are little more than vestiges of past discrimination. For example, in 1971, this Court unanimously found no substantial relationship between a state law that favored men over women as executors, and the state's objective of reducing intrafamily controversy. <u>Reed v. Reed</u>, 404 U.S. 71, 77 (1971). In language particularly relevant to the case before this court, the <u>Reed</u> Court expressed its unwillingness to countenance the use of an irrebuttable gender stereotype in lieu of a simple hearing on the merits: **15**

To give a mandatory preference to members of either sex over members of the other, <u>merely to accomplish the elimination of hearings on the merits</u>, is to make the very kind of arbitrary legislative choice forbidden by the Equal Protection Clause of the Fourteenth Amendment; and whatever may be said as to the positive values of avoiding intrafamily controversy, the choice in this context may not lawfully be mandated solely on the basis of sex.

<u>Id.</u> at 76-77 (emphasis added). This Court has also struck down a gender-based distinction in a statute that allocated government benefits to families with dependent children based on the sex of the parent who had lost his or her employment. <u>Califano v. Westcott</u>, 443 U.S. 76, 96 (1979). The statute was struck down because it did not substantially relate to the achievement of the government's objective, which was to allocate resources only to those families truly in need. <u>Id.</u> at 88. In striking down the statute, the <u>Westcott</u> Court apparently recognized — as this Court should, as well — that not every family consists of a wage-earning father and a child-rearing mother.

Congress may make gender-based distinctions if the reason for the distinction is based in fact and not stereotypes. <u>Rostker v. Goldberg</u>, 453 U.S. 57, 67 (1981). In <u>Rostker</u>, the Court held constitutional a statute that exempted women from registering for the military draft, noting that, with respect to military service, men and women were not similarly situated due to another statute: men could serve in combat positions, but women could not. <u>Id.</u> Thus, a statute that exempted women from registering for the draft was substantially related to the government's legitimate goal of

15 Notice how the writer uses long quotes sparingly, and introduces them effectively with a focusing, or "Tom Brokaw" introduction.

providing for an induction system that would produce combat soldiers. Id. The Court specifically noted that its holding was not predicated on antiquated notions about the relative abilities of men and women; rather, the holding was predicated on the objectively verifiable fact that women could not serve in combat roles in the United States armed forces. Id.

The application of the "substantial relationship" test to § 1409(a) is straightforward. **16** In a limited sense, § 1409(a) *is* related to the government's objective of conditioning citizenship on close family ties: § 1409(a) will certainly prevent citizenship from flowing to some children who do not deserve it. The fatal flaw in § 1409(a), though, is that it is overinclusive. Section 1409(a)'s various hurdles exclude from citizenship those children — like Ms. Miller — who are deserving of citizenship under the standards of the statute due to their close family ties with their U.S. citizen parents.

16 This topic sentence is too subtle for a brief. The sentence should signal more strongly what the result will be when the test is applied to the client's case.

The degree to which § 1409(a) is overinclusive is a function of the degree to which the assumptions underlying § 1409(a) are invalid. Thus, because the assumptions underlying § 1409(a) — that paternity is hard to establish reliably and that women and men are destined to occupy different roles — are substantially incorrect, the use of these irrebuttable stereotypes is not substantially related to the government's objective.

The gender stereotypes underlying § 1409(a) are the very sort of archaic generalizations that modern equal protection jurisprudence seeks to eradicate. This court has repeatedly recognized that the government "must not rely on overbroad generalizations about the different talents, capacities, or preferences of males and females." Virginia, 116 S. Ct. at 2276 (citing Weinberger v. Wiesenfeld, 420 U.S. 646, 643, 648 (1975); Califano v. Goldfarb, 430 U.S. 188, 223-24 (1977)). If we as a society have learned anything about gender in the twenty years since Fiallo was decided, it is that women and men may not be conclusively pigeon-holed solely on the basis of their gender.

The facts of this case support this rather obvious conclusion. Ms. Miller is twenty-seven years old. Although she is not a minor, and although she neither needs nor receives the financial support of her father, she and Mr. Miller have a close family relationship. By the terms of the stereotype underlying section 1409(a), all men — including Mr. Miller — irrebuttably do not form close family relationships with their adult "illegitimate" children. To uphold the rationality of this irrebuttable stereotype is to deny the existence of Mr. Miller and those other men who, for whatever reason, form relationships with their "illegitimate" children later in life. To uphold the validity of this irrebuttable stereotype is to deny reality. This Court should reject the validity of this irrebuttable stereotype and acknowledge that there is no substantial relationship between the use of the stereotype and the government's goal of fostering close family relationships.

B. There is no "exceedingly persuasive justification" for the use of an irrebuttable gender stereotype in 8 U.S.C. § 1409(a) because less discriminatory methods would achieve the government's objective.

Even if the irrebuttable gender stereotype codified in section 1409(a) could somehow be found to be substantially related to the government's objective, the statute must still be found unconstitutional because there is no "exceedingly persuasive justification" for the use of that irrebuttable gender stereotype. See Virginia, 116 S. Ct. at 2276. Even if this Court finds that the stereotype is generally valid, Congress need not have made it operate conclusively and irrebuttably, with no safety-valve provision for fathers like Mr. Miller. A *rebuttable* presumption might be justifiable if indi-

17 This subsection would be much more effective if the writer provided support for his assertions and analysis of how the "exceedingly persuasive justification" language has been analyzed in the past.

viduals are given the opportunity to show that they do not fit the mold, but any stereotype that mechanically and permanently penalizes people because of their gender offends the very core of the Constitution's equal protection guarantees. This Court recognized as much in <u>Reed</u>, 404 U.S. at 76-77, and <u>Westcott</u>, 443 U.S. at 90. The Court should recognize that basic truth again today. **17**

IV. 8 U.S.C. § 1409(a) violates the Equal Protection Clause even under an extremely deferential level of scrutiny because Congress had no "facially legitimate and bona fide" reason for using an irrebuttable gender stereotype.

The irrebuttable gender stereotype codified in section 1409(a) is so irrational that it fails even the <u>Fiallo</u> Court's extremely deferential level of scrutiny. As the <u>Fiallo</u> Court itself recognized, this Court's cases "reflect acceptance of a limited judicial responsibility under the Constitution even with respect to the power of Congress to regulate the admission and exclusion of aliens." 430 U.S. at 794 n.5. Even if this Court does not use the <u>Virginia</u> "skeptical scrutiny" standard, there is still ample reason to conclude that section 1409(a) violates the Constitution's equal protection guarantees.

The <u>Fiallo</u> Court held that naturalization legislation is constitutional if Congress had merely a "facially legitimate and bona fide reason" for enacting it. 430 U.S. 792 n.4 (citing <u>Kleindienst v. Mandel</u>, 408 U.S. 753, 770 (1972)). In this test, all that is necessary is that the use of the irrebuttable gender stereotype be legitimate and reasonable. Section 1409(a) fails even this easy examination.

The <u>Fiallo</u> Court assumed that all men are different from all women with respect to their relationships with their "illegitimate" children, referring any concerns about this gender stereotype to Congress. 430 U.S. at 799 n.9. Congress's failure to abandon this gender stereotype in the twenty years since <u>Fiallo</u> was decided has left this Court no choice but to reject it today. This Court has repeatedly held that it is unconstitutional to legislatively assume that one's gender conclusively determines one's personality, noting in 1994 that "[t]oday we reaffirm what, by now, should be axiomatic: Intentional discrimination on the basis of gender by state actors violates the Equal Protection Clause." <u>J.E.B. v. Alabama</u>, 511 U.S. 127, 136-37 (1994); see also <u>Mississippi Univ. for Women v. Hogan</u>, 458 U.S. 718, 725 (1982) ("Care must be taken in ascertaining whether the statutory objective itself reflects archaic and stereotypic notions"); <u>Duren v. Missouri</u>, 439 U.S. 357, 370 (1979) (striking down a state's practice of excluding women from jury service on equal protection grounds where the only rationalization for the practice was based on a stereotype); <u>United States v. Virginia</u>, 116 S. Ct. 2264 (1996).

Furthermore, this Court has previously struck down the perpetual, irrebuttable application of this very stereotype regarding relationships between fathers and their "illegitimate" children. <u>Caban v. Mohammed</u>, 441 U.S. 380, 389 (1979). The <u>Caban</u> Court used equal protection grounds to strike down a statute that distinguished between mothers and fathers of "illegitimate" children based on their presumed relationships with those children after infancy. The Court noted that "[e]ven if unwed mothers as a class were closer to their newborn infants, this generalization concerning parent-child relations would become less acceptable as a basis for legislative distinctions as the age of the child increased." <u>Id.</u> Section 1409(a) does more than legislate on the basis of this stereotype beyond infancy; it applies this stereotype *forever*. Ms. Miller is long past infancy, but the stereotypical assumptions about her relationship with her father govern her to this day.

The irrebuttable gender stereotype that distinguishes between the relative proclivities of men and women towards their offspring is not a "facially legitimate and bona fide reason" for the gender-based distinctions codified in section 1409. As Justice Marshall pointed out in his dissent to <u>Fiallo</u>, "[t]he majority does not even engage in the modest degree of scrutiny required by [<u>Kleindienst</u>]. . . . That failure, I submit, is due to the fact that the statute could not even pass that standard of review." <u>Fiallo</u>, 430 U.S. at 806 n.6 (Marshall, J., dissenting). Justice Marshall was right. Given all that we know about the dangers of irrebuttable gender stereotypes, the stereotype embedded in section 1409(a) is neither facially legitimate nor bona fide.

CONCLUSION

Because the irrebuttable gender stereotype codified in 8 U.S.C. § 1409(a) (1994) violates the equal protection guarantees of the Fifth Amendment to the United States Constitution, this Court should declare § 1409(a) unconstitutional and remove one more vestige of gender discrimination from our laws. The decision of the United States Court of Appeals for the District of Columbia Circuit should be reversed.

Respectfully submitted,

Simon Scholar

_____

Simon J. Scholar
1356 School Street
Metropolis, Ohio
555-555-5555

CERTIFICATE OF SERVICE

This document certifies hand delivery of one copy of this brief to Edward Enemy, 456325 Student Mailboxes, Metropolis, Ohio, on November 3, 1997.

Simon Scholar

_____

Simon Scholar

13

No. 97-7597

IN THE SUPREME COURT OF THE UNITED STATES

FALL TERM, 1998

_____

Patrick Knowles,
        Petitioner,

v.

State of Iowa,
        Respondent.

_____

ON WRIT OF CERTIORARI TO THE SUPREME COURT OF IOWA

_____

BRIEF FOR THE RESPONDENT

_____

Samuel J. Student
1234 School Street
Metropolis, Ohio
555-555-5555

Counsel for the Respondent

QUESTION PRESENTED

Consistent with the Fourth Amendment, can a state promote the interest of officer safety by enacting a statute that gives police officers authorization to conduct a search of a motor vehicle when they issue a citation to a person who has committed an offense that allows arrest?

TABLE OF CONTENTS

TABLE OF AUTHORITIES

IN THE SUPREME COURT OF THE UNITED STATES

No. 97-7597

Patrick George Knowles,
Petitioner,

v.

State of Iowa,
Respondent.

ON WRIT OF CERTIORARI TO THE SUPREME COURT OF IOWA

BRIEF FOR THE RESPONDENT

OPINIONS BELOW

The opinion of the Supreme Court of Iowa, affirming the denial of the petitioner's motion to suppress, is reported at 569 N.W.2d 601 (Iowa 1997). The opinion of the Iowa District Court, Fifth Judicial District, County of Jasper, denying the Petitioner's motion to suppress, is reported in the Record at page 20. The judgment entries of the Iowa District Court, Fifth Judicial District, County of Jasper, convicting and sentencing Petitioner Patrick George Knowles, are reported in the Record at pages 26 and 30, respectively. **1**

1 If a decision below is reported in the record and in a published source, you should list both. The goal is to give the court information that will allow it to find the opinions easily.

JURISDICTION

The judgment of the Iowa Supreme Court was entered on October 22, 1997. The petition for the writ of certiorari was filed on January 20, 1998, and this Court granted the Petition on March 23, 1998. The jurisdiction of this Court rests on 28 U.S.C. § 1257 (1994).

STATUTORY AND CONSTITUTIONAL PROVISIONS INVOLVED **2**

2 Note how this section is labeled according to its contents.

The Fourth Amendment to the United States Constitution provides in pertinent part that "no warrants shall issue, but upon probable cause, supported by Oath or affirmation, and particularly describing the place to be searched, and the persons or things to be seized."

Iowa Code § 805.1(4) (1995) provides: "The issuance of a citation in lieu of ar-

1

rest or in lieu of continued custody does not affect the officer's authority to conduct an otherwise lawful search."

STANDARD OF REVIEW

The Iowa Supreme Court did not err as a matter of law when it held that the search of Patrick Knowles's automobile was valid under the Fourth Amendment. The questions of reasonable suspicion and probable cause to make a warrantless search are questions of law that may be reviewed de novo. Ornelas v. United States, 517 U.S. 690, 691 (1996). **3**

3 Because this standard of review is not particularly helpful to the respondent's argument, it is handled with a minimum of fuss. Check local rules to see if the standard of review should be in the argument or in a separate section.

STATEMENT OF THE CASE

This Court is being asked to determine the constitutionality of Iowa Code § 805.14, which allows an officer to conduct a search similar to a search incident to arrest when the officer issues a citation **4** in lieu of the arrest. Iowa Code § 805.14 (1995); Record 21.

4 Throughout, the author uses the more abstract, formal-sounding "citation" instead of the more concrete, casual-sounding "ticket." A "search incident to a citation" sounds much more reasonable than a "search incident to a ticket."

In March, 1996, in Jasper County, Iowa, Newton Police Officer Ronald J. Cook observed petitioner Patrick George Knowles traveling in his automobile at a high rate of speed. Record 12. Officer Cook conducted a radar reading on Knowles's automobile and observed that Knowles was traveling at 43 miles per hour in a 25 mile-per-hour zone. Record 12-13. Traveling at 43 miles per hour in a 25 mile-per-hour zone is an arrestable offense in the state of Iowa. Record 12-13. **5**

5 The writer emphasizes the petitioner's crime by putting it in a separate paragraph and spending three sentences on it.

Instead of arresting Mr. Knowles, Officer Cook decided to issue a citation in lieu of the arrest. Record 12-13. Following the issuance of the citation, Officer Cook conducted a search of Mr. Knowles's person and of his vehicle. Record 15. Officer Cook testified that his authority for the search came pursuant to Iowa Code § 805.14, which allows an officer issuing a citation in lieu of an arrest the ability to conduct a full search, as if an arrest had been made. Record 16.

Upon conducting his search of Knowles's vehicle, Officer Cook discovered two cotton gloves under the driver's seat. One glove contained a pipe for smoking marijuana, while the other glove contained a quantity of marijuana. Record 16. **6**

6 The writer puts the Petitioner's wrongdoing in a position of emphasis by isolating it in a short paragraph between two longer paragraphs.

Patrick Knowles was brought to trial in Iowa District Court for Jasper County and accused of (a) keeping a controlled substance (marijuana) in a moving vehicle, and (b) possession of a schedule I Controlled Substance, a serious misdemeanor. Record 2, 4. At trial, Patrick Knowles moved to suppress the evidence gathered during the search of his person and of the vehicle, arguing that the search was unconstitutional under the Fourth Amendment to the United States Constitution. Record 6-7. After conducting an evidentiary hearing to consider Knowles's motion to suppress, the district court determined that the Iowa Supreme Court had twice examined the constitutionality of Iowa Code § 805.1(4) and had twice upheld the statute under that constitutional scrutiny. Record 21. The court therefore denied the Motion to Suppress. Id.

Defendant appealed to the Iowa Supreme Court, claiming that the search was unconstitutional under the Fourth Amendment. The Iowa Supreme Court determined that authority for Officer Cook's search was indeed conferred by Iowa Code § 805.1(4). Upon examining the constitutionality of Iowa Code § 805.1(4), the court noted that the statute had already been upheld under challenges brought under the Fourth Amendment and under Article I, Section 8 of the Iowa Constitution. State v.

Knowles, 569 N.W.2d 601, 602 (Iowa 1997). In reconsidering its previous holdings, the Iowa Supreme Court upheld the constitutionality of Iowa Code § 805.1(4), noting that the officer did have the power to make a custodial arrest and conduct a search pursuant to that arrest. The court noted that the concerns over officer safety that justified the search incident to an arrest justified the lesser intrusion presented by the issuance of a citation. Id. at 602. **7**

7 This ending is a little too subtle because the complex structure places demands on the reader. It would be better to end by adding a strong statement such as, "The Court found that the search was constitutional."

SUMMARY OF THE ARGUMENT

The issue before this Court is whether a state may allow an arrest-level search in situations in which an arrest is allowed, but not made. In deciding this issue the Iowa Supreme Court held that the fact that the officer had the authority to arrest — and the authority to conduct a full search incident to that arrest **8** — implied that the officer also had the authority to search when issuing a citation in lieu of that arrest.

8 Use of dashes emphasizes this point.

In deciding the constitutionality of searches under the Fourth Amendment, this Court has articulated several exceptions to the warrant requirement of the Fourth Amendment. One example of such an exception is the warrantless search incident to an arrest. This Court should extend the search incident to an arrest exception to include situations in which the officer is issuing a citation in lieu of an arrest. Three reasons justify this new exception.

First, in articulating the arrest exception to the warrant requirement, this Court has not focused upon the fact of the arrest itself, but upon the underlying policy justifications for allowing a warrantless search incident to an arrest. Because the same policy justifications exist in both an arrest situation and a citation situation, officers facing either situation should be given identical authority to search.

Second, in deciding whether or not to allow a particular warrantless search, this Court has in the past balanced the public interests served by a warrantless search against the extent to which the search will interfere with individual privacy interests. The public interest in officer safety in a citation situation substantially outweighs the search's interference with the privacy interest of licensed drivers.

Finally, this Court should consider the result if such an exception is not allowed. If Iowa police officers are not allowed to conduct a search incident to citation in lieu of arrest, officers will simply use their authority to arrest those they wish to search. They will then be authorized to conduct a full search pursuant to that arrest. An arrest represents a much more significant intrusion into individual privacy than a search incident to a citation.

Accordingly, this Court should find that searches incident to citations issued in lieu of arrest are constitutional, and affirm the decision of the Iowa Supreme Court.

ARGUMENT
I. This Court should extend the search incident to arrest exception to the Fourth Amendment's warrant requirement to include situations in which officers issue a citation in lieu of an arrest.

The Fourth Amendment prohibits searches and seizures conducted without a warrant that was issued based upon probable cause. U.S. Const. Amend. 4. However, this Court has interpreted the Fourth Amendment to permit certain searches and seizures, conducted pending the issuance of a warrant, if some recognized exception to

3

the warrant requirement is present. <u>United States v. Place</u>, 462 U.S. 696, 701 (1983) (holding that the investigative detention of a traveler's bags is permissible on less than probable cause); <u>Vernonia School District 47J v. Acton</u>, 515 U.S. 646, 653 (1995) (noting that "a warrant, however, is not required to establish the reasonableness of every government search, and often when a warrant is not required, neither is probable cause").

The search incident to arrest exception has yet to be extended by this Court to cover the situation in which an officer issues a citation in lieu of an arrest. However, this Court should craft just such an exception for three reasons: (1) the same policy concerns that justify allowing a search incident to an arrest also exist when an officer issues a citation in lieu of an arrest; (2) the public interests advanced by allowing a search incident to a citation greatly outweigh the extent to which this search will interfere with individual privacy; and (3) the alternative to allowing such an exception will be to encourage the Iowa police force to conduct the same searches through a new method — pursuant to full arrests rather than to the issuance of a citation. Accordingly, this Court should affirm the decision of the Iowa Supreme Court.

A. The situation contemplated by Iowa Code § 805.1(4), where an officer issues a citation in lieu of arrest, presents the same policy concerns as when an actual arrest takes place.

Iowa Code § 805.1(4) provides that "[t]he issuance of a citation in lieu of arrest ... does not affect the officer's authority to conduct an otherwise lawful search." Because the issuance of a citation in lieu of arrest presents the same policy concerns as the situation in which an actual arrest takes place, officers should be allowed similar authority to search in both an arrest situation and a citation in lieu of arrest situation.

This Court has established an exception to the Fourth Amendment's warrant requirement when an officer is performing a lawful, custodial arrest of the suspect. See, e.g., <u>Chimel v. California</u>, 395 U.S. 752, 756 (1969). In <u>Chimel</u>, this Court examined the search incident to an arrest exception to the warrant requirement and made note of the two major policy justifications for the search: preserving officer safety and preventing the destruction of evidence by the suspect. <u>Id.</u> at 763. In paying so much attention to the underlying policy concerns that justify a search incident to an arrest, the <u>Chimel</u> Court seems to be saying that it is not the fact of the arrest that gives officers the authority to search; rather, it is the policy concerns that arise when someone is arrested that create the authority to search. See <u>New York v. Belton</u>, 453 U.S. 454, 463 (1981) (Brennan, J., dissenting) (noting the <u>Chimel</u> Court's focus upon the underlying policy justifications for a search incident to arrest). **9**

The argument that it is the actual arrest that provides grounds for the search incident to arrest is countered by the fact that in a search incident to an arrest, the arrest itself need not occur *before* the search takes place. <u>Rawlings v. Kentucky</u>, 448 U.S. 98, 110 (1980) (upholding the constitutionality of a search conducted before a formal arrest had taken place). **10** If this Court is willing to allow a search before the actual arrest takes place, then the fact of the arrest itself must not be the basis for the search incident to that arrest. Instead, the basis must be the underlying policy justifications that arise when an arrest takes place.

This Court has recognized that a search incident to an arrest is justified by (a) the need to preserve officer safety and (b) the fact that an arrest has already com-

9 It would help to know more details about either one of these cases. What issues were these Courts looking at? How did they decide those issues? If certain language particularly reveals the <u>Chimel</u> Court's focus on the policy concerns, it would be helpful to quote that language.

10 This parenthetical is more helpful, but it would be better still if we knew *why* a search before arrest was found to be constitutional.

promised an individual's rights. **11** Because both of these justifications are also present in a citation situation, it necessarily follows that a search incident to a citation is just as reasonable under the Fourth Amendment as a search incident to an arrest. **12**

1. Both an arrest and a citation issued in lieu of arrest present legitimate concerns about officer safety.

Because a citation situation presents the same concerns about officer safety as an arrest situation, officers in either circumstance should have equal authority to search. This Court has specifically identified officer safety as a reason why the search incident to arrest is reasonable under the Fourth Amendment. Chimel v. California, 395 U.S. at 762-63. In articulating why the search incident to arrest is reasonable under the Fourth Amendment, the Chimel Court observed that: "When an arrest is made, it is reasonable for the arresting officer to search the person arrested in order to remove any weapons that the latter might seek to use in order to resist the arrest or effect his escape. Otherwise the officer's safety might well be endangered, and the arrest itself frustrated." Id.

Concerns over officer safety are enough to justify a search incident to arrest even in situations in which the arresting officer had no subjective fear of the defendant and did not need to conduct the search for evidentiary reasons. United States v. Robinson, 414 U.S. 218, 234, 236 (1973). In Robinson, the arresting officer was in the course of arresting the defendant for two violations related to the validity of his driver's license. Id. at 223. While searching the defendant's person, the officer discovered a crumpled cigarette package. Id. Although the officer had no further evidence to gather for the crime of driving with a revoked permit, and although the officer knew that the cigarette package did not contain a weapon, the officer searched the crumpled package and discovered a quantity of heroin. Id.

In finding the search legal, the Court first noted that the reason for the authority to search incident to a lawful arrest depended just as much on the need to disarm the suspect as it did on the need to preserve evidence. Id. at 234. The Court noted that a search incident to arrest could be justified purely by concerns over officer safety — despite the fact that a need to preserve evidence did not exist in that situation. Id. The Court observed that a person arrested for driving with a revoked license is just as likely to possess dangerous weapons as a person arrested for other crimes. Id.

Accordingly, the Robinson Court held that all arrestable offenses present the same level of danger to the arresting officer, noting that "the danger to the police officer flows from the fact of the arrest, and its attendant proximity, stress, and uncertainty, and not from the grounds for arrest." Id., n.5. See also Washington v. Chrisman, 455 U.S. 1, 7 (1982) (noting that "every arrest must be presumed to present a risk of danger to the arresting officer"). After examining relevant Supreme Court precedent, the Robinson Court concluded that it was not necessary to adjudicate every case to determine whether or not the arresting officer had probable cause to perform a particular search. Robinson, 414 U.S. at 235. Rather, the Court held that in light of concerns over officer safety that exist in all arrest situations, any custodial arrest based upon probable cause is automatically a reasonable intrusion under the Fourth Amendment, and no further investigation is required regarding the reasonableness of the officer's search. Id.

The case at bar, where Officer Cook chose to issue a citation in lieu of arrest, presents the same concerns about officer safety as the situation in which an arrest has taken place. Like the defendant in Robinson, Patrick Knowles had committed an arrestable offense. The only difference between Robinson's situation and Patrick

Knowles's situation is Officer Cook's decision not to complete a full custodial arrest. In both an arrest and a citation, the critical variable — the defendant — remains equally blameworthy and equally dangerous to officer safety. If a suspect is "dangerous," he is no less dangerous because the officer has decided not to arrest him or her. See <u>Michigan v. Long</u>, 463 U.S. 1032, 1050 (1983) (upholding the search of the passenger compartment of an automobile during an investigatory stop of the occupant of the vehicle). **13**

In fact, a cited defendant may represent an even greater danger to the officer than someone placed under arrest. An arrested individual will often be handcuffed, so that it will be virtually impossible for him or her to attack the officer. A cited individual, on the other hand, will not be handcuffed and will have his or her hands free to reach for a weapon or to otherwise compromise officer safety. Officer Cook may have had an even greater need to conduct a full search of Patrick Knowles during this citation situation than if he had completed a full arrest.

Since Officer Cook had already issued the citation and had completed his business, Patrick Knowles was free to go. Therefore, it would seem as if an officer safety justification no longer existed for effecting a search of Patrick Knowles and his vehicle, because a reasonable person would not attack an officer in this situation. However, criminals rarely act reasonably, particularly those with the capacity to attack a law officer. Patrick Knowles could have just as easily reached for a weapon and made an attack on Officer Cook after receiving the citation as before he received the citation. Because Officer Cook was still under a substantial threat of danger, even after issuing the citation, his search was reasonable under the Fourth Amendment.

2. Since both an arrest and a citation issued in lieu of arrest already represent a substantial intrusion upon individual liberties, the intrusion presented by a search is justified.

This Court has traditionally justified the search incident to arrest exception by referring to the fact that an arrested person can expect to experience substantial intrusions upon his personal liberties. <u>United States v. Robinson</u>, 414 U.S. at 228. Because the same expectation exists in a citation situation, identical authority to search should also exist.

An arrest allows for more extensive authority to search because the arrestee's individual liberty interests have already been compromised. <u>Id.</u> at 228. In <u>Robinson</u>, this Court observed that broad search powers should be granted incident to arrest because an arrest "is intended to vindicate society's interest in having its laws obeyed." <u>Id.</u> This Court noted that an arrest is "inevitably accompanied by interference with the individual's freedom of movement, whether or not trial or conviction ultimately follow." <u>Id.</u> This "inevitable interference" justifies the additional interference posed by the search incident to the arrest. **14**

The issuance of a citation in lieu of an arrest presents the same types of intrusions as those that accompany an actual arrest. Like an arrest, the citation of Patrick Knowles for excessive speeding "vindicates society's interests in having its laws obeyed." Also like an arrest, a citation of Patrick Knowles would invariably be followed by certain intrusions upon Knowles's individual liberties. An arrest will usually involve a period of detainment and criminal prosecution. The issuance of a citation to Patrick Knowles would have required Knowles to pay a sizable fee and perhaps attend a criminal prosecution proceeding. In many states, multiple citations can result in some loss of driving privileges. The Supreme Court has allowed a warrantless search when a custodial arrest is performed largely because the suspect al-

13 Although there are exceptions, generally, within a section, you should not cite an authority for the first time in the application section. If an authority helps the reader to understand the meaning of the *rule*, it should be introduced during the explanation section. If, on the other hand, an authority helps the reader to understand more about the *facts*, it may be appropriate to bring it up for the first time in the application section.

14 This section makes good points; but it would be even stronger if the author had cited more than one authority. The ratio of ½ page of explanation to a page or more of application is often not a good sign.

ready will be subject to substantial interference with individual liberties; similar intrusions exist when a citation is issued in lieu of an arrest.

In focusing upon the justifications behind the warrantless search incident to arrest instead of the fact of arrest itself, this Court seems to be saying that the custodial arrest exception to the Fourth Amendment's warrant requirement is not justified by the pure fact of arrest, but rather by the concerns that arise from the circumstances that accompany that arrest. The constitutionality of a particular search should not depend upon such an arbitrary distinction as whether a custodial arrest did or did not take place. If another set of facts presents the same concerns and circumstances as an arrest, then the officer presented with those circumstances should have the same authority to search as an officer in an arrest situation. Thus, the search incident to arrest exception should be extended to include searches incident to citations in lieu of arrest.

> **B. The search incident to arrest exception should be extended to cover citations in lieu of arrest because the public interests advanced by such a search substantially outweigh the extent to which such a search intrudes upon individual privacy rights.**

In the past, this Court has applied a balancing test in order to determine whether a particular class of searches is allowable under the Fourth Amendment. **15** Applying this balancing test to the case at bar reveals that this Court should extend the search incident to arrest exception of the warrant requirement to include the class of searches conducted incident to a citation issued in lieu of an arrest.

The Fourth Amendment requires that all searches be reasonable. This Court has established that determining the reasonableness of a particular class of searches requires "balancing the needs of the search against the invasion which the search entails." New Jersey v. T.L.O., 469 U.S. 325, 337 (1984) (applying the balancing test to hold that a school official's search of a student's purse was allowable under the Fourth Amendment). **16** On one side of the balance is the government's need for effective measures to deal with breaches of public order. On the other side is the individual's legitimate expectations of privacy. Id. If the government's public policy needs for a particular class of searches outweighs the degree to which this class of searches interferes with individual privacy rights, then that class of searches should be found to be allowable under the Fourth Amendment. See, e.g., id.

This Court used the balancing test to create a new exception to the Fourth Amendment's warrant requirement in Terry v. Ohio, 392 U.S.1, 20 (1968). In Terry, Officer Martin McFadden conducted a warrantless pat-down of the outer clothing of three defendants who had been behaving suspiciously on a street corner. The pat-downs resulted in the discovery of two firearms. Id. at 7. Evaluating whether or not this search was allowable under the Fourth Amendment, this Court first noted that the case did not involve a search incident to an arrest, pointing out that there is a "distinction in purpose, character, and extent between a search incident to an arrest and a limited search for weapons." Id. at 25-26. Thus, for the search to be constitutional, it would have to be found constitutional under some other exception to the warrant requirement.

This Court noted that the general class of searches involving investigatory stops would have to be evaluated under a reasonableness standard, balancing the governmental interests justifying the search against the level of invasion that the search would entail. Id. at 21. In conducting this balancing, the Terry Court held that the substantial government interests in preventing crime and promoting officer safety outweighed the level of intrusion presented by a limited frisk for weapons, which repre-

15 This is a statement of a legal proposition and should be followed by a citation.

16 This parenthetical would be even better if it reflected the test cited to. The reader wants to know how the Court accomplished the balancing in that case: why did the need of that search outweigh the privacy invasion?

7

sented something less than a full search: "Our evaluation of the proper balance that has to be struck in this type of case leads us to conclude that there must be a narrowly drawn authority to permit a reasonable search for weapons for the protection of the officer." Id. at 27.

Therefore, if the public interests served by a particular class of searches outweigh the level of interference with individual privacy, then that class of searches should be found permissible under the Fourth Amendment. The class of searches that includes the search of Patrick Knowles — searches incident to a citation in lieu of an arrest — should be found to be permissible under the Fourth Amendment. This is so because (a) the search advances legitimate government interests in officer safety, and (b) the search results in a minimal level of interference with personal privacy interests. **17**

1. Allowing a search incident to a citation in lieu of arrest advances the substantial government interest in officer safety.

A warrantless search can only be justified if that search advances some substantial public interest. Compare Terry v. Ohio, 392 U.S. at 22 (upholding the constitutionality of the investigatory stop and frisk, finding that it advanced an "immediate" government interest in preserving officer safety), with Delaware v. Prouse, 440 U.S. 648, 661 (1979) (striking down as unconstitutional the practice of random police stops, which were held to present only a "marginal" contribution to roadside safety). Allowing an officer the ability to search pursuant to a citation in lieu of an arrest serves the legitimate and important governmental interest of promoting officer safety.

This Court has found that it is "too plain for argument" that the public interest in officer safety is "both legitimate and weighty." Pennsylvania v. Mimms, 434 U.S. 106, 110 (1977). In Mimms, the defendant challenged the constitutionality of a search conducted after he had been ordered out of his automobile during a routine traffic stop. Id. at 107. The Mimms Court noted the substantial public interest in preserving the safety of police officers and observed that ordering the suspect out of the car would greatly enhance this interest. **18** The Court observed that "an inordinate risk" faces an officer as he approaches a suspect seated in a vehicle and that ordering the suspect out of the car would lessen the hazard of accidental injury from passing traffic. Id. at 111. In balancing the "legitimate and weighty" public interest in officer safety advanced by the search against the level of private intrusion, the Mimms Court concluded that the search was constitutional, observing that ordering a person out of his car "hardly rose to the level of a 'petty indignity.' " Id. at 111 (quoting Terry v. Ohio, 392 U.S. 1, 17 (1968)). **19**

Maryland v. Wilson, 519 U.S. 408 (1997), is another case in which this Court has described the substantial public interest in officer safety. **20** In Wilson, this Court upheld the constitutionality of a police officer's order for an automobile *passenger* to step out of the car during a traffic stop. Id. at 410, 415. The Wilson Court balanced the "weighty" public interest in officer safety advanced by the officer's order, noting that the passenger had every bit as great a motivation as the driver to employ violence to prevent the officer from uncovering evidence of a more serious crime during the stop. Id. at 413, 414. Ordering a passenger out of the car would diminish the threat to officer safety because the passenger would "be denied access to any weapon which might be concealed in the interior of the passenger compartment." Id.

The search incident to the issuance of a citation for an arrestable offense similarly advances the legitimate public interest in officer safety. When Officer Cook pulled Patrick Knowles over for a traffic violation, he placed himself in just as dangerous a position as the officers in Mimms and Wilson, both of whom also pulled individuals over for a traffic violation. As the Court noted about the traffic stop in Wilson, when

17 Note this effective introduction, in which the writer gives general background about this area of law and then roadmaps the discussion to come.

18 A cite is needed here, as it is every time that the writer notes what a court held, found, believed, stated, etc.

19 Noting the original source of the quotation is appropriate here, because the Mimms Court cited to a case already relied upon. If the source of the quotation were irrelevant to the current discussion, the author could have ended the citation with "(citation omitted)" instead.

20 Compare this relatively ineffective topic sentence — which does little more than announce that this case exists — with the other, more effective topic sentences in this document, that focus on court rules and reasoning.

Officer Cook pulled Patrick Knowles over for speeding, there was a substantial chance that Knowles might employ violence in order to prevent the detection of a more serious crime. The use of a search incident to a citation for an arrestable offense helps alleviate these concerns over officer safety by allowing officers, like Officer Cook, the authority to search for weapons that might be used against them.

2. Conducting a search incident to a citation in lieu of arrest represents a minimal intrusion upon individual privacy rights.

If a particular class of searches is found to advance a substantial public interest, that class of searches will be found to be permissible under the Fourth Amendment if that public interest outweighs the degree of personal intrusion created by the search. See, e.g., New Jersey v. T.L.O., 469 U.S. 325, 337 (1984). The lesser the degree of personal intrusion posed by a particular class of searches, the more likely it is that the search will be permissible under the Fourth Amendment. Compare Maryland v. Wilson, 434 U.S. at 111 (upholding the constitutionality of ordering a suspect out of his car because the level of personal intrusion was "de minimis"), with Delaware v. Prouse, 440 U.S. at 656 (striking down random stops of motorists because the stops were found to be inconvenient, time-consuming, and to substantially interfere with freedom of movement). **21**

An individual's privacy rights depend in part on that individual's reasonable expectations of privacy. Katz v. United States, 389 U.S. 347, 361 (holding that a defendant had a constitutionally-protected expectation of privacy when making calls from a telephone booth). An examination of the factual situations covered by the Iowa Code reveals that any suspect who falls under the search power of § 805.1(4) will invariably have diminished expectations of privacy, and therefore a diminished privacy interest. In addition, a central concern in establishing the level of private invasion created by a search has been "to assure that an individual's expectation of privacy is not subject to arbitrary invasion solely at the unfettered discretion of officers in the field." Brown v. Texas, 443 U.S. 47, 50 (1979) (citing Delaware v. Prouse, 440 U.S. 648, 655-55 (1979)). **22**

A search incident to a citation in lieu of arrest will impose only minimal intrusions upon personal privacy rights for two reasons: (a) the search will occur in instances where there is already a diminished expectations of privacy, and will therefore represent a diminished intrusion into individual privacy rights, and (b) the intrusion into individual rights will be minimized by the fact that officers searching incident to citations in lieu of arrest are bound by specific requirements that severely limit the officers' discretion.

a. Iowa Code § 805.1(4) will most often be applied in situations in which there is already a diminished expectation of privacy. **23**

i. Petitioner's privacy interests were not substantially interfered with because one has a diminished expectation of privacy in a moving vehicle.

Knowles's expectations of privacy were minimal, because Officer Cook's search came pursuant to a citation issued for a speeding violation. This Court has held that privacy expectations are diminished in a moving vehicle. Cardwell v. Lewis, 417 U.S. 583, 590 (1974)

The characteristics of an automobile, and the way in which it is used, result in a lessened expectation of privacy within an automobile. Cardwell, 417 U.S. at 590. In

21 Note how these parentheticals successfully focus on the issue of the level of intrusion, noting how the holding in the case related to that issue, and the facts that supported the result.

22 Even though the writer will be discussing this case later in this section, he could provide a parenthetical here to fulfill the reader's expectations.

23 Ideally, when you create sub-sections within a section, you should have an introductory section to set up the reader's expectations.

24 The use of the sentence opening "In Case-name," is probably the easiest and most effective substantive/orienting transition.
25 Notice how the writer uses a "Tom Brokaw introduction" to encourage the reader to read the quotation.

Cardwell, **24** a search of a suspect's car pursuant to a murder investigation was found to be constitutional, even though the officers did not have a specific warrant for the search of the car. Id. at 583. A key component of the analysis was the Cardwell Court's finding that the search of a vehicle implicated a lesser expectation of privacy: **25**

> One has a lesser expectation of privacy in a motor vehicle because its function is transportation and it seldom serves as one's residence or as the repository of personal effects. A car has little capacity for escaping public scrutiny. It travels the public thoroughfare where both its occupants and its contents are in plain view.

Id. at 589-90.

This Court has also noted the fact of diminished expectation of privacy in a vehicle to justify the use of fixed vehicle checkpoints for detection of illegal aliens. United States v. Martinez-Fuerte, 428 U.S. 543, 562 (1976). In making its decision, the Martinez-Fuerte Court noted that "one's expectations of privacy in an automobile and of freedom in its operation are significantly different from the traditional expectation of privacy." Id. at 558. This Court found that this diminished expectation of privacy, coupled with the reasonableness of the procedures followed in making the stops, made "the resulting intrusion upon the interests of the motorists minimal." Id.

Patrick Knowles had a diminished expectation of privacy when he was stopped for driving his automobile at an illegally high speed. The application of Iowa Code § 805.1(4) presented a minimal intrusion upon Knowles's privacy interests, because his expectations of privacy in a moving vehicle are less than what he might expect in his home or office. Knowles's situation represents the rule rather than the exception, for most citations issued in lieu of arrest are for moving vehicle traffic violations. Thus, this Court should find that searches under the authority of Iowa Code § 805.1(4) do not violate the Fourth Amendment in this case because Patrick Knowles had a diminished expectation of privacy while in his vehicle.

ii. There is a diminished expectation of privacy after having committed an arrestable violation.

Iowa Code § 805.1(4) gives an arresting officer the authority to search only when issuing a citation in lieu of arrest. This limit on authority means that in order to become subject to § 805.1(4), the suspect must have already committed an arrestable offense. Those who are subject to § 805.1(4) have diminished privacy interests, because, as this Court has held, one's expectation of privacy is diminished when engaged in an illegal act. See New York v. Class, 475 U.S. 106, 113 (1986).

A driver's expectation of privacy is diminished when he or she has committed a traffic violation. Class, 475 U.S. at 113. In Class, this Court held that it was constitutional for an officer to reach into an automobile to move papers on the dashboard that were obscuring the vehicle's identification number. Id. In analyzing the expectations of privacy of the vehicle's occupants, the Class Court first noted that they had a diminished expectation of privacy merely as occupants of an automobile. Id. Next, the Court observed that "this [diminished expectation of privacy] is especially true in the case of a driver who has committed a traffic violation." Id. The Class Court found that, because of the suspect's diminished expectations of privacy, the officer's actions were sufficiently unintrusive to be constitutionally permissible under the Fourth Amendment. Id. at 107.

Members of this Court have noted the distinction between the "legitimate" privacy interests of law-abiding individuals and the "subjective" privacy interests of someone engaging in unlawful activity. Katz v. United States, 389 U.S. 347, 361 (1967) (Harlan, J., concurring). In his concurrence in Katz, Justice Harlan argued that those committing illegal acts do not have a privacy interest that is recognized in the eyes of the law: "A burglar plying his trade in a summer cabin during the off-season may have a thoroughly justified subjective expectation of privacy, but it is not one that society is prepared to recognize as 'legitimate.' " Id. at 361 (Harlan, J. concurring). **26**

A "subjective intrusion" upon a law-abiding driver's privacy interests is even constitutional when a police seizure might have the effect of generating "fear and surprise." Michigan v. Sitz, 496 U.S. 444, 452 (1990). In Sitz, this Court noted that the "subjective fear" caused by officers conducting sobriety checkpoints may represent a substantial intrusion upon individual privacy interests. Id. However, it allowed the search, noting that *law-abiding motorists* would experience only "the fear and surprised engendered . . . by the nature of the stop." Id.

The searches authorized by Iowa Code § 805.1(4) are applicable not to *all* motorists, but only to those cited for committing an arrestable offense. When Officer Cook searched Patrick Knowles, he was not searching an innocent motorist, but one who had been recorded driving at almost 20 miles per hour over the posted speed limit. Record 14. **27** Although Knowles may have had a subjective expectation of privacy, it was not a legitimate expectation recognized by the courts. As a person cited for committing an illegal activity, Patrick Knowles had only a minimal expectation of privacy.

Because § 805.1(4) applies only to those who have already been found to have committed an arrestable offense, the searches authorized by § 805.1(4) represent only minimal intrusions into privacy rights.

b. Allowing a search incident to a citation in lieu of arrest is consistent with Brown because it affords police officers very little discretion in deciding whom to search.

An otherwise constitutional search may be found unconstitutional if officers are allowed too much discretion in deciding who to search. Brown v. Texas, 443 U.S. 47, 50 (1979) (citing Delaware v. Prouse, 440 U.S. 648, 654-55 (1979)). Because § 805.1(4) grants Iowa police officers only minimal discretion, this Court should find that it is constitutional.

Searches and seizures that are not carried out pursuant to a plan embodying explicit, neutral limitations on the conduct of individual officers have been found unconstitutional. Delaware v. Prouse, 440 U.S. 648, 663 (1979). In Prouse, this Court found unconstitutional random stops for the general purpose of promoting law enforcement. Id. at 648. The Prouse Court expressed concern over the fact that the stops involved "unconstrained discretion" which is "the evil the court has discerned when in previous cases it has insisted that the discretion of the official in the field be circumscribed, at least to some extent." Id. at 661 (citations omitted).

Searches without particularized suspicion have been found constitutional when strict limits on police discretion were present. Michigan v. Sitz, 496 U.S. 444, 447 (1990). In Sitz, this Court found a highway sobriety checkpoint to be constitutional under the Fourth Amendment. Id. In its reasoning, the Sitz Court first noted that the state had a substantial interest in eradicating the problem of drunken drivers. Id. The Court concluded that the brief stop and questioning at the checkpoint represented only a minimal intrusion into the drivers' privacy interests, noting that the officers could not randomly pull over whomever they chose, but that they instead had to pull every motorist over. Id. at 453.

11

---

26 Notice that every reference to a nonmajority opinion must indicate that fact in a parenthetical.

27 Notice that you should cite to the record *every* time you mention a legally significant fact.

Iowa Code § 805.1(4) creates a substantial check upon the discretion of Iowa police officers. Section 805.1(4) allows an officer to conduct a search *only* when issuing a citation in lieu of an arrest. The officer has the power to stop and search only those suspects who have been observed committing a crime that the legislature deemed serious enough to warrant arrest. The Iowa police are without authority to search those Iowa citizens who obey the law. Patrick Knowles would not have been subjected to a search if he had been obeying Iowa's posted speeding laws.

Like the public interests advanced by a search incident to an arrest, the interests advanced by a search incident to a citation in lieu of an arrest are substantial, and the interference with individual privacy rights is minimal. This Court should extend the exceptions to the warrant requirement to include searches incident to citations in lieu of arrest.

CONCLUSION

Because the search incident to a citation in lieu of an arrest is necessary in order to protect the safety of police officers, this Court should affirm the decision of the Iowa Supreme Court rejecting Petitioner's motion to suppress.

Respectfully submitted,

Samuel J. Student

Samuel J. Student
1234 School Street
Metropolis, Ohio
555-555-5555

CERTIFICATE OF SERVICE

This document certifies hand delivery of one copy of this brief to Olivia Opponent, 12354 Student Mailboxes, Metropolis, Ohio, on November 3, 1998.

Samuel J. Student

Samuel J. Student

12

Index

ORTHO'S All About

Container
Gardening

Written by Sally Roth and Pamela K. Peirce
Photographed by David Goldberg

Meredith₀ Books
Des Moines, Iowa

Ortho® Books
An imprint of Meredith® Books

All About Container Gardening
Editor: Michael McKinley
Contributing Technical Editors: Paul E. Cappiello of
  Bernheim Arboretum and Research Forest,
  Gary R. Keim, Elvin McDonald, Dennis Schrader,
  Steve Titko
Art Director: Tom Wegner
Assistant Art Director: Harijs Priekulis
Copy Chief: Catherine Hamrick
Copy and Production Editor: Terri Fredrickson
Book Production Managers: Pam Kvitne,
  Marjorie J. Schenkelberg
Contributing Copy Editor: Barbara Feller-Roth
Technical Proofreader: Fran Gardner
Contributing Proofreaders: Kathy Roth Eastman,
  JoEllyn Witke
Contributing Illustrator: Mike Eagleton
Contributing Map Illustrator: Jana Fothergill
Contributing Prop/Photo Stylist: Peggy Johnston
Indexer: Donald Glassman
Electronic Production Coordinator: Paula Forest
Editorial and Design Assistants: Kathleen Stevens,
  Karen Schirm

Additional Editorial Contributions from
  Art Rep Services
Director: Chip Nadeau
Designer: lk Design

Meredith® Books
Editor in Chief: James D. Blume
Design Director: Matt Strelecki
Managing Editor: Gregory H. Kayko
Executive Ortho Editor: Larry Erickson

Director, Retail Sales and Marketing: Terry Unsworth
Director, Sales, Special Markets: Rita McMullen
Director, Sales, Premiums: Michael A. Peterson
Director, Sales, Retail: Tom Wierzbicki
Director, Sales, Home & Garden Centers: Ray Wolf
Director, Book Marketing: Brad Elmitt
Director, Operations: George A. Susral
Director, Production: Douglas M. Johnston

Vice President, General Manager: Jamie L. Martin

Meredith Publishing Group
President, Publishing Group: Christopher M. Little
Vice President, Finance & Administration: Max Runciman

Meredith Corporation
Chairman and Chief Executive Officer: William T. Kerr

Chairman of the Executive Committee: E.T. Meredith III

Thanks to
Spectrum Communication Services, Inc.

The container gardens for this book were designed and
  grown by Pamela K. Peirce

The photographer expresses his appreciation to the
  following people for assistance in creating images:
  Berkeley Horticultural Nursery, EuroAmerican
  Propagators, Robert McRoskey, Zach & Pat Coney, Iris
  Goldman, Janet K. Anderson, Sue Carver, Nancy Fisher,
  Auguste Broucaret, Mrs. Fritz H. Grau, Mary Ellen
  Mynatt, Patricia Morgan, Department of Environmental
  Horticulture & Floristry of City College of San Francisco,
  Floorcraft Garden Center, Gardener's Supply, Campbell-
  Thiebaud Gallery, Netherlands Flowerbulb Information
  Center, Planterra Pots and American Designer Pots from
  Fiskars, Ellen Pearce & Linda Aurichio, Mr. & Mrs. R.S.
  Milligan, Smith & Hawken, Tom & Sally Adams, Flower
  Framers by Jay, Maurice Kamins, Callie McRoskey, Holly
  Money-Collins, Berenice Spalding, Alexander
  Montenegro, Allied Arts Guild, Nancy Favier, Fredrick
  Sonenberg & Emil Miland, Bob Clark Garden Designer,
  Bill Milligan Landscaping, Sarah Fitzgerald, John Harvey,
  Cheryl Lisin, Tim Lipinski, Kate Meyer, Gamble Garden,
  Stewart & Laurel Bonn, Red Desert

Additional Photography by:
  (Photographers credited may retain copyright ©
  to the listed photographs.)
L = Left, R = Right, C = Center, B = Bottom, T = Top
John Bessler: p. 11
Pete Krumhardt: p. 7b
Richard Felber: p. 40
Susan Roth (container design by Dennis Schrader): p. 44T
Steve Struse: pp. 10T, 31T

Cover photograph: David Goldberg

All of us at Ortho® Books are dedicated to providing you
with the information and ideas you need to enhance your
home and garden. We welcome your comments and
suggestions about this book. Write to us at:
  Meredith Corporation
  Ortho Books
  1716 Locust St.
  Des Moines, IA 50309–3023

If you would like more information on other Ortho
products, call 800-225-2883 or visit us at www.ortho.com

Note to the Readers: Due to differing conditions, tools,
and individual skills, Meredith Corporation assumes no
responsibility for any damages, injuries suffered, or losses
incurred as a result of following the information published
in this book. Before beginning any project, review the
instructions carefully, and if any doubts or questions remain,
consult local experts or authorities. Because codes and
regulations vary greatly, you always should check with
authorities to ensure that your project complies with all
applicable local codes and regulations. Always read and
observe all of the safety precautions provided by
manufacturers of any tools, equipment, or supplies,
and follow all accepted safety procedures.

CONTAINERS FOR EVERY PURPOSE 4

CONTAINER BASICS 14

CONTAINER GARDENS 32

GALLERY OF CONTAINER PLANTS 64

4

CONTAINERS FOR EVERY PURPOSE

A waterfall of bright orange nasturtiums and vivid petunias spills from a container at eye level. Like other annuals, these bloom in profusion for months, lavishing color against a sunny wall to boost the overall effect of the garden.

Container gardens are the answer to every gardener's dreams. They bring the joys and rewards of gardening home even if the only outdoor space you have is a deck, balcony, or window box. And in the larger landscape, containers are such strong players that they provide instant excitement and make everything around them look better. They add bright color or soothing greenery wherever you need it most, without the investment in time, money, and space that a garden in the ground requires. Satisfying for beginning gardeners as well as the experienced, container gardens are:

EASY: Just fill a container with potting mix and plant it—it's that simple.
FAST: Planting a container garden takes only minutes, and plants fill in quickly.
ECONOMICAL: Containers are limited in scale; creating a satisfying design can be less costly than planning a full-size garden bed.
COMPACT: Container gardening packs a lot of beauty into a small space. It's the perfect solution for gardeners who have limited planting area.
VERSATILE: You can grow nearly any kind of garden in containers. And they're portable, easy to move around as needed.

HOW TO USE THIS BOOK

Container gardens outdoors have such strong personalities that they can shape the daily use of your surroundings as well as improve the look of your home and garden. This chapter surveys the many purposes that containers can serve—from an eye-catching splash of color to a gentle barricade to deter pets. You'll find lots of ideas for using containers to liven up your garden, with plenty of practical tips for deciding where to position your container gardens to make the most of them.

Once you know how you want to use containers in your landscape, turn to "Container Basics" (pages 14–31) for the easy fundamentals of growing plants in a container. There you'll learn how to select a container for style and function, and how to select appropriate plants for the conditions and the effect you want to create. And you'll find out how to fill, plant, and care for a container garden to keep it looking its best.

In "Container Gardens" (pages 32–63) you'll meet dozens of beautiful container gardens in styles to suit every garden and gardener. The plantings were designed and grown by experts who share exactly how you can enjoy the same results. You can re-create the garden with the instructions provided, or use it for inspiration and add your own personal touches. You'll also find tempting designs for specialty gardens of herbs and vegetables, butterfly and hummingbird plants, water gardens, and even fruit trees and bushes.

The final chapter, "Gallery of Container

Its working days at an end, a weathered wheelbarrow planted with petunias delivers a jolt of color. Containers filled with a single color pack a big punch.

Plants" (pages 64–91), introduces more than a hundred of the best plants for containers and provides instructions for use, planting, and care. You'll also find our recommendations for the best cultivars, as well as suggestions for beautiful plant companions.

Combine your own creativity with the seasoned advice offered throughout this book, and your containers will give you a garden you can be proud of.

Balance the height of tall growers with wide-spreading plants beneath them.

THE PRACTICAL SIDE OF CONTAINERS

Plants in pots are more than just pretty—they're downright useful. Use containers to:
■ Define a sitting spot, mark a gateway, or spotlight a path.
■ Bring gardening within easy reach with raised containers secured to a railing, bench, or other waist-high support.
■ Protect treasured plants from your pets' paws by keeping them up high in pots.
■ Distract attention from eyesores with a striking group of pots placed several yards away from a utility pole, doghouse, or neighbor's boat.
■ Hide a low object such as a water spigot, gas meter, or electrical outlet with containers placed in front of it.
■ Block access to areas of the garden with a "wall" of containers.

■ Create a private nook with a screen of tall plants in containers.
■ Corral bamboo and other plants that would spread rampantly in the ground.
■ Coddle plants with special needs for soil, fertilizer, or water that your regular garden can't supply.
■ Solve the problem of what to do with gladiolus, cannas, and other bold plants that can be tricky to integrate into a garden. Instead of trying to find these plants suitable companions, give them a pot of their own where they can shine in the spotlight.
■ Brighten a lull in the perennial border with a few blooming containers slipped into the planting.

BRIMMING WITH VERSATILITY

Fanciful containers call for innovative arrangements— and announce your sense of humor. These plants in a pachyderm are as strong a focal point on an outdoor deck as a piece of sculpture in the living room. They also create a transition that ties the deck to the greenery of the garden beyond.

Versatility and flexibility are the bywords of container gardens. You can set a style, create a mood, or emphasize a color scheme simply by varying the containers and the plants you fill them with. Adding a container instantly livens up the look of your garden. A basket of daffodils and pansies on the step, an urn of aromatic lavender at a curve in the border, or a winter window box filled with boughs of pine and holly or eucalyptus and pepperberry add the finishing touches that make your yard look better and your home look loved.

Even if you never turn a shovel of earth, you can enjoy a bigger garden with plants in pots. You can put container gardens anywhere: on the lawn, in a garden, on your front step, on the paving of a patio, on a deck or balcony, or hanging from an eave or porch post. There's always room for one more.

QUICK CHANGES

Change the mood of your garden in an instant by adding or changing containers. Bring in a container to complement a new garden bench or an arbor. Transport a pot into a nook near the door to brighten your entrance for the holiday season or to welcome visitors with a dash of spring.

The portability of containers lets you make quick changes in the garden, too. Insert a few pots of bright flowers into the perennial bed for an immediate splash of color while you wait out the break between iris and daylilies. For a special event, gather containers into one large-scale grouping on the patio. As long

BEAUTIFYING A PROBLEM SPOT

The most unloved corners of your yard can become places of beauty, thanks to container gardens. Poor drainage, hardpan, caliche, tree roots, and other problems that can frustrate gardeners are no longer a difficulty when the garden doesn't have its roots in the ground. Nestle a group of containers into these areas and you can grow practically anything you like.

If the dry shade beneath a thirsty maple or other tree is the bane of your gardening efforts, try a little

trompe l'oeil trick. Insert 8-inch plastic pots of blooming impatiens or other shade-tolerant plants into the spaces between roots, burying the pots to just below the rim. Water frequently and mulch to conserve moisture. Voilà! Instant garden, and only you know it's containerized.

Neglected areas around your home can also get a facelift with a container garden. Brighten the back steps or the area beside the garage door with a cheerful garden in an imaginative container.

Raised containers are the place to spotlight colorful foliage, such as the leaves of these zonal geraniums.

as you can lift a container (on page 33 you'll discover tricks for maneuvering even large pots), you can move it to another location whenever you like.

CHOOSING STYLE AND SITE

Containers come in styles to suit the mood of any garden, whether it is the casual cottage garden, the dramatic modern landscape, or the formal estate. Keep in mind the style of your garden and use containers that help strengthen that effect. A wooden half barrel works well on a weathered wood deck; a pair of concrete containers better complements a formal brick entryway. Versatile clay pots are adaptable to any style of garden.

Practical and design considerations go hand in hand when you decide where to place containers in your garden. Make sure the containers are within easy reach of the garden hose or within reasonable distance for carrying a watering can. Plan on watering your plantings at least twice a week, more often in hot or dry weather, and position them so that the regular watering they require doesn't become a frustrating chore. If you have rambunctious pets or active children, choose hefty containers that can hold up to hard knocks without toppling or breaking, and place them safely out of the way of flying feet or Frisbees. Your climate affects how you use containers, too. In an area with mild winters, containers are a year-round part of the garden. In the North, only large, weatherproof containers remain part of the garden fixtures in winter.

Think about where you want attention to be focused and how you would like family and friends to make their way through the garden. Use containers to channel interest toward paths, sitting areas, gates, or other garden features you want to highlight. Mark your main entrance with a significant container to let the pizza delivery person or dinner party guests know where the door is.

Selecting containers to mix or match with the style of your home and garden is fun, but let your new gardens do some work, too. Use them to guide traffic through the garden and to shift attention toward a view or distract from an eyesore. Place hefty single containers or groups of pots as boundary markers at the limits of garden spaces—between play area and patio, for instance. Or use a row of containers as a windbreak or privacy screen while your permanent hedge plants grow to decent size.

ROOFTOP GARDENING

Turning a rooftop into a successful garden refuge depends on choosing plants and containers suitable for the concentrated sunlight and heat. Light-colored containers and light-colored mulches, such as gravel, reflect sun, keeping the roots of plants cooler. Plastic pots help slow evaporation.

Plastic pots are also light in weight, an important consideration for a roof. If you're planning on a large container garden, check with an engineer to make sure the roof below can support the added weight (see pages 22 and 24 for tips on reducing the weight of containers).

To retard water loss, slip a smaller pot inside a larger one, allowing an inch or more of space between their walls. Fill your pots with moss rose, petunias, and other plants that tolerate hot, dry soil, or, if your roof is sturdy, use self-watering containers. (You'll find more on self-watering containers and other watering tips on pages 26 and 27.)

No need for your garden to stop where the soil does. Here, a potted cactus and other plants bring the look of the desert right to the wall of a Southwestern abode. Note the small pot of flowers snuggled into the cactus's container to make even more use of the space.

DECORATING OUTDOORS

Good design begins with placing containers in accordance with the same principles you use in planning a satisfying garden. Whether you exactly follow the designs in the following chapters or branch out to play with other plants, you'll discover that container gardening is a great confidence-builder that helps to sharpen your design instincts.

Repeating red geraniums and tuberous begonias creates an irresistible rhythm of color.

COMBINING CONTAINERS

MIX AND MATCH THESE COLORS AND FORMS:

- All shades of natural clay
- Dark green plastic with hand-painted pottery
- Faux terra-cotta with real clay
- Faux terra-cotta with faux or real concrete
- Iron or iron finish with faux or real concrete
- Urns with low, wide bowls
- Rectangular pots with tall, straight-sided pots
- Tall, vertically ribbed pots with low, wide pots
- Baskets with faux or real clay pots

COLOR

The color of the container is as important as the color of the plantings with which you fill it. If you intend to let flowers or foliage attract attention, choose a container that will blend with its background. A clay or naturally stained wooden container against a similarly hued wall fades into the surroundings, whereas a colorful painted planter draws attention. Use terra-cotta, green, black, or other neutral-toned containers in the garden if you want the plants in them to shine without competition from the container.

White or light-colored containers have more visual impact. Place them against dark backgrounds, lawn areas, or garden greenery to show them off.

Follow the same principles with window boxes and planters that stand on the deck or porch or against the house. Colors that contrast sharply with the tone of the house or window trim make the container a strong focal point. Colors that match the hue of their surroundings, whether it's white wooden siding or red brick, turn the container into a background player.

SCALE

Consider carefully the scale of its intended surroundings before selecting a container; appropriate size in keeping with its setting is a crucial but often overlooked criterion for an effective container planting. Containers that are too small for their surroundings become quickly lost in the overall scene, while those that are are too large can overwhelm. Keep your garden composition strong by using a few groups of containers or single large pots instead of many small containers dotted here and there. Highlight the flat-topped posts flanking a garden wall with a pair of good-sized containers, for example, instead of scattering smaller pots along the entire wall.

FORM AND TEXTURE

The shape of containers contributes an element of form to your garden. Handles, fancy rims, ridges, molded wreaths, rusted finishes, and other surface decorations on pots add texture. As with color, you can use the form and texture of containers and the plants you grow in them to contrast or correspond with the rest of the garden. A heavy, plain pot with a large-leaved plant, such as hosta, is a solid character in the garden that lends an air of stability and gives the garden a feeling of maturity. Fanciful urns or painted pots add a lighter, artistic touch to the surroundings.

Use plain containers just as you use plants with large, simple leaves—to anchor an area or provide solid mass in the middle of a finer-textured planting. For example, emphasize the soft texture of a bed of lavender with a large, plain pot set in the center. Use textured containers with airy, small-leaved plants to contrast with bold foliage or plain backgrounds, or to continue a theme of fine-textured plants. A footed iron urn planted with asparagus fern, for example, looks striking against a stark wall, and just as good surrounded by a fine froth of white sweet alyssum.

RHYTHM

Spacing pots or hanging containers at equal distances creates a repetitive rhythm that's impossible for the eye to resist. A lineup of clay pots along the driveway or a quartet of large planters along a fence leads the gaze from one to the next without hesitation. Use this even rhythm to draw garden visitors along a walk or toward a sitting area, sundial, or other destination.

Evenly spacing containers creates a controlled look that's best in a formal or semiformal garden. For an informal rhythm, stagger the placement so that the plants are spaced casually rather than like soldiers.

To reinforce a formal attitude, rely on symmetry. Use the same number and kinds of containers on each side of an entranceway, for example. Asymmetrical arrangements, such as a large pot on one side of the doorway balanced by three smaller ones on the other side, suits a more casual garden style.

ACCENT

Container gardens act as focal points, drawing the eye to their position. Strong contrast, created by color and form and aided by scale, creates a compelling accent. Even a single container that contrasts with its surroundings has a powerful visual draw.

Place a large or light-colored container at the far end of a lawn, and visitors will gravitate toward it. Use a raised container in the center of an herb garden, and the casual beds of herbs will become more focused and organized. Bold-leaved plants of striking form and color, such as New Zealand flax, canna, and hosta, are immediate eye-catchers in large containers.

Use an overturned clay pot or a stack of bricks as a simple prop to raise a container above neighboring plants in a garden for greater visibility. Iron stands, widely available at garden centers, also elevate a container to a position of greater importance.

A dramatic fan of New Zealand flax helps ensure that no one misses this accent, elevated as an ornament above the beds. Delicate Mexican daisy spills over one edge to link the urn to the garden below without obscuring the container.

No shy violets in this high-voltage shade garden of impatiens, lobelia, and golden-leaved hosta. The large, simply shaped leaves of hostas, whether they're plain green or dressed for the party, are an ideal companion for smaller flowers or fine-textured foliage.

CONTAINERS IN THE LANDSCAPE

Use containers to shape your landscape by guiding both the eye and the feet through the garden. These versatile arrangements can highlight an intriguing view, change the visual height of the garden, and even create intimacy by sheltering a sitting space. Depending upon how you place them, containers can serve as invitations to enter an adjoining space or as deterrents to encourage traffic to move in another direction.

SHAPING SPACE

Wide-open spaces may be welcome on the range, but in the garden, intimacy is more appealing. Use containers to suggest a wall—it doesn't need to be solid to be effective—around a dining area or contemplation bench. Mark the boundaries of the children's play area or other outdoor spaces with containers that act as a gateway.

Define pathways for both beauty and actual foot travel by placing containers to mark a corridor. A long lineup isn't necessary; establishing the start and midpoint of the path is all it takes to initiate movement.

Containers help make the transition from garden to house by bringing greenery onto paved areas or porches. Use containers on steps, too, to continue the sweep of the garden toward the house.

Above: This welcoming container garden frames a gateway with colorful 'Purple Wave' petunia and mandevilla in pots and ivy geranium in baskets. The focal urn filled with more 'Purple Wave' petunias and backed by 'Bengal Tiger' canna in pots invites the visitor to enter.

Right: Pots planted with lotus (also called parrot's beak, Lotus berthelotii) beckon a visitor up steps to the front door.

GUIDING TRAFFIC

Dividing up the yard calls for traffic control. The children have their play space, the dog has his exercise area, and the compost heap hides in a back corner. Hedges, flower beds, and other in-ground plantings are the usual devices to break up wide-open spaces into areas for different purposes, but containers can also do the job. Potted trees are a pretty way to define the corners of a sitting area. Tall ornamental grasses and bamboos make a light-textured screen to provide privacy around a patio or pool area. Even low containers, such as boxes filled with lavender or salvias, can serve as a hedge by defining boundaries.

Guiding traffic from one place to the next is another way in which containers can be a big help. Everybody from the meter reader to your pets appreciates a well-defined route through the landscape, and containers are an effective device to mark the trail. Use them to spotlight the beginning of a path or a garden gate or to signal an approaching step or change in surface (grass to wood chips, for example). Group several substantial containers at a bend in a garden path to discourage shortcuts.

ADDING HEIGHT

If your yard is flat, containers can create visual height. Variations in height add vitality to overall garden design, because a garden that causes the eye to move holds more interest than one that's flat. Try containers of bamboo, large cannas, standard-trained roses, small trees, or other tall plants to create a change in level. Or elevate a container by setting it on a stand or post, where it will draw the eye upward from the garden.

For maximum vertical effect, grow vines in the container, supported by a narrow trellis, an upside-down conical tomato cage, or a *tuteur*—a slatted wood or metal tepee support. If you like a lush look, include plants that trail downward to visually connect the planting to the garden or pots below. Let vines drape over the side of a hanging basket, window box, or other high container, or train them up a wall, along a railing, or around a window frame for more greenery against the house.

FASHIONING A FRAME

Vertical boundaries are the trick to framing a view. Think of tall container plantings as the sides of a picture frame. Placed on either side of a view "window"—such as a garden gateway, an opening in a wall or hedge, or even an actual window with a window box— vertical container plantings help to enclose and define a view, calling attention to it and directing the eye. Enclosing a view on at least two sides is most effective—with two vertical elements on opposite sides, or a single vertical element at one side and a horizontal element, such as an extending branch, at the top or bottom of the frame. But even a single tall plant can suggest a frame and help to direct the eye to the view beyond.

CREATING A FOCAL POINT

Container gardens are living sculpture for your yard. A large container or a group of smaller ones makes a beautiful centerpiece for a lawn area or a fine accent for a foundation planting or flower border. In design lingo, this is called a focal point: an element placed so that it becomes the focus of visual attention.

Avoid placing your container smack-dab in the middle of a large expanse of lawn, where it will look dwarfed by the open space around it. Instead, place your container within a smaller area defined by surrounding flower beds, fences, or hedges. Settling the container off-center rather than in the exact middle is usually more pleasing to the eye.

Restraint is the rule when your containers are art in themselves. Bright ceramic pots,

THE SPOTLIGHT EFFECT

Raising plants above the level of the in-ground garden makes them special because they're easier to see. The container itself adds to the appeal of the plants within, too. Its visual weight makes it a focal point in the landscape, no matter what's growing in it. The combination of extra height and eye appeal magnifies the effect of the plants in the pot. In a border garden, for instance, a dozen roses becomes just one part of the beautiful, larger whole. But a single rose in a container can take center stage all by itself. Turn this effect to your advantage by planting unusual or favorite plants in your containers so they get the attention they deserve.

Garden and interior work together for a pretty-in-pink arrangement. Fast-growing annual morning glories twine up strings to frame the window above the cascade of pink petunias.

VINES TO FRAME A WINDOW

These annuals quickly twine up string.

- Cardinal climber (*Ipomoea × sloteri*)
- Cypress vine (*Ipomoea quamoclit*)
- Morning glory (*Ipomoea tricolor*)
- Scarlet runner bean (*Phaseolus coccineus*)
- Spanish flag (*Ipomoea lobata*)
- Sweet pea (*Lathyrus odoratus*)

antique wheelbarrows, and other unusual containers are attention grabbers. Use them to add a lighthearted touch to a patio or to jazz up an entryway, but don't go overboard unless you like the look of a folk art collection.

SPECIALTY CONTAINER GARDENS

Container plantings let you play with special types of gardens in a limited space that can offer very different growing conditions from the rest of your garden. If you live in an arid area but yearn for the sound of moving water, you can create a bubbling spring or a quiet pool without feeling guilty about wasting water. Or you can enjoy the taste of homegrown produce even in an apartment by raising cherry tomatoes in hanging baskets, lettuce in window boxes, and fresh herbs in patio pots. Container gardening gives you the freedom to experiment with new plants without investing a lot of time and money. Because they command special attention, containers also let you show off your collection of cacti, succulents, lavenders, or other favorite plants. You'll find detailed how-tos in the following chapters for creating the specialty gardens that most appeal to you.

Sunny spots without soil are rescued from obscurity by a container collection that stars beautiful succulents.

WATER GARDENS

Water-filled containers are heavy, so choose a site before you pull out the garden hose. Any waterproof container makes a suitable home for water plants, but bigger is better, because large containers let you include more plants. For the most pleasing look, keep your arrangements simple—a single water lily (*Nymphaea*) in a glazed pot, accented by the vertical stems of a rush (*Juncus*) or papyrus (*Cyperus papyrus*), is a more dramatic arrangement than a jumble of eight different aquatic plants fighting for space. Floating water plants such as water lettuce (*Pistia*) or parrot's feather (*Myriophyllum aquaticum*) can drift at will in your container; dwarf water lilies, dwarf lotus (*Nelumbo*), and other aquatics that require soil for their roots are sold in slotted pots that you simply set in your container.

To add the delightful sound of moving water to your container garden, add a small electric recirculating pump, widely available at garden centers or home supply stores. Solar-powered pumps work well in a large container garden that includes open water; the pumps are sold at some retail outlets as well as through catalogs (see pages 56 and 57 for step-by-step instructions on creating a container water garden).

A water lily, an iris, and a few goldfish in a container are all it takes to bring the serenity of water gardening to your deck or patio.

EDIBLES IN CONTAINERS

A patio collection of festive hot peppers, patio-type tomatoes, and eggplant looks attractive—and you can take the crop right to the grill. Growing vegetables in containers adds garden space, eliminates weeding, and puts the plants within easy reach for a quick snack or a meal.

Rich planting mix, regular watering, and supplemental feeding are the keys to growing vegetables in containers. Mulch the surface of the soil with grass clippings or other organic material to conserve moisture.

Lettuce, radishes, beans, and other crops that mature quickly are ideal for container culture, but try any plant you like. Look for bush-type cultivars of squash and cucumbers, or set the container at the foot of a trellis to support the rampant vines.

Dwarf cultivars of fruit trees grow well in extra large containers. Choose dwarf trees of 'Liberty' apple, 'North Star' cherry, or other favorite fruits for a wooden half barrel or other supersize container. (Turn to pages 60, 61, 72, 88, and 89 for more on vegetables and fruits in containers.)

PLANT COLLECTIONS

Containers are the perfect showcase for plant collections. Combine your favorite plants in one spot to focus attention on your darlings. An herb sampler is a likely candidate for a collection—especially culinary herbs, which containers will keep within easy reach for a quick snip of fresh flavor (see pages 58 and 59 for instructions on growing herbs in containers). Scented geraniums are a delight in a container along a path or on a patio, where passersby brush against the foliage and release its delicious aroma. Put roses near nose level, too, by growing them in containers so their luscious blooms can be admired up close.

Plants that may be tricky to grow in garden conditions often thrive in containers, where you can supply customized soil and care. If you like the look of the desert, an assortment of cacti and succulents can feel at home in pots on a sun-drenched patio. Orchids, many of which flourish in filtered light, add an exotic touch under an arbor or on a porch. Azaleas and camellias—difficult to grow where soils are alkaline—are easy in containers, where their need for acid soil can be accommodated.

It takes only a few containers in a sunny spot to bring the pleasures of homegrown produce right to your kitchen door. This tiny spot boasts lettuce, snow peas, alpine strawberries, chives, scallions, carrots, and edible pansies for weeks of delicious harvest.

Dwarf conifer enthusiasts can enjoy a satisfying hobby by gardening in containers. Roses, cacti, citrus, and orchids are only a few of the other collectibles that are ideal for container culture.

CONTAINER BASICS

Colorful, imaginative container gardens are easy to create when you begin with the basics. Regular attention to the details of watering, feeding, and maintenance is what container plants need to keep looking their best.

GROW CONTAINER PLANTS LIKE A PRO

Lush, colorful container gardens start with good basic gardening techniques. Attention to soil, water, food, and light are vital, because your plantings depend on you to provide all their needs. Roots in containers can't reach into surrounding soil to seek the food and water the plants require.

The five secrets of healthy container plants are as simple as common sense.

1. GOOD DRAINAGE: Free-draining planting mix and holes in the container to release excess water are essential to prevent roots from suffocating in waterlogged soil.

2. REGULAR WATERING: Attention to watering is paramount, because planting mix dries out much more quickly than garden soil.

3. FERTILITY: Fertilizer will be needed on a regular basis as water leaches nutrients from the planting mix.

4. APPROPRIATE LIGHT EXPOSURE: Select the plants for your container according to the amount of sun or shade in your site.

5. ENOUGH PLANTING MIX: The potting mix supports root growth, keeps plants stable, and protects the roots from overheating.

To create container gardens that delight your eye, keep design elements in mind, too.

■ **SELECT THE RIGHT-SIZE PLANT.** For the fastest effect, use the biggest plant that will fit. Shallow containers look best with mounding or sprawling plants; upright growers make a low pot look top-heavy. Very large containers need arching or big-leaved plants to visually balance their size.

■ **MAXIMIZE GROWING SPACE.** Every inch counts in a container. Plant tightly, squeezing root balls if needed to shoehorn in plants. Maximize root space by including plants that spill over the edge for more greenery or flowers.

■ **ADD DRAMA WITH BOLD FORM.** Huge leaves, especially shiny ones, or strong, spiky, or arching plant forms make your container garden a guaranteed focal point.

■ **CREATE ROMANCE.** Plants with a mounding form and those that sprawl or trail over the edge make for a softer mood. Use fragrant flowers or foliage for sensory pleasure.

DESIGN LIKE A PRO

The container is as important as the plants it holds. Its form and color set the mood of the finished garden, and its size and shape determine the plants that will look best in it. You'll notice that nearly all of the containers pictured in this chapter include only a single kind of plant. That's because using one type of plant lets you see at a glance how well its form, texture, and color combine with the container of your choice. This chapter will show you how to choose a container that is both practical and aesthetically pleasing, and how to fill it with a plant that complements its design. Once you are confident in your ability to create a simple composition, you'll enjoy moving on to combining different plants in the same container, as shown in the next chapter.

A shady nook is just the right spot for this cascading tuberous begonia. Its electric orange hues provide a dramatic contrast to the bright blue window trim.

CONTAINER CONSIDERATIONS

Your goal is to make the finished container garden look good, fulfill its intended function, and thrive in the site you have selected. Start by choosing an appropriate container for your climate and a plant that suits the container and the growing conditions as well as the intended function. If you live in an area with cold winters, select a container that will stand up to your climate or that you can move to a protected place to prevent chipping and cracking in the cold season. Check the label or the catalog description to find out if a container is weatherproof. In full sun, use plastic or resin containers treated with an ultraviolet (UV) inhibitor to resist fading and other sun damage. In regions with wet winters or humid summers and in coastal gardens, wooden containers need frequent maintenance because of the effects of the climate; plastic or other materials less susceptible to moisture or salt are a better choice.

Think big when buying containers: A common mistake is using a pot that is too small, which looks jarring in its setting. A small pot of flowers may be just the right size to be viewed in the center of a patio table, for instance, but it would look insignificant as an accent at the end of a garden path.

Multiply the effect and give yourself a bigger garden by arranging containers in groups. Anchor the collection with a container of substantial size, for visual weight. Then place smaller pots of coordinated styles and color around and in front of the star. Stagger the heights by elevating background performers on a stack of bricks or an overturned pot, or add dramatic height by placing them on sections of clay drainage pipe, pedestals, or other supports.

COMPATIBLE PLANTS

You control the potting mix, watering, and fertility at all stages of growth for plants in a container. You also control exposure to light and to prevailing wind by the sites you select for placing containers. Be sure the plants you choose are appropriate for the conditions, or find another place if your favorites won't thrive in a certain site.

Fill your pot with plants that complement its style and shape. Use low, mounded plants in shallow containers and taller plants in more vertical containers. Generally, the composition will be aesthetically pleasing if the plants are at least half as tall as the container. Except for trees and trellised vines, plants that are more than double the height of the container often look out of proportion.

Match plants to the setting and the style of the garden as well as the container: hot-colored dahlias for a high-voltage garden, an elegant hosta for a formal yard, or a dramatic canna to accent modern architecture.

The shallow roots of succulents, such as this echeveria, flourish in a container that holds just a few inches of soil.

TERRA-COTTA CONTAINERS

Plain or fancy, big or small, clay pots are versatile containers. Naturally colored clay is the perfect partner for any plant and any style of garden. Glazes add rich color.

The term "terra-cotta" is associated with the classic red color of clay pots, but it means simply "baked earth." Such pots may be of various colors, depending on the clay used to make them. Soft shades of natural beige, brown, pink, and off-white clay look beautiful in a garden of cool colors or pastels. Clay pots may be unglazed or finished with clear or colored glazes or paint.

Terra-cotta containers are hefty, which gives them stability, an advantage in windy locations or with large plants. The weight makes large terra-cotta pots hard to move around once filled, however.

Pots fired at a high temperature last longer than "low-fire" pots. If your supplier doesn't label the pots, identify high-fire wares by their resistance to scratches and a lack of clay dust residue when the pot is handled.

Glazed and unglazed pots can be damaged by freezing winters, which can cause chipping, cracking, or flaking. Bring them inside in cold-winter regions. In borderline areas where the ground may occasionally freeze, bring glazed pots indoors; elevate unglazed pots to be sure they are well-drained and to prevent the container from freezing to the ground.

UNGLAZED CLAY

Unglazed clay pots are among the oldest kinds of containers and still among the most popular, thanks to their low cost and adaptable design. Unglazed clay pots are made in several classic shapes that are simple to incorporate in any style of garden. They are also available in decorated styles for a bit of Southwestern or Mediterranean flair. Terra-cotta may give you years of use, but handle carefully to avoid an accidental knock that could easily break a container.

Porous unglazed clay pots allow air and water to move through their walls. Air can reach plant roots, and fertilizer salts that could damage roots are wicked away. The evaporation of water through the pot also helps to keep roots cool. Porous clay reduces the likelihood of overwatering, but the pots can dry out quickly in sun or wind. Before planting an unglazed pot, spray it thoroughly with water and allow the clay to soak it up. This technique will slow down the initial loss of water from the freshly planted, newly watered container. To further reduce watering with unglazed clay pots, group them together so that their sides are sheltered from the evaporative effect of sun and wind.

GLAZED CLAY

Glazed clay pots add wonderful splashes of color to blend or contrast with the garden. Because of their finish, they cost more than unglazed clay. They are often used to create an Oriental effect, but many are neutral enough in shape and color to work well in other styles of gardens, too. Glazed pots are not porous, so they hold water and fertilizer longer than unglazed containers. Those without drainage holes make fine containers for small water gardens.

SHAPES AND FUNCTIONS

■ English pot: the classic slant-sided clay pot. Slanted sides allow easy removal of plants, and the thickened rim adds strength.
■ Standard pot: a pot as tall as it is wide, good for tap-rooted perennials and other deep-rooted plants.
■ Azalea pot (fern pot, three-quarter pot): a pot three-fourths as tall as wide, excellent for annuals, ferns, azaleas, and other plants with relatively shallow roots.
■ Bulb pot (pan): a pot half as tall as wide, perfect for spring bulbs or for very low-growing plants such as sedums.
■ Long Tom: a pot taller than it is wide and usually rimless; prone to tipping, but good for very deep-rooted plants or as a display for trailing nasturtiums or other vines.
■ Italian pot: a rimless pot with a slightly flared edge, pretty with sweet alyssum and other plants that spill over the edge.

WOODEN CONTAINERS

Wood offers the same advantages to plant roots as unglazed clay, allowing water and air to move through the sides of the container. Wooden containers require more frequent watering but help protect roots from accumulated fertilizer salts and keep roots aerated. They also provide some insulation from extreme temperatures, keeping soil cooler on hot days. In cold-winter areas, soil within the container will freeze, but the wood itself will not be damaged by cold.

Old-fashioned twig-type containers and other rustic wood styles look good in an informal setting. For a large container at low cost, it's hard to beat a wooden half barrel. Dressed up with a smooth painted finish and some decoration, wooden containers fit right in formal gardens, too. The classic white-painted Versailles box, a square container with short legs and small, ball-shaped finials on the four top corners, was traditionally used to hold a citrus tree; it is an elegant container for any tall, formally pruned plant.

Making wooden containers is an ideal project for a novice or skilled do-it-yourselfer. You can design classic window boxes or patio planters with simple lines for just a small investment in time and lumber.

Containers made of redwood, cedar, and cypress are rot-resistant and long-lasting, but because of declining natural stands of these trees, some gardeners prefer to use commercially farmed pine or other softwoods. A coat of wood preservative or paint will extend the life of any wood by retarding decay. Use a wood preservative that does not contain pentachlorophenol (also known as penta), such as Thompson's Water Seal or Cuprinol; they are available in tinted stains as well as a clear finish. Pressure-treated wood can be a good long-lasting alternative, as long as you don't grow edibles in containers made from it.

Lining wooden containers with plastic or galvanized metal will also extend their life. If you use a liner, be sure to punch holes in it to match the container's drainage holes. Paint, preservatives, and liners reduce evaporation through the wood, so water and fertilizer are held longer in the planting mix.

Wood is rugged and often inexpensive. Because large containers provide insulation for plant roots, they are a good choice for permanent plantings in warm or cold climates.

PROTECTING SURFACES UNDER CONTAINERS

Use saucers beneath containers placed on decks, paving, and other surfaces to help prevent rot and stains. Remove standing water that isn't absorbed within an hour from plant saucers by using a turkey baster to suction it up. Raising a container slightly also helps protect the supporting surface from moisture damage, and prevents decay of the bottoms of wooden containers. If your container lacks built-in supports to raise its bottom surface, use bricks or narrow strips of wood to allow air to circulate beneath the pot or its saucer. You can also buy supporting "pot feet" of unglazed or glazed clay in simple shapes or whimsical animal forms. Metal supports are also widely available. Container platforms on rolling casters, which you can buy or make yourself, allow you to move pots about on deck or patio to prevent moisture buildup.

CAST, MOLDED, AND METAL

Some may look like clay, concrete, or other pricey materials, but all of these containers are plastic. The containers with holes near the base, in the second tier from the top, are self-watering pots, with built-in reservoirs that minimize watering chores.

Containers formed in molds are a long-standing tradition in gardening, even though the materials have changed drastically. Once limited to concrete and metal, molded and cast containers today include a staggering variety of plastic products, reconstituted powdered stone, and other innovations that give us a huge selection of durable containers at prices to suit any gardener's wallet. Containers may be called "molded" or "cast," depending on the material and process used. The terms aren't important from a gardening perspective and are often used interchangeably.

CONCRETE

A half century or so ago, concrete was the miracle material for container gardeners. Cheap and versatile, it was poured into molds to form urns, bowls, and giant pots. Gardeners could use the stuff, too, mixing up a batch of concrete from cement, sand, and water to make their own constructions from bought or borrowed molds. Today, concrete yards that specialize in garden ornaments are as popular as they were long ago. New concrete wares are a staple in nurseries and garden centers, and older models are prized when they turn up at flea markets and yard sales.

Concrete containers can carry high price tags. The material is dense and heavy, and the cost reflects the high price of shipping.

Concrete is usually white to gray, although coloring can be added before or after the pot hardens. Give fancier concrete pieces a place of honor on a wall or at an entrance. Large concrete containers are durable in cold-winter areas, a good thing because they are too heavy to move easily.

PLASTICS AND FIBERGLASS

With the advent of plastics, container choices expanded dramatically. Every style from plain pots and hanging baskets to fancy containers indistinguishable from concrete, stone, metal, or terra-cotta are now filling retailers' shelves. Not until you pick one up will you recognize some of these pots as plastic. Depending on the process used to make it, a plastic container may be described as plastic, resin, extruded, or cast, among other terms. Pulverized marble or other stone may be added. Fiberglass is a

RECYCLED PLASTIC PRODUCTS

Window boxes made of milk jugs, flower pots that began their lives as tires—the world of recycled containers is expanding at a rapid clip. Discarded plastics get a new lease on life, thanks to manufacturing processes that break down old products into material that can be reused in a similar form or combined with crushed stone and other materials to create a brand-new look. Recycled plastic containers offer the same benefits as their virgin counterparts, and they are indistinguishable in appearance. Look on the label or read the catalog to find out if your container choices will help turn yesterday's trash into a garden treasure.

No need to remove potted plants from their containers if they'll be hidden within a larger container. Just slip them in as is. Replacement is just as fast when you want a fresh look.

similar lightweight material, slightly higher in price.

Plastic containers have big advantages over other materials:
■ They are lightweight, so they're easy to bring home and to move around.
■ Their walls are practically nonporous, so they retain moisture longer after watering than wood, concrete, or clay.
■ They are made in a range of styles and colors, for extra eye appeal in the garden.
■ Models are available with built-in reservoirs for less frequent watering.
■ Prices are a fraction of the cost of most other containers.
■ Weatherproofing treatments are added by some manufacturers. Check the label or catalog to find containers that are winterproof or made with ultraviolet inhibitors to prevent sun damage.

METAL

Cast-iron urns were a common sight in Victorian gardens, and metal containers in both old-fashioned and modern styles are enjoying a comeback. Lightweight galvanized tin and aluminum containers will last for years in the garden, even in cold winters. Iron can crack in cold weather; it will rust with age and exposure, or you can keep it looking new with a yearly coat of paint. Copper develops a prized greenish coating, or patina, with age and is not damaged by cold weather.

Metal containers can be expensive. Many are art pieces produced in small quantities. For a bargain price, shop hardware and farm supply stores and home centers for galvanized buckets or tubs, which make fine containers.

OTHER KINDS OF CONTAINERS

Your favorite container may be an object never intended to hold plants at all. Wicker baskets are country-fresh with white Marguarite daisies. A festive striped mixing bowl begs for a collection of cacti. Work boots, red wagons, and yes, even the kitchen sink have all seen their glory days in the garden. Use your imagination when you comb garage sales, thrift shops, or your own house.

There is a style of container to suit every garden, and a price for every pocketbook. Finding the perfect container is almost as much fun as filling it. These containers are fashioned from concrete, fiberglass, polyurethane foam, pressed paper, metal, and wire. Look for similar containers and other styles at home centers, discount stores, and specialty shops.

PROS AND CONS OF CONTAINER MATERIALS

Container material	Cost	Weight	Sunproof	Winterproof
Terra-cotta	Low to moderate	Moderate	Yes	No
Clay	Moderate to high	Moderate to heavy	Yes	No
Wood	Low to moderate	Moderate to heavy	Yes	Yes
Concrete	Low to high	Heavy	Yes	Yes, but not always
Plastic	Low to moderate	Light	No (unless specially treated by manufacturer)	No
Fiberglass	Moderate to high	Light	No (unless specially treated by manufacturer)	No
Recycled rubber	Low to moderate	Moderate	No (unless specially treated by manufacturer)	No
Iron	High	Heavy	Yes	Somewhat
Copper	High	Moderate	Yes	Yes, with patina
Galvanized metal	Low	Light to moderate	Yes	Yes

REFINISHING CONTAINERS

WEATHERED IN WEEKS

Moss gives a living patina to clay pots as it colonizes the surface slowly over seasons in the garden. The moss spores drift in, find a foothold on the pot, and begin to spread, eventually cloaking the sides away from direct sunlight in a soft green finish. The process can take years, unless you live in a very moist climate, where a pot can acquire a mossy patina in a single season.

Hasten the effect by providing a hospitable growing medium for moss, which thrives in acid conditions. Slather your container with yogurt, a naturally acidic milk product (for an even quicker effect, mix the yogurt with a handful of ground moss in a blender). Brush on the yogurt thickly, then set the pot in a discreet, deeply shaded corner of the garden. When moss has gotten a solid start, plant the container, being careful not to damage the moss, and move it to a permanent site in shade.

You can give containers a look of antiquity or a brand-new personality by applying special finishes. Decorating pots requires only a couple of hours from start to finish. You don't have to be an artist to come up with appealing results, and it's so simple and quick that children will enjoy it, too.

If you yearn for the look of a long-established garden, try the technique at left to make your containers look as though they've been sitting in the garden gathering moss for decades. They'll green up in several weeks after this treatment.

If you'd rather have the look of an old mossy pot right away, you can create a reasonable facsimile in minutes with a can of fast-drying acrylic paint and a brush. The same paint also allows you to decorate your pots with whatever colors and designs you desire, from classic solid white to high-energy designs in bold colors.

Page through gardening and decorating magazines and catalogs to find inspiration. Notice the colors you find most appealing in decorated containers. Consider carefully the palette that already exists in your garden or on your house, deck, or patio; your finished containers should either complement or contrast—not clash with—the existing color scheme.

Keep in mind that painted pots are high-visibility ornaments in the garden—they stand out among the plants and greenery, drawing the eye. If you position them sparingly, or in groups, they can draw attention to various areas of your yard. If you dot a lot of decorated pots around willy-nilly, you may end up with an effect that is whimsical or cluttered, depending on the eye of the beholder.

THE NATURAL LOOK

Poor plastic—it still gets no respect. Although it's a miracle product, able to be formed into just about any shape or color, natural materials still carry more cachet.

Some plastic containers are obviously of synthetic origin. Their sides may be shiny or their colors not found in nature. Other plastic products are made to imitate the look and texture of stone, iron, clay, and other natural materials. They usually carry a heftier price tag than the unimproved variety.

If your garage holds a stack of shiny plastic pots, or if your budget won't allow many natural-look plastic containers, use paint to disguise your planters and give them the aura of respectability.

■ Spray or brush on a coat of matte-finish polyurethane, which will dull the plastic sheen. This treatment works equally well on white, green, or clay-colored plastics.

■ Spray or brush on a faux finish. You'll find paint in crafts stores and home centers that allows you to apply the speckled look of granite, the subtle texture of sandstone, or other trompe l'oeil effects.

■ Use a semitransparent, dark-colored glaze to streak the pot or darken the areas around grooves and molded decorations. Brush on the glaze, then wipe it off until you have the effect you want.

INSTANT ANTIQUES

Age is a desirable quality, at least when it refers to gardens and the objects in them. A weathered patina, a coating of rust, and darkened crevices or spots of lichen or moss add dollars to the price tags of containers in antiques shops.

With a little ingenuity, you can make practically any clay, concrete, stone, or metal container look old. Faux finishes are your helper in this subterfuge. Scout the paint aisle of any discount store, home center, crafts shop, or similar outlet, and you'll find paint in spray bottles and cans to simulate just about any weathered natural finish you can imagine. You can even try your hand at the Midas touch and turn your cheap plastic pots into containers that shine like mellow old gold.

DESIGNS AND DOODADS

Making containers into objects of art is hard to resist when decorating magazines and TV shows keep putting inspiration in front of us. With acrylic paint and a few brushes, you can transform an ordinary clay container into a Ming Dynasty porcelain, a blue-and-white Delft beauty, a festive Mexican urn, or anything else that strikes your fancy.

You may want to play with designs on paper first, using markers or crayons. If you prefer a speedier approach, you can paint directly on the pot to fancy it up.

For complicated designs, draw the pattern on the container after you give it its base color of paint. Then color in the lines with your brush and acrylic paints, as if you were working in a coloring book.

Waterproof glue will let you affix just about anything to your containers—buttons, seashells, stones, grapevine curlicues, or seedpods, for example. If you plan to put the container in an unsheltered place, consider the effect of weather on the decorations you choose. Peacock feathers may look good on a container on a covered porch, but they'll quickly look bedraggled in the rain and dew out in the open.

PLAYFUL COLOR IN MINUTES

Transform ordinary clay into a fun color accent inexpensively with acrylic paint.

Work outdoors on a day with low humidity. Cover the work surface with newspaper.

Apply a base coat of polyurethane to the outside of the pot. If you plan to paint inside the top rim—which will be visible because the planting mix ends short of the very top of the pot—brush this area with polyurethane also.

When the polyurethane is dry, apply acrylic paint to the sides of the pot, and inside the rim if desired. (You can also keep the top of the rim free of paint, for contrast.) Raise the pot to make it easier to paint the bottom edge.

Be sure the pot you decide to paint is one you won't regret "improving." Plain clay pots are a good starting point because of their relatively low price and classic lines.

POTTING MIX

One cubic foot of potting mix will fill a container 15 inches in diameter and 12 inches deep. If it is dry, moisten the mix before you fill the container; it may take up to an hour for a dry soilless mix to thoroughly absorb water.

The best soils for your containers are highly engineered growing media that contain no native (or mineral) soil at all. Garden soil—even the best topsoil from the garden—compacts too readily and does not hold enough water, nutrients, and air for optimum growth in the limited confines of a container. Garden soil is also frequently contaminated with weed seeds, insects, and disease-producing organisms.

Few things determine container gardening success as much as the choice of a good potting mix. A *standard* mix is a basic potting mix designed to sustain plant growth with little or no enhanced growth capabilities. A *premium* mix includes high-tech additions such as fertilizer, wetting agents, and extra water-holding capacity that take a lot of the guesswork out of container gardening. Check labels carefully; most states require potting mixes to list ingredients in order of volume. Mixes that list only a few ingredients are probably *standard* mixes. Those that list many are generally *premium* mixes.

Potting mix can go by many names— potting soil, soilless mix, container soil, container mix, growing mix, or growing media. For the highest quality, look for brands that supply potting mix to professional growers.

For the greatest success, look for a *premium* potting mix that has the following qualities:

1. HIGH TOTAL POROSITY: Good premium potting mixes achieve a total porosity of 80% or more with a combination of organic matter that soaks up water and nutrients like a sponge, such as *sphagnum peat moss, coir pith* (processed coconut husk), and *composted pine bark;* and inorganic materials that increase drainage and resist compaction, such as *perlite* (extremely light granules of volcanic glass expanded by heat). Some inorganic materials, such as *vermiculite* (mica expanded by heat) and *pumice* (ground volcanic rock), absorb water as well as increase drainage.

2. APPROPRIATE DENSITY OR WEIGHT: For most container gardening, *medium* and *light* soil mixes are best. They have high porosity, are easy to handle, have good rigidity to anchor roots, and are usually heavy enough to prevent pots from toppling. *Heavy* and *medium* mixes should be used for tall plants to keep them upright. *Light* mixes are useful in hanging baskets and window boxes. *Super-light* mixes can be used where weight is especially critical, such as on rooftops, but they are dry and dusty and require special anchoring to keep plants from toppling over.

3. APPROPRIATE PH: The *pH* of the growing medium (measure of acidity and alkalinity) affects the availability of nutrients to plants. Most container plants perform best in a mix that is slightly acidic (pH 5.0–6.5), but some plants, such as azaleas and camellias, prefer a more acid mix. Manufacturers add lime or other substances to adjust the pH of their mix. Always check the label to ensure that the pH of a mix is right for your plants.

4. GOOD WETTABILITY: Oils and waxes that naturally occur in organic materials can cause them to shed water and be difficult to wet thoroughly when they dry out. Good premium mixes will include a *wetting agent* to increase the ability of the mix to absorb water quickly.

5. SUFFICIENT NUTRIENTS: Standard mixes have little or no nutrients, and require the addition of fertilizers before planting. Good premium mixes include a wide array of fertilizers (as many as five kinds in one mix) that combine slow-release pellets with fast-acting water-soluble nutrients at the correct level to promote optimum growth.

6. ABSENCE OF WEED SEEDS, INSECTS, AND DISEASE ORGANISMS: The sphagnum peat, coir pith, and perlite used in the best premium mixes are inherently low in these contaminants. If compost is included, it should be processed by the manufacturer to kill weed seeds, insects, and disease organisms without killing beneficial fungi and bacteria. Soilless mixes should not be sterilized.

FERTILIZING

Regular fertilizing is vital for container plants to perform at their best. Frequent watering rapidly washes nutrients out of the soil. By supplying extra nutrients to your container plants, you will keep them growing vigorously. Commercial products include long-acting timed-release pellets and fast-acting liquid fertilizers. Both will keep your plantings lush.

Follow package instructions carefully to avoid killing your plants with kindness. Toxic salts from too much fertilizer can burn the sensitive tissues of their roots.

FERTILIZER OPTIONS

Timed-release fertilizer pellets are a convenient way to supply an extended nutrient boost. The length of effectiveness can vary depending on temperature and the frequency of rain and watering but is generally several months. Mix timed-release fertilizer into the soil when planting, and renew as recommended on the package.

Water-soluble fertilizers applied when plants are watered provide a reliable and regular dose of nutrients. Mix in a sprinkling can for application. If you are maintaining lots of container plants, buy an inexpensive siphon attachment for the garden hose that will supply fertilizer as you water.

WHEN TO FERTILIZE

Feed regularly with frequent applications, following package directions for container plants. Annuals, perennials, and vegetables generally do best with a weekly or twice-weekly boost of fertilizer; herbs can be fertilized every other week, and trees and shrubs once a month. Taper off at the end of the growing season.

If your fertilizer does not include trace minerals, apply organic fish and kelp products or a complete chemical fertilizer every two to three weeks. If azaleas, hollies, and other plants that thrive in acid soil show yellowing between leaf veins, apply chelated iron to the soil or spray it on the leaves.

If you use a standard potting mix that does not already include fertilizer, add timed-release fertilizer to moistened potting mix at the rate directed on the fertilizer package before you fill containers with the soil. Combine it thoroughly, using a trowel to make sure it is evenly distributed.

READING A FERTILIZER LABEL

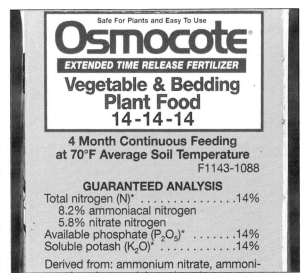

The series of three numbers on a fertilizer label tells you how much nitrogen (N), phosphorus (P), and potassium (K) are supplied by the product. A balanced formula (for example, 14-14-14) is a good, all-purpose choice for a container of flowering plants. A high-nitrogen fertilizer (18-6-12, for example) stimulates leafy growth, just the ticket for foliage plants. A high-phosphorus formula (for example, 10-52-10) won't do as much to boost plant growth but will encourage flowers and fruiting.

The leaves of this plant show salt burn from too much fertilizer. Leaves with yellow or brown edges, curling, loss of color between the veins, or stunted growth often indicate incorrect feeding.

PLANTING

Collect your plants, potting mix, and container on a potting bench, table, or other workspace if the container will be portable. Or plant in place if the container will be too heavy to move when filled.

Open the bag of potting mix; if it is dry, pour in warm water, fold over the bag, and knead. Allow the mix to absorb the water, which can take up to an hour. If you are filling a large container, pour the mix onto a tarpaulin or into a wheelbarrow and add water.

If the container's drainage holes are large, place screening over them to prevent soil from spilling out. The old-fashioned technique of placing broken pot shards at the bottom of containers has been proven undesirable by modern research; this so-called "drainage layer" actually slows drainage instead of improving it.

When the mix is evenly moist, blend in timed-release fertilizer pellets and other amendments if desired. Fill the container half full if you are planting larger plants, or to within a few inches of the rim if you are planting small plants. Set the potted plants into the container to get an idea of how your planned arrangement will look.

WEIGHT REDUCTION

If you are filling a heavy, stable container where weight is a serious problem, such as a large pot or a permanent planter box on a balcony or rooftop, use a light or super-light potting mix, which are readily available and inexpensive. Or you can make your own by combining a standard mix with perlite.

Measure the mix after it is moistened: one part perlite to three parts moist potting soil. Perlite is expensive and dusty; to prevent it from scattering, pour it into a deep container, such as a 5-gallon bucket, then slowly add the potting soil and stir. Whether you buy it or make it yourself, a super-light mix will need more watering than conventional mixes.

Lightweight plastic pots, tall containers with a narrow bottom, or containers in windy areas need weight for stability. Don't use light or super-light potting mix if your container garden needs a heavy base to prevent it from tipping.

OUT OF THE OLD POT

Fill your container one plant at a time, keeping extras in their pots until you're ready to plant them. This will keep their roots moist and undisturbed until transplanting time.

Pop small plants out of their plastic cell packs or pots by pushing on the bottom of the pot while covering the soil surface and supporting the plant between the fingers of your other hand. To get a plant out of a large pot, lay the pot on its side and push firmly against the side. Repeat on the other side, then turn the pot upside down and try to slide the root ball out of the pot. If it resists, use utility shears to cut apart the bottom of the pot and free the roots.

You may find that the roots of each plant are massed into a tangled ball. Gently pull apart the roots to untangle them before planting. If you are planting large plants from gallon-size or bigger pots and you discover that the bottom or sides of the root ball are thick with jumbled roots, make three or four shallow, vertical cuts with a pocket knife around the root ball.

PLANTING VINES IN CONTAINERS

 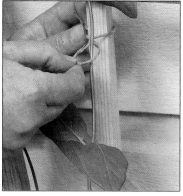

Green garden twine is practically invisible among foliage. Tie twine in a figure-eight shape to form a loose loop. This honeysuckle will soon choose its own supports as its stems begin to grow and twine.

Vines are a quick way to soften a deck railing, balcony, or window box, or to add height in a garden bed. Scarlet runner bean, hyacinth bean, and morning glories are fast-growing climbing annuals; vivid pink mandevilla, fragrant jasmines, and sweet-scented honeysuckles are excellent in containers. Support vines with a trellis inserted in the container or mounted nearby where the twining stems can reach for it, or supply a network of strings. Tie the stems loosely to the new support with soft twine. If the potted plant included a small trellis, gently unwind the vine from the old support and fasten it to the new. Be sure to locate these generally top-heavy containers out of the wind.

INTO THE NEW POT

If you're placing large plants, settle the plant on a layer of potting mix that is deep enough to raise the top of the root ball to about 1 to 3 inches below the rim of the pot. Add other plants of the same size. Pour potting mix around the root balls, pushing it in gently to fill all empty spaces. Keep the original soil surface of the plant at the same height as the final tamped-down potting mix.

For small plants, add potting mix to about 2 inches from the top of the container, then scoop out holes for each root ball. Tuck in each plant and pat down the mix around it.

Always be sure to allow an inch or two at the top of the container to create a reservoir for watering. If you fill the pot to the top with potting mix, water will run over the sides instead of soaking down into the mix.

AFTER PLANTING

When you are finished planting, water with a slow, gentle spray. Fill the pot to the top, letting the water sink in until it drips from the drainage holes. Gently bounce the pot to eliminate air pockets. Add more soil if necessary and water again.

Place portable containers in a shady area out of the wind. Water lightly whenever the surface feels dry. Move to the final location in a couple of days, after plants have recovered from the initial shock of transplanting. If the plants in large containers you planted in place begin to wilt, rig up a shade structure for a few days by draping a towel across lawn chairs placed on the southwest side of the container.

RECYCLED POTTING MIX

Some gardeners save money from year to year by reusing potting mix. When removing plants from containers that have finished their show, empty the used potting mix into a large covered storage bin or trash barrel kept for this purpose, cleaning the soil of large roots and other debris. At planting time, premoisten the potting mix with water to which you have added a mild dish-washing detergent at the rate of 1 tsp. per gallon, which will act as a wetting agent. Mix in a timed-release fertilizer according to package instructions, and use as you would fresh potting soil. Do not reuse potting mix that has been contaminated by insects or disease, or when planting especially disease-prone plants such as orchids or roses.

BASIC PLANTING TECHNIQUES

Step 1: *If you are planting large plants, fill the container half full with moist potting mix. For small plants, fill to within 2 inches of the rim.*

Step 2: *Press firmly on the pot's sides to loosen the plant's roots.*

Step 3: *Tease apart matted roots with your fingers to encourage them to grow into the potting mix.*

Step 4: *Settle the plant in the pot; make sure the top of the root ball is 1 to 2 inches below the rim. Fill in around the plant with potting mix to the top of the root ball.*

Step 5: *Water generously until the potting mix is thoroughly moistened and water runs out drainage holes in the bottom of the pot. If necessary, add more potting mix as it settles.*

WATERING

THE SELF-WATERING CONTAINER

One of the most welcome innovations in container culture, self-watering containers cut down watering chores to as little as once a month. Such an invention sounds priceless, but self-watering plastic containers are not much more expensive than regular plastic pots.

An increasing number of manufacturers market hanging baskets, large and small pots, rolling planters, and even window boxes that contain a built-in reservoir for extra water. Capillary action draws the moisture from the reservoir into the soil above.

Plastic is the material of choice for these containers, which feature simple, classic styling and matte or glossy finishes in white, terra-cotta, deep green, and other colors. The reservoir is invisible from the outside of the container. Some containers incorporate a pipe that extends above the soil level for filling. Others have an access hole at the base of the planter for restocking the reservoir. And add-on reservoirs are available that can turn ordinary pots into self-watering ones. A surprising amount of water can be accommodated. One style of 15-inch-square self-watering pot holds more than 6 quarts.

WATER-HOLDING MATS

Not as dramatic a labor saver as self-watering pots, water-preserving fiber mats also reduce the frequency of container watering. Thin,

Watering is the most frequent chore of container gardening. Devices such as these reduce the effort. Left to right are a self-watering container with an absorbent wick, tubes that carry water to soil from a nearby bowl, an add-on reservoir, and a refillable tube that contains a water-releasing cellulose gel.

flexible mats are impregnated with moisture-absorbing polymer beads. Wetted before use, the mats absorb an astonishing amount of water—one small square of 7 by 7 inches can hold a quart of water—then are placed inside the container before it is filled with potting mix. Place the mat along the sides or bottom of a container, but be sure not to block the drainage holes. As the potting mix dries out, the polymer beads release their moisture to the mix and plant roots. At watering time, the beads are replenished with moisture.

Be sure to check moisture regularly if you use water-conserving devices. It's easy to become forgetful when watering is not a daily task.

WICKS AND CAPILLARY MATS

Any material that absorbs water can help keep containers from drying out. Cotton wicks have been a reliable aid to houseplant enthusiasts for years. The ropelike material protrudes from the bottom of the pot into a bowl or tray of water. The wick absorbs water and transfers it to the soil in the pot. Wicks work well for some outdoor containers, too, but they do not absorb enough water for pots larger than about 8 inches in diameter or those in full sun. For containers with bigger water demands, turn to capillary matting, available at garden centers. Because the matting is visible as it protrudes from the pot, you may want to save it for the times when you must leave your garden for a few days. Or disguise the matting by placing other containers in front.

Cut the matting into strips about 2 inches wide and 8 inches long or longer. Three strips will suffice for a 12-inch-diameter pot; 5 stips for an 18-inch-diameter pot. Add more for larger sizes. Insert the strips at the same time you fill the pot with mix, or poke them through the drainage holes later. Keep the strips in contact with a few inches of potting mix and pull about 6 inches out through the drainage holes (more than one strip can protrude through the same hole). Set a brick or other support into a basin of water and set the pot on top, making sure the strips are in the water. Replenish the reservoir as needed.

Try your best to water regularly, because soilless mixes are difficult to rewet once they have dried out. Should your container get too dry, water will run off immediately without being absorbed, fooling you into thinking that your potting mix has been moistened when in fact it is swiftly shedding water. To solve the problem, soak the pot overnight in a large container of water. If it is impractical to move the pot, tilt it and plug the drainage holes with corks, wads of plastic wrap, or strips of duct tape—anything that will prevent water from pouring out quickly. Then water the container to the brim and let the soil soak up the moisture. Repeat. After water is absorbed, remove the plugs.

Wilting plants can indicate too much water as well as too little. If dry soil is the problem, water generously immediately; plants usually recover within a few hours. If the soil is wet when you poke a finger into it, or if very little water runs out the drainage holes after watering, too much water is likely to be the cause of severe wilting. Raise the container so it drains freely, insert wicking into the drainage holes, and poke twisted sheets of paper towels an inch or two into the soil surface. Replace absorbent materials when saturated. If drainage is impeded, search for the cause before the plant roots drown. Tip or lift pots to see if roots are blocking the drainage holes; if so, slice them away or repot to a larger container. If the soil level has dropped, the potting mix has become compacted and the plant will need repotting. A flat-bottomed container on a flat surface may not allow proper drainage; elevate the container on pot feet or a stand.

POLYMER GEL: PROS AND CONS

Water-holding polymer gel has received much attention, but its use is controversial. In isolation, polymer gel crystals can absorb a lot of moisture, expanding up to 100 times their weight in distilled water. In soil, however, ions decrease the water-holding capacity of polymer gel by as much as 85%. Research shows that at the low rates recommended on product labels and offered in some potting mixes, polymer gel is ineffective in increasing the water available to roots. Organic matter is less expensive, so it can be used in potting mix in much greater quantities than polymer gel to hold far more available water. To be effective, polymer gel must be mixed into potting soil in such high volumes that its expense and excessive shrinkage preclude its use.

DRIP IRRIGATION

Drip irrigation completely eliminates the daily chore of hand-watering containers. It's ideal for forgetful gardeners or for those interested in saving time and labor. A system of thin, flexible tubes carries water to container plants according to a schedule set on an automatic timer. Installing drip irrigation to your containers is much easier than it looks, thanks to kits and specialized parts. A bit of planning and an afternoon of installation is a small price to pay for months of freedom from watering chores.

The theory is simple: A ³⁄₈- or ½-inch polyethylene water supply line connects to your outside faucet, then branches into narrow, flexible, vinyl microtubes that carry water to your containers. Wherever you want water to drip out, you attach an emitter. For small containers, you can use a single emitter; for big pots, a half dozen. A battery-operated timer controls the system, delivering water at the intervals you specify.

Kits are widely available, or you can plan your system on paper and buy only the individual parts you need. Well-stocked home supply stores and garden centers carry a full line of parts.

Choose heavyweight, vinyl microtubing for your system. It is more flexible than the polyethylene type, and it comes in several colors that blend well with containers and other surfaces. You can run the microtubing up the outside of your containers or thread it through a drainage hole to hide it. Suspend it over a hanging basket to drip into the soil mix, or lay it in a circle over the soil surface of large pots.

Relatively inexpensive computerized timers let you water automatically at the same time every day, for the same length of time. You can reset the timer as seasons change; more complicated timers allow you to water groups of containers on different schedules.

In cold-winter areas, you can leave the tubing outside if you install drain valves at low points in the system to flush water from the tubes and prevent damage from ice. Bring the timer inside, though, to protect it from cold weather.

GROOMING AND CARE

Keep an eagle eye on container gardens so you can remove flowers as soon as they fade to keep the arrangement always looking fresh. Use shears to snip off the flower stem close to its junction with leaves that will hide the stub.

on each plant stem. This will encourage new side shoots to sprout, forming a denser plant.

4. TRIM INTO SHAPE: Use pruners to snip back fast-growing plants that are showing signs of unruliness or unattractive bare stems. Or trim for a better shape, cutting back plants in graceful proportion to the container.

5. PRUNE WOODY PLANTS: Keep roses, shrubs, and trees in shape with selective pruning. Remove errant branches and dead wood. Thin fruit trees or flowering shrubs for better bud production.

6. WEED: Weeds are a rarity in container gardens, but be alert for strays and give them the heave-ho at once.

7. MULCH: Cover the soil with an attractive mulch—such as compost, finely shredded bark, sandstone pebbles, or river rock—to conserve water and add a handsome touch to containers that aren't densely planted.

FOR THAT PROFESSIONALLY CARED-FOR LOOK

It's the details that count in a container garden—healthy foliage, fresh flowers, and an attractive soil surface. All it takes is a few minutes a day to keep your container gardens looking nursery-fresh. Follow these swift and easy maintenance steps:

1. DEADHEAD: Remove flowers as soon as they begin to wilt or fade. Your fingers are good tools for pinching off blossoms gone past their prime; shears work well, too.

2. REMOVE UNSIGHTLY FOLIAGE: While you're grooming flowers, attend to the foliage, too. Pinch off dying or yellowed leaves, or any other discolored or disfigured foliage.

3. PINCH FOR COMPACT GROWTH: Prevent the lax and leggy look by pinching out the growing tip and first pair or two of leaves

JUST A TRIM, PLEASE

Regular "haircuts" are one of the best ways to keep containers looking their best. To keep your container garden growing vigorously, snip branching plants back by an inch or two every few weeks. Most plants recover remarkably fast from a trim, pushing out new growth within several days.

Plants that spill or trail over the edges of a container, such as petunia and ornamental sweet potato, may lose leaves near the base of the plant and take on a bare-stemmed, leggy look. To keep them dense and lush, trim back the plant an inch or two about every two weeks, using scissors like a pair of hedge shears. If trailing plants have become scraggly, be ruthless and cut them back by one-third to one-half their length. They'll rebound quickly, pushing out side branches from the formerly bare stems.

OVERWINTERING AND COLD-WEATHER OPTIONS

When freezing winter weather moves in, plants and pots alike suffer the effects. Porous containers made of clay, plastic, metal, and even concrete may chip, crack, or break into pieces after repeated freezes. For controlling winter damage to plants, the temperature of the potting mix is more important than air temperature. Moist potting mix provides some insulation in large containers. But plant roots are much less protected in any container than in the ground.

Here is how you can give your container gardens their best chances at surviving winter:

■ Empty small containers and store them out of the weather.

■ Move tender plants indoors for the winter (be sure they are free of insects). Some tender plants tolerate the relatively low light levels, dry air, and warmth of indoor rooms quite well as houseplants. Others are best on a sunny enclosed porch that remains cool but never freezes.

■ Save valuable permanent plants that are difficult to overwinter in containers, such as roses in Zones 4 and 5, by transplanting them permanently into the ground in late summer or early fall. Buy new ones for containers the next spring.

■ Get to know your garage, enclosed porch, basement, and potting shed—purchase a maximum-minimum thermometer and monitor temperature fluctuations through winter. For many people, an attached garage is an ideal

Keep large, upright plants looking good by trimming selectively, one stem at a time. Cut back the tips of branching plants by an inch or two with sharp pruners or scissors, removing the stem to a point just above a leaf or pair of leaves. Cut back to an outward-facing leaf or flower, so that your cuts are hidden from the main viewing angles.

Overcrowding may affect flowering, as one plant prevents another from receiving sunlight. And overcrowded plants may ruin the effect you intended by distorting the shapes of their neighbors. Thin by removing excess stems with pruners or scissors.

SLIP IN SUBSTITUTES

When flowering plants are past their peak, or when you just want a change, it's out with the old and in with the new. Use a hand trowel to lift out the retirees and transplant them to a garden bed or holding area for rejuvenation. Insert replacement plants in the container for a fresh, new look.

Garden centers and nurseries are stocked with plants in bloom and with foliage plants throughout the gardening season. See page 31 for details on creating and stocking a staging area for your own supply of container candidates that you can use to fill in gaps.

REPOTTING

The roots of shrubs and trees can soon become overcrowded in a container, which causes frequent water stress and need for watering. When you notice that a plant needs watering too often, move it to a bigger pot or trim the roots to keep the plant producing attractive foliage, flowers, or fruit. If you don't want to use a larger pot, rein in the plant by pruning the roots to keep the top growth and roots in

Shrubs, trees, and other woody plants benefit from a root trim at repotting time. Cutting back the roots an inch or two slightly slows the top growth of the plant, a desirable effect for shrubs confined to containers.

balance. Remove the plant from the pot and slice off an inch or two of roots from the bottom and sides of the root ball with pruners or a knife. Replant, using fresh potting mix in the bottom of the pot and around the plant.

PESTS AND DISEASES

With the close attention you give containers, you're bound to quickly notice any signs of pest or disease problems, such as disfigured or discolored foliage or visible pest insects. Control them immediately, as you would in the garden. Remove and discard affected plant parts or plants, handpick insects, and use other controls if necessary. *The Ortho Home Gardener's Problem Solver* is an excellent resource for diagnosing and treating specific problems. It is available wherever quality books are sold.

overwintering environment, dry and cool with temperatures that rarely go below freezing. Use yours to store containers you have emptied as well as those with permanent, dormant plants. It's often the perfect place to store pots of fall-planted bulbs, too.

■ Keep as much contact as possible between permanently planted outdoor containers and bare ground, which is a wonderful source of radiant energy and insulation from chilling winds. Even the difference between a

container sitting on bare ground and a wooden deck can be dramatic. More effective is to sink the container into the ground and cover the top with a layer of mulch, although this can cause the outside of the container to become stained. Lay standard roses on their sides in a trench and cover both top growth and container with a layer of mulch and then soil.

■ Make sure outdoor containers go into winter's freezes with moist potting mix, which is far more

insulating than dry mix.

■ Protect the sides and top of exposed large containers with several layers of bubble wrap, followed by a weatherproof tarp and a final layer of less obtrusive burlap.

■ Make a cylinder of chicken wire around an exposed large pot or tub, about 12 inches taller than the container, with 6 inches or more of space between walls and wire. Fill the space and cover the surface of the container with fallen leaves or straw.

BACKSTAGE

Well-planned facilities make it easier to plant and maintain container gardens. A potting bench that provides a sturdy work surface and space for supplies is the first addition to consider. You can place it in the garage, on a covered porch or patio, against an out-of-the-way fence or wall, or in a potting shed you build just for this purpose. A holding area is also a great convenience for rotating plants as they come into and out of bloom.

THE POTTING BENCH

If you've ever stood up and rubbed your aching back after bending awkwardly to pot a plant, you'll appreciate a potting bench. Potting benches, which consist of a rectangular table with attached shelves above the table and sometimes beneath as well, are made for stand-up work. The work surface is the same height as a kitchen counter, so you won't have to bend or stoop while planting your containers.

You can design and build your own potting bench, hire a carpenter, or buy a kit at home supply stores, garden centers or through mail-order catalogs. Expect to pay at least $100 for a basic model. Those made of rot-resistant cedar, cypress, or other specialty woods are pricier than pine, but they are longer-lasting and can even be used outdoors for years.

Invest in a higher quality bench rather than starting with a flimsier bargain model. As with any wood product, look for sturdy construction details: substantial lumber instead of plywood or

Every gardener's dream, a potting bench adds convenience and saves your back from bending to plant and transplant. A simple, sturdy bench is a project even an inexperienced carpenter can build. Having supplies near at hand to a comfortable workplace eliminates backache as well as unnecessary trips to collect pots, planting mix, or tools.

POTTING BENCH ESSENTIALS

Now that you have a place to keep everything within easy reach, here are the supplies and tools you will need at the potting bench:
- Covered bins or garbage cans to hold potting mix, perlite, mulch, and fertilizers.
- Decorative containers to hold finished gardens.
- Potting mix to fill containers.
- Plastic pots of various sizes to start seeds or hold plants removed from containers.
- Seed-starting mix for grow-your-own plants.
- Labels and an indelible pen to identify started seeds.
- Sprinkling can.

- Fertilizer.
- Measuring cup to measure fertilizer.
- Watering wand with fine-spray nozzle.
- Empty buckets to hold excess potting mix during planting or to moisten potting mix.
- Trowel for planting and transplanting.
- Pruners for grooming container arrangements.
- Scissors to thin and shear small-stemmed plants.
- Journal to note planting dates, varieties, and thoughts.
- Whisk broom or brush for clearing the work surface of soil and other debris.
- Stakes and twist ties, raffia, string, and other ties.

1×4s, and screws or bolts at the joints instead of nails.

Place your bench in a roofed area or in a potting shed. Make sure a source of water is nearby. The garage is often an ideal location, especially when it is attached to the house. Access is convenient to both house and garden, and storage space, water, and electrical outlets are often easy to arrange. The moderate winter temperature of an attached garage—especially near the wall where it attaches to the house—makes it ideal for overwintering potted bulbs and dormant container gardens.

THE POTTING SHED

A small outbuilding dedicated to potting up plants is a highly useful addition to any garden. A potting shed also can add a touch of fun to the garden. Decorated with a coat of paint, a colorful door, fancy trim, and other finishing touches, a potting shed looks like a charming little storybook cottage come to life.

In a potting shed, you can start seeds, transplant seedlings to larger pots, arrange gardens in your containers, and corral extra pots, planters, and supplies all in one central location where you can be as messy as you like.

You can make a potting shed out of an all-purpose storage shed or yard barn, or buy a potting shed kit from a home supply store or mail-order catalog. It should be big enough to accommodate a potting bench, or you can add your own high table and shelves, either by doing it yourself or hiring a carpenter.

THE STAGING AREA

Dedicate part of your garden to a staging area, which will serve as both nursery for young plants and rest home for old ones. This is the backstage arena, where plants get ready for their star turn in your containers.

A corner behind the house or garage is a convenient staging area, because storage space for pots, soil, and tools will be close at hand. Choose a spot close to a water faucet. Keep part of the staging area free of grass, so that you don't have to move pots for mowing. Lay thick sections of newspaper over existing lawn, then cover with weed-barrier landscaping cloth and finish with a 2-inch layer of gravel, bark, or wood chips.

Use the staging area to start seeds and cuttings and grow plants to blooming size. Annuals bloom in as little as eight weeks; most perennials flower the second year after sowing.
■ Sow annuals in pots to avoid setbacks caused by digging up transplants from garden soil, or sow directly in the final container. Hold them

in the staging area until they are ready to burst into full glory.
■ Sow perennial seeds in a nursery bed, then transplant to plastic pots when plants emerge from dormancy in their second year. They will be ready to slip into your container gardens at bloom time. In warm-winter areas, sow perennials in 6-inch plastic pots where they can grow without disturbance until it is time to transplant them.
■ Start cuttings of perennials and shrubs in a bed in the staging area. Transplant to gallon-size pots in early spring of their second year.

A staging area also serves as a rest home for plants that you retire from containers when they are past their prime. Transplant perennials to a staging area bed after their bloom period or when you empty containers in the fall. The next spring, pot them up again and hold them until they are ready for another turn in a container. Use the staging area to refresh plants that may have suffered from neglect or become lank and leggy in containers by cutting them back by a third to a half, transplanting to a staging area bed, and watering well.

Above: With a covering of lattice and the addition of French doors, a simple potting shed purchased at a home center becomes a beautiful garden focal point. Note the fence behind which masks a staging area.

Below: Turn an unused corner near a building into a holding zone for potted plants. You can use this staging area to bring perennials into bloom, refresh those you retired from arrangements, or pamper seedlings to planting size.

CONTAINER GARDENS

Combining plants in containers is creative fun. Now that you know the basics of planning and planting a simple, single-plant container garden, it's time to free your artistic side and experiment. Recreate the gardens in this chapter or use them as inspiration for your own ideas.

MAKING GOOD CHOICES

Start with plants that will thrive in the conditions of the site, and make sure all plants in the container have similar cultural needs. Put petunias with other sun-loving plants, for instance, instead of trying to make them grow in a shady pot of ferns. Then move on to more artful considerations.

COLOR: Color reinforces the rhythm of a garden and can be a strong accent.

■ Decide whether the container should echo or contrast with nearby in-ground plantings.

■ A single-color planting is more attention-grabbing than a mix of colors.

■ Keep viewing range in mind. Red, yellow, orange, hot pink, magenta, and white flowers shine from a distance; cool blues and purples and delicate pastels are best admired up close.

FORM: Combine a variety of plant postures for a more interesting arrangement.

■ Use spiky or upright plants to balance the height of a container and add vertical interest.

■ Mounded plants are ideal for filling the middle ground of the arrangement, to contrast with upright or trailing plants.

■ Let relaxed, sprawling plants spill over the edges to make a transition to the surrounding garden and visually soften the container.

TEXTURE: Use contrasting textures to add excitement.

■ Mix big, plain leaves with wispy or lacier textures.

■ Partner glossy leaves with velvety or crinkled ones.

■ Choose plants with flower or foliage texture that contrasts with nearby in-ground plantings.

Contrasting colors bring out the best of both worlds. Icy lime-green 'Envy' zinnias and 'Margarita' sweet potato vines amplify the heat of orange-striped 'Mr. Majestic' marigolds and warm-toned terra-cotta pots.

HOW TO PLANT MIXED CONTAINERS

Work on a flat surface that is large enough to hold plants, tools, potting mix, and container. A patio table or potting bench (see pages 30 and 31) is ideal because you won't have to bend and stoop. Cover surfaces with a plastic drop cloth to make cleanup easier.

ASSEMBLE SUPPLIES: You will also need tools for planting and a ready supply of water. Your hands make excellent tools for scooping planting holes. A hand trowel also works well. A narrow-bladed trowel is handy for wiggling plants into tight quarters.

Use pruners to snip roots or stems or cut through plastic pots to free stubborn roots. An empty bucket is useful for holding extra potting mix that you remove while planting.

ARRANGE PLANTS: If you're using a design in this book, follow the suggestions for composing the arrangement. For original designs, arrange the potted plants until you are pleased with their look. Young plants will fill out; place them close so you have a better idea of how their color, form, and texture will look beside their neighbors when full-grown.

Place plants according to how the container is viewed. Your aim is to keep plants visible. In a large pot out in the open, put tall plants in the middle so that the container looks attractive from all angles. In containers against a wall or fence, put tall plants at the rear.

FILL THE CONTAINER: Select an appropriate planting mix (see page 22) and review the planting instructions on pages 24 and 25. Plant the container from big to little: plants with the deepest root ball first, followed in order by those with shallower roots. Pour in a few inches of potting mix, remove the first plant from its pot, and settle it into the container, scooping out mix if you need a deeper hole. Fill in around the plant with more potting mix and plants with shallower roots.

Set plants as close together as you can, squishing the root balls if necessary. The extra fertilizer and water you supply will compensate for the limited growing space.

If you change your mind about the arrangement, it's easy to make changes at planting time. Slip your hand or a trowel beneath the root ball to lift the plant, then gently set it aside while you reposition its planting hole. Water generously when done.

BACK-SAVING SUGGESTIONS

Filled containers are surprisingly heavy and awkward to move without damaging the plants. Save yourself chiropractor visits by doing the final planting in place in large containers, or use mechanical aids and ingenuity to move hefty pots.

- Before moving a heavy container across the yard on a wagon or handcart, position wide boards or plywood over lawn areas and soft paths to prevent ruts.
- Tilt the pot and slowly roll it, keeping it at an angle and letting the bottom edge serve as a "wheel."
- To move containers on paved surfaces, place a plant trolley on casters beneath the pot before you fill it.
- Drag moderate-sized containers on a child's plastic sled.
- Use a garden cart or yard wagon to move large containers. Enlist a helper to lift the pot onto the cart.
- Rent a refrigerator dolly. Tip the pot and slide the edge of the dolly underneath, then strap the pot tightly before moving it.

Settle the plant with the deepest root ball into the container first. Fill in around it with potting mix to the depth of the plant with the next-deepest root ball.

Tamp the mix with your fingers after placing a plant. Lightweight, soilless potting mixes may settle after watering; top off with more potting mix if needed.

The result: one half-gallon pot of cordyline, three 4-inch pots of variegated potato vine, and three 4-inch pots of ivy geranium have been planted in a 16-inch terra-cotta pot.

HANGING POTS

To disguise the bare sides and bottom of a solid hanging pot, use exuberant trailing plants. This 12-inch, self-watering, plastic hanging pot was planted with two 4-inch plants of Brachycome 'City Lights', two 4-inch plants of Bacopa 'Snowstorm', and one 4-inch plant of Asparagus densiflorus 'Sprengeri' in the center.

■ For high visibility, choose flowers and foliage that contrast with the background of the location where the container will hang.

■ Group three pots at staggered heights for more impact.

■ Place hanging pots with fine-textured foliage and small-flowered plants where they will be seen up close.

■ Avoid using tall plants in hanging containers; they will look ungainly.

■ Cut back cascading plants, removing several inches of each stem's length, as soon as they show signs of legginess, straggly growth, or bare stems.

■ To reduce watering chores, insert a water-holding mat impregnated with polymer beads before adding potting mix.

■ Set another container beneath a hanging pot to benefit from the runoff of water and liquid fertilizer.

Hanging container gardens provide a quick splash of color in areas where an in-ground garden would be impossible—on the deck, on the porch, or next to the front door. For rapid effect, you can pick up an already planted plastic pot at any garden center and enjoy months of bloom. But by investing a bit of time, you can have the pleasure of creating a custom arrangement that accents the color of your house, puts fragrance at nose height, or makes your sitting spaces as inviting as your garden.

H anging pots command attention because of their height, which brings the garden to eye level. Place the pots thoughtfully to make the most of these accent pieces, and keep them in tip-top shape with daily care.

Hanging gardens flourish in solid-sided pots of plastic and other materials. Look for flat-backed containers to hang against a wall or to decorate a privacy fence.

Left: It's easy to refill the reservoir of a self-watering container with a sprinkling can that has a narrow spout.

Right: Use the power of a pulley to easily lower a hanging container at watering time.

FUNCTIONAL POTS

Pots with solid sides and a solid bottom require less watering than openwork baskets, because they slow the evaporation that causes the soil to dry out. Plastic pots are the most familiar hanging garden containers, and they are popular for good reasons—they are inexpensive, lightweight, and easy to plant and maintain. Look for self-watering pots with a built-in reservoir. Pots made of clay, resin, metal, and other solid materials also work well for a hanging garden. Innovative hangers, available at garden centers and through catalogs, allow you to quickly convert classic clay or clay-look pots to hanging containers. The drawback to hanging pots is that, unlike baskets, only the top can be planted. Disguise the sides with vines and other cascading foliage and flowers. White or light-colored pots, which reflect sunlight, help keep the soil moist and cool, but green pots that blend with foliage are less obtrusive.

HANG IT UP

The hook or bracket that holds your hanging garden can be inconspicuous or a decorative asset. Visit a home supply store, garden center, or nursery to find hangers in a myriad of styles, colors, and materials. Antique shops and flea markets may also have just the hook. Select hardware that complements the style of your house: a white gingerbread bracket for a Victorian home, a sleek angled hanger for a modern ranch, a wrought-iron holder for a farmhouse. Make sure the bracket is sturdy enough to hold the heavy weight of a freshly watered container. Attach it to a wall, post, or other support with screws instead of nails, which can pull out under the weight.

Above: Lacy texture backs a profusion of warm-colored flowers in a single plastic hanging pot. Two 4-inch pots of golden bidens (Bidens ferulifolia *'Goldmarie'*) *and one 4-inch pot each of* Calibrachoa *'Cherry Red' and 'Terra Cotta' have grown to almost completely hide the green 12-inch plastic pot. Although the diameter of the container is rather small, the overall garden is wide because the plants arch out.*

Above: Hanging pots tend to tip because of their small bases. Rest the container in a flat-bottomed pot or bucket for more stability while planting.

A swivel at the end of a hook allows a hanging pot to rotate in the wind instead of swinging and makes it a simple job to turn the pot for deadheading or other maintenance.

WATERING HANGING POTS

Water your hanging pots daily unless they are large ones hung in full shade, or unless they contain succulents or other nonthirsty plants. Because of the height of hanging containers, you'll want a system that delivers water in a slow but steady stream to allow the potting mix to soak it up without excessive runoff. Self-watering pots are a boon to busy gardeners, and they also protect plants in sunny sites from suffering when you're not home to water. A watering wand attached to the end of your garden hose makes the chore easier by extending your reach and eliminating the need to fill and lift a sprinkling can; be sure to look for one with a shut-off valve. Drip irrigation emitters attached to thin vinyl tubing are a permanent labor-saving solution, but the tubing can be hard to camouflage in its approach from the faucet.

HANGING BASKETS

Sphagnum moss in open half baskets gives these twin gardens a natural look, with no containers visible. 'Accent White' impatiens contrasts with lavender edging lobelia, white-variegated 'Glacier' English ivy, and the weathered wood of a fence, making a cool but strong focal point. As the ivy planted around the sides and bottom of the basket grows, it will trail downward so that the gardens look gracefully proportioned against the wooden fence.

Overflowing with flowers and foliage from all sides, hanging baskets let you create a lavish garden in a very small space. Their elevated position immediately draws the eye, so choose their location as carefully as you would when hanging a painting. You'll also want to design the planting to create a feeling of abundance.

■ Position plants in the basket so that their fullest sides face outward.
■ Snuggle edging lobelia, sweet alyssum, and other sprawling plants around the rim beneath larger leaves of other plants. Their stems will spill over the rim to find growing space.
■ Use neutral gray-leaved plants as fillers between bright colors.
■ Use a potting mix with high water-holding capacity to fill the central space of baskets; hanging baskets can be difficult to rewet if you let them dry out.
■ Choose plants with large blossoms, vivid color, and bold leaves or dramatic form in hanging baskets that will be viewed from a distance.
■ Select plants with an arching form instead of strongly vertical growth for a more graceful effect.
■ Reinforce the romance of a hanging basket with long, trailing vines, such as variegated periwinkle (*Vinca major* 'Variegata') or trailing nasturtiums, which may grow 3 feet or more.
■ Camouflage plain plastic hanging pots by removing the hanger and slipping the planted pot into a natural woven basket hung from chains attached to the rim with S hooks at three equidistant points.

Use a heavy-duty plastic trash bag to line the back of a wire half basket, which will protect the wall upon which the container will hang from moisture. The liner and wire grid will be hidden when the sphagnum moss is added.

Line the basket with a thick layer of moistened sphagnum moss, laying pieces inside of the frame and pushing them through to the outside. Overlap and compress securely. You will fill the center with potting mix as you plant.

Cut a slit through the moss to insert a plant into the side or bottom of the basket. Carefully snug the moss back into place around the plant and add potting soil to the level of the plant roots. Repeat with several more plants, as shown here with 'Glacier' English ivy (Hedera helix). Apply liquid fertilizer to the leaves each time you water.

Containers with open sides of widely spaced wire, wrought iron, or other materials give you more planting room. You can plant the sides and even the bottom of the container instead of only the top, increasing the number of the plants in the arrangement and enhancing the overall effect of the hanging garden.

Showcase plants that deserve close attention in a hanging basket near a sitting area. For the most pleasing form, choose low growers, short upright plants, fountain shapes, and sprawlers or draping vines.

LINING MATERIALS

Hanging baskets must be lined to retain the potting mix within their slatted, woven, or grid-work sides. Sphagnum moss makes an excellent liner if your container has widely spaced grids. Preformed mats of light brown, fibrous mesh are widely available for lining open-sided pots; they may be made from coconut palm fiber (coir), sisal, or synthetic fiber. In wicker baskets and other hanging containers constructed with tightly woven sides, the liner will be hidden by the basket itself.

Hanging baskets allow significant evaporation. Plants on the perimeter of the basket, whose roots are closest to the drying effects of outside air, need particular attention so that they don't dry out. Use a houseplant watering can with a skinny spout to direct water through the slit in the liner into the root area.

PLANTS FOR HANGING BASKETS AND POTS

FLOWERS FOR SHADE:	**FLOWERS FOR SUN:**
Begonia	Calibrachoa
Bellflower	Edging lobelia
Fuchsia	Fan flower
Impatiens	Ivy geranium
Pansies, violas	Lantana
Primrose	Petunia

FOLIAGE FOR SHADE:	**FOLIAGE FOR SUN:**
Coleus	Asparagus fern
English ivy	Dusty miller
Ferns	Licorice plant
Periwinkle (Vinca minor)	Sweet potato vine
	Vinca (Vinca major)
Spider plant	Winter creeper
Swedish ivy	euonymus

Brighten a shady nook with a hanging basket of tuberous begonias in warm colors. Smaller yellow monkey flowers (Mimulus) echo the color theme; maidenhair fern and spider plant liberated from their houseplant roles contribute sprays of greenery.

Tough, matted coconut fiber, called coir, is a long-lasting, natural-looking liner. Overlap sections as necessary to settle firmly in your container.

Use pruners to remove excess liner material, and to cut slits through the liner to plant the sides of the container.

Holding the root ball securely, insert a plant through the coir. Push it firmly into the potting mix, then pull the liner together around the plant's stem.

After the sides are planted, place larger plants in the top and add potting mix around them. The wire frame will help support the begonias.

SEASONAL DRAMA

Make a container garden look fresh in every season by combining permanent plants with a few changing players.

■ Anchor the planting with permanent plants in three basic forms: spiky, mounding, and spilling over the edge.
■ Include strong textural contrast in foliage as well as flowers.
■ Take advantage of garden center plants, available in full bloom and prime condition, to add instant color to the display.
■ Replace temporary plants as soon as their floral display diminishes noticeably.
■ Use plants that are seasonally appropriate in your region—for instance, russet chrysanthemums in fall instead of spring.
■ Buy perennial plants in bud and hold them until they are just beginning to open before slipping them into the container. Perennials bought at the peak of bloom fade fast.
■ Add a plant with large flowers to make the container garden a strong focal point.
■ Determine the main vantage point before placing permanent plants. If the container will be viewed from all sides, put tall plants in the middle.

Container plantings can change and develop over the seasons just like a garden bed, with a little help from you. For a seasonally changing pot, start with small shrubs, ornamental

'Silver Carpet' lamb's-ears, 'Heavy Metal' switch grass, 'Gulf Stream' heavenly bamboo, and 'Emerald Gaiety' winter creeper euonymus provide a permanent foliage effect in this 24-inch glazed ceramic bowl. In early summer, one Oriental lily and three 4-inch dianthus are slipped in.

PERMANENT PLANTS FOR A SEASONAL PLANTER

Agave (*Agave* spp.)
Blue fescue (*Festuca glauca*)
Boxwood (*Buxus* spp.)
Cordyline (*Cordyline australis*)
Fuchsia (*Fuchsia* spp.)
Heavenly bamboo (*Nandina domestica*)
Hollies, dwarf types (*Ilex* spp.)
Japanese sedge (*Carex morrowii*)
Maiden grass (*Miscanthus sinensis*)
New Zealand flax (*Phormium tenax*)
Pittosporum, dwarf (*Pittosporum tobira* 'Wheeler's Dwarf')
Switch grass (*Panicum virgatum*)
Yucca (*Yucca* spp.)

Use sturdy shears to cut out the bottom of the 4-inch pots of replacement performers. This frees their roots to take up moisture and nutrients from surrounding soil.

grasses, or perennials for foliage or bloom. Leave gaps into which you can slip flowering plants to change the display.

By anchoring a good-sized container with permanent plants, you create a structure similar to that achieved in the garden with shrubs and perennials. Filling in the spaces with temporary accent plants is fast and easy, thanks to place-holding pots that prevent the roots of the permanent plants from filling the empty spaces in the design.

To save space for later additions, sink pots filled with mulch or potting mix into the places where you intend to add plants over the course of the year. Cover the surface of the entire planting with mulch to hide the pots. When you are ready to plant, remove the bottoms of the new replacement pots with shears. Scoop away the mulch, lift the place-saving pots, and sink the replacements, pots and all. Push the root balls into the potting mix to ensure contact, and water well. When blooms fade, replace with the next round. The container shown here incorporates four permanent plants with four temporary planting stations.

In warm-winter climates, make changes year-round. In regions with cold winters, plant in early spring and make changes until frost. Then either empty the pot and winter it in a protected place, or move the pot with its permanent plants to an unheated garage.

TEMPORARY ACCENT PLANTS FOR SEASONAL-CHANGE PLANTERS

These ideas are only a beginning of the possibilities; look for blooming potted plants at garden centers and nurseries.

SPRING:
- One fringed bleeding heart (*Dicentra eximia*) in center, with three pots of forget-me-nots (such as *Myosotis* 'Victoria') in front
- Deep blue pansies and miniature daffodils (such as *Narcissus* 'Tete-a-tete')
- Lungwort (*Pulmonaria* spp.) and pink hyacinth

SUMMER:
- Sweet alyssum (*Lobularia maritima*) and lavender
- Salvias and sages (*Salvia*) and cascading petunias (*Petunia* × *hybrida*) or calibrachoa (*Calibrachoa* spp.)
- Garden verbena (*Verbena* × *hybrida*) and miniature roses

FALL:
- Orange pot marigold (*Calendula*) and purple pansies
- French marigold (*Tagetes patula*) and dwarf blue asters
- Red kalanchoe and small red dahlias

WINTER:
- Hellebores (*Helleborus* spp.) and white or pink pansies
- Winterberry branches (*Ilex verticillata*) and bearberry (*Arctostaphylos uva-ursi*)
- Bergenia (*Bergenia cordifolia*) and white or pink crocus

In fall, the arrangement gets a seasonal makeover with mums and ornamental kale. After they retire, empty pots will hold the stage ready for the next round of performers.

Cheerful daffodils and primroses steal the scene in the same garden in early spring. Like the other seasonal performers, they are potted plants slipped into holes held ready through winter by empty 4-inch pots.

FORMAL SHRUBS

A fancy formal style in which the plant is pruned to a spiral or layers of ball-shaped foliage is known as topiary. Investigate nurseries and garden centers for topiary-trained shrubs, and maintain them with frequent haircuts.

Fashion a formal element with a classically clipped shrub or tree. Add seasonal interest by changing plants at its base.

■ Shear formal plants on a holiday schedule: Memorial Day, Fourth of July, Labor Day.
■ Use a carpenter's level to make sure that flat-topped shrubs are straight.
■ Choose evergreen shrubs in cold climates for a year-round formal accent.
■ Set up stakes and string for straight cuts.
■ Flare the bottom of a nonstandard shrub slightly outward so that sun reaches all branches.
■ Stand back often to check from all sides the regularity of the shape you are creating.
■ Use inexpensive, fast-growing privet as a substitute for boxwood.
■ Visit a nursery to find unusual plants of formal attitude, such as columnar dwarf apples.
■ Fertilize only once a month to keep the shrub from outgrowing its container.

Strong lines and a standard-trained Grecian laurel (*Laurus nobilis*) lend elegance to the formal container planting on page 41. The white-painted wooden box has a stately feel, thanks to its unadorned style and substantial size. Two wooden runners on the bottom of the box lift it to protect the area beneath from moisture and allow water to drain.

The Grecian laurel is frost-tender, so this is an all-season planting in mild areas but a

warm-weather choice for colder regions. In cold climes, overwinter it on a sunporch or any other area with very bright light, or substitute a formally sheared conifer, such as juniper.

FORMAL PRUNING STYLES

Controlled growth is the watchword of a formal planting. The Grecian laurel shown on page 41 is pruned into a standard, a style in which a vertical stem supports a clipped head of foliage or flowers on top. You can find already-trained roses, ivy, ficus, and other plants at nurseries, or you can do your own training with the plant of your choice. Other formal styles you might find at nurseries include topiary trained in the shape of globes, cubes, cones, pyramids, spirals, and even fanciful animal shapes.

FORMAL PLANTERS

Simplicity is always in style in a formal garden. Look for containers with straight lines, which echo the defined edges of beds and walkways. Square-sided boxes and rectangular patio planters have a solid dignity that works well with the structure of this style of garden.

Curving urns and more fanciful containers can also be incorporated into a formal garden, as a contrast to the strict regimentation of the design. To make effective use of a small container in a formal garden, elevate a pot on a post or column, or use a pair of matching containers atop a wall to flank a gate.

GOOD CONTAINER SHRUBS FOR FORMAL PRUNING

■ Arborvitae (*Thuja* spp.)
■ Azalea (*Rhododendron* spp.)
■ Barberry (*Berberis* spp.)
■ Boxwood (*Buxus* spp.)
■ Citrus (*Citrus* spp.)
■ Ficus (*Ficus benjamina*)
■ Hemlock (*Tsuga canadensis*)
■ Junipers (*Juniperus* spp.)
■ Privet (*Ligustrum* spp.)
■ Smooth cypress (*Cupressus arizonica* var. *glabra*)

DO-IT-YOURSELF FORMAL PRUNING

Standards and topiaries are pricey plants because of the amount of time and labor required to train them into their unusual shapes. For a low-budget substitute, shear an evergreen, either broad leaf or conifer, to a cone shape.

Columnar junipers and other plants that exhibit a natural pattern of tight, upright growth are also suited for formal containers. Or if you like an artistic challenge, try creating your own topiary design with an evergreen.

Plants pruned to a dense globe shape also lend formality in a container. This style is among the easiest to do yourself, requiring nothing more than patience with the pruners. Boxwood (*Buxus*) or even privet (*Ligustrum*) are likely subjects, because their twiggy branches fill in to create a solid mass after pruning.

In mild climates, this Grecian laurel is a permanent part of the garden. The fragrant, summer-blooming lavender at its base can be replaced with spring or winter bloomers for a seasonal display.

A mix of holly berries, evergreen boughs, and bare, red-twig dogwood branches fills the bottom of the same container in winter, setting the scene for a new season even though this arrangement is in a mild climate. In colder areas, the laurel tree must be moved indoors to escape frost.

Spring is here, say these bright tulips and blue grape hyacinths. The bulbs were prechilled for 10 weeks in a refrigerator, then planted in 6-inch plastic pots in January and kept in a cool spot in the garden. After leaves began to sprout the pots were sunk into this container (see pages 46–49).

SUMMER BOUQUETS

This living bouquet depends on daisies for season-long bloom: 'Irish Eyes' gloriosa daisy, black-eyed Susan, and red blanket flower. Marigolds carry the color lower, where lime-green sweet potato vine and 'Aureum' feverfew glow brightly against their hot-colored neighbors.

A container garden with luxuriant flowers and foliage in soft or bright colors sets a summer mood like an exuberant, just-picked bouquet, but this arrangement will keep on blooming through the season. Here's how to create your own garden "bouquet:"

■ Choose plants that supply the three basic plant forms: spiky, mounding, and spilling.
■ Use pastels to set a quiet mood, bright colors to add excitement.
■ Counter the busy effect of small-flowered, fine-textured plants with a simple container.
■ Select partners that are harmonious variations of a color or textural theme. But be sure to add a dash of contrast to create the tension necessary for a satisfying arrangement.
■ Create a focal point with a splash of bright color or bold foliage. This is especially effective when flower shapes are similar.

Whether your taste leans to soft pastels or strong summer colors, you'll find an abundance of container-worthy flowers to create a long-lasting display. These arrangements use mostly annuals, which bloom heavily from spring until fall.

WARM COLORS, HOT SUMMERS

When summer heat makes spirits sag, a pot of bright flowers is a quick pick-me-up. Daisies highlight the summer planting in a 17-inch glazed ceramic pot shown at left, which is splashed with the golden pinwheels of gloriosa daisy (one plant each of dark-eyed *Rudbeckia hirta* and green-centered *R. hirta* 'Irish Eyes') and warmed with the Indian-blanket reds of a blanket flower (one plant of *Gaillardia* 'Goblin'). One plant of yellow marigold (*Tagetes* 'Disco') and three plants of a redder cultivar, 'Bonanza Spry', continue the warm tones. Dramatic lime-green sweet potato vine foliage (two plants of *Ipomoea batatas* 'Margarita') and chartreuse feverfew (one plant of *Tanacetum parthenium* 'Aureum') add unusual contrast.

COOL IT OFF WITH PASTELS

Bright 'Liberty Light Pink' snapdragon is the focal point of the mostly pastels summer bouquet on page 43. Two 4-inch pots were planted in a 24-inch container and pinched to encourage bushiness and more flowers. They were filled out with a tall clump of 'Lime Green' flowering tobacco (*Nicotiana* 'Lime Green' in two 4-inch pots) partnered with blue cape plumbago (a 1-gallon specimen of *Plumbago auriculata* 'Royal Cape') for height, and softened with a ruff of small daisies. The gentle sulfur-yellow flowers of the coreopsis (*Coreopsis verticillata* 'Moonbeam' in one 4-inch pot) visually separate the blue of the plumbago from the lavender of the Mexican daisy (*Erigeron karvinskianus* 'Moerheimii' in three 4-inch pots). The trailing daisies and arching Mexican feather grass (*Stipa tenuissima*, one 4-inch pot) leave the more upright plants to blend into a romantic melange of soft color.

The pot may look like natural clay, but it is a high-density polyurethane foam guaranteed not to chip, crack, break, fade, or leak for three years. The planter withstands extremes of heat to 140 degrees F and cold to minus 40 degrees F, so it is ideal for any climate. Its clean lines and light color were chosen so as not to overwhelm the pastel bouquet within.

As casual as a cottage garden, this pastel summer arrangement of annuals, perennials, and ornamental grass shows to best effect against a darker background. Tall 'Lime Green' flowering tobacco holds the limelight, partnered with pink snapdragons, yellow 'Moonbeam' coreopsis, lavender Mexican daisies, blue cape plumbago, and a soft tuft of delicate Mexican feather grass.

LIGHT YELLOW FLOWERS

To create a pastel color scheme, select yellow flowers that lean toward moonlight rather than zingy bright or deep-toned yellows that shout rather than whisper. Here are some good choices:
'Happy Returns' daylily (*Hemerocallis*)
'Liberty Yellow' snapdragon (*Antirrhinum*)
'Moonshine' yarrow (*Achillea*)
'Penny Chiffon Yellow' viola (*Viola*)
'Prism Yellow' petunia (*Petunia*)
'Trailing Yellow' calibrachoa (*Calibrachoa*)
'Whirlybird Cream' nasturtium (*Tropaeolum majus*)

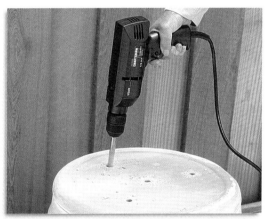

If your container is lacking an escape route for water, use a masonry bit to drill several well-spaced holes about ⅜ to ½ inch in diameter.

CHARTREUSE FLOWERS AND FOLIAGE

CHARTREUSE FLOWERS:
Cushion spurge (*Euphorbia polychroma*)
'Envy Double' zinnia (*Zinnia elegans* 'Envy')
Lady's mantle (*Alchemilla mollis*)
Langsdorff tobacco (*Nicotiana langsdorffii*)
'Lime Green' flowering tobacco (*Nicotiana* 'Lime Green')

CHARTREUSE FOLIAGE:
Golden feverfew (*Tanacetum parthenium* 'Aureum')
'Limelight' helichrysum (*Helichrysum petiolare* 'Limelight')
'Margarita' sweet potato vine (*Ipomoea batatas* 'Margarita')
Yellow moneywort (*Lysimachia nummularia* 'Aurea')

SUMMER FRAGRANCE

Angel's trumpet (*Brugmansia*)
Heliotrope (*Heliotropium arborescens*)
Jasmine (*Jasminum*)
Madagascar jasmine (*Stephanotis floribunda*)
Mignonette (*Reseda odorata*)
Oriental lily (*Lilium* hybrids)
Petunia, especially light colors (*Petunia*)
Stock (*Matthlula*)
Sweet alyssum (*Lobularia maritima*)
Tuberose (*Polianthes tuberosa*)

TROPICAL EFFECT

Think big, bold, and bright for a tropical effect. Depend on dramatic foliage to create the mood.

■ Include one outstanding plant as the focus of the group.
■ Place multiple pots as you would the plants in a single container, using vertical plants to punctuate mounding ones, and fronting the arrangement with plants that spill.
■ Brighten a shady area with colorful foliage and shiny leaves that reflect dim light.
■ Group containers so that they are easily accessible for watering and other care.
■ Use big-leaved squash, leafy corn, and red-stemmed chard in large pots to evoke the tropics, where many vegetables originated.

Tropical arrangements are no place for a delicate touch. Fill your containers with plants that shout for attention with large leaves and unusual foliage. The tropical arrangements for both sun and shade on these pages include a number of pots grouped for a lush, large-scale look. Planting in separate containers gives you the freedom to move plants in and out of the arrangement at will. Find a new candidate on the houseplant counter or at the nursery? Two minutes is all it takes to add another pot to the jungle.

Containers are secondary to plants for ornament in a tropical-look collection. Neutral colors and adequate sizes are the main considerations. Plastic or glazed clay pots gathered in a group help minimize water loss.

Vigorous morning glory vines (Ipomoea) clamber above containers, bringing to mind the twining creepers of the tropical rain forest.

Evoke the sun-drenched tropics with the huge leaves of canna and elephant ear, partnered with exotic, dark-leaved dahlia and 'Blackie' sweet potato vine. Bright pink and red dahlia flowers and a chartreuse 'Margarita' sweet potato vine add more color.

PLANTS FOR A BOLD, TROPICAL LOOK

These plants will grow to good size in a single season.

Angel's trumpet (*Brugmansia; Datura*)
Bamboo (*Bambusa, Phyllostachys*)
Banana (*Musa* and *Ensete*)
Canna (*Canna*)
Castor bean (*Ricinus communis*)
Cordyline (*Cordyline australis*)
Elephant ear (*Colocasia*)
Flowering maple (*Abutilon*)
Fountain grass (*Pennisetum*)
Fuchsia (*Fuchsia triphylla*)
Hosta, large-leaved types (*Hosta*)
Kentia palm (*Howea forsteriana*)
Mandevilla (*Mandevilla*)
Mexican sunflower (*Tithonia rotundifolia*)
New Zealand flax (*Phormium tenax*)
Rubber tree (*Ficus elastica*)

A splash of bright flowers is welcome, but foliage is the backbone of the tropical effect. That doesn't mean your tropical garden will be all green. Coleus, sweet potato vine, canna, and caladium are only a few of the many plants with leaves as flashy as flowers in reds, yellows, chartreuse, and a burgundy so deep it's almost black.

Partner strong colors with equally hearty plants that have big leaves or a bold, upright stance. The huge, furled leaves of cannas give an instant dose of the tropics, as do the giant flags of banana plants (*Musa* and *Ensete*) and the immense spades of elephant ear (*Colocasia esculenta*).

Coleus (*Solenostemon*) is as popular today for foliage color as it was two generations ago. It fills out fast to make mounded layers of beautiful colored foliage, and a rainbow of leaf colors is available. Much newer to the gardening scene, the versatile sweet potato vine (*Ipomoea batatas*) has become an instant favorite. Look for dramatically dark 'Blackie', or 'Margarita', a sprightly chartreuse.

THINK HOUSEPLANTS FOR SHADE

For a shade garden of tropical greenery, turn to these houseplants and arrange them outdoors for the summer.

Bird's-nest fern
Bromeliads
Cast-iron plant
Chinese evergreen
Clivia
Croton
Dracaena

Japanese fatsia
Palms
Split-leaf philodendron
Spotted dumb cane
Staghorn fern
Umbrella plant (*Schefflera*)
Wandering Jew

Splashy foliage sets a tropical mood in shade as houseplants take a holiday. Snowy caladium and a starburst of 'Star Bright' spotted dumb cane light the deep greens of palm and fatsia. Impatiens and coleus add color.

OVERWINTERING BULBS AND RHIZOMES

Tender tropicals and subtropicals rarely survive cold winters, so gardeners in colder zones must take measures to protect dormant bulbs over winter. In most cases, the best way to store them is to simply leave them in the pot and move it to a cool place protected from freezing, such as an unheated garage. Divide them and replant in spring.

If the pot is too big to move, dig up the bulbs or rhizomes of cannas, begonias, and other nonhardy plants after frost kills off the top growth but before the ground freezes. After you dig the bulbs, gently remove or wash away soil, snip off old foliage, and allow the bulbs to dry. Then pack them so that they do not touch each other in slightly damp peat moss or vermiculite in moisture-resistant containers; a plastic sweater box with the top set on loosely is ideal. Keep in a cool place protected from freezing over winter, and replant in spring.

EARLY SPRING

Growing bulbs in a container is an easy way to enjoy lots of spring color, so plan to slip some early bloomers into pots when you add daffodils and other early spring charmers to your garden in autumn.

■ Choose varieties that bloom at or near the same time for concentrated effect.
■ Or combine a succession of bulbs with early spring perennials for longer bloom.
■ Pack small bulbs atop larger ones to fill every inch with color.
■ Give bulbs their needed chill period by planting in fall and keeping the container in a cool place protected from freezing (such as an unheated garage) until spring.
■ Plant some of the same bulbs in nearby garden areas to visually expand the display.

A small number of bulbs makes a big splash when you put them in a pretty pot or a window box. Instead of the 50 narcissus you might need in a garden bed, you'll find that a container looks good with as few as a half dozen bulbs. The large, rectangular container shown on these pages is 31 inches long, 11 inches wide, 8 inches deep, and made of molded plastic. It holds nine 'Quail' narcissus and 15 blue glory-of-the-snow (*Chionodoxa*)

Choose bulbs according to their flowering time to enjoy simultaneous blooms. Wiry-stemmed Iceland poppies and white 'Snow Cap' rockcress add grace notes to this early season garden of multiflowered 'Quail' narcissus and blue glory-of-the-snow.

bulbs, along with a few plants each of Iceland poppies (*Papaver nudicaule*) and 'Snow Cap' rockcress (*Arabis caucasica*).

As with other container plantings, get the fullest effect by planting as closely as you can. Because the tight spacing may reduce the size or numbers of flowers in succeeding years, it's best to plant anew each fall. Include early perennials and annuals to add variety to the form and foliage of the bulbs and to lengthen the display as the early bulbs fade.

If you want to reuse the bulbs after the flowers are finished, move the container to a holding area and continue watering and fertilizing as the bulb foliage fades. After it has yellowed and dried, transplant bulbs and perennials to garden beds, freeing your container for a new display next year. The bulbs should recover and begin blooming again after their second year in the ground.

WHEN TO PLANT BULBS

ZONES 3–5: Plant hardy bulbs in September, October, or November. Bulbs will survive winter outdoors only in containers that are at least 3 feet across and protected from freezing (see pages 28–29). For smaller containers, plant bulbs in fall in 6-inch plastic pots and overwinter them in a cool place (35 to 50 degrees F is ideal) that is protected from freezing, such as an unheated garage. In spring, when bulb growth is beginning to emerge, sink the pots into a larger container and plant blooming annuals and perennials around them. You can also carefully slip the root ball out and plant it without the pot.

ZONES 6–7: Plant bulbs in October, November, or December. The containers can survive winter outdoors if they are at least 2 feet across. Plant pansies with the bulbs in fall, but other blooming annuals and perennials should be added to the container in spring. Or plant smaller containers in spring using the techniques described above for Zones 3–5.

ZONES 8–11: Plant prechilled hardy bulbs (see page 49) in November, December, or January. You can plant cool-season annuals and perennials at the same time you plant the bulbs, placing them in the container first and then settling the bulbs closely around them. Use a light-colored container (dark containers trap heat) and place it in the coolest part of your garden until bulb foliage begins to emerge.

HOW TO LAYER BULBS

Maximize the limited planting space in a container by planting layers of small bulbs over larger ones, as if you were making lasagna. Depending on the bulbs you choose and their recommended planting depths, you can expect to sandwich two or even three layers into a container. The larger bulbs of daffodils go at a depth of 4 to 6 inches, topped by smaller bulbs of miniature daffodils at a depth of 3 to 4 inches, followed by the smallest bulbs, such as glory-of-the-snow, grape hyacinth, and crocus, at 2 to 3 inches. Fill the container with enough potting mix to put the first layer of bulbs at the right depth. Space them more closely than recommended for in-ground planting; the bulbs can even touch each other, but be sure to leave 1 to 2 inches of space between the bulbs and the sides of the container. Cover with an inch or two of soil, then add the next layer of bulbs. Don't worry if you forget exactly where the lower layers are planted; the stouter plants will wiggle their way between any small bulbs on top.

EARLY- TO MIDSEASON BULBS

VERY EARLY
Crocus tommasinianus
Dwarf iris (Iris reticulata)
'February Gold' daffodil
'Rijnveld's Early Sensation' daffodil
Snowdrops (Galanthus)

EARLY
'Beersheba' daffodil
Dutch crocus (Crocus vernus)
Glory-of-the-snow (Chionodoxa)
'King Alfred' daffodil
'Quail' narcissus
'Tete-a-tete' miniature daffodil

EARLY MIDSEASON
'Barrett Browning' narcissus
'Carlton' daffodil
'Dutch Master' daffodil
Fosteriana tulips
Grape hyacinth (Muscari)
Greigii tulips
'Ice Follies' daffodil
Kaufmanniana tulips
Squill (Scilla)

MIDSEASON
Darwin tulips
Dutch hyacinth
Fringed tulips
'Jack Snipe' miniature daffodil
'Minnow' miniature daffodil
'Mount Hood' daffodil

Early-spring perennials keep the container garden looking good after the bulbs retire. The first few buds of bright Iceland poppies (Papaver nudicaule) *open while the daffodils are going strong, as you can see on page 46, but their best show comes later, extending the season of this garden.*

TULIPS FOR SPRING

Treat yourself to a concentrated dose of late-spring color by filling a container with tulips and hyacinths partnered by long-blooming spring annuals and perennials.

■ Make sure that hardy bulbs such as tulips and Dutch hyacinths get the period of cold they need, but protect them from freezing.
■ Buy spring annuals and perennials when they're in bud and bloom to add to the container at the proper time for your area.
■ Heighten textural interest by including plants with foliage that contrasts with the smooth, broad leaves of the bulbs.

■ Select bulbs with different bloom seasons for a longer display.

Tulips steal the show in this planting because of their height and big flowers. The mood of the garden is much softer when only the earlier hyacinths and accessory plants are in bloom. Take advantage of the strong personality of tulips by selecting a color that contrasts sharply with their surroundings. If the container will be viewed against a dark wall or hedge, boost the contrast by planting white, pastel, or bright yellow tulips. If the background is light, skip the delicate colors and plant bright tones or dramatic deep hues.

This container is viewed from the top and all sides, so the plants are arranged to look appealing from any angle. Twenty-four 'Don Quichotte' tulips form the centerpiece, flanked by two clumps of eight hyacinth bulbs and circled by 'Penny Azure Wing' violas and pink 'Galaxy Rose' English daisies, bought in multipacks at a garden center. Four grassy clumps of lilyturf (*Liriope spicata* 'Silver Dragon'), transplanted from 1-gallon plastic pots, punctuate the small flowers.

If you are not using a weatherproof container for the finished arrangement, plant the tulip and hyacinth bulbs the preceding fall in 6-inch plastic pots and keep them moist over winter in a cool place protected from freezing (see page 49). When the bulbs begin to send up their first pointed shoots in spring, carefully slip them out of the plastic pots, keeping the root balls intact, and transplant them to the final container.

To plant the container, begin with the lilyturf. When it is in place, add the bulbs. Fill in with potting mix to the appropriate depth for smaller companion flowers, then plant them.

Other cool-season companions attractive with spring bulbs include pansies (*Viola* × *wittrockiana*), edging lobelia (*Lobelia erinus*), primroses (*Primula* × *polyanthes*, *P. obconica*, *P. malacoides*), and periwinkle (*Vinca minor*).

Tulips and hyacinths seldom perform well a second year after their performance in a pot and are usually grown as annuals. Discard them after blooming is over and replace with new ones the next fall. If you want to try planting them out in the garden, keep them moist after blooming until the foliage yellows and dies back.

'Don Quichotte' tulips burst open in an explosion of color that is echoed by the charming faces of English daisies and violas snuggled around the rim of the pot. The container is a concrete bulb bowl 36 inches in diameter and 12 inches deep. This arrangement is a later version of that shown on page 49. By the time the tulips bloom, the hyacinths are finished, but the silvery lilyturf and the small flowers are still going strong.

CHILLING HARDY BULBS

Most spring-blooming bulbs need 10 to 15 weeks of cold between 35 and 50 degrees F in order to bloom well. Tulips and hyacinths are most demanding of proper winter chilling to initiate flower buds; daffodils are less picky. A few of the more tender bulbs, such as paperwhite narcissus and freesia, perform well with little or no winter chill. If you're not sure which bulbs require winter chill, ask at your local full-service nursery when you buy them.

To chill hardy bulbs, first plant them in the fall in 6-inch plastic pots and potting mix, inserting a plant label in each pot identifying the variety and the date of planting. Be sure the bulbs have excellent drainage; use a fast-draining potting mix and pots with drainage holes. Protect the bulbs from freezing by placing them in an unheated garage or other protected area where temperatures are cool but not freezing. Be sure to keep the pots moist (but not soggy) throughout winter; water is important for root development as well as helpful to protect the bulbs from frost injury.

In Zones 6–7 you can provide proper chilling by overwintering large containers (at least 2 feet in diameter) outdoors, or by sinking small pots of bulbs to their rims in a bed of sand or soil and mulching well.

If you live in Zones 8–11, buy prechilled tulip and hyacinth bulbs or give them the prechilling they need by storing the bulbs for 10 to 15 weeks in the vegetable bin of a refrigerator before planting. Do not store with apples or other ripening fruits and vegetables; these emit ethylene gas, which can have an adverse effect on the bulbs. Since some bulbs are poisonous, prechilling them in your refrigerator is not recommended if you have small children.

If you intend to plant a lot of bulbs each year, consider purchasing a secondhand (but functioning) refrigerator dedicated to this purpose. Besides being excellent for chilling bulbs over winter, a gardener's refrigerator is useful all summer for holding cut flowers while they wait to be arranged, storing extra produce from the vegetable garden, and stratifying certain seeds that require a period of chill before planting.

The tulip and hyacinth bulbs in the arrangement were planted in plastic pots in the fall, chilled for 10 weeks in a refrigerator, then placed in an unheated garage until they began to sprout in spring.

After the chilled bulbs rooted and began to sprout, they were transplanted to a large concrete bowl along with the lilyturf, violas, and English daisies. Pink and blue are the theme for this spring bulb garden; the pointed shoots of tulips-to-come are visible in the center of the container.

LATE-MIDSEASON TO LATE-SEASON BULBS

LATE MIDSEASON
'Baby Moon' miniature daffodil
Double tulips
Hyacinth
'Misty Glen' daffodil
Poet's narcissus
'Primeur' daffodil
Spanish bluebell
Triumph tulips

LATE SEASON
Alliums
Bunch-flowering tulips
'Camelot' daffodil
'Hawera' miniature daffodil
Lily-flowered tulips
Parrot tulips
Rembrandt tulips
'Stainless' daffodil

WINDOW BOX FOR SUMMER

The semiformal attitude of geraniums (four 4-inch pots of **Pelargonium** *'Pinto Red') relaxes into casual dress when accessorized with three 4-inch pots each of 'Bright Red' garden verbena, cascading blue* **Anagallis monellii,** *and white calibrachoa. 'Silver Dust' dusty miller* (**Senecio cineraria**) *in two 4-inch pots adds a mid-height focal point to this all-American window box.*

Window boxes add instant charm. Fill them with annuals that bloom for months or with foliage plants that don't need fussing to keep looking good.

■ Keep things simple with only a few repeated kinds and colors of plants.
■ Place boxes at the windows flanking the front door to signal the entrance.
■ Edge each box with trailing plants for a visual transition to the garden below the window.
■ Fertilize frequently to keep growth healthy and vigorous.
■ Include tall plants to screen an unsightly view from inside the house.
■ Use potting mix with high water-holding capacity, a self-watering window box, or water-holding mats to reduce watering chores.

Old-fashioned favorites, window boxes are timeless additions that beautify your house, link the house to the garden, and give you room to grow more plants. Making a window box is a satisfying project even for a novice, requiring few tools and little expense.

WINDOW BOX CHOICES

Wooden, plastic, clay, or metal boxes are all long-lasting and attractive. Choose a style that complements your house and suits your budget. Most have classic, simple lines suitable for any type of architecture or garden style. Some are ornamented with molded decorations or dressed-up edges and finials. For an English village feel, try a metal hayrack-type window box, with open, curving slats lined with fibrous matting (such as coir) to hold the soil.

Plastic boxes are lighter weight than wood but still need sturdy mounts. Self-watering plastic boxes have a water-holding reservoir beneath the soil. In cold-winter areas, protect clay, plastic, or metal boxes from the weather, just as you would other containers (see pages 28–29). In mild climates, boxes of any material are fine for year-round use.

If your budget is limited or you like doing home projects, make your own wooden boxes. Or use a large metal or plastic window box liner as a box, without slipping it into another container, for an inexpensive alternative.

BUILDING A BOX

A pine box protected by a coat of paint or wood preservative will give you several years of reliable use. Redwood, cypress, and cedar are highly resistant to decay but are more costly. Use screws to join the box instead of nails, which can pull out. A strip of decorative molding (available at any home supply store or lumberyard), nailed along the bottom edges of the box on front and sides, adds a quick, low-cost finishing touch.

Extend the life of a wooden box by installing a metal or plastic liner to hold the soil and protect the wood from moisture. Preformed liners are widely available in various sizes. Choose a size that slips easily into your box with an inch or more of space between liner and wood. You can use more than one liner to better fill a large box. Metal liners tend to rust after a few seasons, whereas plastic ones are impervious to water.

A BIG ENOUGH BOX

Select a box that extends to at least the edges of the window frame. Annuals are usually shallow-rooted, so any box 6 inches deep will give them a comfortable home to spread their roots. Deeper boxes hold more soil; they will be heavier but less prone to drying out quickly. The depth from front to back of the box interior should be enough—at least 5 inches—to allow you to place two ranks of plants in the container: a rear row and a front edging row of lower growers. If the box is 8 inches wide, you can shoehorn in a row of mid-height flowers in the middle. The box shown on these pages is 9½ inches deep, 8 inches wide, and 39 inches long; it was made from one 1×10 finish-grade pine board 8 feet long, plus a 2×2 for the runners and ½-inch plywood for the bottom.

PLANTING AND WATERING

Choose plant colors to contrast with or complement the color of your house or its trim. Bright hues and white flowers show up well at a distance, but even a monochrome green palette will make your domicile more inviting by adding the touch of living plants. For a formal look, avoid trailing plants and use only those with an upright posture.

It's a hot life beneath most windows, where sun is reflected from the glass and the wall of the house absorbs solar heat. Boxes in full sun are likely to need daily watering. You will probably not be able to align the drainage holes of preformed liners with the holes in the outer box, so punch new ones to make sure the soil stays well-drained.

To prevent drain holes from becoming blocked by the window box's supporting shelf, nail a pair of 1-inch or 2-inch-high runners to the bottom of the box to allow open space between the box and the shelf.

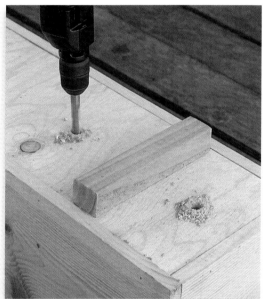

Drill a generous number of ½- to ¾-inch-diameter drain holes into the bottom of the box so that excess water can run off freely after a rain or watering session.

Paint the box with one coat of oil-based primer, then two coats of exterior-grade acrylic latex to protect the wood from moisture and to make the box an ornamental addition to your house. The final color match shown on page 50 was achieved by bringing home sample chips from the paint store.

WINDOW BOX WITH WHITE THEME

This all-white planting features 'White Domino' flowering tobacco, 'Vintage White' stock, 'Sugar Baby' Marguerite daisies, 'Happy Festival' baby's breath, and 'Silver Brocade' dusty-miller (Artemisia stelleriana). The 4-foot fiberglass box has been painted teal to match the house trim. Metal hangers bolt to the house and slip under the lip of the box.

The simplicity of using all-white flowers and silvery foliage can be stunning, but if you prefer another color scheme, you can still follow these suggestions for planning and planting and just use all blue, pink, or yellow flowers, or whatever suits your fancy.

■ Depend on annuals for the longest-lasting floral display.
■ Choose perennials that contribute good foliage or form when they're not in bloom.
■ Paint the box to add accent color to the arrangement.
■ Include several kinds of flower shapes in a single-color planting to add visual interest.
■ Select low-growing plants for an unobstructed view from the window.
■ Snip back sprawling plants as needed to keep growth full and prevent bare-legged stems.
■ For proper window box placement, measure twice, install once.

One look at your elegant, all-white window box arrangement announces to passersby that a person of artistic sensibilities lives within.

They'll never guess that you chose the arrangement as much for its ease as for its beauty! A single-color planting frees you to concentrate on form and texture, so you end up with a combination that satisfies all the basics of design with little effort.

POSITIONING THE BOX

Window box plantings are most appealing when plants reach the glass and even nestle against it. Place your window box so that its top edge is just below the window frame. Avoid the temptation to use the windowsill as a support: it is not designed to bear such a burden. If your windowsill protrudes outward, position the box below the sill.

To make sure your boxes are well-centered and evenly placed from one window to the next, use a measuring tape. Have a helper hold the box at the window so that you can decide on a satisfactory height. Use a level to make sure the windowbox is correctly placed. While your helper holds the box in place, mark the position of the bottom of the box with a short chalk line on the wall. Then

Use a stud finder to locate the supporting structure of the wall. Attach your window box to studs to make sure its weight is well-supported.

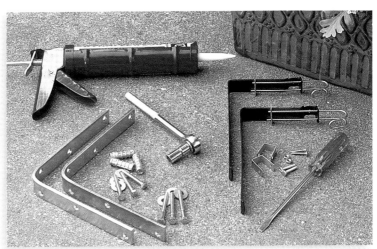

Assemble the hardware and tools you will need to attach the box before you begin mounting it. Use strong brackets and sturdy screws that won't pull loose.

measure the width of the window frame and the width of the box. Subtract the smaller dimension from the larger and divide the remainder in half to determine how far from the edge of the window frame the corners of the box should be. If you have a 30-inch-wide window frame, for example, and your box is 40 inches long, mark a point 5 inches beyond the frame for the outer corners. Use a straightedge to make sure the box aligns horizontally with the window frame, and mark the position of the box on the wall with chalk.

MOUNTING THE BOX

A filled window box is heavy; you will need sturdy hardware to hold it securely in place. You can attach the window box to the wall with brackets, or use a shelf to support it as shown on page 50.

Some brackets, including commonly available L-shaped metal strips, must be attached to both box and wall with screws or bolts. Use them for wooden window boxes that remain in place all year. Attach brackets to the empty box and add liner, potting mix, and plants when it is in place. You can also use this type of bracket to attach a supporting shelf to hold the window box. These brackets are for permanent placement; you won't be able to lift off the box to replant or store it over winter without undoing the mounting. Many brackets are nearly invisible in use, so they allow all the attention to be focused on the box and its arrangement of plants.

Brackets that support the box from beneath are more versatile. Two or three of them, spaced along the box, provide a strong platform for support. Because they are not attached to the box, they are ideal for any type of window box, and for permanent or removable displays. Garden centers and home supply stores stock a wide variety, from plain metal bars with an upturned tip to keep the box from sliding forward, to fanciful creations that add style to the display. Or you can make your own simple or fancy brackets from wood. If you want the brackets to be unobtrusive, use a simple style and paint them the same color as the container.

A box placed tightly against the house can cause moisture damage to the window frame and siding. Prevent problems by mounting the brackets so that the box is held 2 to 3 inches away from the wall to allow air circulation.

TOP 15 WHITE WINDOW BOX PLANTS

Check the label or catalog description to be sure that the plant has white flowers; most of these plants are available in other colors besides white.

African daisy (*Arctotis* spp.)
Begonia (*Begonia* spp.)
Calibrachoa (*Calibrachoa*)
Edging lobelia (*Lobelia erinus*)
Flowering tobacco (*Nicotiana*)
Geranium (*Pelargonium* spp.)
Impatiens (*Impatiens* × *walleriana*)
Ivy Geranium (*Pelargonium* spp.)

Lantana (*Lantana* spp.)
Blue salvia (*Salvia farinacea*)
Moonflower (*Ipomoea alba*)
Pansies (*Viola* × *wittrockiana*)
Petunias (*Petunia* spp.)
Sweet alyssum (*Lobularia maritima*)
Verbena hybrids (*Verbena* × *hybrida*)

SHADE

Practice your design skills by playing with colored foliage and varied form to create a pretty container garden for shade.

■ Use similar pots to unify diverse groupings.
■ Highlight flashy foliage by planting in plain pots that don't compete for attention.
■ Give the eye a strong accent plant to discover first, before the gaze wanders to quieter neighbors.
■ Vary height in a grouped arrangement with pots of different sizes or in elevated positions.
■ Allow access on all sides of the grouping for watering and other care.
■ Depend on variegated and lime green foliage to add light to a shady nook.
■ Spotlight a single eye-catching plant in a small container.

Even a deeply shaded garden can come alive with color. Spark a grouping of plants in a dim corner with the color-rich accents of begonias, which bloom for months, and the fleeting but lovely spires of red, pink, or white astilbe (*Astilbe* × *arendsii*).

Eye-catching foliage is another solution to liven up shade. Notice how magnetic the white-edged leaves of the hostas (*Hosta* 'Wide Brim') are in the arrangement shown below.

Light green leaves like those of silver-edged goutweed (*Aegopodium podagraria* 'Variegatum') at the lower right in the photograph below also bring life to a shady nook, almost as if a shaft of sunlight were penetrating the planting. This perennial is sometimes planted as a ground cover but can become invasive once it's established. If you use it in a container, never set it free!

In the center of the group is a true beauty, Japanese painted fern (*Athyrium nipponicum* 'Pictum'), with a rosette of fronds tinged with red and splashed with silver. Many hardy ferns are indispensible for creating a tropical effect. Other choices might include the evergreen Christmas fern (*Polystichum acrostichoides*), holly fern (*Cyrtomium falcatum*), and soft shield fern (*Polystichum setiferum*).

HOW DEEP IS YOUR SHADE?

Most shade gardens aren't in the dark all day long. As the sun moves through the sky, occasional shafts or patches of sunlight will illuminate various plants in the collection. If this is the case in your chosen site, too, place the plants that prefer partial shade, such as bellflower, in the areas that get the most light. Partial shade, which means an hour or two of direct sun or several hours of dappled sun, greatly expands the possible plant choices for a shade garden.

COLORFUL FOLIAGE AND FLOWERS FOR SHADE CONTAINERS

FOLIAGE
Begonias (*Begonia* × *rex* and angelwing types)
Bergenia (*Bergenia* spp.)
Coleus (*Solenostemon*)
Coral bells (*Heuchera* spp.)
English ivy, variegated or lime green cultivars (*Hedera helix*)
Hostas, variegated, lime green, or blue-gray cultivars (*Hosta* spp.)
Lungwort (*Pulmonaria* spp.)
Ornamental sweet potato (*Ipomoea batatas* 'Blackie' and 'Margarita')

FLOWERS
Astilbe (*Astilbe* hybrids)
Begonia (*Begonia* spp.)
Camellia (*Camellia* spp.)
Fuchsia (*Fuchsia* spp.)
Hellebore (*Helleborus* spp.)
Impatiens (*Impatiens* hybrids)
Lily-of-the-valley (*Convallaria majalis*)
Pansy (*Viola* × *wittrockiana*)

When flower choices are skimpy because of shade, turn to foliage that's striped, splashed with white, or glowing with bright color. White-edged hostas add the spark to this grouping. Potted begonias will bloom nonstop; the tall astilbe can be retired when its plumes of flowers fade. Other interesting foliage plants—a Japanese painted fern, 'Cappuccino' coral bells, and a pot of silver-edged goutweed—add diverse texture and color.

HOT SUN

For success in a hot, dry climate, turn to plants that flourish with minimal moisture. Special adaptations such as the swollen leaves and stems of succulents and cacti allow them to hold their precious reserves for the dry season. Fuzzy or waxy leaves slow down the evaporation of water from the plant, and those sneaky spines deter animals from taking an interest in browsing. If you have an ounce of collector's blood in your veins, beware of cacti and succulents. Acquiring a collection of these plants, which come in an incredible variety of forms and flowers, can be a lifelong obsession.

Many succulents and other arid-country plants—such as yucca, many sedums, and cacti in the genus *Opuntia*—are surprisingly hardy in containers.

A few "normal" flowering plants also thrive in blast furnace conditions. The genus *Salvia*, mostly native to the arid regions of the Americas, is one of the best sources of plants that laugh at drought and heat. Familiar red garden sage, for example, needs less water than most other annuals.

Variegated agave is the star of this full-sun garden. A small specimen springing from a blanket of small-leaved Sedum rubrotinctum *mirrors the larger plant in a stand-alone pot. The bluish leaves of* Senecio mandraliscae *and the near-black leaves of* Aeonium *'Zwartkop' provide dramatic counterpoint, and 'Red Hot Sally' salvia brightens the group with color that attracts hummingbirds from across the garden.*

Mulch succulents and cacti with tiny pebbles or gravel to protect their shallow roots from getting washed out by a deluge of rain or a forceful garden hose. A quarter inch of mulch is adequate and also creates a natural backdrop for these dry-country plants. All pots are unglazed terra-cotta.

CONTAINER PLANTS THAT TAKE THE HEAT

Aeonium 'Zwartkop'
Agaves (*Agave*)
Aloes (*Aloe*)
Bedding geraniums (*Pelargonium*)
Cacti (many species)
Cosmos (*Cosmos*)
Hen and chicks (*Sempervivum*)
Kalanchoes (*Kalanchoe*)

Moss rose (*Portulaca*)
Petunia (*Petunia*)
Salvias (*Salvia*)
Sedums (*Sedum*)
Senecio mandraliscae
Vinca (*Catharanthus*)
Yucca (*Yucca*)
Zinnia (*Zinnia*)

WATER GARDENS

Water lettuce floats serenely on the surface of a garden in a simple glazed pot. Dwarf papyrus contributes contrasting angled texture, and nearby potted plants add a dash of color.

Growing a water garden in a container will let you experiment with new plants and new techniques, but the best reason for this garden is the pleasure that it will give you. Here are some tips to create a successful container water garden:

■ Fill the container with water and wait two days before planting to make sure it is waterproof. If it leaks, seal minor cracks from the inside with aquarium sealant.

■ Top off the container with fresh water as needed to replace any loss to evaporation.

Plants are secondary to this magnificent container, which is itself the initial focus of the arrangement. Plant sparingly so that you can enjoy the sight of some open water between the textural delight of the plants.

■ Remove excess floating plants by lifting them above the water and slicing off unwanted parts with pruners.
■ Feed fish only as much as they eat in five minutes, to prevent fouling the water.
■ Simplify small containers by limiting them to just one or two kinds of plants.
■ In cold areas, overwinter plants indoors in a dishpan or plastic tub of water, placed in a sunny spot. Or buy new plants each year.
■ Keep the surface of the water clean by using an aquarium net to skim off fallen leaves and other debris.

WATERPROOF CONTAINER

Any container that holds water—or can be made to hold water—can be the start of a small, serene water garden.

Finding a container that holds water is easy. Home decor stores are filled with all kinds of possibilities, from kitchen mixing bowls to painted Chinese fishbowls. Antique shops are another good place to seek out an unusual container for your water plants.

To make a leaky container waterproof, seal minor cracks with an aquarium sealant or caulk labeled for use underwater. Plug drainage holes with a rubber-gasketed, stainless-steel bolt or a piece of liner spread with caulk. Use flexible liner to waterproof wooden and other leaky containers, poking it carefully into all recesses inside the container, then affixing the liner's edges to the container with aquarium sealant or staples.

Depth is important because you will be adding plants in pots to the container. Visit a garden center or nursery to get an idea of the size of the pots of the plants you like. A small starter plant of grassy reeds may come in a 4-inch pot, whereas a ready-to-bloom lotus or water lily can come in a 2- or 3-gallon-size container. For parrot's feather, water lettuce, and other floating aquatic plants, the depth of the container is not important because their roots trail freely in the water. Select a container at least 6 inches deep for small or floating plants, or as deep a container as you can find for large plants such as pickerel weed and cattails.

PLANTS

More garden centers and nurseries are featuring water plants as they become increasingly popular. A container water garden can be a year-round asset in mild regions and a temporary beauty in colder areas.

Viewing the water itself is a big part of the charm. Use restraint when adding plants, and monitor their growth so that you can scoop out or clip back any that get out of bounds. Quiet stretches of water between the greenery make a small pool look serene.

Remember the basics of design when choosing plants. Complement low, flat-leaved types with upright, spiky rushes or iris for a dramatic effect. In a very small garden, try a single type of plant for satisfying simplicity.

Choose plants in keeping with the scale of your container. Miniature water lilies, fairy moss (*Azolla caroliniana*), miniature cattail (*Typha minima*), water-loving iris (such as *Iris laevigata*), or whirly-stemmed rush (*Juncus effusus* 'Spiralis') are excellent for growing in container water gardens. Plants that trail over the edges, such as parrot's feather (*Myriophyllum aquaticum*) with its feathery leaves, also work well.

FISH

If you want fish in your water garden, you'll have to balance the plants' need for sun with the fishes' need for oxygen. Water heated by sunlight quickly becomes depleted of oxygen. Position your water garden where it gets afternoon shade. Keep a thermometer in the water, and never let the water get warmer than 85 degrees F. If fish surface to gasp for air, aerate the water immediately. You can use a small battery-powered aeration pump or an air stone, a device connected to a small external pump and placed in the pool.

FOUNTAINS

Small fountains add appealing water music to outdoor spaces and also help oxygenate the water in a container. Most fountains are electrically powered; you will need to run a cord from an outside outlet for power. Solar-powered fountains are ideal for a large container water garden in the sun. Avoid big, high sprays; most floating plants don't like their leaves splashed. You'll need only the smallest of pumps—a bubbler is a good choice. It should allow you to adjust the spray to the right size for the container. To determine the pump size you'll need, measure the container volume by filling it from 5-gallon buckets. When you install the pump, securely seat it in the container; some pumps come with suction feet which are meant to adhere to the bottom of the container. Run the cord over the back of the container where it will be obscured by the plantings, or bury it under gravel.

Plug drainage holes with a rubber-gasketed, stainless-steel bolt or a piece of liner spread with caulk. Seal any minor cracks with caulk or brush on water garden sealant.

To grow fish and plants, add an aquarium bubbler or a spitter fountain to oxygenate the water. Conceal the cord, and plug it into a ground-fault-interrupted outlet.

Fill the container with water. Place bricks that will raise the level of the pots of aquatic plants. Before planting or stocking with fish, let the water sit for five to seven days.

Add potted plants on supports so that the tops of the pots will be below the water surface. Then add floating plants.

Allow fish to adjust gradually to the water temperature by leaving them in their original water in a plastic bag. After 10 minutes, release the fish.

HERB GARDENS

Snappy meals are just a pinch away when you grow herbs near the kitchen. They take to container culture readily.

■ Snip herbs often to keep them vigorous and looking good; dry or freeze extra clippings.
■ Experiment with a few new herbs every year to expand your palate.
■ Replace mints yearly with a pot of new cuttings or a young plant. Older plants die out or get leggy quickly in containers.

Herbs flourish in container culture, and their combined textures meld into a collection that's pretty as well as practical. Add a dash of color to the container planting with pansies, chives, calendulas, and other plants with edible blossoms. Salads will never be the same.

Start with the herbs you use the most. Parsley, basil, thyme, rosemary, and oregano figure in many favorite dishes from pasta to pizza. Visit the herb section of a nursery or garden center and you'll find dozens for adding flavor to your family dinners. Choose your favorites by using the sniff test.

Herb gardens lend themselves to themes. If you're a fan of Mexican cooking, grow your own salsa ingredients and plenty of hot peppers. For Italian cooking, oregano,

Pot marigolds look so pretty in container herb gardens that it seems a shame to eat them. But try them in potato dishes or salads for their color and subtle flavor. To learn how to grow specific herbs in containers, see page 74.

Stoop to sniff a chive blossom and you'll notice it smells sweet rather than oniony. Sprinkled in a salad or scattered atop a bowl of soup, however, the purple florets add the slight spicy tang of true chive taste.

EDIBLE FLOWERS FOR CONTAINERS

Small, bright blossoms and petals add a colorful confetti touch to food. Most flowers are fairly bland tasting; their piquancy comes from the fun of eating flowers rather than from their flavor. Violets, roses, and pansies smell much more sweet than they taste. Nasturtiums, however, are delightfully peppery, like the best Dijon mustard. Here is a list of some favorite edible flowers:

Borage (*Borago officinalis*)
Calendula (*Calendula officinalis*)
Chives (*Allium schoenoprasum*)
Daylilies (*Hemerocallis* spp.)
Lavender (*Lavandula* spp.)
Mints (*Mentha* spp.)
Nasturtium (*Tropaeolum majus*)
Pansy and violet (*Viola* spp.)
Roses (*Rosa* spp.)
Sage (*Salvia* spp.)
Tulips (*Tulipa* spp.)

BRINGING HERBS INDOORS FOR THE WINTER

Indoor life is hard on herbs, and only a few will thrive, even on the sunniest south-facing windowsill. Chives, garlic, parsley, rosemary, and thyme are more adaptable to winter windowsill culture than other herbs, although rosemary is susceptible to mildew.

Except for rosemary, cut back established plants to about 3 to 4 inches before bringing them indoors. Repot if necessary, or just bring them inside in the same container.

rosemary, parsley, marjoram and basil are the basics, plus garlic, whose green tops are as flavorful as the bulbs.

Like other plants, herbs may be perennial or annual. Potted perennials are inexpensive and the best way to start a permanent collection. Annuals are fast-growing from seed sown directly in the container. Basil, dill, and cilantro are easy to grow from seed; you can sow successive crops for ready replacements after a crop is harvested.

Most herbs are tough plants that thrive in well-drained soil and soak up heat without suffering, exactly the conditions found in a container garden. Frequent snipping and pinching don't slow down the plants—in fact, they stimulate dense, quick regrowth.

You can grow herb gardens in one or two big containers or in smaller pots grouped together. To add variety to the height of the planting, place some of the pots on overturned clay pots or other supports. Design your garden according to the dictates of your appetite: No matter what herbs you put together, they're bound to look good. Be sure the plants are easy to reach for picking. Put those you use most in front, where they're accessible for instant snipping.

PLANTING A STRAWBERRY POT WITH HERBS AND EDIBLE FLOWERS

Urn-shaped containers with planting pockets in their sides and an open top are commonly called strawberry pots, because they were once popular for growing strawberries in a small space. They are a good way to grow a lot of plants in a limited area, but the pocket areas dry out swiftly and are difficult to keep moist without waterlogging the rest of the potting mix. They also bear the full brunt of the sun on the plant roots. Thyme, oregano, and some other herbs thrive in such hot, dry conditions.

To plant a strawberry pot, fill the container with moist potting mix to the level of the lowest pockets, then settle small plants into the side pockets. With one hand on the outside of the pot and the other on the inside, push the roots as deep into the pocket as you can, then tamp the soil. Add more potting mix as needed, spooning it into place and patting it in firmly. Then fill the container to the next level of planting pockets and repeat.

Planting a trailing nasturtium in a strawberry pot.

VEGETABLES AND FRUITS

This container garden is good enough to eat— and within easy reach for picking. Many favorite vegetables adapt to a life of confinement. Yields may be reduced, but it's hard to beat the convenience of tomatoes, lettuce, peppers, and herbs just steps from the kitchen door. For a guide to cultivating specific vegetables in containers, see pages 88–89 in the "Gallery of Container Plants."

No more weeding if you move your vegetable patch to pots on the patio! Even fruit trees yield a crop in a container. Roomy pots are the key.

■ Big is better: Use large containers to help keep soil cool.
■ Fertilize food crops more generously than flowers.
■ Group containers to reduce evaporation.
■ Place edibles within easy reach for picking on the spur of the moment.
■ Try cherry tomatoes or yellow mini-pear tomatoes on the patio, and let guests pick their own hors d'oeuvres.
■ Fill window boxes with pretty ruffled lettuce.
■ Insulate containers of fruit trees and bushes in cold winters with a wire cage stuffed with dry leaves.

Whether your edible garden is perched on a balcony or an addition to in-ground plantings, container gardening gives you growing space for fresh vegetables and mouthwatering fruit—offering a satisfying harvest without the work

of weeding. A container vegetable garden is ideal for children who will enjoy the close-up look at their plants.

Fast-maturing lettuce and salad greens and heat-loving crops such as tomatoes and peppers flourish in the light soil and fast drainage of a container. Blueberries, cherries, nectarines, and other fruit trees and bushes make good patio plants, contributing significant stature and the fun of collecting a handful of tasty fruit.

DWARF FRUITS FOR CONTAINERS

Fruit trees are classified by size according to the rootstock onto which the cultivar is grafted. Dwarf rootstocks yield short trees, sized just right for container culture. All varieties of favored fruits are available in downsized cultivars. Some bush fruits also take to container culture. For more details on growing fruits in containers, see page 72.

A wooden half barrel or other large container is ideal for dwarf fruit trees and shrubs. Smaller shrubs can be accommodated in a 3-gallon container. If you have to bend roots to fit the container, it's too small.

GROW UP

Vining and trailing vegetable plants can grow like Jack's beanstalk, so make sure you're prepared to offer solid support that hoists them up instead of out. Train vines of squash, cucumbers, and pole beans along a railing or fence, or install a tepee or trellis for them to climb. Gently move young vines to the support and tie them loosely into place with short pieces of soft twine or cloth. Stake tomatoes with sturdy canes inserted deep into the container, or tie their stems to a nearby fence or trellis.

Install supports at the time you plant the containers, even though they will tower over the young plants. This avoids the root damage that can be caused by poking poles into the soil when the plant is more mature. When plants are confined to pots, every root counts toward supplying the food and water the plant needs to ensure a good harvest.

Insert poles for beans to climb, then push the large seeds about an inch into the moist planting mix. They'll sprout in just a few days.

Gently pull apart the tangled roots of peppers and other vegetable plants before scooping out a hole and setting them into the soil.

Labels are handy for jogging the memory, and they add a touch of country charm to vegetable container gardens.

ROOM TO GROW

Ample root space is the key to success with edibles. A big container holds enough potting mix for fast-growing plant roots and also provides insulation from heat. Select a pot whose size fits the plant you have in mind: Tomatoes, with their lush top growth, need more space than one jalapeño pepper plant.

Wooden boxes, half barrels, and plastic household tubs provide lots of growing room at low cost. Use pots that hold about a half gallon of potting mix for small plants, such as a single pepper.

Your planting can be pretty as well as useful. Lettuce, with its frilly green or red leaves, is an appealing accent, and the fruits of tomatoes, peppers, and eggplant offer splashes of color.

CARING FOR EDIBLES

Flowers and foliage plants are more forgiving than food plants when it comes to maintenance. Forget to water your tomatoes, and it may take them quite a while to recover from your neglect. Dropped flower buds and immature fruits are a common consequence of unreliable watering.

Water and fertilizer determine the size of the crop and the size of the individual fruits or vegetables. Enrich your potting mix with aged manure or slow-release fertilizer and replenish frequently. Water extra-generously, at least once a day in summer. Use a mist nozzle on your hose to drench the foliage, too (but never in full sun). This will invigorate the plant and help prevent pest problems. Mulch the soil surface with dried grass clippings or other organic material to help conserve moisture and prevent the sun's heat from stressing plant roots. Monitor the plants for insects or diseases just as you would in the garden.

SALAD IN A CONTAINER

Toss your salad when you plant the seeds by growing a mix of lettuces or a "mesclun" mix of familiar and unusual greens. Such mixes sell for premium prices at supermarkets and restaurants but mature in as little as three weeks from seed sown directly in a container.

The picking is easy because you won't have to worry about weeds being mixed with your greens. A few slices just above root level with a pair of scissors, and the makings of tonight's dinner salad are in your hands. The shorn plants will quickly sprout new growth for another harvest.

BUTTERFLY GARDENS

This butterfly garden packs in the purple with Aster cordifolius *'Little Carlow', 'Marine' heliotrope, 'Surfinia' petunias, and* Verbena tenuiscerta *'Edith'.* Tall Cleome *'White Queen' and an edging of 'Snow Crystals' sweet alyssum brighten with white.*

GARDENING IN WOODEN BARRELS

Recycled or brand-new half barrels hold a lot of potting mix that can support a lot of plants. The wood and the soil mass help insulate roots from heat and cold, making barrels good for permanent plantings. Use barrels for planting dwarf trees and shrubs; tomatoes, squash, and other vigorous vegetables; and flower gardens of perennials, annuals, bulbs, and herbs. If you are growing plants in a barrel where weight is a problem, reduce weight by using light or super-light potting mix (see page 22).

To tighten the hoops of a half barrel, turn it upside down and tap the hoops downward with a chisel and hammer.

While the barrel is inverted, hammer several broad-headed nails above each hoop to hold it in place.

B ring butterflies into close viewing range by planting a container of long-blooming, nectar-filled flowers.

■ Daisy-shaped flowers almost always attract butterflies.
■ Rely on annuals for flowers from spring to fall.
■ Snuggle in perennials without removing their pots; replace when bloom is finished.
■ Plant in layers: vining vertically, standing upright, mounding, and spilling over the edge.
■ Attract butterflies with purple flowers.
■ Deadhead every few days to keep plants producing new blooms.
■ Guarantee customers by including butterfly bush (*Buddleia davidii*).

Butterflies are drawn to an expanse of flowers, but a container garden will tempt them to investigate if other plantings are nearby. Use the largest container you can find for your garden, or group several pots to make a bigger display. A wooden half barrel like that used in the design at left will accommodate a variety of plants of different heights and habits, so that the blooming extends through the entire spring-to-fall butterfly season.

Depend on long-blooming annuals, and augment the planting with perennials or shrubs. Butterflies visit flowers of all colors, but purple seems to be particularly attractive.

Mix and match flower and plant forms so that they complement and contrast with one another. When perennials finish their bloom season, lift and replace them with new plants for continued butterfly appeal.

BUTTERFLY PLANTS FOR CONTAINERS

Ageratum (*Ageratum houstonianum*)
Aster (*Aster* spp.)
'Autumn Joy' sedum (*Sedum* 'Autumn Joy')
Blazing star (*Liatris* spp.)
Bluebeard (*Caryopteris* × *clandonensis*)
Butterfly bush (*Buddleia davidii*)
Cosmos (*Cosmos* spp.)
Heliotrope (*Heliotropium arborescens*)
Lantana (*Lantana* spp.)
Pentas (*Pentas* spp.)
Petunias (*Petunia* × *hybrida*)
Purple coneflower (*Echinacea purpurea*)
Russian sage (*Perovskia atriplicifolia*)
Sweet alyssum (*Lobularia maritima*)
Verbena (*Verbena* spp.)
Zinnia (*Zinnia* spp.)

HUMMINGBIRD GARDENS

Hummingbirds are easy to attract to a container garden of their favored flowers. Plants of staggered heights and habits let you pack in more flowers.

■ Splash the planting with plenty of red, plus orange and bright pink, as a beacon for passing hummingbirds.
■ Use plants with tube-shaped blossoms for the most appeal.
■ Keep color coming from spring to fall with a foundation of annuals.
■ Add a trellis for a red-flowered annual vine or long-blooming honeysuckle.
■ Place the container near a bench, patio, or porch where you can watch the traffic.
■ A wooden half barrel insulates the roots of permanent plants to help them survive cold winters.

The deep red-orange trumpet blooms of 'Gartenmeister Bonstedt' fuchsia, a long-blooming tender perennial shrub, are a beacon to hungry hummingbirds.

Unlike butterflies, hummingbirds don't need a big planting to feel at ease. They will happily visit even a single nectar flower in a small pot. A hanging basket of fuchsias on a shady porch, for instance, will bring them within arm's length. But a large garden will keep them lingering longer so you have time to get a better view.

The design shown here entices hummingbirds with the vivid colors of deep pink, dwarf 'Liberty Pink' canna, brilliant red-orange 'Dainty' fuchsia, a long-flowering climbing honeysuckle (*Lonicera × brownii* 'Dropmore Scarlet'), and late-blooming *Salvia greggii* 'Coral'. Stems of multicolored 'Confetti' lantana and licorice plant (*Helichrysum petiolare*) stretch out near the bottom of the grouping for balance. Layering the plants increases the number of types you can grow.

Choose plants with an extended bloom season when planting a hummingbird container. Annuals blossom nonstop for months. Perennials have a shorter season but are useful for adding a weightier feel to the design. Flowering vines, grown on a trellis, require little actual space in the container.

Red, orange-red, and deep pink are the colors dear to a hungry hummingbird's heart. Once hummingbirds discover the container, they will happily feed at flowers of any color, as long as the blossoms hold nectar accessible to their long bills and there is enough space around the blooms for the birds to hover.

HUMMINGBIRD PLANTS FOR CONTAINERS

Butterfly bush (*Buddleia davidii*)
Cardinal climber (*Ipomoea × sloteri*)
Culinary sage (*Salvia officinalis*)
Cypress vine (*Ipomoea quamoclit*)
Daylilies (*Hemerocallis* hybrids)
Fuchsias (*Fuchsia* hybrids)
Geraniums (*Pelargonium* hybrids)
Honeysuckles (*Lonicera* spp.)
Lilies (*Lilium* spp.)
Red sage and other salvias (*Salvia splendens* and other species and cultivars)
Zinnia (*Zinnia elegans*)

Just getting started, this hummingbird garden will fill out and cover the trellis with nectar-filled honeysuckle blooms that attract the tiny birds year after year. Cannas, lantana, fuchsia, and coral Salvia greggii make it a multilayered planting that can satisfy several hummingbirds at once.

GALLERY
OF CONTAINER PLANTS

The following pages contain some of the most beautiful and best-adapted plants for growing in containers. There are bold tropicals and delicate shade plants, harbingers of spring and plants to color your fall garden. Try them, experiment with combinations, and use what you have learned in this book to try plants not mentioned here.

Each plant description in this gallery begins with a photograph of a representative species or cultivar and a summary of important features, including hardiness.

The "Uses" section will help you choose plants for particular kinds of containers and help you decide whether to grow them alone or with other plants. In many cases, we provide suggestions for suitable companions.

"Siting and Care" gives the basic information you need to grow each plant in a container garden, including the type of potting mix, how often to fertilize, how moist to keep the soil, and how much sun a plant needs or tolerates. Special needs are also described, such as deadheading, pruning, or winter protection.

"Selected Varieties and Related Species" tells how to choose varieties of each plant for container gardens. In general, the most compact plant varieties are the ones best adapted for containers.

Remember that most plants, especially annuals and small perennials, can survive in a container for a season. Experiment and enjoy!

Impatiens comes in a profusion of cultivars with flowers in many colors and forms; some varieties have multicolored foliage. This double red is from the 'Confection' series. Turn to page 76 for more about this versatile shade plant.

HARDINESS IN CONTAINERS

Most plants can be grown successfully outdoors in containers for the summer. If you want them to survive over winter, however, hardiness is a critical issue.

The range of USDA Hardiness Zones given for trees, shrubs, vines, and perennials is for plants grown in the ground. As a rule, assume that you lose about two zones of hardiness in unprotected containers. To locate the USDA Zone in which you garden, turn to the map on page 93.

Because hardiness in containers differs so markedly from hardiness in the ground, each entry includes an additional container hardiness rating based on research conducted by Dr. Paul Cappiello over many years, primarily at the University of Maine. The plants in this gallery are divided into four hardiness groups based on the minimum soil temperature a plant can withstand:

Hardiness Group A: Plants that cannot withstand freezing; if the soil mass freezes, the plant will be killed.
Hardiness Group B: Plants that can withstand minor freezing (the soil remains frozen for two nights or less).
Hardiness Group C: Plants that can withstand freezing if the temperature of the soil does not drop below 20 degrees F.
Hardiness Group D: Plants that can withstand soil temperatures below 20 degrees F but not below 5 degrees F.

Remember that many things can influence the cold hardiness of a container plant besides temperature, including the duration of low temperatures, the frequency of freeze-thaw cycles, the health of the plant, the size and insulating property of the container, and the amount of moisture in the potting mix. When the hardiness of a plant is in question, see information on timing and protection under "Siting and Care" in the plant's description, or refer to pages 28–29 and 45 for additional overwintering tips.

AGAPANTHUS SPP.

Ag-uh-PAN-thus

African lily, Lily-of-the-Nile

3'
2'

- Summer blooms
- Blue or white flowers
- Handsome foliage
- Zones 7–11; Hardiness Group A

Exotic spherical flower heads on tall, bare stems are dramatic in containers.

USES: Plant a dwarf variety alone in a 10- to 12-inch container, a full-size plant in a pot 15 to 20 inches across. Plant tightly if you cannot overwinter it; give more room if it can live from year to year.

SITING AND CARE: Use low-compaction potting mix with moderate fertility. Give partial shade in hot climates, sun where summers are cool, moderate water. Where not hardy, winter in a cool room by a north window or in a location that will be above freezing and receive some light. Divide in early spring, but only every several years; the plants bloom best when they are somewhat root-bound.

SELECTED VARIETIES: All varieties are suitable for containers. Dwarf hybrids 'Peter Pan', 'Rancho White', and 'Tinkerbell' have flower stems less than 2 feet tall. 'Tinkerbell' has white-variegated leaves; 'Rancho White' has white flowers. 'Headbourne Hybrids' are hardy to Zone 6 but go dormant in winter. They reach 2½ to 3 feet tall.

Agapanthus *'Peter Pan'*

ARGYRANTHEMUM SPP.

ar-gee-RAN-theh-mum

Marguerite

2'
3'

- Long-blooming summer daisies
- White, pink, or yellow 1- to 2½-inch flowers
- New compact varieties available
- Zones 9–11; Hardiness Group A

Short-lived perennials where they are hardy, fast-growing Marguerites are also useful as summer annuals in cold climates.

USES: Give full-size Marguerites at least a 10-inch pot. Short varieties can be grown in smaller pots, window boxes, or hanging baskets. Try with ivy geraniums and calibrachoa.

SITING AND CARE: Grow in full sun. Provide good drainage, regular water, light feeding. Deadhead and cut back often, but lightly, to encourage fresh blooms and bushy form. Not suited to the Deep South.

SELECTED VARIETIES AND RELATED SPECIES: 'Silver Leaf' offers 1½-inch white flowers and silver-green leaves on a 2- to 3-foot plant with good pest resistance. The new Cobbity Daisy series ranges from 8 to 16 inches tall and includes single and double flowers in white or pink.

Argyranthemum *'Silver Leaf'*

ARTEMISIA SPP.

ar-teh-MISS-ee-uh

Wormwood, Dusty-miller

3'
3'

- Silvery gray leaves
- No-fuss plant
- Perennial beauty
- Zones 5–8; Hardiness Group C

Icy hued artemisia blends well with all colors. It is indispensable for an all-white planting.

USES: Grow in window boxes, mixed bouquets, or hanging baskets. It's beautiful with pale yellow coreopsis and deep blue sage.

SITING AND CARE: Plant in moderately fertile potting mix with excellent drainage. Grow in full sun. Fertilize lightly once a month and remove flowers as they form. Prune unruly growth as needed. Good in a hot, sunny location but cannot tolerate soggy soil.

SELECTED SPECIES AND VARIETIES: Feathery-leaved 'Powis Castle' (*Artemisia* × 'Powis Castle') is mounding, with woody branches that will reach over the sides of containers. It reaches 2 to 3 feet high and wide. It is hardy in Zones 5–8 (to Zone 11 in the West), and tolerates humid heat well. Elegantly lobed leaves of *A. stelleriana* 'Silver Brocade' cascade gracefully from a 1-foot plant. It is hardy in Zones 4–7 (to Zone 11 in the West).

Artemisia stelleriana *'Silver Brocade'*

BAMBUSA SPP., PHYLLOSTACHYS SPP., SASA SPP.

bam-BOO-suh,
fil-oh-STAY-kus, SAS-uh

Bamboo

Phyllostachys aurea

8'

3'

- ■ Elegant, tropical effect
- ■ Fast-growing and easy
- ■ Some species hardy in Zones 5–10; Hardiness Group C. Others are tropical plants

The many species of grass known as bamboo share an exotic appearance, with polished, woody canes and leaves set at angles.
USES: Bamboo is best used alone in a pot. Plant dwarf types in pots as small as 9 inches, others in large, sturdy pots or barrels. Tall bamboos make good screens. Bamboo grows quickly; rapidly expanding roots can break pots.

SITING AND CARE: Grow in low-compaction potting mix with good drainage. Most bamboos thrive in sun, but some require partial shade. Protect from drying wind. Keep moist. Fertilize with high-nitrogen fertilizer monthly, or less often to limit growth. Cut out dead and unattractive canes, and cut back plants that get too tall. Repot when roots become pot-bound. Where not hardy, bamboo can overwinter in a bright room at just above freezing.
SELECTED SPECIES: Hundreds available, many are hardy. Golden bamboo (*Phyllostachys aurea*), black bamboo (*P. nigra*), and the dwarf *Sasa* spp. are hardy in Zones 5–10. *Bambusa* spp. are mostly tropical.

BEGONIA SPP.

bee-GOH-nee-uh

Begonia

Begonia × tuberhybrida 'Nonstop Salmon Pink'

8"

9"

- ■ Vivid color for shade
- ■ Flowers all summer
- ■ Tender perennials; Hardiness Group A

Bedding begonia (*Begonia semperflorens-cultorum*) bears small flowers in white, pink, and red. Flowers of tuberous begonia (*B. × tuberhybrida*) are up to 6 inches across, in white, pink, red, yellow, and orange. Both have varieties that are either upright or trailing.
USES: Grow in pots, window boxes, or hanging baskets, alone or with other shade-loving plants such as ferns and fuchsias.
SITING AND CARE: Begonias thrive in shade but tolerate sun

in cool weather. Plant in fertile, humus-rich, well-drained potting mix. Keep tuberous begonias moist; water bedding begonias moderately. Feed both lightly every two weeks. Bring inside as houseplants in cold winters. Lift dormant tuberous begonia tubers and store them over winter (see page 45).
SELECTED VARIETIES: Bedding begonias in the 'Cocktail Hybrids' series have bronze leaves; the 'Wings Hybrids' series has extra-large flowers. Both are 12 inches tall and bloom in many colors. Look for tuberous begonias in double forms that resemble roses. The popular 'Nonstop Hybrids' series has profuse 3- to 4-inch flowers.

BUXUS SPP.

BUK-sus

Boxwood, Box

Buxus sempervirens

4'

4'

- ■ Bright green, small-leaved shrub
- ■ Perfect for pruning into formal shapes
- ■ Leaves are evergreen
- ■ Zones 6–8; Hardiness Group C

Dwarf varieties of this popular hedge plant lend a formal air to container gardens.
USES: Slow-growing and dense, this shrub is ideal for formal shapes and topiary. Best potted alone. Use a container slightly larger than the nursery pot, moving to a larger container as the plant grows.
SITING AND CARE: Grow where protected from wind, in part shade

if summer is hot. Use moderately fertile, well-drained, low-compaction potting mix. Keep moist, and fertilize monthly in warm seasons. Prune to shape in spring and early summer. To overwinter where borderline, see page 28.
SELECTED VARIETIES: Check local nurseries for species and varieties recommended for your area. *B. sempervirens* 'Suffruticosa' reaches 4 to 5 feet in Zones 6–8 (to 9 in the West). *B. sempervirens* 'Northern Find' and *B. microphylla* 'Wintergreen' are hardy in Zones 5–8 (to 11 in the West). Most tolerant of heat and humidity is *B. microphylla japonica* (hardy in Zones 6–9, to 11 in the West).

CALADIUM X HORTULANUM

kuh-LAY-dee-um hor-too-LAY-num

Caladium

2'
2'

- Grown for its colorful leaves
- Tropical look for shade gardens
- Tender perennial; Hardiness Group A

The large, heart-shaped leaves of this exotic plant always include green but are netted, blotched, or spotted with white, pink, or red.
USES: Grow alone in an 8- to 10- inch pot, or mix with other shade plants such as impatiens and ferns in pots or window boxes.
SITING AND CARE: Except for sun-tolerant varieties, caladium is best in shade. Needs a well-drained, moisture-retentive soil, ample water, and monthly feeding while growing. Thrives only in humid locations where temperatures rarely drop below 60 degrees F at night. Set out tubers or plants in late spring or after soil is warm. To overwinter dormant tubers see page 45.
SELECTED VARIETIES: 'Freida Hemple' and 'Postman Joyner' have a green edge and a red center. 'Candidum' and the dwarf 'Candidum Jr.' are white with green veins. 'Carolyn Whorton' is pink and green. 'Fire Chief', 'Rosebud', and 'White Queen' tolerate sun.

Caladium *'Candidum'*

CAMELLIA SPP.

kuh-MEEL-lee-uh

Camellia

10'
6'

- Glossy, evergreen leaves
- Large red, pink, or white flowers
- Zones 8–11; Hardiness Group B

These elegant shrubs bear splendid flowers in fall, winter, or spring.
USES: Grow alone or surround with low plants such as Swedish ivy or periwinkle. Group informally or use two to flank a doorway.
SITING AND CARE: Use humus-rich, slightly acidic potting mix. Grow in part shade; plants tolerate less sun in winter and should be protected from strong wind. Feed monthly and keep constantly moist. Remove and discard any flowers with brown petals. Prune to shape after flowering.
SELECTED VARIETIES AND RELATED SPECIES: Fall-blooming *C. sasanqua* is denser and smaller than *C. japonica* and a better choice for containers. Check locally for recommended varieties. Hybrids derived from *C. oleifera*, such as *C.* 'Polar Ice' (white, double), 'Winter's Charm' (pink, peony form), and 'Winter's Star' (lavender pink, single), are fall-blooming and hardy to Zone 6 (Hardiness Group C).

Camellia japonica *'Nuccio's Gem'*

CAMPANULA SPP.

kam-PAN-you-luh

Bellflower, Harebell

12"
24"

- Blue or white flowers
- Creepers and trailers drape from pots
- Zones 3–9; Hardiness Group C

Any bellflower can be grown in a pot. Trailing types are most useful.
USES: Grow trailing types in mixed plantings or alone in pots, window boxes, and hanging pots.
SITING AND CARE: Most ground cover bellflowers are best in partial shade unless summers are cool. They need a moderately fertile, moist potting mix with excellent drainage, and grow best where night temperatures are below 70 degrees F.
SELECTED SPECIES: Serbian bellflower (*C. poscharskyana*) is hardy in Zones 3–7 in the East, to 11 in the West. Dalmatian bellflower (*C. portenschlagiana*, formerly *C. muralis*) is hardy in Zones 4–8 in the East, to 11 in the West, and tolerates full sun. Carpathian bellflower (*C. carpatica*) 'Blue Clips' and 'White Clips' form mounds 8 to 12 inches tall. They are hardy in Zones 3–9. Italian bellflower (*C. isophylla*), which is hardy only to Zone 7 (Hardiness Group B), can also be used in an indoor hanging basket.

Campanula poscharskyana *'Alba'*

CANNA SPP.

KAN-na

Canna

Canna 'Lucifer'

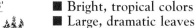

3'

2'

- Bright, tropical colors
- Large, dramatic leaves
- Flowers from midsummer to fall
- Zones 8–11; Hardiness Group B

Dwarf varieties of this plant, which grow 2 to 3 feet high, are more useful for containers. Full-size varieties can reach 6 feet or more. Broad leaves may be green, red, or variegated. Flowers are red, pink, orange, yellow, or bicolored.

USES: Best in a pot 15 inches or more deep. Grow alone or in mixed plantings. Lantana and ornamental sweet potato are good companions.

SITING AND CARE: Give canna fertile potting mix, ample water, and a hot, sunny location. Remove spent flowers and cut each flower stem to the ground after all its flowers have bloomed. Where winter temperatures stay above 30 degrees F, leave in the pot, dividing every year. Where it's colder, overwinter pot in a cool, frost-free place or dig rhizomes after the first frost and store (see page 45).

SELECTED VARIETIES: 'Tropicanna' has orange flowers and leaves striped with red, yellow, and green. 'Pretoria' has orange flowers and leaves striped with yellow and green. 'Cleopatra' bears red-speckled yellow blooms atop burgundy-streaked leaves. 'Pfitzer's Dwarf Hybrids' grow to 2½ feet tall.

CHRYSANTHEMUM SPP.

kri-SAN-theh-mum

Chrysanthemum, Garden mum

Chrysanthemum 'Pelee'

2'

2'

- Bright fall flowers
- Blooms often survive fall frosts
- Zones 5–9; Hardiness Group B

From late summer until hard frost, these vivid flowers appear in hues from white, yellow, and pink to bronze, burgundy, and red.

USES: Grow these colorful, bushy or mounded plants alone in a pot or in mixed plantings. Avoid crowding the roots. Combine with licorice plant and Mexican feather grass.

SITING AND CARE: Grow in full sun. Use moderately fertile potting mix; water regularly and feed weekly. Pinch off stem tips until July 15 in the North, August 15 in the South, to keep plants low and increase the number of flower buds. Leaving stems on plants will enhance hardiness if you plan to protect and overwinter them. Where hardy, divide in spring and repot the divisions.

SELECTED VARIETIES: Choose cushion varieties for low mounds, or taller types for upright plants. Shop locally for varieties hardy in your area—early bloomers in the North, later bloomers in the South. Florist's mums, often blooming out of season, are usually late-blooming types. They are not hardy enough for northern gardens but are handy in any climate for seasonal color.

CLEMATIS SPP.

KLEH-muh-tiss

Clematis

Clematis × jackmannii

6'

2'

- Leaf stems twine; use trellis or netting
- Enchanting flowers
- Some varieties bloom all summer
- Zones 3–8, to 10 in the West; Hardiness Group C

Clematis flowers, which may be white, pink, purple, red, or yellow, are followed by decorative seedpods. Some hybrids have 10-inch flowers.

USES: Grow in clay pots or wooden tubs at least 18 inches deep, alone or with shallow-rooted plants such as lamb's-ears. Three different cultivars in a 24-inch pot are lovely.

SITING AND CARE: Clematis likes cool roots; choose a container that insulates the soil from heat. Ideally, locate the container in shade, the top of the plant in sun to part shade. Support on a trellis or on netting attached to a wall or fence, or on a tepee inserted in the pot. Use a humus-rich potting mix with excellent drainage. Keep it moist, but not soggy, and fertilize monthly during growth. Mulch well. Pruning varies according to species. The rule: Prune after blooming, but only when necessary.

SELECTED VARIETIES AND SPECIES: The small size of the large-flowered hybrids makes them best for containers. Excellent long-blooming hybrids include 'Niobe' (red), 'Marie Boisselot' (white), and 'Royal Velvet' (deep purple).

CORDYLINE AUSTRALIS

KOR-dih-leen aus-TRAY-lis

Cordyline

2'
2'

- Bold, structural foliage plant
- Tropical appearance
- Zones 8–11; Hardiness Group A

This 40-foot tropical tree is grown as a summer annual in cold climates. Purchased at a foot or so tall, it becomes fuller and grows to 2 feet tall even in short northern summers. It is sometimes incorrectly labeled *Dracaena indivisa*.

USES: Grow alone or with other sun-loving plants, such as geranium (*Pelargonium* spp.) or verbena.

SITING AND CARE: Plant in full sun, using moderately fertile potting mix. Water moderately and fertilize monthly. Cordyline is most often replaced each spring but may be overwintered indoors. Let the root ball dry out, then keep the plant in a bright, cool place (36 to 50 degrees F). In moderate winters, plants left outdoors may regrow from frost-damaged stumps, producing a multi-trunked plant. If a plant seems to be outgrowing its container, repot it in early spring.

SELECTED VARIETIES: In addition to the green version of *Cordyline australis,* look for a white-striped one, 'Variegata', and another with leaves purple at their bases and underneath, 'Purpurea'.

Cordyline australis

COREOPSIS SPP.

kor-ee-OP-sis

Coreopsis

2'
2'

- Cheerful yellow or pink flowers
- Upright or spreading
- Tough, easy perennial
- Zones 3–9; Hardiness Group C

Coreopsis is a no-fuss container plant popular for all-summer color.

USES: Grow coreopsis with other flowers in pots or window boxes. White cosmos and blue asters are lovely companions.

SITING AND CARE: Plant in full sun in moderately fertile potting mix with very good drainage. Fertilize lightly once a month, and water moderately. For upright types, cut back stems of spent flowers to next bud or leaf. Shear spreading types periodically for rebloom.

SELECTED SPECIES AND VARIETIES: *C. grandiflora* (Zones 5–9, to 11 in the West) has 2-inch, bright yellow flowers on bare stems. Varieties range from 9 inches to 3 feet tall. Airy threadleaf coreopsis (*C. verticillata*) (Zones 3–9, to 11 in the West) is a low, spreading plant with ferny foliage. 'Zagreb' bears 1-inch golden yellow flowers; the flowers of 'Moonbeam' are pale yellow. *C. rosea* is similar but has pink flowers and is hardy in Zones 4–8 (to 11 in the West).

Coreopsis verticillata 'Moonbeam'

COSMOS SPP.

KOZ-mohs

Cosmos

36"
24"

- Graceful blooms
- Free-flowering summer through fall
- Deadheading keeps the blooms coming
- Fast-growing and easy
- Annual; Hardiness Group A

C. bipinnatus blooms in white, pink, or magenta; *C. sulphureus* in yellow to scarlet tones. Finely divided leaves give both species a delicate look even when they are covered with blooms.

USES: Fill a pot with either species for a color statement, or use in mixed containers. Dwarf types work better in small containers or window boxes. Try pink ones with blue scabiosa and white trailing lantana, yellow to scarlet ones with signet marigolds.

SITING AND CARE: Plant in full sun in moderately fertile, well-drained potting mix and fertilize lightly once a month. Keep moist but never soggy. Deadhead to a bud stem or to a leaf.

SELECTED SPECIES AND VARIETIES: *C. bipinnatus* has white to magenta blooms 3 to 4 inches wide and may reach 5 feet tall. Short varieties include the 1½- to 2-foot-tall 'Sonata Hybrids' series. *C. sulphureus* has 2- to 3-inch flowers. 'Bright Lights' blooms yellow, orange, and red on plants to 2½ feet tall. 'Ladybird', only a foot tall, includes bicolored flowers.

Cosmos bipinnatus 'Sonata Hybrids'

DAHLIA SPP.

DAH-lee-uh

Dahlia

- Large, bright flowers
- Blooms midsummer to fall
- Wide range of plant and flower sizes
- Zones 8–11; Hardiness Group A

Flower colors include white, yellow, pink, orange, red, burgundy, and many bicolors. Flower forms include single, cactus-flowered, and others.
USES: Grow midsize dahlias (3 to 4 feet tall) alone in 12-inch-deep containers or in large mixed containers. Use bedding types (12 to 16 inches tall) in mixed pots and window boxes 8 to 10 inches deep.

SITING AND CARE: Requires full sun and protection from strong wind. Stake tall plants at planting. Grow in moderately fertile potting mix, fertilize lightly every two weeks, and keep moist. Pinch stem tips of young plants to encourage bushiness. Cut spent flowers to keep blooms coming. Where not hardy, or to divide roots, dig and store them over winter (see page 45). Or store pots in frost-free location and divide in spring.
SELECTED VARIETIES: Varieties under 4 feet with blooms less than 4 inches across are best for containers. Bedding types include 'Figaro Hybrids Improved' (12 inches) and 'Rigoletto Hybrids' (12 to 16 inches).

Dahlia *'Gallery Hybrids' series*

ERIGERON KARVINSKIANUS

eh-RIH-juh-rawn kar-vin-ski-AN-us

Mexican daisy

- Small white, pink, or pale lavender daisies
- Fine-textured foliage
- Blooms spring to fall
- Zones 8–11; Hardiness Group B

Mexican daisy is charming when spilling over the lip of a pot.
USES: This is an ideal plant to grow in any container at the edges of a mixed planting, in a hanging pot or window box, or as a ground cover around a taller plant such as New Zealand flax. Beautiful with Marguerites and flowering tobacco.
SITING AND CARE: Plant in full sun. Use moderately fertile potting mix and feed lightly twice a month.

Withstands drought but fills in and blooms best if it is kept moderately moist. Where hardy, cut back in early spring to remove dead stems and encourage fresh growth.
SELECTED VARIETIES AND RELATED SPECIES: Flowers of the species open white and fade to pink. 'Moerheimii' has lavender flowers. Many hybrid cultivars with larger flowers are available (often listed as *E. speciosus*), with 1- to 2-inch double or semidouble flowers in bright pink, rose, purple, and lavender. All are hardy in Zones 2–7 (Hardiness Group C). 'Black Sea' is purple, 2 feet; 'Prosperity' is lavender-blue, 18 inches; 'Foerster's Leibling' is pink, 18 inches.

Erigeron karvinskianus

EUONYMUS FORTUNEI

you-ON-ih-mus for-TOO-nee-eye

Winter creeper euonymus

- Hardy climber, shrub, or ground cover
- May be evergreen
- Variegated varieties add interest
- Zones 5–9; Hardiness Group C

This fine-textured foliage plant can be effective in a container for months or, where hardy, for years.
USES: Plant alone or with other small shrubs, perennials, ornamental grasses, or bulbs. Most varieties will creep down a pot edge or, if planted next to a wall, will climb.
SITING AND CARE: Plant variegated forms in sun or part

shade; others tolerate more shade. Avoid winter winds. Grow in moderately fertile potting mix with good drainage. Fertilize monthly, water moderately, and prune as desired to shape.
SELECTED VARIETIES: 'Colorata' is a low, creeping form with dark green leaves that turn maroon in winter. 'Emerald Gaiety' has white-edged leaves, pink-edged in winter; 'Emerald 'n' Gold' has yellow-edged leaves, all-pink in winter. Both are spreading and shrubby to about 3 feet tall. *Euonymus fortunei* 'Vegetus' forms a 5-foot shrub or climbs a wall. It fruits freely, bearing small pods that open in fall to reveal orange seeds.

Euonymus fortunei *'Emerald Gaiety'*

Ferns

- Elegantly divided foliage
- Most thrive in part to full shade
- Hardiness varies by species

A fern's lacy fronds fill the spaces between more colorful plants. Some ferns are upright, others drape.

USES: Use small ferns in hanging baskets, mixed pots, or window boxes with impatiens, begonias, or coleus. Large ones are handsome alone in a hanging pot.

SITING AND CARE: Best in shade to part shade, although some tolerate full sun if kept watered. Use moderately fertile potting mix high in organic matter. Keep moist and fertilize lightly once a month. Overwinter tender ferns indoors in a bright, humid location out of direct sun.

Nephrolepis exaltata 'Bostoniensis'

FERNS FOR CONTAINERS

Common Name (Scientific Name)	Hardiness Zones	Height and Width	Container Pot Depth	Notes
Button fern *Pellaea rotundifolia*	8–10 Group A	6"×8"	6–8"	Round leaflets; nice in small mixed plantings; filtered shade, or sun with midday shade
Christmas fern *Polystichum acrostichoides*	3–8 Group C	18"×36"	8–12"	Rather narrow, dark green, leathery leaflets remain green in winter; best in shade
Holly fern *Cyrtomium falcatum*	6–10 Group A	12"×40"	8–12"	Broad, shiny leaflets remind some of holly; part to full shade, deciduous in colder climates
Japanese painted fern *Athyrium nipponicum* 'Pictum'	5–8 Group B	18"×24"	6–10"	Maroon stems; deciduous leaves are gray-green with paler gray patterns; grow in shade
Maidenhair fern *Adiantum spp.*	8–10 Group A	12"×16"	4–10"	Delicate fronds tremble in the least breeze; part to full shade; needs high humidity
Soft shield fern *Polystichum setiferum*	6–9 Group B	48"×36"	10–14"	Soft, lacy, bright green leaves; best in shade; fancy-leaved varieties sold as "English fern"
Squirrel's foot fern *Davallia trichomanoides*	9–11 Group A	15"×15"	8–12"	Fronds grow on furry brown rhizomes; good alone in a hanging basket; part shade
Sword fern, ladder fern *Nephrolepis cordifolia*	9–11 Group A	32"×60"	8–14"	Like a dwarf Boston fern; shade, more sun if well-watered
Sword fern, Boston fern *Nephrolepis exaltata*	10–11 Group A	24"×36"	8–16"	Best in shade, but tolerates sun where the climate is humid
Western sword fern *Polystichum munitum*	3–11 Group B	36"×48"	10–14"	Ideal in the West, where it is well-adapted; dark green, leathery leaflets; best in shade

---

FRAGARIA HYBRIDS

fruh-GAY-ree-uh

Strawberry

12"
18"

- Tasty berries; some have colorful flowers
- Attractive foliage
- Suited to most climates
- Zones 4–10; Hardiness Group C

These are charming plants for containers, and a taste of fresh strawberry is a fine reward.

USES: For best production, plant hybrid berries in containers at least 8 inches deep, and grow 8 inches apart. However, you will get some berries if you plant in the pockets of a strawberry jar or in mixed plantings. Try hybrid strawberries in a window box with petunias. Grow three alpine strawberry plants in a 10-inch azalea pot (see page 16).

SITING AND CARE: Hybrid strawberries need full sun; alpine strawberries grow best in partial shade. Both thrive in fertile, well-drained potting mix with ample moisture. Fertilize every two weeks while they are growing and bearing.

SELECTED VARIETIES: For container gardens, choose everbearing, day-neutral, hybrid strawberries; they will bear fruit all spring and summer. Check at local nurseries for the best varieties for your area. 'Pink Panda' has showy pink flowers, rarely bears fruit. Alpine strawberries, both red- and white-fruited varieties, bear small, intensely flavored fruit all summer.

Strawberry 'Fresca'

Fruit trees

■ Delicious fruit in small spaces
■ Fragrant blossoms scent the air
■ Dwarf varieties are suited to containers
■ Hardiness varies by species

Valencia orange

Dwarf 'Granny Smith' apple

'Winter Banana' apple

Dwarf fruit trees let you create your own Eden on a patio or roof. Although small in stature they produce full-size, full-flavor fruit.
USES: Grow fruit trees alone in large clay or wooden containers. Pruned as espaliers, fruit trees can grow flat against walls or fences.
SITING AND CARE: Plant bare-root or small potted plants in containers that are slightly wider than their roots; move to larger, more permanent containers the following year. The final container should be at least 18 inches across and 18 inches deep, and may be up to the size of a half barrel. Pot or repot while plants are dormant. Use a fertile, well-drained potting mix that will resist compaction and provide ample water and fertilizer. All fruit trees appreciate an organic mulch on the soil surface. Every two to three years, when trees begin to require watering more than once a day, they need to be root-pruned. Dig them while they are dormant, and shave off an inch of soil and roots at the sides and bottom of the root ball. Prune the top slightly at the same time, to balance the root-pruning. Return to the same container, adding fresh potting mix to replace what you have removed, and soak thoroughly.

For convenience in root-pruning, some gardeners construct wooden boxes that can be taken apart easily by removing screws. Attached casters or a plant dolly are also convenient so that the large containers can be easily moved.
DECIDUOUS FRUIT TREES: Many favorite deciduous fruit tree varieties are available as grafted dwarfs. These are growing on a rootstock that keeps the plant small but doesn't affect fruit quality. On the other hand, genetic dwarfs remain small on their own roots. Although both can succeed in containers, genetic dwarfs resist temperature changes better, are less prone to wind damage, and often bear more fruit. Available genetic dwarfs include apple, apricot, nectarine, peach, and cherry.

Fertilize deciduous trees weekly when they begin to leaf out and grow, then taper off in midsummer. Provide full sun when the trees are in leaf. In the ground, most deciduous fruit trees are hardy to Zone 5 (Hardiness Group B). Apricot and pie cherry are hardy to Zone 4, and some apple varieties are hardy to Zone 3 (Hardiness Group C). Where they are not hardy, deciduous fruit trees can be stored in a cool but protected place or wrapped in insulating material over winter. Where winters are mild, be sure to select a variety that will produce in a low-chill area. Refer to a book on pruning for guidance in pruning your deciduous fruit trees and thinning their fruit. Genetic dwarfs require little pruning but may require fruit thinning.
CITRUS FRUIT TREES: Citrus are also available as both grafted and genetic dwarfs, with genetic dwarfs offering better adaptation to life in containers. Hardiness varies slightly among types of citrus, but most cannot tolerate temperatures below freezing (Hardiness Group B). Citrus trees need ample water and fertilizer. Refer to information on special citrus fertilizer packages for timing and amounts. Citrus requires full sun in summer, half-day sun in winter. Where not hardy, citrus should be brought indoors in winter and kept near a sunny window. When moving trees indoors for the winter or outdoors for the summer, avoid shock from rapid changes in temperature and light. Where summers are cool, fruits may lack sweetness, making lemons and limes the best choices. Consult local nurseries or mail-order citrus retailers for advice in choosing types and varieties for your situation. Citrus doesn't require pruning but may be pruned lightly to maintain an attractive shape.
POLLINATION: Deciduous fruit trees and citrus depend on bees for pollination. If citrus is blooming indoors, use a small brush to transfer pollen from the stamens of some flowers to the pistils of others. In addition, some kinds of fruit trees need cross-pollination by flowers of another variety to produce well or at all. Neighborhood trees can sometimes serve as pollinators. If you want to be sure, however, ask about this when you buy the trees, and purchase at least two pollen-compatible varieties of each species that needs cross-pollination.

FUCHSIA HYBRIDS

FEW-shuh

Fuchsia

2'
3'

- Colorful blossoms dangle on arching stems
- Attractive to hummingbirds
- Best in part shade
- Zones 8–11; Hardiness Group A

The intriguing flowers of fuchsia are white, pink, red, lavender, or purple, including bicolors.

USES: Grow cascading types in hanging pots or baskets, upright forms in pots or window boxes. They are lovely underplanted with ivy or sweet potato vine.

SITING AND CARE: Plant in spring in humus-rich, neutral to slightly acid, well-drained potting mix. Keep moist and fertilize lightly every two weeks. Most types grow best in part shade in a cool, moist climate, but some tolerate more sun, heat, and dry air. Pinch off branch tips early in the season to encourage bushiness. Where not hardy, discard in fall, or overwinter in a cool, dark spot, then cut back last year's shoots in spring.

SELECTED VARIETIES: Hybrids sold locally are most likely to succeed in your climate.

'Gartenmeister Bonstedt', with 2-inch-long, tubular, orange-red flowers, tolerates more heat. *F. magellanica* (Zones 7–11) is 3 to 8 feet tall with many small blossoms.

Fuchsia *'Gartenmeister Bonstedt'*

HEDERA HELIX

HEAD-er-uh HEE-lix

English ivy

3'
1'

- Evergreen leaves
- Cascading or climbing vines
- Many variations in leaf variegation and form
- Zones 5–9 (to 11 in the West); Hardiness Group C

This versatile evergreen vine climbs with rootlets that adhere to smooth surfaces.

USES: Grown alone, ivy can drape or be trained to create topiaries (as shown in plant profile at left). It can also be grown with other plants in hanging pots or baskets, mixed pots, or window boxes, but in time it will crowd small, less aggressive plants, or compete with the roots of shrubs or trees. Grow in annual planters with pansies, impatiens, or spring bulbs.

SITING AND CARE: Grow in part to full shade in fertile, well-drained potting mix. Water regularly to keep moist; fertilize lightly once a month. Rearrange or prune errant stems to suit your purposes. Where not hardy, ivy can be overwintered as a houseplant in a cool, bright room.

SELECTED VARIETIES: Popular cultivars include 'Needlepoint' (green leaves with narrow, pointed lobes), 'Glacier' (green, white, and gray-green), and 'Goldheart' (yellow blotch in the center of a green leaf).

Hedera helix *'Adam'*

HELICHRYSUM PETIOLARE

he-lih-KRIH-sum pet-ee-oh-LAH-ray

Licorice plant

2'
5'

- Small, woolly leaves
- Spreading habit
- Stems and leaves in shades of silver, green
- Zones 10–11; Hardiness Group A

Licorice plant has little licorice scent, but its small leaves and pale colors create a charming mosaic with contrasting leaves and flowers.

USES: This plant is beautiful arching through other plants, such as ivy geraniums or petunias, in hanging pots or baskets, in window boxes, or other containers.

SITING AND CARE: Most kinds need full sun, but 'Limelight' has better color if grown in light to part shade. Plant in spring in average potting mix with good drainage. Withstands dry soil when established but tolerates regular watering. Fertilize lightly once a month. Prune to remove branches growing in unattractive directions.

SELECTED VARIETIES AND RELATED SPECIES: The species has gray-green leaves. Two-toned leaves of 'Variegatum' are gray-green and light green. 'Limelight' has pale chartreuse leaves. *Plecostachys serphyllifolia*, often sold as dwarf licorice plant, is similar but with smaller gray-green leaves.

Helichrysum petiolare *'Variegatum'*

Herbs

- Seasonings handy to the kitchen
- Attractive plants
- Some have showy flowers
- Hardiness varies by species

Many herbs used in cooking are easy to grow in containers. Clip them for use as needed while still enjoying their beauty.

Italian parsley

USES: Grow one kind alone in a pot, mix several in the same pot, or combine with ornamentals. (Always grow mints and lemon balm in their own containers; they are too aggressive with other plants.) Herbs can be used in hanging baskets, strawberry pots, or window boxes.

SITING AND CARE: Most herbs grow best in full sun for at least half the day. Some need fertile potting mix and ample water; others thrive in less fertile soil that is kept barely moist. If you are combining herbs in mixed containers, it is best to grow those with similar needs together.

In areas with mild winters, some perennial herbs can grow year-round in containers outdoors. If hardiness is in question, sink the planted containers in the ground, then cover the plants with organic mulch. Where herbs are not hardy outside, bring them indoors for the winter. Prune in fall or winter.

French tarragon

Culinary thyme

HERBS FOR CONTAINERS

Common Name (Scientific Name)	Plant Type	Hardiness Zones	Sun	Water	Fertilizer	Plant Height	Pot Depth (Minimum)	Notes
Basil (*Ocimum basilicum*)	Ann.	Group A	S	Moist	Ample	8–30"	9"	Plant in spring; needs warm weather
Chives (*Allium schoenoprasum*)	Per.	3–11 Group C	S/PS	Moist	Ample	12–24"	9"	Cut flower stems to increase leaf production
Dill (*Anethum graveolens*)	Ann.	Group A	S	Moist	Mod.	24–60"	12"	Grow from seed in spring
French tarragon (*Artemisia dracunculus* 'Sativa')	Per.	3–11 Group C	S	Mod.	Mod.	12–36"	9"	French tarragon is much more flavorful than Russian
Garden sage (*Salvia officinalis*)	Per.	2–11 Group C	S	Mod.	Mod.	18–24"	9"	Some are purple-leaved or yellow-variegated
Garden thyme (*Thymus vulgaris*)	Per.	5–11 Group B	S	Mod.	Mod.	6–12"	9"	Some are yellow- or white-variegated
Greek oregano (*Origanum heracleoticum*)	Per.	5–11 Group B	S	Mod.	Mod.	12–36"	9"	To find best scent, smell plant before purchase
Lemon balm (*Melissa officinalis*)	Per.	5–11 Group B	S/PS	Moist	Ample	24–36"	9"	Spreads fast, grow alone; cut back after flowering
Lavender (*Lavandula* spp.)	Per.	6–11 Group B	S	Mod.	Low	8–48"	12"	Don't overwater; English lavender is hardy to Zone 6
Marjoram (*Origanum majorana*)	Per.	9–11 Group A	S	Moist	Ample	12–24"	9"	Where not hardy, grow as a summer annual
Mints (*Mentha* spp.)	Per.	5–11 Group B	S/PS	Moist	Ample	12–24"	9"	Grow each kind alone; they spread by runners
Parsley (*Petroselinum crispum*)	Bienn.	Group B	S/PS	Moist	Ample	6–12"	9"	Best in cool weather; harvest before it blooms
Rosemary (*Rosmarinus officinalis*)	Per.	7–11 Group B	S	Mod.	Low/mod.	10–72"	9–12"	Some are creeping, others upright; 'Arp' to Zone 6

HEUCHERA SPP.

HYOO-keh-ruh

Coral bells

20"
20"

- Bright sprays attract hummingbirds
- Tidy mounds of foliage
- Hybrids offer dark foliage colors
- Zones 3–8 (to 11 in the West); Hardiness Group C

Coral bells is grown for its tall stems topped with sprays of bright flowers. Newer hybrids with colorful leaves often have less showy white flowers.

USES: Handsome alone in a pot or in mixed plantings. Purple-leaved hybrids contrast nicely with green, silvery, or chartreuse foliage and pastel flowers, such as pink impatiens and 'Silvery Sunproof' lilyturf.

SITING AND CARE: Grow in full sun, part shade where summers are warm, in fertile, well-drained potting mix. Keep moist and fertilize lightly once a month. Remove spent flower stems to encourage longer bloom. In cold winters, plant out in fall, or bury pots in mulch over winter to prevent frost-heaving.

SELECTED VARIETIES: *H. sanguinea* forms neat mounds of green leaves, with red, pink, or white flowers on 10- to 20-inch stems. Among the new purple-leaved hybrids are *H. micrantha* 'Palace Purple', 'Chocolate Ruffles' (ruffled edge), and 'Pewter Veil' (gray tones).

Heuchera *'Mt. St. Helens'*

HOSTA SPP.

HOSS-tuh

Hosta

2'
3'

- Dramatic leaves, many variegated forms
- Attractive mid-season flowers
- Easy, winter-hardy plants
- Zones 3–8; Hardiness Group C

Hosta leaves vary from blue-green to yellow-green, often variegated or textured. Plants may be from less than 8 inches to several feet wide.

USES: Grow large hostas alone, smaller ones alone or in mixed pots. Attractive with ferns and begonias.

SITING AND CARE: Yellow-green types need part sun for best color, blue-green ones tolerate shade. Use fertile, well-drained potting mix, moderate water. Fertilize lightly every month. Containers can be overwintered in an unheated garage, or sunk into a bed and mulched.

SELECTED VARIETIES: Thousands of varieties provide nearly infinite choice. Three popular ones are 'Blue Wedgwood', a blue-leaved form that grows 18 inches tall and 30 inches wide; 'Gold Standard', with gold leaves edged in dark green on plants that are 15 inches tall and 2 feet wide; and 'Francee', with olive green leaves edged with white on plants 15 inches tall and 3 feet wide. All three have lavender blooms.

Hosta *'Wide Brim'*

HYACINTHUS ORIENTALIS

high-uh-SIN-thus or-ee-en-TAHL-iss

Dutch hyacinth

12"
6"

- Bright, midspring blossoms
- Strong, sweet fragrance
- Reliable, hardy bulbs
- Zones 3–7, best as annual in Zones 8–11; Hardiness Group D

The fat "drumstick" heads of Dutch hyacinth are made up of small single or double flowers in white, yellow, pink, blue, or purple.

USES: Mass five or more hyacinths of the same color in a bulb pot. Combine with other spring bulbs or with pansies and forget-me-nots.

SITING AND CARE: Plant in fertile, well-drained potting mix. Set bulbs with sides nearly touching and tops just below the surface. Grow in full sun. Keep barely moist until shoots emerge, then keep moist. After bloom, taper off watering; dig when dormant, and plant in the garden at the correct time for your climate. In mild-winter areas, discard, or prechill before replanting.

SELECTED VARIETIES: 'Gipsy Queen' (peach) is a relatively new variety. 'L'Innocence' (white), 'City of Haarlem' (pale yellow), and 'Delft Blue' are other popular varieties.

Hyacinthus *'Lady Derby' (pink)* and *'Blue Jacket' (purple)*

ILEX SPP.

EYE-leks

Holly

Ilex cornuta *'Burfordi'*

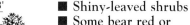

3'
3'

- Shiny-leaved shrubs
- Some bear red or yellow berries
- Hardiness varies

Holly offers some fine choices for containers—hardy plants with a dense covering of attractive leaves. **USES:** Plant alone or underplant with ground covers and bulbs. Evergreen hollies are good subjects to train as a standard or a topiary. **SITING AND CARE:** Plant in sun to shade, using slightly acidic, well-drained potting mix that resists compaction. Fertilize in late winter. Keep moderately moist during the growing season, barely moist in winter. Prune in late winter, before spring growth begins. Where it is not hardy outdoors, holly may be moved indoors and kept moist. **SELECTED VARIETIES AND SPECIES:** Japanese Holly (*I. crenata*) is hardy in Zones 5–7, 11 in the West, Hardiness Group C. It has small, evergreen leaves similar to boxwood. Evergreen Chinese holly (*I. cornuta*) grows in Zones 7–9 (to 10 in the West), Hardiness Group B. It includes 'Dwarf Burford' (red berries) and the berryless 'Carissa' and 'Rotunda'. Blue holly (*I.* × *meserveae*) is a good hardy evergreen in Zones 5–9 (to 11 in the West), Hardiness Group B. Female plants bear red berries if a male pollinator is present.

IMPATIENS HYBRIDS

im-PAY-shens

Impatiens

Impatiens *'Accent Pink'*

12"
10"

- Low, bright bloomers for shade
- Long summer bloom
- Some have burgundy or variegated leaves
- America's favorite annual for shade; Hardiness Group A

Common impatiens, or busy Lizzie (*I. walleriana*), lights up shady spots with pink, orange, white, lavender, scarlet, or bicolor flowers. The larger-flowered New Guinea impatiens adds tropical flair. **USES:** Grow in hanging containers, window boxes, or pots, alone or with other plants. Some drape, others mound. Excellent with hostas, ferns.

SITING AND CARE: Impatiens needs part shade in cool weather, full shade where weather is hot. Grow in moist but well-drained potting mix, feed twice a month until late summer, and keep moist but not wet. To encourage bushy growth, pinch branch tips of young plants. Later, cut back leggy plants; they will rebloom in a few weeks. **SELECTED VARIETIES:** 'Accent Hybrids' (4 to 8 inches) are dwarf; 'Mosaic Hybrids' (to 12 inches) have pastel, shimmery centers. 'Victorian Rose' flowers look like miniature pink roses. New Guinea hybrids grow to 15 inches, are more robust, perform well in sun, and often have variegated or red leaves.

IPOMOEA HYBRIDS

ih-poh-MEE-uh

Morning glory

Ipomoea *'Star of Yalta'*

10'
3'

- Twining vine for pole, trellis, or railing
- Bright flowers are 3 inches or more across
- Blooms summer to frost
- Easy, vigorous annual; Hardiness Group A

Morning glory suggests old-time gardens and country byways. Now available in red, purple, white, and bicolor streaks and swirls as well as classic blue. **USES:** Try several morning glory plants in a 10-inch pot in which you have set three bamboo poles tied together at the top. Alternatively, let them climb a nearby trellis, fence, or railing.

SITING AND CARE: Plant seeds in spring; nick seeds, then soak overnight to encourage germination. Use potting mix with moderate fertility and excellent drainage. Select a relatively small container; limited root space will stimulate blooming. Place container in full sun, water lightly, and feed lightly once a month. **SELECTED VARIETIES AND RELATED SPECIES:** *I. tricolor* 'Heavenly Blue' is sky blue with a white throat, while the flowers of 'Pearly Gates' are pure white. *I. nil* 'Scarlett O'Hara' has crimson flowers. Mixed color hybrids include 'Mt. Fuji' (mixed pinwheel-patterned bicolors) and 'Early Call'.

IPOMOEA BATATAS

ih-poh-MEE-uh buh-TAY-tas

Sweet potato vine

6" 7'

- Decorative leaves
- Vigorous, easy-to-grow filler and spiller
- Zones 9 to 11; tender perennial. Hardiness Group B

These recently introduced vines delight with their different foliage colors and shapes. They are less than a foot tall, but can cascade to several feet long.

USES: Ideal for draping from hanging baskets or spilling over the edge of mixed plantings, or filling a pot alone as part of a container group. Combine them with cannas, zinnias, or cascading petunias.

SITING AND CARE: Plant sweet potato vine in spring, in sun or part shade, in moderately fertile, well-drained potting mix. Keep moist and fertilize once a month. Pinch tips to limit the length of vines.

SELECTED VARIETIES: 'Blackie' has dark purple, almost black, deeply lobed leaves. The leaves of 'Margarita' are bright chartreuse, heart-shaped, up to 8 inches long. 'Terrace Lime' is similar but more compact. 'Pink Frost' is a compact plant with deeply lobed leaves rarely more than 2 inches long, tricolored in light green, lavender, and white.

Ipomoea batatas 'Blackie'

LANTANA SPP.

lan-TAN-uh

Lantana

3' 5'

- Covered with bright blossoms spring to fall
- Mounding or trailing varieties
- Zones 7 or 8–11; Hardiness Group A

Verbena-like flower clusters cover these tropical plants. The blooms in each cluster may be purple, white, yellow, orange, pink, or red, often with several colors together.

USES: Plant in all kinds of containers, using cascading forms in hanging pots and at pot edges. May be trained into a standard. A red or yellow variety with 'Blackie' sweet potato vine is outstanding.

SITING AND CARE: Grow lantana in full sun in moderately fertile, well-drained potting mix. For best bloom, keep just moist and feed only lightly. Pinch off stem tips early to encourage branching. Where lantana is hardy, prune back in spring to encourage new growth.

SELECTED VARIETIES: 'Purple Swirl' (medium purple flowers) and 'White Lightning' (pure white) are trailing varieties of *L. montevidensis*. 'Patriot Rainbow' is a compact, mounding lantana with flower heads in a mixture of yellow, orange, red, and purple. *L. camara* 'Confetti', a low, mounding type, has yellow, coral, and purple flowers.

Lantana 'Spreading Sunset'

LAURUS NOBILIS

LAW-russ NO-bill-iss

Grecian laurel, Sweet bay

7' 4'

- Scented leaves used in cooking
- Evergreen; good for formal pruning
- Tolerates hot weather
- Zones 8–9 (to 11 in the West); Hardiness Group B

This evergreen shrub or small tree looks good all year. Clip a leaf now and then to season a dish, or dry leaves after routine pruning and store them in an airtight jar.

USES: Grow alone in a large pot or surround it with shallow-rooted plants such as lavender, sweet alyssum, or spring bulbs. Can be pruned to a standard, a narrow pyramid, or a broad oval.

SITING AND CARE: Best in full sun to part shade. Plant in average potting mix with very good drainage. Keep moderately moist and feed lightly from spring to midsummer. Pinch off actively growing stem tips to shape plant and encourage branching. Prune to shape and limit size in late winter, before growth begins. Where not hardy, bay laurel can overwinter in a bright indoor place or a dark, cool place where it is kept barely moist.

SELECTED VARIETIES: 'Saratoga' is resistant to psyllids, insect pests that often trouble bay laurel.

Laurus nobilis

LILIUM SPP.

LIL-ee-um

Lily

36" ... 12"

- Blossoms up to 8 inches across
- Tall, elegant plants
- Some are fragrant
- Zones 5–8; Hardiness Group B

Oriental lily 'Stargazer'

Seductive flowers in white, pink, orange, yellow, lavender, or scarlet.
USES: Plant alone (five bulbs to a 15-inch pot) or in larger mixed pots. Lovely with Mexican daisy or edging lobelia. Two- to 4-foot varieties are easiest to grow in pots, but taller ones are dramatic.
SITING AND CARE: Best in sun with some afternoon shade. Plant bulbs in fall in fertile, well-drained potting mix high in organic matter.

Provide stakes for taller kinds. Overwinter fall-planted pots in a cool spot protected from freezing, and keep moderately moist until top growth appears. Move outdoors and keep moist until the plant dies back after blooming. Then plant in the garden in late fall to early spring, or overwinter as noted above.
SELECTED VARIETIES AND SPECIES: Fragrant Oriental hybrids are hardy in Zones 5–8 (to 11 in the West), Hardiness Group B. Asiatic hybrids are hardy in Zones 4–8 (to 11 in the West). Dramatic regal lilies (*L. regale*) reach 5 feet tall (Zones 4–7, to 11 in the West) and are fragrant. Both Asiatic and regal lilies are in Hardiness Group C.

LIRIOPE SPP.

lih-RYE-oh-pee

Lilyturf

2' ... 2'

- Gracefully arching green or variegated leaves
- Spikes of blue, lavender, or white flowers
- Easy to grow
- Zones 5–9 (to 11 in the West); Hardiness Group C

Liriope muscari 'Majestic'

Lilyturf blooms in late summer but is handsome in all seasons. It is untroubled by pests, heat, humidity.
USES: Show off a variegated type alone in a pot or use any kind in mixed plantings.
SITING AND CARE: Use moderately fertile, slightly acidic

potting mix with good drainage. Grows best in partial shade. Keep moist until roots are established, then water moderately. Cut flower stems after bloom, and trim back cold-damaged leaves in late winter.
SELECTED VARIETIES: All are good in containers. 'Majestic' has dark green leaves to 2 feet tall, dark violet flowers. 'Silvery Sunproof' leaves are striped in yellow that becomes almost white in full sun. It grows to 18 inches tall and has lavender flowers. 'Silvery Midget' has white, variegated leaves only 8 inches tall. The similar mondo grass (*Ophiopogon planiscapus*) boasts a dramatic black-leaved cultivar, 'Nigrescens' (Hardiness Group B).

LOBELIA ERINUS

loh-BEE-lee-uh er-RYE-nuss

Edging lobelia

4" ... 6"

- Blue, lavender, or white blooms cover low plants
- Mounding or trailing forms
- Annual that blooms spring to fall; Hardiness Group A

Lobelia erinus 'Riviera Lilac'

Deep blue-flowered forms are best-known, but light blue, crimson, lavender, or white forms are also attractive.
USES: Mounding varieties make tidy edging for mixed containers; trailing ones drape over the edge of pots, window boxes, or hanging pots and baskets. Try bright blue edging lobelia with zinnias and dusty miller (*Senecio cineraria*).

SITING AND CARE: Plant in spring in fertile, well-drained potting mix. Keep moist. Edging lobelia will tolerate full sun during cool springs or summers; otherwise, give afternoon shade to full shade. Hot summers will cause plants to decline, but they will revive when weather turns cool again. Shear back lightly when first blooms fade to encourage more flowers.
SELECTED VARIETIES: 'Crystal Palace' has deep blue flowers and bronzy leaves on compact, 4-inch plants. 'Riviera Hybrids' series is early and includes lilac, sky blue, and bicolors, 4 to 6 inches tall. 'Cascade Hybrids' series is trailing and available in several colors.

LOBULARIA MARITIMA

lob-you-LAY-ree-uh mah-RIH-tih-muh

Sweet alyssum

4"
 10"

- Low, billowy clouds of small blossoms
- Flowers often sweetly fragrant
- Tolerates infertile soils
- Fast-growing annual; Hardiness Group A

Narrow leaves are all but hidden by a mass of blooms on a plant that is usually less than 6 inches tall. Classic sweet alyssum is white, but pink, rose, lavender, violet, and apricot flowers are also available.

USES: Tuck sweet alyssum into hanging pots and baskets or at the edge of mixed pots and window boxes. It is extremely versatile, ideal to mix with other low-growing flowers, such as pansies and dianthus, or with taller flowers or shrubs.

SITING AND CARE: Plant in moderately fertile potting mix in containers that will grow in light shade or full sun. Keep moist. After the first flush of bloom, cut plant back by half to encourage rebloom. Plants will decline in high temperatures.

SELECTED VARIETIES: 'Carpet of Snow' is white-flowered, spreading, 4 inches tall. The 'Easter Basket Hybrids' series is spreading, in rose-red, violet-blue, white, and peach-apricot, to 4 inches tall.

Lobularia maritima *'Carpet of Snow'*

LONICERA SPP.

lon-ISS-er-uh

Honeysuckle

9'

 4'

- Fast-growing perennial vine
- Bright flowers most of the summer
- Some kinds attract hummingbirds
- Zones 4–9 (to 11 in the West); Hardiness Group C

Honeysuckle twines prettily on a trellis or along wires on a wall. It's effective trained as a standard.

USES: Plant in a pot at least 12 inches in diameter; move to a half barrel as it matures. Or plant in a large mixed container with sweet alyssum or trailing lantana.

SITING AND CARE: Plant in full or part sun using fertile potting mix. Water moderately, but never let the soil dry completely. Fertilize monthly in spring and summer. Trim branches that get out of bounds, and prune side branches to 6 to 8 inches in late winter. Where not hardy in containers, overwinter in an unheated garage.

SELECTED SPECIES: Trumpet honeysuckle (*L. sempervirens*) has orange to scarlet tubular flowers and scarlet fruit. Flowers of 'Goldflame' honeysuckle (*L. × heckrottii*) are fragrant and bicolored gold and coral pink. Avoid Japanese honeysuckle (*L. japonica*); birds spread it, and it becomes a weed.

Lonicera brownii *'Dropmore Scarlet'*

MANDEVILLA SPP.

man-deh-VIL-ah

Mandevilla

7'

 2'

- Fast-growing vine
- Showy pink or red flowers all summer
- Large, shiny, dark green leaves
- Tropical perennial; Hardiness Group A

This twining climber needs a trellis or other support. It grows up to 15 feet in a season.

USES: Plant mandevilla alone, or with a flowering ground cover such as trailing fan flower or verbena, in a 12- to 15-inch-diameter pot.

SITING AND CARE: Thrives in heat; plant in spring in a warm, sunny spot. Use fertile potting mix and fertilize every two to three weeks. Early in the season, pinch off stem tips to encourage branching. Where not hardy, cut back and overwinter in a sunny window. Or grow as an annual from a new plant each year. Where hardy, prune heavily in late winter to encourage new growth.

SELECTED VARIETIES: M. × *amoena* 'Alice du Pont' is most common. It has medium pink flowers with a darker throat. M. *sanderi* 'Red Riding Hood' has red flowers with a yellow throat. It reaches 4 to 6 feet and can be grown in a hanging pot.

Mandevilla *'Alice du Pont'*

MUSA ACUMINATA

MEW-suh uh-kyu-mih-NAY-tuh

Dwarf banana tree

8' / 8'

- Tropical drama
- Large leaves may be variegated
- Can reach 6 to 9 feet in a season
- Perennial in Zones 10–11; Hardiness Group A

Musa acuminata *'Sumatrana'*

A dwarf banana tree makes a large, exotic statement. It may bloom in the second year, and fruit is possible, though unlikely.
USES: Plant alone or with a low shallow-rooted plant such as cigar flower (*Cuphea ignea*). Group with pots containing palms or canna.
SITING AND CARE: Plant in fertile, moisture-retentive potting mix in a sunny, warm, humid site out of strong wind. (Some tearing of the leaves is normal, but strong winds will shred them.) Keep moist, but never water into the crown of leaves. Fertilize monthly during summer using a high-potassium fertilizer. Overwinter indoors in a heated sunroom or other bright place, watering moderately. Repot every one to two years, in spring.
SELECTED VARIETIES AND RELATED SPECIES: 'Dwarf Cavendish' has green leaves. 'Sumatrana' has leaves with burgundy blotches. Other variegated-leaved forms exist. Red Abyssinian banana (*Ensete ventricosum* 'Maurelii') is also a good container subject.

MUSCARI

mus-KAH-ree

Grape hyacinth

6" / 6"

- Blue, white, violet blooms in mid-spring
- Fall-planted bulbs
- Zones 4–8 (to Zone 11 in the West); Hardiness Group C

Muscari armeniacum

Grape hyacinth, which looks like a tiny Dutch hyacinth, blooms in blue, violet, pure white, and even pale pink.
USES: Tuck under shrubs that are growing in containers. Mix with other spring bulbs or with spring-blooming flowers such as primrose or English daisy.
SITING AND CARE: Plant in fertile, well-drained potting mix. Set bulbs an inch or so apart, with tops an inch below the surface. Grow in full sun or light shade. Keep barely moist until shoots emerge, then keep moist. These small bulbs may live from year to year in a container or can be dug after leaves die back and planted in the garden.
SELECTED VARIETIES AND RELATED SPECIES: M. *armeniacum* has cobalt blue flowers; 'Blue Spike' is less traditional, with larger, double flowers. M. *botryoides* 'Album' has pure white flowers. All three are 6 inches tall. Fringe hyacinth (M. *comosum*) has feathery blue flowers on stems that reach a foot or more.

NANDINA DOMESTICA

nan-DEEN-uh doh-MESS-tih-kuh

Heavenly bamboo

4' / 4'

- Elegant, bamboo-like effect
- Lacy foliage, white flowers, red berries
- Good fall color
- Zones 6–9 (to Zone 11 in the West); Hardiness Group C

Nandina domestica *'Gulfstream'*

The canelike form of this graceful plant is reminiscent of bamboo. Young leaves have a rosy blush, mature to medium green, then turn purplish or red in fall or winter. Some varieties produce red berries if plants cross-pollinate.
USES: Use dwarf varieties alone or in mixed plantings. It is lovely with lilyturf and impatiens.
SITING AND CARE: This plant thrives in sun or shade, with more vivid leaf colors in sun. Plant in fertile potting mix and fertilize monthly when growing. Best with ample water but can tolerate less. Limit height by pruning oldest canes to the ground. Where not hardy, store container in a dark, cool place through winter dormancy. If roots are still alive, plant should regrow in spring.
SELECTED VARIETIES: 'Gulfstream' reaches 4 feet tall, with bluish-green leaves; 'Harbor Dwarf' grows to 24 inches tall. Both have good form and fall color. 'Compacta' grows to 4 feet with particularly lacy foliage.

NARCISSUS

nahr-SIS-sus

Daffodil, Jonquil

15"
6"

- Cheery spring flowers
- Yellow, white, pink, peach, or orange, often bicolored
- Easy-care bulbs
- Zones 3–7 (to Zone 11 in the West); Hardiness Group C

These fragrant spring harbingers are available in many forms and colors.
USES: Mass them alone, or combine with other spring flowers, such as Iceland poppies or pansies, using techniques for mixing bulbs and other flowers that are suited to your climate (see page 46).

SITING AND CARE: Plant in fertile, well-drained potting mix. Set bulbs with sides nearly touching and tops just below the surface. Keep barely moist until shoots emerge, then keep moist and grow in full sun. After bloom, taper off watering as leaves die back, then replant in the garden in fall.

SELECTED VARIETIES: Classic yellow trumpets such as 'King Alfred' are good choices. 'Thalia' is pure white. 'Tete-a-tete' is early, yellow, and only 6 inches tall. 'Salome' has a pink trumpet and white petals. Jonquilla and Tazetta types are less hardy, and most likely to survive winters in Zones 8 and 9.

Narcissus *'Quail' (yellow)* and *'White Lion' (white)*

NICOTIANA SPP.

nih-koh-she-AY-nuh

Flowering tobacco

2'
1'

- Wide color range
- Some kinds are sweetly scented
- Long bloom period
- Tender perennial; Hardiness Group A

These tobacco relatives bloom in crimson, red, lavender, pink, peach, white, and chartreuse.
USES: Plant tall types alone, tall or short ones in mixed plantings.

SITING AND CARE: Grow in fertile, well-drained potting mix in light shade or, where weather is cool or humid, in full sun. Fertilize monthly. Water regularly, especially in hot weather. Prune out flower stems that have finished blooming.
SELECTED VARIETIES: Some kinds are fragrant, especially in the evening, such as *N. alata* (to 5 feet tall with white flowers). 'Sensation Hybrids' offer fragrant flowers on 3-foot plants. 'Domino Hybrids' (12 to 18 inches tall) and 'Merlin Hybrids' (to 12 inches tall) offer a wide range of colors. Green-flowering tobacco (*N. langsdorffii*) is 3 to 4 feet tall with small chartreuse bells. It blooms from early summer to frost. Woodland tobacco (*N. sylvestris*) has open sprays of pendulous, fragrant white blossoms on 5-foot plants.

Nicotiana alata *'Lime Green'*

PAPAVER SPP.

pah-PAY-ver

Poppy

20"
8"

- Large flowers in warm colors or white
- Silky, translucent, crinkled petals
- Spring or early summer bloom
- Zones 2–7; Hardiness Group C

Magnificent, large flowers in bold colors are stunning for accent. The perennial Oriental poppy provides a brief but transient show.
USES: Plant an Oriental poppy alone in a 10-inch pot. Set several Iceland poppies in an 8-inch pot or grow in mixed pots or window boxes with blue lobelia.
SITING AND CARE: Plant in full sun in moderately fertile, well-drained potting mix. Keep moist. Divide Oriental poppy after it dies down in late summer, but only when overcrowded.
SELECTED VARIETIES AND RELATED SPECIES: Oriental poppy (*P. orientale*) is best in Zones 2–7 (to 9 in the West). In addition to the classic red or deep orange, look for white, peach, shell pink, and bicolors. Most have a dark blotch at the base of each petal. Iceland poppy (*P. nudicaule*, Hardiness Group B), is often grown as a cool-season annual in mild-winter gardens. It is available in mixes of white, yellow, orange, and pink. Popular mixes are 'Champagne Bubbles' (12 inches tall) and 'Oregon Rainbow' (15 to 20 inches).

Papaver nudicaule *'Wonderland'*

PELARGONIUM SPP.

pel-ar-GOH-nee-um

Geranium

15"
15"

Pelargonium *'Pinto Red'*

- One of the easiest flowers to grow
- Blooms all summer
- Some have variegated leaves
- Tender perennial in Zones 9–11; Hardiness Group A

Geraniums survive with little care, but with extra attention they pay dividends of outstanding beauty.
USES: Grow zonal geranium or ivy geranium alone or in mixed pots or window boxes. Ivy geranium is also suited for hanging pots or baskets.
SITING AND CARE: Plant in fertile, well-draining soil in a sunny spot. Pinch tips from stems of young plants to encourage branching. Water moderately and fertilize twice a month in spring and summer. Cut spent flower stems. Where not hardy, allow soil to dry somewhat, then grow indoors in a sunny window. Cut back by one-third in winter and repot as growth begins.
SELECTED VARIETIES: Zonal geraniums are upright, with globe-shaped flower heads in white, pink, salmon, or red, including bicolors. The round leaves may be marked with rings of burgundy, yellow, red, white, or several of these colors. Ivy geraniums have ivy-like green leaves (some with white markings) and flowers that are pink, salmon, red, lavender, purple, or white.

PENNISETUM SETACEUM 'RUBRUM'

pen-eh-SEE-tum se-TAY-see-um

Purple fountain grass

3'
2'

Pennisetum setaceum *'Rubrum'*

- Arching, burgundy leaves
- Airy, rose-colored flower heads
- Evergreen where hardy
- Zones 8–11; Hardiness Group B

This versatile grass blends with pastel, meadowy flowers or with vivid tropical ones. Where not hardy, it turns straw-beige in winter.
USES: Handsome grown alone or in mixed pots. Center it and underplant with a ground cover such as trailing lantana, or put it at the back of the pot with upright flowers such as bedding dahlias in front and spillers such as sweet potato vine at the front edge.
SITING AND CARE: Grow in full sun in moderately fertile potting mix. Fertilize every two weeks. Water generously, never letting soil dry out. Where hardy, cut back in late winter before new growth.
SELECTED VARIETIES: The variety 'Rubrum' (also known as 'Cupreum' and 'Purpureum') grows 3 to 4 feet tall. 'Rubrum Compactum', also sold as 'Cupreum Compactum' and 'Eaton Canyon', grows to only 30 inches tall. Both are good choices as these varieties only rarely set seed. (In mild-winter areas, seed-setting types can become weeds.)

PETUNIA HYBRIDS

pe-TOO-nee-uh

Petunia

2'
2'

Petunia *'Celebrity Pink Morn'*

- Bright, showy, all-summer flowers
- Often fragrant
- Mounding and trailing forms
- Easy-care annual; Hardiness Group A

Petunias are available in many flower colors and forms—pastel or vivid, solid-colored, striped, edged, or veined; single, double, or ruffled.
USES: Grow petunias alone, mixed with other flowers, or around potted trees or shrubs. Trailing types spill 2 feet or more over hanging baskets, pots, or window boxes.
SITING AND CARE: Plant after last frost in full sun to part shade. Keep moist and fertilize lightly every two weeks. If plants become untidy, cut stems back by half.
SELECTED VARIETIES AND RELATED SPECIES: Choices are legion. The 'Celebrity Hybrids' series offers compact, mounded plants to 2½ feet tall. 'Razzle Dazzle Hybrids' offers white-striped blossoms on 1-foot mounds. The Wave Hybrids™ series is only 6 inches tall but drapes 3 to 5 feet from container edges. Other fine trailing series are 'Supertunia Hybrids' and Surfinia Hybrids. Similar *Calibrachoa* spp., sold under the trade name Million Bells, has small, petunia-shaped blossoms. It comes in upright and trailing forms.

PHORMIUM SPP.

(FORM-ee-um)

New Zealand flax

7'
- Bold, fan-shaped plant
- Striped and colored leaves
- Zones 8–11; Hardiness Group B

4'

Eye-catching, sword-shaped leaves are this plant's showy feature, ranging from plain green, bronze, or cerise through various striped forms that include yellow, cream, bronze, red, apricot, or pink, in various combinations.

USES: Pot alone or underplant with draping plants, such as verbena or Mexican daisy. It is used much like cordyline to provide accent.
SITING AND CARE: Plant in moderately fertile potting mix that will drain well. Best in full sun, or part shade in warm climates. Water amply and fertilize weekly until late summer. Tolerates wind, hot or cool weather, and more water or less, but not the heat and humidity of the South. Cut out dead leaves as needed. Where not hardy, overwinter at 50 degrees F in a bright location, or in a dark, cool place, watering little.
SELECTED VARIETIES: The leaves of 'Apricot Queen' and *P. tenax* 'Yellow Wave' have green edges with colored centers. 'Bronze Baby' is 2 to 2½ feet tall with purplish-bronze leaves. 'Tom Thumb' has bronze-edged green leaves, to 18 inches. 'Jack Spratt', with bronzy leaves, is only 1 foot tall.

Phormium *'Guardsman'*

PLECTRANTHUS SPP.

plek-TRAN-thus

Swedish ivy

15"
- Attractive foliage, some kinds variegated
- Draping habit softens container edges
- Tender perennial often used as annual bedding and houseplant
- Hardiness Group A

24"

Swedish ivy spills charmingly over the sides of containers, its branches growing up to a yard long.

USES: Use in all kinds of containers to provide contrast to plants grown for flowers. Combines well with geraniums or impatiens.
SITING AND CARE: Grow in sun or shade in fertile potting mix and feed lightly every two weeks. Water moderately. Pinch off stem tips to increase branching and trim back branches that are growing in unattractive directions. Overwinter as a houseplant in a bright, cool room, or root cuttings for the next growing season in potting mix. Small white flowers can be pinched back to keep attention on foliage.
SELECTED VARIETIES:
P. madagascariensis has fleshy green leaves 1¼ to 1½ inches long. 'Variegated Mintleaf' has white-edged leaves and a faint minty smell. *P. forsteri* has hairy leaves 2½ to 4 inches long. 'Marginatus' leaves have creamy-white edges.

Plectranthus madagascariensis *'Variegated Mintleaf'*

PRIMULA X POLYANTHA

PRIM-you-luh paul-ee-AN-thuh

Polyanthus primrose

6"
- Upward-facing flowers in vivid colors
- Easy-care, cool-season bloomer
- Zones 3–8; Hardiness Group C

8"

These cheerful plants boast white, yellow, pink, red, lavender, or blue-violet flowers; some are bicolored with yellow centers.
USES: Mass in a low, wide container for a bedding effect, or plant at the edge of window boxes or mixed pots. They're beautiful with narcissus or other spring bulbs.
SITING AND CARE: Grow in part shade in spring, shade in warmer weather. Use fertile, well-drained potting mix. Keep moist and fertilize lightly every two weeks while blooming. In mild-winter areas of the West, it blooms all winter into spring. Where winters are cold, plant in containers in early spring.
SELECTED VARIETIES AND RELATED SPECIES: 'Pacific Giants Hybrids' (to 12 inches tall); 'Wanda Hybrids' (to 6 inches, some with bronzy leaves); 'Joker Hybrids' and 'Dreamer Hybrids' (3 to 4 inches). Florist's primroses, such as fairy primose (*P. malacoides*) and obconica primrose (*P. obconica*), are also lovely in spring containers.

Primula *'Pacific Giants Hybrids'*, red and scarlet shades

RHODODENDRON SPP.

row-doh-DEN-drun

Rhododendron, Azalea

Evergreen azalea 'Lorna'

- Billows of mid- to late spring blooms
- Shrubs range from 1 foot to more than 6 feet tall
- Both evergreen and deciduous types
- Many are hardy in Zones 5–9 (to Zone 10 in the West); Hardiness Group C

Rhododendron flowers are most commonly white, pink, red, or lavender. Some yellow and orange varieties are available.

USES: Best alone in a pot or a wooden container. The largest varieties require up to a 24-inch container; the smallest azaleas will be fine in a 10-inch pot. Group with hostas, ferns, or holly.

SITING AND CARE: Use a humus-rich, well-drained, slightly acidic potting mix. Provide light shade where summers are cool, more shade where summers are hot or when overwintering outdoors. Use acid-type fertilizer according to the directions provided with it. Cut off faded flowers and, just after blooming, prune lightly to shape plant. Depending on hardiness, overwinter unprotected, wrapped in insulating material, or indoors.

SELECTED VARIETIES: Hundreds to choose from. Select small- to medium-size ones for containers. Check at local nurseries for varieties best for your area. Tender Vireya rhododendrons winter well indoors. 'Northern Lights' is hardy to Zone 3.

ROSA

RO-zuh

Rose

- Favorite garden flowers
- Often sweetly fragrant
- Many bloom all summer
- Zones 5–9; Hardiness Group C

Available in a multitude of colors and flower forms, roses are outstanding subjects for containers.

'Little Charm' miniature rose

USES: Best grown alone in a large pot, tub, or wooden barrel. Shallow-rooted annuals, such as sweet alyssum or pansies, make attractive ground covers. Cascading forms are suitable for use in hanging pots.

SITING AND CARE: Locate in full sun at least half the day. Plant in fertile, well-drained potting mix. Plant miniature roses in containers 12 to 18 inches in diameter and larger roses in containers at least 18 to 24 inches in diameter. Keep moist, watering at ground level to avoid wetting leaves. Fertilize lightly every week to 10 days while growing. In cold climates, stop fertilizing in late July; where winters are mild, fertilize through August.

In Zones 9–11, leave roses in containers outside all winter. In colder climates, overwinter in an unheated garage or other protected location where the temperature will not drop below 10 degrees F.

About every three years, roses in containers will need root pruning. At the same time that you prune the top, remove the plant from its container and shave 2 to 3 inches of roots from the sides and bottom of the root ball. Return it to the same container, adding fresh potting mix as needed. Water well.

SELECTED VARIETIES: Hybrid tea roses produce large blooms, but the plant itself is often unappealing in a container. Better choices are miniatures, polyanthas, floribundas, shrub, ground cover, standard, and patio roses. Consult your local nursery for roses best suited to your climate. Look for disease resistance and summer-long blooming.

The following are some popular and easy-care choices: 'Bonica' is a disease-resistant landscape shrub with a spreading habit 3 to 4 feet high and shell pink flowers. Heaviest bloom is in spring and fall. 'Carefree Beauty' is a 4- to 5-foot upright shrub with fragrant pink blossoms all summer. 'Europeana' is a floribunda with brilliant red flowers all summer on upright 2- to 3-foot plants; it is often available grafted as a standard. The Flower Carpet Hybrids include wide-spreading, everblooming ground cover roses 2 feet high. 'Iceberg' is a floribunda with fragrant, pure white flowers all summer on rounded, 3- to 4-foot shrubs. 'Rise 'n' Shine' is an upright, 2-foot miniature with yellow flowers all summer. 'Sweet Chariot' is a 1½-foot cascading, everblooming miniature with fragrant, violet-pink flowers. It is lovely in hanging baskets and is disease-resistant. 'The Fairy' is one of the most popular of all roses, and for good reason: it is a highly disease-resistant polyantha rose that produces loads of pink blossoms nonstop all summer on neat, rounded, 2- to 3-foot plants.

SALVIA SPP.

SAL-vee-uh

Ornamental sage

18"
10"

- Bright flower spikes
- Hummingbird plants
- Good for hot climates
- Perennials and annuals; most are in Hardiness Group B

These plants offer dependably long bloom in a wide range of colors.
USES: Combine with annuals, perennials, and grasses in pots or window boxes. Try scarlet sage with fan flower and dusty miller.

SITING AND CARE: Most sages grow best in full sun, but can tolerate light shade. Plant in well-drained potting mix—fertile for annuals, moderately fertile for perennials. Keep annual sages moist, perennials slightly less so. Feed annual sages lightly each week; give perennials a moderate feeding monthly. Cut spent flower stems to encourage repeat blooms.
SELECTED VARIETIES AND RELATED SPECIES: Annual scarlet sage (S. splendens) blooms in red, peach, yellow, white, or purple. Choose dwarf varieties such as 'Firecracker Hybrids' (10 to 12 inches). Annual blue salvia (S. farinacea) blooms in blue or white.

S. × sylvestris 'May Night' is a perennial (Zones 4–8) with deep violet spires. Many tender sages are grown as perennials in areas with mild winters or as annuals elsewhere.

Salvia farinacea 'Victoria Blue'

SCAEVOLA SPP.

scuh-VOH-luh

Fan flower

10"
24"

- Covered with blue or white flowers
- Thrives in sun, heat
- Easy to grow— no deadheading necessary
- Zones 10–11; Hardiness Group A

These small, fan-shaped flowers open all summer long on mounded or cascading plants.

USES: Plant creeping varieties in hanging baskets or pots, or at the edges of window boxes and other mixed containers. Excellent in a hanging basket with ivy geraniums or bidens, or under roses. Plant mounded varieties alone.
SITING AND CARE: Plant in fertile, well-drained potting mix. Place in a sunny location, feed lightly once a week, and keep moist. Spent flowers shrivel and fall without deadheading, but as the season progresses, you may want to cut back any leggy stems to encourage branching.
SELECTED VARIETIES: Creeping varieties include 'New Wonder' (deep blue-violet flowers nearly

an inch across), 'White Charm' (white flowers nearly an inch across), and 'Sun Fan' (½-inch, light blue flowers). 'Blue Shamrock' forms a bushy ball 10 to 14 inches tall covered with intense blue, 1-inch blossoms.

Scaevola aemula 'New Wonder'

SENECIO CINERARIA

suh-NEE-see-oh sin-uhr-AIR-ee-uh

Dusty miller

10"
6"

- Whorls of velvety, silver leaves
- Upright growth habit
- Often grown as an annual
- Zones 8–11; Hardiness Group A

This is one of many species known commonly as "dusty miller." The silvery leaves are nearly white.
USES: Plant among upright flowering plants in mixed pots and

window boxes. Mix with flowering plants similar to it in height, such as upright verbenas or petunias. Or grow in front of taller plants.
SITING AND CARE: Grow in full sun in well-drained potting mix. Water and fertilize moderately. Overwatering or high humidity can encourage fungus infections. Plant is often discarded at the end of summer but can be overwintered in mild climates; may bloom the second year. Pinch out the flower stems to keep attention on leaves.
SELECTED VARIETIES: Several varieties with different leaf forms are available. 'Cirrus' has broad, finely toothed leaves; the leaves of 'Alice' are deeply cut. 'Silverdust'

has lacy, finely divided leaves.

Senecio cineraria 'Silverdust'

SOLENOSTEMON SCUTELLARIOIDES

so-len-OSS-teh-mun skoo-tul-lair-ee-OYD-eez

Coleus

Solenostemon *'Alabama Sunset'*

24"
12"

- Leaves in bright, fantasy colors
- Some have handsomely frilled edges
- Easy to grow from cuttings or seed
- Zones 10–11, annual everywhere; Hardiness Group A

The color range of this bright foliage plant includes yellow, chartreuse, green, pink, red, violet, burgundy, and nearly black. The leaves may be solid or variegated.
USES: Grow a specimen alone in an 8- to 15-inch pot or use in mixed plantings with flowers or foliage that repeat or contrast with its

colors. Ferns, fuchsia, and impatiens are good companions. Cascading varieties work well in hanging pots.
SITING AND CARE: Coleus thrives in shade, and most kinds tolerate sun as well. Plant in spring in fertile, well-drained potting mix. Fertilize weekly with a high-nitrogen fertilizer and keep moist. Pinch stem tips as needed to increase bushiness, and remove flower spikes to highlight leaves. Overwinter indoors, taking cuttings to plant the following spring.
SELECTED VARIETIES: Choose by sight from many new cutting-grown cultivars to get the coloration that you like best. Plants grown from seed are highly variable.

STACHYS BYZANTINA

STAY-kiss biz-uhn-TEEN-uh

Lamb's-ears

Stachys byzantina *'Silver Carpet'*

18"
24"

- Soft, furry leaves
- Spreads and drapes over pot edges
- Bloomless varieties available
- Zones 4–7 (to 10 in the West); Hardiness Group C

Plant lamb's-ears where you can touch its velvety leaves. The cool-colored foliage tones down mixed plantings of warm-hued flowers or harmonizes with blue or white ones.
USES: Plant lamb's-ears in window boxes or mixed pots either with blooming plants or combined with perennial shrubs and ornamental grasses with contrasting foliage.

SITING AND CARE: Lamb's-ears takes heat well but not high humidity. Grow in full sun or light shade in moderately fertile potting mix that is kept moist but not wet. It doesn't need much fertilizer but will tolerate what you give other plants. Remove leaves that wither and decay—check especially in damp weather. Where hardy, plant in the garden in fall. Remove dead leaves in early spring and divide plants that have become too large.
SELECTED VARIETIES: Nonblooming varieties, such as 'Silver Carpet', are best to keep attention on the attractive foliage. 'Big Ears' has large leaves and is the most tolerant of hot, humid weather.

Stipa tenuissima

STIPA TENUISSIMA

STEE-puh ten-you-ISS-ih-muh

Mexican feather grass

30"
20"

- Upright shocks of fine-textured grass
- Turns gold in fall
- Zones 7–11, annual in Zones 3–6; Hardiness Group A

Sometimes called ponytail grass, the upright, arching leaves are a bright, clear green in spring. Both the leaves and the feathery flower heads turn light gold by late summer.
USES: Grow alone in a pot or urn

about 8 inches in diameter. Or underplant with succulents, perennials, or small annuals.
SITING AND CARE: Grow in full sun to light shade, planting it in moderately fertile potting mix. Water moderately, letting the mix dry somewhat between waterings. Where hardy, it may resow. To reduce resowing, cut back plants or remove them at the end of the growing season.
SELECTED VARIETIES AND RELATED SPECIES: A related species, giant feather grass (*Stipa gigantea*), reaches 6 feet tall when it is in bloom. It is too tall for most container plantings but is dramatic in a half barrel with sunflowers and *Verbena bonariensis*.

TAGETES

tuh-JEE-teez

Marigold

12"

12"

- Bright, sunny flowers
- Long blooming season
- One kind has edible blossoms
- Dependable annuals; Hardiness Group A

Available in a range of warm colors, bicolors, and a near-white, in various heights and flower sizes; indispensable for summer color.

USES: Mass shorter varieties of marigolds in a wide pot for a bedding effect, or mix them with other annuals in window boxes or container bouquets. They are dramatic combined with other tropicals, such as canna and coleus.

SITING AND CARE: Plant in full sun in moderately fertile, well-drained potting mix. Keep moderately moist. Pinch off stem tips when plant is young to increase bushiness, and remove spent flowers all season for more bloom.

SELECTED VARIETIES AND RELATED SPECIES: French marigolds range from 6 to 18 inches tall with flowers an inch or so in diameter; 'Mr. Majestic' bears electric red-and-yellow pinwheel flowers on 12-inch mounding plants. African marigolds, which grow 1 to 3 feet tall and have bigger blooms, are useful in larger containers; the 'Antigua' series comes in orange, gold, and primrose and grows 10 to 12 inches tall. Signet marigold (*T. tenuifolia*), which forms an airy mound 6 to 8 inches tall covered with small, edible flowers, is also charming.

Tagetes tenuifolia *'Gem Hybrid'*

TULIPA HYBRIDS

TOO-lih-puh

Tulip

15"

6"

- Brilliant spring color
- Wide array of flower forms
- Easy-to-grow bulbs
- Zones 4–7 (best as annuals in Zones 8–11); Hardiness Group C

Available in a wide range of colors and in plain or fancy flower forms.

USES: Mass one variety of tulips in a pot or, alternatively, combine with other spring bloomers, such as forget-me-nots, pansies, or primroses.

SITING AND CARE: Plant in fertile, well-drained potting mix. Set bulbs with sides nearly touching and tops just below the surface. Grow short varieties in a shallow "bulb pot," but, for stability, use tall pots for tall varieties. Grow in full sun. Keep barely moist until shoots emerge, then keep moist. After bloom, taper off watering; dig when dormant, and plant in the garden at the correct time for your climate. In

Tulip 'Dreaming Maid' (lavender), 'Meissner Porzellan' (pink and white), and 'Passionale' (purple)

mild-winter areas, discard, or prechill before replanting.

SELECTED VARIETIES: Unusual forms and colors include red-and-yellow Flame Series, the variegated-leaved *Tulipa praestans* 'Unicum', and lily-flowered tulips. Species tulips, especially the *kaufmanniana* or *greigii* types, are excellent for early spring blooms and attractive, long-lasting, variegated foliage. Good early-blooming varieties for containers include 'Orange Emperor', 'Toronto', and 'Apricot

Beauty'. Recommended midseason varieties include 'Pink Impression' and the variegated-leaved 'New Design'. Excellent late-season tulips for containers include 'Temple of Beauty', the yellow, lily-flowered 'West Point', and double varieties such as creamy pink 'Angelique' and the feathery, pale-lavender, peony-flowered 'Lilac Perfection'.

Vegetables

- Enjoy a harvest on your deck or patio
- Fun for children to watch and pick the crops
- Most are annuals; Hardiness Group A

Vegetables are rewarding container plants, providing a handy source of salad greens or other fresh delicacies. Even a few vegetables

Tomato 'Better Boy' VFN Hybrid

Pepper 'Red Beauty Hybrid'

give the feeling of completing the age-old cycle from seed to table. Children enjoy watching vegetables grow, and vegetables in containers provide a focus for close-up examination. Combine vegetables with flowers to add beauty and color to their more utilitarian charm.

USES: If production is your goal, give vegetables plenty of root room and don't crowd the plants together. Consult the chart on page 89 for appropriate container depth and distance between plants. If your main goal is an attractive planting rather than production, you can crowd plants together more closely, or mix them with flowers. Use young, leafy vegetables, such as lettuce, chard, or kale, in mixed planters with flowers and herbs for a temporary display, and harvest them when they outgrow the planting. Some tomato varieties, often called "patio" types, are suitable for hanging pots.

SITING AND CARE: For best production, grow vegetables in an adequate volume of fertile, well-drained potting mix. Make sure the plants are not crowded and the container is deep enough for the kind of vegetable you are growing. Economical containers are half and quarter barrels or homemade wooden boxes. Although you can grow shallow-rooted crops such as lettuce or spinach in deep containers, you can save money by using shallow containers for these crops.

Use a fertilizer containing as much or more nitrogen as phosphorus (such as a 14-14-14 fertilizer) if you are growing crops from which you plan to harvest the leaves, but use one with less nitrogen than phosphorus (such as 5-10-10) for fruiting crops such as beans, tomatoes, and peppers. Fertilize by using a timed-release fertilizer when you are planting or weekly applications of half-strength liquid fertilizer as the plants grow. Keep moist. Except while they are young seedlings or recent transplants, most vegetables are best watered at ground level; water on leaves may encourage disease.

Cool-season vegetables, which include most of those grown for

their leaves or roots, do best when daily temperatures reach only 55 to 75 degrees F. Where summers are hot, they are grown either in early spring or as weather cools at the end of summer. Gardeners with cool summer weather can grow some or all of them throughout the summer. Where winters are mild, many of these crops can be grown into fall and winter.

Warm-season vegetables, which include most of those grown for their fruits or seeds, do best when temperatures average 65 to 95 degrees F. They thrive in warm summers but may need afternoon shade if the weather is very hot. In the desert Southwest and in Florida, they may do best planted to mature in early spring and fall. In climates with short or cool summers, gardeners choose early or cool-tolerant varieties of these crops in order to be able to grow them at all.

Some fruits and vegetables are best grown on trellises or given poles for support. Put these crops on the north side of your container garden so they won't shade shorter plants. You can attach wooden trellises, or a nylon trellis on a wooden frame, to a container, or insert bamboo poles in the potting mix.

Miniature vegetables are smaller-than-normal plants that still have flavorful crops. These are useful if you don't have room for containers large enough for full-size crops. Some of the most useful are round carrots (for shallow pots), miniature lettuces, and bush pumpkins. Patio tomatoes can provide heavy crops of small but tasty tomatoes even in an 8-inch hanging pot.

Lettuce 'Oak Leaf', 'Frecklles', 'Red Sails', and 'Black Seeded Simpson'

VEGETABLES FOR CONTAINERS

Common Name (Scientific Name)	Cool or Warm Season Crop	Minimum and Ample Container Depths	Distance Apart of Seeds	Depth to Plant Seed	Distance Apart (After Thinning)	Notes
Bean, bush* (*Phaseolus vulgaris*)	Warm	10–15"	1½–2"	1–1½"	4"	Does not need support; keep picked to keep plants bearing
Bean, pole* (*Phaseolus vulgaris*)	Warm	12–18"	2-3"	1–1½"	6"	Requires a 6' trellis or poles; keep picked to keep plants bearing
Beet (*Beta vulgaris* ssp. *vulgaris*)	Cool	8–12"	1"	½–1"	2–3"	Often best pulled at 1" or so in diameter; replant for another crop
Carrot (*Daucus carota*)	Cool	6–9" (short) 12–16" (long)	½"	¼–½"	2–3"	Plant seeds in place; carrots don't form good roots after transplanting
Chard, Swiss* (*Beta vulgaris* ssp. *flavescens*)	Cool	10–12"	1-2"	1"	6–10"	Harvest over a long period by eating outer leaves, letting inner ones grow
Cucumber* (*Cucumis sativus*)	Warm	12–18"	3"	1"	4–8"	Best on a 4' trellis; keep picked, or production will stop
Lettuce, looseleaf* (*Lactuca sativa*)	Cool	8–12"	1"	¼"	6–8"	Harvest a few outer leaves at a time, or take the whole plant
Lettuce, looseleaf, miniature* (*Lactuca sativa*)	Cool	6–10"	1"	¼"	4–6"	Usually harvested by pulling entire plant
Melon* (*Cucumis melo*)	Warm	16–18"	3"	1"	18–24"	Attach to a strong wooden trellis; support fruits in soft cloth slings
Onion (scallions)*** (*Allium fistulosum*)	Cool	8–10"	1-2"	3"	1–2"	Use sets (small bulbs); plant every two weeks for continuous supply
Onion (bulbs)*** (*Allium cepa*)	Cool	8–12"	3"	¼"	3–4"	Plant sets 4-6 weeks before average last frost; dig when tops die down
Pea, bush or pole (*Pisum sativum*)	Cool	12–14"	1"	1–2"	2–4"	Pole peas require a 4-6 foot trellis; snap peas can be eaten raw
Pepper** (*Capsicum annuum annuum*)	Warm	15–18"	2"	¼"	15-24"	Use bell peppers green, or, where summer is long, ripen to red or yellow
Pepper, compact varieties** (*Capsicum annuum annuum*)	Warm	10–12"	2"	¼"	12-18"	Many small, hot peppers have smaller plants than the larger, mild ones
Potato*** (*Solanum tuberosum*)	Cool	12–18"	8–10"	4"(see note)	8–10"	Plant 8" below top of pot; cover with 4" of soil, 4" more in three weeks
Pumpkin (*Cucurbita pepo*)	Warm	16–18"	2"	1–1½"	24"	Try bush pumpkins or vining ones with miniature fruit (see Melon)
Radish (*Raphanus sativus*)	Cool	6–8"	1"	½"	1–2"	Thin by pulling and eating largest roots; let others grow more
Radish, long (*Raphanus sativus*)	Cool	6–12"	1"	½"	1–3"	Some long kinds can be spring-planted; others are for summer
Spinach (*Spinacia oleracea*)	Cool	8–12"	1"	½"	3–4"	Needs very fertile soil high in nitrogen, and ample water
Squash (summer)* (*Cucurbita pepo*)	Warm	16–18"	3"	1	18–24"	Keep picked to avoid large, tough fruits and keep plant bearing
Tomato (indeterminate, tall)** (*Lycopersicon esculentum*)	Warm	15–24"	1–2"	½"	18–24"	Needs support—stakes or trellis; attach plant to support as it grows; harvest tomatoes all season.
Tomato (determinate, short)** (*Lycopersicon esculentum*)	Warm	12–18"	1–2"	½"	15–18"	Short plants, but some support is still a help; protect from winds; harvest lasts only one to two weeks
Tomato, patio type** (*Lycopersicon esculentum*)	Warm	8–10"	1–2"	½"	8–15"	These are small enough to use in a hanging pot; fruit is small

*Often grown from purchased plants, but easy from seed; **Most often grown from purchased plant; ***Use sets, small bulbs, etc.

VERBENA HYBRIDS

ver-BEE-nuh

Garden verbena

- Sheets of intense or pastel colors
- Blooms all summer
- Spilling or arching
- Zones 6–11; Hardiness Group B

Verbena 'Tapien Pink' and 'Tapien Blue Violet'

Verbena has masses of summer-long color in nearly every hue but yellow. **USES:** Most kinds of verbena arch or spill over the sides of containers. Use in hanging pots, window boxes, and mixed pots. Combine with petunia, bidens, or licorice plant. **SITING AND CARE:** Verbena requires full sun and tolerates heat. Plant in fertile, well-drained potting mix; feed lightly every two weeks, and provide moderate water. When stems are through blooming, cut back to the next flower bud, or lightly shear plants. Often grown as an annual, even where hardy. **SELECTED VARIETIES AND RELATED SPECIES:** 'Imagination Hybrids' (purple), *V. tenuisecta* 'Edith' (lavender-pink), and *V. canadensis* 'Homestead Purple' (fragrant, resists humidity) are spreading cultivars. 'Peaches and Cream' is somewhat more upright. 'Temari Hybrids' (trailing) and the Tapien series (slightly more upright) are available in many colors. *V. bonariensis* bears 3- to 4-foot stems topped with purple flowers. It is hardy in Zones 7–11 (Hardiness Group A).

VINCA SPP.

VIN-ka

Periwinkle, Vinca

- Small flowers on trailing stems
- Blooms spring to fall
- Evergreen leaves; some kinds variegated
- Hardiness varies according to species

Vinca major 'Variegata'

Vinca major and *Vinca minor* have slightly different qualities, but both add charm and grace to containers. **USES:** *V. minor*, the smaller plant, is excellent in spring plantings. Use it in hanging pots or in mixed plantings with bulbs and other spring flowers. Both kinds combine well with summer flowers in mixed pots, window boxes, or urns. **SITING AND CARE:** Both species are best in light to part shade where summers are hot, but they can tolerate sun in cool weather. Plant in moderately fertile to fertile, well-drained potting mix and keep moist. Trim back branches that grow too long. If plants overwinter, cut them back in early spring to stimulate new growth. **SELECTED VARIETIES:** *V. major* (hardy in Zones 7–11; Hardiness Group B) bears lavender-blue flowers 1 to 2 inches across. Flowers of *V. minor*, hardy in Zones 4–9, to 11 in the West (Hardiness Group C), are an inch across and available in white as well as various shades of blue and purple. Both species have white- or yellow-variegated cultivars.

VIOLA SPP.

vy-OH-luh

Pansy, viola, Johnny-jump-up

- Long-blooming flowers in many colors
- Most bloom best in cool weather
- Edible flowers
- Hardiness varies; Hardiness Group C

Viola 'Penny Azure Wings'

Pansies (*V. × wittrockiana*) and violas (*V. cornuta* and *V. tricolor*) bloom in white, yellow, pink, orange, scarlet, and various shades of purple, including nearly black. Some are bicolored and tricolored. **USES:** All types are beautiful massed alone in a wide pot, and in mixed plantings in window boxes, pots, or hanging pots and baskets. Combine with spring bulbs, stock, flowering tobacco, and *Vinca minor*; or with herbs and leafy vegetables. **SITING AND CARE:** Plant in sun or light shade in spring or fall. Use fertile, well-drained potting mix; feed lightly every two weeks and keep moist. Remove spent flowers. In areas with mild winters and cool summers, they bloom nearly all year. **SELECTED VARIETIES AND RELATED SPECIES:** Many cultivars are available. 'Crystal Bowl Hybrids' pansies and 'Sorbet Hybrids' violas are particularly heat-tolerant. Hardy violets (*V. odorata*, Zones 6–9, to 11 in the West, or *V. labradorica*, Zones 3–8, to 11 in the West) are good under shrubs or vines in containers.

YUCCA FILAMENTOSA

YUH-kuh fil-uh-men-TOW-suh

Yucca, Adam's needle

6'

3'

- Dramatic, spiky form
- Fragrant white flowers in summer
- Southwest or tropical look
- Zones 5–11; Hardiness Group C

Yucca provides architectural drama and is long-lived in the garden. The flower stems can reach 6 feet high.

USES: Best as a specimen alone in a container. Use in groupings with containers of sun-loving annuals, succulents, or tropical plants.

SITING AND CARE: Locate in full sun. Has sharp leaf tips, so keep away from paths and where children play. Grow in moderately fertile, well-drained potting mix or in cactus mix. Water amply and feed twice a month. Remove any dead or unsightly leaves. Cut off spent flower stalks. In cold winters, containers may be overwintered in a bright, indoor location at 41 to 50 degrees F. Water little in winter.

SELECTED VARIETIES: 'Bright Edge' has leaves with broad yellow margins; leaves of 'Golden Sword' have yellow centers. 'Variegata' is blue-green with white edges. The leaves have a pink tinge in winter.

Yucca filamentosa *'Bright Edge'*

ZANTEDESCHIA SPP.

zan-tuh-DEE-shee-uh

Calla lily

3'

2'

- Elegant spring and summer flowers
- New hybrids in many flower colors
- Zones 8–11, elsewhere dig and store rhizomes; Hardiness Group A

Calla lilies bloom in white, yellow, orange, pink, lavender, purple, and a range of buffs and mauves. Their flowers, shaped like curved funnels, stand above arrow-shaped leaves.

USES: Grow several calla rhizomes alone in a container, with impatiens or pansies, or in large mixed pots.

SITING AND CARE: Using fertile potting mix, plant in fall in Zones 8–11 (keeping just moist over the winter); plant in early spring north of Zone 8. Provide light shade or afternoon shade in the Southeast, full sun elsewhere. Keep moist and fertilize every two weeks until end of bloom period. In Zones 10 and 11, overwinter outdoors in containers. Otherwise, keep in pots or dig rhizomes and store over winter in a cool, frost-free place (see page 45).

SELECTED VARIETIES AND RELATED SPECIES: Shorter types, such as the many named hybrids that are less than one to two feet tall, are ideal for containers. *Z. elliotiana* is 2 feet tall with yellow flowers. *Z. rehmannii*, to 2 feet tall, has pale to bright pink flowers.

Zantedeschia *'Gem Rose'*

ZINNIA ELEGANS

ZIN-ee-uh

Zinnia

24"

8"

- Carnival-bright summer blossoms
- Thrives in heat
- Flowers all summer
- Sturdy annual; Hardiness Group A

Zinnias range in height from 6 inches to more than 3 feet, in flower size from less than 1 inch to more than 4 inches across, and in color from white, ivory, and green to yellow, orange, pink, and red.

USES: Grow alone massed in a wide pot, or mixed in window boxes or bouquets with other annuals such as petunias or verbena.

SITING AND CARE: Plant in fertile, well-drained potting mix. Grow in full sun, or part shade in hot areas. Zinnias tolerate considerable heat. Keep moist but water at the base of the plants to discourage mildew. Fertilize monthly. Deadhead to encourage continuous blooming.

SELECTED VARIETIES AND RELATED SPECIES: Best for containers are midsize, bushy types, which include 'Peter Pan Hybrids' (12 to 14 inches tall) and 'Dreamland Hybrids' (10 to 12 inches). Unusual colors include chartreuse 'Envy' (30 inches) and striped 'Candy Cane Hybrids' (17 inches). *Z. haageana* is a 1- to 2-foot tall plant with an abundance of orange, yellow, or mahogany flowers.

Zinnia *'Peter Pan Hybrids'*

CONTAINER GARDENING RESOURCES

B & D Lilies
P.O. Box 2007
Port Townsend, WA 98368
360-765-4341
www.bdlilies.com
Many kinds of lily bulbs.

Charley's Greenhouse Supply
17979 State Route 536
Mount Vernon, WA 98273-3269
800-322-4707
www.charleysgreenhouse.com
Greenhouses and a wide variety
of accessories, supplies, and tools.

Dutch Gardens
P.O. Box 200
Adelphia, NJ 07710-0200
800-818-3861
www.dutchgardens.com
A wide selection of spring and
summer bulbs, and perennial flowers.

Earthmade Quality Products
3301 Steck Avenue
Austin, TX 78757
800-843-1819
www.earthmade.com
Many kinds of containers, container
gardening accessories, and tools.

Four Winds Growers
P.O. Box 3538
Fremont, CA 94539
510-656-2591
www.fourwindsgrowers.com
Dwarf citrus trees.

Gardener's Supply Company
128 Intervale Road
Burlington, VT 05401
800-863-1700
www.gardeners.com
Containers and container accessories,
including self-watering pots, hanging
plant pulleys, devices to reduce the
need for water, and small-scale drip
irrigation systems.

Jackson & Perkins
#1 Rose Lane
Medford, OR 97501
800-872-7673
www.jacksonandperkins.com
Containers and container accessories,
roses (including miniatures), and
many other plants.

Kinsman Company
P.O. Box 428
Pipersville, PA 18947
800-733-4146
www.kinsmangarden.com
Chambers English planters in many
styles (black metal frames with coir
liners), as well as many other kinds
of containers and accessories.

Lilypons Water Gardens
6800 Lilypons Road, Box 10
Buckeystown, MD 21717-0010
800-999-5459
www.lilypons.com
Plants, fish, and equipment for water
gardens. Catalog includes tips for
water gardeners.

Logee's Greenhouses
141 North Street
Danielson, CT 06239-1939
888-330-8038
www.logees.com
Tropical and subtropical plants. Most
are suitable for year-round container
gardens in mild climates. In cold
winter climates, use for summer
gardens and winter them indoors, in
sunrooms, or greenhouses. Includes
citrus, begonias, and hibiscus.

Park Seed
1 Parkton Avenue
Greenwood, SC 29647-0001
800-845-3369
www.parkseed.com
A seed company that also offers
a wide selection of perennials,
flowering shrubs, bulbs, and vines.

Simple Gardens
615 Old Cemetery Road
Richmond, VT 05477
800-351-2438
www.simplegardens.com
Year-round containers, water garden
bowls, watering aids, other container
garden accessories, and water garden
plants.

Smith and Hawken
P.O. Box 431
Milwaukee, WI 53201-0431
800-776-3336
www.smithandhawken.com
Containers, accessories, and tools.

Stokes Tropicals
P.O. Box 9868
New Iberia, LA 70562-9868
800-624-9706
www.stokestropicals.com
Tropical plants, most suitable for
containers. Includes many bananas,
cannas, gingers, and ginger relatives.

The Urban Farmer Store
2833 Vicente Street
San Francisco, CA 94116
800-753-3747
www.urbanfarmerstore.com
Drip irrigation supplies sold through
an informative catalog.

Van Englen Inc.
23 Tulip Drive
Bantam, CT 06750-1631
860-567-8734
www.vanenglen.com
Fall bulbs, lilies, and amaryllis.

Van Ness Water Gardens
2460 North Euclid Avenue
Upland, CA 91784-1199
800-205-2425
www.vnwg.com
Plants and equipment for water
gardens; informative catalog provides
tips for water gardeners.

Wayside Gardens
1 Garden Lane
Hodges, SC 29695-0001
800-845-1124
www.waysidegardens.com
Perennials, bulbs, shrubs, and vines.

White Flower Farm
P.O. Box 50
Litchfield, CT 06759-0500
800-503-9624
www.whiteflowerfarm.com
Perennials, annuals, bulbs, vines,
shrubs, and containers.

Windowbox Gardening
www.windowbox.com
A plant search feature, the
"Floracle", gives full information on
growing specific plants in containers.
The online shop, "The Balcony
Store", offers containers and other
supplies.

USDA PLANT HARDINESS ZONE MAP

This map of climate zones helps you select plants for your garden that will survive a typical winter in your region. The United States Department of Agriculture (USDA) developed the map, basing the zones on the lowest recorded temperatures across North America. Zone 1 is the coldest area and Zone 11 is the warmest.

Plants are classified by the coldest temperature and zone they can endure. For example, plants hardy to Zone 6 survive where winter temperatures drop to –10° F. Those hardy to Zone 8 die long before it's that cold. These plants may grow in colder regions but must be replaced each year. Plants rated for a range of hardiness zones can usually survive winter in the coldest region as well as tolerate the summer heat of the warmest one.

To find your hardiness zone, note the approximate location of your community on the map, then match the color band marking that area to the key.

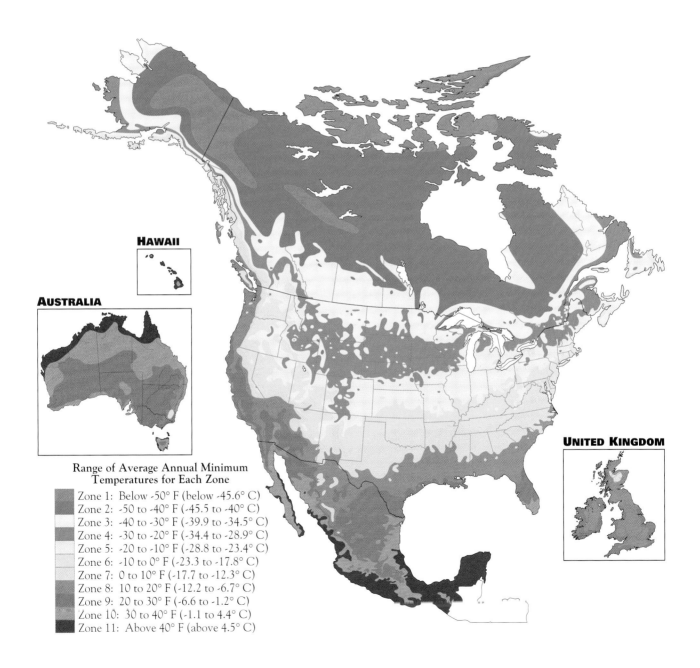

HAWAII

AUSTRALIA

UNITED KINGDOM

Range of Average Annual Minimum Temperatures for Each Zone

Zone 1: Below -50° F (below -45.6° C)
Zone 2: -50 to -40° F (-45.5 to -40° C)
Zone 3: -40 to -30° F (-39.9 to -34.5° C)
Zone 4: -30 to -20° F (-34.4 to -28.9° C)
Zone 5: -20 to -10° F (-28.8 to -23.4° C)
Zone 6: -10 to 0° F (-23.3 to -17.8° C)
Zone 7: 0 to 10° F (-17.7 to -12.3° C)
Zone 8: 10 to 20° F (-12.2 to -6.7° C)
Zone 9: 20 to 30° F (-6.6 to -1.2° C)
Zone 10: 30 to 40° F (-1.1 to 4.4° C)
Zone 11: Above 40° F (above 4.5° C)

INDEX

A number in boldface indicates a photograph or illustration. An asterisk following a number (*) indicates a descriptive entry in the "Gallery of Container Plants."

METRIC CONVERSIONS

U.S. Units to Metric Equivalents			Metric Units to U.S. Equivalents		
To Convert From	Multiply By	To Get	To Convert From	Multiply By	To Get
Inches	25.4	Millimeters	Millimeters	0.0394	Inches
Inches	2.54	Centimeters	Centimeters	0.3937	Inches
Feet	30.48	Centimeters	Centimeters	0.0328	Feet
Feet	0.3048	Meters	Meters	3.2808	Feet
Yards	0.9144	Meters	Meters	1.0936	Yards
Square inches	6.4516	Square centimeters	Square centimeters	0.1550	Square inches
Square feet	0.0929	Square meters	Square meters	10.764	Square feet
Square yards	0.8361	Square meters	Square meters	1.1960	Square yards
Acres	0.4047	Hectares	Hectares	2.4711	Acres
Cubic inches	16.387	Cubic centimeters	Cubic centimeters	0.0610	Cubic inches
Cubic feet	0.0283	Cubic meters	Cubic meters	35.315	Cubic feet
Cubic feet	28.316	Liters	Liters	0.0353	Cubic feet
Cubic yards	0.7646	Cubic meters	Cubic meters	1.308	Cubic yards
Cubic yards	764.55	Liters	Liters	0.0013	Cubic yards

To convert from degrees Fahrenheit (F) to degrees Celsius (C), first subtract 32, then multiply by $\frac{5}{9}$.

To convert from degrees Celsius to degrees Fahrenheit, multiply by $\frac{9}{5}$, then add 32.